Westminster's World

WESTMINSTER'S WORLD

Understanding Political Roles

DONALD D. SEARING

Harvard University Press
Cambridge, Massachusetts
London, England
1994

Library of Congress Cataloging-in-Publication Data

Searing, Donald.
Westminster's world : understanding political roles /
Donald D. Searing.
p. cm.
Includes bibliographical references and index.
ISBN 0-674-95072-0 (alk. paper)
1. Great Britain. Parliament. House of Commons. 2. Great
Britain. Parliament. House of Commons—Leadership.
3. Legislators—Great Britain—Interviews. 4. Great Britain—
Politics and Government—1964–1979. I. Title.
JN677.S43 1993
328.41'0731'0922—dc20
93-25088
CIP

For my mother and father

CONTENTS

PREFACE

This is a study of eight political roles in the British House of Commons. Four are informal, backbench roles: Policy Advocates, Ministerial Aspirants, Constituency Members, and Parliament Men. The other four are formal, leadership roles: Parliamentary Private Secretaries, Whips, Junior Ministers, and Ministers. My reconstructions of these roles and their subtypes, and my explorations of the institutional constraints and individual choices that shape them, are designed to advance our understanding of political life at Westminster during the eventful decade of the 1970s. They are also designed, more generally, to advance our understanding of the careers of politicians and to reinvigorate the study of politicians' roles by showing how motivational role theory can be used to examine the impact of goals and incentives upon behavior. These general aims constitute the study's principal contribution to the field of comparative politics. Nevertheless, they have been, so to speak, subordinated to substance—because I have written this book first and foremost as an interpretation of British political life at Westminster.

Since academic studies have devoted so much more attention to Parliament's institutional structure than to its politicians, I have tried to redress the balance by focusing on the Members of the British House of Commons and especially on aspects of their political culture that guide them in their careers. Both Emile Durkheim and Max Weber distinguished between institutional structure and culture; and, ever since, scholarly interest has tilted

back and forth between these two topics.[1] The culture of parliaments constitutes a substantial portion of the political culture of politicians. It has three
principal components. One is ideology, which consists of values and policy
beliefs. Another is norms, some constitutional, others purely parliamentary.
The third is political roles—the subject of this book. Political roles are central to the system of symbols that condition behavior and experience at
Westminster. And yet they are themselves conditioned by the institution.
Political roles are the place where individual choices meet institutional constraints. They deserve to be examined carefully. They deserve what Clifford
Geertz called thick descriptions.[2] They also deserve what I would call con-
vincing explanations.

The thick descriptions and convincing explanations that I have in mind
are macroanalytic but mainly microanalytic, naturalistic but mainly interpretative, quantitative but mainly qualitative. Hence, while I propose to address macroanalytic concerns about the distributions of roles and their institutional contexts, I want mainly to see what can be learned through a
microanalytic analysis of the desires, beliefs, and behaviors that define these
roles in the minds of their players. Likewise, while I propose to address
causal explanations about the sources and consequences of these roles, I
propose mainly to construct interpretative explanations about their statics
and dynamics. And, while I shall use quantitative analysis, for it has greatly
helped me to reconstruct the roles, I have deliberately kept such analyses
simple and secondary to the qualitative character of the study. Thus, I have
blended in this book several different strategies of inquiry that used to be
regarded as incompatible but that are in fact quite compatible and reinforcing.[3] The mix is, I believe, particularly well suited for analyzing topics such
as authority, power, duty, ambition, and representation—topics that will
be addressed in the book's chapters.[4]

Parliament and parliamentary roles have a special prominence in Britain's
political imagery.[5] The British typically characterize their system as a parliamentary government rather than as a democracy. The prominence of parliamentary roles is reflected in the surprising popularity of political biographies
and memoirs, and in the considerable attention devoted to the lives of politicians in the political weeklies, the national press, public affairs programs,
and journalistic commentaries.[6] Equally striking, and more surprising, is the
way that the study of politicians has been neglected by social scientists, partially because politicians are less accessible to us than are members of the
electorate, partially because we are better trained to study institutions than
to study individuals.[7] One of the most fruitful ways to focus the study of
political institutions on individuals is to use the concept of roles, since roles
are constructed by such institutions and, at the same time, reconstructed by

the politicians who play them and use them to pursue their goals. This is a desirable direction for the "new institutionalism" to take and an opportunity to achieve a long-overdue integration of sociological and economic perspectives. It is also analogous to the approach to history pursued by Sir Lewis Namier, who, when he sought to understand a time and a place, tried first to understand the purposeful behavior of the principal actors he found on the stage.[8]

My task is more difficult than Namier's, because I lack centuries of hindsight and shelves of commentaries. But it is also easier, because I have been able to speak with the principal actors involved. Thus, most of the best-known political figures of the 1970s were interviewed for this study. My associates and I talked, for example, with Cabinet Ministers like Margaret Thatcher, Peter Walker, and James Prior, and with Shadow Ministers like Harold Wilson, Barbara Castle, and Denis Healey. We talked with rising stars such as Michael Heseltine and Norman Tebbit on the Conservative side of the House, and with David Owen and Roy Hattersley on the Labour side. We talked with outsiders destined to become insiders like Michael Foot, and with former insiders like Enoch Powell, who were on their way into exile. We talked with Neil Kinnock, Cecil Parkinson, and John Smith, leaders for the next decade, and with many of those who would eventually rise to the top with them. These were some of the most helpful and articulate people we interviewed. What they had to say about their roles and those of their colleagues constitutes the basis for the chapters on leadership in Part II of this book. Some of their views are already in the public domain, for these are the politicians who are most likely to do the media interviews and to write books and articles about their experiences.

Much less well known are the views of the vast majority of Westminster's backbenchers who shape Parliament's roles but are less likely to discuss them in print or in broadcasts. Thus, we talked with trade unionists, Knights of the Shires, and small businessmen. We interviewed those who came to Parliament from the pits, and those who came from the country houses and banks. We also interviewed most of the Members who were women, and the "Father of the House" and the "Baby of the House," too. We interviewed Members who were well past retirement age as well as those who were just starting out on the road. Some were part-timers who didn't have much to say, but others were more informative and entertaining than their better-known colleagues. Only by virtue of their collective contribution can we be confident that the backbench roles reconstructed in Part I are not just those of the show horses but also those of the vast majority of MPs who work behind the scenes.

This book was first conceived as an introductory chapter for a study of the political education of Members of Parliament. It soon became clear, however, that this study of the origins of roles presupposed a study of their content: that to explain satisfactorily how roles were learned, it would be necessary first to explain interpretatively the roles that were being learned. As the work developed, I realized that the transcribed material on these roles was far richer than I had thought. This impression was reinforced by Edward Crowe's dissertation on the four general backbench roles.[9] His comprehensive analysis aroused my interest in the subtypes that lay beneath these general roles and convinced me that, to make proper sense of those subtypes, it would be necessary to burrow deep into the interviews with a qualitative study. I decided to investigate the matter, and to investigate as well Westminster's leadership roles, partly because the transcribed discussions about them proved much too fascinating to pass over, partly because I found that their structure as "position" roles offered a fundamental and instructive contrast to the "preference" roles on the backbenches. Thus a little chapter became a big book.

Since the project began, it has been aided by many generous institutions and individuals. I would like to thank the National Science Foundation, the John Simon Guggenheim Foundation, and the National Endowment for the Humanities for supporting various stages of data collection, transcription, coding, analysis, and further data collection. And I would like to thank Ivor Crewe and Jeffrey Obler for their comments on the manuscript. Important acknowledgments are also due to members of the Department of Political Science and the Institute for Research in Social Science of the University of North Carolina, Chapel Hill, and above all to my wife, Pamela Johnston Conover, without whose love and support this book might never have been completed. In London, the Royal Institute of International Affairs made available to us meeting rooms and facilities at Chatham House over a period of several years. I am grateful to them and also to the staff at the Palace of Westminster, particularly to the policemen assigned to the Central Lobby at the time and to Mr. Stole, who was assigned to the House of Lords. They helped care for our equipment and helped care for us in many little ways that made a big difference as the months wore on and the second winter of late-night sittings set in. The project's most important debts are, however, owed to the University of Essex, to its then Vice Chancellor, Albert Sloman, and to the Department of Government, which housed the project for three years and intermittently thereafter, and supported it with supplies, administrative assistance, and a great deal of advice and encouragement.

The project's most indispensable individuals were the other members of my interviewing team: Elizabeth Crighton, Christopher Game, Janet Morgan, and Pamela Poulter. Had it not been for their tact and subtlety, we would never have achieved interviews of the quality that will be apparent in the quotations. Had it not been for their energy and patience, we would never have achieved the very high response rate that has made possible the detailed analyses of the subtypes and, thereby, this book itself. The study's success also had much to do with the skills of its principal administrative secretaries, Sue Brookes and Nancy Tupper-Cary, who scheduled and rescheduled the interviews and organized, supervised, and proofed the work of a pool of part-time typists who transcribed the interview tapes. These laborious transcriptions were produced mainly by M. Longhurst, J. D. Ellacott, Irene Warner, and Janet Parkin. The first chapters of the manuscript were typed and retyped by Elizabeth Taylor and Julie Daniel, whose accuracy and amused reactions to some of the material helped keep up my spirits as I despaired over the growing length of the book.

I would like to thank as well the following Members of Parliament whose guidance proved essential to the study's progress. They gave us exceptional help and encouragement, for which I am deeply grateful: Humphrey Atkins, Bernard Braine, Hugh Brown, Anthony Buck, Sydney Chapman, Patrick Cormack, Anthony Crosland, G. Burnaby Drayson, William Hamling, Walter Harrison, Michael Heseltine, Patrick Jenkin, Marcus Kimball, Richard Leonard, Maurice Macmillan, Michael Meacher, Ernle Money, Patrick McNair-Wilson, James Tinn, and Shirley Williams. There is a still larger group of Members whose insights, frankness, and generosity with their time contributed significantly to whatever authenticity the study may have. Where we have got it right, it is usually due to their articulate explanations: John Davies, Sir Geoffrey De Frietas, Hugh Dykes, Tom Ellis, Michael Fidler, Nigel Fisher, Ted Garrett, John Gorst, Sir Harwood Harrison, Alan Haselhurst, John E. B. Hill, Douglas Houghton, Denis Howell, Cledwyn Hughes, John Jennings, Neil Kinnock, Sir Harry Legge-Bourke, Joan Lestor, Arthur Lewis, Michael McNair-Wilson, Ian Mikardo, Connie Monks, John Pardoe, Merlyn Rees, Ernest Perry, Reginald Prentice, Ivor Richard, Albert Roberts, Rafton Pounder, Sam Silkin, Julius Silverman, Geoffrey Johnson Smith, Harold Soref, H. Keith Speed, George Thomas, George Thomson, Peter Walker, George Wallace, and Bernard Weatherhill.

I have saved for last the fondest obligations, which are to my colleagues at the University of Essex who over the years became my friends, taught me about British politics and about Britain, introduced me to many British academics and nonacademics, taught me about good wine and good food, about real holidays and amusing dinner parties, about wonderful walks through the countryside, about kindness, generosity, sensibility, reliability, and trust. We have, since I first arrived with my family for a two-year stay in 1971, grown together into middle age and watched our children grow into adulthood. I could never have sustained either the research or myself for so long without their help. Perhaps they suspect that one not unimportant reason for my continuing interest in the study of British politics has been the excuse it gives me to return each year to Ireton Road in Colchester to rejoin them and renew our friendship: Anthony Barker and Lisa Barker, Jean Blondel, Michele Blondel and Tess Blondel, Ian Budge and Judith Budge, Ivor Crewe and Jill Crewe, Mary Frank and Peter Frank, Anthony King and Jan King, Virginia Sapiro and Graham Wilson.

If there is "a good read" in this book (and I very much hope that there is), it begins at the beginning of Chapter 2. That is where all non-political scientists should head forthwith, because the first chapter is devoted to professional nuts and bolts. It introduces the analytic framework that, if the work has been done the way I intended, is present but not prominent in the subsequent chapters, where Westminster's roles are reconstructed from the viewpoints of those who play them. I have made their viewpoints—the viewpoints of Members of Parliament—the touchstones for my interpretative explanations, because I believe that Peter Winch's wise advice about studying monks applies equally well to studying Members: "A [monk's] social relations with his fellows are permeated with his ideas about reality . . . it would be impossible to give more than a superficial account of those relations without taking into account the . . . ideas around which the monk's life revolves."[10]

INTRODUCTION: ROLES, RULES, AND RATIONALITY

> Each man makes his own role; that's
> what it comes to, you know.
>
> Labour backbencher

Who now writes about roles? Among others: sociologists, novelists, anthropologists, poets, psychologists, journalists, playwrights, and historians. The noun "role," which has been used since the seventeenth century, is a word that we cannot do without. And yet political scientists have done without it for nearly a decade. Articles continue to be produced on the topic, but they aren't much discussed. There aren't any major research projects under way on political roles. Nor are there signs of significant innovations in theory and method. It seems difficult to believe that studies of political roles actually dominated our research on politicians during the 1960s and early 1970s.

It is puzzling that professional interest in this area has declined, because roles are such prominent concepts in the everyday thinking of the politicians we study, quite regardless of what they might pick up second-hand from social science analyses. Politicians use roles in their relationships with one another. For central to the thinking that they bring to their relationships are conceptions of how typical people in typical positions (e.g., Minister, Whip, or backbencher) are expected to behave. Because so many ordinary people similarly use this concept to organize their experience, it has become well established throughout the social sciences and, with the exception of political science, continues to be studied vigorously.[1] Why the exception? There are, I think, three principal reasons that our discipline's interest in political roles has recently gone into eclipse. The first concerns intellectual fashion: a change in interdisciplinary tastes from sociological imports, which include roles, to economic imports, which do not. The second concerns conceptual confusion: a disenchantment with towers of babble constructed in the service of role "theories" that weren't theories after all. The third reason concerns consequences for behavior: there weren't any, or at least so it seemed at the time.

Perhaps these three reasons are enough to accept the eclipse and not try to recover the study of roles for the study of politicians. But I don't think so, principally because I believe that the roles of politicians are much too important to be overlooked. They are central concepts in the symbolic worlds of the people we study. They are also central concepts for the "new institutionalism" that has recently been emerging in political science.[2] Furthermore, and more forcefully, I believe that all three reasons for the neglect are unconvincing. Let us begin by examining each of them in turn and taking stock of several decades of research on politicians' roles, in order to clear the ground for a new motivational approach to the subject. This approach builds on what went before and satisfies some of the objections that came afterward by being more rational, less muddled, and better oriented to behavior.

Homo politicus, Homo sociologicus, or Homo economicus?

The recent march from *Homo sociologicus* to *Homo economicus* is more of an explanation of the decline of research on roles than a justification for it. This, the first of our three reasons behind the eclipse, will be difficult to dismiss as unconvincing, because it is as much a matter of changes in intellectual interest as of argument. Still, there is an argument here that needs to be addressed by putting it in the perspective of the relative significance of formal rules, informal rules, and individual preferences.

Before the Second World War, classic political views of political institutions were more widely held in political science than they are today, even now that we have brought the state back in. Political scientists and political philosophers emphasized that institutional structures greatly constrained the conduct of politics by shaping the motives and conduct of politicians. They stressed particularly the importance of formal rules such as constitutions, laws, contracts, and other institutional arrangements, stable formal rules that guided individual behavior and thereby secured order in the political world.[3] *Homo politicus* made history, but he made it on stages constructed by constitution makers and controlled by formal rules.

By contrast, the decades after the war, and especially the 1960s and early

1970s, witnessed the rejection of this formalistic political institutionalism and its replacement by new sociological perspectives. This sociological era of research on politicians turned the discipline's attention away from formal rules and toward the informal rules of political organizations, toward norms and roles that were said to guide behavior more directly.[4] But what was at first a set of creative and stimulating ideas became increasingly rigid and "sociologistic" as parliaments became characterized as highly structured institutions that, by determining their norms and roles, determined the behavior of their members.

Today, this sociological emphasis on informal rules is still one of two recognizable perspectives in the study of legislative behavior. The second, which took the lead from the mid-1970s and is now intellectually dominant in the United States, is associated with economic models of individual behavior, with models that are purposive, models that stress the significance of neither formal rules nor informal rules but, instead, of individual preferences and choices.[5] Thus, the informal rules, the norms and roles of *Homo sociologicus,* have been pushed aside by the reasons of *Homo economicus,* by a new interest in the preferences and calculations of individual politicians. Yet, just as the sociological approaches were shortsighted in giving short shrift to such individual preferences or goals, so the new economic models underestimate the significance of institutional contexts. Politicians, they seem to suggest, calculate their self-interests and act upon them in a vacuum.

Rules, roles, and reasons—these are ingredients that March and Olsen have proposed to blend in the new institutionalism.[6] This new perspective on the relationship between institutions and individuals has been emerging since the late 1980s and has come to be regarded as the new wave in legislative studies. It seeks to synthesize the political and sociological theses about rules with the economic antithesis about reasons. Formal and informal rules, March and Olsen argue, do indeed constitute very important institutional constraints on the behavior of politicians. At the same time, however, politicians are purposive actors who pursue their individual preferences or goals. They calculate and they compromise as they adapt to their situations. The new institutionalism offers fertile ground for the study of rational norms and rational roles, that is to say, norms and roles that are both framed by institutional rules and shaped by individual preferences. But the new institutionalism has thus far focused its investigations mainly on formal rules rather than on the informal rules whereby norms and roles play their parts.

This concentration on formal rules seems odd, not least because the study of organizations is currently moving in the other direction and has always, in fact, shifted back and forth between the formal and the informal. It has always recognized the significance of each and also their interdependence. Let us remind ourselves of the distinctions involved. The formal structure of an organization is found in its constitutional code, which defines lines of authority and divisions of work by specifying the organization's principal offices and their principal duties and responsibilities. These formal rules always differ, as Herbert Simon long ago taught us, from the organization's actual operations because they can never fully specify or be fully consistent with all the relationships, attitudes, and behaviors that must be developed if the organization is to run smoothly.[7]

The informal structure of an organization refers to these relationships, attitudes, and behaviors that are not fully specified in the formal scheme. Informal rules are critical to an organization, for it is not possible to operate without them. Every organization, therefore, develops and maintains a structure of informal rules. And the principal components of these informal rules are norms and roles.[8] The relationship between the formal and the informal is reciprocal and complex. The most obvious connection is that the formal rules set boundaries for the informal rules and thereby guide informal relationships along lines that are appropriate for pursuing the organization's goals. Perhaps the current resistance to studying informal rules like norms and roles reflects a reluctance to return to the sociological models that were set aside to pursue the new economic perspectives. Perhaps it is also due to the fact that many of the "new institutionalists" are rational choice theorists whose models favor explicit rules of the game that politicians can take into account in calculating how they might best achieve their preferences. For rational choice theorists, rules, are "the strategic context in which optimizing behavior takes place."[9] This characterization fits formal rules better than informal rules, which, in fact, often drive out calculational conduct and replace it with what March and Olsen call a disposition to pursue normatively appropriate behavior.[10] All the more reason, then, to reemphasize the importance of informal rules and to press the point that without them the new institutionalism may turn out, like its predecessors, to be rather more sectarian than synthetic.

It is a question of the relative significance of individual preferences, formal rules, and informal rules. From the new economic models, we have learned to take individual preferences and calculations very seriously. And those who have taken them most seriously are now reintroducing formal political rules such as constitutional and other institutional codes. *Homo economicus* is being reunited with *Homo politicus*. But what about the informal rules? Handicapped by a distaste for calculation, *Homo sociologicus* remains unwelcome because of further doubts about the political significance of informal rules, doubts that linger from our discipline's experience in studying relationships among norms, roles, and political behavior. With regard to roles, I shall address this matter below. But as for norms, if Jon Elster's recent arguments haven't convinced skeptics of the considerable significance of these informal rules, then perhaps the data in Table 1.1 will.[11]

The point is that informal rules are extremely effective in shaping the behavior of politicians—and therefore cannot be overlooked. Table 1.1 refers to collective responsibility rules in the House of Commons, rules that apply, conveniently for our present purposes, formally in one situation and informally in another. Thus, the formal rule of collective responsibility, which is a long-standing and important constitutional doctrine, applies to Members of the Government. It says, among other things, that if they wish to vote against government policy, they must first resign from the Government and return to the backbenches. By contrast, the informal rule of collective responsibility, which applies to Opposition Front Bench Spokesmen, has no constitutional or formal standing. It is instead a norm that has developed during the postwar period, a norm that says if they wish to vote against their party's policy, they too should first resign their leadership positions and return to the backbenches.[12]

The relative influence of formal and informal rules can be explored in

Table 1.1 Cross-votes by formal and informal rules of collective responsibility, in percent

	Conservatives*		Labour*	
Cross-votes	Formal collective responsibility applies (members of the government)	Collective responsibility does not apply (backbenchers)	Informal collective responsibility applies (opposition front bench spokesmen)	Collective responsibility does not apply (backbenchers)
None	100	39	62	23
One	0	22	20	29
Two or more	0	39	18	48
Total	100	100	100	100
	(N = 42)	(N = 202)	(N = 50)	(N = 174)

Note: Cross-votes are votes cast against the stated policy of one's government (for Conservatives in this case) or one's parliamentary party (for Labour).

*$p \leq .001$. Since this is not a probability sample, conventional significance tests are not, strictly speaking, appropriate. Nevertheless, they will be reported to give a general sense of the strength or weakness of associations. Given the very large proportion of the population sampled, these tests will usually be extremely conservative indicators.

Table 1.1 by comparing the number of cross-votes cast by Members of the Government, who are under the *formal* collective responsibility rule, and the number cast by Opposition Front Bench Spokesmen, who are under the *informal* collective responsibility rule, with the number of cross-votes cast by their respective backbenchers, who are not encumbered by either of these constraints. To be sure, the formal rule of collective responsibility has the strongest absolute effects over the behavior of those Conservatives to whom it applies—there are no deviations. But the informal rule of collective responsibility is impressive as well. In fact, it ensures that nearly three times as many of Labour's Opposition Front Bench Spokesmen as compared to the party's backbenchers refrain from cross-voting—a ratio that exceeds the parallel ratio between Conservatives.[13]

The new institutionalism seeks to free politicians from their utilitarian cocoons and send them back into the institutional contexts where they work and pursue their goals. Yet, important as formal and informal rules may be, it is necessary to remember that individual preferences are active too. Indeed, the unfortunate sociological history of role theory's "oversocialized" analyses should caution us against tilting the enterprise too far back toward the institutional side. The reintegration of the formal institutional rules of the prewar period with the informal rules of the postwar sociological decades can be done without losing sight of what has been learned more recently by looking through economic spectacles. What is needed is a new conception of roles that is sensitive to the interplay between institutional frameworks and individual preferences—and to the fact that this balance between framework and preference varies greatly from one role to another.

The best way to understand political institutions is to understand the interaction between such rules and reasons, between the constraints of institutional frameworks and the preferences or goals of individual members. And there is no place where such rules and reasons come together more clearly than in an institution's roles. This leads directly to the motivational approach. But first it is necessary to dispose of the remaining two objections to role analysis itself.

Conceptual Confusion

Another reason that the discipline set the study of roles aside was weariness with the conceptual confusion surrounding role theories—which were themselves eventually unmasked as untheories. However, this reason too can be shown to be unconvincing, in this case by clearing up the clutter. The task can be accomplished in three steps: (a) by sending most of the neologisms down the memory holes of history; (b) by clarifying why role theory is not a theory and cannot be a theory; and (c) by ordering and interpreting the existing literature, and particularly the existing empirical studies, so that we can see where we have been and where we need to go.

Efforts to study roles in the most general terms have produced some of the most spectacular scholasticism in the social sciences.[14] This has been created by many different scholars studying many different roles from the perspective of many different disciplines. Although it is appropriate to develop different definitions for different research purposes, conceptual pluralism was turned into pandemonium by an extraordinary passion for neologisms that often contained very peculiar assumptions about the determinants of behavior.[15] "Role" as a noun was modified by long lists of adjectives to create concepts like these: covert roles, complementary roles, reciprocal roles, contextualized roles, personalized roles. "Role" as an adjective was used to produce more of the same, such as role visibility, role enactments, role sets, role integration, role networks.

I have suggested that role theory is not a theory. What is usually called role theory are frameworks that consist of topics, concepts, and assumptions. There are in such frameworks no sets of statements that explain why or how phenomena occur. There are, in short, no general role theories.[16] The difficulty is that this quest for a general theory of roles has always been fundamentally misguided and as unlikely to produce satisfying results as would be a quest for a general theory of holes. The phenomena in question, roles or holes, are so utterly polymorphic that the only general statements applicable to all of them are likely to be as general (and as useless) as this: "The general principle is clear: the more persons have their preferences and needs met in role relationships, the more satisfied they are in those relationships."[17] The most promising path to explanation is not a search for a single general role theory, but instead a series of quests for particular explanations about particular types of roles in particular types of institutional contexts.

Finally, it is necessary to bring some order to decades of seemingly discursive literature so that we can build constructively rather than simply continue to muddle through. Fortunately, the waters have cleared somewhat since political scientists last looked; and it has become apparent that most studies have more or less proceeded under one or more of the frameworks summarized in Table 1.2. Each framework concentrates on a different aspect of the subject. Thus, the structural approach highlights connections between institutions and roles. The interactional approach focuses on the processes through which roles are learned. And the motivational approach focuses on the content of roles and particularly on the goals and incentives that drive them.

Just as parliamentary and legislative studies do not neatly sort themselves

Table 1.2 Approaches to studying the roles of politicians

Approach	Principal topics	Preferred research methods	Examples[a]
Structural	Sets of norms linked to performance of institutional functions	Structured interviews with large numbers of respondents, using both open- and closed-ended questions to examine norms	Wahlke, Eulau, Buchanan, and Ferguson; Davidson; Newton; Jewell and Patterson; Converse and Pierce
Interactional	Interaction in specific settings; negotiation and learning of roles	Participant observation or in-depth studies with manageable numbers of respondents	Huitt; Manley; Fenno; Cain, Ferejohn and Fiorina
Motivational	Description of roles emphasizing the influence of goals and incentives	Semistructured interviews with moderate-sized samples; preference for tape-recording responses	Matthews; Barber; Woshinsky; King; Aberbach, Putnam, and Rockman; Payne

a. Joel D. Aberbach, Robert D. Putnam, and Bert A. Rockman, *Bureaucrats and Politicians in Western Democracies* (Cambridge, Mass.: Harvard University Press, 1981); James David Barber, *The Lawmakers: Recruitment and Adaptation to Legislative Life* (New Haven: Yale University Press, 1965); Bruce E. Cain, John A. Ferejohn, and Morris P. Fiorina, "The House Is Not a Home: British MPs in Their Constituencies," *Legislative Studies Quarterly* 4,4 (November 1979), 501–523; Philip E. Converse and Roy Pierce, *Political Representation in France* (Cambridge, Mass.: Harvard University Press, 1986); Roger H. Davidson, *The Role of the Congressman* (New York: Bobbs-Merrill, 1969); Richard F. Fenno, "U.S. House Members in Their Constituencies," *American Political Science Review* 73, 1 (September 1977), 883–917; Ralph K. Huitt, "The Outsider in the Senate: An Alternative Role," *American Political Science Review* 55, 3 (September 1961), 566–575; Malcolm E. Jewell and Samuel C. Patterson, *The Legislative Process in the United States,* 3rd ed. (New York: Random House, 1977); Anthony King, *British Members of Parliament: A Self-Portrait* (London: Macmillan, 1974); John F. Manley, "Wilbur D. Mills: A Study in Congressional Influence," *American Political Science Review* 63, 2 (June 1969), 442–464; Donald R. Matthews, *U.S. Senators and Their World* (New York: Random House, 1960); K. Newton, "Role Orientations and Their Sources among Elected Representatives in English Local Politics," *Journal of Politics* 36, 3 (August 1974), 615–636; James L. Payne, "Show Horses and Work Horses in the United States House of Representatives," *Polity* 12, 3 (Spring 1980), 428–456; John Wahlke, Heinz Eulau, William Buchanan, and Leroy Ferguson, *The Legislative System* (New York: Wiley, 1962); Oliver H. Woshinsky, *The French Deputy* (Lexington, Mass.: D. C. Heath and Co., 1973).

into the sociological and economic traditions discussed above, neither do they neatly sort themselves into these three approaches to role analysis. Most efforts have been eclectic, and many authors will be uncomfortable with seeing their work categorized in this way. Nevertheless, I believe that there are three identifiable streams of research on the roles of politicians, each influenced more by one of the three approaches than by the others. The studies within each stream share many features with one another and at least several important features with the general approach under whose umbrella I have gathered them together.[18]

THE STRUCTURAL APPROACH

The structural approach, an application of structural-functional analysis, was developed under the guidance of Linton, Merton, Znaniecki, and Parsons.[19] It emphasizes the dominance of institutions over individuals and treats roles as constructs that are maintained by institutions and have little to do with individual preferences.[20] Individuals are presented with roles that are built into an institution's structure, roles that will continue to exist whether or not these individuals choose to play them.

The main difficulty with the structural approach as an all-purpose strategy for studying roles is that it introduces, through its definitions, two important but unacceptable assumptions. The first is that there will normally be widespread consensus about how any given role should be played. Actually, such consensus varies enormously from one role to another. It is a variable.[21] The second unacceptable assumption is that the individual's role-related attitudes and behaviors are determined by the expectations of his or her associates. Again, the power of such expectations is surely a variable that differs across different roles and institutions.[22] By the mid-1970s, this emphasis on conformity had cost the structural framework its position as the dominant approach to role analysis.[23] Ironically, however, the most important contemporary contribution of the structural approach continues to be its emphasis on what it has always overemphasized: that roles are deeply embedded in institutions that structure both the range of roles available and how particular roles are to be played. The structural approach takes structure seriously.

THE INTERACTIONAL APPROACH

The interactional approach is part of the symbolic interactionist tradition that traces its intellectual roots back to the Scottish Moral Philosophers of the eighteenth century.[24] This perspective was adapted for contemporary social science by George Herbert Mead and is associated with the influential empirical work of Turner, Blumer, and Goffman.[25] Symbolic interactionism derives its unusual name from its assumption that symbols, or meanings, emerge from processes of social interaction and serve as powerful forces in shaping behavior. Thus, roles are seen as sets of informal rules created and recreated through interactions and especially through negotiations between individuals and their associates.[26]

Symbolic interactionists concentrate so much on these social psychological negotiations that they have been criticized for being "psychologistic," for making exactly the opposite error to that made by the structuralists: for neglecting the broader institutional contexts within which such negotiations occur.[27] It is striking, therefore, that this approach, which gives so much attention to how people construct the rules that govern their behavior, nevertheless still locks up its subjects in social cages. But that is exactly what symbolic interactionism does, because it does not adequately credit people with their own independent standpoints, with their own preferences and incentives outside the flow of interaction in which they are immersed at any given time.[28] The psychologistic cage, in fact, turns out to be sociologistic. Society produces individuals through role relationships that reshape them constantly. Compared with structural frameworks, these interactional cages are much smaller (encounters rather than institutions); but they are sociologistic cages nonetheless, not psychologistic.[29] Still, the chief contribution of the interactional approach remains its emphasis on the facts that individuals participate in defining their own roles, that these roles have many variations, and that they are usually undergoing change.[30]

THE MOTIVATIONAL APPROACH

Unlike its counterparts, the motivational framework has not been unfolded in abstract theoretical discussions. It is instead found in empirical studies of politicians' roles and in the minds of the politicians themselves. After we consider the third objection to role analysis, the objection based on behavior, I will return to this motivational approach to develop it more fully in the context of the new institutionalism, for this is the approach that will be applied in this book. For the present, several distinctive features will suffice. First of all, many of the career goals and emotional incentives that politicians use in adapting to their institutions are, the motivational approach assumes, acquired before they take up their posts. Second, this approach stresses that rationality is a dominant feature of the parliamentary institutions in which the roles of politicians are embedded. Third, rationality in the thinking of politicians is believed to afford them perspectives and agendas that are independent of their current interactions.

Thus, when Cayrol, Parodi, and Ysmal asked French deputies to define their roles, they defined them in terms of what they did.[31] The motivational approach suggests that the best way to understand the roles of politicians is to try to see them as they do.[32] This is what Heady's study of the roles of British Ministers was designed to capture: "a Minister's-eye view of his job." Heady's semistructured interviews focused on recognizable outlooks and patterns of conduct. The first question he put to his Ministers was, "What are the most important tasks a Minister has to perform?" They told him about their "priorities" and "role conceptions."[33] Since this goal-oriented outlook is the way that politicians usually characterize their own roles, it should not be surprising to find the same tack being taken by many political commentators and historians.[34] When Sir Lewis Namier constructed his influential account of the roles played by eighteenth-century MPs, he paid very close attention to their motivations.[35]

The roles in motivational studies are very much like the "purposive roles" of Wahlke and his associates, roles driven by a politician's main purposes.[36] These images of politicians as rational, goal-oriented actors are incorporated in role typologies and in the variables that underlie them. Matthews' study of United States Senators, for instance, used the criteria of status and accomplishments to generate types with strong purposive characteristics, types such as Patrician and Agitator.[37] Jewell regards as leading examples of purposive studies many of the same ones that I am characterizing here as motivational, including work by Wahlke and associates, Woshinsky, Barber, and Davidson.[38] His inclusion of Woshinsky and Barber's studies is particularly noteworthy because they are more explicitly motivational than the other two and demonstrate how purposive roles fit within a more fully developed motivational framework.

Reasons shape role choices and interpretations in Woshinsky's study of fifty French deputies. Woshinsky draws heavily upon Barber, who also emphasizes that politicians shape their own roles.[39] Indeed, one of the most striking characteristics of Barber's study is the artful way in which it focuses on the individual without losing sight of the institutional context. This was the principal aim of his investigation: to examine how politicians with different individual characteristics adapt to legislative institutions. Barber's incentive-based study can be contrasted with the work of Richard Fenno, who has likewise paid close attention to motivations but has emphasized instead cognitive goals. This interest in goals was developed furthest in *Congressmen in Committees,* where Fenno dismantled purposive roles to investigate the specific "personal political goals" within them, goals like influence in the House and reelection.[40]

The great strength of the motivational studies is that they try to take careful account of political reality as it is experienced by the politicians who construct it. Thus, they favor the meaning of the role concept in ordinary language: *the part one plays in an event or a process.* To reconstruct such roles satisfactorily, it makes good sense to try to understand them as they are understood by their players, as dynamic interactions between rules and reasons, between institutional constraints and individual preferences.

Consequences for Behavior

The third unconvincing reason behind the neglect of role research in political science was disappointment over the failure to connect role-related attitudes to behavior.[41] Under the aegis of the structural approach, early studies introduced the role concept as a key that would unlock the door between institutional structure and individual behavior. But as it turned out, measures of the structurally defined roles of "delegate" and "trustee," the two most widely studied roles in the literature, failed to yield the anticipated relationships. Most studies found no positive results. And one study found that delegates were, paradoxically, much less likely than were trustees to vote their constituents' wishes.[42] Definitely disappointing. But the conclusion drawn (that roles are in general unrelated to behavior and are therefore trivial matters that need not be investigated) was wholly unconvincing, because it was based on peculiar claims and concepts.

What was peculiar about the claims was the assumption that roles must be insignificant unless they are linked clearly to decision-taking activities such as voting or putting down Questions, as opposed to, say, deliberative activities such as political thinking or political conversation.[43] Surely mental constructs like roles can be politically significant without directly affecting how politicians vote. Still, it would be encouraging to see some impact on decision-taking activities too, on traditional measures of political behavior. But much of that was missed entirely because of the concepts in terms of which these tests were conceived. One difficulty was the failure to distinguish between position roles and preference roles. Another was to mistake the usual measures of delegates and trustees for measures of roles that exist in the minds of most politicians.

Parliaments are structured by networks of positions such as Whip, Parliamentary Private Secretary, Minister, and backbencher. Position roles are associated with positions that require the performance of many specific duties and responsibilities. Preference roles, by contrast, are associated with positions that require the performance of few specific duties and responsibilities. Now it must seem obvious, once it is stated, that position roles, like the roles of Whips, Parliamentary Private Secretaries, and Ministers in Britain, are typically as chock-full of behavior as they are politically important. No one would suggest that links might not exist between position roles like these and traditional forms of behavior. As part of their roles, Whips, for example, are required to roam the House touching base with Members, to attend committees and take notes for the Chief Whip, and to sit in the Chamber and help the Speaker activate procedure. Parliamentary Private Secretaries are not required to do nearly as much. But no one would suggest that they do nothing. In the same vein, Ministers vote a lot, for they are required to do so. They also answer Questions and make statements at the Despatch Box. They listen in committees. They seek support in corridors. And they drink with backbenchers in Westminster's bars. Surely the conclusion that roles are unrelated to behavior does not apply to position roles like these at all.

Instead, the conclusion could only conceivably be applied to preference roles associated with positions like that of the backbencher, positions where very little specific behavior is actually required of incumbents, where there are very few duties and responsibilities that incumbents *must* do but very many they *might* (or might not) do. Associated with the position of the backbencher, for instance, are the preference roles of Constituency Member, Parliament Man, Policy Advocate, and Ministerial Aspirant. Many of the roles that have been examined in survey-based studies of politicians are preference roles like these. And they have nearly as much to do with the preferences of the role players as with the established rules of the institution. These are the sorts of roles, presumably, to which the conclusion about the lack of connections between roles and behavior was intended to apply.

But this conclusion was drawn from data on delegates and trustees, from constructs that existed in the minds of many social scientists rather than in the minds of many of the politicians we studied. Moreover, the items used to tap these constructs look, in retrospect, less like measures of roles than like measures of a very specific norm or decision rule. Thus, the representational "roles" of delegates and trustees were assessed with a question about whether representatives should be guided primarily by their constituents or by their own judgments. Now such a norm could indeed be the pivot of a full-blown role. But in that case, the politicians who play the role would, in their minds and their conduct, associate the norm with a package of desires, beliefs, and behaviors typical of people who play this part—which apparently they did not do.

These representational roles of ours were at the time the most widely investigated in the discipline. But they may not have been theirs: they may not have corresponded to the structure or the content of the roles that existed in the minds of the people we were studying.[44] Nevertheless, they weren't even unrelated to behavior. Later and closer looks suggested that the failure to connect them to behavior may have been due to the fact that other variables were involved in the relationships. Hence, one reaction to the negative findings was to reconceptualize the representational role concept.[45] Another was to look more carefully for the relationships to behavior. Eventually, these links were found by focusing on salient policy issues where cues from the district were consistent. They were also found by taking account of the fact that the constituencies politicians think about may vary from issue to issue.[46] In sum, the overall empirical results do not look so disappointing after all. But they were disappointing at the time. And, coming on the edge of the march from sociological to economic models, and on top of disenchantments with conceptual muddles, the early findings about this *norm* helped to lock up the study of political *roles* in the cupboard.

The motivational approach suggests that by directing our concepts and measures toward roles as politicians themselves conceive of them, we will be in the best possible position to explain the behavior that is inherent in such roles. It will be unnecessary to concern ourselves with position roles like the role of the Minister, since I assume that by now no one would suggest that what Ministers think about the parts they are playing has nothing to do with their conduct. Instead we shall focus our attention on preference roles, on roles that are grounded as much in the preferences of the individual as in the rules of the institution.

From this perspective, as the motivational preference roles are reconstructed in the following chapters, we shall see numerous examples of relationships between desires and beliefs on the one side and behaviors on the other. We shall see Ideologues who promote propaganda, Generalists who barrage the executive with Oral and Written Questions, and Specialists who immerse themselves in Select Committees. We shall find Constituency Members at their surgeries (advice bureaus) and local factories, and Parliament Men back at the House. Other backbenchers will be expressing their preference roles by dissenting in the division lobbies, developing convivial contacts in the corridors, or witnessing history in the Chamber. Many of the desires, beliefs, and behaviors in these preference roles, moreover, are inherently intertwined—so much so that where we do not find relationships between a role's hypothesized desires and beliefs on the one side and behaviors on the other, the most appropriate inference may be not that the two sides are, in general, unrelated, but that we have got the wrong desires and beliefs.

I hope that enough has been said to render unconvincing this third reason for the neglect of interest in political roles, as unconvincing as the first and second reasons. Still, it is not sufficient simply to counter the chief objections. What is needed is a new agenda that will help us to build on what was done during the 1960s and 1970s and also to improve upon it.

The Motivational Approach and Situational Analysis

The motivational approach offers the most promising framework with which to proceed. Its chief recommendation is that it encourages the reconstruction of political roles as they are understood by their players. Moreover, it builds on studies of purposive roles by articulating what has been implicit in such studies and by adding those elements that are necessary to give them their proper due.

CONSTRAIN AND ENABLE

Thus, the motivational approach incorporates insights from both the sociological (structural and interactional) and the economic traditions. It integrates these two traditions by recognizing that the roles of politicians are embedded in institutional contexts while, at the same time, treating the role players as purposive actors with independent standpoints. This integration of sociological and economic perspectives reflects, therefore, a recognition that political roles both constrain their actors and enable them.[47] Hence, the motivational approach brings *Homo sociologicus* and *Homo economicus* into a flexible framework suitable for studying *Homo politicus*.

The image of people as conformists, the image of *Homo sociologicus*, is surely needed in some form to account for the fact that roles do greatly constrain their actors. Systems of constitutional and other formal rules specify the principal positions around which roles develop. The positions of Whip, Minister, and backbencher exist in Parliament, for example, because formal rules create them. The politicians who take up such positions, however, help to create the corresponding roles, which then become part of the institution's informal structure. Such roles vary greatly in the degree to which they are determined by the institution's formal structure. The most clearly defined and highly constrained are, as we have seen, the position roles for which the scripts are officially written in the many duties and responsibilities that are assigned to them. While the scripts of these formal roles always leave some room for interpretation, they specify not only the many tasks to be performed but also the chief goals that constitute the roles' motivational cores.

Preference roles, by contrast, are much less constrained by the institution and therefore more easily shaped by the preferences of the role players. As

informal roles, they allow considerably more scope for interpretation. Notice, however, that even on Westminster's backbenches, where the formal
rules specify very few duties and responsibilities, the roles shaped by individual preferences are far fewer than the number of backbenchers involved,
and predate and postdate the individuals who play them. In fact, only four
major preference roles are associated with the position of the backbencher,
each framed by one of Parliament's institutional tasks: checking the executive (Policy Advocates); maintaining institutional structures (Parliament
Men); making Ministers (Ministerial Aspirants); and redressing grievances
(Constituency Members). Backbenchers make their roles with a view to
making themselves useful in the established framework of roles that they
find at Westminster. They pass over some of these roles, adopt others, and
then interpret and modify them to suit their preferences. They certainly do
make their own roles, but they make them in and for Westminster's world.
They certainly can do whatever they like—but they don't.

Still, roles also enable their players. Position and preference roles enable
them to pursue their individual goals. The motivational approach makes
room for this rationality and also takes account of it by providing for an
independent standpoint, for a quiet place within the bustle of interaction
where the actors' own preferences can shape their role choices and interpretations. Here it draws upon economic models, for these are the models that,
more than any others in the social sciences, recognize the autonomy of the
individual self in individualistic cultures like our own and thereby afford
actors independent standpoints. In traditional societies, the self was usually
defined by social identities (cousin, member of a certain village) that could
never be stripped away to discover the "real me." In our modern world,
however, the self has become increasingly distinct from the particular roles
it may be playing at any given time and increasingly able to understand,
evaluate, choose among, and reshape these roles to suit its private agenda.[48]

And yet, as Hollis and Smith point out, the very narrow economic definition of rationality is too narrow for the study of political roles; having *Homo
economicus* do calculations will not give us what we need.[49] If the new institutionalism is to be truly a synthesis, it needs a rationality principle that is
less constricting and more like rationality as understood in ordinary language: the exercise of reason in the service of desire. Hume taught us that
only desire can supply the motivation for which reason seeks paths to satisfaction. The difficulty with economic models is that their much needed emphasis on cognition and calculation sometimes obscures the wide variety of
desires that constitute and reshape our goals—and also our judgments about
which courses of action will most effectively satisfy these goals. Nonetheless,

rational principles of the kind we need can be found in some of the same roots from which economists have taken their cues.[50]

SITUATIONAL ANALYSIS

Thus, the situational analysis that was originally recommended to the social sciences by Popper and Weber and recently reconstructed by James Farr[51] is a particularly robust framework for the new institutionalism and the motivational approach. I have used it in this book to bring in institutions, bring back rationality, and integrate naturalistic and interpretative strategies of inquiry. Situational analysis, in Farr's reconstruction, consists of two central components: the *situational model* and the *rationality principle*. The situational model includes an account of the institutional environment in which the action takes place and an account of the problem situation in which the role players find themselves. The problem situation is the key, for this is the account of the relevant institutional rules, formal and informal, and of the desires and beliefs of the actors. Situations in which politicians find themselves range from the typical to the unique. Role constructs are built around typical situations. They suggest how, in such situations, politicians typically think and act.

The rationality principle here is a methodological assumption (albeit examined wherever possible as an empirical hypothesis) that we make in order to complete the explanation of politicians' role behavior. In the absence of evidence to the contrary, we assume that our subjects are acting purposefully. And we therefore explain their role behavior, as has been done in the motivational sections of the following chapters, by providing an account that suggests how this behavior is "logically" connected to the desires and beliefs that are characteristic of their roles, that is to say, by showing how the behavior is "adequate to the situation" *as the actors understand the situation*. This method works best when we can study the actor's own explanations of his or her behavior directly through either transcribed interviews or historical materials. And the assumption makes sense because, as economic models remind us, politicians are indeed usually rational even when they are not the egoistic, calculating utility maximizers of economic theory.

The purpose of the rationality principle is to help us reconstruct the reasons or rationales that actors actually have for acting as they do. The task requires a definition of rationality that is more philosophical than economic. Something like the following: a "coherent set of desires and beliefs that lead the actors to act as they do in the given situation."[52] This rationality presumes that actors have the ability to analyze and shape roles in accordance with their own desires. Thus, politicians bring to Westminster personal goals that they modify through experience and that lead them to particular roles. In these roles, they interpret and combine characteristic desires (career goals and emotional incentives) with beliefs (about how Parliament works, for instance) and with typical patterns of behavior. These patterns of behavior are usually understood by the actors as being *inherent* in the desires and beliefs that give rise to them. It is inappropriate, therefore, to model the dynamics of such roles primarily as calculating processes.[53] In fact, much of the thinking involved is heuristic reasoning, and much of the behavior is more rule-driven than optimizing. Even when politicians seem to be undertaking cost-benefit analyses of their career choices, they may be constructing instead rationalizations for dispositions at which they have already arrived, rationally.[54]

The nature of this connection between desires and beliefs on the one hand, and actions on the other, has often divided proponents of interpretative and naturalistic social science.[55] The dominant view at present is that such connections are not causal, or if they are to be considered causal, then the appropriate concept of causality is different from that used in the natural sciences. This distinction makes an important difference, for the dominant view would have us place a premium on understanding the reasons of the role players as they themselves understand them, while nesting the interpretative enterprise (and the study of roles) at the center of a framework of naturalistic explanation.

This view of reasonable people adapting to the rules of institutions is very much the way that politicians themselves think about their roles.[56] They think about them as we think about individual characters: not as "bundles of autonomous traits" but rather as "organized conceptions," as patterns, as configurations of goals, attitudes, and behaviors that are characteristic of people in particular positions.[57] This conception of political roles provides the basis for the synthesis we have been pursuing between reasons and rules, for this is a conception of reasonable actors pursuing preferences in roles shaped by institutional structures. It is depicted in Figure 1.1. It is fortified by our interview transcripts which suggest that British politicians use the term "role" to refer to the part one plays in an event or process and conceive of these parts as organized conceptions, as patterns of interrelated characteristics.

Political roles, then, are particular patterns of interrelated *goals, attitudes,* and *behaviors* that are characteristic of people in particular positions. These three terms are used by politicians and by political scientists who try to make sense of the world at Westminster. Politicians also use the terms that

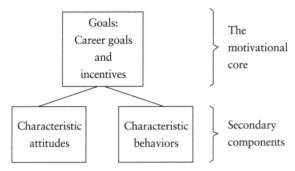

Figure 1.1 The motivational approach:
Principal components of politicians' roles

philosophers prefer—"desires," "beliefs," and "actions." In the motivational approach, goals constitute the core of roles because they constitute the motivational drive. They include both *career goals* and *emotional incentives* since, as Charles Taylor puts it, "our actions are ordinarily characterized by the purposes sought and explained by desires, feelings, emotions."[58] The career goals are usually focused on the institution. Indeed, they are often defined by the institution or at least defined with an eye to the institution's structure. They have therefore sometimes been characterized as cognitive goals and sometimes as institutional goals. Emotional incentives, by contrast, are usually focused on the individual role player; and, because they are likely to be defined by him or her, they are sometimes called personal incentives.

Cognitive career goals play a prominent part in parliamentary roles, since the thinking that politicians do about their careers is relatively more conscious and strategic than in many other areas of their experience. The more established and institutionalized a role is, the more likely the balance between its career goals and emotional incentives will be weighted on the cognitive side. Thus, position roles are more cognitively controlled than are preference roles; more of what their role players do and think is formally specified by institutional rules about which they are more aware and analytic. In very highly institutionalized position roles, like that of the Minister, preference-oriented subtypes can also be rooted in assigned responsibilities that all players must perform. Nonetheless, even in the most highly institutionalized position roles, emotional incentives are intertwined with the cognitive career goals and play a very important part in their interpretation and application. Emotional incentives are the principal energizing forces in all parliamentary roles.

The nature of the relationship between the career goals and the emotional incentives is that the emotional incentives provide the "passion"; they intensify the striving that is inherent in the career goals.[59] Their contribution is more obvious, and even more influential, in preference roles where very few duties and responsibilities are formally specified. The career goal of representation, for example, orients Constituency Members' thinking about their roles. But it is substantially shaped as well as energized by two emotional incentives, a sense of duty and a sense of competence, with which it is closely related in the minds of the role players. Actually, three types of relationships between career goals and emotional incentives are apparent in the parliamentary roles we shall examine. Thus, emotional incentives not only intensify the striving in the career goals, and not only shape the interpretations and applications of these goals; they also in some cases precede the goals and structure choices among them. Some Constituency Members, for instance, clearly came to Westminster with the desire to fulfill a sense of duty or a sense of competence and chose the career goal of constituency service, in part, on this basis.

As politicians play roles, they modify their existing goals and develop new ones in order to adapt to institutional environments and problem situations. This learning process occurs slowly in reaction to new experiences and becomes part of their evolving interpretations of their roles. It proceeds through both sociological "sublimation" and economic "calculation." Thus, in the motivational approach, the preferences of politicians are not treated as wholly exogenous to the institutional context, as they are in economic models. There are, as we shall see, just too many examples of MPs who explain convincingly how they adjust their utilities to their changing career situations.[60] Those unable to do this, they will tell us, run the risk of "souring their souls."

At the same time, of course, political actors adjust their existing roles or take up new ones to suit changes in their goals, a process that has a much better fit with economic than with sociological perspectives. Ministerial Aspirants, for instance, are strong on ambition and often manage to reshape their backbench roles with strategies that "make a mark," that "strengthen their positions" and help ensure that when the time comes to be judged, their goals will be fulfilled. Career goals and emotional incentives are equally important factors in choices among backbench roles and in choices about whether or not to take up offers of leadership roles. There is nothing very complicated about it: people seek out roles whose typical goals seem compatible with their own personal goals. Thus, backbenchers with a strong desire for influence will be attracted to the role of the Policy Advocate; and, among them, those whose emotional incentives include a taste for action and diversity will tend to play this role in the key of the Generalist.

Now let us consider the relationships between a role's motivational core and the attitudes and behaviors that politicians typically associate with it. To pursue the Constituency Member as an example, a typical attitude would be the belief that "the redress of grievances is extremely important." A typical behavior would be "spending a great deal of time in the constituency." Like the relationships within the motivational core, the relationships between the core and these attitudes and behaviors are subject to investigation rather than fixed by definition. They also vary in strength from one role to another and from one individual to another, notwithstanding that the collective pattern defines the role. Specific behaviors are included as integral parts of the roles because that is how politicians themselves see it.[61]

Here too the motivational approach expects to find independent standpoints and rationality. It expects that the roles politicians construct around their goals will usually be constructed reasonably. This is ensured by the role players themselves, who assess and reassess their goals and adopt appropriate attitudes and behaviors. They evaluate the outcomes of their performances and, in this light, adjust both the goals and the attitudes and behaviors. All these ongoing adjustments are constrained by institutional structures that restrict greatly the range as well as the interpretations of the evolving roles. Yet, within these constraints, important adjustments are created by rational actors whose motivations include more than self-interest and whose rationality is more familiar to philosophers than to economists.[62] In sum, the roles of politicians are dynamic and adaptive patterns of goals, attitudes, and behaviors.

The Motivational Approach and Explanation

Interpretative explanations work well with the motivational approach and with the new institutionalism, because their two dominant features fit perfectly with these research programs: a focus on *rules,* and a focus on *choice.*[63] Thus, interpretative explanations are associated more than anything else with an interest in formal and informal rules and how these rules are followed. And interpretative explanations are equally concerned with the phenomena of individual choice, intention, and meaning, with the connections among desires, beliefs, and actions.

EXPLAINING ROLES

Most of the explanations in the following chapters are interpretative ones that provide accounts of role behavior by providing accounts of the rules and reasoned choices that are embedded in roles. We make our reconstructions of such roles intelligible by *identifying and describing* these rules and reasoned choices—in other words, we *explain* the roles by identifying and describing the relevant sets of characteristic desires, beliefs, and behaviors and their interconnections. The point requires emphasis, because many political scientists are unfamiliar with thinking about explanation in this way: from the viewpoint of contemporary work in the philosophy of social science, the best explanation of a political role would be an essentially descriptive account that renders the role intelligible by identifying its principal desires, beliefs, and behaviors and the connections among them. The weakness in much research on political roles is not, as charged, that it has been too descriptive, but rather that much of this description has been done through the lenses of standardized cross-national concepts that are too far removed from the roles in the minds of particular politicians to explain those roles successfully. Thus, this book, which is essentially descriptive, is at the same time essentially explanatory. But how are its interpretative microexplanations related to naturalistic macrotheoretical frameworks?

When we focus on roles and look inside them to analyze their components (desires, beliefs, and behaviors), we are usually dealing with "person facts" and interpretative explanations. But when we treat these roles as dependent or independent variables, we are usually dealing with them as "group facts" and using naturalistic explanations. These interpretative and naturalistic enterprises are complementary in that the findings of each provide matters for inquiry by the other: "inquiries in the one perspective move to the boundaries of the other and hand over the work."[64] A role's attitudinal components (desires and beliefs) can be thought of as proximate attitudes intertwined with behavior. The reconstruction of these proximate attitudes and behaviors constitutes an interpretative explanation. Now one of the most important ways that this interpretative explanation becomes nested in more-naturalistic macroexplanations is by constructing generalizations that link it back to more-contingent systemic factors that structure the experiences through which the attitudes are learned. Investigations of these origins of roles help us to explain them more fully. We also explain them more fully by investigating their consequences.

ORIGINS AND CONSEQUENCES

Thus, although this book concentrates on person facts and interpretative explanations, its findings—the roles it reconstructs—can become group facts that raise questions for naturalistic explanations, questions about the systemic and institutional *origins* of these roles and questions about their systemic and institutional *consequences*. "Intention" is the focus of interpretative explanations, whereas "causation" is the focus of naturalistic explanations. I shall explore these matters throughout the chapters and particularly in the conclusion, where I consider changes in the distribution of parliamentary roles over time and relationships between them and institutional rules. Here, suffice it to provide several illustrations from naturalistic explanations that are offered in the book. First, roles as dependent variables: the rise of the Welfare State, a systemic change on the origins side, has altered the distribution of backbench roles by increasing the number of Constituency Members. Likewise, roles as independent variables: an increase in the intensity of personal ambition in ministerial roles has contributed to constitutional changes and triggered a movement for constitutional reform.

Moreover, it should be clear from these sketches of naturalistic explanations that they frequently presuppose interpretative explanations. For in order to explain satisfactorily how systemic changes modify particular roles, or how changes in particular roles promote institutional consequences, it is necessary to have as part of the naturalistic explanation an interpretative account of the roles' principal desires, beliefs, and behaviors. The behavior of political actors may not always be at the center of macroanalytic explanations of systems, institutional structures, or policy outputs—but it usually is, if not explicitly then implicitly.[65] Thus, we need to know something substantial about the nature of constituency member roles in order to explain how the rise of the Welfare State could lead politicians to the personal career goals that would lead them to these roles; we need to know something substantial about the nature of ministerial roles in order to explain why increases in the intensity of particular desires within these roles might lead to constitutional misdemeanors and reform movements.

It does not, however, seem to work the other way round. Interpretative explanations do not presuppose naturalistic explanations in the same way that the latter presuppose the former. Nevertheless, they need them. For studies of political roles to do nothing beyond identifying sets of characteristic desires, beliefs, and behaviors would constitute a politically myopic research enterprise. Political roles derive their political significance from the institutional contexts in which they are embedded. When we miss the contexts, we miss the significance.

The Motivational Approach and Comparative Politics

Despite nearly half a century of exhortations on behalf of cross-national analysis, the field of comparative politics remains dominated by single-country studies. Perhaps it is time to wonder whether there may be some sound theoretical reasons for this state of affairs. Perhaps it is time to wonder how, despite its parochial avoidance of cross-national research designs, the sub-field of American politics has managed to produce so many successful systematic explanations.

We need cross-national analysis to alert us to potentially important concepts and relationships. We also need it to probe variables that do not vary within single countries. And we very much need it to ascertain the usually modest range of nations across which our usually modest theories may more or less apply. But we do not need cross-national analysis either to construct or to test convincing explanations of most important aspects of political behavior—including explanations of the person facts in political roles—which are usually pursued most effectively through single-country research designs that are contextually rich and that look more across historical time than across national boundaries.

CASES FOR COVERING LAWS?

The most committed cross-nationalists among us characterize single-country studies as case studies and depreciate their significance by assigning to them the role of generating the occasional hypothesis that can then be "tested" in cross-national research projects.[66] This argument is based on two mistakes. The first identifies comparative politics *qua* comparative politics with such cross-national projects (which is not what most scholars who study comparative politics do) and thereby underestimates the importance of contextually rich analysis (which is exactly what most scholars who study comparative politics do). The second mistake is to justify the first mistake by outdated views from the philosophy of social science, views that identify satisfactory explanation only with naturalistic explanation (which has no law-like generalizations to show for itself after four decades in the study of politicians' roles) rather than with interpretative explanation (which has by contrast produced many convincing motivational accounts that are overlooked in the bootless search for a general theory of roles).

In the field of comparative political behavior, we are still mesmerized by the goals of Popper-Hempel covering law explanation. Thus, we assume as a matter of course that where no comprehensive theories are hovering overhead, no satisfactory social scientific explanations can be found.[67] Moreover, in order to contribute to the construction of these theoretical chimeras, we long ago set aside our early interest in "purposive roles," the precursors of the motivational roles that have been developed in this study. The enormous variety of such roles made them seem intractable for cross-national analysis;[68] so we set them aside in favor of roles, like trustees and delegates, that were standardized by what seemed at the time to be more theoretically oriented concerns.

In the natural sciences, advances have often been made by realizing that everyday descriptive categories, like those politicians use to characterize their roles, are impediments to discovering generalizations and need to be replaced by more theoretically standardized concepts. But in the social sciences we must work, at least initially, with the descriptive categories that we find in everyday life, because these concepts are usually part of the motivational structure of the actors whose behavior we are trying to explain. Indeed they are often the most important part of the explanation. Thus the role concepts in the minds of our politicians are the concepts that best explain their behavior. If we as observers wish to use other concepts for theoretical reasons, including reasons of cross-national comparability, we must somehow relate our role concepts to theirs—otherwise we may miss the phenomena that are actually doing the explanatory work.[69]

Given the way that we thought about theory during the 1950s and 1960s, the only explanations that seemed appropriate for roles as person facts were the same sorts of naturalistic explanations that were indeed appropriate for roles as group facts. The result was that we rarely gave the great variety in politicians' roles the attention it deserved and overlooked a very important message that it might have suggested to us: the great variety in politicians' roles across relatively similar parliamentary contexts suggests that these roles are quite dependent upon the choices and actions of the people who play them. This is a powerful argument for a motivational approach that combines sociological constraint with economic choice to offer two results. The first and most important is the interpretative explanation of the principal roles that politicians actually play in liberal democratic states. A good map of these roles is much needed for modern democratic theory and for comparative policy analysis. Such a map is also needed to construct the slightly abstracted role concepts that may be both "related to theirs" and suitable for cross-national naturalistic analyses of origins and consequences.

But precisely because the roles of politicians differ so much across relatively similar parliamentary contexts, even our naturalistic explanations of their origins and consequences seem likely to be quite contextually bound and limited to a relatively small number of countries.[70] They are, moreover, likely to be modest frame theories, whose value lies more in the perspective they provide for particular explanations of particular cases than in their pretensions as grand intellectual constructions from which hypotheses might be "derived." It should be sobering to reflect on the fact that after so many decades of digging, we have turned up so very few true nontrivial statements about politicians' roles that apply universally across, as committed cross-nationalists used to say, both space and time. These are some of the reasons that what we have been calling role theories during these same decades are not sets of law-like generalizations but instead only sets of assumptions, concepts, and topics for investigation.

With interpretative explanations, by contrast, the contextual-boundedness of the roles of politicians is not a difficulty; it only reinforces the rationale for seeking to identify and understand the situations of these actors in the way that they do themselves, for using so far as possible their own language and concepts. We need to do this because in the motivational approach the center of our explanatory target is an account that shows how the actor's behavior is, in his or her mind, the rational thing to do in the actor's situation. And we need to understand the institutional context in order to understand how the actor understands the situation. In sum, skepticism about the goal of constructing universalistic role theories in no way suggests skepticism about the enterprise of comparative politics or about social scientific explanations of role phenomena—only about how that enterprise and those explanations have for several decades been defined.

GETTING IT RIGHT

The motivational approach uses the thinking of the role players as its point of departure because this keeps us close to the world in which we seek to reconstruct their roles with explanations that will be convincing to them and to us. But how can we know whether a particular reconstruction of a political role's typical desires, beliefs, and behaviors is true? Verification is a major problem in interpretative inquiries that are purely qualitative, for without quantitative analysis and dependent and independent variables, it is difficult to choose confidently among competing interpretations.[71]

Some commentators argue that the only basis for choice here is "Cartesian intelligibility," that is to say, epistemological rationalism, which they regard as a fundamental and powerful starting point.[72] This will not, however, satisfy most comparative political scientists, who, even if they do not demand cross-national tests, will count such role constructs as knowledge only if there is evidence independent of our psychological feeling that they seem right, are intelligible, or make sense. In fact, although the motivational approach to the study of politicians' roles is mainly qualitative, it is not purely qualitative, for in the context of verification it looks beyond Cartesian intelligibility to the familar empirical procedures of political behavior research.

Interpretative accounts of roles do, in the first instance, win considerable certification when they seem intelligible to those who are familiar with the institutional worlds they purport to explain. It is said to be characteristic of such explanations that while they may fascinate outside observers, they may also seem banal to the actors whose everyday world is being reconstructed on paper.[73] Indeed, Cartesian certification requires such banality. I will therefore be pleased when MPs say "nothing new here" to the reconstructions of roles with which they are most familiar. But it also requires "more of the same"—more statements, more quotations, more information to make the interpretations as persuasive as they can be in their own terms.[74] Hence, each chapter includes both considerable detail about each role and many quotations from Members of Parliament. An old Yiddish proverb cautions that " 'for example' is no proof." Nevertheless, "for example" can be persuasive.

At the same time, these accounts of parliamentary roles are typological abstractions and may always seem to other observers, who view the same targets from a different viewpoint, to have missed the mark. Such accounts therefore require further certification. I have tried to provide some of this not through cross-national analysis (which is better at probing theories than at explaining cases) but rather through a series of quantitative contextual analyses. These were conducted frequently as the roles were being constructed in order to determine how widespread a particular desire, belief, or behavior was among the members of an emerging role type, and also to investigate whether empirical implications of some of the emerging interpretations were well founded. Similarly, once the roles were constructed, they were treated as hypotheses: relationships among their component attitudes and behaviors were examined through quantitative analysis, which was used as well to explore their relationships with some of their origins and consequences. These methodological procedures are described more fully in Appendix B. What is important to emphasize here is that, contrary to the claims of the antiscience lobby in the social sciences, interpretative explanation can and should rely on quantitative methods to question its reconstructions of purposive behavior. In fact, these can be exercises in falsification, efforts at "regulating our acceptance or rejection of the description of the situation."[75]

The successful pursuit of motivational research designs presupposes that it is possible to develop from what politicians tell us a reasonably accurate reconstruction of their viewpoints. This presupposes, in turn, that they understand their roles reasonably well. Of course most of us most of the time are only vaguely aware of why we do what we do.[76] Yet, politicians reflect self-consciously on their principal political roles because such roles are the frameworks of their careers. Most MPs are, for example, extraordinarily articulate about their roles and are prepared to talk about them with interviewers just as they do with colleagues. What they have to say is a rich and subtle source of data. It draws attention to a rule that all of us who study politicians would do well to stencil on our briefcases: If one wants to know why politicians do something, the most sensible way *to begin* the investigation is by asking them about their conduct and listening very carefully to what they have to say.

What they have to say should be enough to convince us that the synthesis proposed by the new institutionalism is much too good an idea to leave to rational choice theories that stuff it into the procrustean beds of their utility maximization models. Lord Wigg is the only real politician I know whose strategic exploitation of informal rules resembles anything like the images conjured up by such models—and he was regarded by his colleagues as an eccentric, whose machinations they dubbed "Wiggery-Pokery."[77] March and Olsen have clarified the discipline's long march from the formal rules of *Homo politicus,* to the informal rules of *Homo sociologicus,* to the "unruled" *Homo economicus*—from one form of tunnel vision to another.[78] These alternative images of political actors were built into paradigms that led us to study particular topics and to think about those topics in particular and sometimes peculiar ways. Each time, we have survived the distortions and learned much more about the political world than we knew before. Still, the time seems long overdue for the sort of synthesis that March and Olsen have suggested, a genuine synthesis of rules and reasons that recognizes the importance of understanding the interactions between them. The political roles of politicians is a subject where these interactions can be seen with special clarity, a subject that points directly to motivational frameworks which, compared to their alternatives, are more rational, less muddled, better oriented to behavior—and well suited for investigating how rules and reasons interact to create political roles that are much too important to continue to be overlooked.

The Political Stage

Roles and rules change slowly. Thus, although this is a book about the principal roles in the House of Commons during the 1970s, the basic structure of these roles has remained remarkably stable throughout the postwar period and, indeed, throughout the century.[79] The institutional changes that have occurred since our interviews were concluded are the establishment of a new system of backbench Select Committees in 1979, the growth of the lobbying industry, larger allowances, and, most recently, the televising of Parliament. There have been systemic changes too. The evolution of parliamentary roles in response to these changes will be analyzed in the concluding chapter, where we will consider as well some of their origins and consequences and the institutional contexts in which they are embedded.

But before we begin, we need to consider briefly the political context that was putting pressure on Westminster's roles during the years we were discussing them with their players. This was a decade that made Parliament a busier place than it had been for some time and turned its parliamentary parties away from the political center.[80]

There were throughout the period signs that new attitudes toward authority in the society outside were trickling into Westminster. Party leaders with sensitive antennae were saying that these changes had become most noticeable in the orientations of the 1966 intake. The new MPs seemed irreverent about Parliament's traditions and impatient with its established procedures.[81] They also seemed more professional than their predecessors and increasingly keen on parliamentary reform to invigorate backbench activity and influence.[82] The focus of their push toward the "professionalization" of parliamentary roles was the creation of effective specialist committees. And, when a few such committees were created, but only to have their reports ignored, the traditionally quiescent backbenchers protested loudly. They were less willing than their predecessors had been to serve as cannon fodder in the division lobbies and Standing Committees.[83] Even the traditions of quiet civility in the Palace of Westminster seemed threatened as the Member for Mid-Ulster, Bernadette Devlin, shouted "murdering hypocrite" and physically assaulted the Home Secretary at the Despatch Box.

Thus, the 1970–71 session of Parliament, the session just before our interviews began, was dominated by acrimonious disputes over the new Conservative Government's Industrial Relations Bill to regulate the trade unions. The Common Market was also at the top of the Government's agenda. But the major explosion of that session was undoubtedly the announcement in February that Britain's best-known blue-chip company, Rolls Royce, had crashed and that the Heath Government had agreed to nationalize parts of it. Both the politicians and the public were stunned. It was the beginning of troubles that would strengthen backbenchers, weaken Whips, and eventually replace Edward Heath as party leader with Margaret Thatcher in 1975. This U-turn, and the U-turns that followed it, were prompted by grave concerns over unemployment, which by July 1971 was higher than at any time since 1940. Employers as well as trade unions declared it intolerable. "Crisis," *The Times* said, "is hardly too strong a word."[84] "Callous indifference," the Leader of the Opposition said, was behind the Government's free-market dogmatism. But the Government had already turned. By the spring of 1972, while our interviews were under way, it engaged the Trade Union Congress and the Confederation of British Industries in consultations that *The Daily Telegraph* described as a return to the consensus politics of the 1960s.[85]

If tensions were high in the Conservative Parliamentary Party, they were higher still on the Labour side. Essays published by the Fabian Society claimed that the previous Labour Government had left Britain more unequal in 1970 than it had been in 1964. The forces of the Left were emboldened by the fact that the largest trade unions were now led by Jack Jones and Hugh Scanlon, who were prepared to use their considerable influence to press the Parliamentary Labour Party leftward. Soon, the possibility of a party split was widely discussed and taken seriously. Pro-European moderates were, it was rumored, about to break off to form a new center party in alliance with the Liberals. This was the beginning of the fissure that would lead right-wing Labour MPs, at the end of the decade, to create the Social Democratic Party.

Such was the setting in which Members of Parliament played their roles and explained to us their situations. Tension and irritability were high during this session, tension due to pressures for increased influence, irritability due to rebellions in the division lobbies, intensification of the political struggle, and movements that were driving both parties away from the electoral center.

BACKBENCH ROLES

It seems a reasonable thing to say
What their condition was, the full array
Of each of them as it appeared to me
According to profession and degree.

Chaucer, Prologue to *The Canterbury Tales*

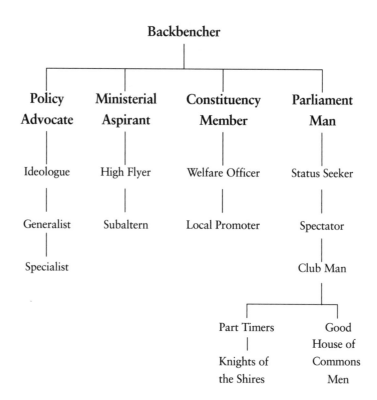

Backbencher

Policy Advocate — Ministerial Aspirant — Constituency Member — Parliament Man

Ideologue | High Flyer | Welfare Officer | Status Seeker

Generalist | Subaltern | Local Promoter | Spectator

Specialist | | | Club Man

Part Timers | Good House of Commons Men

Knights of the Shires

BACKBENCH ROLES IN PARLIAMENT

THE INSTITUTIONAL structure of Parliament contains a network of formal positions with which roles are associated. In Part II I examine Parliament's leadership positions and the roles associated with them, such as the position and general role of the Minister. Here I examine the position of the backbencher—but not the *general role* of the backbencher, for such a role would be too abstract, too shapeless, and too distant from the everyday experience of MPs. Instead, I consider the four backbench preference roles that are associated with this position: Policy Advocates, Ministerial Aspirants, Constituency Members, and Parliament Men.

Thus, the backbencher's position, in contrast to most leadership positions, is associated with several distinct roles rather than with only one. Because the position of backbencher entails so few duties and responsibilities, the general role of the backbencher is poorly crystallized and constrained. Because there are so few duties and responsibilities that *must* be done, there are so many that *might* be done. "So many duties and responsibilities," worried a new Member. "If you ask me to define the job . . . I would say he is a cross between a barrister, a solicitor, a vicar, a doctor, a personnel manager of a large works . . . so many things to do." And so much choice. No wonder backbenchers say that they make their own roles. But what is more remarkable is that out of all this flexibility emerges not hundreds of different backbench roles, but instead only the four distinct roles and their subtypes that are listed on the facing page. This reflects the fact that even backbench flexibility is framed by institutional constraints.[1] Hence, Members are able to understand the performances of their colleagues as variations on familiar roles that help everyone make sense of political life at Westminster.[2] Even these four backbench preference roles may still at times seem somewhat shapeless. But they are far less so than the general role of the backbencher, for they are far closer to the actual experiences of Members on the backbenches.

The construction of backbench preference roles is constrained by responsibilities associated with the position of the backbencher, particularly responsibilities related to the principal goals of the House of Commons. In fact, preference roles have sometimes been used to characterize and compare parliaments, because such roles are embedded in established parliamentary goals.[3] From this perspective, it is not surprising that another coder and I independently identified in the transcripts the same four major backbench roles.[4] Nor is it surprising that these roles resemble those frequently mentioned by British Members of Parliament and political commentators.[5]

Textbook accounts of Parliament's principal goals begin with "supporting and criticizing the Executive," a task that includes the duties of approving

expenditure and taxation and examining the national accounts.[6] These are
the responsibilities around which backbench *Policy Advocates* construct
their roles. The "recruitment and grooming of Ministers" was regarded by
Walter Bagehot as the most important goal of all, particularly because aspiring Ministers spend such long apprenticeships at Westminster.[7] *Ministerial
Aspirants,* of course, are those who concentrate on being selected. The third
and best-known goal of the Commons is the "redress of grievances,"
whereby problems once laid before the Crown are now taken up with the
Crown's Ministers. This enterprise is the chief concern of *Constituency
Members.* The fourth backbench role, that of the *Parliament Man,* is linked
to the somewhat more nebulous goal of "institutional support." Parliament
Men encourage camaraderie, chair committees, protect privileges, and organize amenities.

Parliament's goals are pursued through formal and informal rules that
define the essential tasks that need to be performed. And these tasks, in turn,
structure both the variety and the content of backbench roles. Here are the
institutional constraints. Constitutional rules, for example, require Parliament to produce Ministers—and backbenchers therefore produce Ministerial Aspirants. But, as we shall see, backbenchers have created several quite
different interpretations of the role of the Ministerial Aspirant. Backbench
roles, by contrast with leadership roles, enable their players more than they
constrain them. All backbenchers have their own desires and beliefs that
they use to "make their own roles." Indeed, the more I immersed myself in
the transcripts, the more flexibility I found in the institutional frameworks
within which backbenchers pursue their aims. There exist a quite remarkable number of role types and subtypes tethered to the single position of
backbencher in the House of Commons.

Each of the following chapters explicates one major backbench preference
role and its subtypes. And, in each chapter, three interrelated themes are
carried through. The first is to explain the role as it is understood by its
players in sufficient detail to understand it ourselves and to facilitate explaining its origins and consequences. The second theme uses the role as a
window for viewing the institutional matrix in which it is embedded. The
third theme explores general questions for the study of comparative politics,
questions that have relevance beyond these particular roles in the British
House of Commons. Unfortunately, there is not something of this sort to
be learned from every role and subtype, but there is from most of them—
and much of this material is summarized in the book's conclusion.

POLICY ADVOCATES:
CHECKING THE EXECUTIVE

It's little grains of sand and little drops
of water all the time.

Sir Harry Legge-Bourke

In 1876, Trollope's Mr. Wharton, "a Tory of the old school, . . . abhorred in his heart the class of politicians to whom politics was a *profession* rather than a *creed*." Today it is a bit of both. Yet the significance of this fact is insufficiently appreciated. Many accounts of the House of Commons still portray it as a parliament that debates rather than legislates, as an agreeable club full of clever amateurs, as a body of sheep under the spell of party discipline. These images no longer fit the reality. Responding to growth in the size and complexity of British government, the House of Commons became, by the end of the 1970s, oriented toward legislative intervention, dominated by professional politicians, and increasingly rebellious and influential.[1] Policy Advocates led this transformation and thereby established their approach as the predominant role on Westminster's backbenches.

Institutionalization

Roles are embedded in institutional contexts. And, with the rise of the administrative state, "institutionalization" gained ground at Westminster. The Conservatives were the first to establish specialized subject committees, which, after 1945, expanded into the backbench structure that exists today.[2] On the Labour side, a similar committee scheme was introduced, which evolved into its present form by 1976. The aim of this specialization was to help backbenchers inform themselves about particular topics and influence their party leaders. In the same vein, a new type of Select Committee developed during the 1960s and 1970s to study major policy areas and was eventually given serious powers of investigation to shadow the principal departments of state.[3] These Select Committees have proved surprisingly active and critical, like the Policy Advocates who run them and whose efforts are changing the House of Commons from a gothic club into a highly institutionalized and active organization.

The changes are both a response to the professionalization of parliamentary roles and a stimulus to their further professionalization. As the dialogue became more academic on the Labour side, the number of working-class MPs declined. As the dialogue became more managerial in Conservative ranks, Knights of the Shires slipped into the background.[4] There has been much comment about the fading of the amateur politician and the growing commitment to politics as a vocation. By 1971, William Whitelaw, Leader of the House of Commons, explained to a gathering of MPs and journalists that the character of the House had been modified. It was a busier place, and its members were younger, better educated, and harder working. They were more likely to come from the professions, to spend longer hours at Westminster, and to expect politics to provide more career opportunities than it had in the past. They expected better committees, better staff assistance, better salaries, better travel allowances—and more influence.[5]

There has always been confusion and controversy about the appropriateness of characterizing as professions many different occupations and vocations.[6] In Chapter 10 I develop the argument that political life in Parliament today is a vocation that has become increasingly professional. In this chapter I show why Policy Advocates, particularly the most energetic ones, are so often regarded by their colleagues as the archetype of the professional politician at Westminster. Policy Advocates are full-time, service oriented, and determined to convert the House from an amateur assembly into an efficient and effective institution.

Influence

Policy Advocates have more in common with Ministerial Aspirants, the subjects of the next chapter, than either group has with Constituency Members or Parliament Men. In fact, Constituency Members and Parliament Men belittle the bustling Policy Advocates they encounter in corridors and committees. Advocates "have an exaggerated sense of their own importance," it is said; these backbenchers who think they influence policy have "an overgrand idea of themselves." "Actually," they further explain to outsiders, "policy decisions are taken by Ministers," who tell backbenchers about these decisions only after the fact. Despite the cynicism of their colleagues, the paramount aim of Policy Advocates is indeed "to influence government policy." And they "do honestly believe" that they are effective. For them, influence is the beginning and the end of the exercise: "I very much like being in the corridors of power. If you are not going to walk up and down the corridors and do something, you are wasting your time."[7]

How much influence do they actually have? Eager young Advocates certainly produce enough hyperbole to make one wonder whether they are deceiving themselves: "I have, together with only half a dozen colleagues, the power . . . to totally change the immediate course of history in the nation." And some still talk this way after thirteen years' experience: "I've set out to influence the destiny of this country to the best of my ability in accordance with my principles and ideals." Nevertheless, backbenchers are at the minimum an important pressure group whose support the Government must keep. And while they may have less clout than particular pressure groups on particular issues, their pressure extends over all the issues, not just a few.[8] To retain their support, moreover, Ministers do take account of their views, "provided you are prepared to keep on with things," and provided you are prepared to be patient, "for it may be months afterward . . . before you see any results." Sensible Policy Advocates do not expect dramatic results, but they do expect modest successes: "One doesn't influence events as much as one would like to think, but one can get little things done. A very wise guy, I'll tell you who it was—Henry Legge-Bourke, the Chairman of the '22 until recently—said to me once, 'It is no good thinking you can build castles here, or knock down windmills.' He said, 'it's little grains of sand and little drops of water all the time. That's what you can hope to achieve.' And I think that's absolutely right."

Perhaps backbench influence is so often underestimated because key backbench forums such as the weekly meetings of the Parliamentary Labour Party (PLP) or the 1922 Committee seem more like sounding boards than like power centers. PLP meetings are frank and acrimonious; but everyone is aware that the potential sting of hostile votes is greatly diminished by the presence and "payroll votes" of frontbenchers. Similarly, the 1922 Committee, the Conservative Private Members' Committee, is not expected to be much of a channel for influence, although the atmosphere of its meetings is reported back to appropriate Ministers.

In fact, backbench influence flourishes behind the scenes, especially when policy is being formulated, for Ministers find it easier to compromise with backbenchers privately before matters are presented formally to the House.[9]

Policy Advocates know this and therefore are most "interested in seeking to influence policies that Governments are going to pursue." The process works through anticipatory reactions. White Papers and Green Papers, for instance, have been used by Governments to test opinion in areas where they would like to legislate but to which they are not yet firmly committed. This gives Ministers time to learn about backbench views and, by anticipating them, adjust the formulation of policies so as to avoid unnecessary storms and battles. That's why, Advocates argue, "you rarely see the Government defeated. . . . It tends to formulate its policy in response to our pressures." I shall return to these actions and reactions when I explore the characteristic behaviors in the Policy Advocate's subroles. Here, the important point is that Advocates have much more influence than many people suppose, influence that has been increasing since the early 1960s.

Faith in the efficacy of the Policy Advocate's role is important to backbenchers who aim "to be able to express an opinion and to be able to bring influence to bear." Their numbers have grown in recent years, as has their conviction that influence is a proper trade and that Constituency Members and Parliament Men are another kind of MP altogether. To many Policy Advocates, the constituency is something of "a distraction," for they are "not the kind of blokes who think first, last, and always about their constituents." Another way of putting it is that "the nation or the world has got to be your constituency . . . because you really can't spend your life talking about Tolpuddle on the Marsh." They can't see spending their lives as Parliament Men either. They realize that other Members enjoy this, "but it's a great pity because there are quite a lot of reasonably intelligent people in Parliament who ought to be *working* instead of sitting in the Chamber listening to somebody else." Still less are they in Parliament "merely to be a member of an agreeable club," because "there just isn't time."

There just isn't time because Policy Advocates are dead set on "doing something that matters in life and particularly in politics." Helping constituents isn't enough. Being at Westminster isn't enough. Advocates want to change things; they want to achieve results.

Distribution

Policy Advocates believe that the backbencher's "main role, prime role, indeed in many ways the only important role, is as a spokesman in this place, without any executive responsibility whatsoever, for influencing policy in national affairs."[10] This is the principal focus of interest for 136 backbenchers whose transcribed discussions suggest several obvious subtypes. The criterion that best differentiates these subtypes is generality-specificity, which runs from interest in many general goals to interest in a few policy areas. Thus, some Policy Advocates become Ideologues; some become Generalists; and some follow the advice of the Great and the Good, all of whom seem to have said something like, "Specialise in two subjects!"

Ideologues are recognized by their absorption with abstract political values and by their efforts to promote such values through propaganda. They say that they are different from "your typical politician because he has no basic principles." This focuses attention on the content of their discourse rather than its form and reflects what Members themselves mean when they use the term "Ideologue" to describe a colleague. Ideologues, and Generalists and Specialists too, were coded and then coded further on a four-point scale (very strong, strong, moderate, weak) according to the consistency and strength of their responses.

Like Ideologues, Generalists "don't really think that MPs should be highly skilled and well-versed experts in specialist subjects." But, unlike Ideologues, Generalists' primary interests lie in concrete issues rather than in abstract political values. They see the proper backbench role as being "sort of jurymen who exercise their judgements at given times and over a wide range of issues." They have been identified by the range of their interests: more than three policy areas or three areas that either are defined broadly or are quite distinct from one another. Specialists believe, by contrast, that to influence the Executive, "you've obviously got to narrow your range of interests" and give yourself time "to do your homework." They have been coded as those Policy Advocates who concentrate their attention on fewer than three policy areas or on three areas that either are defined narrowly or are closely integrated with one another.[11] Specialists assume that knowledge provides the springboard for influence, that backbenchers must make the Executive "sit up and take notice—and that you won't do it by getting bright ideas in your bath."

The proportions of Ideologues, Generalists, and Specialists are reported in Table 2.1, as is the breakdown by political party. There are very few Ideologues because there are very few pure and simple "fundamentalists" on the backbenches. The coding criterion I have used emphasizes the content of the respondent's discourse over its form and style and thereby puts the premium upon "whether you are a reformist or a fundamentalist in the Labour Party, well, inside of the Conservative Party too, whether you are a reformist or a fundamentalist." "I'm a fundamentalist" is a position taken, purely and simply, by only a small number of Policy Advocates, since only a small number of those who think abstractly think primarily about abstractions.[12]

Specialists are clearly the dominant subtype among Policy Advocates.

Table 2.1 Policy Advocates: Subtypes, and subtypes by political party

| | All Policy Advocates | | Political party* | | | |
| | | | Conservative | | Labour | |
Subtype	N	%	N	%	N	%
Ideologues	(7)	5	(2)	3	(5)	9
Generalists	(48)	35	(25)	32	(19)	35
Specialists	(81)	60	(51)	65	(30)	56
Total	(136)	100	(78)	100	(54)	100

*$p = .19$

There are eighty-one of them in the sample, which means approximately one hundred in the House—more than enough to give the Executive a difficult time. Debates in the Chamber may be becoming less well attended, but they are at the same time becoming better informed. "You cannot, just for the interest of it, sit and listen to all the debates of all the others," Specialists say, not "if you are really to study your own subject." Professionalization makes specialization the preferred approach. And the reasons seem, to Specialists, perfectly straightforward: "As governments become more complicated, the necessity for an MP, if he wants to get anywhere, to specialise has become more and more."

Generalists, who constitute 35 percent of the Policy Advocates, disagree. They prefer the role of "a kind of freewheeling, freelancing trouble shooter." They are "not so interested in being able to say 'I did that'" when "that" is merely a minor modification of government policy. Instead, Generalists are "much more concerned that I myself should be able to say to myself that I have . . . played a part in things which are important." They are interested in the "opportunity," in the "platform" that "gives one a chance to voice, and to press for, and to argue for, and to fight for things which you care about," such as "a United Europe, abortion, church affairs, family planning, education, and foreign policy generally of course."

Table 2.1 also reports a distribution by political party which reveals that the Conservative and Labour patterns are not so very different. Similar recruitment and socialization processes produce, on each side of the House, similar proportions of Ideologues, Generalists, and Specialists. Still, the very modest interparty differences that surface in this table grow among the "strong" and "very strong" representatives of each subtype. For instance, among the strong and very strong Specialists, Conservatives outnumber Labour by nearly three to one.[13]

Now that we have mapped the role of the Policy Advocate by focusing on the career goals in its motivational core, it is time to reconstruct the full-blown subtypes by examining the attitudes and behaviors that characterize Ideologues, Generalists, and Specialists.

Ideologues

There are not many Ideologues in the House of Commons. And, compared with Generalists and Specialists, there isn't much to be said about them either. Ideologues pursue grand objectives through political analysis and propaganda. But so few of their colleagues share their fundamentalist tastes that they occasionally resign themselves to having a pint with Ideologues from the other side—who are as amused with the situation as they are. Hence, at the time of our interviews, the Conservative Parliamentary Party was surprised to find its traditional unity disturbed by a growing struggle between Left and Right. The focus of this struggle was Enoch Powell, who, despite having been "frozen out" of the party's inner circles, was successfully stirring up ideological concerns.[14]

ABSTRACTIONS

The Ideologues' predominant interest in abstract political ideas sets them apart from their colleagues, for very few Policy Advocates, let alone other backbenchers, would characterize their chief career goal as "to contribute to new ideas" or continue to talk about such ideas for twenty minutes without ever discussing a single concrete policy issue. Ideologues do it easily. They begin, for instance, by positing "socialism as the only solution to most of the problems that we're faced with today." But instead of talking about these problems, they pass on to reflections about how rapidly the solutions may come ("I don't think, as I did as a young man, that there will be a miraculous change overnight") or about the role of the Soviet Union in the historical process: "I was appalled when I learned about the repression in Soviet Russia. . . . But there are signs of a new society emerging from this terrible situation. I don't think it will be necessary for our country to go through that process. That's one thing that we have to thank the Russian Revolution for." This is a response to a question about the principal duties and responsibilities of the MP, the same question that led other backbenchers to talk about constituency work, parliamentary interests, or policy projects. Ideologues talk instead about ideas and describe the part they play in terms of their beliefs: "I have very powerful socialist ideas, and I was a socialist theoretician in the Movement. . . . I was a Young Trotskyite in my time. . . . But I find the Communist Party much more realistic politically these days . . . because my background is really a Marxian background, my approach to socialism is through the scientific road of Marxian understanding—not in the vulgarised way of people who masquerade, who parade themselves as Marxists."

This active member of the Tribune Group sees his role as an MP as that of a politician whose main concern is ideas, in his case Marxist ideas. Most Labour Ideologues are concerned with the concepts and theories of socialism. There are a few, however, who construct their role in much the same style but with the mortar of other notions such as liberty: "I think that the most important role of an MP is to recognize that what is paramount is the expansion of liberties . . . to be on guard and vigilant forever against those activities in society which impinge upon the liberties, the freedoms."

For Conservative Ideologues, who are mainly Tory populists, "the most important responsibility of being an MP is really to be on the side, as it were, of the people against the Establishment." They are irritated with the Establishment and with their colleagues who "want to be Establishment figures for their own promotion and advancement." They, by contrast, want to be on the side of the people because they see the people as their allies; they believe that "the people in the country are often to the Right of the party." "I think the man in the pub, generally, is a very sensible fellow." Unlike most left-wing MPs, they display a taste for the particular, but for particular *anecdotes* to illustrate their abstract principles. "And I'll give you an example of this":

> When I was at Oxford, my own university, the other day . . . I was passing Balliol and the most awful collection of International Socialists and Marxists marched out chanting and clenching their fists. And I happened to notice two splendid men digging a hole in the road. And I always talk to men who dig a hole in the road. And I said, looking at these awful roughs, "Oughtn't they ought to be locked up?" "Of course they should, sir," they said. [chuckle] And you see the working class who didn't have these opportunities can't understand why people who get this handed to them on a plate should then abuse it. And of course they dislike ill manners very much.

Although most Conservative Ideologues take the propagation of Tory populism as their principal goal ("And so that's my role: standing up for the country and representing ordinary people"), there are other ideological garments in the party wardrobe. These include authority: "We simply must have it. . . . And I think there always will be those who lead and always those who will follow." And also subversion, "which is, of course, much more widespread than people realise." Several of their topics sound as though they easily could become specific, but specificity is restricted again mainly to the personal pronoun and the illustrative anecdote: "I was delighted that Alec Home arrested all those Russian spies and sent them packing. I'm just waiting for the day when they arrest some other people in this country who, I believe, by means of strikes and some other things are trying to cause confusion in the country."[15]

ACTIVITY: PROPAGANDA

Deciding where one stands politically is an important activity that characterizes Ideologues. But what else do Ideologues do? They aren't very interested in constituency work and don't talk much about their constituencies or cases. They aren't especially interested in Parliament as an institution either and hardly ever talk about its web of history or about its housekeeping functions. Moreover, they are not at all keen about many of the activities that are pursued by their fellow Policy Advocates, Generalists, and Specialists: "I'm not a great asker of Questions. . . . I don't go to any of the subject groups within the Parliamentary Labour Party. I don't spend much time on these Anglo-French, Anglo-What-Have-You groups in the Inter-Parliamentary Union . . . or on the Committee for Science and Technology, or the House of Commons Motor Club. None of this interests me very much."

What interests Ideologues are ideas. And, beyond discovering, savoring, and reconstructing political ideas, the most characteristic activity that Ideologues pursue is the propagation of their favorite themes through propaganda in Parliament, in the country, and wherever opportunities arise. "These are, from my perspective, the most important duties and responsibilities of an MP: putting forward right-wing views." Or left-wing views: "to develop concepts of the Left, to try and define, to use this place to define what we're all about and to project ideas." Some thinkers project ideas, Ideologues explain, through essays and books, an approach that is used successfully by several MPs. But MPs also "get other opportunities which are not available to outsiders." At their disposal they have Parliament's facilities and forums as well as platforms and press attention in the country. They exploit these opportunities energetically.

The House of Commons offers them resources for research and adversaries for arguments. Ideologues find the House of Commons Library an invaluable source for information that will enable them to put forward their views effectively. Armed with these weapons, they needn't go far to find forums in the Palace of Westminster where their views can be expressed forcefully. "It would indeed be very frustrating to have such strong views and be able to do nothing about it." Doing something about it means attacking "the outrageous treatment of Rhodesia on Thursday (I am immersed over Rhodesia)" and, on Friday, "denouncing the appalling postal service in this country about which my constituents are much exercised." The point of making these speeches against things is "not so much to influence Government, Labour or Tory," but "instead to play an influential role in the world of ideas." Ideologues set out to influence the climate of opinion at Westminster and, in particular, within their parliamentary party.

Projecting ideas in Parliament can help project them outside. Yet Ideologues aren't satisfied with the amplification from Westminster's precincts, because, usually, "a backbencher's speech is not given more than a few lines in the press." They wish to influence both "a general public attitude" and "a general attitude in our own Movement or party" through "the Word," printed and spoken. Thus, they write letters to the press: "I write to them every two or three months. Lately, two of my letters have been first in *The Times*." They write journalistic articles: "I've written quite a bit. I even write in the *Morning Star*." They lecture to party groups ("from a political education point of view . . . the party is povertystricken from a political education point of view") and to students at universities: "This coming Saturday I shall be in some forum at Essex University. I wouldn't ever be on that unless I was an MP." And they "accept most invitations to television and sound broadcasts. I have done about half a dozen so far and, again, judging by the mail one receives, one does get one's views across."[16]

Ideologues want to believe "that if you know what you are talking about, and feel deeply, people will always listen." It is, they explain, "a fact of life that an MP is given a serious hearing in all the sober councils of the country." Yet, some Ideologues are less energetic than others and are not inclined to visit all the country's sober councils. They prefer to remain at Westminster and dispense their ideas to whomsoever they encounter, including grateful academics whose interviews they fill with comments like this response to our role item: "In my opinion capitalism, at the end, is bound to fail . . . we've seen it in history. . . . Capitalism will never guarantee that no child is ever thwarted. . . . But I don't think our people are right for communistic socialism. . . . Now that doesn't mean . . ." Another, who finds the propaganda tiresome, finds that the behavior that suits his role best is simply to sit back and await the revolution:

I think that the people will feel a new power in their own unity, in their own demands for justice and not simply ask for it from Parliament. . . . I think they'll realise that they have some power outside, that power for instance in the U.C.S. and the miners' strike . . . these lessons are not lost on the people. And something similar will happen to Parliament . . . there will be extra-Parliamentary action, revolutionary action on the part of the people in the event of a war or economic collapse. I've always had that idea, and of course events are more and more . . . justifying those thoughts that I had in early life.

Self-justification is indeed one of the attractions around which Ideologues construct their roles. But there are others too. These emotional incentives are subtle and difficult to unravel. Since all we have to go on is what Ideologues tell us in the transcripts, we must not presume to poke around very much in their personalities. Yet some of what they say explicitly is quite clear and convincing: individuality, rectitude, and hubris are the incentives they talk about most often. Intertwined with the career goal of projecting abstract political ideals, these incentives will complete our account of the motivational core of their roles.

INCENTIVES: INDIVIDUALITY, RECTITUDE, HUBRIS

Individuality, a desire to distinguish oneself from one's associates, to see oneself as singular or even unique, is an idiosyncratic motive among Ideologues, since those who like to stand alone are outnumbered by the team players who operate through groups such as Tribune or the Monday Club. Those who do stand alone, however, are quite articulate about what they are doing. They are choosing the singularity of independence over the lowest common denominator of collective action: "I am very much an outsider within my party in the House," a right-wing Conservative observes. "I am fundamentally independent-minded in everything. . . . I believe that individuals get much further than groups. I think that groups ruin individuals." Groups, because of the lowest common denominator they express, "miss many matters . . . because they don't want to upset people. . . . And if you are going to tell the truth, you must upset people."

Ideologues are determined to discover the truth, hold fast the truth, and tell the truth. And they are irritated with a Parliament that threatens to blur their vision, weaken their conviction, and muffle their message: "Society's defence mechanisms are built into Parliament to prevent it" from serving as a force for radical change. Thus, a left-wing miner complained that he was suspicious of the place because, "as Karl Marx said, 'you can expect socialism as much to emerge from the House of Commons as you can expect to get sausages out of a sewing machine.' "[17] Some Ideologues dislike the House because it is a forum for compromise; and some dislike their colleagues because they are compromisers and opportunists: "There are a lot of curious people . . . lawyers, like that, looking for some enhancement to their silk and their court prowess." Ideologues are especially wary of the club atmosphere, because its attractions, they suspect, smother individuality and commitments to abstract ideals.[18]

Rectitude, a feeling of integrity, honesty, or uprightness, is the emotional incentive that Ideologues talk about most. In both the Labour and Conservative parties they say, and seem to enjoy saying, "I'd much rather be right than successful." This quotation is from one of Westminster's most right-wing Tories, who uses it to explain why he has given up on ministerial ambitions. Unless one is prepared to compromise one's principles more than one should do, he believes, there is "no chance, no chance at all," of attaining office. Ideologues who are left-wing socialists concur and would apply to their party's electoral strategies this moral that they have learned themselves as individuals. Being right is preferable to being in office because it is, some say, impossible to exercise power and not be corrupted.

Ideologues are politicians of conscience: intellectual honesty and self-justification are prominent themes in their thoughts and conversations. This is particularly true on the Left, where Ideologues care very much about whether they or their less ideological colleagues are the truer, "deeper socialists." They derive satisfaction from being the keepers of the party's conscience, from being the ones who press principles to the forefront of the party's mind and who remind the world "what the parliamentary struggle is all about." Also characteristic of the Left is a strong concern with consistency as a measure of self-justification: I am a genuine socialist, for I am consistently "faithful and true to the basic ideas which brought the Labour Party into being;" I am an honest socialist, for I consistently advocate the same ideals in the House that I advocate outside; I am a steadfast socialist, for the principles I argue with people about today are consistent with, "indeed, are exactly the principles and arguments I was conducting in my teens and in my twenties."

Beyond integrity and honesty, rectitude encompasses a feeling of uprightness that comes from "exercising a little pressure to remove what you consider injustices." Ideologues are more sensitive than many of their colleagues to issues of justice and injustice. They assume that "there are so many evils in society that require political remedies," and assume that they are the ones whose "objective in politics has to be to try and change them." Fighting evil is a righteous vocation for politicians who sometimes become self-consciously, and sometimes intolerantly, contemptuous of "pragmatists who, in order to succeed, try to remain in the centre of politics." Such people, they say, "like [Harold] Wilson . . . who believed in the origins of his own pragmatism," lack the rectitude earned through consistency in the political struggle. Such people are "destructive to the Movement" and more irritating even than their traditional political enemies, who at least believe in some principles and with whom, therefore, one at least knows where one stands.

Hubris, expressed through desires to attract attention and occasionally through delusions of grandeur, is another incentive that energizes the Ideologues' role. They see themselves "reaching a very wide public, where, judging by the mail one receives, one does get one's views across." Others believe that they shape the evolution of political culture by developing "in words the ideas that are beginning to crystallize . . . in the society in which we live." And still others concentrate on the party: "I don't think I'm boasting if I say if you study the speeches I was making in the party . . . you can see where the thoughts have come from—many of them. And it was nice when I saw the Prime Minister coming out in the party political broadcasts with ideas I had argued and put across to colleagues and so on."

Although Ideologues assume that they will never be Cabinet Ministers, they feel that, by virtue of their potential power to bring down the Government, they are sometimes "in a position to make decisions of fundamental importance and with untold repercussions." At the Marxist end of the spectrum, Ideologues can also see themselves as handmaidens to inevitable historical processes. This sort of hubris surfaces in the suggestions, heard more frequently than one might expect from both Conservative and Labour Ideologues, "that I have prophesied in my time, both in writing and in speech, every ill that has befallen this country—and therefore my conscience is always clear."

Through propaganda in the country, in the parties, and in Parliament, Ideologues aim to influence the way that the influential think and thereby influence the general direction of government policy. The other Policy Advocates, Generalists and Specialists, share this desire to influence decisions of national and international importance, but they approach the task more directly.

Generalists

Thus, Generalists, who represent approximately one-third of all Policy Advocates, are much more concerned with concrete issues than with political ideals. Generalists are usually not, however, drawn to the details of particular policies, for they resist "the idea of specialization which . . . one is urged to engage in." Specialization seems inappropriate because the policy problems they find at Westminster appear to them to be "interlaced in a spider's web in which one comes in touch with various strands of the web, but cannot afford to get really enmeshed in them."

Generalists, then, prefer to define their role as more like that of the well-informed commentator than the well-versed expert. This is what many of them believe most MPs should ideally be: "almost, if you like, sort of jurymen, people who exercise their judgments at given times on given issues." The specialist subject, they say, comes up only once a year—but MPs must exercise their judgments hundreds of times before and afterward. "And that's why some of the best MPs are not those who claim to be experts." The most attractive topics are not, moreover, the little things but rather "the subjects of global importance," the "big issues" like divorce, abortion, or the Common Market. Parliament "is not about the little things; it's about big things. It's about how the nation should be run. . . . It's the great issues with which Parliament should really be concerned."

JACK OF ALL TRADES

The Generalist is a jack of all trades and master of none. He defends the variety of his interests as appropriate for the flow of parliamentary activity that requires one to redirect one's attention year to year ("This year it has certainly been broadcasting, education, and Rhodesia . . . but these things come and go"), or month to month, or even occasionally day to day: "I never know from one day, or one hour, to the next what one is going to be called upon to do." Extreme Generalists take the shotgun approach exemplified by this Conservative anti-Marketeer who, in response to our first role question, listed as his policy interests state steel, radio pirates, finance, motorways, antitrust laws, unemployment, Canada, small-business administration, and "What else am I interested in? The other things, I've forgotten what they are. Anyway, that's the general drift." Some Generalists complain about being caught up in a lot of last-minute, furious adrenalin-pumping projects. But others find the variety and the pace of change breathlessly exciting: "I am interested in industrial relations. I am interested in foreign affairs. And I am interested in science and technology. . . . Therefore I am on committees. Therefore that brings travel. This in turn brings you in touch with industry. . . . I'm full-time . . . time to serve the people, time to influence legislation, time to keep in touch with the world outside. I'm in constant touch with life and therefore reacting to it in terms of whatever interests I may have. . . . I'm getting great stimulus now from . . . you're dealing with a subject . . . then you go on to something new. You can do it!"

The Generalist's pursuit of important policy issues often leads him or her to current events, to "the subject uppermost at the time." The goal is to get involved in whatever one "feels is of vital importance to the life of the country," in whatever seem to be "the major questions of the day." And so they become "instant experts" on currency parities, or the floating exchange rate, or African developments, or the Northern Ireland position. When important matters are for the moment lacking, some try to create their own by "taking the opportunity of raising matters which seem to me to be important. For example, the plane crash a few weeks ago. I thought the interviewing of the young stewardess on television was absolutely appalling, a bloody disgrace. . . . I was so annoyed about it I came straight down here and put a Question to the Minister." Many Generalists would be quick to dissociate themselves from "those who think as soon as there is a disaster or a crash somewhere, that the best thing to do is have a debate about it." But they would be criticizing only this particular criterion of importance, not the general concern that they all share, the concern for involvement in political matters of great moment.

ACTIVITY: BEAT THE DRUM

Generalists stir coals and beat drums. They see their characteristic behavior as reacting to the Government on the one side and rousing their parliamentary colleagues (or groups outside) on the other—and avoiding committee work, especially backbench party committees, which "I find boring, fatuous, and nearly useless in a Parliamentary setting." The sort of committee work that they particularly dislike is the long, hard slog behind the scenes, the sort of work that requires perpetual patience, perseverance, attention to detail, and a lot less excitement than they desire.

Instead, Generalists prefer to be in and around the Chamber, where they can criticize Ministers and launch ideas. Although many backbenchers drift away from the Chamber to pursue specialized work in committees, Generalists are drawn there by the opportunity to criticize the Executive, a task they think "frightfully important" and not at all overdone. Indeed, this criticism is what many see as the essence of their role, as their principal duty and responsibility: "Well, as I conceive them [duties and responsibilities], it is to act as a gadfly, to keep stinging the Executive to do the things that you consider necessary, to keep the Executive under constant supervision."

The other main attraction of the Chamber is that it can be used as a launching pad for ideas. Generalists like to put forward ideas that might move Ministers and stimulate legislation: "I had a talk with the Minister about it beforehand. . . . I stood up . . . it was a four-minute speech, and the Minister intervened and said, 'Yes, the British Government would be more than prepared to start discussions with the Australian Government.'" They enjoy the opportunity to put down Questions to be answered by Ministers. Some put down hundreds each year. Answers to Written Questions are used to collect information for policy campaigns. Answers to Oral Questions are given by Ministers who must be prepared to deal with supplementary Oral Questions of which they have no prior notice. These supplementary Oral Questions enable Generalists to "put to a Minister, from the Prime Minister down to the most Junior Minister," a point of view, an opinion, an idea, a suggestion. Generalists believe "that in some way the message may get through," and that they are therefore engaged in an instrumental exercise as well as an expressive one.

Generalists also use Adjournment Debates to react and rouse, to criticize, and to pursue policy modifications. At the end of each day's business, half an hour is allotted to a discussion that is initiated by a backbencher: "So I had the whole of the debate devoted to pollution, you know, and I led the debate for half an hour. Well, you know, you get a terrific amount of satisfaction out of that." Most Adjournment Debates address specific constituency matters, but approximately one out of three focuses on national issues like pollution or unemployment.[19] Although the audience may sometimes be small ("the Deputy Speaker, the Minister, myself, two Whips, and a Hansard reporter, and that's all"), the debate goes into Hansard; and the occasional success compensates for the many failures and convinces Generalists that this undertaking is worth a try. Others are convinced that "you can do far more . . . speaking outside the House, taking part in discussions, and so on, than you can do in." They do a lot of it and would like to think, as does this leader of his party's pro-EEC forces, that such talks have "had some effect in molding the sort of world that I want there to be." Whereas Ideologues prefer to address the general public, Generalists seek out individuals and organizations in the fields of their current interests, because "they can help you do your job" by providing valuable ammunition, and "you can help them" by being their spokesman at Westminster.

Another way to beat drums is to exploit the Ten Minute Rule: "You give a speech for ten minutes after Question Time, Tuesday and Wednesday, and you explain the kind of legislation you want to introduce, and the Speaker asks the House if permission is granted." If permission is granted, then the

Generalist can have the Bill printed and circulated. "So what I do, I promote a Ten Minute Rule Bill, print it, and then I start campaigning. . . . I use one session for propaganda, and then reintroduce it, and that's how I've been lucky getting progress with Ten Minute Bills—changing the laws of the country, that's what it involves, you see." According to Sir Gerald Nabarro, an energetic Generalist who used the Ten Minute Rule more than most, this procedure is primarily "a device, and a very good one too, for publicising a Member's legislative intent or propagating a Member's views" rather than for initiating measures that will reach the statute book. Hence, many Generalists are skeptical about the efficacy of this procedure and look instead to Private Members' Bills.[20]

PRIVATE MEMBERS' BILLS

The annual ballot for Private Members' Bills attracts Generalists, and all the best-known gadflies dream of making their mark in this way: "I did succeed in getting implanted health warnings on all cigarette packs. . . . I have, over the years, promoted a great deal of Private Members' legislation, including clean air, including coroners, including thermal insulation of industrial buildings, including oil standards. And I've attempted legislation which has made a lasting mark on the subject of renal transplantation and the process of securing cadaver kidneys and implanting them in live human beings in order to save life."

At the time of the interviews, twelve days were allotted for Private Members' Bills. On these days, all Fridays, twenty-five MPs who had won the privilege by ballot could initiate legislation.[21] Now and then such legislation succeeds by the Government taking up the Bill as its own. Usually, however, the Government remains uncommitted. And, very occasionally, Private Members' Bills catch it unawares: "I involved the Government in a technical defeat on food prices . . . on a Private Members' motion. The Government were caught napping and daren't vote against it." But the fact remains that very few Private Members' Bills can be introduced in a session, and far fewer actually pass. The obstacles are fortuitous and formidable: winning the opportunity to introduce the Bill; drafting the Bill satisfactorily; keeping the House in session; guiding the Bill through Standing Committee; avoiding filibusters; and, perhaps most important of all, securing the Government's support or at least benevolent neutrality.[22] Even successful originators of Private Members' Bills ("I've put four on the Statute Book myself") emphasize that all of this requires an enormous amount of effort and time: "a quite interesting small matter which has taken me twenty years to win—just won it."

Given the strong interest that Generalists have in Private Members' Bills, they should be expected to support strongly proposals that would make these Bills easier to achieve.[23] Table 2.2 compares the beliefs of Generalists with those of other Advocate subtypes. The topic is a proposal to reduce obstacles to Private Members' Bills. Most backbenchers endorse this idea, but not all of them are ready to "agree without reservation," the response labeled in Table 2.2 as "very favorable." Those who have reservations are concerned about the costs of expanding these initiatives and are skeptical about the value of the enterprise.

Contrary to what one might expect, Policy Advocates are not, as a group, more vigorous supporters of this type of legislation than are other backbenchers. When analyzed all together, Advocates are not outstanding, because their different subtypes disagree about the most-appropriate strategies for backbench influence. Thus, enthusiasm for Private Members' Bills among the Specialists falls below the backbench mean and provides a counterweight to the Ideologues and Generalists who respond as anticipated. Table 2.2 reports the data by these subtypes.

Ideologues are usually uninterested in little campaigns to achieve modest policy gains. But what attracts them nevertheless to Private Members' Bills is that such Bills occasionally draw considerable publicity and can thereby project ideas. Generalists, by contrast, would be pleased to make any mark, even a small one, on the tablets of history. Several are tempted by grandiose visions: "We make the laws here, and you can change them all as I have

Table 2.2   Attitude toward Private Members' Bills by Policy Advocate subtypes, in percent

	Policy Advocate subtype*				
Attitude	Ideologue	Strong Generalist	Weak Generalist	Weak Specialist	Strong Specialist
Very favorable	67	59	58	39	25
Less than very favorable	33	41	42	62	75
Total	100	100	100	101	100
	(N = 6)	(N = 22)	(N = 19)	(N = 39)	(N = 20)

Q. There should be fewer obstacles to Private Members' Bills. (Agree/disagree)
*$p \leq .05$

done myself, quite frequently, changed the laws by promoting Private Member's Bills." But most see Private Members' Bills as a technique for launching particular policy proposals or for modifying existing statutes on subjects such as pornography laws, gaming laws, or other areas of domestic legislation.

Specialists are skeptical. Even weak Specialists offer 20 percent fewer endorsements than do the Generalists; and only one out of four strong Specialists is strong on this strategy. Instead, Specialists prefer working through party committees, all-party groups, Select Committees, and personal contacts with Ministers to generate steady pressure behind the scenes. They are skeptical about the likelihood of success and even about the value of what can be achieved by Private Members' Bills:[24] "I was greeted on my first day here by an elderly peer who had been a Member. And he said, 'You will remember me, won't you?' I said, 'Well, I'm afraid I don't.' And he said, 'Ah, well, I was the man who introduced a Bill to limit the use of flick knives.' Well, he'd obviously got tremendous satisfaction out of having produced this Bill, a Private Members' Bill that nobody else had ever heard of, and probably was the least significant of Bills."

MOTIVATIONS: GADFLIES AND PEACOCKS

As the gadfly stings the cow, so the Generalist checks the Executive. Generalists are familiar with this analogy, "to act as a gadfly, to keep stinging the Executive to do the things that you consider necessary, to keep the Executive under constant supervision." Checking Executives is, they claim, "far and away the most important duty . . . undoubtedly the most important thing in any Member's life."[25] They enjoy scrutinizing legislation. But they also enjoy the animation and agitation involved in harassing the beast, in "constantly questioning the Executive, constantly denying them the right to take decisions and do things without justifying it all the way down the line." The principal goals of the Generalist are to make the Government defend itself publicly and to test the mettle of individual Ministers.

The fact that the Government must defend itself keeps Ministers and civil servants on their toes. The way that the Government defends itself affects its reputation at Westminster and its popularity with the public.[26] This check on Executive power is "very important, because the Executives are always encroaching. . . . That part of Parliament which is not part of the Executive therefore has a role to play scrutinizing the actual Executive, keeping it within bounds. . . . Year by year, unfortunately, it seems to be a losing battle, like Venice which sinks an inch every year." But it is a battle that

Generalists obviously enjoy fighting. And although they are more energetic in checking Executives from the other side of the House than from their own side, some see a struggle between backbenchers and Executives that rivals the struggle between the parties.[27] In fact, the exuberance with which such Generalists pursue Executives evokes images of the House before the rise of party discipline. One of them, who practices what he preaches, puts it this way: "I personally have adopted the attitude that my role was, is, and will always be to oppose the Executive when I think the Executive needs to be opposed, to attack Ministers and their departments when I think they deserve to be attacked, irrespective of party or politics."

The attacks on Ministers test their mettle as administrators and debaters and keep their departments on edge. The cut and thrust serves to remind Ministers that they are "human beings, that they are fallible, and that lots of mistakes and misjudgements are bound to happen. . . . It's very good they should be constantly reminded of this fact." A few Generalists, like this young Tory, are plainly looking for a fight: "I fight *all* Ministers, on any terms, with knives. And I'm not one of those who think the clever thing to do is to be nice to all Ministers . . . to hell with them." But most are just peppery and combative, pleasantly disputatious people who enjoy stirring coals and beating drums. It all seems so natural to them that they are puzzled by people who lack their clamorous dispositions: "I have known Members who have literally come in, and except for saying 'Please close the window' or 'Please get me a piece of paper,' they literally say and do nothing and never oppose the Executive or take an active part at all!"

Best known to the public are those Generalists, sometimes referred to as "peacocks," whose performances are suffused with both vanity and service: "Well, I think being in politics is a good way to massage one's vanity. It is very nice to see one's name in the newspapers. I'm not too ashamed of that . . . it's a mixture of vanity and service, and it varies in proportion with every politician." For the vanity, there is something to be had from standing up in the Chamber and making a speech about national affairs. But the greater satisfactions come from national audiences, from the press or radio or television, where millions of people may read or hear the "Media Member's" views.[28] Gratification lies not simply in the fame, in the fact that one's name is known, but also in the acclaim that may accompany it, such as appreciative letters from around the country. Public acclaim offers "very great pleasure indeed." Thus, "I'm often accused of being a publicist," protested one of the champion backbench publicists. "In fact, I do not publicize myself at all. Er, people are deeply interested in what I am doing, and regard me as, um, an original, they're prepared to interest themselves in it. . . . I mean I love people. . . . I love them all, and by and large they love me."[29]

Generalists use publicity to illuminate problems and stimulate solutions by persuading people and mobilizing support. Through publicity flows influence, and the greater the publicity, the greater the potential influence. The key to winning is "to put the thing simply and colourfully." To get the point across with the greatest force, "you use a little poetic license." Generalists are "propagandists in the best sense of the word, people who try to influence public opinion through Parliament." To the skeptics, they argue, persuasively, that this role is "very important. You can't dismiss Jesus Christ. . . . A friend once said to me, 'The Trades Council doesn't matter, it has no power, they are just propagandists.' And I pointed out that Jesus Christ had no power; he was just a propagandist. And therefore I think it is a vital role." Vanity and service are not necessarily such an unappealing mixture unless the vanity, in the shape of self-publicity, so dominates the service as to undermine it. Motives are always mixed.

What is clear is that all Generalists, gadflies and peacocks alike, seek influence over concrete policy. Like Ideologues, they want to shape the way people think. But unlike Ideologues, they concentrate on alternatives rather than on assumptions. Like Specialists, they want tangible results. But unlike Specialists, they concentrate on many targets rather than on only a few. Indeed, some Generalists define their responsibilities so broadly that they "think the real role of a Member of Parliament is to look after the way of life of the nation . . . to be a Member, primarily, for the whole of the United Kingdom rather than just for one's constituency." Most of them, however, focus their energies more than this and concentrate on the agendas that already exist in their Parliament and in their parties.

Thus, they believe that they can influence policy by discussing policy. Such discussions, they say, are the backbencher's most important responsibility: "to be a part of a sort of marching forward, left foot, right foot . . . process for the development of a common mind with people in Parliament . . . of their attitudes to problems, policies, priorities."[30] Politicians are effective to the extent that they can persuade other politicians of their points of view. This process of opinion formation defines the attitudes that Parliament eventually adopts about things, defines the scope and the room within which the Government must then operate.

The case they make is a fascinating one from which political scientists have much to learn. If decisions can be shaped by influencing the decision takers, they say, then these decisions can also be shaped by influencing those who influence the decision takers. Members of the party, collectively, influence the party leaders who become Ministers. Hence, if you play a "role in shaping policy views within your party . . . you do in fact have enormous influence; you do play a very big part in actually changing the nature of our society." Generalists believe that the direction in which a party moves is affected by deliberation and discussion, in the House and outside it, where "one is simultaneously sharpening up your own ideas and getting your ideas across to your colleagues." They believe in the force of reasoned argument and tell themselves and others that "if you've got a valid point, sooner or later that valid point will get through."

Generalists are strongly motivated by the pursuit of influence, the career goal round which they construct their roles. "The thing that I am really concerned about," said a new and energetic Conservative backbencher, "is . . . to feel that I've done certain things that have played a part in things which are important, you know. This is a personal thing and not a public thing at all." Playing a part may involve direct influence; but more often the influence will be indirect, for "the levers of power here are all remote control as far as backbenchers are concerned." In either case, it will always involve persuading associates: "There is nothing better than sitting down with half a dozen other people who hold different views from your own, and getting them eventually to agree . . . influencing one's colleagues and peers and persuading them to adopt one's own point of view."[31] The satisfaction comes from the awareness that one has played a part and influenced one's associates. This sort of influence is cumulative and difficult to demonstrate convincingly, for it is, Generalists say, more "like a maze" than like a row of dominoes. Therefore, although it may be difficult to measure the contributions of particular backbenchers in particular cases, the cumulative impact of their efforts cannot be denied—a point that is very important to them and taught through tales like the story of the Mediterranean oarsmen: "Well, you might say to someone who was rowing one of these ancient vessels you see pictures of in the Mediterranean, where there's about 150 oarsmen, 'How important is the role of any individual oarsman at the oar?' If I stopped, nobody would notice. But if we all stopped, everybody would notice."

And yet the motivational core of their role must involve more than the pursuit of influence, for Generalists will have been told time and time again that the most effective path to influence is built by specialization and laid down behind the scenes. Why are they Generalists? What other desires are involved? Part of the answer is that they relish the action and the diversity offered by generalist roles. This disposition can also be seen in their attitudes toward the House as an institution: "I don't see myself as being in the House of Commons simply because it's a nice social club. I see it more in terms of either doing something or, you know, not being there at all. . . . The great opportunity it offers *to do things* by involving yourself in situations, looking at problems." Generalists are concerned much more with instrumental activities than with atmosphere, as this Tory Reformer makes coldly clear: "I've heard many MPs say (I used to think it was a joke), 'Oh this is the best club,' and when they'd been beaten and returned, 'Oh I'm so delighted to be back in the club again.' But, quite frankly, I think those are the ones who don't do a lot of parliamentary work."

The pursuit of influence has promoted professionalization in the postwar House of Commons. And where Generalists follow full-time the trails of influence, they encounter action and diversity. They like the action, for they are the sort of people who find it difficult to stand aside and watch decisions being taken by others. They also like the diversity. They don't at all mind the discontinuities in their role and, instead, find it exhilarating to jump from one topic to another. These incentives anchor their interpretation of the search for influence in an environment where practically everybody else seems to be specializing. The strength of the role's motivational core was expressed by this reluctant Generalist as follows: "I keep trying to stop it. I can't: it's like my hair going grey. My problem is an unquenchable thirst for what goes on in the House, and the House is an all-round place. There's something different every day."[32]

Specialists

Among backbenchers, policy advocacy has become the dominant approach to the job. And among Policy Advocates, Specialists have become the principal subtype, a subtype frequently characterized as the most professional of Westminster's new professional politicians. In the same vein, David Judge has found a striking relationship between degree of specialization and commitment to politics as a career.[33] The magnitude of specialization at Westminster must not, however, be exaggerated. Specialists may constitute a majority of Policy Advocates, but they remain a minority among backbenchers and in the House as a whole. Besides, only a few of them are genuine experts in their subjects. The rest are knowledgeable, but lack the depth and analytic order displayed by the civil servants and academics in their fields.

Yet Specialists are politicians, not civil servants or academics, and the softer specialization they develop is suited to their goals. They aim to influence policy—carefully, quietly, persistently, and effectively—"in very small, localised, specialised fields." They assume that influence is won in such fields, and that the Generalist "who tries to be a jack of all trades in this place is not only riding for a fall, he also bears less influence than he would like to think, even than the general public for that matter." The General-

Purpose MP, Specialists say, spreads himself or herself too thin. He may win publicity in the country, but he doesn't win anything in the House: "I think the need in this is not to be a Nabarro. You keep your powder dry and use it only when (a) you think it is really important, (b) when you think you can win." According to Parliament's Specialists, "the General-Purpose MP is a No-Purpose MP."

How many subjects do Specialists take up? Novices seek guidance in anecdotes and quotations from sages of the recent past. They hear, for example: "And Dalton used to say, 'Specialise in two subjects.' And I think that's good advice." The theme is repeated by senior backbenchers who have never doubted for a moment that "the absolutely essential thing if you want to get anywhere is to be knowledgeable, to decide what are the two, conceivably three, subjects that you will really try to master, and then read, study, inform yourself about them." Our coding criterion for Specialists therefore identified those Policy Advocates who concentrated their attention on fewer than three policy areas or on three areas that were either defined narrowly or integrated closely with one another.

ACTIVITY: RESEARCH AND LEVERAGE

Although Specialists, like Generalists, use Question Time and Adjournment Debates, they say that they don't spend much time in the Chamber, for "if you are really to study your own subject, you cannot just for the interest of it sit and listen to all the debates of all the others." Instead, they concentrate on research and leverage, on gathering information and then applying pressure behind the scenes where they believe it will do the most good.

Information about one's special subject is gathered from newspapers, which Specialists scan daily for articles, and from site visits to domestic facilities or to foreign countries. While important books in the field are read, and research is done in the House of Commons Library, Specialists seek current and first-hand knowledge, much of which comes from contact with organizations and individuals outside Parliament. Thus, the Specialist attends many functions over the weekend because "he wants to have his feet firmly on the ground outside the Palace of Westminster. He wants to have plenty of contacts outside so he can know what they think." If he specializes in problems of the handicapped, for instance, he will be found at events such as a demonstration of a partial-hearing unit for a primary school. Specialists also keep in touch with pressure groups, "like the Disablement Income Group, who are always trying to get one to do something for them." On the committee stage of a Bill, such organizations may offer draft amend-

ments or even provide daily briefings. Some Specialists become so involved
with outside groups that they serve as officers of organizations like the National Council of Civil Liberties or the Footpath and Open Spaces Preserva-
tion Society. Moreover, when the need has existed, several have helped to
found their own pressure groups such as Amnesty International or the Mental Health Research Fund.[34]

Contacts with key individuals in the field can be very useful too, particularly for collecting inside information. It is desirable in industrial relations,
for instance, to maintain contacts with informants in trade unions or business associations "like the Engineering Employers Federation or the Small
Business Association, with people who are involved in industrial relations."
In this way, one accumulates sets of knowledgeable acquaintances: "And I
automatically know, when a subject's coming up, who to ask round for a
drink. He's the man who will tell me (providing that I don't ever say that
I've seen him) what is going to make my speech effective."[35] Often these are
people the Specialist has met after entering Parliament.

Besides gathering information through newspapers, site visits, and outside
contacts, Specialists look to Select Committees for some of the ammunition
they seek. Select Committees attract them because they create an incentive
to keep up with one's subject. They also provide an unusual opportunity to
grill Ministers and civil servants. Select Committees are created to deal with
specific topics and come in two types. One type, such as the Public Accounts
Committee or Select Committee on Statutory Instruments, reviews reports
from expert staff and is usually not controversial. The other type, like the
Select Committee on National Industries, conducts its own inquiries and
can be very controversial.[36] Specialists want these committees to matter.
They want to "have no doubt at all," as a member of the Expenditure Committee explained, "that I am working in effective company, that I make an
effective contribution alongside the other effective contributions, and that
our report will stand scrutiny for many years to come as a work worth
undertaking and effectively discharged."[37] Specialists are committee men.
They aim, through their committee work, to influence government policy.

Although Select Committees later became somewhat more effective, at
the time of the interviews they were doing little more than irritating Ministers and departments.[38] Their promise was great, but their impact did not
yet warrant the ministerial meddling to manipulate their rules and membership that would be seen by the 1990s.[39] In fact, their impact at the time
seemed scarcely more than that of all-party groups like the Committee on
Slavery and Primitive Peoples. All-party groups do not carry out investigations with the assistance of specialist advisors; nor do they produce reports

with policy recommendations to the Government. Yet they do occasionally make a mark upon both party policy and government policy. Several Common Market pressure groups certainly did so, as did the Disablement Income Group, for example. Even the Commonwealth Parliamentary Association, which is usually seen as merely a pleasant diversion and an excuse for travel abroad ("I think I've visited every Commonwealth country in my time"), has been also used by several Specialists as a launching pad for influence.[40]

Backbench party committees are like all-party groups in that their meetings are attended not just by Specialists but by many different types of Members. Yet, more than the all-party groups, they are used by Specialists, particularly by Conservative Specialists, as major staging posts for campaigns to shape party policy and governmental programs. Older Members don't attend them very much and say that they are really "for those on the way up." Cynical Members don't attend them very much either and are likely to dismiss such committees as occupational therapy for MPs with little else to do. Other backbenchers attend "whenever there is a row." And Specialists keep them going, because the main function of these committees is to serve as sounding boards for backbench opinion, to reflect suggestions, and to react to information from the party leadership.

When the Conservatives are in Government, for instance, the officers of their backbench committees expect to exert some influence and are often able to do so. They invite Ministers to come along and explain policies. What makes it worthwhile, "if you specialise in any particular area," is that "you can make of it what you wish"—because these are private meetings where backbenchers feel freer to air their views than they do in the Chamber or the 1922 Committee.[41] It is mainly on the Conservative side that Specialists "think there is a great opportunity for backbenchers to influence decisions through party committees." And it was mainly during the 1960s and 1970s that these committees became significant sounding boards for the Conservative leadership, particularly when the party was in Government and when backbenchers had opportunities to influence decisions before such decisions were formally taken.[42]

Thus, before announcing their decisions publicly, Conservative Ministers frequently discuss with their party committee the measures they have in mind and thereby collect backbenchers' views. Led by their Specialists, the party committees seek to modify ministerial attitudes by "acquainting Ministers with what is intolerable," with what backbenchers will not stand. Officers of these committees have regular contact with Ministers and believe "that they certainly listen to what I have to say." Such officers are often ex-Ministers or backbench barons who are flattered but not surprised by the occasional comment from a senior civil servant that acknowledges their status and importance.

"The specialist groups (backbench party committees) are important for Conservatives for policy and upward mobility," an envious Labour Specialist observed, "but in the Labour Party they are unimportant for either purpose. Hence, no one goes." This assumption was widely held among Labour backbenchers, though the Trade Union Group was cited as an exception.[43] Actually, Conservatives may overestimate the influence of their backbench party committees, and Labour may underestimate the influence of theirs, partially because Labour's groups work better in Opposition than in Government. In Opposition, Labour's backbench party groups collect information and discuss policy and do have some impact on the formulation of party aims.[44] But in Government, Labour's Specialists say they tend to promote their projects through less-formal channels. Still, they do speak out at the weekly meetings of the Parliamentary Labour Party (PLP), which are often very frank and acrimonious. They also seek to shape party policy through the National Executive Committee (NEC), which offers an extraparliamentary platform for influence.[45]

Specialists regard committee work as their most important duty because they believe that it is their most important formal opportunity for exercising influence. After backbench party committees for Conservatives, and perhaps NEC committees for Labour Members, many look to Parliament's Standing Committees, which scrutinize legislation, as a place where they might get "hold of a subject which you think you know a bit about, and then either alone or in conjunction with a colleague, being able to . . . alter policy." On Standing Committees, this requires getting the Minister to change his mind "by getting amendments carried through to a major Bill—and you get a kick out of that." It is, of course, much more easily said than done, and much more easily done in Government than in Opposition, for Ministers may be inclined to give something to their own backbenchers when the latter make a convincing case. Besides, even if they don't give away anything publicly, they may "make sympathetic noises" and later introduce the changes themselves, quietly.

SELECTING SUBJECTS

The activities of Specialists concentrate on research and leverage, on gathering information and applying pressure to influence those who are influential in particular policy areas. But why are they concerned with one policy area more than another? How do they choose their subjects? A few Specialists select them strategically, but most discover them inadvertently in the course of their work in Westminster, Whitehall, or the constituency.

Those who choose their topics strategically look for areas that are neglected by backbenchers in their party. One such area on the Conservative side is "the social service field. . . . I've chosen very much to specialise in this field . . . because there aren't too many of us who do." A neglected subject on the Labour side is defense policy. Because Conservative experts in the social services and Labour experts in defense policy are scarce, they are in demand—and consequently in a position to exercise more influence than might otherwise be the case. This approach is clever, but it is also dangerous because it runs the risks of heterodoxy: "I'm a bit out on a limb as far as the Labour Party's concerned. One's work on defence can completely change one's mind about defence people."[46]

Most Specialists are not so calculating and instead simply take up opportunities that come their way. When backbenchers make new outside contacts, for example, one thing leads to another as experiences and interests become intertwined. Or MPs who have acquired some expertise in Government may subsequently work these topics on the backbenches. As Ministers, they may have been asked to take up a subject about which they know next to nothing. So they plunge in; and their investments produce a store of information that, later on the backbenches, only needs to be updated periodically to be effective, thereby reducing research and conserving time. It is not surprising, therefore, to find former Ministers of Defense writing, as backbenchers, occasional papers on the subject. In the same vein, backbenchers who have served as Parliamentary Private Secretaries (PPSs) to the Secretary of State for Education find, for example, that for years afterward, "my interests have been education, particularly the provision of better facilities, longer facilities for those who were hitherto leaving school at age fifteen."

Most Ministers and PPSs, however, are not at their posts long enough to develop the sort of investments that make today's duties tomorrow's specializations. They are as likely, much like their other colleagues, to develop the special interests that they originally brought with them to Parliament. The best-known example of this is the barrister who is "interested in legal subjects, not so much criminal law as commercial law," because that is what he practiced for twenty years before he entered the House. This pattern fits a wide range of occupations: exporters who are interested in trade with those parts of the world about which they have previous knowledge and experience; physicians who concentrate on "health matters and allied subjects"; former colonial civil servants whose major interest "for many years now" has been race relations; former headmasters of grammar schools who find that "the thing I probably feel strongest about is education." Furthermore, these preparliamentary interests are not solely occupational. There are Specialists with lifelong interests in music, though with no professional experience, who see themselves as guardians of the Scottish BBC Symphony Orchestra. There are Specialists who "have always been interested in welfare matters" in their communities. And there are Specialists who grew up abroad and have always been concerned "about conflicts between the races."

Second in importance after preparliamentary interests is the MP's constituency work: "I think one tends to take an interest in matters that particularly affect one's constituency. I've got one of the largest agricultural seats in the country, and I suppose that agriculture is one of my main interests." Or it might be defense: "I had to learn all about this (it was something new to me) because of my constituency being the naval port and the majority of my constituents employed in the dockyard. Naturally, I had to learn all about defence as quickly as I could." Constituency-related topics are usually linked to occupations such as shipbuilding, mining, motorcars, steel works, or fishing. But even when one's constituency does not provide an obvious subject (most do not), work with individual constituents can sometimes stimulate specialization in particular topics. Problems raised by their constituents have immersed Policy Advocates in Britain's foreign policy toward Barbados or Bangladesh or toward domestic-policy topics such as pensions or disablement. The experiences are idiosyncratic, as are the Specialists' reactions to them. One irreverent Conservative became immersed in Home Office affairs in this way:

> A large number of my supporters, admirable people in every possible way, seem to think that most of the ills of society can be cured by flogging people . . . "Bring back the birch." . . . And I used to be assailed with accusations that the Conservative Government was not being sufficiently firm with criminal elements in society. . . . So I said, "Well, look, I will go and have a look and see what goes on, and then let you have my considered opinion." And I spent a couple of years going around all the penal institutions in the country. And as a result of it I formed certain views . . . and I put them into a little book, which solved two problems: it enabled me to know what I thought; and it also enabled me always to answer people who raised this with me. I say, "Go and read my book." It wraps up the conversation very promptly because they don't want to have to buy it!

Up to this point I have constructed an account of the Specialists' characteristic attitudes and behaviors. I have also explored how they choose their
subjects. But to understand Specialists satisfactorily, we need to know more
about their career goals and emotional incentives and about how these motivations differ from those of other backbenchers, especially from those of
other Policy Advocates.

DESIRES: INFLUENCE, ACHIEVEMENT, SELF-IMPORTANCE

The principal career goal of the Specialist is "to do": to influence, to achieve,
and, at the same time, to feel important. It is their dominant concern with
influence that distinguishes Specialists from other backbenchers and brack-
ets them with Ideologues and Generalists. But it is their dogged devotion
to effective influence that distinguishes them from Ideologues, who are less
interested in concrete issues, and from Generalists, who are less interested
in the details of particular policies. Specialists immerse themselves in issues
and details because they are convinced that this is the only sure way "to
bring about the things in which you have believed."

Backbenchers often define what they *are* by talking about what they *are
not*. Thus, Specialists define their role by telling us that "an MP clearly isn't
merely a Welfare Officer [Constituency Member] . . . equally also he isn't
merely a member of an agreeable club [Parliament Man], or, still less, he
isn't merely a member of a debating society [Generalist]. He is there to have
his share in *influencing* events." This is the Specialist's theme: "doing," organizing and achieving policy innovations. "I'm not a talker," explained a
busy former Junior Minister on the Conservative side. "I'm a doer." What
attracts them is not the expectation of shaping ideas, nor the anticipation
of excitement and publicity. What attracts them is "the ability to do, the
opportunity given to do things." By frequent use of the verb "to do," Specialists make it known that, unlike some other backbenchers, they take their
role very seriously, avoid theatrical or convivial distractions, and work carefully, quietly, and persistently to influence the influential.[47]

Their goal is "to get things through," to make a contribution to the life
of the country by influencing the Acts of Parliament about which they are
knowledgeable. And, in getting things through, they say that they are much
more interested in the results than the credits, much more interested in the
outcomes than the publicity: "The only public relations I use is to bring
pressure to try to get the thing through." Therefore, Specialists tend to make
only the occasional speech—for which they have usually "worked on it,
worked out the ideas," gathered the information very carefully. They are

convinced that the "glittery bit of oratory" in the Chamber doesn't do much good. "I've always been a bit of a technocrat I suppose," one of them said, and therefore, he explained, he is most comfortable behind the scenes presenting views to Ministers in offices, corridors, division lobbies, or the Smoking Room. Successful Specialists are as modest about their ends as they are dogged about their means. They have learned to "be content sometimes with rather small returns." The secret is to think small but seriously, for though the results may not be grand, they do affect national policy.

The satisfactions that Specialists find in this modest influence can be heard in their descriptions of the strategies by which they pursue it. To the same role questions that other backbenchers answer by chronicling constituents' dilemmas or by describing parliamentary dramas, Specialists respond by reviewing the rules of thumb they follow "to influence, to get something done." Since backbenchers don't have power, the first of these rules is to influence those who do.[48] Another is to keep one's policy objectives specific. Specialists concentrate on subjects "where there is something in particular that you want to put right." They do not try to influence the broad flow of policy but rather to have highly focused concerns so that "when there is an opportunity of . . . hammering another nail in, one is always ready to do it." It is in the concrete and the particular that influence is most likely to succeed. "In fact, anybody in my view who tries to be a jack of all trades in this place is not only riding for a fall, he bears less influence than he would like to think, even less than the general public for that matter." Being specific requires gathering detailed information. Being specific requires narrowing one's interests and concentrating one's time. Specialists willingly bear the costs in time, energy, and parochialism because, unlike Generalists, they want to do more than merely check the Executive. They want to scrutinize it: "I think it's very important that the Executive should first of all be challenged and then, over and beyond that, *scrutinized*. And a Member can do that through the Parliamentary Question . . . he can do it more effectively through committee work, especially in view of the evolution of the committee system in the House on specialist lines. . . . What I think is the most important function of the Member of Parliament is to scrutinize and influence the work of the Executive."

The most effective way to influence the Executive is through anticipatory action. Anticipatory action involves group pressure, individual pressure, and threats of rebellion—all applied *before* the Executive has taken a firm public stand on the matter in question. "I'm more interested," one Specialist explained, "in influencing policies which Governments are *going to pursue*." Specialists believe that "it's a cumulative effect," that influence is best exercised in the context of group campaigns. Everyone is aware that individual influence, in contrast to group-driven pressure, can occasionally be effective: "There is the sort of single star, who is also essential to the working of Parliament." "But," most Specialists would add, "you should remember when talking to me that I am one of the team-working MPs." Behind the pressure is the threat of rebellion.[49] "No Government can stay in power unless it keeps its backbenchers with it. . . . The influence of the 1922 Committee collectively is immense." Party leaders are especially vulnerable when they are in Government and when the internal pressure is combined with pressure from powerful outside interests.[50] Specialists also believe that threats of rebellion are most successful when used sparingly (since persistent rebels tend to be ignored) and that such threats have, in recent years, become increasingly effective.

Sense of achievement, an important emotional incentive, is closely intertwined with the Specialist's more cognitive dedication to influence: "I find most satisfying the undoubted fact that one does make an impact. . . . I consider it an achievement to have some effect on policy." Here the stimulus is focused not so much on experiencing the processes of influence as on contemplating the results: "I'm not interested in playing party games; I'm interested in something achieved." The link between achievement and influence is the policy modification, the something that is done. Thus, the doing is bracketed by achievement on the one side and by influence on the other: "I've always wanted to achieve things. I've always wanted to get something done. I've always wanted to influence."

When Specialists discuss influence, they celebrate the strategies by which it is pursued. When they discuss achievement, they are more likely to savor the significance of the results. Stories about such results are for them the equivalent of the Constituency Members' tales about cases resolved on behalf of their constituents. "The Government have now announced that they are going to do away with the levy grant system in industrial training," the Specialist tells us. "I consider this a great personal achievement." And he recounts, at length, both the nature of the achievement and the circumstances that made it desirable. These stories are trophies, symbols to others and reminders to Specialists themselves of what they have accomplished in their roles. "I rather like to count up the sort of achievements that one's persisted in," said a former Junior Minister and active committee man; "at the end of the day you count them up, you know, . . . issues that have made progress because of my pressing."

Achievements are most satisfying when one is convinced of the significance both of the decisions and of one's impact upon them. Unfortunately, it isn't always so easy to be convinced. Some decisions, such as joining the EEC, are obviously very important; others, such as the regulation of motion sickness pills, are obviously very much less important. But the significance of the vast majority of policy decisions is often ambiguous—which may be why Specialists dwell so much on their desire to affect things "that *really matter . . .* things that *really matter* in national policy." Furthermore, it is even more disconcerting to find that "you can never say for certain what the end effects of *your* actions are." Some Specialists find that "the uncertainty of it has a certain amount of thrill." But most find this "rather frustrating and unsatisfying. Even if something comes about which you have been agitating for . . . you can never say for sure that it was due to your action." "You see," the barrister reflects, "if I'm in court and I get a client acquitted . . . I say, 'Well, I've done that.' But in politics you can very rarely say as much."

This concern with effectiveness sometimes makes Specialists impatient with Westminster's club-like atmosphere and with those who, like Spectators, are content to watch rather than to do. "I don't particularly like Parliament, not really," said one of the more impatient among them. "Instead, I *use* it." The club-like atmosphere reduces efficiency. And there is precious little time to enjoy it anyway, for "when one comes here one wants to get down to it. . . . It's quite impossible to do the club sort of thing." There isn't time for developing close friendships either. Besides, Specialists need allies more than they need friends. Parliament's "Doers" will not be lulled into lethargy by the gothic club: "It's *doing* that matters. . . . At a very early age I learnt the frustrations of being a very well-placed Spectator—and they're awful." "Effectiveness" means achieving changes in a Bill either during preparliamentary stages, when backbenchers on the Government side have the best shot, or during the committee and report stages, when Opposition backbenchers have an opportunity too. During these stages, Specialists are "quite convinced that the determined backbencher, on fairly narrow but important themes, can achieve results."[51]

Some of the older Members are weak Specialists whose stories about successful influence are largely a remembrance of things past. This is particularly true of former Ministers who, while awaiting retirement, serve on committees to use their specialized knowledge but cannot overlook the contrasts with their previous positions, for "if you've been a Minister, you've been in the middle of it. And quite frankly I'm not so interested in playing cowboys and Indians now." Their colleagues seem to understand, and to overlook their grumbling about how achieving things directly by exercising power, as opposed to indirectly by influencing the influential, was "the highlight" of their careers and "the only really interesting aspect of political life."

Some tired ex-Ministers, and some energetic eager beavers too, say they are also motivated by a sense of self-importance that comes from dealing in influence behind the scenes. It is a "sense of satisfaction that one gets out of being involved in politics at this level. Some people might call it 'ego'. . . they're probably right. There's a degree of egotism in it I suppose." It is pleasing to realize, they point out, that one has influenced Government policy by influencing senior Ministers; it is pleasing to feel that "one's advice is sought and taken." Indeed, "A senior chap in the F.O. [Foreign Office] said, 'We regard you as the most important chap in our affairs after the Foreign Secretary.'" At the same time, one is also aware that "we exaggerate the significance of the role because . . . it's part of our narcissism. . . . We really believe that when we've passed an Act, we've altered people's personal lives. And I say that as someone who has passed more legislation than most people."

There is an obvious incentive involved in having people listen to you "with keen interest and, if not admiration, at least respect"[52] because you have detailed knowledge. When you have such knowledge from having served successfully behind the scenes, "there is a satisfaction in being a sort of minor authority on something, you know, when you go back to the constituency." More important than appreciation in the constituency is appreciation in the House. Specialists very much want to be taken seriously: "Some Members on both sides tend to be dismissed by Ministers, and quite properly. Other Members . . . are taken seriously. Even though the Minister . . . may not accept the argument . . . you nevertheless know that you are being taken seriously as a Member—and that is very important." Specialists secure this sense of importance through their dogged devotion to effective influence, through patient research and persistent pressure. They take themselves seriously, enjoy being taken seriously by others, and find it difficult to understand why Ideologues and Generalists don't play the role of Policy Advocate their way.

Consequences for Behavior

Many investigations that have sought to link preference roles (usually representational roles defined by structural approaches) to behavior have yielded mixed results. This section examines relationships between the preference roles of Generalists and Specialists and behavior associated with institutionalization in the House of Commons: allocations of time, Oral and Written Questions, and participation in Select Committees.

ALLOCATIONS OF TIME

Generalists and Specialists see themselves as busy professionals for whom time is a precious resource. Since they pursue influence with such different strategies, they should be expected to allocate their time differently depending on the suitability of particular arenas to their particular aims. The data in Table 2.3 are the respondents' own estimates of the number of hours they spend in each setting during "an average week."

Differences among role types should not be very large, because all MPs spend some time in each place, and the distinction between Generalists and Specialists will be only one among many different variables that determine the allocations. Nevertheless, there are substantial differences in behavior. Generalists are nearly twice as likely as Specialists to spend fifty or more hours per week at Westminster. They express their commitment to politics as a career by bustling about the House and involving themselves in all the exciting campaigns. Specialists, by contrast, use the House more selectively and do much of their work through contacts with organizations and individuals outside Parliament. The gap between Generalists and Specialists is greatest in the Labour Party, where Policy Advocates are known as Westminster's "eager beavers" and where the omnipresent Generalists contribute most to this reputation.

Table 2.3 Allocations of time by Policy Advocate subtypes, in percent

Time allocated*	Total at Westminster		In the Chamber		In lobby, dining room, etc.	
	Generalists	Specialists	Generalists	Specialists	Generalists	Specialists
High	43	24	21	12	21	05
Moderate	50	55	68	68	39	36
Low	07	21	11	21	39	60
Total	100	100	100	101	99	101
	(N = 28)	(N = 42)	(N = 28)	(N = 43)	(N = 28)	(N = 42)

*At Westminster: high = 50 or more hours per week; moderate = 39–49; low = 11–29. ($p = .02$)
In the Chamber: high = 15 or more hours per week; moderate = 5–14; low = 1–4. ($p = .08$)
In lobby, dining room, etc.: high = 20 or more hours per week; moderate = 10–19; low = 0–9. ($p = .02$)

To criticize Ministers and launch ideas, Generalists need to be in the Chamber and around the lobbies and dining rooms. And, although the result is not statistically significant at the .05 level, Generalists are nearly twice as likely as Specialists to attend the Chamber for fifteen or more hours per week. Everyone will consider attending for Prime Minister's Questions, important debates, or dramatic confrontations. But Generalists are also drawn to the Chamber by the opportunity to attack the Executive, a task that many of them regard as their principal duty and responsibility. The other side of the Generalist's strategy, using the House as a launching pad for ideas, sends them into the lobbies, dining rooms, and other areas of the House where they are four times as likely as Specialists to be frequently found. This contrast appears in both parties but is more pronounced on the Labour side.

QUESTIONS IN PARLIAMENT

Table 2.4 analyzes Oral and Written Questions put down by backbenchers between 1970 and 1973. The range in this behavior is enormous: some backbenchers put down none at all, some around 150, and several, such as Arthur Lewis, "the undisputed champion" of Question Time, over 1,000.[53] Since Oral Questions afford an opportunity for criticism and publicity, an opportunity to be both gadfly and peacock at the same time, Generalists should again be expected to do more than their share.[54] They do. They are twice as likely as Specialists to ask many Oral Questions and particularly likely to ask "peg questions" on which almost any supplementary Question can be hung.[55] When they table these a fortnight in advance, some Generalists do not know exactly what their supplementary will be. They wait and see what crises appear in the media and then select their topic on this basis.

Table 2.4 Oral and Written Questions by Policy Advocate subtypes, in percent

	Oral Questions		Written Questions	
Questions*	Generalists	Specialists	Generalists	Specialists
Many	69	38	85	44
Few	31	62	15	56
Total	100	100	100	100
	(N = 39)	(N = 68)	(N = 39)	(N = 68)

*Oral Questions: many = more than 10; few = 0–9. ($p \le .001$)
Written Questions: many = more than 50; few = 0–49. ($p \le .001$)

The difference between Generalists and Specialists is only slightly stronger on the Labour than on the Conservative side. This reflects the fact that not all Oral Questions are critical of the Executive. Some, in fact, are regularly tabled by Government backbenchers to make friendly points that will enable Ministers to show themselves and their departments in a favorable light.

Another indication of institutionalization in Parliament is that the number of Written Questions rose from twenty-two per day in 1960–61 to ninety-eight per day in 1971–72.[56] Written Questions are sometimes said to be put down not for pressure and publicity but instead to collect information or to put a case to a Minister in a way that might produce a reasonable response. Thus, it is somewhat surprising that, with Written Questions, Generalists are again so much more likely than Specialists to be among the most active questioners, sufficiently so on the Labour side to generate a correlation of .90 (gamma) at the .01 level of significance. The fact that this difference is so pronounced even for the party in Opposition reinforces Judge's point that Written Questions too can sting the Government and attract backbench attention.[57]

The widely noted sparsity of convincing links between role variables and behavioral variables in structural and interactionist studies makes it desirable to investigate this relationship further. Thus, the multiple regression analyses reported in Table 2.5 assess the impact of the role variable upon

Table 2.5 Regressions of Oral and Written Questions on selected independent variables

Independent variable	Oral Questions		Written Questions	
	Beta	F ratio	Beta	F ratio
Role	−.218	(4.75)*	−.218	(8.92)**
Attendance	.210	(3.16)	.265	(5.73)*
Marginality	−.109	(1.08)	.020	(0.01)
Tenure	.049	(0.20)	−.108	(1.08)
Party	.035	(0.11)	.052	(0.29)
R	.355		.478	
R^2	.126		.228	
R^2 (adjusted)	.081		.188	

$*p \leq .05$
$**p \leq .01$

Questions in the context of other independent variables that might reasonably be assumed to be involved.

The dependent variables, "Oral Questions" and "Written Questions," are measured as they were before. "Role" (Generalist-Specialist) is entered as a dummy variable. "Attendance" is measured by the total number of divisions in which R participated during the period 1970–1973 and is introduced as an indicator of a general disposition toward activity that should encompass Questions as well as other instrumental behaviors. "Marginality" is the difference between the winner's percentage of the total vote and that of the candidate who came second. It has been included in the equation because, like "tenure" (length of service) and "party," it is likely to structure both the inclination and the time available for putting Questions. The standard regression coefficients, beta weights, reported in Table 2.5 show the impact of each independent variable upon Oral Questions and Written Questions when the remaining independent variables are controlled statistically to remove confounding effects. It can readily be seen that the only independent variables exerting a substantial force are role and attendance. The Generalists and the assiduous attenders are most involved in Questions both Oral and Written. But the striking finding is that the role variable here outperforms all others including standard workhorses such as electoral security (marginality) and party.

PARTICIPATION IN SELECT COMMITTEES

If Generalists occupy the Chamber and the lobbies and take the lead at Question Time, it is the Specialists who should be expected to dominate Select Committees, for these committees conduct inquiries about particular subjects and construct informed judgments about policy programs. The data in Table 2.6 were gathered from published sources and include only those Select Committees that met for five or more sittings in 1972–73. Approximately one out of three backbenchers served on at least one such committee. Although membership in Select Committees should differ by role type with Specialists out in front, the differences might be attenuated by the fact that the committees were at the time relatively new, relatively weak in influence, and on the whole relatively obscure, that is to say, not as attractive to methodical influence seekers as they became after the reorganization of 1979.

Nevertheless, Specialists are committee people and are disposed to devote a great deal of energy to parliamentary affairs. Table 2.6 shows that they are nearly twice as likely as Generalists to participate in Select Committees. This difference in behavior is, however, entirely owing to the situation in

Table 2.6 Participation in Select Committees by Policy Advocate subtypes, by party, in percent

Committee membership	All Policy Advocates*		Conservative*		Labour**	
	Specialists	Generalists	Specialists	Generalists	Specialists	Generalists
Member	49	26	59	22	27	42
Nonmember	52	74	41	78	73	58
Total	101	100	100	100	100	100
	(N = 68)	(N = 39)	(N = 46)	(N = 23)	(N = 22)	(N = 12)

* $p \le .01$
** $p = .20$

the Conservative Party, whose Specialists are nearly three times more likely than Generalists to attend Select Committees. On the Labour side, by contrast, there is much less optimism about the effectiveness of these bodies. Here the pattern of behavior is reversed, leaving Generalists as more likely than Specialists to join the select committee bandwagon.

Insubordinate Inclinations

The role of the Policy Advocate attracts more than its share of backbenchers with "unruly humors." Nearly all the mavericks and eccentrics who become best known to the public—Willie Hamilton, Enoch Powell, Irene Ward, or Dennis Skinner, for instance[58]—are backbenchers who are involved in policy advocacy at Westminster. Their numbers are small, but their impatience with authority amplifies one of this role's underlying themes.

As Policy Advocates, mavericks are occasionally unrestrained and irresponsible, and frequently frolicsome, energetic, and aggressive. All five adjectives fit well one of Labour's most famous mavericks, who has already characterized his role as "is, and will always be . . . to attack Ministers and their departments . . . irrespective of party or politics." Some mavericks in our sample had been on the attack for a long time (several since Suez) and, like Humphry Berkeley, had many amusing stories about clashes with Whips and other authorities.[59] And some in our sample are still at it today.[60]

Others claimed that they were quite happy to be regarded as eccentrics. "It's a curious idiosyncracy of the British character," said one of the Conservative Party's best-known eccentrics, "that they like people who are eccentric. Now I am a member of the eccentric club. That doesn't mean I am an eccentric, either mentally or otherwise, but people regard me as an eccentric; some people regard me as a nut case—because they think I'm too original and sensational and different." But perhaps he isn't so very different. Like other Policy Advocates, he is vigorously pursuing policy goals. He has practical aims and uses eccentricity to draw attention to his projects. He and others like him see themselves as independent personalities, "an outsider within my party in the House." "I am fundamentally independent-minded in everything," says a Tory imperialist from whom we have also heard earlier. "I believe that individuals get much further than groups." "Now that Independent Members have been eliminated, we must replace them by Members of robust independence."[61] Independence and impatience with authority are themes to which they return again and again. They stand alone. They are ready to clash with colleagues on issues. And, like Richard Crossman's Sydney Silverman and Tam Dalyell,[62] they are not disposed to toe any lines: "I am essentially a loner, a loner and an individualistic Member apart, who does not believe in being guided by party doctrine or party Whip. I know my own Conservative philosophy much better than may be dictated to me by the whims and the nuances of party politicians even within my own party and sitting in established party committees."

Such unruly desires do not sustain consistent loyalty and obedience to party leaders. Fortunately for the parliamentary parties, most Policy Advocates are neither mavericks nor eccentrics. Yet, many of them share a little of the individualistic impatience that their parties' mavericks and eccentrics feel toward authority. Policy Advocates believe they know better than most others, at least on a few subjects, about the proper path for the party parade. And when the troops are led in other directions, they develop an understandable urge to dissent and even occasionally to kick over the traces in the division lobbies. Thus, when backbenchers were asked to agree or disagree with the statement that "MPs owe consistent loyalty and obedience to party leaders," the Policy Advocates expressed more reserve toward authority than did others, a reserve that decreased from Ideologues to Generalists to Specialists. Whereas only approximately one out of three other backbenchers were cautious about how much loyalty and obedience party leaders deserve, two out of three Ideologues held such views. Generalists likewise felt that at least occasionally it should be their "job to chart the path in the fields in which they are interested." And half of them were prepared to consider "bucking the Whip," "swallowing hard," and "saying no." Specialists, by contrast, appeared more willing to go along, for Specialists are by nature disposed to work quietly within the system.

Mavericks and eccentrics who become Policy Advocates earn their reputations by carrying the comparatively well crystallized preference roles of the Policy Advocate to extremes. They tend to regard their performances as legitimate, albeit vivid, interpretations of established types. All Ideologues, for instance, are interested in principles and ideals. Among them, those who become most strongly determined "to influence the destiny of this country . . . in accordance with my principles and ideals," are those most likely to cast themselves as mavericks prepared to defy "all the pressures, to stand for what they believe in." Similarly, all Generalists are in the business of checking the Executive. Among them, those who become most impatient with authority, who "never, never let loose until I have secured justice, often involving head-on collisions with the bureaucracy," are those most likely to become mavericks prepared to identify party leaders with the Establishment and "think the most important responsibility of being an MP is to be on the side, as it were, of the people against the Establishment."

In this way, mavericks and eccentrics are enabled by the role of the Policy Advocate to preach and practice intensely what they believe. They adapt the role to suit their preferences. They like it too. They like it because it puts them in the midst of things when "there's a row brewing." They like it because they enjoy "attacking and complaining too. And that gives me a great deal of satisfaction." They like it because it affords the opportunity of "being a rebel. This has given me the greatest pleasure of all. O.K., I'm in hot water with my party. . . . But I've enjoyed being a rebel, because if one is not a rebel, one becomes just a mere cipher. . . . But by being a rebel, and always likely to turn back and either snap or bite . . . this is [the] thing that I value most."

Mavericks and eccentrics are only a small minority among Policy Advocates, but their actions magnify and thereby help us to understand what other MPs regard as a characteristic trademark of the species: they often take themselves very seriously indeed. Thus, one of our "extremists" "enjoys and obtains gratification . . . from guiding the destinies of men." Another sees himself "in a position to make decisions of fundamental importance and with untold repercussions." And a third reports, by way of both self-mockery and self-disclosure, that "there are times when I'd like to be Lord Protector."

Sources of Role Choice

In an increasingly institutionalized House of Commons, it is easy to understand why most backbenchers regard policy advocacy as part of the job. But why do some backbenchers, the Policy Advocates, make this the pivot of their duties and responsibilities? Their decisions are a function of individual characteristics on the one side and opportunities and demands on the other.

The principal individual characteristics involved are the backbenchers' own goals, that is to say, their own career goals and emotional incentives. These are modified through experience in the role at the same time that they are shaping the individual's interpretation of the role. But such goals are often held prior to taking up roles and often point a backbencher toward one role rather than another. There is nothing very complicated about it: people seek out roles with core goals that are compatible with their own desires. Thus, backbenchers with a strong interest in influencing government policy are drawn toward the role of the Policy Advocate and, depending on their other preferences and emotional incentives, will develop this role in the key of the Ideologue, Generalist, or Specialist. The Policy Advocate's goals have already been explored extensively. There is, however, another individual characteristic that deserves some attention: ideology.

It would be surprising if ideology dominated the choices among backbench roles, although it would be more surprising still if it were not involved at all in these decisions. Thus, there is little reason to expect *particular* political values to be strongly involved with professional roles like that of the Policy Advocate, which are found in both major political parties and not associated with promoting *particular* party-political programs. That they are not strongly involved here was the conclusion of an exercise in which MPs were asked to rank-order a set of thirty-six political values arranged in four lists of nine items each.[63] There was little difference between the outlooks expressed by Policy Advocates and those expressed by other backbenchers. And yet, many Policy Advocates plainly regard politics, *pace* Trollope's Mr. Wharton, as a creed as well as a profession. They show many signs of being more dogmatic than has often been supposed. Most obviously, they are often attracted to their roles because they care a good deal about political aims and policies. Compared to their colleagues, then, Policy Advocates should stand nearer the poles rather than the midpoints of their parties' political spectrums. To investigate this possibility, backbenchers within each party were classified by ideological reputation: Left, Center, or Right.[64] And these data do indeed show a tendency for Policy Advocates to cluster at the poles rather than at the midpoints. The pattern is present in both parties and for both Generalists and Specialists.[65]

Opportunities and demands, the other variables in the equation, affect time. And Policy Advocates need time. They need time to gather information, to prepare strategies and speeches, and to seek influence on public platforms, within parties, and behind the scenes. Their chief distraction, the principal competing claim on their time, comes from constituency demands. "The most difficult thing is to give yourself time from all the distractions— the constituents, the letters, the personal cases—time to work out in your mind, as best you can, some of the problems of government in which you may actually have a share of the responsibility. . . . We are returned here to influence policy. And you cannot influence policy unless you give yourself time." When constituency demands are light, there is more time to pursue advocacy in national affairs. When they are especially heavy, backbenchers feel pressured toward the alternative role of the Constituency Member. The heaviest casework comes from constituencies that are heterogeneous in their class compositions and include a broader range of problems than those arising in comparatively homogeneous working-class or middle-class areas. To examine the impact of these opportunities and demands, proportions of Policy Advocates were therefore plotted across constituency class compositions (measured by percentage of nonmanual workers). The results show that the proportion of Policy Advocates does indeed decrease as constituency class composition becomes increasingly heterogeneous. Moreover, this pattern holds when electoral security is controlled. It also holds for both parties and, within parties, especially for Specialists. Specialists require a great deal of time to develop their expertise and extend their influence. Generalists, by contrast, are better able to ride hobby horses while at the same time managing moderate constituency workloads.

If a low level of constituency demands enhances the opportunity to practice policy advocacy, then electoral security might have similar effects. The expectation here would be that the safer the seat, the greater the proportion of Policy Advocates, because the safer the seat, the greater the opportunity to devote time to national affairs. Using "Marginality" as the measure of safeness of seat, the data tend to support this expectation too, although only very weakly. Among Labour MPs, the pattern is pronounced: the proportions of Policy Advocates increase steadily from 22 percent in the most marginal seats to 44 percent in the safest constituencies. But Conservatives follow a curvilinear pattern whereby advocacy peaks in the middle ranges of electoral security. Again it is the Specialists, the Policy Advocates who might be most hindered by heavy constituency demands, who display the relationship most strongly.

Sir Lewis Namier's eighteenth-century MPs played many of the same preference roles that appear in Trollope's nineteenth-century political novels. But neither the Parliaments of Namier nor those of Trollope include Policy Advocates among their role types, because Policy Advocates are associated with the rise of the complex Administrative State in the twentieth century and with professionalization in the House of Commons. It is the growth in legislation and the growing potential for modifying it that have created this script and made it attractive to career-oriented backbenchers. The determination of Policy Advocates to influence government policy forges roles that resemble those of the Ministerial Aspirant but are very different from those of Constituency Members or Parliament Men.

MPs regard policy advocacy as a major mode of backbench work, which nearly everyone practices at one time or another. They are familiar with the labels that I have used for the subtypes and can usually recognize an Ideologue, a Generalist, or a Specialist when they see one. Moreover, these roles are fairly well defined, for MPs have a fairly clear idea about their characteristic responsibilities. Thus, Ideologues concentrate on propaganda at Westminster and in the country. Generalists stir coals and beat drums. Specialists pursue research and leverage behind the scenes. These are the usual expectations. Yet, contrary to sociological versions of role theory, such expectations, even when clear and well established, do not "determine" the way these roles are played. They only sketch out the scripts for scenes set by the institution's more formal rules. The rest is done by individual desires, by the career goals and emotional incentives that shape roles and subtypes and guarantee considerable variation within as well as among them.

One of the most obvious variations is in depth of involvement. Strong tendencies to merge role and self-image are reflected in statements such as "I *am* a right-wing politician" or "I *am* an originator." This absorption is reflected in the puzzlement that Ideologues express about "MPs who are nonpolitical Members of Parliament. How the hell they ever got here I don't know." Equally engaged are the Generalists and Specialists who feel that "one's working hours, apart from anything else, put one in a rather special category here. I don't think I ever work less than 65 hours a week, and it's very often over 80." At the less-involved end of this dimension, one finds Ideologues waiting for the revolution, Generalists remembering things past, and Specialists who are "part-time, amateur" Members.

Although not so obvious as the variations in psychological involvement, the most peculiar characteristic of Policy Advocates is undoubtedly the weakness of their ambitions for ministerial office. This must seem odd, because the principal concern of Policy Advocates is to influence and modify policy. Yet Advocates insist that they live their lives day by day and that "there's loads of things to do without having ambitions." They work very hard to make effective contributions, but not to achieve ministerial office. Why?

Part of the explanation lies in the choices that these individuals have made about their careers. And part of it lies in situations created by the structure of parliamentary career ladders. On the individual side, there are Policy Advocates who simply doubt their ability to be successful Ministers: "I've never satisfied myself that I deserve to be here, never, oh that's true, that's true. You see, I read the history of the House and I know the men of tremendous stature that's been here and still are here, and I know I'll never measure up with them." Others are avoiding disappointments: "I've seen so much unhappiness in this place [among position seekers] that I've got a complete contentment just in my present role." More than a few say something like this—and most of them sound as though they mean it. Still others, as we have seen, would "much rather be right than successful," or assume that no Cabinet would stand them, or even take a certain pride in turning away from their party's top posts. And some are simply so busy outside Parliament and so specialized inside it that they turn down opportunities in fields in which they are not really interested.

Unfavorable positions on career ladders can also dampen aspirations. Many Advocates are backbenchers who were poorly placed. For example, those who enter Parliament in their late forties or early fifties find that they are too old to get started and that they would be foolish to spend much time regretting this state of affairs. Far better to take a positive view and turn to doing what can be done, to influencing the influential.[66] Those who enter earlier but don't reach the ladder's lower rungs by the age of 50 usually accept the situation, for they recognize that "they are not likely to put a chap into a junior post at 54." Several years further on, some find that they are just too tired ("too much of a burden . . . I couldn't possibly do another job"), while others redirect their ambition at this stage and look to what is still realistically attainable, such as positions in the EEC or chairmanships of Select Committees.

Even moderately ambitious Policy Advocates are uncommon. They tend to be young, new Members who, for the moment, are not terribly interested in office because they believe that they have years ahead of them, and that there is no need to rush. They may, for a while, feel some self-confidence based on past successes, like this very young and very new Tory Advocate who has "always found in my life that one has been offered things to do," or like his colleague who has "always entered at the top or I've got to the top very quickly." Neither of them could imagine that it wouldn't someday happen again. But it didn't. The first left the House. The second stayed to complain that I "don't think I'm ever likely to become a Minister . . . and I don't know why." Another in the same boat knew very well why: "I took a line which was unlikely to endear me to the way in which things were going, shall we say, a slightly broader line on education and a rather blacker line on Commonwealth affairs." Suggestions of frustrated ambition can be heard behind the words through which such Policy Advocates present their roles.

Still, even the most frustrated Advocates usually make a virtue of a necessity and enjoy exerting whatever influence they can. They know that their influence is limited, but they also know that its returns are genuine, that it helps shape the context and content of public policy. Perhaps above all, they come to appreciate Westminster's distinction between influence and power, a distinction that has structured the directions in which they have shaped their roles. This distinction was put best by Sir Harry Legge-Bourke, a popular chairman of the 1922 Committee who was frequently quoted on the subject by his colleagues:

> I have very often been asked by chaps who have never been into Parliament what they ought to do about coming in. I always ask them first of all to make up their minds whether they seek power or influence, because the two things are very different. There are some who want office and are ambitious from their career point of view. There are others who prefer to get into a position where they can exercise influence on those who have power. To me, it's a much more sophisticated thing to exercise influence than it is to use power. And to me the fascinating part of politics is the building up of influence and the directing of influence. This is the sort of person I am.

And this is the sort of role that Policy Advocates play.

MINISTERIAL ASPIRANTS:
ANTICIPATORY SOCIALIZATION

We'll know you in several years' time.
So it doesn't matter how you try to
hide what you are really like. We will know.

Chief Whip to Aspirant

When Harold Macmillan said that there were only four good reasons to be in the House of Commons—to become Prime Minister, Chancellor of the Exchequer, Foreign Secretary, or Home Secretary—he was giving voice to the visions of Ministerial Aspirants whose "dreams of office and power" drift through the corridors of the Palace of Westminster.

In the eighteenth century, Ministerial Aspirants were a small minority in Parliament, for offices were few and much of political life was a matter of indifference for most Members.[1] Two hundred years later, the rise of the Administrative State created many more opportunities for office and stimulated processes of professionalization that turned the eighteenth-century pattern round by reducing to a minority the former majority of politically indifferent Members. Institutional structure is important. But it is equally important to remember that backbench preference roles are rationally selected and interpreted by backbenchers. No one has sufficient time and energy to pursue vigorously all backbench roles at once. Everyone therefore gives some roles predominance over others by choosing among them on the basis of their goals. Thus, the essential difference between Policy Advocates and Ministerial Aspirants is captured in the contrast between the goals expressed in Legge-Bourke's remarks celebrating the art of influence, with which we left Chapter 2, and the goals expressed in the following comments from an ambitious Labour Member: "What is enjoyable about politics? Power and the exercise of power, which I find absolutely delightful. If I thought for one moment I was going to spend forty years in the House of Commons and never exercise power again, I would find it an absolutely dreadful and appalling and arid prospect."[2]

The role of the Ministerial Aspirant informs us about how future Ministers are nurtured and selected in the House of Commons. From this viewpoint, the most striking characteristic of the role of the Ministerial Aspirant is that even those backbenchers who have played it successfully in the recent past are so very uncertain about how it is most successfully played. This pervasive uncertainty can be seen plainly in Julian Critchley's efforts to put down on paper for his ambitious colleagues some rules of thumb about how best to succeed as a Ministerial Aspirant in the post-1970 Conservative Party.[3] Despite Critchley's skills as a social observer and his inside views as a Conservative MP, the advice is remarkably vague. His rules of thumb are insightful, clever, and amusing—but not clear. In other types of organizations, this sort of ambiguity is peculiar to aspirants who lack mentors and therefore have little contact with those who ultimately will judge their performances.[4] But in the House of Commons, it is found even among Ministerial Aspirants who have mentors. The role is simply not well defined.

That is in itself curious but not extraordinary. What is, from the perspective of role theory, extraordinary is that the expectations held by others about how this role should be played are every bit as powerful as they are ambiguous. In other words, Ministerial Aspirants are not as free as it might seem they would be to play their parts as they please. Hence, when they talk about their role, they spend far more time than do other types of backbenchers worrying about what exactly it is and about superiors whose criteria they must discover in order to play the role successfully: "I look to see if there is any distinctive pattern," one explained, but "it doesn't seem to fit into any pattern. . . . Indeed there's 630 Members here . . . if *you* can find how to do it, we'd be only too pleased to read the manual." Gatekeepers not only determine the skills that Ministerial Aspirants need to fit themselves for higher positions; they also possess the authority to determine who has acquired them. Thus, many Aspirants are keenly aware both of the power of such expectations and of being judged: "And Francis Pym [Conservative Chief Whip] said this to me, it was the second night, he gave me dinner and he said, 'We'll know you in several years' time. So it doesn't matter how you try to hide what you are really like. We will know.' And they do know! . . . You see, John Biffin amazed me. He told me that Enoch has a view about me . . . that's surprising. I mean, I just find it surprising . . . I don't know why, it's a surprise to me." Apparently the Chief Whip and other Conservative frontbenchers liked what they saw, for Francis Pym's young dinner companion became a High Flyer who rose rapidly, all the way to the Cabinet. And yet he did not, even in retrospect, understand what exactly he had done right. What he did understand was that he had been judged constantly—and that his career's trajectory had been determined by the power of his superiors' expectations.

Distributions

Outsiders nearly always overestimate the proportion of MPs who carry a Minister's baton in their knapsacks. To count up those who are ambitious, one must of course include the frontbenchers, who, along with Whips, constitute approximately 20 percent of the House. But the rest are backbenchers, three-fourths of whom aren't terribly interested, at least not enough to make the role of Ministerial Aspirant the principal focus for their attitudes and activities. They are, they say, either too busy, too old, too tired, or too eccentric for the race.

What about the proportion among new Members? On the face of it, the odds must seem difficult, but not necessarily discouraging. At some time during their careers, nearly one out of three MPs will, in fact, attain a position above the rank of backbencher. Citing odds like these, a new Tory explained that he could afford to be ambitious and even impatient in his desire to become a senior Minister; a new Labour Member said that if he didn't go somewhere by age 33, he would expect to lose his hair, by 40 to want to leave, and by 50, if still there, to lose interest altogether. Not surprisingly, there are more Ministerial Aspirants among new MPs than among their older colleagues. What is noteworthy, however, is the wide range of variation. Some declare frankly that "I wouldn't be here if I didn't want ministerial office." Some say that their ambition, while substantial, is not terribly powerful. Others keep the fires burning lower still and qualify their aspirations with comments about how, although they hope it comes, "it's a terribly bad thing to want preferment all the time. It's very bad for one's character apart from anything else."

These variations point the way to subtypes within the role of the Ministerial Aspirant. The subtypes among Policy Advocates, Constituency Members, and Parliament Men have been defined in terms of distinctive strategies and activities for playing those roles. But the role of the Ministerial Aspirant is not so well crystallized. And we cannot simply rely upon the behavioral distinction, which is often made in the House, between those who "bow" and those who "kick" their way to the top, because there are far too few pure kickers or bowers in the sample.

Instead, subtypes distinguish themselves by another characteristic that is goal related, prominent in the transcripts, and salient to Members of Parliament: the level of position sought. Thus, some Aspirants aim to become senior Ministers, some leave the question quite open, and some are plainly pursuing junior office. These variations in the levels of our Aspirants' desires correspond closely to their degrees of ambition. That is to say, the High Flyers usually express stronger ambition than do members of the Mixed group, who may avoid specifying a rank but who, in turn, sound more ambitious than the Subalterns, whose sights are set on the office of Junior Minister. Despite the room for problems of validity in this classification, it has the considerable advantage of being familiar to MPs, who themselves regularly use the label "High Flyer," albeit "Subaltern" was used more by Trollope's Members than by their successors today. Most important, this classification partitions Aspirants into types that differ in motivations, attitudes, and behaviors. They were therefore coded into these categories as well as by the intensity of their ambitions.[5]

The key criterion for identifying High Flyers is their focus on positions above Undersecretary or Parliamentary Secretary. Also coded as High Flyers were those Aspirants who may not have named a specific position such as Foreign Secretary, but who nonetheless made their goals known (e.g., "the frontbench"). By contrast, the Mixed category is more heterogeneous and residual. These were the Aspirants who focused their ambition on "being involved in Government," without specifying the level of involvement. Some were relatively straightforward ("an administrative appointment"), some were vague ("virtually anything that's offered, within reason"), and some were obscure ("everybody just wants to use their ability the best they can"). All of them, however, made it plain that they were indeed devoting their energies to seeking office.[6] The Subalterns, who saw themselves as future Junior Ministers, usually expressed their aims more explicitly: "I would be surprised if I didn't get junior ministerial office sometime," "the lower echelon," "a minor job." Several harbored hopes that further steps would not be completely ruled out. But the majority were more pessimistic, or realistic: "I am quite ready to believe that I wouldn't advance from junior office." The distribution of Ministerial Aspirants among these three subtypes is shown in Table 3.1.

If the number of High Flyers, or indeed of all Ministerial Aspirants (82 out of 521 MPs), seems unrealistically small, it must be remembered that we are examining only the backbenchers. Many other ambitious MPs are already holding positions on the Government side or shadowing them from the Opposition. Among backbench Aspirants, it can be seen that nearly

Table 3.1 Ministerial Aspirants: Subtypes, and subtypes by political party

			Political party*			
	All Aspirants		Conservative		Labour	
Subtype	N	%	N	%	N	%
High Flyer	(35)	43	(15)	38	(20)	48
Mixed	(28)	34	(15)	38	(13)	31
Subaltern	(19)	23	(10)	25	(9)	21
Total	(82)	100	(40)	101	(42)	100

*$p = .65$

twice as many are oriented toward becoming full Ministers compared to those who look to the junior posts. Four out of ten have set their sights on the top of the tree. Furthermore, this proportion will probably increase over the long run, for the Mixed type includes many Aspirants who will eventually go for the top too. Party controls show that Conservative and Labour MPs are again much alike. A few more Labour than Conservative Aspirants do aspire to senior positions,[7] but the difference is small and may be due, in part, to the fact that Labour was in Opposition during our interviews: high hopes are easily entertained on the outside.

Note that Subalterns show no signs of being High Flyers in disguise, of quietly harboring ambitious, long-term plans. In fact, most of them are, compared to the High Flyers, a different breed of politician that plays the role of the Ministerial Aspirant in a different key. Subalterns and High Flyers display distinctive patterns of beliefs and actions that arise from differences in their career goals and emotional incentives.

Goals: Modalities of Ambition

HIGH FLYERS

High Flyers tend to be young, policy oriented, and professional. Exemplars from the early 1970s would include Cecil Parkinson, Neil Kinnock, and Nicholas Scott. Such newcomers propose to make a career in politics, don't see much point to being at Westminster otherwise, and foresee a turn at Secretary of State as an appropriate reward for their efforts. Their youth, they believe, greatly enhances their opportunities; and many assume that they will feel like failures if they do not someday attain high office. Policy interests are closely wedded to these ambitions, because, they tell themselves and others, their goal is not simply a personal desire for office but also a desire for power over policies, power to make, power to do, power to achieve desirable results.

Some, however, appear hungry mainly for power as an end in itself, like the High Flyer who lectured us about the desirability of moving ever "upwards" and about the wonders of having "the driving force within" to do so successfully. Another spoke much the same way about his quest for the post of Secretary of State for Education, "the most worthwhile ambition any man could possibly have." Neither attained office during the ensuing years, but others did who seemed similarly driven. The intensity with which these extreme cases express their views draws attention to a common denominator among High Flyers: they are ambitious people, and proud of it. They say, frankly and with conviction, that their principal career goal is to climb the ministerial ladder; that they would certainly like to sit on the frontbench; and that they will indeed finish up as senior Ministers some day. Their frankness in our nonattributable interviews should not be mistaken for ingenuousness or naiveté. The fact is that most of them *did* succeed, including this candid newcomer who arrived by way of Cambridge and the Young Conservatives:

> Oh yes, I would like to get into the Government. I'd like to do an executive job in Government. Being one of the crowd, even in the sense of being one of this extremely pleasant and privileged crowd, is not enough. I like to be sort of doing things. I like to have specific problems to tackle where I have got the, you know, the wherewithal, the information, the backing, the staff, and so on, to be able to get on with things. This is what life's about as far as I'm concerned. I don't like to be sort of standing around idly as it were. I like to get my teeth into something. And I'd certainly very much like to have government responsibility some day.

The impact of political ambition upon career mobility in Parliament is very strong indeed. A recent study by Stuart Elaine Macdonald, which measures ambition with the same variables that constitute the motivational core of the role of the Ministerial Aspirant, demonstrates convincingly that ambitious Members do succeed much more often and much more rapidly than do their less ambitious colleagues.[8] Macdonald's findings are well worth reviewing here because they are based on an analysis of the data used in this chapter.

The career goal of ambition is essentially a desire for advancement. Yet, despite the fact that this goal is so specific and "intention-like," and therefore likely to be related to strategic behavior, its relationship to "recruitment" has rarely been investigated. It is certainly possible that politicians might, in general, be recruited to higher posts quite regardless of how strongly they themselves try to advance. The opposite is also plausible: that this desire to advance might play a critical mediating role in the Ministerial Aspirant's success or failure. The question, "Does ambition make a difference?" is, furthermore, an excellent example of a naturalistic puzzle, the solution to which requires stepping beyond interpretative methods to statistical and causal analysis. Peter Winch and others have made a persuasive case for interpretative methodology in the social sciences. But they have not been persuasive in their claims that this method can stand alone without other types of data and strategies of inquiry.[9] Thus, we do need to interpret qualitative data in order to understand what ambition means to our subjects. But we also want to know about ambition's consequences—and to know that, we need to know quantitatively and statistically whether or not ambition affects attainment.

To test the impact of political ambition, Macdonald coded, for all MPs interviewed in this study, all promotions between 1972–73, when they were interviewed (and when their ambitions were examined), and 1986. Using rates of upward mobility from one leadership position to another as the dependent variable, she introduced as independent variables education (number of years), age (at entry), and tenure (year of intake), as well as political ambition. The results, reported in Table 3.2, show that political ambition has a consistent and strong positive effect on promotions from the backbenches to the positions of PPS, Assistant Whip, Senior Whip, and Junior Minister. To become a PPS, it also helps to have entered the House recently and at a young age. To become a Junior Minister, it helps to have entered at a young age and, in this case, to have more education. But, across the board, it is political ambition that performs most strongly and consistently in explaining rates of promotion from the backbenches to these offices. The backbenchers who are most ambitious for ministerial office are the ones who are most likely to win rapid advancement in their careers.

It is remarkable that so many High Flyers are so confident about their chances of someday enjoying governmental responsibility. It is more remarkable that the most confident among them so often turn out to be the most successful. These are the backbenchers who, before the end of their first year in the House, have already been noticed as promising ministerial material for the future. They are young, articulate, convivial, intelligent, and

Table 3.2 Impact of political ambition on promotion rates from backbencher

		Type of transition: from backbencher to		
Variable	PPS	Assistant Whip	Senior Whip	Junior Minister
(Constant)	−2.5380*	−6.4150*	−4.9510**	−2.5260**
Ambition	.0736*	.1715*	.1697**	.1627*
Education	.0697	−.0646	−.1187	−.1648**
Age at entry	−.0570*	.0393	.0522	−.0530*
Year of intake	.0224**	−.0007	−.0425	−.0111
Chi sq. (4 df)	78.41*	13.76*	5.47	60.03*
N of cases	493	493	493	493
N of changes	207	36	16	83

Source: Stuart Elaine Macdonald, "Political Ambition and Attainment: A Dynamic Analysis of Parliamentary Careers," Ph.D. diss., University of Michigan, 1987.
Note: Entries are unstandardized parameter estimates.
*$p \leq .01$
**$p \leq .05$

self-assured. They know that they "compare favourably" with their colleagues, that time is on their side, and that they will not for very many more years "sit on my backside on the backbenches." They also know that achieving *government* positions, as opposed to achieving the frontbench, which can be done in Opposition, "is a bit of a lottery." Their party, for instance, may not be in Government during their critical career years (35–45), when winning a first post is most important and most likely. Nor can they know for certain who will be leading their party at that critical time and taking the decisions about appointments. Nonetheless, it is very satisfying to have been noticed so early on. This helps maintain the self-esteem needed to sustain oneself in the race and to sustain a view of one's chances as "quite good, since you ask," and "actually, I think about two to one on."

Others feel that they must work harder to win from their colleagues recognition as someone who is likely to succeed. They seek, first of all, to avoid the trap of being labeled a "clever outsider," which handicaps writers like Julian Critchley and professors like John Mackintosh, who, Critchley observed, "made the best speeches in the Commons but only from the back-bench."[10] They study career patterns and plan carefully their apprenticeships as best they can, given the ambiguous information available. Actually, they calculate more carefully than is generally realized. These calculations include the variables of age, length of service, the timing and probable outcome of elections, and the preferences of probable party leaders. At the same time, they seek to alert Westminster to the fact that they are committed and serious apprentices. Some Labour Aspirants try to make this point heard by overemphasizing it: "I mean politics is all I care about . . . like a painter who wants to paint all the time. . . . I want to be a politician all the time. And that's what being an MP means." Among Conservatives, by contrast, overdoing the "committed" image can be counterproductive ("the kiss of death, really"), albeit one must still see that one is viewed as a "serious" politician.[11] Thus, a Conservative "amateur" who at Oxford had been "regarded by the athletes as an intellectual and by the intellectuals as an athlete" explained how he learned that the age of the amateur at Westminster had come to an end. It was at a dinner party where half the other guests were Members of the Government and he was the youngest backbencher present: "What an impressive collection of people. But they *are really* professionals. For instance, I'm a keen skier, and I said that I'd spoken to the Speaker (it was the week of the Budget) and asked him if I could be called early because it was the European Parliamentary Ski Races at the weekend. . . . And they were genuinely affronted that I could *even consider* saying to the Speaker, you know, that I wanted to go skiing. . . . They are professionals, you see, and they don't think it is a game. And I just wonder . . . I think, I think I have this terrific ability to squander my efforts."

MIXED TYPES

Ministerial Aspirants in the Mixed category also dream about office and power, but they are not clearly focused, nor are their goals as ambitious as those of the High Flyers. "It's always said," reflected one, "that everybody who goes into politics must need be dreadfully ambitious. I'm not entirely sure. Quite honestly, I believe that you can go too far . . . you can so dedicate yourself to this place, and politics, that you can stop living as a normal human being." Yet, he is forty-three and not about to pass up any opportunities: "If, for example, you know, I thought I might get on, obviously I'd take it."

They are prepared to take whatever is offered, within reason. "I wouldn't venture . . . I just can't tell" they say. "It's all a matter of luck. You lose your seat in the next election; you get struck down by a bus; your party could be out of office for 20 years. . . . And you, you just can't tell, you can't tell, you can't tell." Some can't tell because they are new Members still adjusting to the House, still testing the waters. They "may in another year's time want to push further ahead"; but their goals have not yet pointed them toward particular strategies: "You asked a straight question and you get an honest answer—as long as you promise not to reveal it. I would like to be in the Government. I'm in this House because I think, vainly or otherwise, that I've got a contribution to make. . . . I do wish to attain some position, yes. But obviously one can't yet particularise . . . any position would be a challenge."

Others have decided that they are not High Flyers, but neither are they ready to accept that junior office will be their limit. They do not make any secret of the fact that they would like to be involved in Government. But when it comes to "just what sort of office one could hope for," they turn the discussion to departments and topics rather than to levels of positions. One such Aspirant, for example, had been a successful young chairman of a major education committee in local government and "um, would like to occupy national office in the education field." Another had extensive experience with the housing problems that face local authorities: "Housing would be my scene." These are the fields where they have contributions to make. "But how party leaders will recognize this is, well you know, it's not for me to say."

Still others refuse, for a variety of idiosyncratic reasons, to admit much more than that they are available. And even this they prefer to admit obliquely: "I mean if one believes that one has a contribution to make on behalf of one's constituents, on behalf of the country, if one is in a position to enhance that contribution, one would be a fool and a knave to say that he wouldn't take it." They play their cards close to the chest and resist being cajoled into saying anything beyond what feels general and safe ("I'm a doer as opposed to a thinker. And therefore one's ambitions would veer towards an administrative appointment. I would like to be able to put my ideas into practice"). "The penny will either drop or it won't," others say enigmatically. But when they lower their guard a little, the confidence and conviction often comes through: "Well, I've always found that I've succeeded so far in life. . . . And I see no reason to feel that the same won't happen again."

This Mixed group also stands out, compared to other Ministerial Aspirants, by its stronger interest in policy advocacy. Perhaps they are working to cover career bets about which they are uncertain. But whatever the explanation, they talk a good deal about goals such as getting amendments accepted and notching up small changes in the law. They talk about how they are elected as representatives rather than as delegates and are there ultimately to use their judgment. A few even express delusions of grandeur about it all: "One indeed can alter the course of history. . . . I don't think there is any doubt about that." But fewer still would be mistaken for Policy Advocates. They aren't Policy Advocates, because the principal focus around which they construct their roles is not policy advocacy but instead getting a foot on the ladder. And this produces different patterns of desires, beliefs, and behaviors. They have much less in common with the Policy Advocate than they do with the High Flyer who has "taken up politics with the express desire of getting his foot upon a rung of the ladder of promotion."[12] Their principal aim is to climb.

SUBALTERNS

Subalterns, the dictionary tells us, are officers whose duty it is to assist superior officers in their administrative work. And, compared to Aspirants in the Mixed category, aspiring backbench Subalterns are much easier to recognize. These are the MPs who propose to become Junior Ministers. Like High Flyers, they construct their roles as apprenticeships. But, unlike High Flyers, they do not plan to rise very far above the backbenches. Moreover, they are often refreshingly realistic about their capabilities and convincingly content about their situations. For instance: "Well, I suppose in my place, assuming that I was in the House for 30 years and the Labour Party was in power for its normal ration of that, let us say one-third off and on, then I would be disappointed and I think surprised if I didn't get junior ministerial office sometime. But I am quite ready to believe that I wouldn't advance from junior office."

Reasons for the realism, and possibly for some of the contentment, are based on assessments of age, energy, and talent. Age is very important because it is widely supposed that if by the age of fifty one hasn't gotten on the ladder, there is little chance of climbing to the highest rungs. At the same time, it is not unreasonable "to think my chances ought to be moderately good of being a Junior Minister one day—provided I don't get too old in the meantime." Any factor, such as being out of favor with the party's leaders, that extends the waiting time is discouraging, because one's biological clock forever ticks away.[13] With regard to energy, Subalterns claim that they had no intense driving force to become MPs in the first place; it just happened. Nor do they feel much driving force now to become Ministers. If that happens too, fine, they will be very pleased. But if it doesn't, they won't be terribly disappointed, because they won't have invested much energy in the enterprise. This lack of intensity is often linked to a modest view of one's talents "as a kind of ordinary, average, intelligent kind of backbench MP who might someday make an average, decent Junior Minister, and that's the sort of limit." No Ministerial Aspirant who talks this way has been to university. When they compare themselves to the clever, young High Flyers, they lower their sights and, like this former hotel manager, hope to "be given a chance, be given an opportunity, at some stage or other, of being a Parliamentary Secretary or something like that."[14]

They try to be realistic about their opportunities too, because "only a few are going to get through to this." All the more reason, then, to take the attitude that, "if office is coming to you, it will come, and the only way you can deal with it is to prepare yourself as you go along; and if it doesn't come, well, make a good job of being a backbencher." Most realistic of all are the prudent people who plan carefully to avoid unnecessary disappointments. They set their sights no further than the next step ahead so that, if they don't make it, the rebuff is minimized. They minimize failure by managing ambition.[15] They seek to restrain themselves from developing "an overwhelming ambition which, if unfulfilled, results almost always in a great feeling of bitterness, and you sour your soul." These modest Subalterns are uneasy about projecting their chances across an entire career. Instead, they prefer to plan in the now and near. And, not being gamblers, they are unwilling to let themselves think that they can be happy only on the frontbench. Hence, they talk less about the challenges than about the safety nets: "I think that you can only come into the House thinking that being a backbencher is something that you can do properly for the rest of your life."

That may be why Subalterns take a stronger interest in constituency affairs than do other Ministerial Aspirants. Several sound very much like Constituency Members: "I hold regular surgeries within the constituency every week. I think you've got to do this. And I think you, you've got to help your constituents as much as you can, with the case work. . . . That's one aspect of a Member's job." But when stressing the constituency side, they don't stress it enough to blend in with the Constituency Members, for they nevertheless see this as a secondary aspect of their work. Perhaps the Subalterns are simply the sort of people who take all their responsibilities seriously. Certainly they are "pleased to be here. I mean, well, after all, I mean my own case, I graduated from Leeds University I suppose in 1957, and I got here within nine years . . . one is secretly pleased about that." It may not be, moreover, that their ambition is so very feeble, but rather that they prefer to take things one step at a time: "I mean when one was fighting as a candidate, the summit of your ambitions was to get 'MP' after your name. Now you've got 'MP' after your name, you want to become a Junior Minister. This is a natural progression, and it's a reflection of life in general." Actually this is a reflection of their own distinctive approach to life in general. Like the High Flyers, they calculate as carefully as they can and try to take all relevant factors into account. One Scot, for example, explained at length why his best chance was at the Scottish Office, and that he was therefore preparing himself to be the "sort of general factotum" for whom they would be looking.

PROMOTION AND PERCEPTION

Intertwined with the goals of Ministerial Aspirants are their beliefs about the ambitions of their colleagues, for they are very conscious of competing in a race. "It's funny," a young High Flyer said, "I mean something is pushing us. I don't know what it is, but there are 637 potential Prime Ministers." Of course that is an exaggeration. But are Ministerial Aspirants more likely than other backbenchers to exaggerate in this way, and thereby perhaps pump up their adrenalin for the duration of the contest?

Some insights about these perceptions can be gleaned indirectly from data on reasons for refraining from cross-voting, that is to say, from voting with the other side. Backbenchers reviewed a list of nine possible reasons for refraining from cross-voting (e.g., "basic agreement with party leaders' positions," "potential criticism from constituency association") and were asked to rank them in what they believed to be their order of importance for *most of their colleagues*. One of these reasons was "hope of future promotion to ministerial or Shadow Cabinet position." Table 3.3 presents their beliefs about the importance of this motivation, which are closely related to their beliefs about the competitiveness of the race for office.[16]

Ministerial Aspirants do indeed overestimate the ambitions of their colleagues. They are more likely than other backbenchers to "suppose everyone would be interested in office," or at least to assume that the hope of future promotion is significant enough for enough other MPs to assure a competitive race. This perceptual error occurs for both Labour and Conservative MPs, although it is stronger on the Conservative side of the House, where Aspirants ask rhetorically: "I mean, what do people come here for? . . . I mean, you obviously hope, since politics is about power . . ."

The table also suggests that the higher the Aspirant's own aspirations, the greater the tendency to believe that others pursue similar goals. Thus, 72 percent of the High Flyers seem ready to assume that "if we went into Gov-

Table 3.3 Judgments about colleagues' interest in promotion by Ministerial
Aspirant subtypes, in percent

Judgment	Aspirant subtype*			Other backbenchers
	High Flyer	Mixed	Subaltern	
Significant motivation	72	63	56	42
Not a significant motivation	28	38	44	58
Total	100	101	100	100
	(N = 32)	(N = 24)	(N = 18)	(N = 217)

Q. Compared with other countries, the British system shows MPs voting very closely on party lines—we are therefore interested in the reasons why most MPs vote with their party. Could you write number 1 alongside the reason which, in your view, best explains why most (R's party) MPs refrain from cross-voting most of the time? Then write 2 beside the reason which seems next in importance, and so on down to 9 for the least-plausible explanation. (Reason: hope of future promotion to ministerial or shadow cabinet position)

*Aspirants v. other backbenchers ($p \le .001$)

ernment," a very high proportion of our colleagues would "be by the telephone waiting for that call." The Mixed group produces an intermediate response of 63 percent. And even the views of the Subalterns reflect the force of the motivational core of their roles. Some of them say they wish that ambition weren't so pervasive. Nevertheless, they also tend to believe that this is the way of the world: "I think it would be a good thing if more Members didn't want to be Ministers, or didn't care whether they became Ministers or not. . . . If the House were as it should be, then getting ministerial office wouldn't be the only way in which a Member can see himself not wasting the whole of his bloody life. But that is the way it is."

Ministerial Aspirants seem particularly eager to assume that Policy Advocates, their closest kindred spirits on the backbenches, are as interested in office as they are themselves. That assumption is incorrect. Nor are Ministerial Aspirants simply power-charged versions of their influence-oriented associates. Although Aspirants and Advocates have much in common, there are sharp distinctions between these two roles.

Characteristic Beliefs and Behaviors: Contrasts with Policy Advocates

Ministerial Aspirants are usually less specialized than those Policy Advocates who are Specialists, less interested in little campaigns than those who are Generalists, and slightly more interested than either group in constituency work. It all fits together nicely with the Aspirants' goals and, by helping us understand what they do, begins to fill out the pattern of their roles.

SPECIALIZATION

Ministerial Aspirants suspect that narrow specialization might prove a handicap in pursuing their aims. Although the evidence for this is none too clear, they base their judgments on comments from senior Members such as this very successful Specialist who never did become a Minister: "Well I set my sights on thinking that one had to more or less specialise. And I was eventually told by Iain Macleod that I had 'overspecialised,' you know, from the point of view of my own selfish advancement." At the same time, Aspirants hear the standard advice to backbenchers to specialize in two or three subjects. So they naturally examine the examples they see around them to try to sort out the situation. It doesn't take long. "What was Harold Wilson's specialty?" asked a Labour MP who was discussing this subject. "What was Hugh Gaitskell's? What are Michael Foot's, Tony Crosland's? Let's look at the people who've made it to the top. 'Young man, specialise!' What did these characters specialise in? Nothing."[17]

Observations like these lead Aspirants, as we shall see in the analysis below, to stretch out a bit, to make themselves capable of contributing in a number of areas. "When I came here," a High Flyer explained, "I rather took the view that I knew quite a bit about housing, and therefore in fact the first year I was here I spent more time on the *education* side than perhaps anything else. And the second year I spent more time on *health and social security*. . . . And also on *unemployment*." Even the relatively specialized Ministerial Aspirants tend to be less specialized than Policy Advocates who are Specialists. Like these Specialists, Ministerial Aspirants want to influence policy and know that they need some expertise in order to do this successfully. But, unlike the Specialists, they ultimately care more about power than about influence; and in the competition to attain power, although specialization helps ("I think it's very important to develop a technical expertise in certain areas, to be taken seriously as an individual at all"), it also handicaps. When specialization is carried too far, Aspirants become identified with particular hobby horses and risk riding on the backbenches rather than running in the race.

INFLUENCE AND POWER

Just as Ministerial Aspirants are less likely than Specialists to ride hobby horses, they are also less interested than Generalists, the other principal type of Policy Advocate, in little campaigns to modify policy: "I find that so much in the House of Commons is completely trivial, a lot of routine," they complain after a few years in the trenches. The influence that really interests them is more general and associated with power, the goal by which they set their sights. Thus, their discussions of influence are frequently abstract ("to influence the course of events" or "to influence life for the better") and concern contexts rather than specific cases or concrete details.[18] Of course they are pleased when departments of state respond to their protestations about one matter or another. But that isn't, for them, nearly enough, because they are so very aware that "MPs don't have power." They like the influence, but they long for the power, they long to be in office themselves. Unlike Advocates, their thoughts about influence are dominated by thoughts about power as they work back and forth between the two perspectives: "to have an influence on some of the problems which I mentioned early on would intrigue me enormously. I've developed a certain affection for the Home Office, however. And the Home Office is one which seems to have so many of the thorny problems and such a poor reputation with many colleagues actually simply because it does end up often with some of the rough stuff and the unpleasant little problems. I'd be very interested to sort of be there and try to help improve the image and do things better."

But whether they adopt Westminster's distinction between influence and power, or whether they make the two notions interchangeable, nearly all Ministerial Aspirants are fascinated by the general subject. The exercise of power is an art, they claim, "the most demanding art there is. It's much more comprehensive. . . . Not only is it more comprehensive, but it's much more important in the sense that it affects a much wider range of activities in the nation and a much wider range of people in the nation." As a former Chairman of the Young Conservatives reported, it was reading political biographies "that inspired me to move into politics . . . the thought that, in fact, it's only in Westminster that you can get to grips with power as such." It is the potential to shape the course of events that brings many of them into politics and, added a former Labour Agent, "keeps me in politics even through the rough times."

When asked directly about their own interests in influencing the actions of others, they can be very frank: "It's perfectly true. I'd be a fool to deny it because I like to influence people and policy." Most of their colleagues don't deny it, but they don't talk about it so much either. By contrast, influence and power permeate the transcripts of Ministerial Aspirants. When they talk about their colleagues, for example, they talk about deriving a sense of achievement from getting them to rethink their views. When they talk about their constituencies, they talk about how influential they can be in dealing with constituency problems. When they talk about Parliament, they talk about meeting Ministers in the Smoking Room, trudging with them through division lobbies, dining with them in the evenings.[19] Policy Advocates want influence, but Ministerial Aspirants want more. They are not satisfied with modest successes in modifying policies, because, unlike Advocates, they dream of office and power. Not only is backbench influence too weak for their taste, "but the number of occasions on which one influences things are very few and far between unless you're a very important chap." Their goal is to become a very important chap.

The way that Ministerial Aspirants talk about ambition is as striking as the frankness with which they acknowledge its importance to them. First of all, they don't like to think that they seek office "primarily for reasons of *personal* ambition." Nor do they like to think that they seek it primarily for the undoubted status it confers. And neither do they seek it primarily, they say, to satisfy some psychological need to control the actions of others. Instead, they would like to think that the primary goal driving their dreams is a public-spirited one: to achieve the opportunity to implement good public policy. This ideal was said to be expressed best during the 1960s and 1970s by the conduct of Sir Alec Douglas-Home, "whose inheritance and upbringing," his biographer wrote, "carved the word [duty] on every panel of his character."[20] They would like to think that they are motivated not so much to use power for "personal ambition," but rather "to use power for good, that's the way to go, and . . . you might be able to achieve something."[21] Hence, for Aspirants, the only satisfactory success comes with the acquisition of office, for only then are they in a position to implement ideas "on a grand scale." Their true satisfactions lie in the future: "The attractions of a political career are that *eventually,* after one has gained a position of some stature or importance, one has a chance to put over one's views, influence people, and ultimately to make decisions. But obviously that's for me some time ahead."

For the present, there is always advocacy to keep one busy and draw attention to one's talents. For most Aspirants, advocacy is a means to the end of attaining offices that will make possible still more effective advocacy. But for some who are less committed to their roles and less confident about their futures, mainly members of the Mixed and Subaltern subtypes, advocacy also offers an insurance policy. If in the end office doesn't come, it won't be such a difficult transition to the role of the Policy Advocate, for the Aspirant will be familiar with the effects of water upon stones: "the capacity for a Member to jerk departments of state into rethinking obsolete

or inconsistent policies is very considerable as long as the Member concerned has the quality of pertinacity—you have to keep on, it's the water
dripping on the stone." Besides, everyone finds it satisfying to get "more
concessions from the Government than practically any other committee has
got for decades I should think."

CONSTITUENCIES

If, compared to Advocates, Aspirants are less interested in little policy campaigns, they are somewhat more interested in solving constituency problems
and "helping people who are in a mess." They accent the constituency side,
in part, because compared to Policy Advocates they are often younger,
fresher, and closer to the flush of their first electoral success. In the same
vein, they may simply not yet have had time to learn how to manage the
constituency work effectively: "One is coping with the shoal of stuff that
comes along from the constituency. From surgeries and from correspondence you get an enormous number of personal problems . . . and these take
quite a lot of time to deal with." Their approach to constituency work reveals distinctive patterns that dovetail with their aims.

Thus, Ministerial Aspirants regard power and influence as primary ("at
the end of the road, this is what we're here for") but "also think that the
constituency duties are very important." They talk about their constituencies more than anyone else except Constituency Members. Yet most of this
is quite general talk about how representing the constituency is "in a way"
one of the most important duties. In fact, it is uncommon to hear an Aspirant
discussing, in detail, any specific cases. They speak sincerely about "articulating the views of your constituents . . . enabling them to get answers they
wouldn't perhaps know themselves." But one quickly gets the impression
that the constituency itself is not their main concern. One also gets the impression that many of them do not particularly relish the individual cases.
For example: "I had literally a girl who wrote to me the day before yesterday, she had been in correspondence with a firm for two years about a skirt
costing two pounds, and she didn't like the cut of it, or she thought it was
immodest . . . and would I please deal with the firm for her?—that's not
what we're here for!!!"

Instead, Ministerial Aspirants emphasize educating and inspiring their
constituents. The constituency, they say, is a wonderfully convenient po-
dium for practicing leadership, for putting views before the people and trying "to persuade them that something or other is a good idea." You can
raise their horizons, teach them "to be internationalists and not chauvinists,

and this sort of thing." You can get the Government's message across or the Opposition's criticism heard. By being approachable and responsive, you may even be able to help, in a small way, to strengthen the legitimacy of the nation's political institutions: "If it gets around the constituency that the Member is active and perhaps idealistic and very involved . . . I think people feel pleased about it. You know, I think Jack Kennedy did this for the country. You can, you can, we can play that role." These images suggest a shepherd guiding his or her flock—or an aspiring Minister's-eye view of constituents and constituencies. What such images leave out is the ambivalence that Aspirants feel, since their constituencies provide not just audiences but also problems demanding precious time.[22] As Ministerial Aspirants review their constituency work, they make it clear that "the constituency was not, let me say quite openly, my central motivation in coming here." Constituency work is important, but it is "more important to be associated with particular things in this place so that people say, 'Ah, yes, defence, he's the man who will say something on that.' And I don't think I've done that yet"—because he is too new and has been devoting too much of his time to constituency chores.

Where the constituency side can help with promotion is when one's actions make a mark and secure a base. When Aspirants talk about "making a mark" through their constituency activities, they are talking about being noticed by their constituents. For instance, Toby Jessel, a youthful Tory MP in the 1970 intake, attracted his constituents' attention by requesting a change in the departure routes of aircraft leaving Heathrow Airport so as to move the heaviest-decibel levels from over their homes to over his.[23] But some of them also believe that, so long as they don't become identified as "good Constituency Members," making such marks can very occasionally attract the attention of party leaders who may have constituencies in the same general area or who may, as in the case of Jessel, read about it in *The Times*. Nevertheless, the main function of "making a mark constituency-wise" is to "ensure that one's base is sound." Young Ministerial Aspirants may not be in the safest of seats. They will already have sorted out what kind of part they wish to play on the backbenches: their main priority will be to achieve office. But they must, at the same time, "try and become a bit of a good Constituency Member," because "if you win a seat for the first time, particularly if you win a marginal, you've got to get your base right. And therefore in your first Parliament you put what over your parliamentary career in hindsight would appear to be an overemphasis on your constituency duties." A Conservative Subaltern put it this way: "The thing at the moment is still satisfying my constituents. . . . But the reason why one should come here is to try and influence policy. . . . And it's this that I now want to devote myself to rather more."

If the Subalterns resemble Policy Advocates when they discuss influence, they quickly reverse this impression when they turn to constituency work. More than the High Flyers, they believe that "you don't realise before you get here how important the constituent, the constituency is to the whole Parliament, how much you are allowed here to actually raise constituency matters, however small and limited and narrow they are." This point impresses them all the more if and when they become discouraged and begin to dampen the fires of their ambitions. A new Labour entrant, for example, "came in very ambitious hoping eventually that . . . I could perhaps become a Junior Minister, eventually, in the long term." But "now, however, my ideas have changed"—and, while he believes that he still has "a fairly good chance" for office in the future, he is growing increasingly pessimistic about it. So he has thrown himself into his constituency work and says he is beginning to feel that "if you can deal with constituents' complaints and difficulties, then you have done your basic job as an MP." Some Subalterns have been or may soon become Constituency Members.

Most Ministerial Aspirants, however, compartmentalize their constituency work. They regard it as significant but for the most part as separate from their principal interests and activities at Westminster: "I would always put the constituency side on a high plane, but it is very separate. Within the Palace of Westminster, I think that at the moment I have achieved a reasonable balance," the fulcrum of which is the desire to achieve ministerial office. By comparing these Aspirants with the Policy Advocates, we have foreshadowed some of the strategies through which they pursue their goals.

Characteristic Beliefs and Behaviors: Strategies for Advancement

Since the proper mix of strategies for achieving promotion is a mystery, Aspirants get little guidance in their roles. Their work on the backbenches seems like such a haphazard process of training and selection that they have difficulty thinking it through: "I think it's such a haphazard system, it's difficult to know what contribution . . . training on the backbenches makes. I think in some ways it does sort you out. . . . It is curious how the place does somehow sort people out. But if *you* can find some rules to the game, *we'd* be delighted to find out, to read about them." Ministerial Aspirants may not know exactly what the expectations are, but they do know that their time on the backbenches is regarded by their colleagues as a "necessary part of the experience and training if one's going to do a ministerial job." They also know that they will be judged on how well they perform this ambiguous apprenticeship.[24]

What is clear is that Aspirants must somehow "make a mark," "make a reasonable impression" in the House, become "a fairly readily recognisable backbencher," and avoid at the same time putting "my foot in it, you know." Hence, they seek strategies that will "strengthen my position" when the time comes to be judged, strategies through which they might prepare themselves, consolidate their knowledge of the workings of the House, and build up contacts, all with a view to being selected for higher responsibilities. Aspirants develop rough ideas about which actions are useful and which are not. These "dos" and "don'ts," upon which there is no convincing consensus, but which nevertheless structure the role of the Ministerial Aspirant, include the following: Do: speak regularly in the House, seek convivial contacts, and pay attention to committees. Don't: become too specialized or too rebellious.

STEADY SPEECHES

The Ministerial Aspirants of the eighteenth century, Sir Lewis Namier's "Politicians," pursued their goals by attending Parliament regularly and by focusing on eloquence and debate.[25] In the nineteenth century, their successors likewise paid careful attention to language, for through language one inspires trust, and "it is the trust which such men inspire which makes them so serviceable"[26] Today, speaking in the House still wins recognition; provided it is well done, this can significantly improve an Aspirant's prospects: "I hope that one can just make sufficient impact with making speeches in the House. I think one has to do that. I now sort of intend to try and make some more, to do a little bit more to improve my striking rate."[27]

The difficulty is to discover how to do it properly. One wants to create a reputation, but not the wrong sort of reputation. New Aspirants, therefore, look before they leap. It makes sense to "bide my time . . . and concentrate on gaining particular experience before making, um, general pontifications." This is institutionalized in the ritual of the Maiden Speech and in the advice to wait till you know how to avoid putting your foot in your mouth—knowledge that many in this ambitious generation apparently acquired in the span of a few weeks. After the Maiden Speech, new Ministerial Aspirants are in the swim, where a few obvious rules apply. They are advised, first of all, to avoid overly frequent interventions in debate, particularly when their party is in Government, for this can disturb government timetables and also disturb government Ministers whose good will one needs to maximize one's prospects for office.[28] Another word to the wise suggests that ambitious young backbenchers would do well to follow the lead of Norman Tebbit and concentrate on tormenting the brutes opposite rather than attacking their own side.[29] It is simply imprudent to harass the notables on one's own front bench over major or even minor items of party policy.[30] Furthermore, speaking at public meetings and debates outside the House as well as within its precincts can be very helpful. It is difficult to develop a national reputation before being appointed to office. But it doesn't hurt at all if you become identified by the media as an articulate representative of particular party views so that you are asked to present those views in television programs and in radio broadcasts.

Finally, although it is wise to become known for distinctive views in your speeches, it is extremely unwise to become known as an eccentric or, worse yet, as an ideologue or faction-fighter: "Above all, the ambitious Member should avoid becoming identified with one wing or other of the party. The aspirant for office should travel lightly, unweighed down by obvious ideological baggage. He should find the party's centre of gravity and sit on it."[31] To weigh this advice, we made the same analysis of ideological reputations for Ministerial Aspirants as we did for Policy Advocates. Compared to the Policy Advocates, who stand near the wings of their parties, Ministerial Aspirants were indeed more likely to be found near their parties' centers.

CONVIVIAL CONTACTS

Ministerial Aspirants also hear that it is useful to make convivial contacts. In the Labour Party, this comes through as advice to avoid appearing aloof: "I mean if he's an aloof type of person, not in touch, not communicating with others, I think this can be a very dangerous thing." Since Labour is more puritanical than the Conservative Party, its MPs' aloofness is more likely to be overcome in the Tea Room than in Westminster's bars. The occasional pint is fine, but too much time spent sipping spirits invites negative comments. The Conservative version of convivial contacts suggests that Aspirants "must be clubbable. It was Harold Macmillan's view that there were only two rooms in the Palace of Westminster worth visiting, the Chamber and the Smoking Room." Yet, trying to be too clubbable can be counterproductive: "Then you've got the opportunist, at the drop of a hat, you know, always looking, uh, they're talking to you, but they're looking over their shoulder to see if there's anybody more important to talk to. Er, they sort of suck up and so on." It can also make the clubbable actors uncomfortable themselves: "I mean I hate going round trying to cast a sort of sickly smile in the direction of everyone you think that counts." It makes them feel self conscious: "But I'm a, I'm a, I was told by a colleague yesterday that he regards me as a very 'cultivating' person. He said, 'You're all very, all very easy going on the surface, but you know exactly where you're going.' I said, 'I don't . . . I've never made a decision of that kind before.' "

Nevertheless, most find it perfectly natural and extremely agreeable, especially the fortunate few who are invited to join one of the Conservative Party's dining clubs: "I'm a member of a small dining club where we dine in each other's homes (we have a mutual interest in economic affairs). In fact, six of the twelve are now in the Government. But we're not a pressure group—we are the whole spectrum. So it's a good cross-section. And they came here about three weeks ago."

DILIGENT COMMITTEE WORK

"Do pay attention to committee work," young Aspirants are counseled. Committee work deserves attention because of the "satisfaction and creativeness that goes with making decisions. . . . And you can," this Subaltern continues, "feel at least that you, you're doing something useful." You may be doing something useful for your career as well. Backbench party committees, for example, are "constantly bringing particular items to the notice of Ministers"; and backbench members of such committees sometimes "have direct contact, constant contact with those Ministers related to that particular committee." Here is an obvious opportunity, particularly in the Conservative Party, for Ministerial Aspirants to capture the attention of their superiors. To ensure that the impression they make is favorable, they "try to be dutiful in attendance" and to be seen doing "a constructive job of work," or at least appearing, "you know, eager-beaver to do work."

It does no harm if one is able to participate with sufficient skill and energy to become elected as an officer of one of these backbench party committees, because such positions move Ministerial Aspirants a little closer to the ladders they seek to climb.[32] Standing Committees likewise provide opportunities for recognition. During the committee and report stages of major pieces of legislation, Aspirants may be asked to assume some responsibility for details, to move amendments, or to work for a time as the close confidant of senior members of their party.[33]

BEHAVIOR: SPECIALIZATION

I have already suggested that, to maximize their opportunities for recognition, Ministerial Aspirants accept the advice to specialize—not to overspecialize, but to specialize. They are aware that this will help them achieve influence and also appear well informed in their contributions. Topics are chosen carefully by those most anxious to get on; but this doesn't preclude building upon one's background: "When I first came in, I was asked what did I want to specialise in. . . . Well, predominantly I'm an economist. . . . So things like the economics of shipbuilding and shipping, regional problems, these I must be involved in." Just as important as building up one's knowledge is becoming *known* as someone who is knowledgeable. A new, progressive Tory High Flyer learned, "or am learning I think, the need to specialise. There is so much coming up, you've got to be ruthless at turning aside from it . . . researching for the particular subjects you want to be knowledgeable about—and *to be known* to be knowledgeable about."

Aspirants talk this way. But to what extent do they actually behave this way? How much do they actually specialize and, in particular, pursue moderate specialization? To investigate this matter, the Aspirants were coded along an eight-point scale from "very specialized" to "very unspecialized." These codes were based upon their discussions of policy interests in response to the questions that they were asked about their roles, and also upon their responses to the same direct questions about policy interests that were used to code subtypes among Policy Advocates in Chapter 2. This procedure concentrated on the number of issue areas mentioned but also took account of their scope (e.g., "foreign affairs" versus "aviation supply").[34] The data were then cross-tabulated by the Ministerial Aspirant's three subtypes—High Flyers, Mixed, and Subalterns—to produce the results reported in Table 3.4.

In reading their responses to the role questions, one is struck by how very much less talkative Ministerial Aspirants are about specific policy concerns than are the Policy Advocates. What I propose to explore with the Table, however, is, first of all, the relationship between ambition and specialization. Ministerial Aspirants do specialize. And the more ambitious they are, the more likely they are to do so. Thus, a majority of each subtype is specialized, but the High Flyers are considerably more specialized than the other subtypes, more likely to "concentrate on certain areas and understand them in depth and become an expert—in political terms of being an expert, which is not being an expert in real terms."

But to what extent do Ministerial Aspirants pursue *moderate* specialization? Consider this new Welsh backbencher who describes his areas as "agri-

Table 3.4 Degree of specialization in political issues by Ministerial Aspirant subtypes

| | Subtype* | | | | | |
| | High Flyer | | Mixed | | Subaltern | |
Degree of specialization	N	%	N	%	N	%
Specialized	(28)	82	(16)	57	(9)	47
Unspecialized	(6)	18	(12)	43	(10)	53
Total	(34)	100	(28)	100	(19)	100
Moderate specialization I	(21)	62	(14)	50	(8)	42
Moderate specialization II	(23)	68	(17)	61	(12)	63

*p ≤ .05

culture, Welsh affairs, and regional development . . . that's my field. Anything outside that field, although I'm interested in it, I don't think I'm capable enough to look at it." The scope of his field would count as weak specialization by our standards. Weak and moderate specialization comes closest to fitting the strategically informed model for appropriate conduct: specialize without becoming too specialized. The proportions of weak and moderate specialization (moderate specialization I) for each subtype of Aspirant, as reported in Table 3.4, show that most Ministerial Aspirants, but particularly the more ambitious among them, do indeed develop their interests along these lines.[35]

In the same vein, one further reshuffling of the data narrows the gaps among the three subtypes. Moderate specialization II adds to moderate specialization I the category of "unspecialized, weak." Since the Mixed and Subaltern subtypes are less devoted than the High Flyers to reading the runes for promotion, they may miss the optimal specialization mark by at least one level, most likely in the direction of "unspecialized, weak" (two to four issue areas) rather than strong specialization. By adding in this additional category to create moderate specialization II, we boost substantially the proportions of the Mixed and Subaltern subtypes who behave as though they are on track. There are now approximately two out of three Aspirants in each subtype who seem to be following the advice to specialize without becoming overspecialized. It is a difficult balance to strike: specialized enough to be noticed, but not specialized enough to be pigeonholed. It runs from the former PPS who still works on education but has added to this an interest in "race relations and immigration, employment and foreign affairs" to his colleagues who concentrate on "Home Office, and consumer affairs" or on "communications and anything to do with the Middle East."

MAVERICKS AND MADAME MAX

The final item of strategic advice by which Ministerial Aspirants adjust their actions is, again, not at all as clear as they would like. This concerns the advisability of being deferential to the party's leaders and, above all, of avoiding the label "maverick." And yet, Aspirants ask, if impertinence disqualifies people from high office, how then are we to explain those frontbenchers who most certainly were mavericks during their backbench apprenticeships? Was Trollope's Madame Max entirely incorrect when she told her friend Phineas Finn, "As far as I can understand the way of things in your Government, the Aspirants to office succeed chiefly by making themselves uncommonly unpleasant to those who are in power. If a man can hit hard enough he is sure to be taken into the Elysium of the Treasury Bench— not that he may hit others, but that he may cease to hit those that are there. I don't think men are chosen because they are useful."[36] Madame Max Goesler was exaggerating, being amusing to make a point. Her point was that there exists an informal rule whereby prickly mavericks suffer poor promotion prospects, but that to this rule are attached many exceptions who rise by virtue of their exceptional behavior rather than despite it. Today it is often said that the situation is much the same, albeit the exceptions seem more exceptional.

High Flyers scrutinize these exceptions for clues about the limits of tolerance, about the combinations of "kicking" and "bowing" that will be acceptable and successful. Kicking, as Madame Max observed, does indeed sometimes produce an invitation to join the Government ("not that he may hit others, but that he may cease to hit those that are there"), for joining the Government requires accepting the constitutional convention of collective responsibility, which includes a vow of silence: Members of the Government must either support its policies by voice and vote, or resign.[37] Surely most Junior Ministers are chosen because they are useful. But to give Madame Max her due, there are in every Government Junior Ministers whose "usefulness" was enhanced by their difficult dispositions: "In my own position, for example, I followed a *very* independent line. The last vote I took part in as a backbencher was against the Government. . . . I voted against prescription charges in the summer and then went off on holiday and came back a Minister."

Besides their awareness of this twist to the doctrine of collective responsibility, ambitious mavericks may also believe they have a chance based upon the well-established respect in the House for an independence like John Biffin's that reflects strength, conviction, and intellect. Their assumptions are fueled by examples of notable cases, such as Harold Wilson, who was not the most docile backbencher but who nonetheless climbed the greasy pole. At the same time, even the most sanguine maverick knows that kicking is a dangerous strategy, for what today seems a sign of healthy independence may tomorrow look much less acceptable. Thus rose and fell John Biffin, who, when sacked by Margaret Thatcher, was characterized by her press secretary as "semi-detached." And thus it was the one-time "undocile" but more durable Harold Wilson who, as Prime Minister, addressed a meeting of the Parliamentary Labour Party as follows: "All I say is 'Watch it.' Every dog is allowed one bite, but a different view is taken of a dog that goes on biting all the time. If there are doubts that the dog is biting not because of the dictates of conscience but because he is considered vicious, then things happen to that dog. He may not get his licence renewed when it falls due."

It is extremely unusual for licenses not to be renewed, but not so unusual for mavericks to be locked out. Even in the Conservative Party, which is more tolerant than Labour, Ministerial Aspirants have been cautioned that if they feel they absolutely must revolt, they should do so on no more than one subject at a time. They seem to have taken this advice to heart. When Macdonald investigated the impact of ambition upon cross-voting among the 1970 intake of MPs, she found that ambitious Conservative backbenchers were considerably less likely than their less ambitious colleagues to risk more than a few cross-votes.[38] The constraining effects of ambition upon this behavior can be seen in the regression reported in Table 3.5. Here the strongest and only significant independent variable affecting cross-voting among Conservative backbenchers in the 1970–1974 Parliament is political ambition, a variable that, interestingly enough, behaved in the opposite way for Labour backbenchers whose party was in turmoil at the time and also in Opposition. Macdonald further showed that, as the years passed for those who were passed by, the constraining power of ambition weakened considerably.

Whips can live with an occasional conscientious rebellion more easily than they can live with congenital rebels.[39] Many Conservative Ministerial Aspirants risked a conscientious rebellion or two during their first four years at Westminster, but few rebelled enough to risk becoming known as rebels. One who did, and who had been tipped as a High Flyer, began down this path when he felt obliged to organize a particular backbench rebellion

Table 3.5 Effects of political ambition on the cross-voting behavior of
backbenchers, 1970–1974

Independent variable	Conservative (N = 42)	Labour (N = 38)
Political ambition	−.28*	.22
Age	−.09	.22
Former office holder	.20	−.04
Length of tenure	−.02	−.05

Source: Stuart Elaine Macdonald, "Political Ambition and Attainment: A Dynamic
Analysis of Parliamentary Careers," Ph.D. diss., University of Michigan, 1987: 182.
  Note: Entries are standardized regression coefficients.
  *$p \leq .05$

against his Government. As one thing led to another, he got caught up in
similar projects till this affected his entire attitude, "because I don't believe,
in the first place, that a Government ought to have done the stupid things
that they were embarking on. So it gave me no great satisfaction to prevent
my Government from being stupid." Colleagues began to doubt that he ever
would fly up. And he never did. Neither did this older Labour Subaltern
who just couldn't restrain himself from voting "against a Government that
I was sent here to support. I voted against the Labour Party on prescription
charges . . . on the increase of school meals . . . on the Industrial Relations
Bill. And that's just three." When interviewed, he was still hoping to make
Junior Minister some day, but recognized that the only way to do it now
would be "if I were to trim my views."

Whatever may be said for kicking, it is certainly safer to bow, safer to
swallow hard and "realise that you're lobby fodder, and if you want a rise
you keep quiet and you offer to help when required." Thus, Ministerial
Aspirants are sometimes caricatured as modern versions of Mr. Bott, who
"was a tuft hunter and a toady, but he did not know that he was doing
amiss in seeking to rise by tuft hunting and toadying . . . he believed that
he was progressing in public life by the proper and usual means."[40] Tuft
hunters seek the company of important people. Toadies are fawning flatter-
ers. Surely more tuft-hunting toadies attain office than do troublemakers.
Yet, the important point is that both these colorful interpretations of the
role of the Ministerial Aspirant are exceptional. Most Aspirants are neither
tuft-hunting toadies nor troublemakers. They seek a middle ground whose
boundaries are unmarked, unstable, and subject to changing calculations
based upon the most recent cases of success and failure in the race.

Taking the Role of the Minister

Up to this point, I have explored the motivational core of the Ministerial Aspirant's role and examined some of the beliefs and behaviors that are closely associated with it. But what is most distinctive about this role is its "teleological" character. Unlike backbenchers who are Policy Advocates, Constituency Members, or Parliament Men, Ministerial Aspirants are preparing themselves to become something other than backbenchers. Like Aristotle's famous example of the young horses, part of their natures can best be understood by thinking about what they will in the future grow to be. Thus, some Ministerial Aspirants try to anticipate their frontbench futures by "taking the role" of the Minister, by trying to understand that role as Ministers understand it, by adopting some of its essential perspectives.

INEXPERIENCE AND EXPLORATION

"Taking the role" of the Minister requires considerable observation and experience. And the newest Aspirants haven't yet had time. Like this High Flyer, they frankly admit that "I don't know what a good Minister is like because I haven't seen a Minister at close quarters. . . . I, I haven't seen, and I'm speaking really here from sort of theoretical knowledge."

He and his colleagues were asked about characteristics that make a Minister good at his job and were encouraged to discuss this subject at some length. But even with the experience of a year or so, most Aspirants are not yet sufficiently comfortable in their own roles or sufficiently in control of their own schedules to have studied and understood what makes Ministers tick: "I think breadth of vision and all those other qualities I mentioned for a Member," said a young Tory as he fussed with his diary, "an understanding of people, I suppose, as well as policies." He hasn't thought much yet about differences between good Ministers and good Members. And, at this stage, even those who have thought about it still see Ministers as distant figures with generally positive features, with whom one has occasional dealings: "Above everything else . . . I think it's a question of one's own dealings with him. In one's own dealings with Ministers one eventually finds Ministers whom one can trust."[41]

Thus, unseasoned High Flyers talk about the role of the Minister as something possessed by a distant "Them" rather than as something close to "Me." And they talk about Them not so much in terms of characteristics required for success in office, but more in terms of how They react to Me. A good Minister is one who is receptive to Me, who shows "receptiveness in receiving representations . . . in the receptiveness he displays to points made by the Member." A good Minister is one who is respectful of Me, one who "is approachable. He must be ready to see Members. He must be prepared to take trouble with their individual grievances. . . . He must instill in his civil servants an attitude of respect for Members."

It is not only the unseasoned who fail to show convincing signs of "taking the role" of Minister. Many experienced Subalterns also see Ministers as people who act upon them rather than as people in whose shoes they can imagine themselves, and through whose eyes they try to view Westminster's world. These Subalterns have been around long enough to know about the principal duties and responsibilities of Ministers. The fact that they do not "take the role" has less to do with lack of information than with modest goals. After waiting in the wings for eight years, this graying Subaltern is tired himself and beginning to wonder how Ministers manage to do it all anyway: "Well, Ministers have obviously got to be good in the Chamber, very patient and good at debate, and really to have done his homework and to know his briefs and so on. I often wonder how Ministers can do all those things. . . . Awfully good Minister if you can do all that." Clearly some Subalterns who are aiming for minor posts simply have not thought of themselves as full-blown Ministers. Instead, they hope that the latter will "treat one as quite somebody . . . don't just make you feel an ignorant twit of a backbencher."

This preliminary look at Ministerial Aspirants who do not take the role of the Minister can help us spot those who do. The first sign of a desire to take the role appears when Aspirants begin to evaluate it critically. One day they find that frontbenchers look less Olympian than they did before: "After I'd seen some of our Shadow Spokesmen on the frontbench, I wondered how they ever came into any position," said a young Labour Aspirant reflecting on eighteen months' experience. "You know, there are people who are far better on the backbenches. I mean a person like Timothy Raison," for example. Raison was widely cited as a High Flyer because of his impressive performances: he spoke well and was singularly well informed about his subjects. Skill in debate is a salient criterion, for this is the principal context in which Aspirants observe Ministers whom they rarely have the opportunity to observe in their departments. One of their first observations is that some Ministers who are said to be good in the department are not so good in the House: "I think that delivery at the Despatch Box is an essential quality . . . there are many Ministers who have made a good job within the Ministry, who have been bloody awful at the Despatch Box." Having in this way brought Them a little closer to Me, Aspirants begin quite naturally to wonder how they themselves might do the job: "I mean I could make a better show than Julian Amery," one confided. "I mean, you know, he's a complete balls-up every time he gets on."

On several topics in the transcripts, Ministerial Aspirants can be seen scrutinizing Ministers' performances, understanding them, and, occasionally, trying on aspects of ministerial outlooks, aspects they associate with the worlds to which they aspire.[42] These include style and sensitivity, Machiavellianism, dealing with the other side, and thinking administratively. To "take the role" of the Minister is to imagine oneself in his or her place, to empathize with his or her problems, and to see the world the way he or she sees it. More than any of their backbench colleagues, Ministerial Aspirants are preparing themselves for positions they do not at present hold.

STYLE AND SENSITIVITY

Careful study of frontbench performances can reveal some of the system's subtleties—for example, style: "Crosland . . . he's quite good at strategy, less good at presenting himself. . . . Callaghan or Macleod are good at presenting what they're doing even if what they're doing isn't all that good." And this next High Flyer's use of the pronoun "you" helps him feel closer to the action he is interpreting than do most of the Aspirants from whom we have heard so far: "I think you've got to make a good impression in the House of Commons. . . . And if you succeed in that, you can get away with quite a lot."

A successful style requires sensitivity to the moods of the House. The good Minister, Aspirants say, is particularly sensitive to signs that his own backbenchers may be "unhappy about something, and that's the real thing to worry about if you're a Minister—if you're advocating a policy and your own people are unhappy about it—to be sensitive to that and pick it up," and also "to be able to make the right noises at least so that you can carry the vote at that stage." They study not just the rhythms of the collectivity's moods, but also the relationships in the Chamber between leader and led. Although few of them would put it this way, they study the social psychology of leadership.[43] "He certainly isn't a good Minister," they say, "unless he has antennae," unless he can sense "the feeling of the House. This is where I'm sure many people in all governments fall down. . . . But there's no doubt that if you can feel the way the House is feeling, you will achieve what you want very much more easily." Style involves making "the right noises." Sensitivity involves empathizing with the audience sufficiently to know what "the right noises" are. The House, astute Aspirants learn, is regarded by those most skilled in influencing it as a living organism: they try "to feel the mood of the House and react to it." Aspirants learn by watching Ministers cajole this sensitive creature. And sometimes they fear that this ability to "take the mood of the House" is a "personal quality" they cannot easily learn: "There are certain personal qualities which it is desirable to have . . . taking the mood of the House. . . . John Davies has been destroyed as a Minister through his inability to do this. Dennis Healey was an extremely unsuccessful Minister in the House simply because of his utter inability to sense the mood of the House of Commons and adjust himself to it."

Taking the role of the Minister involves adopting some of its typical beliefs. This process was characterized by Robert Merton as "anticipatory socialization," as adopting attitudes of the group to which an actor aspires in order to become more acceptable to this group and to facilitate adjustment upon joining it.[44] Thus, Ministerial Aspirants, like Ministers, learn to talk about the House as a person with moods and reactions. But this talk is also common among other backbenchers. More peculiar to Ministerial Aspirants are signs of sensitivity to what they take to be their Ministers' basic policy orientations. Responding to a question about solutions to unemployment, for example, Conservative Ministers strongly favored *indirect* state intervention, fiscal measures such as stimulating demand. And Conservative Aspirants were considerably more likely than other Conservative backbenchers to favor indirect intervention along these same lines. On the Labour side, frontbenchers were disposed toward *direct* state planning to guarantee full employment—as were Labour Aspirants, more so than other Labour backbenchers.

MACHIAVELLIANISM

Ministers are rarely as Machiavellian as those who study Ministers suppose. Nonetheless, it would not be at all surprising if Ministerial Aspirants attributed a little Machiavellianism to their leaders and adopted a little of these outlooks themselves.

"I believe that more Members of Parliament should stick more rigidly by their principles and not be put off," said a determined Aspirant with a strong distaste for compromise. "If in fact I stick by the principles that I've got," he continued, "I will get there. . . . Certainly I don't intend to indulge in any of the rather unfortunate methods that are used by some Members of the House to achieve a post or office." He didn't, and he didn't get there. Hugh Gaitskell, by contrast, didn't and *did* get there—but was often criticized for failing to excite and rouse the party's supporters. Crossman is supposed to have said of him that "he lacked the toughness or capacity for self-deceit which was needed in a party leader," and to have commented after his replacement by Harold Wilson, "at last we have a leader who can lie."[45] The attitudes of "highly principled" Aspirants sound unministerial, for "the characteristic he [a good Minister] shouldn't have is stubbornness . . . another characteristic he shouldn't have is pomposity." Twice as many Ministerial Aspirants as other backbenchers disagree with the statement in the study's mailback questionnaire that "one should take action only when sure it is morally right." This result holds for both Conservative and Labour MPs and for all three subtypes of Aspirants. Moreover, those with the strongest ambitions, the High Flyers, reject the statement most strongly.

Even a benign Machiavellianism cautions against defining political issues as matters of principle. It also involves an ability to be convincing about most cases, even weak ones, "the ability to put over a convincing case at the Despatch Box—that's almost the exclusive criteria. . . . Convincing in terms of reasonable presentation . . . even if your case is weak; that's important." What counts most is the *impression* one makes on the House and, through the House, on the electorate. Ministers are able to do well by appearing to have more mastery of a subject than they actually do. What counts with the House, according to many High Flyers, "is really the impression that one is master of one's department." Thus, Subalterns feel that although they are not brilliant themselves, self-confidence and decisiveness may be sufficient to see them through: "He need not necessarily be absolutely expert or brilliant . . . as long as he's a man who can create confidence in his decision making. He must also be able to make clear-cut decisions. You often get a lot of intellectuals who can theorize, but when they get a Ministry, they don't have command of their civil servants. . . . [The key to being a good Minister] is to be able *to put over* the facts."

All this presupposes sensitivity to the art of the possible, weighing "up the arguments placed before him by his officials as against what his political guts tell him and what his colleagues and the House tell him . . . so that he doesn't make a first-rate political gaff." Ministers must assess good policy against the political temperature of the House and the country. They must be prepared to "think electorally" and assess the probable impact of alternative policies upon voting behavior. All politicians think about electoral implications, but Ministers, Aspirants have noticed, think about them more than most. So some of these Aspirants sensitize their electoral antennae too. On the question of unemployment, an explosive political issue for the Heath Government, Conservative Aspirants were three times as likely as other Conservative backbenchers to make electoral considerations central themes in their discussions.[46]

Machiavellianism involves managing impressions, and that requires managing oneself. Self-control underlies the polished performances of accomplished actors. The Minister that some Aspirants are trying to become is the Minister who "never loses his temper," who is able to remain polite and patient and not become rattled. Such Ministers are said "to have got a manner at the Despatch Box." It is a way of doing things that enchants one's own backbenchers and amuses those on the other side. Some Ministers are very good at this and others aren't. John Peyton, for instance, was said always to get a hearing and occasionally "to get away with murder. He usually has them all roaring with laughter—and he is denationalizing Thomas Cook's and all those subjects." This is the "rosy glow theory" (a phrase attributed to Michael Foot) of parliamentary persuasion. James Callaghan was identified as one of its premier practitioners: "When Uncle Jim gets up to speak, a 'rosy glow' descends on the Chamber." It is produced by "the manner" one presents when one is speaking, by "the physical gestures, the way his body moves . . . a sense of humour helps. . . . If he can combine seriousness with a sense of humour."[47]

THE OTHER SIDE

Ministers usually try to work amicably with the Opposition, for otherwise they risk confrontations that can delay their Bills or even derail their careers. The most ambitious Aspirants have apparently adopted beliefs that are consistent with this orientation. A mailback item that focused on giving the Opposition its due[48] produced little difference between Ministerial Aspirants and other backbenchers; but among Aspirants, High Flyers were three times as likely as Subalterns to endorse it without reservation. High Flyers try to be partisan without riding roughshod over the Opposition. They try to respond favorably to sensible ideas from the other side because they realize that "a Minister that can understand the Opposition point of view and is sympathetic to it will get a much better hearing than someone who tries to shout them down." When they become Ministers, they will be "quite prepared," they say, "to concede where generally it is believed there is a weak line" and "to take on board ideas that are generally thought to be good."

In the same vein, Ministers must recognize and be seen to recognize the legitimacy of Opposition campaigns in Parliament, even when these campaigns frustrate their plans. It is prudent to remind themselves and their colleagues that the Opposition's legitimate constitutional role is "to allow nothing to go by unquestioned and to cause the maximum amount of inconvenience to those who carry out policies." This is another attitude that some Ministerial Aspirants take up by way of anticipating the role of Minister.

Thus, although Aspirants and other backbenchers share similar views toward a mailback item on this subject,[49] once again High Flyers are more than twice as likely as Subalterns to accept, without reservation, that the duty of the Opposition is to oppose and that good Ministers should not humiliate their opponents as they skewer them.

THINKING ADMINISTRATIVELY

Even the greenest Aspirants show considerable concern about the administrative side of ministerial roles, because it is more difficult to understand the unseen activities in Whitehall than to view the public performances at Westminster.

The Minister, they say, must strike a balance between "the arguments placed before him by his officials . . . and what his colleagues and the House tell him." He must strike a balance between the time he devotes to administration and the time he devotes to the House. Effective administration will help him in the House, for "the House does sense when a Minister is running his department well, and this helps and eases his relations with Members. That's part of the criteria on which he is judged." Moreover, the House tries to distinguish between those Ministers who, because they have a grip on their departments, can deal with the difficult supplementary questions and those who are merely riding departmental briefs with the whispers of civil servants in their ears. Aspirants absorb whatever information they can about the administrative side of the job and its relationship to the performances they see in the Chamber and upstairs in committee.[50] They focus more than their colleagues do on Whitehall and think more about things they think Ministers think about, such as "what really matters is the struggle with other Ministers over departmental resources."

The ministerial attitude that Aspirants absorb more than any other is uneasiness about the influence of senior civil servants. Indeed, they tend to overdo it by becoming more uneasy about this influence than most frontbenchers are. They become extremely concerned that the Minister "should be *in charge* of his department, um, rather than the civil servants in charge of the department." If knowledge is power, then senior civil servants must be very powerful, for they have the knowledge—and Ministers must strive to keep them "*on tap* rather than on top." Ministers must seek to "inspire the people who are really running it. I mean if they feel proud of their Minister's performance at the Box, that the Minister is getting the message over, then the people who really are at the shop-end perform well. I mean ours [sic] is essentially a missionary role." The role is not yet his, but this High

Flyer thinks he knows a lot about it. He knows that it requires sustained attention to detail, and that Ministers who do not have speeches drafted according to their own detailed directives will become mere "performers rather than playwrights in the department." To keep civil servants on tap rather than on top, Ministers likewise need to control their own diaries and appointments as well as their own telephone calls.

Aspirants absorb all this information about ministerial roles and adopt some of the outlooks associated with them. They also adopt some of the prejudices, including a view of "the House which most Ministers must regard as really a bit of a nuisance and relatively unimportant."

A Bit of a Nuisance

Signs of impatience with colleagues and irritation with the House, especially with its club-like character, are not difficult to find. Fellowship is an uneasy companion to competition; and Ministerial Aspirants are engaged in competition, competition for office: "I'm sorry, but one is in politics to exercise power, not to enjoy friendships." The more avid among them are, as we have seen, kept on edge by the feeling that "the competition for ministerial office is very strong." "Competition is very hot," new High Flyers say as they explore their roles and assess their prospects.

They expect a little conflict, because they find that the competition inherent in their roles generates personal frictions. Most accept these frictions, and a few relish them. "I don't think this is a place you can develop friendships and close relations. I think that is the pity of it," lamented a High Flyer from Oxford and the Law Courts; "to start with you really can't place trust in terms of friendships in anybody. I am speaking now of one's *own* party." He has found, and other Aspirants echo his feelings, that "it's a rather unpleasant place from that point of view, pretty cut-throat." Conviviality is necessary in order to make the right contacts at the right time. But there is a difference between fraternization and friendship. The difference is affection and trust, which competition discourages. "I think this is why," reflects another Aspirant, "why people at the top, I mean if you consider people like Healey and Jenkins, they would have very few close friends I would have thought—and not because they are odd people, but because it's very difficult . . . you can't." Nor can you with the other side, with members of the other parties;[51] although in cynical moments, Ministerial Aspirants may wonder whether "it wouldn't be all that much of an exaggeration, you know, in politics to say that 'enemies' are a term that you keep for your friends. . . . This is because of the nature of politics. Politics is the last bit of totally unreleased, uncontrolled jungle, in any country, always. . . . We are rivals with each other. And that's why, of course, one can often have a more natural relationship with Members on the other side than with Members on one's own side."

Backbenchers who play different roles use different nouns to characterize their colleagues. Parliament Men call them friends. Policy Advocates call them allies. But Ministerial Aspirants are more likely to call them rivals. They are also more likely to express negative feelings about the House of Commons as an institution.

Responses to the question in Table 3.6 were transcribed and coded on a five-point scale of positive and negative feelings toward the House of Commons. The "negative" entries combine the two lowest points on the scale, while the "positive" category covers points 1–3. The data suggest that Ministerial Aspirants do indeed have comparatively ambivalent feelings about the House of Commons as an institution. Parliament is, for them, an arena for ambition and achievement. And they are, Subalterns and High Flyers alike, nearly twice as likely as other backbenchers to express negative feelings toward the House, a pattern that holds across both the Conservative and Labour parties.[52]

Ministerial Aspirants make us think of Policy Advocates, for they too are concerned about the making of policy. There is, however, an important distinction between the career goals and emotional incentives involved, a distinction that motivates these backbenchers to create roles that are more complementary than overlapping. It centers on Legge-Bourke's contrast between

Table 3.6 Views of the House of Commons by Ministerial Aspirant subtypes, in percent

View	Aspirant subtype*			Other backbenchers
	High Flyer	Mixed	Subaltern	
Negative	40	30	42	21
Positive	60	70	58	79
Total	100	100	100	100
	(N = 35)	(N = 27)	(N = 19)	(N = 247)

Q. The House of Commons has been described as having the atmosphere of a "gothic club"—as stuffy, lifeless, and out-of-date. Do you think this description is true?

*Aspirants v. other backbenchers ($p \leq .01$)

influence and power, between seeking to influence those who have the power to take decisions and seeking to become a decision taker oneself, a person who exercises power directly.

To attain office, Ministerial Aspirants try to construct roles that will constitute successful apprenticeships; but the task is difficult because the guideposts are not clearly defined. The fact that Members frequently use the labels "Aspirant" and "High Flyer" in their conversations creates the illusion that this role's duties and responsibilities are reasonably well understood. But the connotations linked to these labels are, in fact, fewer than for most others. The dense cloud cover here resembles what we shall later see surrounding the "Good House of Commons Man." Ministerial Aspirants are not quite sure what they should try to be, because, in part, their colleagues are not quite sure what they want them to be.

The dilemma is compounded by an awareness that the expectations of these colleagues are very powerful indeed. They may be vague, yet they will nevertheless determine whether the Aspirant's performance succeeds or fails. MPs believe that the House forms a collective judgment about the character of all its Members. For Aspirants, this collective judgment focuses on their suitability for ministerial office. But far more important than these collective opinions (albeit strongly influenced by them) are the views held by Ministers and Whips. Moreover, as the country has come to pay less attention to its parliamentary actors than it once did, it has become correspondingly more difficult than it once was to achieve office by building a reputation outside the House. Hence, "the aspirant for office hopes to catch the eye of the Premier or of a senior Minister and to make his wider reputation after he has been appointed."[53]

Parliaments are not, in this respect, so very different from other institutions. Upwardly mobile members of most organizations are judged by their peers and, more consequentially, by their superiors—that is to say, by the counterparts of Ministers and Whips. Likewise, when the expectations held by such superiors are vague, then in most organizations the pressure builds and, along with it, the anxiety and the tension.[54] In the House of Commons they say, "We will know." Among the things that "We" will know is whether the newcomer should be taken seriously as an Aspirant and, if so, what level of ambition and performance might reasonably be expected from him or her. Out of these assessments, High Flyers will emerge self-assured and clear-headed about their desires for office. They will have more information about the career ladder and about their prospects than will members of the Mixed group, who, even after several years, may still be probing the possibilities. Subalterns, the third subtype, will develop modest appraisals of their capabilities and opportunities. They will be pleased to think of themselves as Junior Ministers and, while they are waiting, pleased to pursue modest constituency work and advocacy.

The Subalterns remind us of Policy Advocates when they discuss advocacy and of Constituency Members when they discuss their constituencies; but, as with other Ministerial Aspirants, their career goals strongly color these outlooks. Thus, compared to Advocates, they are more absorbed by the subjects of power and attaining power, an absorption reflected in their overestimation of their colleagues' ambitions. Even those who apparently want junior office more for policy goals than for personal goals still want these offices very much indeed—and therefore are more likely than Policy Advocates to pursue advocacy instrumentally and to prefer general influence to minor campaigns. Their distinctive motivations show through as well in constituency work when they think more about inspiring constituents collectively than about servicing them individually. They regard the constituency as a place to make a mark and secure a base and, once that is done, as a place to fence in so that they can look beyond it to wider horizons.

Ministerial Aspirants concentrate on office and on the strategies by which it might be attained. They study these matters carefully because the rules are so uncertain. They try to make regular, though not too regular, speeches in the House and to attack political enemies rather than allies. They try to be convivial with their colleagues and with their superiors, whom they try to impress by competence and diligence in committees. They want to seem serious, though not too serious, so they specialize but don't overspecialize, which might handicap them as people of narrow vision. They also avoid the maverick's mantle, for though they are aware of examples that support the theories of Madame Max, they see many more mavericks sitting behind the ministerial frontbenches of Westminster than behind the ministerial desks of Whitehall.

Aspirants also prepare themselves to be Ministers by "taking the role," by trying out characteristic outlooks and beginning to think about the role of the Minister as a role for Me rather than only for Them. This takes time and trouble to think through; and many never learn very much about ministerial roles till they are themselves in office. Others, however, learn the significance of style in the Chamber and of sensitivity to the moods of the House. They also begin to think a little like Ministers, or as they suppose Ministers think: Machiavellian enough to be convincing when cases are weak; controlled enough to be an accomplished actor; realistic enough to work with opponents from the other side and to control civil servants and departments.

Ministerial Aspirants look to the future because "you know it dawns on you very early on that really there's not much point in being a backbencher forever." They package their motivations in plans to promote policies by achieving office and power. And they appear to be deferential to the House and its moods while, beneath the surface, their ambition grows ("the job itself teaches you . . . the ambition as it were") and their love affair with the House grows tiresome. The role of the Ministerial Aspirant is confusing because it is so anticipatory and so uncertain. Yet, easy as it is to see the hypocrisies, it is equally easy to see the ideals that, although they may be more difficult to live up to in our era of professional politicians, are still not so very different from those exemplified a century ago by the esteemed Duke of St. Bungay:

> Through his long life he had either been in office, or in such a position that men were sure he would soon return to it. He had taken it, when it had come, willingly, and had always left it without a regret. As a man cuts in and out at a whist table, and enjoys both the game and the rest from the game, so had the Duke of St. Bungay been well pleased in either position. . . . He had been ambitious, but moderately ambitious, and his ambition had been gratified. It never occurred to him to be unhappy because he or his party were beaten on a measure. When President of the Council he could do his duty and enjoy London life. When in Opposition, he could linger in Italy til May and devote his leisure to his trees and his bullocks. He was always esteemed, always self-satisfied, and always Duke of St. Bungay.[55]

CONSTITUENCY MEMBERS:
REDRESS OF GRIEVANCES

> Nobody knows me here. But I am exceedingly
> well known in the constituency.
> Welfare Officer

In many Western democracies, national representatives provide a wide range of local constituency services. Recently there has been a surge in studies of these services in both Britain and the United States. The American research has focused on the electoral advantages that incumbents may gain from such activities.[1] But studies in Britain have been more likely to address, by contrast, the topic of representation.[2] This is because constituency service is regarded as a more central aspect of representation in Britain than it is in the United States.[3] Indeed, the most familiar backbench role in the House of Commons today is the role of the Constituency Member, whose players, it is said, represent by making representations to central government about their constituents' personal cases and collective problems.

Constituency Representation

The role of the Constituency Member, which immerses backbenchers in the small disputes and difficulties of their constituents, must seem a peculiar occupation for members of a parliament that is so nationally oriented. The House of Commons is not a congress of local ambassadors. Representatives are not required to live in their constituencies; and they often enter politics at the national level rather than working up, as the Americans are more likely to do, from the grass roots. Moreover, as Peter Pulzer once observed, the so-called elitist theory of how democracy should work actually describes rather well the way democracy does work in Britain.[4] The Constitution is unwritten, there is no domestic judicial review, and between elections there are few formal controls on the Executive. Certainly the public isn't much involved: there are more active members of the Royal Society for the Protection of Birds than of all political parties combined. Nor are the political authorities eager to involve the public. Indeed, their uneasiness about active citizen participation surfaces at Westminster in sympathy for Official Secrets Acts and Privy Councillors' oaths, and in assumptions that the Great, if not always Good, can nearly always be trusted. What point is there, then, to MPs becoming absorbed with constituency affairs? The point, and it is an important one, is the redress of grievances, the constituency aspect of representation that concerns acting as an agent to protect and advance the interests of ordinary citizens. Embedded in a system of formal and informal rules, this practice has long been interwoven with British concepts of representative and responsible government and regarded as a source of legitimacy and a check on the Executive.[5] There are 650 Members of Parliament, each in a sufficiently small constituency so that people with grievances can realistically think about going to see their MP. Although many of their grievances are trivial matters, many are not; and even the trivial ones may indicate areas where policy is wrong and needs to be put right.[6] Each week, Ministers receive from MPs up to sixteen thousand letters. The volume is great and the pressure is steady, especially upon government departments that deal regularly with the public.

It is sometimes forgotten that the redress of grievances was Parliament's original function and, for centuries, the only important function performed by MPs. Thus, the origins of the role of the Constituency Member can easily be traced back to the end of the thirteenth century, to early parliaments that were more like courts of justice than like legislative assemblies. These were places for petitioning for favors and for righting wrongs, places where the "parleying" was mainly about legal matters. Some of the rolls of these early parliaments are filled with nothing but *Placita et petitiones,* trials of causes and petitions for redress.[7] Indeed, after a parliament had been summoned, the first step in holding it was to proclaim publicly the date by which petitions should be submitted by all those who wished to submit them. Eventually, Members of Parliament linked this redress of grievances to the granting of supply, to the promise of financial aid to the Crown, which was the main purpose for Parliament that the King had in mind.

For hundreds of years, high policy was addressed elsewhere, while the Commons concentrated on representing local matters arising from unsatisfactory administrative, fiscal, or social circumstances. During the eighteenth and nineteenth centuries, however, the role of the Constituency Member became dormant. There was still a steady stream of petitions and private Bills, but regular contact with the electorate was deemed improper except during campaigns, and voters were encouraged to regard MPs as statesmen who debated and deliberated over the great issues of the day rather than as local ombudsmen.[8] The modern role of the Constituency Member is, in fact, a new version of a very old role that had been neglected for some time. It was revived by the demands of the Welfare State and refurbished by the backbenchers who set out most enthusiastically to meet those demands. Labour MPs began to retrieve the role between the wars, and during the postwar period it became a familiar fixture.[9] "What the public sees" today, according to a newly elected MP, "is a sort of local ombudsman, a social service man who is there to intervene on their behalf, and to battle with government departments and to rectify wrongs." The fit between this ancient parliamentary role and the needs of the modern Welfare State helps explain why nearly all MPs today, including those in the highest ministerial offices, do at least a little constituency service. But some Members of Parliament meet much more fully the public's expectations and make constituency work the principal preoccupation of their careers.

These are the Constituency Members, whose role is one of the best known and best defined on the backbenches. Constituency Members are as easily recognized as Ministerial Aspirants and as clear as Policy Advocates about their priorities: "Looking after my constituents, that's the most important" or "serving one's constituency is the most important role. . . . Yes, that's the major task." They explain their aims by contrasting them with the alternatives. Thus, "to me the most important part of being an MP is not so much roving the world on international affairs, important as that may be," nor is it "preparing an important speech to deliver in the House of Commons." Moreover, "I have no pretensions to sit on the Government benches. I've no ambition."[10] The comparative clarity of their role is reflected in the fact that its name is so widely used at Westminster, albeit its players are not so widely respected as are the Aspirants and Advocates. This gives the role a twist that Constituency Members themselves sometimes joke about.[11] The same sentiments that lead them genuinely to insist "that the little man in your constituency who needs help, his needs should come first," are occasionally accompanied by stories that suggest a little irony: "A fellow's been fiddling his income tax for some astronomic sum, and in the last resort came to me to try to smooth things over. And I told him to go to hell. And he's quite happy, gone to hell, he's had an honest answer from on high and he'll have to pay up. So even if you give a bad answer, provided it's an honest answer, they're satisfied. And if your client is satisfied, you too can be satisfied."

Subtypes and Distribution

Within this preference role of Constituency Member live two distinct subtypes that differ in their outlooks and conduct: Welfare Officers and Local Promoters. Nearly all Constituency Members are inclined one of these ways, but several give each equal attention and have therefore been assigned to an intermediate category, "Mixed." The criterion used in this coding would be familiar to MPs and informed observers alike: representations on behalf of *individual* constituents or on behalf of the constituency's *collective* concerns. Welfare Officers are those whose primary focus falls on individual constituents and their difficulties with housing, pensions, or whatever problems they may bring to the surgery. By contrast, Local Promoters concentrate primarily on collective concerns of the constituency as a whole, or of sectors within it, on matters such as industrial development, unemployment, or securing a road bypass.[12]

Constituency Members are typically depicted in the press as Welfare Officers, and Table 4.1 indicates that three out of four of them fit this description. Devoted to casework with individuals, these are the MPs for whom "the most important duty of all is to give your unreserved and unremitting attention to your constituents." The same themes are developed by respondents in the Mixed category, but these backbenchers also give a prominent place to collective constituency matters. Many Constituency Members might object that, in fact, they desire to do both, and that the 9 percent for this

Table 4.1 Constituency Members: Subtypes, and subtypes by political party

| | All Constituency Members | | Political party* | | | |
| | | | Conservative | | Labour | |
Subtype	N	%	N	%	N	%
Welfare Officers	(64)	75	(25)	68	(37)	82
Mixed	(8)	09	(3)	08	(4)	09
Local Promoters	(13)	15	(9)	24	(4)	09
Total	(85)	99	(37)	100	(45)	100

*p ≤ .05

category is misleading. Yet, most of them direct their energies much more to one side than to the other. The other side is that of the Local Promoters, a significant minority among Constituency Members (15 percent), who speak very little about the personal problems of individual constituents and instead develop a constituency-wide perspective ("My predecessor was . . . a bloody awful Constituency Member. . . . And all the things, every sort of service, was in a terribly bad state as a result") or even a regional perspective. But the most notable fact about Local Promoters is that so many of them dislike and denigrate the welfare officer role. As one devoted Local Promoter, a senior Conservative backbencher, put it, "There is a danger of becoming a sort of local Welfare Officer . . . writing to the local council and saying, 'Look here, Mrs. Snooks ought to have a house because she's got this trouble and five children'—when it ought to go to the local authority." This attitude underlines the importance of distinguishing between the subtypes within the role of the Constituency Member. Both Welfare Officers and Local Promoters are Constituency Members, but they are different sorts of Constituency Members, one of which would prefer not to be so closely associated with the other.

It is unusual to find very large partisan differences in distributions of parliamentary roles.[13] And Labour MPs are only slightly more likely than Conservatives to choose the role of Constituency Member as their principal job.[14] The partisan contrasts between the subtypes in Table 4.1 are greater: 82 percent of Labour's Constituency Members are Welfare Officers, compared to 68 percent among the Conservatives, who are more likely than their Labour counterparts to emerge as Local Promoters. These data understate the difference somewhat, since Labour's strength is disproportionately concentrated among the "very strong" Welfare Officers, where they outnumber Conservatives by four to one.[15] Nevertheless, the great majority of Conservative Constituency Members are Welfare Officers too, although they tend to think about their welfare work in broader frameworks: "Churchill once said that you must put your country first, your constituency second, and your party third. . . . The Member of Parliament is a kind of last court of appeal for the individual. . . . If you have a particular constituent's problem, you have a duty to do what you can for them, though never a duty to press a case to the extent where what you're doing is obviously not in the interests of the country as a whole."

Before proceeding to explore the characteristic activities and attitudes of these two types of Constituency Members, it is necessary to stress that all MPs do some constituency work much of the time. Those who are not singled out here as Constituency Members, because constituency service is not their primary concern, may do perfectly satisfactory work for their constituents. Some Policy Advocates and Ministerial Aspirants, for example, engage in active constituency service and are more active than "weak" Constituency Members who may not pursue other roles very much but don't pursue their own principal role very much either. Actually, the amount of time devoted to constituency casework by the average backbencher increased throughout the 1970s and 1980s.[16] Whether or not this trend has increased the proportion of Constituency Members on the backbenches, however, is not known.

Activities in the Constituency

In the constituencies, Welfare Officers and Local Promoters develop contrasting styles of constituency service that are more easily distinguished than are their activities at Westminster. To investigate their characteristic beliefs and behaviors in the constituencies, therefore, the two types are considered separately. Unfortunately, it is not so easy to illustrate these types with familiar names, for the names are not familiar. Alexander Eadie, Joseph Hiley, James Johnson, and Simon Wingfield Digby, for example, are exceedingly well known in their constituencies, but not in the nation at large.

WELFARE OFFICERS

The Welfare Officers' most appreciated service is talking with constituents at the surgery or advice bureau. Nearly all MPs hold surgeries. Approximately 80 percent did so in 1960; 90 percent by 1970; and the proportions are probably still higher today.[17] Labour MPs tend to hold them more often than Conservatives, and Welfare Officers hold them more often than anyone else. Whereas Policy Advocates or Ministerial Aspirants may have a surgery once or twice a month, most Welfare Officers see their constituents each week. They advertise in the local newspaper and open the doors on a Friday or Saturday morning to install themselves, for as long as it takes, in a centrally located meeting room or office.[18] It usually takes two to three hours to listen to the ten to twenty constituents ("from half past nine to half past twelve, your agent stacks them up"), many of whom are older, working class, and not very articulate. Hence, the most successful Welfare Officers are the good listeners, like this Conservative MP: "They are nervous because it's an ordeal for them to have to come and sit and see you. And what you have got to try and do is make them feel relaxed, because if you scare them, they are never going to tell you what they want to tell you, they will mumble on about something and then walk out, and they haven't really told you. . . . You have got to try in a short space of time to, to get their confidence and get them to open up."

But the surgery is only one event in the Welfare Officers' weekend, for they are more likely than other MPs to be in their constituencies and make themselves generally available throughout Saturday and Sunday, something that "the old school" rarely did: "My predecessor was one of the old school . . . he never had surgeries. He went up to the constituency about twice a year for the annual general meeting and the annual dinner or something such as this." By contrast, "I'm there whenever they feel, whenever they need me . . . whatever problem they have they can come and see me." Many live in their constituencies, which allows them to work while they are attending to their families: "I live in the middle of my constituency and I sort of go home every Friday and literally do another two days' work." Others live just outside their constituencies, near enough for people to "come and see me and say, 'Well this is wrong, take it up next week.'" And those who don't live there spend a great deal of time in the constituency nevertheless ("Last year I spent 98 nights in Birmingham"). The aim is to be available always: "I'm always available on the phone, at home, to my constituents. I personally don't believe in Members of Parliament being ex-directory. . . . It may be inconvenient at times to be too readily available, but I think this is one of the prices of the job."

Through promotional activities, some of the "very strong" Welfare Officers boost awareness of their services and the level of demand for them.[19] Whereas ordinary Welfare Officers wait for cases to come to them, the aggressive members of the species set out to find people in need, people who normally wouldn't contact their Member of Parliament. Several take mobile surgeries around the constituency each week.[20] And one even scrapped his surgeries altogether and went instead to seek casework at pubs, clubs, and shopping centers: "And I make my way there, usually getting to each one once every three weeks or so. I pick up my casework that way."

Some visit their constituents at home ("I make a point of visiting the home of everybody who ever contacted me. . . . It does keep your feet on the ground") and make a special point of visiting those who cannot come to them, like the "old lady who's eighty-three years old. She lost her husband and was at the suicide point. And frankly it was nothing that I couldn't sort out in ten minutes' phone call to the manager of the Department of Health and Social Security. I slipped out and made a telephone call and went back and was able to reassure her." During the weekend, they pursue their representations with local civil servants and with the local authority and its representatives; they make phone calls, write letters, and act as facilitators to see that the system works properly and that those who need help get it: "The help is there, but either they're not aware it's there, or they don't know how to get it. And I see my job as to get it for them. I work very closely with my social workers and the social services in my constituency."

Difficulties for which constituents seek their MP's help are a mixture of matters concerning local government, central government, and private institutions and individuals. By far the most common problem is housing. Nearly all Welfare Officers spend a great deal of time trying to sort it out: "If you follow the impression and information you get from your constituents," complained a reluctant Welfare Officer, "housing is really the only problem that matters in this country. . . . I devote a vast amount of time to it, I should think nearly half of my working life." Several spend more time on it than that. One of them, whose constituency has been undergoing extensive urban development, has "thousands of families being disturbed and moved. And I've got to look after them. My local council's got to look after them. And we work as a team and try to get the best possible deal for them. This has dominated all the years I've been in Parliament." The local council is involved because the difficulty usually concerns availability of council houses administered by the local housing authority. MPs who are not Welfare Officers are tempted, therefore, to advise constituents to take their complaints to the local council.[21] But Welfare Officers, by contrast, take it up themselves with the explanation that "the individual seems to want his Member of Parliament to look at the problem, not his local councillor who might be living around the corner from him."[22]

Pension problems concern the central government and can be more complicated, as in the case of the ex-Army Sergeant Major who had retired from the Army at forty-five, took another job that would last twenty years, and was refused permission to commute part of his pension in order to buy a house. The Minister of Defense had taken a paternalistic view and had decided that it would be much better for him to have his pension. So his MP took up the case: "And I said this chap's not a boozy, brainless type. This chap has three 'A' levels and has taken a highly technical job and knows how to arrange his own affairs better than you know how to arrange them." Some Welfare Officers make pension problems their specialty. A Labour Member describes "the strength of my constituency representation as the cases of old-age pensioners, people who've been unjustly treated by the government department. I mean in those cases I don't hesitate, I put the full pressure on to give the kind of return that I think the constituent is entitled to have." In fact, he seeks out people who are unaware that they are entitled to pensions, such as the old man with a war injury to whom he explained: "Now people like you ought to have a pension. You gave your service to your country. Go home and get your papers and bring them back." As a result of negotiations with the department, the old man, who was eighty, was awarded a lump-sum payment of four hundred pounds.

Tax and social security matters are also common cases that require redress from departments of central government. One Labour Welfare Officer worked for over a year to get a few pounds back from the Inland Revenue, which, he believed, had treated his constituent unfairly. In a similar case involving a Chelsea Pensioner, "somebody in the income tax office had made a mistake, and he had underpaid about fifty pounds, and they were going to make him pay it in one fell swoop. And the old boy couldn't do this, he was scared to death, he was in his seventies. He came to me and I managed to help him." Another Welfare Officer cited the example of a seventy-five-year-old woman who was told by the Social Security that they had overpaid her for three years and now wanted 105 pounds back, 105 pounds she didn't have. It took only one letter to resolve: "I wrote to the Social Security and said, 'But this is monstrous that you should, by any stretch of the imagination, ask an old lady who's reaching the fag end of her life, you're causing a great deal of distress.' "

Occasionally, Welfare Officers take up private problems that would be regarded as peculiar responsibilities for representatives even in the most populistic democracies. Thus, it is unusual, but not all that unusual, to hear how they have dealt personally with cases of mental illness or attempted suicide: "One woman had attempted suicide twice, and by weekly visits to her home, to her children, her confidence was built up. I deliberately tried to do this. And eventually with the police we caught the husband who was trying to kill her. . . . People might argue that that's the social worker's job, but the strange, fascinating thing about an MP is that if an MP steps in, confidence steps up." These amateur social workers are usually Labour MPs; Conservatives prefer to regard themselves as local ombudsmen even when, in the age of the Welfare State, this draws them into small matters, such as the case of a constituent who couldn't read or write and was having terrible trouble with the Gas Board. "She complained that there was something wrong with the meter, and they treated her very badly. The poor old soul was worried silly. . . . And I got on to them. And the result of it is that far from her owing them money, they owe her money." It might be a private business whose boss has unfairly treated one of his employees. Or it might be a schoolgirl refused a refund when she returned unsatisfactory goods. In such cases, "the MP with his House of Commons notepaper" may have a go, and may prove more effective than a trade union official or a solicitor. Often the problem is more private still and requires not action but only sympathetic listening: "They come along just to talk to somebody and unburden themselves."

LOCAL PROMOTERS

Local Promoters have two obvious characteristics. The first, illustrated by this quick quip, is that they don't think of themselves as social workers: "Well, as I said, and unfortunately was reported in my local paper as saying, 'One only gets contacted by the *mad* and the *bad*.' And a man came up to me in the street and said, '*Which* am I?' I said, 'Well, *both!*' But you do get problems from the mad and the bad. The great broad mass of one's constituents are worthy, excellent, plodding, competent people who get on with their own life and get a telephone, and get a divorce, and get whatever else they want without bothering me." Their other obvious characteristic is that they frequently hail from Scotland, Wales, Northern Ireland, or the North West, from areas with distinctive needs and problems that require thinking about "not only my constituency, but the city of Liverpool, and even Merseyside, or the North West region." As a Scot put it, "You've got to be on the watch for something, you know, that's going to have an effect on your part of the world." "I do what I can," said another Promoter, "to see that my area of Wales gets its fair share of jobs and transport and all the rest of the things that are going." Yet this regional patriotism is mainly background and context. Most of the problems that Local Promoters pursue are rooted in their constituencies.

The strength of the constituency service rendered by Local Promoters lies not with making representations about individual difficulties but with the constituency's collective needs, which may be economic, environmental, or social. Thus, when Promoters talk about what they do in their constituencies, they are less likely to discuss surgeries than to review visits to local factories ("I consider it part of my job to be in each of those factories at least once in the year"), disablement centers, comprehensive schools, hospitals, or other institutions. At all these places, they seek information about the broad range of contributions being made and about the needs in areas where they might be of help. "Last year I did every other day through the whole of September," reported a Labour Promoter, "in meeting chief officials of my local borough council, visiting, looking at things. Two days with education, two days with social service, looking at old-folks homes, looking at what was being done about the health centre provision, family planning, development housing, new schemes, conversions, improvements, health schemes."[23]

Their work also involves local party activity, "which I would deeply miss. I'm very much involved with my local party and with a number of other local parties in the Midlands." All MPs are expected to aid the local party organization between elections by making political speeches and attending political dances, bazaars, and meetings on the weekends.[24] Yet, Promoters do more than the minimum of this sort of thing and gladly accept as well a part in nonpartisan functions such as opening a showroom for the South of Scotland Electricity Board or giving speeches about delinquency or the environment. This keeps them in touch with "all the various local organisations that are contacting you." One way of looking at it is that, "in his constituency," the MP "should be a catalyst to make sure that all the organisations that make up a constituency, work. And if they don't work, he should make representation to them." Welfare Officers do some of these things too, but they are less likely to think of themselves as community catalysts.

Throughout the 1970s, unemployment was among the most pressing collective constituency concerns. Labour Promoters worried about its demoralizing psychological effects. Conservatives worried also about cheating and about the quality of the statistics. But both took it seriously. It would be difficult not to take it seriously when, following the sudden collapse of a major firm, "half of my constituency was likely to be unemployed." In some areas, like Northumberland, this had long been the dominant problem: "When I went there, there were thirty thousand mining jobs in Northumberland . . . and now we'll be lucky if there's thirteen thousand. It's a full time job in itself, the question of the rundown of the industry and all the upheaval, social, economic, and industrial, that it caused." One Local Promoter, who had experience in building and property development, claimed to have played a significant part in making his town, which was previously "considered to be on the way out," into "one of the most prosperous towns on the South Coast. . . . It happened to be that my experience of building and property development and the like has been applied. And we've got, our unemployment figures used to be one of the highest in the area and are now one of the lowest." Most Promoters, however, were still fighting to reduce unemployment, a problem they tended to discuss less in terms of individual cases than in terms of statistics and strategies for improving the area's economic health.

Chief among these strategies was improving the constituency's industrial base. This might involve "the attraction of new industry . . . to bring firms to the constituency where only coal was the source of employment before. Ronsons, Wilkinson Sword, Glaxo, Commercial Plastics, Alcan Aluminum, pulp mill. So you can get a pretty clear picture of what I've been doing in the last ten years." Or it might involve "mounting a joint effort between the trade unions, and the constituency, and myself . . . to save this particular plant," which is in danger of being closed down. It can also be done by securing government investment, grants of money for shipyards or steel mills, aircraft orders for local firms, or by meeting with the Minister to see that oil rigs are built in "my part of the world" rather than somewhere else.[25] Doing "a good job for the industries in your area" brings work for your constituents and general prosperity. And to achieve this, some Promoters are prepared to travel out into the wider world to win "an order coming to my constituency worth sixty million pounds. These are the things for which one's got to fight, for which one's got to be in touch with the management, the unions, the whole range of the industrial process."

The quality of life is also affected by the provision of health and recreational services. More than a few MPs claim to have kept open or improved a hospital in their constituencies. But perhaps one of the most satisfying projects, and for that reason one that conveys well the civic and service-oriented character of the role, is the work of this Local Promoter who helped to develop a park:

> We have a very large park in Portsmouth that was gifted by the government to Admiral Keele to commemorate his great victory. His successors didn't want it and the Portsmouth Corporation bought it. Since that time the park was practically never used in spite of the fact that it was a colossal size of a park—it's something like 750 acres. . . . You had a mile to walk, all the way up, before you could sit down on the grass or get a seat of any kind because there were railings all the way up. So naturally hardly anybody used it. I persuaded the Council to pull down these railings and provide seats all the way up and to spend something like twenty-five thousand pounds on developing this remarkable park. And now there are more people [who] go there from Portsmouth on a good weekend than now go to the seaside. So that when I walk up to that park, as I often do, I get quite a kick out of seeing all these people enjoying themselves.

The subject of planning decisions is a magnet for Local Promoters; and they are drawn to the larger schemes. A Lancashire MP, who characterized his role immediately "as a good Constituency Member," illustrated this claim by describing his elaborate efforts to guide the course of development of the Lancashire New Town. A more common concern than developing new towns is dealing with decay in old ones, old industrial towns that have "got to be brought back to life and made into decent places where people are proud to live. If I can help towards that end, then I would say I have fulfilled an ambition. I want nothing else." Less grand, but more common still, are campaigns for road improvements such as a by-pass. These can take "a very long time. When I came in I tried to fight for a by-pass for one of my towns. Well, now I've got it—it's taken over 37 years." When won, they therefore bring a "marvelous moment of satisfaction: on May the first we are going to see the Minister and get the announcement on the new Chelmsford by-pass."

Finally, there is a large residual category of special local matters that Promoters pursue: proposing an amendment to help horses; creating a register of disabled people in the constituency ("which did a lot for them by making the authorities aware of them"); seeing that an equipment failure at the local fun-fair is properly investigated: "I'm engaged now in trying to discover who is responsible for insuring the safety and, you know, seeing the departments do something about it. There are always a few things like this that are going on." Promoters expect to help with a wide range of local matters because they are regarded by their constituents, and tend to regard themselves, "as some sort of civic leader who should take a responsible role in the community of eighty thousand people—a purely local point of view."

Consequences for Behavior

Many studies seeking to link preference roles to behavior have been unsuccessful. But the motivational approach seeks to reconstruct roles that inherently involve relationships with behavior. This section examines relationships between the role conceptions of Constituency Members and their conduct in two arenas, the constituency and the House of Commons.

TIME IN THE CONSTITUENCY

Listening, being available to help, promoting local improvements, seeing that the system works properly, all these activities require spending a good deal of time in the constituency. Since constituency representation concerns redressing grievances and promoting local interests, "time in the constituency" becomes a key behavioral variable for those who play the constituency member role.[26] The interview's mailback questionnaire asked respondents to estimate the number of hours they spent, during an average week, on various political activities. Some found this difficult; some said there were no "average weeks." But sixty Constituency Members did supply the estimates. The hours per week they devoted to "constituency and party work" in their constituencies provide the data for Table 4.2.

All MPs have constituents, and all MPs encounter individual and collective problems to which some response is required; it is difficult to ignore old-age pensioners driven to distraction by the Social Security; it is difficult to ignore five hundred seaside landladies going bankrupt because of a clause in the recent Fire Precautions Act; and it is imprudent to ignore one's local party association when it requests a little attention and attendance at local functions. The difference between Constituency Members and non-Constituency Members is that the former do *more* than the latter. Since it is an extra effort rather than a unique one that defines Constituency Members, differences between the time they spend in the constituency and the time spent by other backbenchers should be noticeable but not immense. Results fit that expectation. The correlation is .18 across a range from 0 to 48 hours per week. At the top of the range, Constituency Members outnumber non-Constituency Members two to one, a proportion that is nearly reversed among those who spend fewer than 10 hours per week in their constituencies.

This relationship supports the notion that this role encompasses this behavior, that those who think of themselves as Constituency Members are

Table 4.2 Time in the constituency by backbench role, by distance from Westminster

Hours per week	Role type*		Distance from Westminster	
	Non-Constituency Members (%)	Constituency Members (%)		
0–9	44	28	I	II
10–14	37	35	North,	Wales,
15–48	18	37	Scotland	North West,
			.06 (.35)	Yorkshire
Total	99	100		.13 (.14)
	(N = 174)	(N = 60)		
			III	IV
			Southwest,	London,
			West Midlands,	South East,
			East Midlands	East Anglia
			.30 (.01)	.35 (.001)

*Tau *b* = .18 (.01)

also likely to spend the most time in their constituencies. Such results are not "tautological," as is sometimes alleged. There is nothing redundant about finding that politicians who express certain self-conceptions behave in a manner that is consistent with those self-conceptions. Politicians don't always do so, nor do we always assess their self-conceptions accurately. We should, in fact, be very pleased, in the wake of so many studies in which "delegates" did not behave like delegates by voting their constituents' wishes, that we have succeeded in generating preference roles like that of the Constituency Member whose players do behave like Constituency Members by tending to their constituents.

Moreover, the results in Table 4.2 can be strengthened considerably by adding to the analysis the following condition: the shorter the distance between the constituency and Westminster, the stronger the relationship between the role and the behavior. Backbenchers whose constituencies are in Scotland, for example, can get there only on weekends—whether they are Constituency Members or not. But MPs whose constituencies are in London have a choice about how to allocate their weekdays as well.[27] To take account of distance from the House, four concentric circles were drawn on a map of Britain's regions; four regional groupings (I–IV in Table 4.2) were thereby created, each one a shorter commute from Westminster than the next. Comparing from far to near, from I to IV, the correlations suggest that distance makes an enormous difference. Thus, the relationship between constituency member roles and time spent in the constituency is insignificant in the North and in Scotland. But it rises in three steps to reach .35 for East Anglia, the South East, and, of course, London, where a backbencher can, if so desired, be "in my constituency four or five times a week. . . . I can leave the House at 4 o'clock, I can be at an old-age pensioners' tea party at 4:30, I can cut the cake and be back here by 6 o'clock."

The history of skepticism about links between role variables and behavioral variables makes it desirable to investigate this relationship further. Thus, the multiple regression analysis reported in Table 4.3 assesses the impact of the role variable in the context of other independent variables that are widely believed to be involved.

The dependent variable, "time in constituency," is measured as it was before. "Role" (Constituency Member/non-Constituency Member) is entered as a dummy variable. Electoral security ("marginality"), constituency location ("distance"), and the political value "security" have been included in the equation.[28] I have added "party," also a dummy variable, and length of service ("tenure") because other studies have found them to be related to constituency work.[29] Interitem correlations among these independent

Table 4.3 Regression of time in the constituency on selected independent
variables

Independent variable	Beta	F ratio
Role	.230	(11.44)*
Tenure	−.182	(6.91)**
Marginality	−.083	(1.37)
Party	.079	(1.15)
Distance	−.023	(0.11)
Value-security	.008	(0.02)
R	.326	
R^2	.106	
R^2 (adjusted)	.080	

*$p \leq .001$
**$p \leq .01$

variables are sufficiently low to minimize the danger of multicollinearity.
The standardized regression coefficients, beta weights, show the impact of
each independent variable upon time spent in the constituency when the
remaining independent variables are controlled statistically to remove confounding effects. It can readily be seen that the only independent variables
exerting a substantial force are role and tenure. It is the Constituency Members and the recently elected backbenchers who spend the most time in their
constituencies. But the striking finding is that the role variable here again
outperforms all the others, including standard workhorses such as electoral
security (marginality) and political party.[30]

We now turn to an example of behavior that is not usually considered a
part of the role's definition but is nonetheless related to it.

CROSS-VOTING

At Westminster, cross-voting (voting with the other side) has much more
to do with policy goals than with representational roles. Indirectly, however,
representation can become involved because disrespect for the representation that Constituency Members pursue irritates them and may make them
less loyal to their parliamentary parties than they might otherwise be. This
hypothesis contradicts the traditional ballast thesis that casts Constituency
Members as the most reliable troops on the backbenches. It is not difficult

to find examples of Constituency Members who take the view that "my function in the House of Commons is to support my party, which I do religiously." But are Constituency Members, in general, more disposed toward solidarity and collective action than their backbench colleagues, or are they more likely to bolt?

The ballast thesis overlooks the disdain and underestimates the resentments. In fact, many activities appreciated in the constituencies are depreciated at Westminster. "You know," remarked a Policy Advocate, "to say that he or she was 'a Very Good Constituency Member,' what that really means is that *you don't count* in the House of Commons." And what that means was made clear by an embarrassing incident that occurred in a Members' telephone booth to Mr. Hugh McCartney, Labour MP for Dumbartonshire and Constituency Member. Not recognizing him as a Member, Sir Gerald Nabarro, a Policy Advocate and maverick, did not, contrary to one version of the encounter, pound Mr. McCartney on the chest. But he did, according to Mr. McCartney, bar his way and send for a policeman, who, according to Sir Gerald, "scratched his head, looked in the House of Commons reference book, said he thought the man might be a Member, and after much thumbing through the book arrived at East Dumbartonshire." Sir Gerald thought Mr. McCartney "might be a stranger of evil intent," possibly connected to the IRA, and concluded in his comments to the press, "The face of a Member which is unknown to an attendant and permanent official of the House and unknown to me must be very insignificant indeed."[31]

Part of this disdain carries over from the nineteenth century, when the role of the Constituency Member lay dormant and MPs were admired as politicians who debated and took stands on the great issues of the day. But another part arises from strongly ambivalent feelings about new aspects of the role that appear trivial to those who do not play it full time. The Local Promoter's representations are on the whole accepted because these pursuits fit best the role's ancient traditions. They are not so very different from the type of constituency problems addressed in the fourteenth and fifteenth centuries, such as granting local charters and privileges, intrusions of alien merchants and traders in an area, impediments in the river Thames.[32] The Welfare Officer, by contrast, runs together these ombudsman-like tasks with the concerns of the social worker. At best, this social work dimension means helping people with genuine policy-related problems. At worst, it means commiseration over blocked drains. And it is the social work aspects of the role that draw the most disdain from colleagues who feel that the image of the MP is being trivialized.

Welfare Officers apologize for it: "Some people are going to say, 'Aye, well old Joe was just a Welfare Officer.' But there's a case on the weekend, two old folks who couldn't even get warm in bed." Local Promoters, as we have already seen, try to make it clear that this is not *their* interpretation of the role. And non-Constituency Members sometimes sneer: "Notice, by the way," remarked an aggressive Ministerial Aspirant, "that I don't put the stress on seeing that all the toilets are working in your constituency, or that the pedestrian crossings are painted in the right place and all the rest of it. I think that's the least of an MP's responsibility. His main function is down here. He ought to have some brains, and he ought to have some knowledge of public affairs." Constituency Members get the message. Their reactions sound awkward and resentful,[33] particularly those of Conservative Welfare Officers, since on the Labour side the role's social work aspects draw less disdain. Thus, on a mailback item, Constituency Members expressed slightly more negative views of their colleagues than did non-Constituency Members; Welfare Officers were more sour still; and the most negative perspectives were offered by Conservative Welfare Officers. When one of them explained to his senior colleagues his conviction that Welfare Officers are what the country wants, "they looked slightly shocked."

Table 4.4 compares the number of cross-votes cast between 1970 and 1973 by Constituency Members and by non-Constituency Members. The resentments that Constituency Members occasionally feel can be expressed by occasionally kicking over the traces with a cross-vote. The table suggests that Constituency Members may indeed be slightly more likely to cross-vote than non-Constituency Members. The "all" columns show a difference of only 8 percent, but this is in the opposite direction from that predicted by the ballast thesis. Party controls uncover more-convincing results. Thus, the ballast thesis is not overturned in the Labour Party—but in the "Conservative" columns, Constituency Members are nearly twice as likely as non-Constituency Members to be delinquent. The correlation for Conservative Constituency Members is .21 (.01) and slightly higher than that for Conservative Welfare Officers. This may be why some Conservative Welfare Officers, who feel they are regarded as "second-class Members," don't spend so much time in the Smoking Room ("this silly nonsense") and would really prefer to spend most of their time in the constituency. They look fondly to the constituency, to the place where their talents are truly appreciated: "the contacts in the constituency more than anything, going round to all the people one knows in every town and village. And it becomes more and more satisfying as time goes on I think." And Westminster becomes less and less satisfying. Many of them eventually find that "I haven't seen myself as having achieved very much in political terms in the House, on the general political level,

Table 4.4 Backbenchers: Cross-votes by backbench role by political party, in percent

	All*		Labour		Conservative**	
Cross-votes	Non-Constituency Members	Constituency Members	Non-Constituency Members	Constituency Members	Non-Constituency Members	Constituency Members
None	36	28	21	28	45	22
One	25	25	30	28	23	22
Two or more	39	47	50	44	32	56
Total	100	100	101	100	100	100
	(N = 249)	(N = 85)	(N = 105)	(N = 45)	(N = 140)	(N = 36)

*$p \le .10$
**$p \le .01$

since I've been here," and eventually turn to the constituency, to the arena where their efforts seem most effective and most appreciated.

Relationships between role conceptions and conduct in the constituency and at Westminster have been uncovered by concentrating on characteristic desires, beliefs, and actions. The following sections add further information about activities at Westminster and about Constituency Members' outlooks. They thereby complete the interpretative explanation of this role and prepare the next phase of the investigation, which asks why backbenchers take it up in the first place.

Activities at Westminster

Constituency Members achieve moderate scores on the policy advocate role because at Westminster they must pursue advocacy in constituency-related matters. Some Welfare Officers become frustrated with it and denounce "the ceremony, the red tape, the bullshit of this place . . . and the photographs of the past, and the whole atmosphere, and the background of this place—it really unnerves me." Even Local Promoters can become irritated by "all the day-to-day flummery." But both Welfare Officers and Local Promoters are there. And there they pursue similar strategies, for whether the constituency problem is individual or collective, the task is basically the same: to secure a particular ruling favorable to a particular person or situation in one's part of the world.

Much of what they hope to achieve for their constituents can be achieved only at Westminster. Their devotion in the House of Commons to constituency matters distinguishes them, even more than the time they spend in their constituencies, from backbenchers who take constituency work seriously but whose primary interests lie in other roles. When Constituency Members speak, they typically speak about constituency affairs, for they may be struggling with more than sixty cases per week, and the number of constituents writing to them at the House is at least double the number who attend surgeries at home.[34] Each morning they spend hours responding to letters seeking redress of grievances from departments like Health and Social Security that, under the Welfare State, have been created to serve the public directly and therefore have more contact with the public than do others.[35] One claims that he receives "3000 to 3500 'Live' letters a year. I define a 'Live' letter as one that doesn't only need acknowledgment, but needs to be sent somewhere else to be dealt with and then needs at least one other reply when things are finalised." Most Constituency Members have nothing like this many 'Live' letters, but assert nevertheless that "though some people may think I pay too much attention to my mail, I regard it as probably of supreme importance."

Constituency Members must first decide whether the grievance that is presented to them is genuine and whether they can do anything about it. If they choose to pursue it, they may begin by using Question Time to "build up a case" and draw the department's attention to the matter.[36] Tabling a series of Questions for written answer can be even more effective, because "the prospect of a parliamentary Question on an awkward subject does send civil servants into convulsions sometimes. And if a government department has been incompetent or has behaved very badly, a Member of Parliament can blow them straight out of the water." It isn't often possible to blow them out of the water, but it is easy to get a great deal of useful information, because the Government is obliged to give it. At the least, such information can clarify the case and provide a basis for deciding what to do next. Very occasionally, one hits the bull's-eye: "And finally, by persistence, I discovered that they'd *lost the files* in this case, and in another case too—they'd lost the files and weren't doing anything about it!"

Should the case not be resolved to the Member's satisfaction, the next step is to write a letter to the Minister concerned. Such letters are carried directly to the Minister's private office, sent to the relevant section for investigation, reviewed at a high level, and then taken to the Minister for final consideration.[37] In centuries past, it was the threat to withhold supply that drew the authorities' attention to personal cases and local problems. Today it is the constitutional doctrine of the individual responsibility of Ministers. Many Constituency Members believe that if they have a reasonable case, their letter to the Minister will likely produce the proper results. As a Conservative explained, "When I became a Member, I was told by an experienced Member that if I wanted my name in the papers I should ask a Question, but if I wanted something done I should write to the appropriate Minister."[38] Others aren't so sure and suspect that results are unlikely unless "you really create hell, and you're not prepared to take no for an answer."

Yet, if the answer is no, and if the Constituency Member is still dissatisfied, further steps are available. The most important of these, and one that is usually regarded as the last serious recourse, is to arrange an appointment with the Minister in order to press the case personally.[39] "Making noise leads nowhere." But when you approach the Minister properly, "knock on his door and say, 'Look, let's have a talk about this,' " then, "quietly, behind the scenes, something is done." Sometimes it helps to take along a deputation of local businesspeople, shop stewards, or civic leaders. One Local Promoter claimed that his deputation resulted in the reopening of a shipyard that eventually provided more than a thousand jobs. When it is necessary to seek a general policy change in order to resolve a particular constituency problem, Constituency Members may make common cause with other MPs who are experiencing similar problems in their constituencies' paper-making industries or horticultural farming, for example, and together press their case upon the Government.[40] Nearly every Constituency Member has encountered at one time or another something like "the effect of the Fire Precautions Act upon every seaside landlady in my constituency. And, with a lot of other seaside Members, I was able to achieve quite a softening in government policy as it affected our people."

If all this fails, there isn't much more to be done—unless the matter is likely to attract publicity, such as the case involving a bizarre letter from the Department of the Environment to a woman who died after a road accident, informing her of her responsibility for the road repairs that resulted from the accident.[41] It helps particularly if the publicity is likely to have an electoral bite. Then the Member may mount a campaign to capture public opinion and mobilize interest groups to pressure the Government.[42] These efforts are always long shots, but they usually offer a bonus: the MP's supplementaries and speeches will be reported in his local press and his Written Questions may elicit from the Government information that pleases his local party workers and constituents.[43] Another way to attract publicity is to seek an Adjournment Debate. This affords Members fifteen to twenty minutes to discuss a problem in hopes that it will be picked up by a national newspaper or television program. Most Adjournment Debates are moved by backbenchers pursuing, as a last resort, either an individual's complaint or a matter related to economic or other collective constituency concerns.[44] Thus, it may involve a motorized wheelchair denied to a disabled constituent, or a dock-access road that the local authority complains isn't even in the Government's five-year plan. So, "I applied for an Adjournment Debate, and actually got it at ten to five in the morning. And I'm very pleased to say that in the next few weeks my road is starting."[45] Even if the Adjournment Debate doesn't solve the problem, it at least provides ventilation, "the greatest ventilation I would say in the world, the opportunity to ventilate something that you feel is wrong. I've had two Adjournment Debates about matters that affected people in my constituency . . . and after I sat down I thought, 'Well, I may not change the world, but at least I've given it ventilation. And the people I represent will have the satisfaction of knowing that their complaint has been raised in the greatest assembly in the world.'"

Still, Constituency Members' activities at Westminster aren't all investigating and pressing forward constituency cases. Known to their people as

"Good Constituency Members," they may get more than the usual share of visitors to the House of Commons coming up from the constituency. They will serve them as guides around the Palace of Westminster, as dispensers of tickets to the Strangers' Gallery, and, for special guests, as hosts for drinks, dinner, or strawberries and cream on the terrace. Constituency Members like taking care of their constituents and are nearly always pleased to do whatever they can: "A couple of old dears, for example, 'Never been to London before and we do want to go down to Greenwich on the river. Could you book us a couple of seats?' Well, I know I'm the only person in London they know, so of course I go and do it although it's not part of my job."[46]

Sources of Role Choice

It should no longer be difficult to see how the role of the Constituency Member fits into Britain's nationally oriented political system. Members of Parliament have always spoken for local needs and represented by making representations on behalf of their constituents' interests. It is not at all peculiar that most backbenchers regard this as part of the job. But why do some backbenchers, the Constituency Members, make this the dominant theme of their duties and responsibilities? Role choice here is a function of demands and preferences, in this case the demands of constituents who desire services and the preferences of backbenchers who pursue goals.

DEMANDS OF CONSTITUENTS

In the United States, regional variables help explain the constituency services that members of Congress provide because these variables affect the demand for services.[47] Similarly, in Britain demands are said to vary according to whether constituencies are located in the provinces or near London, and whether they are situated in rural areas or in urban areas.

Table 4.5 groups backbenchers' constituencies into the Registrar General's Standard Regions. From these regional groupings, constituencies in London, Glasgow, Edinburgh, and "other major cities" (Birmingham, Leeds, Sheffield, Manchester, Liverpool) have been removed for separate examination. Within each grouping, the table reports the percentage of respondents who have become Constituency Members. Constituencies in Scotland, Wales, the North, and the Midlands tend to be less prosperous than constituencies in the South, and they are believed to demand greater attention from their MPs.[48] The table suggests they get it. The only region outside the South

Table 4.5 Backbenchers: Impact of constituency location upon role choice

Backbench role	Region								Urban area	
	South East and East Anglia	Southwest	North West	Midlands (East and West)	Yorkshire and North	Wales	Scotland	London	Glasgow and Edinburgh	Other major cities
Constituency Members	21	15	13	34	35	31	41	14	33	22
Non-Constituency Members	79	85	86	67	66	69	59	86	66	79
Total	100	100	99	101	101	100	100	100	99	101
	(N = 48)	(N = 20)	(N = 38)	(N = 47)	(N = 46)	(N = 16)	(N = 22)	(N = 57)	(N = 12)	(N = 23)

that has as low a proportion of Constituency Members as southern constituencies is the North West. This pattern holds for both parties.[49]

The common claims about urban-rural effects are more contradictory. It is sometimes argued that demands are greatest in urban constituencies, and that MPs from such constituencies are most likely to choose constituency member roles. But if urban areas have declining industries and decaying housing, rural areas have dispersed populations. These dispersed populations are the basis of a contrary hypothesis, namely that MPs from rural areas are most likely to become Constituency Members because they spend so much time ministering to their far-flung constituents that they become immersed in local society and its problems.

The data in Table 4.5 tend to support the claim that rural areas spawn more than their share of Constituency Members, but they do not support it unambiguously. If we contrast London with the provinces, as is usually done, the rural case seems plausible since London has one of the smallest proportions of Constituency Members in the table. Still, the North West and Southwest regions are just as low and, when the rest of the cities are compared to the regions from which they have been removed, the relationship weakens further. Scotland does have more Constituency Members than its principal cities Glasgow and Edinburgh, but only slightly more. The Midlands and Yorkshire do have higher concentrations of Constituency Members than their "other major cities," but the North West has fewer.[50]

Let us move now from the demands for constituency services to the backbenchers who work hardest at providing them, whose career goals include reelection and representation, and whose emotional incentives include a sense of competence and a sense of duty.

CONDITIONS AND INCENTIVES

Some backbenchers are believed to turn to the role of the Constituency Member in search of compensatory satisfactions after they have failed in their quest for office. "Perhaps it is vanity," confided one such backbencher as he began to discuss his choice of the role of the Constituency Member, "but I don't think I was the only person who thought I was capable of higher office." "All sorts of accidents," a Conservative said; "I might have thought I'd have been given some duty . . . war injury, these things can slow you down." Another Constituency Member, who had years before been a Minister, claimed that, much as he liked his constituency work, it was certainly second best compared with Government, "because there you can not only do this welfare job, perhaps even more effectively, but you can actually make decisions that have an effect on hundreds of thousands of people. And I did. And I was heartbroken when I was sacked. I simply loved it." Still, thwarted ambition isn't a very persuasive general explanation for taking up the role of the Constituency Member, since so many of those who serve as Constituency Members have never been Ministers and had never expected to become Ministers in the first place.

The desire for reelection doesn't seem to be terribly important either, despite the fact that it is regarded as the primary motivation for constituency service in the United States, and has recently been put forward as a significant factor in Britain.[51] This hypothesis about the impact of electoral considerations upon constituency service certainly applies to some MPs ("If you look after the constituency, they will look after you"). But it has not been readily accepted as a generally important factor, because (a) British voters vote for the national party rather than for the individual candidate, and (b) MPs believe that 500 to 1,500 votes is about all they can expect from work as a good Constituency Member.[52] Nevertheless, it deserves to be examined systematically. Table 4.6 groups constituencies by their margins of victory, which reflect various degrees of electoral insecurity. The most familiar definitions of marginal constituencies would fall within the ranges 0–2 and 3–4 percent.

For constituencies at each degree of electoral insecurity, the table reports the proportion of their backbenchers who have adopted the role of Constituency Member. These data make it clear that, in general, safeness of seat has no linear relationship to whether or not backbenchers choose to play this role.[53] Twenty-six percent of those in the most marginal seats cast themselves

Table 4.6 Backbenchers: Impact of electoral security upon role choice

Backbench role	Margin of victory (%)*						
	0–2	3–4	5–8	9–14	15–21	22–31	32–97
Constituency Members	26	30	33	25	21	24	27
Non-Constituency Members	74	71	67	75	79	77	74
Total	100	101	100	100	100	101	101
	(N = 31)	(N = 27)	(N = 30)	(N = 48)	(N = 68)	(N = 63)	(N = 68)

*Margin of victory = difference between winner's percentage of total vote and that of closest rival. $p = .39$.

as Constituency Members, which is actually 1 percent less than those in the safest seats. Thus, although electoral insecurity is surely an incentive for some Constituency Members, it apparently does not function as a force of general significance.[54]

In the same vein, it would be surprising if political values were not involved here as motivating forces, but more surprising still if they controlled the choices. Thus, attempts to use ideology in explaining constituency service in the United States have produced only mixed results.[55] If ideology is important, then the proportion of Constituency Members in ideological groups within the parliamentary parties should vary systematically across each party's political spectrum. But the proportion of Constituency Members hardly differs at all among these groups.[56] Values that play an important part in selecting roles are more likely to be personal and instrumental goals rather than politically charged ones such as capitalism or socialism. Both sorts of items were included in an exercise in which MPs were asked to rank-order, according to their personal preferences, thirty-six values arranged in four lists of nine items each.[57] Correlations between these items and the dummy variable "Constituency Member/non-Constituency Member" show that the relationships are few and modest, and that they include no highly politicized goals at all.

The strongest correlations are with the value "security," which was defined as creating freedom from uncertainty about the future. These are .34 for the role of Constituency Member; .38 for the subtype, Welfare Officer; and .47 for strong Welfare Officer. Although security is not a highly politicized value, it is highly valued by Labour MPs. And it may help explain why Labour backbenchers are somewhat more likely than Conservatives to become Constituency Members, Welfare Officers, and, especially, strong Welfare Officers. The fact that security tops the list provides a clue about the nature of the goals behind this role. Equally intriguing is that "compassion," which was also included on the value inventory, plays no part whatsoever, even for strong Welfare Officers.

I have argued that career goals and emotional incentives are intertwined in the motivational cores of political roles. The value security recalls the principal career goals involved here, the goals of representation, which have been discussed throughout this chapter: redressing constituents' grievances and advocating constituency interests to central government. Reelection goals are salient for some Constituency Members, but the goals of representation dominate the majority's thinking about these matters. The goals of representation are energized by two emotional incentives, sense of competence and sense of duty, with which they are closely related and whose character is foreshadowed by the poor performance of the value compassion. Sense of competence and sense of duty are the emotional incentives that Constituency Members discuss most often when they discuss their work.

A sense of competence can easily be derived from experiences associated with constituency work: developing talents one had before coming to the House, protecting and nurturing people, helping to shape the local community, or even simply putting up a good fight on behalf of one's constituents. Thus, quite a few Constituency Members say they are attracted to their roles by temperament and training, that they are building upon talents they had before they became MPs: "By virtue of my training as a solicitor, I regularly did (for ten years before coming here) a free legal advice service every Friday night. I'm well equipped for this sort of work. I'm equipped by training and experience, and I also rather like it." Similarly, a Methodist minister explained that he had always worked with problems of individual distress and social disorder and that, as he now sees it, his constituency "is really only an enlargement of my parish." The same point was developed by a former personnel officer who claimed that the "greatest satisfaction" he derived "from achieving certain favourable results in what I've done for my constituents" was built upon his apprenticeship in personnel work. It was also voiced by a doctor who "used to get satisfaction from healing or dealing with a very difficult case" and now gets the same sort of satisfaction from dealing with his constituents and their problems. Furthermore, many Constituency Members served in local government before they came to the House and are pleased that they have found a way to investigate many more grievances than they ever could on the local council. The sense of competence is derived from a successful application of one's talents to interpreting an established role in a new environment: "Well I wasn't long in industrial life till I became a social convener, and I found I had to look after people in the workshop. I had to look after people in the trade union. I had to look after people in the shop steward movement. And I've always had to look after people. . . . I live in the heart of my constituency, my home is open for them, my offices which I open every Saturday are queued up with people with problems . . . and I get the best possible deal for each of them."

Looking after people and protecting them provides the central satisfactions. When Welfare Officers talk about helping individuals, it is noticeable that, although they sound like social workers, their conversation suggests not so much compassion as a sense of competence derived from providing people with *security*. "You are their protector," said a Conservative Member with ten years' experience. "You find people going to nationalised industries, to Gas Board, Electricity Board, and in a lot of cases just being brushed aside. And their MP takes it up. . . . And consequently you will find that you can achieve something that the person can't." There is sometimes a hint of paternalism in stories about helping people who are overwhelmed or in a panic—which is why this Conservative Member adds, "I suppose one shouldn't get the satisfaction, but. . . ." He is uneasy about dwelling too much on the sense of competence he enjoys from helping others because, as someone with a strong church background, he seems to believe that such satisfactions might be inappropriate for what he regards as charity work. But good works are done for all sorts of motives, and most people would not regard a sense of competence as the least desirable: "I personally draw great strength from my constituency, and talking to people who rely on you to do something for them gives one immense strength and that's very satisfying."

For some Constituency Members, it is the test of their abilities that makes the role attractive. It is "being able to help them where no one else has helped them." It is writing a letter to a Minister and getting a reply when other people have written dozens and gotten no reply at all. "I can do things that they can't. This is important." "To achieve a satisfactory solution" is "personally satisfying," to get somebody his pension that he's not been getting for a couple of years, or "to get some old lady, who is really desperately hard up, an extra ten bob a week from the Social Security."[58] Others focus more on the importance of the results achieved.[59] "You can literally transform their lives from one of misery to happiness and comfort. . . . It's the fact that I can do so much for individual people. There is nothing else, only individual people in life." They argue that there aren't any satisfactory alternatives to the essential services they perform, that local councillors change frequently, and that constituents insist on their MP "going in on a protective basis . . . the MP seems to bring this confidence." The anguish of the people shows how much one's help is really needed: "Several months ago two old ladies came and they broke down . . . and *I* nearly started crying . . . and they said, 'If you can't help us nobody can and we'll do ourselves in.' I helped them, thank God." And the gratitude of the people shows how much one has achieved: "You're walking along and somebody comes up to you and they take you by the hand and say, 'Thanks very much, Mr. Budge, for helping in that problem. I don't know what would have happened.' There is a *tremendous* amount of satisfaction in this."

While Welfare Officers seek to protect individuals, Local Promoters derive a similar sense of competence from shaping in some small way their part of the world, from serving as local benefactors to communities. Their constituencies become *their* communities as their commitment becomes increasingly strong: "It's a joy to go back and go up into the mountains and the country-side and live the strange and different life that goes on there." Or, "This is my part of the world. I come from Suffolk and there is no question of my having to work my way into the place. . . . I would loathe ever to represent any constituency other than a Suffolk constituency." When one "likes the place so much," there is a special pleasure in improving its roads, winning a new reservoir, attracting new industries, establishing technical colleges and nursery schools, and in promoting the development of the 750-acre park in the center of Plymouth. There is a special pleasure in replacing with new houses "the rat-infested slums where I was brought up." Compared to great matters of state, "these are little things, but they are little things that in fact have done my people an awful lot of good."[60]

Good results are always satisfying. Yet some Constituency Members get just as much satisfaction out of the process of attaining them. "I like a fight," is how one seventy-three-year-old Conservative put it. "I like a battle, I like a fight. . . . When you've had a fight for something in your constituency, you get a joy out of winning the battle, but it's the fight that, I mean they go on for a very long time." In the same vein, a younger Labour MP ex-plained that "I like to get a case where there's somebody pushing people around, and then I get underneath and push back." Many politicians enjoy a good fight, and many Constituency Members savor the moments when, in the interests of justice, they have been able "to literally get hold of a Minister in a corridor and say, 'Well now look here, here's this problem and something *must* be done about it.'" Some are tempted to measure their competence not so much by the number of constituents served as by the respect and responsiveness received from Ministers and from government departments. Others are pleased simply to have had the opportunity to swim against the tide: "I'm very much in politics [the opposite of] what Lord Halifax of the Restoration called a 'Trimmer,'" one of them said. "That is, when the boat leans one way, I go the other. . . . I lose interest in things immediately they have become successful . . . and when the spring comes . . . and they become popular, I shall then be on the other side."

A sense of duty is the second most common emotional incentive found throughout these transcripts. Constituency Members stress that "you don't do things to get people to support you; you do it because it's your job *and your duty* to help everybody." If the redress of grievances is Parliament's most ancient function, today that means "that their Member of Parliament should be their personal ombudsman—he's there to look after their griev-ances and pursue them." His duty is to fight injustice. "I don't like injustice" are words echoed by many: "If there is a real, basic injustice being imposed upon them, you can raise hell about it." Doing one's duty in redressing grievances brings the satisfactions of rectitude and, in this way, doing one's duty brings its own rewards.[61] It is a common observation that people often derive feelings of satisfaction from performing their duty as defined by norms that they accept. And it is also a common observation that these feelings are distinct from the feelings of compassion that arise from acting out of concern.[62]

It should not be surprising, therefore, that Constituency Members regard their surgeries as "a civic service" that is part of their unwritten contract of employment.[63] The tone of their approach can be heard in the insistence that it should be nonpartisan: "I refuse absolutely to use party premises [as a location for the surgery] because I think it could be embarrassing for someone who's a committed Labour voter. . . . It's outside politics what I do on these days." The civic orientations are coupled with the medieval conception of the role "as a lawyer, as an advocate for my constituents, the people I represent." If someone brings him a problem, continues this Constituency Member, he sees it as his duty to represent him, full stop: "I'm not interested in his politics. All I'm interested in is the fact that he lives in my constituency." The same point was made by a Labour Constituency Member whose constituent believed she was being unfairly denied a grant to send her children to fee-paying schools. And so, although this Labour MP very strongly opposed such schools, he felt it was his duty to fight the case, because she was his constituent and "as the law stood she was being denied something to which she was entitled."

In these civic themes the emphasis is on the duty to serve, which, through rectitude again, creates intrinsic rewards. A long-serving country Member, for example, gave a brief review of his villages and the sorts of things he does to help the people who live in them. "One looks at it that way," he said. "I was born and bred in my constituency and it does give one satisfaction to feel that one can be of some small help to some of them when you come up to Westminster." Much can be learned about Constituency Members from their reactions to the post: "And every now and again you do have a success. And my secretary will say, 'It's a lovely post today, you have got three or four thank-you letters.' And, er, it makes you feel good." It feels good because one has done one's duty in taking the trouble to provide a service: "And she wrote me such a sweet letter saying, 'Thank you so much for taking the trouble to look after my small interests.'" Another Constituency Member said that the emotional incentives are much like those of a family doctor of the old-fashioned kind, for "one gets this sense of having helped somebody, and that's the most important thing that one gets out of it." Still another Constituency Member describes his reactions to having successfully helped an elderly, frightened constituent this way: "He was so genuinely pleased, that I felt pleased to have been able to help him." The point they are making is that they do not seek a return beyond the satisfaction of having been of service, and, for the quiet Conservative Welfare Officer who carries this altruism to its logical conclusion, "also the satisfaction I find of not necessarily telling anybody else about it."

The sense of duty is also reflected in characterizations of constituency service as a safety valve and of the Constituency Member as "a priest in a post-Christian society, someone to go and unburden their troubles to him . . . a purely therapeutic sense, a safety valve." The safety valve is needed because "society is so frustrated by the complexity of modern life that this direct link with somebody is very important . . . for people to realise that at the end of the line there's an MP to whom they can make an appeal." Labour's Constituency Members tend to see it in terms of this therapeutic service for individuals, whereas Conservatives seem more worried about dangers facing the political system. Both, however, desire the satisfactions gained from doing their duty to turn the tide: "The fact of being of service . . . an MP who's doing his job properly is fulfilling a tremendously important purpose—making people realise that they have a representative at or close to the seat of power."

It is fortunate that the Constituency Member's principal incentives are easily satisfied: a sense of competence derived from a few hard-fought victories, a sense of duty that provides its own rewards. It is fortunate because the rate of success with constituency cases must sometimes disappoint them. Several MPs claim success rates of one-fourth to one-third, but no one claims more than one-half, and most claim considerably less than that.[64] "The failures are quite considerable because lots of the cases that come to a Member of Parliament have made the rounds before it comes to him . . . failure is probably ninety percent certain. So I can understand that when many Members of Parliament get a success, they feel a great sense of achievement because they may have had a whole battery of failures." Yet, for Constituency Members, even some of the failures can be gratifying: "You are satisfied if you know the reason why you haven't succeeded . . . you learn things which you were not aware of. And out of that you understand the reasons why such and such a thing comes about and just cannot be solved. . . . And that's gratifying to me—as long as you know."

Win or lose, those who try hard can also look forward to respect in the local community. Like electoral considerations, this factor should count as idiosyncratic, because it motivates only a minority. "I am a Constituency

Man," said a member of this minority who was sitting on the terrace of the House of Commons. "Nobody knows me here. But I am exceedingly well known in the constituency. If there was a poll, more people would know me, apart of course from the Prime Minister."[65] Moreover, with respect comes "immediate access to anyone you want in the constituency. If I want to see the Town Clerk, I can see him at very short notice. If I want to see the Director of Housing or Education, I get immediate access, which no one else can do." Another Member claims that only he can get hold of his Chief Constable if somebody has a youngster picked up for hooliganism and put in a cell. He is also "the only man, I suppose, who can say to his Chief Constable, 'Look here, I want to go in this panda car of yours on Saturday night,' which I do occasionally in Rotherham after closing time. . . . No one else is in this unique position I think." Many such Members "don't think it's a great honor to be a carpetbagging MP, no," and are especially pleased to be able "to represent one's native place," for these are the circumstances from which flow respect and standing in the local community.

Overview: Representation and Role Distance

Finally, I would like to consider two matters that together summarize much of the character of the Constituency Member's role. The first, "the focus of representation," probes more deeply than we have done thus far into the cognitive goals at the role's core. The second, "role distance," clarifies some of the ambivalence that surrounds this role and improves our ability to assess it.

THE FOCUS OF REPRESENTATION

Since Constituency Members are the MPs who give representation the greatest attention, it will be instructive to clarify what this concept means and does not mean to them. Long before the role codes were developed, responses to the first two role questions noted in Table 4.7 were scored for themes concerning several functions of parliamentary government. We were searching specifically for instances in which Constituency Members introduced into their discussions of their roles one or more of these aspects of representation: articulating constituents' political opinions; redressing individual constituents' grievances; and advocating constituency interests to central government. The table reports the distribution of these representational roles among Welfare Officers, Local Promoters, and non-Constituency Members.

Table 4.7 Constituency Members: Focus of representation, in percent

	Focus of representation								
	Articulate political opinions			Redress individual grievances*			Advocate constituency interests*		
Centrality of focus	Welfare Officers	Non-Constituency Members	Local Promoters	Welfare Officers	Non-Constituency Members	Local Promoters	Welfare Officers	Non-Constituency Members	Local Promoters
Central to discussion	00	02	08	97	50	39	06	11	54
Present but not central	13	11	08	02	25	31	11	14	23
Not present	88	88	85	02	25	31	83	75	23
Total	101	101	101	101	100	101	100	100	100
	(N = 64)	(N = 249)	(N = 13)	(N = 64)	(N = 249)	(N = 13)	(N = 64)	(N = 249)	(N = 13)

Note: Data derived from responses to these questions: Thinking about your broad role as a Member of Parliament, what are the most important duties and responsibilities involved? Thinking for a moment very broadly about British society, how do your duties and responsibilities fit in with the work of the society as a whole? How important is your work as an MP to the functioning of society as a whole?

*p ≤ .001 (Welfare Officers v. Local Promoters)

In discussing their roles, all Welfare Officers and Local Promoters intro-duce at least one of these themes, usually as a central feature in the conversa-tions. They are indeed concerned with representation. But they are not con-cerned with representing the political opinions of their constituents. The table shows that hardly anyone mentions representing political opinions as part of his or her role. It has been several centuries since a Member of Parlia-ment responded this dismissively, and with impunity, to constituents: "Gen-tlemen, I have received your letter about the excise and I am surprised at your insolence in writing to me at all."[66] But the representation of constit-uents' political opinions has never been at the forefront of the Member of Parliament's attention. The few who have talked about "trying to know what my constituents are thinking" have usually been quick to add, "That doesn't mean I've got to mirror what they are thinking; there's a matter of exercising my judgement."

Political opinions are represented in Britain, but they are represented by a process that typically has a national rather than a constituency focus. That is to say, national rather than constituency-based perspectives on policy are considered—and they are considered by the Government. Ordinary MPs are not customarily expected to articulate the particular policy views of their particular constituents on matters of national or international significance.[67] From a populistic perspective, Britain is an elitist democracy. From a British perspective, representation is nevertheless very much alive and very well. For what Constituency Members believe their constituents really want from representation is "not so much that they particularly want you to put their [policy] views over, but rather that when something goes wrong, there is somebody who will shout for them."

Table 4.7 makes it clear that the modes of representation that most attract Constituency Members are, as would be expected, the redress of constit-uents' grievances and advocating constituency interests to central govern-ment. For all MPs, one of the first definitions of the verb "to represent" is to act as an agent to protect and advance the interests of the individuals and groups on whose behalf one is acting. Of course Welfare Officers do much more than redress individual grievances. But this quickly becomes the dominant theme when they review their roles: 97 percent of them make it central to these discussions. Constituents write to them almost exclusively about personal problems.[68] Their duty seems plain: "not so much represent-ing the political views of constituents at Westminster, because you don't do that, but rather being able to bring the private trouble and complaint of a constituent to the notice of authority and get it put right." Likewise, Local Promoters do far more to represent their part of the world than advocating constituency interests to central government. Nevertheless, nearly eight out of ten discuss their belief in this particular theme when they describe their roles, because bringing industry to Preston or a hospital to Luton frequently involves working with central government.

Welfare Officers and Local Promoters are tribunes who shout for their people. But they shout for their constituents' needs rather than for their political opinions. And they shout at Westminster, where they are most likely to be heard. This pleases constituents, since this is what constituents want them to be doing. This also helps to check the Executive, since when they shout at Westminster, administrators become more sensitive to possible errors or injustices than they might otherwise be.[69] Finally, the fact that Local Promoters are even less likely than the non-Constituency Members in Table 4.7 to make the redress of grievances central to their discussions suggests again that they are establishing distance from aspects of the constituency member role that appeal to their constituents but not to their colleagues.

ROLE DISTANCE

The role of the Constituency Member is one of the best-known backbench roles at Westminster. But it is not one of the best loved. Confusion about the appropriateness of its various modes of individual representation is compounded by criticism from colleagues and "role distance" from players. Thus, the distinction between Welfare Officers and Local Promoters is widely recognized. Yet, further distinctions within these two subtypes are not so clearly understood. Local Promoters, for instance, advocate collective constituency interests, but there is a difference between badgering the Executive at Westminster about local industries and badgering the local council about recreational facilities—a difference between being an ambassador to central government and being a local benefactor. Many Promoters play both ends of the role, but they get the most respect from their colleagues for the ambassadorial efforts.

Welfare Officers face a more difficult situation. They serve as local ombudsmen and perform for individuals what Promoters perform on a collective basis: they seek redress for their constituents by appealing to the authorities.[70] But, at the same time, they serve their constituents as social workers, which at best means helping people with genuine personal problems and at worst means dealing with gas meters, toilets, and drains. Their colleagues at Westminster, who may already be uneasy about the notion of local benefactors, know exactly what they think about this sort of social work. They think it trivializes the image of the MP and tarnishes their own roles in the process. These are the images and activities that make the role of Constituency Member much less respected than the role of Policy Advocate or Ministerial Aspirant. From the very beginning of this chapter, we have been aware of the undercurrents: we have heard Welfare Officers sounding awkward, Local Promoters disdainful, and non-Constituency Members positively caustic. We have also noted the resentments and the occasional cross-votes, particularly among Conservative Welfare Officers. These negative attitudes toward Constituency Members bring out from some of them striking examples of "role distance."[71]

"Role distance" is a neologism created by Erving Goffman to draw attention to cases in which the negative images associated with a role lead people to play it with "disdainful detachment."[72] Most observers cannot distinguish clearly between the roles they see us playing and our identities. Therefore, when negative stereotypes are associated with one of these roles, we may become uneasy and try to let them know that we are not entirely what we at present seem to be. A common strategy for doing this is to adopt a detached stance and to play the role self-consciously.[73] These efforts to neutralize the effects of the negative images associated with roles are frequently expressed, Goffman notes, in jokes, apologies, and explanations. Only a few political roles offer the opportunity to see such performances clearly—and the role of the Constituency Member is one of them.

Joking expresses distance from the negative images through a mocking style that suggests the speaker is mimicking the role rather than playing it earnestly. Etonians sometimes seem to specialize in role distance. They certainly don't specialize in being Welfare Officers. The mocking tale told by this unusual Etonian Welfare Officer is worth a full quotation:

I think truly satisfying the little man is perhaps the most rewarding. Give you an example. Silly old man went to hear a pension tribunal. He was turned down for his pension but he wanted his bus fare to the hearing; and he wrote to me saying it was a damned disgrace that he'd been turned down, and a damned disgrace that he hadn't been given his bus fare. So I got on to the Clerk of the Court, who said, "Well, terribly sorry he was turned down, but he hasn't got a leg to stand on. And doubly sorry, but he was paid his bus fare." So I went back to the old man, "Well, they say you were paid your bus fare." He said, "*I was not.*" So I wrote to the Clerk again and said, "Sorry to come back to you, but this funny old man is absolutely insistent he never got his 4/6d." So the Clerk went out and saw the cashier and wrote back saying, "It's absolutely true, he didn't get his 4/6d. But you see, he was the first case of the morning, and he came to the desk to get his 4/6d, and signed the book for his 4/6d, and then the cashier found he hadn't got 4/6d in the till, so he said come back and see me when your case is over and I'll give you the 4/6d." Silly old man was so angry at being turned down he stumped off without his money. Anyway he got his 4/6d, the fact that he'd been turned down for a pension of 10 pounds didn't worry him, justice was done, and he really was genuinely very, very thrilled over his 4/6d.

Another way to neutralize unwelcome stereotypes is to apologize for them. One Conservative, for example, feels that he is a country Member in a very isolated, inward-looking county, and that "in a county like that, one is, in a sense, too much perhaps a social worker, in a sense perhaps this is not what an MP should be doing, but it is, in practice, what an MP *is* doing. I mean one does find that one can help people." Besides, there really isn't anything else worth doing, for backbenchers have no power at Westminster anyway. "I don't find what's said in Parliament of absorbing interest. . . . It's always so predictable." Work in the Palace of Westminster is boring, whereas work in the constituency seems vital. Another common apology is to complain that so many of the problems are in fact more appropriate for local councillors and to be "hopeful that local government reform may eventually result in the increased prominence of local representatives taking some of this load off us." "If society worked properly, half the things that I do wouldn't be required at all."

The third strategy for dealing with these unwanted images is explanation. Thus, Constituency Members may insist that usual views of their role are outrageously incorrect: "Sometimes you're regarded as a slightly inferior type of Member compared to the Member who is floating off to the Councils of Europe and foreign parts. I *resent* anybody who thinks that a grass-roots Member is a second-class type of Member. I think we've all got something to contribute." Defiance is one way to deal with the situation. Disagreement is another: "People say that a Member of Parliament is a glorified Welfare Officer—all right, there is *nothing wrong* with that. The great thing is that you are able to do it." Many explanations stress the importance of the service to individual constituents: "It may seem trivial, but to the person concerned. . . ." "I look at it this way," said a Constituency Member who had just acknowledged that not many MPs would share his views. "We have 634 Members of Parliament to look after Britain's interests, we've got 71 MPs to look after Scotland's interests, but there's only me to look after my constituency—nobody else." Importance is also demonstrated by reminding listeners that "you ought to be able to deduce after a period, from the pattern of the cases . . . certain conclusions about what's wrong with national politics." Then you are in a position, explained another Constituency Member, to tell the Minister that "either a legal provision or a practice of his department is not helpful, and therefore you get it changed."

Goffman interprets such explanations as defensive reactions and implies that most of them are rationalizations. But surely it is possible that something is wrong with the negative images themselves—and that the explanations are convincing demonstrations of this fact. MPs can indeed get something significant done for the ordinary individual in pensions, tax matters, welfare matters, and housing, explained a senior Conservative backbencher. This is indeed an important test of an MP, he argued persuasively, and certainly no less a contribution than the usual backbencher's contributions to the great debates: "It's very important that this should be respected. . . . There are hundreds of instances every day where people's lives are directly affected by their Members of Parliament. Now this is what democracy is for." The redress of grievances isn't all that democracy is for, but it is undoubtedly central to the theory and practice of representative government.

The House of Commons is a representative institution, and its members perform the function of representation. Central to the British concept of representation is the notion that an MP "is expected to defend and further the interest of his constituents, collectively and individually."[74] Representing by making representations is, in fact, the first of three usages of the term "representative" listed by A. H. Birch in his well-known essay on the Constitution.[75] It is also the core of the role of the Constituency Member.

But is it really representation? Many foreigners tend to associate representation mainly with political opinions and consider the representative's part well played when his policy positions correspond as closely as possible to those of his constituents.[76] From the British perspective, this confounds two dimensions of representation: the national dimension, which focuses on policy opinions, and the constituency dimension, which focuses on redress of grievances. Policy opinions are represented nationally, not by constituency MPs, for it is national views that are aggregated in party policies, tested in general elections, and promoted through party discipline.[77] Of the two dimensions of representation, the constituency-based redress of grievances is certainly the more hallowed by time.

Most MPs take it seriously, and some make it their chief role. This role subsumes two distinct subtypes: Welfare Officers, who assist individual constituents, and Local Promoters, who advance constituency interests. Around these goals, I have reconstructed characteristic attitudes and activities in the constituencies and at Westminster; and I have shown that the backbenchers who choose this role are influenced by constituency demands and by particular political values and internal rewards. Ambitious American politicians may for electoral reasons work their constituency fields, but their British counterparts are more likely to work the corridors of Westminster and leave the role of the Constituency Member to others. The dispositions of these others have been brought into relief by the motivational approach, which has the further advantage of generating role constructs that incorporate behavior. Demonstrating relationships like those between role conceptions and time in the constituency not only probes our accounts of such roles but also advances role theory, because few measures of preference roles have in the past been successfully linked to behavior.

It is always appropriate to remind ourselves that the House of Commons is dominated by the Executive. It does, nevertheless, redress grievances. And this, its most ancient function, has become its most popular, for it allows ordinary citizens, via their MPs, to have their problems considered directly by the highest authorities. Senior Ministers make the replies and thereby continue the tradition of reform by petition, which, during the reigns of the three Edwards, replaced the feudal expression of grievances by the point of the sword.[78] The need for this ancient function has been revived and intensified by the expansion of central government. And flippant comments about drains and pedestrian crossings give a useful role a lopsided portrayal by diverting attention from its genuine importance:

> I think probably the most important thing of all is to serve as a brake on, and as a warning to, bureaucracy. That to my mind is the great importance of the constituency system. Everybody in this country has got an MP to go to. And it's his job to take their protest, if it's a good one, right to the top. And every bureaucrat in the town hall and the local government office is subject to the quite considerable threat: "If they behave like this, I'll go and see my MP"—that's very important. You have got to have an awful lot of government in an advanced society. And the great danger is the tyranny of the bureaucrat. We are the limitations on that tyranny.

PARLIAMENT MEN:
A WINDOW TO THE PAST

I like the House of Commons and I like
all the people in it. They say it's the best
club in the world, and I think this is true.

A Knight of the Shire

Parliament Men, unlike Constituency Members, are not immersed in the process of representation. In fact, they hardly talk about their constituencies at all, which is reflected in their low composite score of 2.8 (out of 9) on constituency member themes. Also unlike Constituency Members, Parliament Men play a role that is neither widely recognized nor well defined. It is not widely recognized because so few Parliament Men are left in the contemporary House of Commons, and their subtypes have grown apart from one another. It is not well defined because this preference role is, in a sense, empty. As the counterweights to Westminster's "eager beavers," Parliament Men are (with one important exception) more notable for what they do *not* do than for what they do—and lack of activity is not readily observed or characterized.

What Parliament Men have in common, therefore, is not a set of activities but instead a goal. This career goal, which has several variations, concentrates the MP's interest upon Parliament as an institution. As a well-known "Good House of Commons Man" put it, "I mean to say I'm interested in the perpetuation of Parliament and the esteem of Parliament." This is a common theme that backbenchers would expect to hear from colleagues like Charles Pannell, Sir Myer Galpern, or Sir Harmar Nicholls. At the same time, Parliament Men differ with regard to the particular aspects of parliamentary life that most attract them. For some, it is the camaraderie; for others, it is just being there; and for the rest, it is the status conferred by membership in this ancient institution.

That there should be so few Parliament Men in the contemporary House seems strange, for this role was common and indeed dominant during earlier eras. Parliament Men were still very familiar as recently as the interwar period, as Sir Samuel Roberts, a Parliament Man whose father had also been a Member, explained in private notes for his family history.[1] After accepting the fact that he was an unlikely Aspirant, but having a private income and a desire to serve, Sir Samuel gradually became a respected senior backbencher, a Chairman of Committees who enjoyed, best of all, pursuing parliamentary friendships, "some for an hour, some for a lifetime."

Sir Samuel was an active backbench Member who joined in the bustle and the camaraderie. By contrast, a more phlegmatic interpretation of this role is offered by Trollope's nineteenth-century Mr. Browborough, who "had been regarded by many as a model Member of Parliament, a man who never spoke, constant in his attendance, who wanted nothing, who had plenty of money . . . to whom a seat in Parliament was the be-all and the end-all of life."[2] But if Parliament Men were better known in the nineteenth century than in the twentieth, their heyday was surely a hundred years earlier still, in the mid-eighteenth-century parliaments described by Sir Lewis Namier.[3] From this perspective, it is not surprising that it was Namier who gave their role the name "Parliament Man," which I have adopted to characterize their twentieth-century descendants. Although the continuity across the centuries is often imperfect, a strong family resemblance persists, particularly if Namier's Parliament Men are considered together with his Country Gentlemen and Social Climbers. These Members were in Parliament from social habit; and, for them, "being there" seemed quite sufficient. If any were very strongly interested in anything, it was less likely to be offices or debates than the status conferred by their positions. Some were "Knights of the Shires" and simply enjoyed having that status confirmed. Others came in search of peerages and preferment. Among their contemporary descendants, such patronage is less of a preoccupation, but there are still MPs drawn to Westminster because, as Namier summarized it for the eighteenth century, "membership of the governing body necessarily distinguishes the man, certainly in his own circle, and opens doors which would otherwise remain shut against him."[4] Parliament Men offer us a view of their institution's past.

Subtypes Distinguished

Only thirty-one Parliament Men can be found among our backbenchers. And yet three distinct interpretations of this role can be seen in their transcripts: Spectators, Club Men, and Status Seekers.

The criterion that identifies Spectators is a primary focus on being "at the center of things" and on watching the political drama unfold rather than seeking to participate actively in policy advocacy or constituency work. Pleasant as this life may seem, explained a jaded member of the subtype, it can become frustrating when one realizes that "one is in a way only a spectator, a privileged spectator, but nonetheless only a spectator." The quiescence of these backbenchers should not, however, be overdone, for although their desires involve more "being" than "doing," they are nonetheless actors in a busy national parliament and, as such, usually have more influence and stronger egos than do their namesakes who have been studied in local government.[5] Club Men, by contrast, tend to be much more active and further distinguish themselves by their absorption in the agreeable atmosphere and collegiality of the House: "I like the House of Commons," said an elderly Conservative with twenty years of service, "and I like all the people in it. They say it's the best club in the world, and I think this is true." Likewise: "One meets people here that one hasn't met before, and one gets to know them—it's a jolly good club." The third subtype, the Status Seekers, are primarily concerned neither with the drama nor with the congenial atmosphere, but instead with what Parliament can do to enhance their status and "visibility" in society. "It's amazing how much attention is focused on us," one Status Seeker began—and then kept returning to this theme throughout his interview. Table 5.1 displays the distribution of these types among Parliament Men and reports as well the distribution within each political party.[6]

Parliament Men are equally divided into Spectators and Club Men. The table also shows that there are extremely few Status Seekers. Many backbenchers seek status, but most of them seek other goals more avidly; very

Table 5.1 Parliament Men: Subtypes, and subtypes by political party

| Subtype | All Parliament Men | | Political party* | | | |
| | | | Conservative | | Labour | |
	N	%	N	%	N	%
Spectators	(14)	45	(7)	33	(7)	70
Club Men	(14)	45	(11)	52	(3)	30
Status Seekers	(3)	10	(3)	14	(0)	00
Total	(31)	100	(21)	99	(10)	100

*$p = .12$ (note the small N)

few make status seeking the principal focus of their careers. Furthermore, like the preference role of the Parliament Man, its two main subtypes, Spectators and Club Men, are rather heterogeneous. Spectators include, for instance, both new Members who approach the political drama with awe and older Members who simply regard it as good theater. Club Men also come in several varieties, including part-timers, who, because they may be active company directors or barristers, spend little time in the House, and Good House of Commons Men, who spend little time anywhere else. Table 5.1 suggests, not surprisingly, that our Parliament Men are more often Conservatives than Labour Members. It also suggests that Conservatives may gravitate disproportionately to the role of the Club Man, whereas Labour MPs may tend to look toward the role of the Spectator. These are, for many of their players, "exit roles," particularly for those who are over sixty years old, thinking of leaving Parliament, and disposed by their preferences toward the club or the political spectacle. Other backbenchers enjoy the club and the spectacle too, but only Parliament Men make them the primary focus of their backbench roles.

Status Seekers

Of all the backbenchers in this study, only three can properly be characterized as Status Seekers. So rare a subtype would not qualify for serious examination were it not for the fact that so many other backbenchers express similar status themes in muted tones. Such politicians are not preoccupied with status, but they do pay attention to it, more than do many people in other walks of life. "Fame is the spur," wrote Julian Critchley; "anyone in public life who tells you differently is not telling the truth."[7] This makes Status Seekers worth considering briefly as a type that casts a common desire into extreme relief and permits us, thereby, to trace tendencies that would be difficult to see in less vivid presentations. For instance, Status Seekers are less immersed in Parliament than are either Spectators or Club Men. Their focus on status leads them to present themselves as marginal Members who are on the fringe, and who are seen by others as on the fringe. Thus, their status goals lead these MPs to look outside the House and to dwell on the fact, as did Namier's "Social Climbers" in the eighteenth century, that the House of Commons "has at all times been one of the great uplifting influences in English social life."[8]

BELIEFS AND BEHAVIORS

In the twentieth century, the century of mass media and mass culture, Status Seekers pursue publicity. It is flattering to be able to attract the attention of national audiences, to project one's name through the press, and to project one's image through television: "I think one enjoys the national publicity that one gets from time to time, and I think one would have to be very unusual not to become a little bit absorbed in this." The opportunity to attract national publicity comes available if "you can raise an issue . . . whatever it happens to be, and find that what you say or do does attract attention through the media." It may be a national issue or it may be a minor matter, such as the successful efforts of one MP to save the life of a disabled child who had been mistreated by her parents and neglected by everyone else: "This was about four days before Easter, and this really sort of hit the headlines you see. And it got in all the national newspapers—here was somebody who'd actually done something." The point is to catch the public imagination. Often this isn't very difficult to do, since compared to parliamentarians in other countries, "we are in the papers quite a lot . . . a story about the wife . . . about how we behave, what we say, the sort of lives we lead." Compared to parliamentarians in other countries, even ordinary backbenchers can step for the moment into the limelight where "I suppose one does enjoy the glamour of it . . . there's no point in denying it." "I have to be quite honest about it," said another, "one can't pretend that one doesn't get a certain pleasure out of being somebody people make a fuss of. . . . I have to admit that when the policemen hold up the traffic for me, and I drive out of New Palace Yard, it's quite a moment."

It is difficult not to notice the policemen holding up the traffic, but only for the Status Seeker is it "quite a moment." It is also quite a moment when Status Seekers have an opportunity to "meet the elite." "To be honest," one said, "what I really enjoy most is the meeting of high-level people from different countries that one would never have met before." Not only can they meet "the chief people from overseas countries," but they can also see people who are in the news at the moment, "and this is enormous, it's immense. I've seen the Prime Minister of India recently; the chairman of Lockheed was here not so long ago; certain American Senators have been here; the P.M. of Sweden was here." And for those who are most preoccupied with status, there are few experiences as rewarding as involvement with established, and preferably ancient, institutions: "Last week I was at the Archbishop's house where I met Cardinal Heenan. I've met the Queen when she came to open a hospital in Manchester. I've met Prince Philip, I've met Princess Margaret and the Duchess of Kent. I've had dinner recently with the Prime Minister. And next Thursday, I'm having dinner with the Speaker." Other important moments are provided by occasional foreign travel, which, while it broadens the mind, also offers uplifting experiences: "I have been twice to the Commonwealth Parliamentary Association Conference. I went to Ottawa, and I went to Kuala Lumpur. I read a paper in Delhi on the office of the Speaker. I've been seven times to the . . . conference in Germany. I've been to the Middle East. I think it's my contacts." And that is the great attraction of the exercise: contacts with the Great and the Good. "I think it's not only going to places," explained a provincial solicitor, "but actually meeting people whose opinion counts—something I'd never get a chance to do outside."

MOTIVATIONS

Since only three Status Seekers are under the microscope, our information is insufficient to allow us to probe very much the nature of this role and particularly to speculate about its chief emotional incentives. Nevertheless, all three of these Status Seekers exhibit a striking theme that sets them apart from other Parliament Men: resentment. None of them is fascinated, as are Spectators, with the spectacle. They may notice it, but they are not fascinated by it: "Parliament gives you a front seat at the opening of Parliament and, you know, various things that are on—you know, *for the fleeting moment,* you'll have a good seat." Nor are they enamored, as are Club Men, with the club: "There aren't any deep friendships in competition with all the young ones." Instead, they tend to see Parliament instrumentally, in terms of what it can do for their image or for their "access to most things and most people . . . something which is incredibly valuable." Actually, try as one might to understand them sympathetically, it is difficult to avoid the impression that these Status Seekers, who wish so much to win respect, to achieve a certain status, are resentful misfits and sometimes bitterly resentful misfits. "I'm very much on the fringe of the parliamentary party," one of them complained, and then proceeded, as did the others, to flog the insiders.

Some of this resentment is directed toward colleagues on the backbenches: "I mean the general level. . . . And the general disarray in terms of how Members dress themselves, and their approach to the hobnobbing," he continued in the third person, "makes it clear that the respect they get from the public these days is every bit as low as they deserve." But most of their resentment is reserved for the authorities who interfere with the modest importance that Status Seekers hope to enjoy: "Government decisions—they're given to people outside before they're given to Parliament. And really you're getting to the point where Parliament is to some extent only tolerated. The Executive carry on and. . . . 'This thing's got to go through Parliament, what a pity.'" There are also signs of thwarted ambition and of special grudges against those party leaders who, they believe, held them back: "One of the reasons very likely that Mr. Heath . . . was able to get to the very highest office . . . is that he was able to keep down the people who were any sort of competition. . . . Never make a man who is personally ambitious Chief Whip, because . . . he can advance himself . . . and he can keep back competition, which is bad."

Still, the House of Commons is useful because it provides the material for scripts and stories that can "uplift" one's status and perhaps, at the same time, deflate a little the noble image of the successful people one resents: "You get more done meeting a Minister while in the next stall in the lavatory than you do in the Chamber, you see." The House is, in the end, a vehicle for attracting attention, "so much attention," "it's amazing how much attention." It is a platform for becoming "somebody people make a fuss of." Unfortunately, Status Seekers find that they are disappointed even by their hard-won status, for "the standing of a Member, of course, in the country is nothing like what it was. There's no question. I mean you were, even in 1950, you were somebody in the community, you were somebody of some significance. Not now."

Spectators

Spectators may be more likely to be Labour than Conservative, but most of them do, and don't do, the same sorts of things. The only obvious party-related difference is in their attitude toward these activities. Thus, Labour Spectators tend to express awe over "just being able to be sitting there listening to the Minister" and "seeing a lot of people, a lot of very brilliant people, at work. . . . I think that's probably it—the pleasure of sort of being there and seeing these people at work that I think is the main thing." Conservatives, by contrast, approach the same scenes as though they expect to be entertained: "The House of Commons never gets dull," a former Conservative Minister said, "because it can be as dramatic as any, more dramatic than any theatre." Many of them say that "there is a drama about this place," and point out that "people will queue up for hours to be in the gallery to see something that you can walk in the House and see." They talk about the "excitement of the meetings of a new Parliament, of a Government's announcing its plans for the ensuing twelve months"; and they talk about "the discussion, the tradition, and the sense of history" associated with all these performances.

BEING THERE

Beyond "the perpetuation of Parliament and the esteem of Parliament," the Spectator's principal career goal is simply to be there. "It isn't the money," a Labour Member explained, "it really isn't. It's the genuine feeling of being there. . . . I just like being there when it happens." The significance that Spectators attribute to observing the scene is captured in the phrase "being in the centre of things." Everyone feels a certain excitement about being in the center of things, but Spectators feel it much more than most: "You are there!" they exclaim. "You *know* you're at the centre of affairs." "The Hub" is another metaphor that expresses the same message: "When you are near the hub of things you don't ever like to be away from the hub of things." To a particularly enthusiastic Spectator from Yorkshire, "it's very much like being at Wembly for a Cup Final. Other people are watching it on television; they're seeing it precisely, probably better, getting a better picture of it, but they've not got the atmosphere."[9]

It is this atmosphere that makes it so exciting, for Spectators are not watching a play, an imitation of life. They are watching instead a real-life drama, parts of which will be recorded in the nation's political history. "Well, after all, when you look at it, it's not much of a job," claimed one Spectator who was talking about the peculiar fascination of being at Westminster. "The hours are funny," he continued, "a lot of responsibility. . . . So what it is, . . . I'll tell you what I think it is: I think one gets tremendous satisfaction out of the consciousness that you are in the web of history being spun." Spectators like to believe that "this is where it's all happening, and that's why one feels that, you know, you can see it happening," for they like to believe that they are witnesses to history. They are "able to pop in and listen to the Prime Minister answering questions on all the great affairs of the world." And it is especially exciting "when some kind of crisis happens" and you find yourself "sitting there listening to the Minister making a major statement say on, one example was the Rolls Royce collapse. You're actually there."

Almost equally attractive to Spectators is the pursuit of inside information: "getting information that might not be available, not readily available, to the general public." Nearly every day brings information that "one wouldn't have on the outside," information about personalities and clashes behind the scenes: "I mean today, down the grapevine, Dennis Skinner was going to have a go at Reggie Maudling in the committee room. . . . Now the fact that one knew this, and that you're privy to these kinds of things, makes the House of Commons, and makes us why we like being here."[10] Spectators also enjoy the idea that they are privy to information *before* it reaches the general public. "It sounds a petty thing," one of them said, "but it's even a satisfaction that I know, sitting here at half past eight tonight, what you won't know till you pick up your newspaper in the morning.

That's small, petty, but, you know, that matters to people." Americans call this addiction inside-dopesterism, and it probably affects a majority of politicians and political commentators on both sides of the Atlantic. But to "hear things first" is more important to Spectators than it is to most of the rest of us. For those who are in the addiction's advanced stages, even a few hours is appreciated: "If there is some major announcement, we hear it here at half past three, before *anyone* else hears it on television news three or six hours later."

Spectators do more than witness history and gather inside information, though these are their most characteristic behaviors. They also meet elites, travel, and collect memories. Spectators are not as thrilled as Status Seekers about meeting notable political figures, but "meeting people, you know, politicians from abroad," has its attractions to those who seek information about "all the great affairs of the world." They aren't big travelers either, but some of them do take "the opportunity, also, of travel, you see—not at your own expense, you see. I've been to Germany and France to see the NATO armies and defenses. I've been on Commonwealth trips to the Bahamas, Barbados. I've been to Singapore. And then on the Inter-Parliamentary Union I've been to Switzerland. I've also been to Uganda." These were, for this elderly provincial journalist, "opportunities that in private life I might not have had." And he talks about them in terms of information, in terms of developing "background . . . all kinds of background from which you draw." From this background, from people met, from events witnessed, Spectators gather their recollections: "Everyone who has been in this place has recollections and memories of the place which others will find interesting . . . to have been here when such and such happened, to have seen Churchill make his last exit from the House, to have heard the declaration of war, the time of Suez, you know these are landmarks in the events of our time, and there is an awful lot of satisfaction to be got from, well, 'I was there to see.'"

Spectators are Parliament Men because they are more interested in the life of the institution than in constituency activities, policy advocacy, or ministerial ambitions. Although there is not much more to be learned about what they do, we can better understand their role by listening to them talk about what they avoid doing.

INACTIVITY AND INDIFFERENCE

They are not Constituency Members. Many Spectators discuss their preference role at length with no more than a passing reference to their constituen-

cies. Some say frankly that they regard the constituency work as a distraction: "I have sixty thousand constituents. If I gave them an hour each of
my time, it would take something like seven hours a day, seven *years*, non-
stop without sleep." And very few refer to particular cases. Instead, they
complain about "communication." "I am vitally concerned about the Common Market," complained a northern MP, "but I can't talk about that in
my area because life for them means 'Improve my condition.' . . . All they
know is the fact that they are living under the conditions under which they
are living. . . . They can't widen their minds." Others, especially Labour
Spectators, complain about how constituency tasks have recently increased
out of all proportion to what they should be, and how the pressure to become "a Welfare Officer detracts, of course, from the amount of attention
he can spend on the national scene."[11]

They do modest constituency service ("I advertise in the local paper when
I may be available, and it's up to them whether they come or not"), but
they talk more about receiving letters at Westminster than about receiving
constituents in the surgery. "Every day in your mail you have human problems," explained a Conservative stockbroker, "people's problems . . . very
important indeed, if you like, for the little man or woman." But that's all
he says about it. Unlike Constituency Members, he doesn't elaborate on
these activities. It is simply a duty, as it is for any MP. And those Spectators
who do discuss their constituency service a bit talk not so much about the
Welfare Officer's social work, but rather about the safety-valve themes that
are typically put forward by Conservative Constituency Members. Thus,
one Labour Spectator mentions the desirability of "making the constituent
feel that there is somebody in London, in Westminster, who is aware of the
problems and has got a sympathetic attitude to them." And one Conservative Spectator mentions the danger that "people feel that they are not involved, that there's 'Them and Us'. . . . We have a useful job to play . . . by
getting it over that there isn't this great division, that we're all in it together."

More Spectators are interested in policy advocacy than in constituency
affairs, but they plainly do not regard this as their principal responsibility
either. A barrister who pursues the occasional campaign pointed out that
"one has got to see [policy advocacy] in a very limited sphere . . . we can
all talk, and we can put our views down, and we can put these to the Minister. It's useful, but it's not actually one of my direct duties." Among his
fellow Spectators, skepticism about the value of such advocacy is widespread. Backbenchers can't really influence the government, they say, for
"this is no longer the centre of decision making. It's away in Whitehall. It's
between Whitehall and the unions and so forth." As another barrister ar-

gued: "I don't think [advocacy is] why I'm in politics. If it was, I'd soon get out because there wouldn't be much purpose to it." The message is that advocacy isn't worth pursuing seriously because it is an achievement-oriented activity that provides too few genuine achievements.

Some Spectators used to be Policy Advocates: "I came into the House with a considerable experience and expertise in the social services. . . . I was a well-known authority on the social services . . . my important responsibilities were helping the Parliamentary Labour Party, or the specialist groups of the Parliamentary Labour Party, understand what the Bills were about." But "I'm not keeping abreast of it now." A few still do keep abreast, but typically their talk sounds more like a mental exercise than like a basis for action: "We should have better schools, we should have a better system of education . . . my interest is in getting better teachers. . . . I'd like to see more nurseries . . . we need, and need badly . . ." But he doesn't seem to be doing anything about it, except to recall that he was "a firm supporter" of a particular Bill "many years ago." This sort of talk is more about "how you can make life better" in general than about specific activities in the Palace of Westminster. The few who do become involved make it clear that their involvement is restricted to special situations, for policy advocacy demands much more time than Spectators wish to devote to little campaigns.

If Spectators are wary of constituency work and policy advocacy, they hardly talk at all about ministerial ambitions. Parliament Men, in general, have weaker aspirations than most other backbenchers. And the comments of Spectators suggest that they have given up hope: "I had that when I came in," one said. "I'll be quite honest on that. Well, I hoped. But I don't see the chance. . . . I'm not terribly upset about that because since I came I have widened my circle . . . I've no terrible burning ambitions." This Member was over fifty, the age after which, if office has not come, it may not come at all. But even the young Spectators take up this text. One in his early forties said that when he came in six years before, he had thought that, as a qualified lawyer, he was remarkably well prepared for office: "I probably thought I was ideal material." Recently, however, he has begun to say that "it wouldn't surprise me in the least if I went through the whole career without ever being offered anything. I'm resigned to it."

He is resigned to it because he has become aware that somehow he just doesn't fit in. Others are resigned to it because "if Harold Wilson formed another Government, I don't think he'd appoint me." But most Parliament Men do not pursue office because they believe that their advanced age would make the likelihood of success ridiculously small: "You've reached an age when you know that you're not going to get any political preferment," so

"I've reached the stage, of course, where I can have no plans." "I've no particular ambition," Spectators say. "I'm 63 just now, so that I retire in two years. This is my last Parliament."[12]

INSTITUTIONAL PATRIOTISM

Spectators have little interest in constituency work, advocacy, or ambition and look instead to the institution and to the dramas through which the institution weaves its webs of history. How, then, do they appraise this House whose stages absorb so much of their attention? And what do they think about the principal performers? Table 5.2 compares Spectators with other backbenchers and with Club Men. Status Seekers are not included because there are only three of them. To examine the Parliament Man's institutional patriotism, this analysis separates out strong positive responses to two different questions, one concerning beliefs about the House; the second, beliefs about colleagues on the other side. Both questions were presented during the interviews and generated discussions that were transcribed and coded along several different dimensions.

Table 5.2 View of House of Commons and of other MPs by Parliament Man's role types, in percent

| View of House and other MPs* | Role type | | Other backbenchers |
	Club Men	Spectators	
View of House of Commons			
Very favorable	43	36	17
Less than very favorable	57	64	83
Total	100	100	100
	(N = 14)	(N = 14)	(N = 297)
View of members of other parties**			
Very favorable	39	23	10
Less than very favorable	62	77	90
Total	100	100	100
	(N = 13)	(N = 13)	(N = 289)

*Q. The House of Commons has been described as having the atmosphere of a "gothic club"—as stuffy, lifeless, and out-of-date. Do you think this description is true? Q. In your experience in Parliament, to what extent can one trust and rely on members of the other parties?

**$p \leq .01$

Perhaps the most important aspect of backbenchers' appraisals of the House of Commons is simply the degree to which their beliefs are positive or negative. "Very favorable" entries represent the strongest positive responses on a five-point scale. The "less than very favorable" entries, to which these are compared, cover everything below what might be described as enchantment. Attitudes toward colleagues in the other parties were tapped by a question about having trust and confidence in these political opponents. Again, the "very favorable" responses represent extremely positive views unblemished by reservations, and the "less than very favorable" category covers everything else on the five-point scale.

Since the number of Spectators and Club Men is so very small, these data must be treated cautiously. On the other hand, confidence in the results is strengthened somewhat by the fact that they point in the same direction on two quite different items. Parliament Men have in common a concern for the well-being of the House as an institution. Involved as they are with Westminster, one would expect them to be particularly strong on institutional patriotism, to be among the most enthusiastic defenders of the House.[13] And indeed Parliament Men are as a group twice as likely as other backbenchers to be captivated by the Commons, a result that holds up for both major parties, though more strongly on the Labour than on the Conservative side.

Table 5.2 shows that, among the subtypes, Club Men are the institution's strongest boosters: "I like the House of Commons, you see. I like the place." They are ever ready to defend their club against its critics: "And I had a critic here just a few weeks ago who was quite disgusted to see only seventy Members in the House. And I said, 'Right,' so I took him upstairs . . . and we had *ten* Standing Committees sitting the same afternoon. . . . They never realise that we have a miniature parliamentary sitting in each Standing Committee." Spectators too are stronger supporters than are other backbenchers; but they are slightly detached in the sense that they are not so deeply involved with the institution's life: "a privileged spectator, but nonetheless a spectator." Some of their colleagues have reservations about the legitimacy of the spectator role,[14] which may lead some of the Spectators to have a few reservations of their own: "It's not such a club as people think."

The institutional patriotism of Parliament Men is further reflected in their views of members of the other parties, views three times more favorable than those of other backbenchers. This result too holds up when party is controlled. And again the table shows that these extremely positive beliefs are more characteristic of Club Men than of Spectators, though Spectators are still twice as positive as other backbenchers. In considering "the other side," it is widely expected that the Good House of Commons Man (a type of Club Man) should not be so intensely partisan that he cannot set his partisanship aside to serve the institution's collective interests.[15] "As far as I'm concerned," runs the approved formula, "I've got many friends on the other side of the House whose political views I disagree with totally but who as individuals I like *very* much. . . . If I like a person, I like a person. . . . And in the House of Commons . . . *you've got a common interest*." Spectators aren't so sure. Although more favorably disposed than some to colleagues on the other side, their irritation with the lack of appreciation for their role is reflected here as well. Thus, several go out of their way to explain that they have just as good friends outside the House, that competition for preferment "can lead to resentment on the part of the one passed over," and that there are experiences that occasionally make one aware of one's peripheral position and skeptical about the clubbable claims: "I don't think one makes an awful lot of friends here . . . I mean . . . I did have a six-weeks' absence when I went to have an operation a couple of years ago, but when I came back nobody noticed that I'd been away. They said, 'Hello, had a good recess?'—because I came back after the Easter Recess. They didn't notice that I hadn't been here for six weeks!"

Signs of ambivalence can also be seen when Spectators discuss the incentives involved in their role. Their reports put them somewhere between the Status Seekers, with whom they share a little discontent and status striving, and the Club Men, with whom they share a desire for affiliation and respect. Their dominant theme is the pursuit of a feeling of importance.

INCENTIVES: VICARIOUS IMPORTANCE

Several Spectators describe their role as a fall-back position, a minimal course of conduct for backbenchers whose ambitions ran into a blank wall. At some point in their careers they found themselves "in rather a sort of backwater" and came to terms with the fact that though they had a "great desire for office," they were just not going to get it. They didn't want to become Constituency Members or Policy Advocates, but they didn't want to leave the House either. Thus, their preferences led them to decide "just to remain a Member . . . that's my burning ambition . . . I am busy enough as it is. And I'm perfectly happy to carry on as I am." Unfortunately, not all of them are perfectly happy about it: "I think there are several ministerships that I could have done as well as those that did them . . . and I must say I resent it slightly that it wasn't offered to me." Their mild discontent and detachment echoes some of the discussions with Status Seekers. And there are a few gentle misfits here as well ("I suspect that I'm far too flippant. I mean this has been said. I mean I know something of the effect I have on people"), a situation that makes them a somewhat less appreciative audience than they might otherwise be.

But when most Spectators discuss their roles, it is not thwarted ambition that comes through so much as a vicarious feeling of importance. Some state it vividly, like this seventy-year-old Member whose reputation in the House is very high: "Well, it's not only a matter of belonging to the club, because I could have gone to the Lords. It is the belief that everything I do is urgent and important." Another elderly Spectator, who is preparing to give up his place at "the centre of things," worries about how difficult it is going to be to deal with "the fact that I am no longer important." This emotional incentive is wrapped in the conviction that "membership of the governing body necessarily distinguishes the man,"[16] or, as our worried Spectator put it: "Most people who come in here develop in a way they would never have developed if they hadn't been in public life. There certainly is a great feel for bringing out the character and capabilities of the public servant." What is it that stimulates this belief and this feeling of importance and self-esteem? Spectators are not protectors of the weak nor benefactors of their communities; nor are they successful policy specialists or holders of governmental office. They are not even active participants in Westminster's world. But they *are there*—and being there nourishes the sense of importance.

It is derived vicariously from association with the Great and the Good. "It is the feeling of the place," explained a former engineer, "in the sense that I am *near* the levers of power." Spectators watch Ministers, listen to Ministers, "and if you're lucky you can ask him a Question." Spectators, like other backbenchers, regularly find themselves in the company of Ministers in the division lobbies, committee rooms, and corridors, in the company perhaps of the Prime Minister in the Smoking Room, in the company occasionally of top industrialists, trade union leaders, bankers, and vice chancellors. It's "the fact that you're actually able to talk first-hand to people who are the principal parties." Being in the center of things makes it difficult not to feel that one is "playing a part in decision making . . . more importantly, the fact that you are helping to make vital decisions." Simply being a part of the political scene makes you feel that "you are in at the beginning of so many things." And, if compared to the Great and the Good, one's role seems minor, it is nevertheless still something to be proud of: "I can always tell my grandchildren I was one of the ones who voted for entry, I was one of the ones in the crucial vote for entering the Common Market. This is what I mean, just having participated, even if it wasn't in any leading position, or if my name wasn't involved." "Membership in the House of Commons distinguishes the man" and strengthens self-esteem by attracting the esteem of others. Spectators speak about the value of "the esteem or otherwise in which one is held by one's own colleagues," a theme most often articulated by those Spectators who have to their credit successful past performances as Ministers or Policy Advocates: "I thought it was very important that I should build up for myself a standing in this House, which I eventually attained."

Those who are unable to attain it in the House find their "great uplifting influence" outside, where "one does get a lot of respect from people . . . and people do look up to you in all forms of life." You impress them with your presence; you impress them with your rhetoric ("You know when to drop your voice, when to raise your voice"); you impress them with what you have to say: "I think this is the important part of going back to your constituency and being able to say, 'Yes, I was there when Bernadette Devlin attacked Reggie Maudling,' this sort of stuff." You become, as one Spectator claimed, "a very leavening, very leavening influence in society," for when people talk to a Member of Parliament, "they can pick his brains, which they'll do if they're sensible," and learn what things are going on. And the "leavening influence," which presumably raises the political awareness of the people, also enhances the image of the provider of this inside information and helps boost his sense of importance:

> When I was a small boy I used to go to football matches at Cranborne Park on Saturday afternoon, in a town in which everybody was interested in what was then a little local team. . . . And it was 3d to go in, and when we didn't have 3d to go in we had a bent railing round the back where we could sneak in. . . . But we used to leave the second the final whistle went, we ran out of that ground and ran as though for our lives, down Beaconsfield Avenue and the next main road. Why? *Because blokes would stop and ask us, "What's the score?"* And we knew, and they didn't, you know. There is something of that in it.

Two other incentives, desires for a sense of competence and for a sense of fellowship, are also mentioned by Spectators, though not as often as they talk about the sense of importance. Being in the House of Commons, "in the centre of things," can make you "confident in your approach." Just being there can be satisfying because it can make you feel useful: "I think it's a great privilege to have the opportunity to be here because being here is to do something useful, and that I like." Besides, "it's quite an achievement just to become a Member of Parliament. Don't let's denigrate the situation." The Spectator's ambition is "just to remain a Member," because being a

Member you feel "that you're a part of it, albeit you may be a minute cog in a big wheel." Yet every wheel requires its cogs, and cogs are therefore useful. "You pick up your *Hansard,* you check the figures . . . you're in the middle of affairs." This sense of competence is also related to being well informed, to "having a knowledge of what is taking place," to being "immediately up-to-date on anything worthwhile that's going." And, as Spectators absorb their information and play their parts with others, a few of them link these experiences to the fellowship, "the companionship, the interest of it." This association between "the fellowship and being at the hub of things" leads us to the Club Men, who, among Parliament Men, are the most respected and the most self-confident about their roles.

Club Men

Club Men, like Spectators, enjoy being there: "Well, I have been very fortunate in my life. I've done about five different things which I have thoroughly enjoyed, and the one I have enjoyed most is being here." What they experience at Westminster is much like what Sir Lewis Namier, with reference to generations of their predecessors, characterized as "that marvelous microcosmos of English social and political life, that extraordinary club, the House of Commons."[17]

But it is more than the political spectacle that they desire. "I like the whole life of it," says a Knight of the Shire, member of the Chairman's Panel, and Good House of Commons Man. What he and his friends mean when they say they like the whole life of it is that they find at Westminster a long-established role that enables the amateur politician to develop a very agreeable life style. Their involvement in the political spectacle is part of this life style, but it is neither its beginning nor its end. In fact, they occasionally make this point by gentle mockery of Spectators and of themselves. Thus, being at "the hub" while "the web of history" is being spun is, according to some of them, really "a *bogus* sense of being in the centre of things"; and although it is amusing to be involved in this way, "one really spends most of one's time trying to get a pair and get out to dinner [chuckle]."

WHAT THEY DO

Club Men are active participants in Westminster's activities. They do talk about *being* in the center of things, but they link this in the same sentence with doing things as well: "Ah, I think . . . the advantage of being at the centre of things *and* all the activity I engage in here." It is this vitality and activity that distinguishes Club Men as a subtype. They enjoy watching the performances, but they are not merely passive observers. Even the part-timers among them have more crowded diaries than do the Spectators; and the full-timers are very busy indeed. Instead of talking vaguely about their interests in the web of history, they express "interests in what happens to be going on." They feel "an attraction to be *in* on all that's going on," behind the scenes as well as on the stage. They like "the curious way in which the House never gets steamed up two days running on the same thing." They especially like it behind the scenes "when suddenly there's a row that blows up out of nothing. And it's an exciting place to be."

Many Club Men "usually sit through Question Time." But if it's dull, "if there's nothing there, there's plenty to do of interest in the library and that sort of thing . . . talking to one's colleagues . . . I never find a dull moment here." They tend to "take the old-fashioned view that the main point of Parliament is to sustain the Government which is in, or to check the Executive." They respond to the whip, vote with the side, take what their colleagues say on trust, do their stint on Standing Committees, and poke thorns in the flesh of the Opposition. Yet, except for the special and important tasks undertaken by those who are Good House of Commons Men, they aren't overactive in any of these areas. What they do mainly is enjoy the company of their friends and acquaintances.

In contrast with the Status Seekers and Spectators, Club Men are not so interested in meeting important people. When they discuss meeting visitors, the emphasis is less on the person's status than on whether or not it's going to be an interesting evening: "You know, . . . the second chap in the Opposition in Malta. Malta is in the news at the moment, and so I shall have an interesting evening talking to him. That interests me, I like doing it, probably lots of people wouldn't, and they wouldn't want to have anything to do with him, you know, they would prefer to do something else. But that I like doing." Club Men talk about meeting interesting visitors, but they talk much more about meeting friends. In fact, for many of them, this is unquestionably their major interest in the House of Commons and, strange as it may seem in the twentieth century, the principal goal that focuses their activities at Westminster. For instance, the Member who just described how he enjoys meeting interesting visitors is the same MP who said earlier that, of the five different things he has done in his life, the one he enjoys most is being in the House of Commons. And now he explains why: "And I think the main reason I enjoy most being here is that I find that there are a lot of my friends that I have had since university days have arrived here as well. There are lots of people I like seeing here that I don't see anywhere else."

When you enter Parliament, according to a Labour Club Man who hadn't been to university, and whose friends hadn't followed him to Westminster, "you lose your local friends, you see, and you can't go back to them. You have lost that friendship and you have to acquire a circle here." Over the years, the circle grows because, even compared to most London clubs, "we really do spend a lot of time here, so there's a lot of time to get to know people and strike up friendships." Making their usual rounds in the Palace of Westminster, Club Men find, more than do other backbenchers, that "one meets people that one hasn't met before, and one gets to know them . . . it's a jolly good club . . . making friends and meeting other people . . . it's a jolly good club." "Strangers" are neither friends nor acquaintances—and the use of this term for visitors to the House helps symbolically to make the "Members" feel solidarity among themselves.[18]

It is no accident that the House of Commons has "got the amenities of a club: Smoke Room, Tea Room, bar, and barber shop." It also has dining rooms, game rooms, television rooms, a library, and a very pleasant terrace. These are the settings in which Club Men develop and play out their interpretations of their role, "meeting Members and talking to them, particularly in the Dining Room and so on, where you've got a bit of time and can talk." The Smoking Room has long been a favorite meeting place for Tories, albeit it has a Labour corner, just as the Tea Room is a favorite haunt for Labour Members who recognize a few tables as Conservative territory. Club Men are also active in House social groups and social events. There are clubs for clay-pigeon shooting, cricket, flying, golf, tennis, painting, yachting, skiing: "I got in for the parliamentary ski race against the Swiss, and you get to know other people on that group as well, and so on. And then you tend to remain friends with the same people." All the time, Club Men find, "you're meeting so many different people in so many different ways, whether it's dances, cocktail parties, sports gatherings, pubs, or clubs." It is their strong interest in the vitality of this social activity that leads them to be unenthusiastic about efforts to provide Members with offices of their own, because once Members are installed in comfortable offices, "you don't see them as much as you used to. I like mixing with people and talking to them. I've never had an office here, I like rubbing shoulders with people and talking to them, and I do my work in the Library." They like the life in all these settings, including what one Chairman of Committees described enthusiastically as "the life in a division," that is to say, the time spent milling about and chatting in the division lobbies.

Club Men are more likely than their colleagues to be found in the other party's favorite haunts, since their interest in fellowship extends to cross-party associations and activities. They "get to be friends right across the board. It doesn't matter which party you're in. I mean I've got as many

friends in the Labour Party and the Liberal Party as I have in my own party."
Club Men are unusual in insisting that "political affiliations don't make any
difference," since they do make a difference to many other backbenchers
who find it difficult to develop friendships with Members in parties besides
their own. Perhaps fewer Club Men than it seems actually have friends on
the other side; there is a sort of informal segregation within the precincts
of the House. Perhaps they are mainly making a point when they so often
go out of their way to assert that "I've got quite a lot of good friends on
the Labour side, a lot of my friends are on the Labour side." From this
perspective, they are also more likely than other backbenchers to speak of
the House as a collective person ("the House makes a judgement," "develops an opinion," "is in an irritable mood") and to claim that "there's such
a, so much together on all sides . . . friends in all parties." When it comes
to friendships, even the strong partisans among Club Men are prepared to
be tolerant: "I certainly find my friends more often on the Right of the Conservative Party . . . being a Member of the Monday Club I find my friends
in that direction. This is not to say that I don't have friends on the other
side. And indeed some of the Opposition socialists are my friends who share
my experiences in some of the work that I do."

Trips abroad are one experience that is widely shared across party lines—
an experience that is often mentioned as the starting point for friendships.
When Club Men talk about "an overseas visit with a group of two or four
or six people," they are, compared with Spectators, less likely to emphasize
the thrill of traveling to the Bahamas than "the pleasure of getting to know
other people in that group well and so on. And then you tend to remain
friends with the same people." Not all Parliament Men like to travel. But
one who doesn't like to travel himself has special reasons for encouraging
other backbenchers to do so, reasons that point to a distinction between
two interpretations of the role of the Club Man at Westminster: "I would
send all the tiresome MPs who want to legislate about things abroad to
Rhodesia to do a study where they can't do any harm . . . all these things
like trips abroad are important—it makes them happy and, well, you know,
think that they are doing something. But it doesn't do any harm." This is
the voice of the part-timer, the Club Man who sees himself as the counterweight to Parliament's eager beavers.

PART-TIMERS AND GOOD HOUSE OF COMMONS MEN

Thus far, we have identified general backbench roles, such as the role of the
Parliament Man, and subtypes within each, such as the role of the Club

Man. It is a tribute to the variability and complex structure of these prefer-ence roles that it is sometimes possible to discern distinct patterns at yet another more particularistic level. Thus, there are two varieties of Club Men, the part-timers, whose commitment is indeed part-time, and the Good House of Commons Men, who keep the ship afloat.

Part-timers include barristers or active company directors with a taste for tradition, as well as Knights of the Shires, who are Parliament Men from the past. Such barristers love the House and the life within it, but they also have busy practices outside and, while they do their duty, "I don't feel the need to be here all the time," or "You know, you have to be here to vote."[19] Similarly, active company directors like this local manufacturer "think one's quite foolish . . . to launch out on some end here which one is highly unlikely to achieve, and abandon the industrial contacts one has outside." Another company director agrees and explains how the House is for him a secondary interest, an important secondary interest because he finds it difficult to make friends in his busy commercial life and, for that reason, values greatly his many friends in the House of Commons—but a secondary interest all the same.[20]

Knights of the Shires are also usually part-timers. For them, membership in the House of Commons is either a family duty or a social habit; and it seems appropriate simply to "be there," though they usually take up one pursuit or another. "I mean I have lots of other things to do other than Parliament, I have a very happy, full life in England anyhow," began one contemporary Knight whose father had also been an MP. "It was sort of assumed that if one hadn't anything else to do, it wasn't a bad sort of occu-pation. Because you've got twenty-two weeks holiday a year, don't you? I mean it was very much approached like that you know." His response to a question about his achievements in Parliament underscores the point: "Well, I have survived for twelve years [chuckle], in these electrifying times [chuckle]." And he develops this, his favorite theme, further as follows: "It's very *nice* to come up to London two or three days a week; you know, to come up from the country, you know, to come up from the country to the centre of things and meet all one's friends. And a lot of my friends who got in with me are now in very responsible jobs. I enjoy the contacts with them immensely. . . . I hunt three days a week, always. Probably hunt four days a week. I don't get any letters anyhow. I only have a secretary part-time. I have one woman, at home, who deals with Parliamentary letters on a Mon-day and that's it."

The Good House of Commons Men, the full-timers, don't seem to mind, though some other backbenchers do.[21] In fact, many Good House of Commons Men value the limited contributions of the part-timers. One of the most respected senior backbenchers in this group explained that since some barristers, accountants, company directors, and others have strong commitments outside the House, "this is all the more reason why we should fill the gaps. . . . These people who can't give us full time have very valuable contributions to make, even in their limited field." A friend of his, also on the Chairman's Panel, added that he himself spends each week four and sometimes five very full days at the House: "I'm not one of those people who want to be off as soon as they can get away." Good House of Commons Men are to the parliament man role what Local Promoters are to the constituency member role: the subtype that receives most of the respect, although part-timers enjoy more esteem than do Welfare Officers. In any event, Good House of Commons Men are full-time and see the House not only as an agreeable club, but also as "a good working place."

The services they perform keep the House running smoothly. Many members of the Speakers' Panel of Chairmen are Good House of Commons Men: "I'm on what's called the Speakers Panel of Chairmen, which means one takes the Chair in the House on certain occasions when it's in committee, and Standing Committees. I always like doing that." This was the position sought by Sir Samuel Roberts after he decided that he was unlikely to get a ministerial post; and it is still regarded as a sensible alternative: "Later on in one's career," said another Club Man who had followed this path, "if you don't become a senior Minister, well then, you tend to fit in, as they say, with the chairmanships here. That's what happened to me."

Most of those to whom it happens tend to be less partisan than their colleagues, or soon become so. The Good House of Commons Man is the counterpoint to the party man.[22] As a Conservative backbencher explained, "I have evolved into being a House of Commons Man rather than a party man . . . when I take the Chair in the House in the Speaker's absence, as a dozen of us are appointed to do, and take the Chairs of Committees, I lose my voting rights." As they devote their energies to the House as an institution, their commitments to Westminster begin to overshadow their commitments to their parties: "I wouldn't give anything to the bloody Labour Party Conference," declared an active House of Commons Man from the Labour side. "And when somebody says, 'Well, this was in the Boilermakers' Resolution,' I say it's bloody time we took notice of what the 'Cabinetmakers' think, not the bloody Boilermakers, you know."

There is a range of committees that attract Club Men who wish to serve the House in this way. One is the Selection Committee: "Again it's more of a House of Commons job . . . to see to it that the sponsors of a Bill have a majority membership [on the committee considering] the Bill. Even though it may be one of the Opposition's Private Members' Bills, we give him the majority on the Bill. So to this extent, this is more of a job of, as I say, the House of Commons than the party." Other committees to which these elder statesmen gravitate are the House of Commons (Services), Register of Members' Interests, Procedure, Broadcasting, and particularly the Committee of Privileges, which has existed since the seventeenth century. Members of the Committee of Privileges, like Charles Pannell, probably the best-known Good House of Commons Man of his generation, are always pleased when they can defend successfully the traditions of the House, as they did at the time of our interviews by deciding that the Member for Berwick-on-Tweed should be referred to as "Mr." Lambton and no longer by his honorary title, "Lord" Lambton.[23] They "enjoy such things as being on the Committee of Privileges and certain things of this kind very much . . . a Member must play his part in Parliament." Such committees are concerned with the domestic or internal administration of the House of Commons and, in the case of the Committee of Privileges, also with the standing of the House in the world outside.[24] Therefore, they attract Members who desire not only to make the House their principal focus of interest, but also to devote their attention to "the perpetuation of Parliament and the esteem of Parliament."[25]

WHAT THEY DON'T DO

Thus, some Club Men are very active in the House of Commons and do a lot of institutional service. There are also things that most Club Men prefer to do only a little, and one of these is constituency work. Like Spectators, Club Men can discuss their roles endlessly with no more than a passing reference to their constituencies. "Your job is to look after the interests of your constituency within the framework of Parliament because you represent everybody in your constituency not just your own party," said one senior Club Man. And that was all he had to say about his constituency in fifty single-spaced pages of transcript. "I think people overplay the hand tremendously," a Knight of the Shire commented about Constituency Members. "I actually find that in my constituency there is never a problem that can't be solved by the regional offices of the various ministries. If you *want* to make yourself busy, you can make a lot of work."

Club Men do not want to make themselves busy with constituency matters. There are some duties to which they must attend. And they realize that constituency work can be important. But what they dislike is that "the

Member of Parliament is becoming too much of a sort of sink-tidy for all the questions that nobody else wants to bother about answering." Moreover, "the constituency chores get a bit boring after I've been here twenty-six years, you know, and they're always the same: you're opening the same bloody horticultural show or whatever it may be, and going to some cricket dinner, you know, year after year and all that. So this really, um, gets a bit dull." The temptation grows, especially for those who enjoy safe seats and supportive associations, to leave most of it to a secretary and concentrate on Westminster: "They allow me to be a national parliamentarian," one of the best-known Good House of Commons Men explained; "they're rather pleased about it . . . I don't say that I consider my constituency job the *least* important—but a lot of that is done by an intelligent secretary, which leaves me free. . . . Populism is a lot of bull, anyway, you know." Just as the Club Man may become more of a House of Commons Man than a party man, so may he become more of a Member of the House than a "Member for Someplace."

Some Club Men are active in constituency service, but even for them this is not a top priority. During their interviews they virtually never, for instance, discuss individual cases or make specific references to advice bureaus or to writing letters. Instead, like Spectators, they speak vaguely about their utility as communicators and safety valves. "I tell the Government what the people are thinking," is a typical comment. "I think you're a very good safety valve. They've got somebody to go to. If they hadn't somebody to go to, they'd explode from time to time." This MP attends to his constituency "after attending to all the other things . . . and the smooth running of the House of Commons. I have the same duty that we all have to attend to my constituency. And, in that respect, I spend a lot of time." He does go and listen. But what he hears from his constituents, and what he does about what he hears, is of comparatively little interest to him in his political life.

Although Club Men resemble Spectators in their beliefs about constituency service, there is a noticeable difference between these two subtypes when it comes to policy advocacy. Vigorous advocacy sometimes irritates Club Men, and they criticize it more sharply than do Spectators. They warm to their critique with comments like "I don't feel such a tremendous urge to implement things now. I sometimes feel a great urge to *stop* something happening." They wish to stop things from happening because they believe that the modern state is too involved in planning, rationalizing, and changing Britain. Echoing the Knights of the Shires, they argue that there is far too much policy mongering and legislation: "It's the fault of all Governments," a Conservative Club Man complained, "far too much legislation, far too much tinkering. I mean, I think Ted Heath should have done the Common Market, say, the Industrial Relations Act, and that's that, and make everything else work well—instead of nothing but blinking change which everyone is fed up with, and quite right too."[26]

They criticize Governments for doing too much and denigrate Policy Advocates for tilting at windmills. There is no point to advocacy they imply, because advocacy scores no points: "There are so many other areas of power" that the House is less important than it used to be. Besides, everyone knows that backbenchers' speeches, eloquent though they may be, have no effect: "It took me about five or six years to discover that the great speeches that I'd delivered on foreign affairs or on the Budget really had no effect." Policy Advocates like to think they are at one end of a two-way influence channel to the Government, but Club Men mock this idea: "I don't think we influence them very much. I mean you are 'The Way' [chuckle], you are 'The Way,' 'the two-way communication channel,' and you are 'The Way,' dribbling ideas through [chuckle]." Policy Advocates promote professionalization and seek to pull Parliament away from its past. One of their pet projects has been the creation of Select Committees to probe areas of government policy, to investigate like American congressional committees, and to publish recommendations. Club Men mock these efforts too: "Those Select Committees are all balls. They are purely occupational therapy for Members of the Parliament who haven't got enough to do; and I won't sit on them. That's a waste of time. Take the Select Committee on Agriculture. We didn't have any guidelines, any effect on policy. It was purely, in fact, a tool of civil servants. I was Secretary of another one of the damn things until 1968 . . . I think it takes ten years or more to realise that they are occupational therapy."

To Club Men who have been Ministers, backbench advocacy seems especially trivial and tedious. Thus, a former Cabinet Minister finds "I get very bored with the boring things now." Another explains that really "this is not quite so fascinating when you've actually been a Minister yourself because then you see that the real point of politics is to exercise power, and you can't exercise power as a Member of Parliament, you can only exercise influence." The chief goals of the Club Men do not include "power or influence—I think, actually, that I had more on the GLC [Greater London Council] as a committee chairman than I do as a backbencher here." This point is made most directly by the part-timers who are active company directors, who value power and influence but don't seek them in the House of Commons: "as a backbench Member of Parliament I certainly influence the actions of others very much *less* than I do in my capacity as Chairman of this company. Most certainly I have a stronger influence here."

As Parliament becomes increasingly professional, Club Men increasingly stick to their institutional service. They don't expect to play a part in the great debates. As one of them, an aristocratic bank director, explained, "I used to be extremely well informed, for instance, about nuclear power plants and that sort of thing, but I've forgotten it all, and therefore I don't take part in debates because I'm so out-of-date." Those who do dabble mention interests such as "the sort of trade union thing" and talk about attending backbench committees or ginger (advocacy) groups; but the work to which they refer is occasional or pursued "much too long really. I must give it up." Similarly, the campaigns they mention are often constituency-related rather than specialized, matters like "playing a part in getting the third London airport to be sited at Foulness." And many of the stories turn out to be about accomplishments and activities in the past: "I certainly enjoy having the two Private Members' Bills that I piloted through, for example." "In my early days, the matter of river pollution was a predominant issue in my constituency . . . I had to fight hard to . . ."

On the subject of ambition, Club Men sound neither as hopeless nor as bitter as some of the Spectators, for they include in their ranks more former Ministers, respected senior backbenchers, and people with satisfying lives outside Westminster. When it comes to office, they explain frankly and without any obvious irritation, "Oh no, I'm too old now, you know." Or, "I don't think so because I've got to an age where one can't expect any more." Or, "No, really there's no time." And several say they simply aren't that sort of chap. Knights of the Shires weren't particularly interested in attaining office in the eighteenth century,[27] and they still aren't: "No, I'm not that sort of chap. Unfortunately, my wife tells me that I should be." They don't seek office now and, contrary to the assumptions of both Lord Acton and rational choice theorists, didn't when they were younger either: "I am not ambitious to go beyond where I am now, and that is understandable because of my age. But in fact I never have been. I just wanted to serve as a Member of Parliament and not to be in the Government as a Minister, Junior Minister, or a Whip."[28]

Those of us who study politicians have always found it difficult to accept that some of them are not avid office-seekers. But when the middle-aged businessman says that the Prime Minister "should be looking for some new blood and some youngsters in junior office to prepare for the future"; when the successful barrister says, "Never. I've never wanted office here. I'm a busy and a rich man"; and when the Good House of Commons Man says, "No, I'm quite happy to do what I'm doing"—they certainly sound as though they mean it. When one encounters aspirations here, they are usually aspirations for positions like Speaker or Chairman or Deputy Chairman of

Ways and Means, for a place on the Committee of Privileges, or perhaps for "office in the 1922 Committee." Furthermore, the part-timers are not even interested in these posts: it wouldn't work, "unless I spend a lot more time in Parliament." In fact, "I wouldn't dream of it. . . . I'm a senior partner in a firm that's been going on for a couple of hundred years, and I wouldn't let down all the people I look after and am responsible for." These part-timers include "gentlemen" who are not "players" but who believe nonetheless that they have a very useful function to perform at Westminster: keeping Parliament anchored in the real world, as their hyperactive colleagues rush about from one side of the deck to the other. A middle-aged Knight of the Shire from whom we have heard before sets the tone: "It tis nice to come up to London, up from the country, several days a week. But I think I shall really stay only until my children . . . uh, I've obviously got to remain in London while my children are just sort of leaving school and coming out. But I don't want to go on having to come to London much longer. I really honestly feel I will have done my duty after twenty years."

INSTITUTIONAL CONSERVATISM

Parliament Men find constituency chores boring, advocacy misguided, and office seeking inappropriate. But they are concerned about the House of Commons as an institution and about its traditions. This is the focus that holds their subtypes together. Nearly all of them, and particularly the Club Men, feel strong institutional patriotism. Nearly all of them, and particularly the Club Men again, should likewise be expected to support strong institutional conservatism. Compared to other backbenchers, Parliament Men should be less willing to change established institutional arrangements and more willing to censure disregard for procedural conventions and rules.

The data in Table 5.3 are derived from responses to the mailback questionnaire that Members completed after their interviews. Parliamentary reform had been a lively topic for a decade, and those who opposed the reformers were usually institutional conservatives. Everything seemed threatened with modernization, as MPs grumbled about the new trendy House of Commons Christmas card and the "calamitous" functional design for a new parliamentary office building opposite the Big Ben tower.[29] In the same vein, many aspects of procedural conventions and informal rules were under attack as a consequence of the tilt against authority in the wider world and the demands for a new efficiency at Westminster. Thus, blocking such attacks on conventions and rules could also reasonably be interpreted as an expression of institutional conservatism. Since it is necessary to separate

Table 5.3 Attitude toward changing institutional structures and skirting procedures by Parliament Man's role types, in percent

	Role type		
Attitude*	Club Men	Other backbenchers	Spectators
Changing structure**			
Oppose	100	57	39
Support	0	43	62
Total	100	100	101
	(N = 10)	(N = 234)	(N = 13)
Skirting procedures***			
Oppose	80	53	39
Support	20	47	62
Total	100	100	100
	(N = 10)	(N = 250)	(N = 13)

*Q. The British parliamentary system has been left unchanged for too long [agree/disagree]. Q. To get things done, it is often necessary for an MP to overlook procedural conventions and informal rules [agree/disagree].
**$p \leq .01$
***$p \leq .13$ (note the small N)

the responses of the Club Men from those of Spectators, the number of backbenchers in each category becomes so small that the results must be taken with several grains of salt. At the same time, some confidence can be derived again from the fact that the responses to the two different questions are very much the same.

Without controls for subtypes, Parliament Men would appear to be only a little more institutionally conservative than other backbenchers. But by controlling for the subtypes, as is done in Table 5.3, we can see that it is the Club Men, and not the Spectators, who seem to be the principal defenders of existing arrangements. Every one of them opposes changing the structure. And eight out of ten also oppose overlooking the rules. Their general orientation was captured best by this member of the Speaker's Panel who, throughout his interview, repeated again and again that "it's a marvelous, fascinating place that works very well." The contrast between the Club Men and the Spectators makes these results particularly striking, for whereas Club Men are twice as likely as other backbenchers to oppose changes, Spectators stand on the opposite side of the line. Nearly two-thirds of them wouldn't at all mind some of the institutional tinkering that Club Men fear.

Let us consider several post hoc speculations about the Spectators' attitudes. Their transcripts demonstrate that, like the Club Men, they are primarily interested in the institution. But, unlike the Club Men, they are more interested in its theater than in its traditions. And some reforms that threaten the traditions might, in fact, improve the theater. At the time of the interviews, the most controversial reform was the proposal to bring television cameras into the Chamber. This Club Man's reaction summarizes the story: "Television is the great enemy of Parliament. . . . The presentation of news and public affairs on television is done mostly from the point of view of entertainment . . . and therefore what we do would tend to become completely trivialized. . . . The people who provide the views on television have got to be entertainers . . . and the views are black and white . . . because the dicey shades of grey are dull."[30] Another possible post hoc explanation for the Spectators' attitude is that many of them do not receive the respect that they believe they deserve. They do not get nearly as much respect as do Club Men, even part-time Club Men like Knights of the Shires. It would be surprising if they weren't at least a little resentful toward an institution that fails to take them as seriously as they would like. They might, in their own way, cherish the House, but that doesn't require defending everything about an institution that has, in its own way, disappointed them.

In sum, Club Men are determined to do things as they have been done in the past. For them, "the rationale for the way we do things here is how Members of Parliament have done it many times." Spectators, who are more interested in watching things get done—and the more dramatic the production, the better—seem less concerned that nothing be changed or disturbed. Throughout the 1970s, Ministers and Policy Advocates were accused of tinkering with the parliamentary rules of the game.[31] Spectators apparently worry less about this sort of thing than do Club Men, who "feel that the standard is slipping," who are very aware that "the whole of Parliament very largely runs by convention," and whose constant theme is "to uphold, if you like, the dignity of the House."

INCENTIVES: AFFILIATION, AVOCATION, RESPECT

Most of the emotional incentives that drive the role of the Parliament Man have been suggested in the review of what they do and don't do. It should be clear by this point, for example, that they are not driven by a burning desire for influence. One of the workhorses among senior Club Men put it this way: "I don't know that it gives me any particular satisfaction to tell the Minister that he must take a clause out of his Bill. It's a part of a day's work sometimes, but I wouldn't say that it sends me home rejoicing unless it was something of vital importance, that the world had been saved or something." The most common incentives are, instead, those found in the notes that Sir Samuel Roberts, our interwar Parliament Man, made for his family history: affiliation, avocation, and respect. "The best thing of all about the House," Sir Samuel wrote, "was the opportunity of making friends, some for an hour, some for a lifetime."[32] Second, "it gave me plenty of work to do." And finally, it provided the satisfaction of becoming "a highly respected old Private Member."

The emotional incentive that Club Men discuss most is the desire for affiliation, which has been found in studies of politicians in other countries to be less uncommon than one might expect.[33] More than any other group in the House, Club Men appreciate Westminster's agreeable social life. They are pleasant to interview and pleasant to be with because, as they like to say, "I'm the convivial sort. And I like people, I get on well with most of them." And if they didn't have the House of Commons, "it would be a sort of political loneliness where I'd be sitting at home watching television and reading . . . I'd miss the contact with people." That was a Good House of Commons Man speaking; but, in this respect, his views are very difficult to distinguish from those of part-timers like the active company director who finds "it's fun to have friends here, and an agreeable social life mixed up with the work, you know . . . I like, I like the House of Commons," or the Knights of the Shires who think, "It's very *nice* to come up to London two or three days a week; you know, to come . . . up from the country to the centre of things and meet all one's friends . . . I enjoy the contacts with them immensely."

Club Men enjoy Westminster a great deal and talk about its attractions far more than do other backbenchers. They don't forget that there is a life outside. In fact, many of them enjoy a very active life outside. But what draws them to the House has much to do with the simple pleasure that Sir Samuel took in "the opportunity of making friends" in the "best club in Europe." "This is what is really the challenge of politics—people," a contemporary Club Man said. "In Durham, I suppose in Yorkshire as well," he continued, "we've got a saying, 'There's nowt funnier than folk.' This is what makes them so fascinating." For others, particularly those who have been to public schools, it "is the tremendous camaraderie amongst you all. We may all be mad, I suppose, I don't know, but there is a camaraderie . . . the camaraderie of the people that you've sweated through committees with, been cooped up in committee rooms, and so on and so forth." Over the years, Club Men find not only "that one's friends here are good and there's a sense of common cause which is fun," but also that it is like being at school: "Well, it's like being at school. I suppose people use that expression because it is . . . it's a way of life," a way of life that reminds them of the sort of camaraderie and companionship associated with having been "a member of a rugger fifteen, a rowing eight."

For this uniquely "anticlub" Club Man, even irritating his companions is a pleasure: "Well, I think I enjoy most at the moment, because of my great age, deflating people. You see, I listen to a conversation, say between three other people at a table in the Dining Room . . . say on this Jenkins business which arose yesterday. I said, 'Yes, a very good speech, but I've heard it so many times before.' You see, and then I proceeded to lay down . . . my reasons—and I must tell you they all shut up! I get a kick out of that." He isn't as convivial as many of his colleagues, but he shares their view that "they say it's the best club in the world, and I think this is true."[34]

It also keeps you going. Another incentive that Club Men say they find in their role is the avocation it provides: it keeps them busy with important activities that need to be done. This is particularly apparent in the transcripts of the full-timers, one of whom, when he was out of the House for five years, missed most "the simple fact that I wasn't as busy as I was previously." Others describe the club as a place "where they don't have to listen to things they don't want people to tell them," and can instead "argue amongst ourselves rather than be argued at by our friends and neighbors and constituents." In short, the role offers a minor occupation, a distraction, a tonic against boredom. It becomes for some of the most clubbable Parliament Men very difficult to do without unless one can find "something very secure and dedicated one can put in its place. I think this is a reason why Members of Parliament hang on so long. I'd find it very difficult to replace this job. I don't know how I shall." "We full-timers need this," another explained. "And this is why it would be a greater loss to me to leave here because it is more my life than it is for some . . . if I were to leave this place I would feel quite lost, because it is so much of one's life. I rarely get home before midnight." Part-timers have weaker commitments and a lighter touch. But they too can find in the role an attractive avocation, attractive because it offers a useful job and an escape from boredom. First, a nineteenth-century illustration from Trollope: "If he be an idle man with a large fortune it may be nice to have a place to go."[35] Then one from a member of our sample: "What other useful job can you do. I mean it is. If you look at it: if you've got a nice home and live in the country, and want to help a little, it's a jolly good job. You get twenty-two weeks holiday a year, and you have a nice constituency, and it does keep you going, it does, it's a marvelous life . . . a Conservative politician, provided you've got some, that you don't have to earn your own living, I mean, you know, a Conservative politician with a nice constituency and lovely holidays, it's marvelous, it's great fun."

The Club Man's emotional incentives also include a desire to be respected, albeit this desire is expressed in different tones from those used by the Spectator. Club Men are more self-confident than Spectators; they can command the respect of their colleagues, and they know it. But respect requires reconfirmation. And this reconfirmation is gained from "being on the Speaker's Panel and the responsibility that that's brought, and the unique corner, niche if you care to call it that, that it's given me in this House. And the regard and respect of good camaraderie that it's brought to me has more than compensated for many of the frustrations involved."[36] Most Club Men regard themselves as successful; and, while they like to see their status reconfirmed, they can afford to be more relaxed about it than Spectators seem to be. They are aware "that I know the chap who will make the decision, and I can go along to him and say, 'Now you really are making a hash of this one.' " They are aware that "I mean, you know, I'm on the biggest committee, the top committee." They are aware that being on the Speaker's Panel of Chairmen, for instance, is "something that can only happen to a very small number of people in their lifetime here." Another member of the Speaker's Panel describes a situation that illustrates both the confirmation and the confidence, and also an amusing exception to the rule that Club Men are politicians who have given up on power altogether: "I always like . . . taking the Chair in the House . . . doing that is I feel not an achievement but an experience. It's rather nice to preside over the House of Commons and think if you press an order for a division you send off all sorts of important people [chuckle]."

Parliament Men focus their attitudes and activities on the House of Commons as an institution. The eighteenth century may have been their heyday, but only very recently have they become such a small minority on the backbenches. Thus, they were familiar figures throughout the nineteenth century and were still a presence as late as the interwar period. The modern players of this traditional backbench role have been divided into three subtypes: Status Seekers, of which there are extremely few; Spectators, who are more likely to be Labour than Conservative; and Club Men, who help keep the institution ticking over.

Status Seekers are marginal members, prickly people whose interest in the House of Commons concerns mainly the opportunity it provides to puff up their images. Happily, very few backbenchers make this their principal role, although a substantial minority echoes the sentiments in more tolerable tones. Such echoes can be heard particularly among Spectators who don't do much in the constituency or in advocacy, and don't have much hope about achieving office either. Instead, they are at Westminster mainly for the feeling of importance it gives them and for the sense of competence they derive from being small cogs in a big machine. Yet the House isn't really their home, for though they certainly aren't misfits like the Status Seekers, their role isn't much appreciated either, and they are more ambivalent about the institution than they appear at first glance to be.

Club Men, the third subtype, are the most interesting of the lot. They are the genuine institutional patriots and institutional conservatives and, probably because they embody traditional aspects of the parliament man role, they tend to be more respected by their colleagues than do either the Status Seekers or the Spectators. There are two varieties of Club Men, part-timers and Good House of Commons Men, both of whom sound confident and pleased with their roles. Like Spectators, Club Men are not keen on constituency chores and are pleased to delegate them whenever they can. But compared to Spectators, they have a stronger dislike for policy advocacy, because they think there is too much legislation, and because they find the eager beavers irritating as well as amusing. The eager beavers are irritating because their activities threaten to disturb Westminster's traditions and its agreeable atmosphere—and it is this agreeable atmosphere that keeps Club Men going and satisfies their desires for affiliation.

The role of the Parliament Man draws attention to two variables: the clarity of established expectations and the power of established expectations. What stimulates us to think about both is the fact that the proportion of eccentrics in the parliament man role is very high, even higher than among Policy Advocates. This might be evident already from the composite portraits I have presented of Status Seekers, Spectators, and Club Men. Individual examples make the point more vividly. Status Seekers, for instance, include the working-class Tory who, monocle in place, meets Ministers in lavatories, characterizes himself as "on the fringe of your Powells and your Heaths," and would like to see Parliament, "which started in a pub," become more of a pub-like place in which he might feel more comfortable. Spectators include the curious Yorkshire journalist who claims to know "exactly what people are thinking," talks about journeying to Germany, France, or Barbados "not at your own expense, you see," and sits on the edge of his bench gesticulating in a hyperactive manner that suggests he is about to dash off to these foreign parts at any moment.

Eccentrics abound among Club Men too, particularly among the part-timers. One of them is surely the rich, crotchety Labour businessman, the anticlub Club Man who characterizes himself as a happy bully who loves to deflate and discomfit his colleagues. The label "eccentric" is today applied as well to Knights of the Shires, the archetypal Parliament Men; for today, Knights of the Shires sound just a little anachronistic as they make their amusing comments about the tiresome MPs who always want to legislate, about Select Committees that are occupational therapy, and about how if you "want to help a little, it's a jolly good job." In fact, this chapter has information about the few remaining Knights only because one of them decided that, since he and his friends avoided interviews like the plague, their role was not being properly portrayed. He therefore sought me out and very kindly introduced me round to make sure that I met his friends as well.

The English usually tolerate eccentrics and sometimes celebrate them. Certainly there have always been eccentrics in the House of Commons. But why is the proportion so high among Parliament Men in particular? Two reasons seem plausible. First of all, there are extremely few established expectations for how Parliament Men should behave. Their roles lack clarity. They are residual roles and therefore very poorly crystallized. Increasingly, these have become "exit" roles taken up by Members who have lost interest in constituency work, advocacy, or office seeking. Thus, backbenchers choose the role of the Parliament Man for many different reasons: status or importance or affiliation on the individual side; outside interests or age or even incompetence on the opportunities side. Their interpretations of the role are therefore very singular: their subtypes have subtypes, and variety is the principal impression they make upon the observer. Parliament Men can be full-time or part-time, involved or detached, in Chamber or in committee, angry about the institution or enraptured by it.

The second reason for the high proportion of eccentrics playing the role of Parliament Man is closely related to the first. Not only are there very few clear expectations established for this role, but, in sharp contrast to the situation with Ministerial Aspirants, the power of these expectations, the force they might exert upon their players, is extremely weak. Since Parliament Men are so undefined in Westminster's world, very few backbenchers, Ministers, or members of the public care much about how Parliament Men play their roles. There does exist a subtype that is well established and well respected. Thus, the Good House of Commons Man represents the most valued mode in which the role of Parliament Man is played. Everyone knows, and more or less appreciates, that the Good House of Commons Man is full-time, chairs committees, defends the institution, and helps with services and accommodations. But the fact that this "sub-subrole" is played by such a small number of backbenchers only underscores the point that the expectations involved are likely to be few and weak.

Parliament Men differ from Constituency Members more than they do from the players of any other backbench role. They differ first, of course, by the arena to which they devote their primary attention: Constituency Members are more at home in their constituencies, whereas Parliament Men prefer their House of Commons. But equally striking is the degree to which their roles differ in crystallization. The role of the Constituency Member is one of the most clearly defined on the backbenches. It has a name that is recognized by constituents and Members of Parliament alike. Even its subtypes, Welfare Officers and Local Promoters, are well known, as are the duties and responsibilities that are expected of them. By contrast, the role of the Parliament Man is one of the least clearly defined that backbenchers can play. Its subtypes are recognizable, but except for the Good House of Commons Man, not widely recognized—and Good House of Commons Men, like Harold Gurden or Sir Ronald Russell, would be recognized only within Westminster's precincts. Beyond the fact that Parliament Men all focus primarily on the House as an institution, variety is the strongest impression that they create.

Actually, not just the role of Parliament Man but *all* of the backbench preference roles we have examined seem less constrained than is usually assumed by either structural or interactionist approaches to the subject. Even the Constituency Member, the clearest backbench role, offers vast opportunities for developing interpretations to suit individual preferences. It is often suggested theoretically that the greatest constraints in complex organizations are imposed upon followers rather than upon leaders, upon those at the bottom rather than upon those at the top of institutional hierarchies. Obviously this generalization does not apply to roles in the House of Commons, for the House of Commons is a hierarchical institution that offers much more choice below decks than above. Thus it was a backbencher, rather than a role theorist, who captured most succinctly the spirit of these situations: "Each man makes his own role; that's what it comes to, you know."

LEADERSHIP ROLES

All the world's a stage,
And all the men and women merely players:
They have their exits and their entrances;
And one man in his time plays many parts.

Shakespeare, *As You Like It*

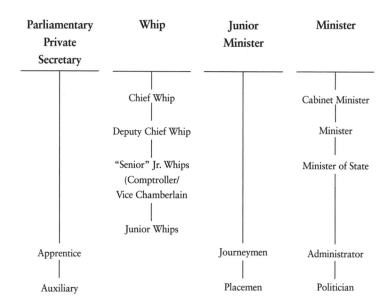

Parliamentary Private Secretary	Whip	Junior Minister	Minister
	Chief Whip		Cabinet Minister
	Deputy Chief Whip		Minister
	"Senior" Jr. Whips (Comptroller/ Vice Chamberlain		Minister of State
	Junior Whips		
Apprentice		Journeymen	Administrator
Auxiliary		Placemen	Politician

LEADERSHIP ROLES IN PARLIAMENT

AT WESTMINSTER nearly everything seems divided along party lines. But with parliamentary roles, the division lies less between the parties than between the frontbenches and the backbenches, between the roles that count as Members of the Government or Opposition Front Bench Spokesmen and the roles that do not. This was explained by a "Minister Designate" as follows: "One of the great things that isn't generally realized outside is that there are *two entirely separate situations* here. There is the Minister and the Minister Designate, and the Minister in Opposition and the Minister Designate in Opposition—who are one stream of people, the Executive and the Shadow Executive. And then there's another stream of people, the ordinary backbenchers who serve on the party committees and may in a highly specialist way be involved in policy making."

The "separate situations" are created by the rules of British parliamentary government that both distinguish the Executive from Parliament and allow it to control Parliament. The Executive thereby becomes the "buckle" that connects the Ministries with Parliament. Ministers manage Ministries, and they manage Parliament. They have two offices, one in Whitehall, one in Westminster. And their positions have two distinct sides, each embedded in a distinct institutional context. These contexts are connected by sets of informal and formal rules. The most important informal rules see to it that most Members of the Government, particularly those in key positions, will also be Members of the House of Commons with constituencies and voting privileges—and roots in Westminster. The most important formal rules make the Executive's right to govern dependent upon retaining the confidence of the House. Thus, the structure of the situation ensures that Ministers come to Westminster to present their departments and themselves. It also ensures, as we shall see, that they come not so much to plead with Parliament as to preside over it.

Frontbench roles are far better defined than backbench roles because the parliamentary parties care far more about how frontbench roles are performed. The proper performance of these roles is critical for winning power and for exercising it effectively. Hence, frontbench roles are fastened to well-defined positions that prescribe how their parts are to be played by specifying their principal goals, beliefs, and behaviors. A "well-defined" position is one to which many specific duties and responsibilities are assigned. Such assignments make Parliament's leadership roles "position" roles that are highly crystallized and constrained.[1] The positions of Parliamentary Private Secretary, Whip, Junior Minister, and Minister are each equivalent to the position of the backbencher in that each refers to just *one position* in Parliament's institutional structure. But none of these leadership positions has associated with it anything like the four main preference roles and their twelve subtypes that are associated with the position of the backbencher.

Moreover, everyone knows exactly who the Parliamentary Private Secretaries, Whips, Junior Ministers, and Ministers are. There is no need to develop a special methodology to identify them. Their names can be read in published lists. We can proceed, therefore, by carrying the motivational approach directly to the transcripts. Parliamentary Private Secretaries and Whips were asked about their duties and responsibilities and about their relationships with Ministers and backbenchers. They were also asked about the value of their work as an apprenticeship for ministerial office. Junior Ministers and Ministers were likewise questioned about the principal duties and responsibilities of their roles, particularly with regard to performances at Westminster. They discussed the significance of reputations in the House and how the House could be used as a "sounding board" for developing policy. They also talked about how they managed constituents, interest groups, the other side, their workloads, and their own political ambitions.

As I listened to them, however, I came to realize that even highly constrained position roles like these have their variations, that even where institutional rules trump individual goals, they cannot drive them out of the picture entirely. Leadership positions allow incumbents some space to make their own roles, to use their own reasoned judgments to construct their own interpretations according to their own individual preferences.[2] I have tried to reconstruct these interpretations and to probe my reconstructions with quantitative analyses. And, again, I have tried not just to construct interpretative explanations of these leadership roles but also to suggest naturalistic explanations for some of their origins and consequences. In addition, the following chapters explore role conflict, which refers to disagreements about how a role should be performed, and role overload, which refers to situations in which there are too many responsibilities and too little time to fulfill them.

Reconstructing frontbench position roles will help us understand how Parliament is both cajoled and controlled. And when Parliamentary Private Secretaries, Whips, Junior Ministers, and Ministers are located in the structure of this institution, we will have completed our examination of the roles, rules, and reasons that characterize Westminster's world.

PARLIAMENTARY
PRIVATE SECRETARIES:
FAGGING AT FORTY

I've never been one, and I'm not the sort.
Not a PPS

The first fact that is usually reported about Parliamentary Private Secretaries is that their position has no official standing.[1] The title Parliamentary Private Secretary is not found either in the Constitution or in legislation. This is not an official position in the Government; nor is it an official post in the House; nor does it command additional salary on top of the MP's salary. Nevertheless, the title refers to a well-established place in the leadership hierarchy: the first rung on the ladder leading from the backbenches to the Cabinet. Everyone at Westminster knows what a Parliamentary Private Secretary is. And everyone refers to this position by its initials, PPS.

The second fact usually reported about Parliamentary Private Secretaries is that their duties and responsibilities are defined by Ministers and defined differently among Ministers: "It's very much a matter for the Minister how he uses his PPS. Some PPSs are almost an additional Junior Minister in the department. Others hardly go to the department at all." And likewise in the House: "Sometimes the PPS fixes pairs and runs errands for his Minister and nothing more . . . and other times he's his highly confidential advisor." Nevertheless, the role does have a common core, one created by the constitutional connections between Government and Parliament. The doctrines of ministerial responsibility, collective and individual, compel Ministers to maintain channels of communication with backbenchers. Such channels include Parliamentary Private Secretaries, whose roles are, as we shall see, considerably more constrained than the roles of the backbencher, but considerably less constrained than the roles of the Whip with which they are often compared. The core is captured in two familiar phrases: "the Minister's eyes and ears" and "the Minister's dogsbody."

Parliamentary Private Secretaries are attached to individual Ministers rather than to departments. Those doing "double duty," as one out of three of our PPSs were doing, serve two Ministers in the same department, albeit one of them will nearly always be senior to the other and the PPS's primary commitment will nearly always be to him. A few PPSs have carried on after their Minister has left the scene, but normally the service is to the ministerial person rather than to the ministerial position, so much so that it is common for PPSs to follow their Ministers from post to post. During our interviews, one devoted PPS, Sir Clive Bossom, even followed his Minister into retirement.[2] The personal flavor of the relationship is conveyed in the remarks of this elderly PPS who has served his master for nearly a decade:

> And he said, "Well, this time I'm going to Technology. I'd like you to come with me again." I said, "I'd be only too flattered, of course." Well, five weeks later Iain Macleod died. And then he said he'd been appointed to the Common Market. I said, "I couldn't possibly join in the Common Market because I'm not sure I'm in favor of it." It was my election address. I said I would only vote for the Common Market if I was satisfied that the terms were right. "Well," he said, "that's damn funny. Look at my election address." His was the same. So I felt perfectly qualified, if those were his terms, to continue to operate with him.

The role of the PPS gradually became institutionalized after the turn of the century. And the number of PPSs gradually increased till, by 1960, nearly every Cabinet Minister who was not a peer, and most Ministers of State who were not peers, had their own PPSs, their own unpaid personal assistants.[3] The number of Parliamentary Private Secretaries has not, however, increased since 1960, despite a very steep climb in the number of Ministers appointed and therefore available to be served.[4] This is due to the concern, often expressed at Westminster, most pointedly by the Select Committee on Offices of Profit, that increasing the number of Parliamentary Private Secretaries increases the number of MPs whose criticism of the Government is muted—and thereby strengthens the Government's hold over the House.[5] From the perspective of those who are not Members of the Government, Ministers and PPSs are both part of the same "payroll vote," even if Parliamentary Private Secretaries are unpaid. They are on their way up and on the Government side of the fence. But they are the lowest stratum of appointees, "dogsbodies" too. This points to the role's most singular feature: it projects two quite different images, one dignified, the other derogatory. The dignified image is the "Minister's apprentice," a backbencher on his way to bigger and better things. The derogatory image is the "dogsbody," a "Minister's fag" who will not be promoted but will nonetheless serve as errand-runner and political batman.[6]

All PPSs recognize that their role has these two faces; and many wish therefore to "play" the role of Minister's apprentice while "playing at" the role of dogsbody. To play a role suggests a serious attitude and a serious involvement, whereas playing at a role suggests a situation of make-believe that is associated with the concept of role distance.[7] The typical Parliamentary Private Secretary has been identified as a candidate for bigger and better things but is required to perform tasks that are uncharacteristic of the offices to which he aspires, tasks that may be seen as demeaning. In order to advance, he must perform them effectively. Yet, while doing so he may seek to make clear, to himself and to others, that he does not possess the traits of character that might be attributed to someone who helps the Minister on with his coat. Such tasks are mainly associated with only one of the role's three principal goals: lightening the ministerial load. Its other two goals are politically and constitutionally more important: communicating with backbenchers and learning the ministerial trade.

Facilitating communication between Ministers and backbenchers is the Parliamentary Private Secretary's most politically significant responsibility. Thus, he makes himself available to backbenchers to explain the Minister's views and to convey their problems back to the Minister. This PPS has been through the role once before and understands it well: "A PPS's principal job of course is in the House as the 'link man' between her Minister and the backbenches. And it's her job to see that her Minister gets well informed. It's her job to see that backbenchers who've got a beef about something have the chance of a word with him. It's her job all the time to see that she is keeping her Minister in touch with what members of the party committee, and those who are interested in the particular subject of her department, are thinking, worrying about, keeping her Minister in touch with what pressures are building up before they actually burst forth." So "he's a 'link man,' really"—as another PPS, who was a former Whip, also put it.

Whips are link men too. And commentators often bracket the two roles together. PPSs do not disagree with this comparison so much as disregard it. Not even the two former Whips among our PPSs brought it up, despite having many opportunities to do so. The reason that this comparison isn't salient to Parliamentary Private Secretaries illuminates the nature of their

contribution to communication, and their status too. While the PPS is casually communicating information about one particular subject and one particular Minister, the Whips "have this very *important* function of finding
out what the party *as a whole* thinks about issues and getting the message
across." Moreover, Whips have so many other important responsibilities:
"they make the party machine tick over in the House . . . they are the orga-
nizers of parliamentary business." They seem so much more busy and so
much more important than PPSs.[8] Descriptions of career ladders may count
the positions of Parliamentary Private Secretaries and Whips as equal bottom rungs. But most PPSs regard Whips as more involved and more influential.

The third career goal in the motivational core of the Parliamentary Private
Secretary's role is learning the ministerial trade. Those Parliamentary Private
Secretaries who are Minister's apprentices are expected to observe closely
how the Minister manages both his department and the House. This is an
apprenticeship that, again, PPSs share with the Whips. And just as some
PPSs envy the Whips their more professional approach to communication,
they also suspect that the Whips' promotion prospects are, at least on the
Conservative side, somewhat better than their own: "I think it's almost possible to say, if you become a PPS, 'Oh, jolly good recognition,' but it doesn't
mean to say that you are going to go from there to sort of fill the ranks of
a Junior Minister one day. . . . I think under this Prime Minister particular
importance is attached to the Whip's Office. And I think you might get
brought into the Whip's Office fairly early on as a distinct sort of first step."

"All PPSs don't become Junior Ministers." But then not all PPSs expect
to become Junior Ministers either. Some see themselves as Apprentices, and
some do not.

Subtypes and Distributions

Since the role of the Parliamentary Private Secretary is not as constrained
as the role of the Whip, it can be played in a variety of ways. But because
the role of the Parliamentary Private Secretary is not nearly as unconstrained
as are backbench roles, its subtypes are fewer and are fashioned more by
the expectations of superiors than by the preferences of players. The results
are two different types of "Minister's eyes and ears in the House," Apprentices and Auxiliaries, which are familiar to backbenchers, Ministers, and
PPSs alike.

APPRENTICES

"The House of Commons is the college, if you like, from which the Ministry is picked," explained the confident young Apprentice who was singled out in the London diaries as this year's rising star. "I'm not a Minister and may never be, but I serve now as a Parliamentary Private Secretary, you know. And if I ever do become a Minister, I certainly would regard this as an apprenticeship, a way of learning the job of being a senior politician." All Apprentices regard their work as an apprenticeship and tend to be eager and energetic as well as ambitious. Many have a nose for power and would prefer to be "a PPS to a Minister who has considerable personal influence . . . whose influence extends beyond his own department . . . a Cabinet Minister." Unfortunately, as Table 6.1 suggests, Cabinet Ministers would rather be served by Auxiliaries than by Apprentices; and most Parliamentary Private Secretaries must therefore learn the trade below the top.

Their principal goal, they say, is to see how "the Ministerial side of it" operates. If they are lucky, for instance, they may be able to help their Minister conduct "at least one Bill the whole way through the House, through the committee stage, the report stage, and the lot." They would also like to acquire a first-hand understanding "of the border area between Parliament and Government . . . and one sees this essential interlocking between the Whitehall work and the Westminster work—this has been the most interesting thing, and takes a good deal of time." It takes time and patience, particularly to get a glimpse of how government works from the Whitehall side, for Whitehall does not welcome these eager observers, who therefore try to exploit every available opportunity: "I can't go regularly to the Ministry, but particularly at crisis times I'm able to get over there to try to help the Minister with odds and ends."

There one sees the relationships between civil servants and Ministers, "how the machine works and how stuff is fed into the Minister and how he takes deputations and all this sort of thing." The point is to observe the Minister and to make your own judgments for future reference: "You see how he's influenced by civil servants, you are able to evaluate the advice given by civil servants because you can then judge the effect of that advice on the Minister. I think it's an invaluable experience if your Minister allows you to see the way in which he operates . . . if you're allowed to evaluate what he does and the advice he receives and the way he translates that in political action—and I think it's a tremendous experience."[9] A few very fortunate PPSs are treated by their Ministers almost like Junior Ministers, the next rung up the ladder, or at least like those Junior Ministers who are confined to minimal responsibilities. At the other end of the spectrum are the Ministers who "hardly use their PPSs in their departments at all because the nature of their job is not worrying enough or interesting enough for that to be necessary."

The ideal situation is to work for a Minister who becomes your mentor. It is a great advantage to develop a personal relationship with a senior Minister, to take part in conversations with him, travel with him, feel as though one is being guided by experienced hands. "It's very much of a personal relationship. It was because I admired and liked Tony Crosland long before I became his PPS, that I was glad to do this and got a lot of satisfaction out of doing it." In the best of all possible worlds, mentors become patrons and facilitate the Apprentice's promotion. The danger, of course, is that much then depends on whether the Minister's own fortunes rise or fall. Senior Ministers are the safest bet, but there are always potential shipwrecks over which one has no control: "I was PPS to three senior Ministers all of whom were sacked. . . . No hard feelings about that, but they all went, and I haven't been a PPS since." Nor was he promoted.

Apprentices emphasize that the role of the PPS is an apprenticeship: "If one has no desire for ministerial office, obviously one wouldn't be interested in being a PPS." But they are speaking for themselves, not for the Auxiliaries, who, as Table 6.1 shows, constitute one out of four PPSs. And just as Local Promoters do not like to be mistaken for Welfare Officers, so Apprentices wish to distinguish themselves from Auxiliaries, about whom they sometimes speak a little unkindly: "You do get the older style PPS, old age and so on, who may be a person who has been bypassed for everything else."

Apprentices and Auxiliaries are easy to spot. They were identified by their

Table 6.1 Parliamentary Private Secretaries: Subtypes by age, tenure, and rank served

Subtype	N	Average age	Average tenure	Rank served*	
				Cabinet (%)	Non-Cabinet (%)
Apprentice	(27)	40	4	30	70
Auxiliary	(10)	51	9	70	30
Total				100	100

*$p \leq .05$

responses to questions about the role of the PPS, its significance as an apprenticeship, and their ambitions for achieving promotion. Those who had ambitions and described their role as an apprenticeship for ministerial office were counted as Apprentices; those who had no further ambitions and described their role not as an apprenticeship but rather as a matter of giving service were counted as Auxiliaries.[10]

The table reports on the twenty-seven Apprentices and ten Auxiliaries on the Government side who were interviewed for the study. It can readily be seen that the typical Apprentice is, by Westminster's reckoning, very young. The average age is forty; and more than half are between the ages of thirty-three and forty-one. Apprentices are also newcomers. Their average number of years in the House is only four, with nearly all of them at less than six. Furthermore, there is an "apprenticeship" for Apprentices who serve Cabinet Ministers. All those who do so are somewhat older than the others, or somewhat longer in tenure's tooth. At the lower end of the ministerial hierarchy, only Apprentices serve Junior Ministers exclusively; and it is mainly Apprentices who do double duty by serving, at the same time, both a Junior Minister and a senior Minister in the same department.

AUXILIARIES

Auxiliaries are older than Apprentices. Their average age is fifty-one, with six out of ten over fifty. Compared to Apprentices, they also have twice the tenure, as can be seen in Table 6.1. Nearly all of them have been at Westminster for at least eight seasons. Auxiliaries have experience, which is why Members of the Cabinet prefer them. And Auxiliaries prefer Members of the Cabinet. If they aren't going to get office themselves, they are at least going to get close to power: "I think if you're a PPS to a senior Minister," said one, "this is tremendously useful because obviously you get a feeling of being in the Government. I doubt if this is true if you're a PPS to a Junior Minister." Seven out of ten Auxiliaries serve Cabinet Ministers, while the others serve full Ministers outside the Cabinet.

Auxiliaries are not being groomed for office. They are not Apprentices: "Serving as a PPS of course is one of the things which . . . often leads to ministerial office. But there are plenty of exceptions to that, er, including myself," noted an Auxiliary who had been in the House for thirteen years and was no longer a promising young man. "There are exceptions, and clearly there are people like myself who are PPSs to Cabinet Ministers who are not themselves going to be Ministers." They seek intrinsic satisfactions from the role rather than instrumental opportunities. Auxiliaries concentrate on the goal of helping senior Ministers. "It's a matter of giving service, as I see it . . . you give your service." Several, when they were "newish Members," played the role of the Apprentice and sought "to learn the ministerial ropes." But that was "the first time round." Then they didn't rise, stayed out of it for a while, and eventually returned with a new approach: "This last time of course it's been slightly different."

Auxiliaries "spend very little time at the Ministry." Because they are not being groomed for ministerial office, they focus on Westminster, "and I confine myself almost entirely to the aspect of the relation of the Minister to the MPs." This serves the needs of Cabinet Ministers, who very much need to maintain good relations with backbenchers in the House, and very much need a PPS who is "somebody with a fair knowledge of the workings of the House and who might be able to be of assistance." Thus, the typical Auxiliary is likely to be a quiet, older man who desires to perform a useful service because he has a talent for working with MPs at Westminster or a talent in the subject area itself. Some become friends and confidants to the Ministers they serve. Such friendships are rarely equal but can nevertheless be very satisfying. Thus, among the most satisfied PPSs are "older Members who are taken in really by the Minister as confidants." Three out of ten Auxiliaries called themselves confidants or described themselves as friends and advisors. Cabinet Ministers, they said, can be indiscreet when they know their PPSs well enough to "let their hair down" and "kick around ideas." For the seasoned Auxiliary, this is the role's promise, the prize that offers a dignity and a satisfaction to match that of the Apprentice who has found a mentor to promote his or her career: "I mean there are a number of people who become PPSs to Junior Ministers or to Ministers who don't use their PPSs in this sort of way. But if you are going to use your PPS as somebody who has no axe to grind, somebody who can jump up and say, 'Don't you think that's not really the thing for us to have done?' or 'Don't you think the Government ought to do this?' If you're going to use him in that sort of way (which is a much more interesting way for him), then he ought to be somebody who has at least learned the ropes and established himself in the House."

Nearly always he is someone who has at least established himself in the House: "I almost feel I'm the 'Father' of Parliamentary Private Secretaries, I've been at it so long." But most Parliamentary Private Secretaries aren't at it for very long at all.[11] The overwhelming majority serve for three years or less, and most serve for no more than two.[12] These data fit the assumption at Westminster that PPSs who are in harness for a short period of time are Apprentices—who either quickly move up to become Junior Ministers or quickly leave the role behind. Those who stay (the 10 percent or more who serve at least five years) are usually Auxiliaries, a few of whom even come back for a second go.

SPECIAL CASES

"The Prime Minister's PPS," other PPSs told us, "enjoys a rather special position." This is the only PPS job "which is really different from the others," they said, for the PPS to the Prime Minister is usually a very influential player.[13] "He really is a very, very important person indeed in the party," because he has the attention of the Leader, and because he "works very closely with the Whips, obviously particularly with the Chief Whip." Compared to other PPSs, his involvement is magnified by his association with the Prime Minister's "sort of entourage the whole time, pretty well everything he does. If he goes abroad, one goes with him; whereas a PPS under normal circumstances does most of his work in the House." This involvement is also raised from the level of arranging a few appointments and meetings to the level of responsibilities normally associated with an aide-de-camp. Thus, he may be charged with seeing that "the P.M. gets to all his meetings" and, once there, "that he doesn't get too cornered," with seeing that he doesn't miss that person or this person, and with ensuring that, after they return to London, everyone they met "gets the necessary letters."

The eyes-and-ears take on a new significance because these are now eyes and ears for "the man on the throne." Like other PPSs, the PPS to the Prime Minister tries "to keep him informed about the attitudes of the party over major problems," in this case, major problems across the board. Thus, his PPS must be alert for politically dangerous developments wherever these may crop up and "at the same time be able to sort of tell one's own colleagues here what his reception was like in Singapore, how things worked out there, and sort of feeding it both ways to some extent." The PPS to the Prime Minister enjoys the top position in an informal hierarchy among PPSs: "Your status is determined by the rank of your Minister and by your relationship with him,"[14] although this hierarchy is not very well crystallized: "I mean obviously somebody who is a PPS to a Cabinet Minister is considered senior to small fry such as myself," volunteered a PPS who was serving two Undersecretaries at the time. Service near the top is valued because it associates one with power and because it is almost always "an important and interesting job in itself."

The other special case is the Opposition PPS, the Parliamentary Private Secretary to a Shadow Minister. This position is special because the "Minister" who is served is not a Minister, and the liaison undertaken by his PPS is not a liaison between Government and Parliament. When increases in the number of the Government's Parliamentary Private Secretaries were checked by constitutional considerations during the 1960s, the role's further developments began to be found in Opposition, albeit, "in Opposition it means very little to be a PPS, very little indeed. I mean it's not even formally recognized as a position"; nor were the players listed in published sources during the 1970s. Those I stumbled upon in the course of my interviews with Opposition backbenchers[15] had age and tenure characteristics very similar to those of the Governmental Apprentices. In fact, every Shadow PPS saw his or her role as that of a Shadow Apprentice. It had been suggested to them, they explained, "on more than one occasion," that the Shadow Minister or even the Leader might like to have the Shadow PPS in the team at some point.[16]

Since Shadow Ministers have no departments of their own, Shadow PPSs cannot explore the Whitehall side of ministerial life and so instead pursue idiosyncratic activities. One served as his master's campaign manager in the PLP's leadership election. Another traveled to New Zealand to gather views about the impact of EEC membership on that country's trade with Britain.[17] At the same time they also pursue many familiar duties and responsibilities: discussing issues with the Shadow Minister, helping with constituency correspondence, handling the odd meeting, listening in at strategy sessions, turning up at Question Time when it's the Shadow Minister's subject. But, unfortunately, "not much more than that. It's terribly informal."

Characteristic Attitudes and Activities

Comparisons with Whips and with Junior Ministers indicate the poles between which are found the PPS's performances. "It varies enormously from department to department," they say over and over again; "and it depends very much on the plans of the Minister." But there is nevertheless a common core, at the center of which lies the goal of facilitating communication: PPSs are expected to be on the alert at Westminster for backbench views that might concern their Ministers and departments.

TWO-WAY COMMUNICATION AT WESTMINSTER

Auxiliaries concentrate on communication at Westminster rather than poking around the Ministry. They therefore have time for other issue interests in the House and for other activities outside. Apprentices, by contrast, deal with communication at the House and then go on to do whatever they are permitted to do at the Ministry, where, unfortunately, they are never permitted to do as much as they would like: "I wouldn't say it's anything very special as an apprenticeship." The real work is the communication back at the House. Both Auxiliaries and Apprentices focus their attention on Westminster.

"Keeping the Minister *au fait* with opinion on the backbenches" isn't such a difficult job, because backbenchers themselves seek out PPSs. It is standard practice to approach the Parliamentary Private Secretary before putting down awkward Questions or bothering a Minister about minor constituency matters.[18] "Backbenchers regularly use the PPS as a channel to the Ministers," a very busy Auxiliary explained. "I think they do this because they appreciate the sheer demands on the time of the Minister, and they don't want to feel that Ministers are being button-holed every five minutes when they're moving about the House. . . . On minor matters, the MP will go to the PPS and say, 'Could you have a word with the Minister about this for me?'" And where the relationship between the PPS and the Minister is believed to be close, backbenchers will be more open about telling the PPS what he needs to know.

But to carry the House successfully, Ministers must dig behind even these requests and complaints. They therefore send back their Parliamentary Private Secretaries "to pick up the gossip a little bit more to feed back to one's Minister and to pick up a little bit more the currents of opinion that are going round on matters affecting the Home Office." These probes can become sensitive, for PPSs can stir up among backbenchers some of the same irritations that Whips raise: "You may be suspected by them because you're trying to listen in to find out what they're thinking about."[19] Many Ministers also expect their Parliamentary Private Secretaries to keep abreast of Opposition thinking and alert the Minister to possible arguments with which he or she may be assailed: "I mean very often Peter Walker wants to find out what people in the Opposition are thinking about a certain thing, so I go round and talk to them, or if they want to pass impressions to him they ask me to do it."

The point is to speak truth to power, "to make sure that if there is criticism going round of Michael Heseltine that he knows about it. And he's worried about that. He's got to carry the House." It is very desirable for the Minister to have a frank relationship with his PPS, for if he is wise he will want his PPS to brief him fully about discontents that backbenchers may feel toward his policies or conduct. It takes a certain amount of courage, and perhaps a little chutzpah, to tell "the Minister (and I think there are some Ministers who need to be told perhaps more than others) *exactly* how Parliament, their own colleagues, and other people outside, see them. And, you know, suggesting ways in which they might improve their communications." The value of frankness is another incentive that leads Cabinet Ministers (who need it most) to prefer Auxiliaries over Apprentices. Mindful of the Minister's influence over their promotion prospects, Apprentices may be too sycophantic to sit their Ministers down after the ten o'clock vote and tell them the things that they don't want to hear but need to know.

To test the atmosphere, Parliamentary Private Secretaries spend a considerable amount of time in social areas such as the lobbies and dining rooms: "I think you are useful to a Minister because if you sit in the Smoking Room, or talk to people in the lobbies or anywhere in the House, at meals, you can report back the general feeling, not only about his department but also what the general feeling of the party is."[20] Auxiliaries like to describe this responsibility as facilitating "the backbench demand for greater participation . . . Members of Parliament want greater participation in the decision-making process. And they use the PPS as their connecting link between the Minister, the government department, and Parliament itself. So I get many Members coming to me and saying, 'I believe such and such a thing is in the pipeline. I would like you to know that if it is, I'm very disturbed.' "

Another and perhaps more essential setting for gathering information is the backbench party committee, especially on the Conservative side of the House. Ministers expect their Parliamentary Private Secretaries to keep in touch with the officers of the backbench committees that focus on the department's topics, to attend these committees regularly, to take notes, and to report back.[21] PPSs likewise attend regularly the weekly meetings of the Conservative backbench 1922 Committee in order to survey the general atmosphere; but the backbench party committees are the most important source for up-to-date information about backbenchers' views. This becomes burdensome for those whose masters, like the Chancellor of the Exchequer, have interests across the board and expect their PPSs to "keep an eye on what's going on amongst them all." Such PPSs can be very busy indeed:

> As PPS to Geoffrey Rippon I attend every committee which involves anything to do with the Common Market. So my average is about five committees every day. . . . It is an unusual situation . . . impossible, in fact, because I sometimes must attend two meetings at the same time, two committees at the same time. I go to the opening of one, find a colleague I can trust, or another PPS, and say, "Look, I've got to go to the Forestry Committee. Would you mind giving me a report on what's happened because I've got to report to my Minister?" This last year nearly all the committees had the EEC somewhere on the agenda.

It has sometimes been said that Parliamentary Private Secretaries serve as officers of backbench party committees when their party is in Government, but there was no evidence of this during the 1970s. Quite the contrary. Our PPSs claimed that there is an informal rule under which "as a PPS I cannot be an officer of any such committees." They attend them regularly; but they attend them as representatives of the Government. They may have been officers in the past ("I was Vice Chairman of the Conservative Party's Employment Committee"), but they are not now, "because I'm now PPS to the Secretary of State for Employment and so I had to resign that."[22]

A more direct contribution to backbench participation is the PPS's responsibility to arrange appointments with the Minister for backbenchers who wish to pursue a policy matter or discuss a constituency case. These invitations are issued mainly to backbenchers who are threatening to behave awkwardly: "Maybe he's against some particular measure Peter's bringing in. Well, then I suggest they have a little chat together, and I arrange that." Apprentices see it as just another chore. But for Auxiliaries this can offer an opportunity to serve as a political impresario: "If I fail to persuade him I go and see John and I say, 'Look, so and so's got hold of the wrong end of the stick, and I think you could have a little chat with him and he'll better understand it.' And I bring him along, and try to take him to John's room at a suitable moment. . . . That's been my job, you see, that's why I'm more than happy being, er, happy being, er—which has been fascinating."

Parliamentary Private Secretaries spend much more time collecting information from backbenchers than telling backbenchers how it is. Still, "If somebody's made (as often happens) a stupid statement, a quite incorrect statement . . . afterwards I say to him, 'You know, that wasn't quite right.' And I try to persuade him, you know, that his facts are wrong." Backbenchers may simply want some explanation as to why some particular decision has been taken, or what the procedure is, or whether it is a subject on which the Minister could reasonably be asked to intervene. "This does look to me as though it's a matter for your Ministry. Is it?" or "This seems an absolute pig's ear of a decision, but maybe there's more to this than I realise?" Finally, the role involves not only persuading and dispensing explanations, but also pouring oil on troubled waters and placating the irate: "A senior backbencher rang my Minister very late one night and said, 'See here, I've heard rumours that you are about to announce some decisions on the third London airport, decisions with which I will be profoundly disappointed. Tomorrow I am going to give a radio interview on the subject.' Well, they rang me late that night (I was in bed) to say they had told Mr. X to ring me and that I would explain it all to him. I was able to placate him—which I did rather successfully."

The Parliamentary Private Secretary's behaviors that facilitate communication also involve explaining the Minister's position to the press. This may require letters to the editor "to set the record straight," as when Harold Wilson's PPS responded at length to Bernard Levin's criticisms of Wilson's performance as Leader of the Opposition. It may also require using personal contacts, as when the PPS has a friend who is an influential political journalist ("we were at Oxford together"): "and so contact was made and Willie Whitelaw had talks with him about the publication of ——, which came out a few weeks ago." In addition, the PPS may be instructed to seek out lobby correspondents who can be useful "channels to the public," channels for leaks to prepare the public for difficult announcements, channels for campaigns to amplify the Minister's themes by providing inside information on a nonattribution basis.[23]

PPSs attend the Standing Committees that consider Bills from their Minister's department. At these sessions, they may serve as supplementary Whips but are more likely to serve by sitting behind their Ministers and looking frustrated because they are unable to say anything. Their contribution is to help the Minister communicate enough to prevent revolts but not so much as to slow down the progress of his or her Bill. This drags on "week after week, and you can't write your letters or fill in your diary as other people tend to do when they're on committees if they're not interested in the subject. You've got to pay attention to every syllable that's uttered. It's damnable! You can't say a thing for yourself"—unless the Minister gives you permission, which rarely happens, but when it does it's like a breath of fresh air: "And so I was *actually* able to speak. And that's the only time I've spoken on a Standing Committee, because I've never been on a Standing Committee as anything but a PPS."

Parliamentary Private Secretaries facilitate communication wherever they go. In general, most of their role's beliefs and behaviors are played out within the precincts of the Palace of Westminster. Still, the exceptions to this rule are numerous enough to require that some notice be taken of them.

COMMUNICATION OUTSIDE WESTMINSTER

Communication outside Westminster "is not really my job," PPSs say. Many Ministers would regard such activities as dangerous, for PPSs are associated with their Ministers, and political views that they express in the country might be mistaken for the Ministers' own. Parliamentary Private Secretaries are, therefore, usually confined to Westminster.

Sometimes, however, they are given unusual ad hoc assignments, such as when Lord Chandos, as Colonial Secretary, used his PPS, Hugh Fraser, to undertake missions as his unofficial agent during the Mau Mau troubles in Kenya. More often, they are simply asked to stand in for the Minister at functions such as memorial services or to accompany the Minister at conferences abroad and receptions at home. Then, "a Parliamentary Private Secretary to a Minister ought to have big ears. . . . If you are with the Minister of Power, you meet people at the National Coal Board, the Central Electricity Generating Board, and you take note of their desires and convey them to the Minister." Occasionally, a PPS finds that he is "invited by some outside group or body or company or organisation, er, to some function, because I'm the Chancellor's PPS and they want to keep in touch with me." Several bring to their posts outside contacts that are useful to their masters. The Attorney General's PPS, for example, brought extensive contacts with colleagues at the Bar, "and the Attorney General attaches great importance to this . . . part of his duty . . . is to keep in touch with the profession."

Three out of ten PPSs work on some form of communication outside Westminster. Well-informed Auxiliaries are especially likely to be involved in such activities. Instead of spending time in Whitehall, they spend time outside where their contacts may prove especially useful to Ministers who are new and green: "And so I was more or less inducting him," explained a former managing director of one of the companies with which the Minister would soon be dealing; "six months to explain the industry to him and explaining him to the industry." "Oh indeed yes, yes," said another Auxiliary, "Chambers of Commerce, Chambers of Trade, the Institute of Chartered Accounts—I've had to keep a permanent contact with them." Sometimes it is just because the PPS is so well informed, such as this old hand at local government and development:

> Well, now normally I would be doing the job adequately if I kept in touch with the House of Commons and opinion amongst Members here. But I do in fact keep in touch with opinion outside. There are two means of doing this . . . through the public associations of local authorities who are joined together in the Rural District Council Association, the County Council Association. One keeps in touch with those in a respectful manner because they are really the people who are running the show . . . I go to them and ask them for their view and find out what they think and what the implications of such and such a thing may be.

Opposition PPSs are freer to pursue such activities because they are not subject to some of the formal role's constraints. What they say in the world outside is less likely to embarrass "the boss," and cannot embarrass a department. Nearly all Opposition PPSs are, therefore, quite active outside. They organize meetings, for instance, with all sorts of groups involved in their Shadow Minister's policy area to try to keep him up-to-date. In fact, such responsibilities are regarded as part of the role in Opposition. Thus, the PPS to the Shadow Minister for Health and Social Security keeps "in touch with as many people as possible who influence health and social security." And her involvement in these field activities sometimes goes beyond collecting information.[24] The PPS to the Shadow Minister for the Environment served energetically on the Executive Committee of the Association of London Housing Estates. The PPS to the Shadow Minister for Trade and Industry involved himself with the Upper Clyde Shipbuilders and Rolls Royce problems.

LIGHTENING THE LOAD AT WESTMINSTER

The Parliamentary Private Secretary's activities that lighten ministerial loads include some of the role's most attractive and least attractive aspects. These activities bring PPSs into proximity with power but, at the same time, make them feel as though they are fagging at forty.

At Westminster, the PPS is expected to keep track of the Minister's schedule and see "that he is aware that he's got to be in the Chamber to listen to a Question or answer a debate . . . keep him apprised of meetings and delegations and how the House is going on a particular day. I mean . . . you can't expect a Minister to sit watching the telly to see whether they're going to be required." It is also the PPS's job to arrange pairs so that the Minister can be away from the House on official business.[25] All PPSs also run errands. They are expected to help their Ministers during debates and Questions on the floor of the House of Commons by serving (in front of the eyes of the assembled House) as messenger boys. When the Minister is on duty in the Chamber, his Parliamentary Private Secretary sits behind him passing messages and remaining alert to the Minister's civil servants in the box at the end of the Chamber, who may have information to convey: "I mean if . . . he's stuck for an answer, you nip along to the officials' box and you try and get the answer for him quick so that he can employ the argument." In the same vein, the PPS must be ready to run messages throughout the Palace of Westminster and make quick calls to the department.

But most Parliamentary Private Secretaries have greater responsibilities. When the Minister is to answer Oral Questions in the Chamber, it is the duty of his PPS to watch the procedure carefully and make sure that the

Minister does not embarrass himself, to note which Questions are coming up and whether the MP who tabled them is in the Chamber. Just before Question Time begins, the PPS usually meets with the Minister and his officials to discuss difficult Questions that may be put. The most important duties, however, concern Oral Questions that seem designed to obscure supplementaries on which the Minister might become impaled. "So I have fairly frequent contact with the Clerk's Office on Parliamentary Questions who may ring up and say, 'Well, really, we're absolutely baffled as to what this Question means.'" Then the PPS may approach the Member who has put down the Question in order to find out more about it. Tact is essential because backbenchers regard Question Time as their opportunity to test the Minister's mettle and check the Executive. Hence, the PPS must give the impression that his master does not wish to undermine the exercise but simply wants to prepare helpful responses: "And if somebody puts a Question down and you read it and you say, 'Well what is it the man is really asking about?' And I think it's a perfectly useful service for the PPS to say, 'You've got a Question down on this, we want to give you as helpful an answer as possible, what particular aspect of it are you searching for?' . . . And then in the most elementary form you can ask the Member what he, what he, what he is really, what information it is he's after."

If the Minister wishes to make an announcement, he may send his PPS to find a backbencher willing to ask a prearranged Question and thereby give the Minister the opportunity.[26] This too is a delicate assignment because backbenchers regard "planted" Questions as attempts by Ministers to vault over the conventions of vigorous opposition and ministerial accountability. The PPS will emphasize, therefore, that this particular request is appropriate because the Minister wishes to announce important new information where it should be announced—in the House rather than in the press.

LIGHTENING THE LOAD IN THE DEPARTMENT?

PPSs keep in touch with civil servants who work in the Minister's Private Office on appointments and matters that are coming up in the House. But many of them, and not just Auxiliaries, say they "spend very little time at the Ministry." References to helping out at the Ministry are found more in academic commentaries about PPSs than in their own accounts of their roles. Eager as Apprentices are to enter this inner sanctum, once inside, the first thing they may be asked to do is "to pop back to the House of Commons to give the Minister's constituents cups of tea when they've come down to Westminster . . . find tickets for them in the Gallery." And, on their next visit to the department, likely as not they will be directed toward yet another aspect of life at Westminster: "And the Ministry involves me in a lot of the, er, how Questions, the whole business of how Questions are dealt with in the civil service."

A fortunate few are allowed to look in on "some of the lesser policy matters that aren't confidential," and may be given a small office and access to a small amount of "inside" information.[27] With this base, they can be in the department more often than most of their colleagues and can spend some time informing themselves about particular areas of policy. They may also be asked to help prepare a parliamentary speech or serve as a personal assistant in policy negotiations with other departments. Although these delights are few and far between, there have always been PPSs who have successfully integrated themselves into informal circles of advisors.[28] Some have even had access to Cabinet papers and papers of Cabinet Committees. At the opposite end of the spectrum a few PPSs have nothing but telephone contact with the department about the Minister's schedule. Most fall somewhere in between, depending, once again, "almost entirely on the wishes of the Minister, on the Minister's evaluation of the 'soundness' of his PPS, and on his own confidence and style. It also varies by department."

Contacts with civil servants in the department can be awkward because the Parliamentary Private Secretary has no authority there. Still, these are precisely the contacts that eager young Apprentices want to explore: "My contacts with the civil servants at the Home Office . . . it's getting quite good!" They aren't able to be demanding. And they don't want to be deferential. One way to handle it is to play the role of the Apprentice quite literally and invite a tutorial relationship: "I've set out to learn something about the subjects concerned," said the rising political son of a successful political father, and "have been regularly around to the Undersecretary, the Principal Undersecretary, and others in the department to find out about their subjects."

It is difficult because Parliamentary Private Secretaries have no formal connections with civil servants at all ("There's actually no reason why they should talk to me, but in fact they do, and I think I've established a relationship"). And civil servants seem to prefer it that way: "I understand that the Permanent Secretary has said, 'No, you don't haggle things in here, if the Minister wants to trust his PPS, fine, but none of my civil servants are going to pass papers to him.' " Whether or not this particular story is correct, most PPSs believe such stories. They also have their David and Goliath tales: "I mean the PPS to ——— was marvelous. I mean . . . he had part of the department terrified. You know, he was fond of saying, 'My job is to liaise with the backbenchers, and they bloody well want to know this—so *you* find it out.' He had a beautiful personality, he could get away with things." Among the civil servants, Parliamentary Private Secretaries "are very small fry. I mean you aren't of any importance, and nobody takes any notice of what you say because you aren't a Minister." The situation breeds irritation: "The relationship between a PPS and the civil service is one of complete hostility. And the civil service in fact do the very best they can to ignore him. He truly has no status other than that given to him by the Minister. And the civil service take full advantage of this. If I might say a word on the civil service. . . . I don't find them to be constructive-orientated. . . . They'd rather use anonymity as a means of either doing no job at all or only doing half a job. . . . They are negatively orientated. And I don't find the relationship satisfactory at all."

APPRENTICESHIPS FOR GOVERNMENT

The role of the Parliamentary Private Secretary is structured by three institutionally defined goals: facilitating communication, lightening the ministerial load, and learning the ministerial trade. The third of these, which is an apprenticeship goal, concerns learning by doing. And the principal activities involved are mainly those we have already examined.

Not all Parliamentary Private Secretaries see themselves as Apprentices. But those who do usually believe that the key learning experiences will be found in Whitehall rather than Westminster, that what's needed "primarily is a feel for Government and how it works rather than for the House." Unfortunately, they too spend far more time in the House than in the Ministry. What they learn there may be more important than they realize. For instance, their position in the two-way flow of communication offers insights into the system, the dangers, the moods of the House. And the tact that their role requires further sensitizes them to Westminster's folkways. This knowledge, often tacit, can be acquired through other experiences, through serving as a Whip, for example. But however learned, future Ministers need to learn it because Ministers need to understand the House. They need to know how to listen to backbenchers and how to sense dangers before they come into sight.

Other aspects of the two-way flow of communication are instructive as well. Keeping abreast of Opposition thinking makes Parliamentary Private Secretaries aware that it helps to have working relationships with the other side. Difficulties in telling Ministers what they don't want to hear sensitizes the PPS to the dangers of distorted political vision. Observing backbench party committees reveals how backbenchers organize to pressure Ministers. And explaining the Minister's thinking to these backbenchers helps teach a PPS why politics is the art of the possible and why sometimes half a loaf is better than none. Likewise, explaining the Minister's position to the press highlights the utility of the formal press release and perhaps also the inspired leak. There is even something to be learned from the tedium of sitting behind one's Minister in Standing Committee: the importance of strategic silence as well as strategic reasonableness toward the other side for getting one's business through expeditiously.

Fagging at Westminster can be instructive too. Keeping track of his Minister's schedule gives the PPS a good idea about what such schedules are like. Passing messages to the frontbench affords a Minister's-eye view of the Chamber. "This is one of the things that happens to a PPS, because he's got to sit behind his Minister on all sorts of occasions when, as an individual, he wouldn't be there. So you do see various sorts of debates. . . . You see all the processes." Sometimes fagging is little more than a demeaning initiation into the guild. But prompting at Question Time and helping Ministers prepare for Question Time is always very serious business. Here Parliamentary Private Secretaries learn how the game works and how dangerous it can be for Ministers who have not learned how to bell the cat.

Apprentices like to spend time in the Ministry even when they are assigned to work there on the Minister's constituency affairs or parliamentary Questions, to work on matters related to duties as *Parliamentary* Private Secretaries. Being in the Ministry gives them the opportunity to learn by observation. They learn how Ministers deal with constituents by watching Ministers deal with constituents. They learn how Ministers deal with Parliamentary Questions by observing how Parliamentary Questions are processed and answered. PPSs never see as much of Whitehall as they would like. But they see enough to observe the vast differences in deference shown there to the Minister and to themselves. As a result of the little humiliations, some become more determined to reach the top than they were before. And all become aware that the quality of their training depends greatly upon the dispositions of the Minister to whom they have been apprenticed: "It's very fortunate if you're Parliamentary Private Secretary to someone who takes an interest in you. This is the thing. You can be a Parliamentary Private Secretary to a man that doesn't take a damned bit of interest in you. . . . There are certain Ministers who will use them as apprentices and regard it as an apprenticeship to becoming a Minister. . . . The lucky young men in the House today are those who are Parliamentary Private Secretaries to bright, intelligent, helpful Ministers."

Constraints and Conformity

Parliamentary Private Secretaries are backbenchers, not Members of the Government. Yet governmental constraints are put upon their roles by extending to them the doctrine of collective responsibility.

SILENCE AND CENSORSHIP

Collective responsibility requires that Ministers not publicly criticize Government decisions. If they propose to do so, they are expected to resign first. During the 1970s, this doctrine sagged under the apparent impunity enjoyed by some dissident Ministers; but it was, at the same time, extended to Parliamentary Private Secretaries. The rationale was "simple logic": "just as the Minister's responsibility focuses on his Government, so the PPS's responsibility focuses on his Minister." And by virtue of this two-step flow of responsibility, the PPS became obliged, "more or less," to support the Government or to resign.[29] But because the PPS is not a Member of the Government, the justification for applying collective responsibility to his or her role derives loyalty to the Government entirely from personal loyalty to the Minister. It certainly sounds peculiar, even when expressed by PPSs who firmly believe "that that is right. Because very often whilst a policy may not come under the purview of his Minister, it may nevertheless be a cabinet decision. And if it is a cabinet decision, it is a decision of the whole Cabinet, of whom his Minister is one of them. Therefore if he starts kicking over the traces about a decision that is in fact a cabinet decision, he is in a sense criticizing his own Minister. So I feel if there is anything important like that, then he should consider well whether he should continue to be a PPS." Not all Parliamentary Private Secretaries accept the argument so readily. And since Ministers are often uncertain about it as well, there is some ambiguity about what PPSs should do.

There is, however, no ambiguity about collective responsibility's single most annoying constraint: those who play the role of Parliamentary Private Secretary must not speak in the House on subjects related to their Minister's department. This rule is straightforward and airtight: "And of course you can't speak about your own Minister's subjects, nor can you put down Questions about it," which would be another form of speech. The further rationale here is that PPSs may have access to confidential information. And even if they don't, they may be assumed by others to do so. In any event, they always have access to their Ministers' private comments and thoughts. Were they to speak publicly on departmental affairs, therefore, it would be unclear whether they were expressing departmental views or simply their own private opinions.[30] This could embarrass the department, make the relationship between the PPS and his Minister difficult, and possibly lead to breaches of trust.[31]

It isn't easy, especially when it is a subject in which the PPS has a special interest. PPSs make do by pursuing such subjects quietly, by making the most of what they pick up behind the scenes, and by pursuing other subjects in which they are also interested. It is most difficult for Welsh and Scottish MPs who serve Ministers in the Welsh and Scottish Offices, for nearly everything that interests them may fall within their department's scope and thus "debar me from talking about all the subjects that I know really well. . . . I cannot speak about Wales. And I would like to speak. And so I have to negotiate every time I want to speak on Wales, or even on a constituency matter, with my Secretary of State to see how far I can go."

Opposition PPSs, who are not so constrained, are very active in their contributions. On Oral Questions put down between 1970 and 1973, for instance, Opposition PPSs exceeded other backbenchers in their party by more than 50 percent. Government PPSs are not as active, for they must confine themselves to subjects that are not covered by their Ministers' departments. Nonetheless, during the same period they did ask Questions at a rate similar to that of the other backbenchers on their own side. In sum, the role's restrictions on asking parliamentary Questions are irritating but not sufficiently serious to make Parliamentary Private Secretaries vulnerable to the sort of criticisms that some Ministers and Whips get from their constituencies. There are problems for Scottish and Welsh MPs. But for most other PPSs, these can be handled by "taking your constituents into your confidence and saying, 'Look, I've got this job, I mean it prevents me from saying what I want to say for a period of time, and you must understand this.'"

PPSs worry more about being unable to pursue the issue interests that they have chosen as their specialization: "Very difficult. I used to go regularly to Chatham House and the Institute of Strategic Studies, but I find I seldom manage to get there now. . . . The subjects in which I can continue to take an interest are very narrow." It is a question of time, but also a question of censorship. Parliamentary Private Secretaries are most likely to feel aggrieved when they are censored on topics that are far from their Ministers' subject, when their roles exclude them from pursuing Early Day Motions, cross-voting, abstaining, or even simply stirring up a few coals, that is to say, from activities that are the prerogatives of other backbenchers.

They are expected to be more loyal than ordinary backbenchers in all these areas, but the rules are not precise. Some believe that if you sign Early

Day Motions, "well, you couldn't continue." Hasn't the Chief Whip told them to consult him first? Any public dissent could easily be misinterpreted, so the reasoning goes, as indicating that the dissenter's Minister disagrees with Government policy but has been overruled and silenced.[32] Yet PPSs wonder why it is not feasible for them simply to say in such circumstances, "I'm speaking just for myself," and to be believed. The scope of informal collective responsibility isn't very clear. Political journalists have reported that Parliamentary Private Secretaries must support the Government when they speak on nondepartmental topics, and that even constructive criticism is only "just about permissible."[33] But PPSs say it varies much more than that, both by the degree of dissent and by the arena where such dissent is presented. Certainly major attacks are not acceptable: "I think if I made a rip-roaring speech against the Government, well I'd probably stop being a PPS."

The key word is "restraint," restraint particularly in criticizing other Ministers and their departments, for these Ministers may long remember the stings and may even have a word with the young wasp's master. It was sometimes said during our interviews that the constraints were being relaxed.[34] Yet everyone seemed to have different interpretations. Perhaps closest to the mark was *The Spectator*'s political commentator "Tom Puzzle," who, using the example of then Conservative PPS Nick Scott, suggested that PPSs who wished to move up should exercise great care in publicly criticizing their own side. Scott hadn't moved up when expected, and this was attributed to his forceful attack on the Prime Minister's policy of arms for South Africa.[35]

BEHAVIOR: CROSS-VOTING AND CONFORMITY

Under the "two-step" interpretation of collective responsibility, "it is taken for granted that you will normally support your Government"; "there is a general assumption, yes, that you will obviously vote for your party, for your party's policies." PPSs are expected to be there when the payroll vote is called up.

A PPS has to have an extremely good reason for going against the party Whip, because "well, you don't want to weaken the Government in any way." Quite apart from endangering your own career, the system itself can break down: "Parties when they're in Government get their legislation through by having unity and achieving a majority vote consistently, and that's important." In discussing cross-voting and abstaining, PPSs put forward general arguments like these—but none of them puts forward the doctrine of collective responsibility. It's unpleasant to dwell on unpleasant subjects. It's also easy to overlook an ambiguous doctrine.[36] The ambiguity affords encouragement: most take the view that "the House would be none the worse for a little freer voting," including a little freer voting by themselves. The extent to which their conduct is successfully constrained can be seen in Table 6.2, which compares the cross-votes of Parliamentary Private Secretaries with those of other backbenchers between 1970 and 1973. These results may inflate slightly the cross-votes of PPSs, because several PPSs did not serve in their posts throughout all the months covered by the data.

PPSs believe that one or two cross-votes on constituency matters or even on very minor policy matters can register a legitimate protest and be done without any great harm. Three or more cross-votes, however, make independent spirits look like mavericks whose dispositions are probably incompatible with the role of a Parliamentary Private Secretary. The data are consistent with these rules of thumb. Parliamentary Private Secretaries are much less likely to cross-vote than are other backbenchers. Two-thirds never set foot into the other side's division lobbies, compared to less than a third of other backbenchers. And most PPSs who cross-vote do so only once or twice. Collective responsibility does not control them as effectively as it does Members of the Government. But it does keep them behind other backbenchers. These constraints are illuminated further by the behavior of Opposition PPSs, to whom the informal doctrine of collective responsibility does not apply: there is no difference at all between their cross-voting and cross-voting by other backbenchers in their party.

Conformity in the division lobbies is characteristic behavior for those who would play the role of the PPS. How much conformity depends above all, as with public speeches, on how closely the matter lies to the scope of one's

Table 6.2 Cross-voting of Parliamentary Private Secretaries and other backbenchers, in percent

Cross-votes	Other backbenchers*	PPS*
None	29	67
One or two	37	23
Three or more	34	10
Total	100	100
	(N = 345)	(N = 39)

*$p \leq .001$

department. "I mean if this was over a matter which concerned one's own department, then I think one would naturally feel obliged to resign as a PPS. If it was a matter that did not concern one's department directly, I would say that one wouldn't feel obliged to resign as a PPS—but one might be obliged to do so by the party machine." There were many stories about chats with the Chief Whip: "On that occasion I saw the Chief Whip and said, 'Look, I'm voting against the Government and that's that.' And he said, 'Well, what's it about?' And I told him, and he said, 'Well, that's all right.' In other circumstances I could see it would, uh, you know, you are expected to support the Government."[37]

Many new Parliamentary Private Secretaries are energetic, independent spirits. How do they manage to live with the role's constraints? One common explanation cites socialization but doesn't explain how it works: "It is quite remarkable that the most rebellious Members who arrive here, within certainly a year, sometimes even within six months, are completely part of the Establishment. . . . It's the system. It's nothing visible. Now you tell me how it happens. You tell me what the sanctions and controls are." We asked what would happen to a Parliamentary Private Secretary who began, one day, to disregard important informal rules and conventions. Not surprisingly, the answer was that "his Minister would tell him to push off." A prickly Parliamentary Private Secretary would be unable "to connect" with backbenchers. He would lose his utility as a two-way channel of communication: "Well, I think that if you were thought to be an outrageous Member of Parliament . . . the first thing that would happen would be that your Minister would drop you because you wouldn't be any good to him. You join the PPS system mainly to get around, to be on talking terms with other Members, and to rather act as eyes and ears and be able to keep him posted on what people are thinking about his policies. So you would be useless as a PPS if everybody thought you were a . . . chap . . . that nobody would want to talk to."

Opposition PPSs need not be quite so restrained. In fact, there were several whom it was difficult to imagine in the role of Government PPS at all: "I've probably blissfully broken all the traditions. I think all this is nonsense . . . I'm only here to represent my constituents and represent people in general. And if I can get . . . some degree of socialism into British society, then if I've got to tramp on traditions, be it ermine cloak or somebody's snuff box, then so be it." The rest were at least as independent as other backbenchers. In Opposition, PPSs tend to think and act very much like the other backbenchers in their parliamentary parties.

The role of the Parliamentary Private Secretary is difficult because "you are part of the Government in one way, but you're not getting access to any paper, you're not getting any of the privileges . . . that a Minister is given." "You can't sign motions," you can't speak on department matters, you can't criticize the Government, and you can't cross-vote either.[38] It isn't easy, particularly for Apprentices. They are the pick of the litter and usually include vigorous, independent backbenchers who are disposed to make it "absolutely clear" that, "at the end of the day, if you don't want me to be a rubber stamp, then I've got to have that freedom." They must learn to live with less freedom than they would like.

Role Distance

The most intriguing feature of the role of the Parliamentary Private Secretary is that it embodies two contradictory images: in the words of William James, an "actual image" and a "potential image."[39] The actual image is the Minister's fag. The potential image is the future Minister. PPSs would prefer, of course, to project the potential image to outsiders. Outsiders see this image, but they also see the Minister's fag. Commentaries by academics, for example, describe PPSs as apprentices, but they also describe their tasks as fetching and carrying, which are undignified pursuits for reasonably successful forty-year-old MPs. Likewise, journalists characterize the PPS as "at best an aide-de-camp and at worst a dogsbody." How can they distance themselves from the image of the dogsbody?

Role distance is the antithesis of deep involvement in or "identification" with a role.[40] Instead of taking in all the role's images as part of one's self-image, one seeks to insulate the "self" from those aspects of the role that seem disagreeable. This is done by hinting to others that, though one may be performing the tasks assigned, one is not really the sort of person for whom such tasks are suitable. These expressions of role distance are usually tailored to the audience.[41] Thus, Parliamentary Private Secretaries might be expected to express role distance least before Ministers (enough to reveal the future Minister within the fag, but not so much as to seem a sour servant) and most before backbench colleagues, in order to escape the image of the fag and maintain their respect.

Backbenchers will not easily be convinced. At least they seem unwilling to edit out the negative image of the dogsbody and have the wool pulled over their eyes: "It's an overrated job"; "A dogsbody . . . he dives between the Minister and the Bench and the Box"; "No hard feelings about this, but there are an awful lot of useless people who become PPSs and quite a lot of useful backbenchers that never do." They know that many MPs become

Ministers without ever suffering through this particular apprenticeship. And many of them think that "a PPS is a total *nonjob*":

> I was never a PPS, but I did spend four weeks as an acting PPS when someone's PPS was away. And on one occasion . . . I was beckoned across by some of the civil service officials sitting in the box at the side . . . she wasn't making a speech, she was out of the Chamber, she was in her room, and the civil servant in the box said, "The Minister would like a ham sandwich and a glass of milk taken to her room." So I took it, but I thought, "My God, I'll never . . ." and subsequently I was asked by two Ministers to be their PPS but declined. And I don't think there is any point in being a PPS unless it's a Minister to whom you are very close as a person and have a lot of respect for. But to be just any Minister's office boy is a total waste of time.

It isn't a waste of time. But it is potentially humiliating: "I would have thought that it can be very humiliating . . . you have to conform to what your Minister says and does, you are really a servant to him." Tam Dalyell, for instance, was described in print by his ministerial master as "the most devoted, kind, good PPS as well as a very nice lodger who cooks my breakfast when Anne isn't here."[42] Or: "What does a PPS do? . . . If I happened to be an Undersecretary of State for Scotland and you were my PPS, all that you would do would be to go down to see if my tickets were all right for the train tonight, or go and get my bag, or if there's anybody wanting to come and see me. . . . It's maybe good enough training for a young lad, but I think it's a humiliating experience for a mature man to be a PPS to anybody."

But the surprising fact is that if Parliamentary Private Secretaries feel humiliated, many of them are very good at hiding it; and only a few seem to deploy role distance to deal with the discomfort. Quite the contrary: the typical Parliamentary Private Secretary appears to thrive on his or her role and to play it with what can only be described as ebullient enthusiasm. "I love it," said a new PPS who was cheerfully throwing himself into parliamentary life; "the only consequence I regret is that the pressure of certain things prevents one from doing some of the other things." "I'm always in this building by nine o'clock at the very latest," reported another Apprentice, "and I very rarely arrive back at my flat before midnight, very rarely. . . . It's a way of life, it's not just a job. . . . And I rather like it." These are not humiliated, anxiety-ridden dogsbodies.

Why don't they seem more humiliated? Why aren't there more expressions of role distance? It's not that they are unaware of the negative "actual" images that color how others see them. They can describe, cheerfully, their role in exactly the same way: "You're very much a dogsbody, you're not a chap of any great importance"; "You are really a bag carrier par excellence"; "Well, a PPS is the sort of, um, I suppose you could say lowest form of governmental existence." "Servile," they admit; "unintellectual," they say. And yet many of them say it with such pleasant equanimity. There are, I think, two reasons that role distance is not so apparent here as might be anticipated. The first is that the role of the Parliamentary Private Secretary is transitory. As we saw earlier, most MPs hold it for no more than two years. Thus, they are aware, all the time, that very soon they will either rise up or move out, either become Junior Ministers or exchange the bag carrying for the freedom of the backbenches. If it is necessary to do a brief stint as a PPS, well, it has its attractions, and besides, "quite frankly, I don't see myself as being PPS to Michael Heseltine forever."

The other reason that so many are able "to enjoy the ride" is that, as with Constituency Members, the negative images mainly damage the lesser and less numerous subtype, the Auxiliary. Apprentices, by contrast, tell themselves that they are candidates for the Ministry and that, if they must stoop to conquer, only a select few are invited to stoop. Apprentices like to talk so much about their activities in the department because, in part, these are the activities that distinguish them from the Auxiliaries. Most Parliamentary Private Secretaries are not awash with discomfort and role distance because they are Apprentices for whom the little humiliations are not so humiliating. This interpretation was investigated by reviewing the interview transcripts for signs of "apologies" and "tensions" that might be associated with feelings of humiliation.[43] The prediction is that Auxiliaries will feel more humiliation and will therefore express more apologies and tensions than will Apprentices. The results are reported in Table 6.3.

The table indicates that Auxiliaries are indeed much more likely than Apprentices to express tensions and to apologize for the role of the Parliamentary Private Secretary. Thus, seven out of ten Auxiliaries talked about task-related tensions ("I think it does produce tension, yes"), whereas only seven out of twenty-seven Apprentices did so. It is mainly the Auxiliaries who describe the role as "a tension-making job. There's no doubt about it . . . one of the first requirements . . . is to have the right temperament and the right digestion." They complain about how there are "occasions when everything seems to bear in on one." They speak about "heavy days," and about how "I, I, I don't sleep very well." One said that he was ill most of the past year because of the "terrible strain." And another explained how "it's the mental worry where the trouble comes. . . . I don't experience too

Table 6.3 Indicators of role distance among Parliamentary Private Secretaries by subtypes, by percent

	Indicator			
	Apologies*		Tensions**	
Presence of indicator	Apprentice	Auxiliary	Apprentice	Auxiliary
Present	19	60	26	70
Not present	81	40	74	30
Total	100	100	100	100
	(N = 27)	(N = 10)	(N = 27)	(N = 10)

*$p \leq .05$
**$p \leq .01$

much of this kind of tension now because I've learnt to control it." "It suits me," the Apprentices say by contrast; "the thing that it hits hardest is not one's sleep as much as one's social life." Apprentices sleep very well ("Oh God, I sleep like a log"). And when they don't, it isn't because they are tense over humiliations, but because they'd rather be awake: "One sleeps less than most other members of the community, I think, but that's because one is busy, not because one is unable to sleep. It's no great problem with me."

Just as tensions can arise from feelings of humiliation, so apologies can express a role distance created to fend off such humiliations. The apologies are more convincing indicators than the tensions, for they are closer to the phenomenon itself. Thus, apologies can themselves be expressions of role distance, poses of disdainful detachment. Six out of ten Auxiliaries expressed role distance in this way, whereas only five out of twenty-seven Apprentices did the same—and one of them was mocking the Auxiliaries more than himself: "The ideal thing is to . . . not just be somebody who says to the Minister, you know, 'I've arranged a pair for you on Wednesday night.' And I'm grateful to say that the latter doesn't arise as far as I'm concerned. I'm jolly lucky actually."

Role distance is expressed through self-deprecating jokes that say it can't be so bad if I can laugh about it with you: "My youngest daughter describes me as 'the Minister's Fag'! . . . this is a fair description. . . . It's not a full description, but it is a part of it." The same message is also conveyed through humble images: "So I'm of the—the—the—the first category. I am really a 'companion.' I always felt that because of my age and, er, somebody that they liked having around. And I looked after them." But role distance is expressed most frequently through apologetic explanations. Thus, one Auxiliary signed on only because "I couldn't afford to have a Minister's job. I have to rely on the income from my business. And I couldn't do without that without considerable embarrassment, financial embarrassment." Another Auxiliary "never" had and "wouldn't" have wanted to be a PPS, till the right Minister, Minister X, "came to me and said, 'Would you be my PPS?'" It is only because "he's such a fascinating politician, indeed man, that you know I would have happily given up any post to have this privilege of working with him."

The expectations and reactions of other people can not only affect how we define our roles but also how we define our identities, because we tend to incorporate some of the roles we play into our views of ourselves.[44] That statement describes a social learning process. It also describes a potential threat. Disagreeable expectations for how we should behave can threaten the way we would like to see ourselves. And so we construct strategies to remind the world and thereby ourselves that this role as generally understood does not accurately characterize the "real me." Thus, Auxiliaries want to be seen as Auxiliaries, not as fags. Apprentices, by contrast, project themselves as future Ministers, and the more they do so the less likely they are to be embarrassed by their role, because the "actual image" becomes, from their viewpoint, merely an instrumental and minor part of what they are about. In sum, signs of role distance are more common among Auxiliaries than among Apprentices because Auxiliaries have more serious problems to overcome. They have no obvious excuses for being dogsbodies, whereas Apprentices have taken up the role as a temporary, instrumental exercise.

It is also noteworthy that Apprentices sometimes "play at" being Ministers.[45] This tendency to "take the role" of the Minister, to become involved with the role through "anticipatory socialization," is a striking antithesis to role distance. It is more difficult for Apprentices than it is for backbench Ministerial Aspirants, who sometimes do the same thing, because Apprentices are in a position where they may do or say something that could embarrass their Minister or department. This makes them even more conscious than are Ministerial Aspirants of being watched and tested. The temptation to take the role is strong, because it's such "a fascinating thing, you're already dealing with central issues of policy, you're dealing with people making decisions, senior Ministers, senior civil servants." In fact, it is difficult not to experiment with the role of the Minister, if only mentally and occasionally, because the role of the PPS licenses Apprentices to do so. As part of their training, they are expected to absorb attitudes and learn behaviors that will facilitate their adjustment to the Ministry, should they eventually join it.

More Behavior

The Parliamentary Private Secretary's position role may not be an official leadership role, but it has assigned to it both a title and a series of responsibilities. These responsibilities prescribe certain behaviors. And since the behaviors are obviously performed, it would make no sense to ask whether this role's attitudinal components are, in fact, related to behavior. As a general query, that question is appropriate more for probing the validity of interpretative accounts of preference roles than for position roles like that of the PPS.

PPSs behave like PPSs. Table 6.2 showed they were less likely than other backbenchers to cross-vote. Quite apart from academic debates in role theory about links between beliefs and behavior, this conduct is important because it is central to the role of the PPS as understood by its players—and therefore central to our reconstruction of it. Other characteristic behaviors include voting regularly and attending party committees.[46]

VOTING REGULARLY

The same informal doctrine of collective responsibility that discourages PPSs from cross-voting encourages them to vote regularly and regularly to attend the House. "In general, a PPS, particularly a PPS to a senior Minister, is expected to obey party Whips meticulously," lamented one who found this difficult, "and also to be more scrupulous than most about his attendance."

Table 6.4 reports the number of divisions between 1970 and 1973 in which Parliamentary Private Secretaries and other backbenchers voted. The

Table 6.4 Parliamentary Private Secretaries: Frequency of voting at Westminster

Divisions, 1970–1973	Other backbenchers* (%)	Parliamentary Private Secretaries* (%)
0–699	37	8
700–799	38	33
800–899	20	41
900–999	5	18
Total	100	100
	(N = 345)	(N = 39)

*$p \leq .001$

differences between these two groups are likely reduced somewhat by the fact that the data cover several months during which some PPSs were still ordinary backbenchers. But the behavior of the PPSs is nevertheless very distinctive. They may be the (unpaid) tail end of the "payroll vote," but they are still much more likely to come along than are their party's other backbenchers. Controls for Government and Opposition, however, show that this pattern applies only on the Government's side of the House. The frequency with which Opposition PPSs troop through the division lobbies is no different from that of other backbenchers in their party, showing again that the role of the PPS is not as institutionalized in Opposition as it is in Government.

ATTENDING PARTY COMMITTEES

Attending backbench party committees where departmental matters are being discussed is another of the principal behaviors expected of all Apprentices and Auxiliaries. First, there is the 1922 Committee, the "Committee of the Whole" for Conservative backbenchers, where "anybody can raise anything, and therefore I nearly always go to that, you know, to see if anything's raised . . . said about him or his department." During the interviews, PPSs filled in forms that listed all committees and requested rates of attendance for each. Since no attendance records are kept at most backbench committees, such self-estimates are the only way to gather these data. The results show that Parliamentary Private Secretaries attend assiduously their party's weekly general meetings (the 1922 or the PLP), where criticisms and cues relevant to their Minister's work might come up. Ninety-seven percent say they go to "almost all" or "many." They seek the same sort of information, albeit in a more specialized way, at the backbench party committees that study topics related to their departments' work. It is all part of the two-way flow, "acting as the liaison between the Chancellor and the House, in a two-way direction . . . the main body I am in touch with is the party's Finance Committee. And I must go to every meeting of that—compulsory!" Most don't go to every meeting, but seven out of ten report that they go to "almost all" of them. And eight out of ten claim to visit "almost all" or "many."

Parliamentary Private Secretaries behave distinctively even if not very differently from other backbenchers. "You are a PPS in your own subject . . . but you're backbench in the ordinary way on the others. And therefore . . . on the others, you do much the same as anybody else." But not exactly the same. Take backbench committees in areas outside the department's responsibilities, for example. Young, ambitious Conservative backbenchers like to attend these "whenever there is a row." But PPSs don't always have the time. Some of the committees they might like to attend may have scheduling conflicts with some of those they must attend. Thus, few find that they can pursue actively more than two interests beyond the department's area. Only Opposition PPSs can afford to be all over the map. They have more time because they have fewer duties and responsibilities. Parliamentary Private Secretaries were similarly asked to estimate the time they allocated to constituency and party work outside Westminster. This picture too fits the pattern. PPSs behave distinctively but not all that differently: fewer are found at the highest levels of activity but, like other backbenchers, about half put in ten or more hours per week.

Sources of Role Choice

Role choices are structured by opportunities and incentives, by the intersection of the institution's rules and the individual's goals. PPSs are, like most people on the leadership side of the fence, "recruited" to their roles, which means that their "opportunities" mainly involve being selected. But, compared to other leadership roles, this selection process is not very rigorous, because the PPS is not very essential to the effectiveness of the institutional machine.

Parliamentary Private Secretaries are often selected personally by their Ministers. This gives Ministers the opportunity to choose kindred spirits who will feel free to warn them when they are creating trouble for themselves in the House.[47] But "he [also] has to get the Prime Minister's, which means the Chief Whip's, approval." Ministers select and the Chief Whip consults. When Ministers have no personal favorites, the Chief may suggest some names and, if one seems acceptable, make the offer himself: "And the Chief Whip called me in and said, you know, 'What about it?' So I accepted."[48] The Whips keep lists of new Members who are performing well in the Chamber or in committee and who seem diligent and loyal. They also keep lists of mavericks and discourage Ministers from choosing them.

OPPORTUNITIES: PARLIAMENTARY AND PERSONAL ATTRIBUTES

The pool from which PPSs are drawn is far smaller than the entire backbench. For some posts, it is very small indeed.[49] Nevertheless, there are selection criteria, the first of which is length of service. And "it really depends on how the Minister intends to use you. I mean there are a number of people who become PPSs very rapidly after they come in," largely to Ministers who are looking for an Apprentice. "But if you are going to use your PPS as [an Auxiliary-confidant], then he ought to be somebody who has at least learned the ropes and established himself in the House." For Apprentices, then, Ministers and Whips look to the fresh recruits. Some say "it is a mistake to start off as a PPS immediately," a mistake for the PPS because he doesn't have time to establish himself as an independent backbencher, a mistake for the Minister because inexperienced PPSs don't know enough about the House to be useful eyes and ears. Yet newcomers who are asked are often flattered and agree to have a go: "I was fortunate enough to be asked to be a Parliamentary Private Secretary very quickly, within four weeks of being here. . . . I was a little diffident about accepting. I wondered really whether I could possibly have enough of an inkling of the place, enough knowledge of colleagues, to be able to be of use to the people I was going to serve. But I was persuaded that this diffidence was natural . . . that I should do the job, so I did."

The new backbenchers who are most likely to be noticed by Ministers and Whips are the ones who are active in the Chamber and the backbench committees—a second parliamentary attribute that is used frequently. In the Chamber they may have spoken thoughtfully or attacked effectively. In backbench party committees their diligence may have won them election as secretaries or vice chairmen. Work on the right Conservative backbench committees can be a useful apprenticeship for Ministerial Office. But those who are tapped usually give it up for the role of the PPS. Table 6.5 lists for all respondents who were serving or had served as PPSs the positions they left to become Parliamentary Private Secretaries.[50]

The table reminds us that the position of Parliamentary Private Secretary is indeed the first step on the ladder that reaches from the backbenches to

Table 6.5 Parliamentary Private Secretaries: Prior positions, in percent

| Party | N | Prior position* | | | | Total |
		Backbencher	Committee officer	Whip	Junior OFBS**	
Conservative	(99)	82	14	3	1	(100)
Labour	(87)	87	5	8	0	(100)

*Includes all respondents who were serving or had served as PPSs.
**OFBS = Opposition Front Bench Spokesman.

the Cabinet, for the vast majority of PPSs are appointed directly from the backbenches. But after this, on the Conservative side they come from among the officers of backbench committees.[51] A good example is Nicholas Scott, who was vice chairman of the Conservative Party's Employment Committee. In this position, he had regular contact with Robert Carr, who was Secretary of State for Employment and who eventually asked Scott to be his PPS. A few also move over from the Whips' Offices, but only from the roles of junior Whips. Senior Whips are much more likely to become Junior Ministers. Curiously, one Conservative PPS, an Auxiliary, came from a posting as an Opposition Front Bench Spokesman.[52] Another unusual path is that of the Opposition PPS who follows his master from Shadow Cabinet to Cabinet, or the Government PPS who makes the reverse journey.

Specialization is believed to improve one's chances, because speeches on special subjects sometimes trigger the first appointment: "I'd made several speeches on building and housing," explained this fifty-year-old Auxiliary, and "just prior to ———'s being appointed the Minister for Housing . . . they wrote and asked me to be his PPS. I'd never met him. And he said, 'My God, you know what you're talking about—come and be my PPS.' " Thirty-year-old Apprentices who deliver impressive speeches on a particular topic have also been invited to serve. There are, in fact, many examples of matches between a backbencher's subject interests and his or her first post as PPS: lawyers to the Law Officers, farmers to Agriculture, even Post Office employees to the Postmaster General. Beyond special subjects, the Whips look for good attendance in the House and loyalty in the division lobbies. They also look for ideological soundness, which seems to mean staying away from extremes and exhibiting "bottom."

All these parliamentary attributes may be reviewed in recruiting PPSs, but they are rarely reviewed systematically. The same applies to social background characteristics. Among them, education and age are the most obvious. When Ministers and Whips look for Apprentices, they look for well-educated backbenchers who are in their late thirties or early forties; when they look for Auxiliaries, they concentrate on backbenchers who are nearer fifty. Most PPSs, of course, are Apprentices. And it has long been thought desirable to start them out young.[53] But beyond age and education, it is difficult to find any clear patterns in social background characteristics. There seems to be even less systematic or even careful attention given to personal attributes, although Members and political journalists have occasionally pointed to types like the steady plodder, the ebullient extrovert, and the Machiavellian. Plodders are said to be selected as Auxiliaries and ebullient extroverts as Apprentices, while the calm, controlled Machiavellians are presumably candidates for both roles. Many such off-the-cuff observations have been made about desired personal attributes, but none very persuasively.[54]

MOTIVATIONS: AMBITION AND AVOCATION

Even the newest and greenest backbenchers soon learn that the role of the PPS entails a bundle of little irritations and humiliations. Why then do they take it up when it is offered?

Apprentices are attracted because one of the role's principal goals is training for ministerial office: "If you are a good PPS and do your job well and effectively, and show good judgement in the advice you give to your master, then you would stand a good chance of becoming a Junior Minister." The role's most important incentive is ambition, a *desire* for office. The role of the PPS lures ambitious backbenchers by its promise of enhanced promotion prospects. What "PPS" really stands for, they say, is "Patently Promotable Servants." And yet they have their doubts. Just as they worry about the potential humiliations, so they worry about exactly how much it helps: "Well I suppose the rewards are a vague expectation that good behaviour might eventually be rewarded by promotion to the general ministerial ranks," mused an Apprentice who had recently accepted an offer, "but I wonder whether the PPS's chances of promotion to ministerial rank are, in all honesty, significantly higher than those of any backbench Member of Parliament. Sometimes I don't think so. Sometimes I don't think you'll find any evidence for that."

What evidence do *they* actually consider? All around them are examples of recent career moves, which they analyze in two ways, retrospectively and prospectively. The retrospective approach begins with today's "leaders, and if you trace their background you see how many were PPSs . . . you see a sort of progression, a chart you might say." By contrast, the prospective approach begins with yesterday's PPSs to see how many eventually became Junior Ministers: "I'm told that about half eventually made it."

Most use the retrospective approach because, although the alternative prospective approach is more reliable, it would require the laborious collection of information like Philip Buck's data on MPs elected between 1918 and 1955.[55] Nevertheless, there are prospectively oriented backbenchers who do try to assess the fortunes at least of those serving Members who they are aware were once PPSs. Had these prospectively oriented backbenchers been able to gather "complete" information at the time of our interviews, they would have found that 53 percent of the former Conservative Parliamentary

Private Secretaries who were still walking around Westminster eventually attained ministerial office.[56] Yet even these "complete" prospective data on serving MPs have serious biases: the failures in their generation are surely more likely than the successes to have left the House; and the Auxiliaries among "the failures" never expected to rise anyway. No wonder inquiring backbenchers are most likely to apply the retrospective method to an important group for whom information is available: senior Ministers and senior Opposition Front Bench Spokesmen.

Table 6.6 reports on the proportions of serving senior Ministers and senior Opposition Front Bench Spokesmen who once served as Parliamentary Private Secretaries. Although these data were checked and corrected by the interviewees themselves, they too have their problems.[57] Still, when backbenchers study the frontbenches, this is roughly what they see. The proportions who served as PPSs are similar in both parties: 43 and 45 percent, about 10 percent lower than less easily attainable prospective estimates about proportions of former PPSs who have risen. These tea leaves might suggest that the promotion prospects of a PPS are better than those of the average backbencher, but only slightly better—which is indeed the conclusion that our interviewees told us they had reached themselves.

There are other incentives too. The title "PPS," for instance, offers a modest honor or status. "Some people say it's the first rung on the ladder . . . people regard it as a debut of their formal career." It guarantees recognition, even if it can't guarantee promotion. The fact that one has been asked announces that one has been singled out as "officer material."[58] Another incentive is the opportunity to get close to power by rubbing elbows with the powerful. This attracts those who are attracted by power: "One of the things that inspired me to move into politics was the thought that it's in fact only

Table 6.6 Promotion prospects for Parliamentary Private Secretaries, in percent: Retrospective view from the backbenches

	Present position	
Prior service as a PPS	Senior Ministers (Conservative)	Senior OFBS (Labour)
Served as a PPS	43	45
Did not serve as a PPS	57	55
Total	100	100
	(N = 28)	(N = 28)

through Westminster that you can get to grips with power. . . . I think I sort of picked this idea up from the political biographies that I read." A related incentive is the (largely unrealistic) hope that one might occasionally find in the role of the PPS a few grams of the influence one seeks. These hopes may be planted by misinterpretations of conversations with Apprentices who like to think that they are "in on at least some important political decisions" and who like to feel now and then that they do "accomplish something . . . by access to Ministers and by trying to influence things."

The incentives for Apprentices are mainly instrumental and focused on future promotion. Since Auxiliaries, by contrast, are not climbing anywhere else, their desires focus on matters that are more intrinsic to the role's activities. "A PPS really is a lot of work for no reward," said our oldest and most experienced Auxiliary—"except the satisfaction you get out of *doing your job*." Auxiliaries take up the role because they want to be involved, even in a very minor way.[59] It is "purely personal," they explain, the excitement of being "in" on the political scene when big decisions are coming up. For them, the role of the PPS offers an opportunity to become "part of the machinery of the House. There are all sorts of people who are very active in the House whom you never hear anything about, such as Harold Gurden [a Parliament Man], for example, who is tremendously important to everybody because he's the one who selects you for committees and so on, but nobody ever hears of him outside. Similarly, PPSs are part of the machinery of Government and are very much behind the scenes."

The Auxiliaries sound like Parliament Men. They talk about friendship and camaraderie. They talk about being there and watching great events unfold. And several even confide that their role "carries a tremendous amount of weight in all spheres." They are, in effect, Parliament Men with seats inside the circle. They are there to watch, but they are also there to give their service, which they are pleased to do: "I just like being here and helping Maurice MacMillan." ("His ambition, I take it, does not go beyond a desire to be a parliamentary flunkey to a big man," it was said of Trollope's Mr. Bott, who served as PPS to the Chancellor of the Exchequer.)[60] The difference between Auxiliaries and Parliament Men is that the former have personal contact with power. The role offers them a sense of doing something constructive as part of the Executive rather than simply observing the Executive as part of the House.

Parliamentary Private Secretaries are relegated to the footnotes of British politics as "the lowest stratum of political appointees."[61] They receive no salary and are not officially recognized either in the Constitution or in legislation. Yet their position has been established for a century, and their role has become familiar and routinized. It includes the contrasting images of the Minister's apprentice and the Minister's fag. Both images are always associated with the role, and the role's players are always coping with both images.

Outside of a few cases like PPSs to the Prime Minister or to some Cabinet Ministers, the role of the PPS is a part-time occupation. Parliamentary Private Secretaries spend long hours in the House, but they don't have endless work to do there. Moreover, since they aren't formally Members of the Government, they can participate like other backbenchers in areas beyond the borders of their departments. They don't have a great deal of spare time, but they have enough to dabble, if they are Auxiliaries, as Parliament Men or even as Constituency Members and, if they are Apprentices, to pursue at least one issue of interest beyond their role assignments. These Apprentices are active, ambitious people who would like to do even more of this sort of thing if they could. It is surely revealing that when PPSs talk about their lives at Westminster and about their satisfactions and dissatisfactions, a substantial minority talks hardly at all, until asked explicitly, about the role of the PPS or about the duties and responsibilities associated with it. In response to exactly the same sort of indirect questions, Ministers, by contrast, talk about being Ministers and about little else.

Despite considerable variations in the way that the role of the PPS is played, the power of others' expectations about how it should be played is pervasive and obvious. The key to this apparent inconsistency lies in the fact that "at the end of the day, every PPS has to attune himself to what his particular Minister wants to make of him." Thus, it turns out that the variations owe less to the individuality of the role players than to the existence of so many script editors. Ministers differ a great deal in what they want their PPSs to do. Some want to involve them in the department's work, whereas others want only to be helped on with their coats. Yet, the role of the PPS is becoming increasingly institutionalized. Its responsibilities are growing, and it is displaying more uniform patterns than in the past. Moreover, in the course of its evolution, the role's dominant subtype, the Apprentice, has begun to look a little less like a Whip and a little more like a Junior Minister.

WHIPS: MANAGING MEMBERS

> Oh it's too crude. If anybody thinks that I am
> able to say to Gerald Nabarro, "Well, come on,
> into the No Lobby," they've got a completely
> wrong idea of how it is done.
>
> Conservative Whip

Since so few formal duties and responsibilities are assigned to backbenchers, they are provided with little more than a desk and a half-time secretary. Since so many formal duties and responsibilities are assigned to Whips, they are provided with abundant accommodations and staff support. Their roles are important. They are the gears of the parliamentary machine. And they are fixed in a compact institutional structure.

Thus, Government Whips work out of two sets of offices, one at No. 12 Downing Street, the other in the House of Commons. From Downing Street, the Chief Whip maintains close contact with Ministers, especially the Prime Minister, whom he sees nearly every day. He works under the portraits of his predecessors and, except for their eyes, passes unseen through a series of interconnecting doors to the Prime Minister's residence at No. 10. The House of Commons is only a few hundred yards away; and here the Government Whips, and the Opposition Whips, fill their suites of rooms with energy, industry, information, and intrigue. Each Whip's Office employs a staff, which in Government includes a Private Secretary backed by several permanent civil servants. There are also "runners" who deliver messages, keep track of division records, and collect information about routine pairing arrangements.[1]

A hierarchy of titles and salaries announces the pecking order among the role's positional subtypes. Except for the top posts of Chief Whip and Deputy Chief Whip, advancement up this formal hierarchy usually proceeds by seniority. The Conservative Chief Whip is appointed from above; the Labour Chief Whip is elected from below (by the Parliamentary Labour Party); yet each is directly responsible to the party's Leader. The Chief Whip therefore commands a special presence: Junior Whips follow him about, laugh at his banter, and, when by themselves, joke about the possibility of his overhearing their backstage comments. He may be well liked, but he is not one of the lads: "Bob Mellish is the great *father* figure, yes, a great father figure." The Deputy Chief Whip, his second in command, handles most of the routine matters and "manages the rest of the team."

In Opposition, "the rest of the team" all play the role of Assistant Whip. Although aware of their standing by seniority, these Whips are not formally differentiated, except for one who receives on top of his MP's salary another salary as a paid official of the House. He thereby becomes "third in line, if you like, in the Whips' Office." The pecking order for the Government's Junior Whips is better crystallized, as can be seen by comparing Tables 7.1 and 7.2 (pp. 246–248). Her Majesty's Household Officers, the roles of Comptroller and Vice Chamberlain, together form the first stratum under the Deputy Chief Whip, who is likewise a Household Officer (Treasurer). The Comptroller of the Household has an edge on the Vice Chamberlain and is frequently described as "number three in the Government Whips' Office." After the Vice Chamberlain of the Household come five Lord Commissioners of the Treasury, who have even less to do with the Treasury than the Household Officers have with the Royal Household. ("Stupid title, people write to me thinking I'm something to do with the Treasury. And somebody called me Lord —— the other day.") Still, the title announces that one has advanced a step beyond the role of the Assistant Whip, who sits at the bottom of this ladder.

Like other Members of the Government, all Government Whips receive an additional stipend on top of their basic salary as Members of Parliament. The size of this stipend reflects their standing. The Chief Whip's standing is obvious: not only is he quartered at Downing Street, but his pay is the same as that of his neighbor the Chancellor of the Exchequer. All other Whips, including the Deputy Chief Whip, are paid much less, but they *are* paid—unlike the Parliamentary Private Secretaries, with whom they are sometimes compared. The Deputy Chief Whip earned at the time of the interviews five hundred pounds less than a Junior Minister, while everyone else in the Whips' Office earned a thousand pounds less than that. Most organizations likewise pay supervisors (Whips) significantly less than junior executives (Junior Ministers). At Westminster, such distinctions are further reflected in the fact that although Whips frequently become Junior Ministers, Junior Ministers rarely become Whips.[2]

Career goals structure these roles. But unlike the situation with backbenchers, the goals are specified more by the institution than by the role players. Hence, the principal subtypes of the Whip's role are positional in the sense that they are defined by responsibilities assigned to a subset of formal positions. The responsibilities are many and varied, but most can be subsumed under the Whip's three principal goals:[3] *liaison,* promoting party cohesion through two-way communications that inform Ministers about backbench concerns and pour oil on troubled waters; *management,* organizing Government business, activating procedure, and organizing the parliamentary parties; and *discipline,* ensuring satisfactory support in the division lobbies by building authority, cajoling backbenchers, and dispensing reprimands and rewards.

Liaison and Management

Many organizations assign both directive and supportive goals to the same roles. The Whips' Office instead divides these responsibilities between the Chief Whip and Deputy Chief Whip on the one hand and Junior Whips on the other.

CHIEF AND DEPUTY CHIEF

As Patronage Secretary, the Chief Whip arranges backbenchers' comforts and political futures. But he spends most of his time arranging the affairs of the House. The core of this responsibility is planning the timetable for Government business. These plans are sensitive and time consuming, because he must take into account evolving backbench views and postpone matters or move them forward so as to ensure that the Government maintains its majority in the division lobbies.

Part of the strength of the Chief Whip's role is drawn from his liaison duties between the Cabinet and the parliamentary party. Described by Francis Pym as the Prime Minister's "Principal Political Advisor," he wields the power of information, for he is better briefed than anyone else on both Cabinet attitudes and backbench opinions. Each day he explains Cabinet attitudes to backbenchers and sends notes to Ministers identifying backbenchers who object to policies or tactics being pursued and suggesting which modifications, if any, may be advisable.[4] Each day he is expected to assess whether particular policies are likely to be acceptable and, if rebellion is in the wind, to gauge how far it will go. He is expected to predict division outcomes. He is also expected to forecast behavior on the Opposition side.

The Chief Whip's main sources of data are the detailed reports of his Junior Whips, who, each day, carefully monitor backbench views:

> It is the role of the Whip to know, before they know themselves, what Members are thinking. The Whips' Office is a remarkable intelligence operation; in fact, the best I've ever seen. . . . The Chief Whip calls a Whips' meeting and says, "Well, we propose to do so and so. What will the party say?" And if you're any good as a Whip, you ought to be able to say, "Well of my thirty-five, twenty-five will be in favour, no trouble; five we'll have to persuade them a bit, but they'll be all right; and the other five, I don't know but I'll find out."

As managing director of the Whips' Office, the Chief also monopolizes contacts outside the House: besides attending Cabinet Meetings, he negotiates with broadcasting authorities and may maintain informal relations with the extraparliamentary party.[5] His contacts with the opposite side are important too. In fact, the two Chief Whips together constitute "the usual channels." They "make the place tick over" by working with the Leader and the Shadow Leader of the House to direct the flow of parliamentary activity. The Chiefs confer about each week's program and then discuss with their Cabinet or Shadow Cabinet the order of business they have negotiated and the whipping proposals they have planned. Afterward, these plans are explained to the Junior Whips and announced to the party's MPs. As the week's activities unfold, the usual channels may meet again to adjust schedules, divisions, and adjournment times.

While the Chief Whip negotiates, the Deputy Chief Whip runs the shop. He organizes and coordinates the work of Junior Whips, which includes assigning them to party committees and Standing Committees: "I'm really the office foreman, if you like. My job is to say, 'You go to this one, and you go to that one, and you go to the other and then come back and tell me what happened.'" His role also includes looking after minor patronage for backbenchers, such as delegations, assignments to Select Committees, accommodations (who gets which office), and Court and Garden parties. And he deals with whatever backbench difficulties Junior Whips are unable to handle.

Although the Deputy Chief Whip is primarily concerned with office matters, his role requires him to reach outside the office as well. Thus, he is often on the telephone with Ministers or their Civil Servants and is expected to be in close touch with his counterpart on the other side: "I see him every day. We get on pretty well together, and he tells me a whole lot of things, and I tell him a whole lot of things, which I know perfectly well that neither of us ever repeats—and that makes it much easier for us to get on in our particular job." Together, the Deputy Chiefs arrange delegations, trips abroad, hospitality, and the occasional political bargain. Only the Speaker, who actually lives in the Palace of Westminster, spends more time there than the Deputy Chief Whip.

"SENIOR" JUNIOR WHIPS

The Deputy Chief Whip on the Government side holds the title of Treasurer of H.M. Household. Two other "senior" Whips are similarly distinguished: the Comptroller of the Household and the Vice Chamberlain. There are occasions when each of them is required to be in contact with the Palace or to appear there, but these titles are essentially ceremonial, for most of the work assigned to their roles is in the Whips' Office.[6]

And most of their work in the Whips' Office is "on the organizational side" of the House, so much so that the Comptroller and the Vice Chamberlain usually have little time to follow specialized policy subjects or attend backbench committees, as can be seen from Table 7.1. Instead, they ease the Deputy Chief Whip's burden by taking up responsibilities for accommodations, telephoning messages to Ministers' private offices, setting up Standing Committees, choosing Members for Select Committees, contacting Central Office or Transport House, or even bringing Young Conservatives to Westminster to meet and exchange views with MPs. One of them is usually charged as well with the sensitive task of watching Private Members' Bills and Motions in order to identify cases in which backbenchers need to be dissuaded from undermining party policy. One of them usually also oversees the preparation of the Documentary Whip, which is delivered to MPs on Thursdays. This outlines the coming week's program and, as a calendar of events, calls attention to special meetings, party committees, and all-party groups. But its primary purpose is to announce debates and divisions that are underscored with one, two, or three lines. One line requests but does not require attendance; two lines require attendance but permit pairs and excused absences; three lines announce that the leadership considers the matter "vital" and that pairs will not normally be allowed.

Pairing refers to the practice in which one Member from each side agrees not to vote on a given day so that either or both can be absent from the House without affecting the outcome of divisions. The "senior" Junior Whip who is assigned to the arduous position of the Pairing Whip approves and records these arrangements, and increases thereby the leadership's patronage and control. Members normally ring one another to arrange pairs after receiving the Documentary Whip.[7] Since the Pairing Whip cannot see every-one individually, these pairing compacts are normally brought in by his mes-sengers and accepted automatically. But not always—and herein lies the role's potential for patronage and control. When pairs rise above a certain number for a day, the Pairing Whip refuses to grant any more without spe-cial permission. Then Members who wish pairs must personally explain their reasons to him. They may also have to plead their case before higher authority, the Deputy Chief Whip or the Chief Whip.[8] The Pairing Whip polices the system and sees that the compacts are honored. He meets with his assistants after divisions to review how MPs voted and to identify those who were absent unpaired or without an approved excuse.

JUNIOR WHIPS

Each party appoints approximately ten Junior Whips as first-line supervi-sors. Of these, the five most senior in the Government team are distinguished by the title Lord Commissioners of the Treasury. But despite this distinction, the roles of all Junior Whips share much the same characteristic attitudes and behaviors. Compared to senior colleagues, their outside contacts are limited. They are immersed in the two-way communication of Westminster's world, where they bear primary responsibility for the party's unity. Thus, the Junior Whip's role sends him or her out to discuss with backbenchers the substance of issues, the importance of tactics, and the shape of the week's agenda: "You tell your colleagues what's happening, how it's structured for the day, the practice and pattern of each day's events, the debate, the con-tents of the debate." Friendly and approachable, these Whips are prepared to pass on information, to be good listeners, to help backbenchers overcome inconveniences, and to assist with personal problems. The rhythm of their activity is structured by the area assignments, subject assignments, and spe-cial responsibilities described in Tables 7.1 and 7.2.

Compared to the roles of backbenchers, and even to the role of the PPS, there is an absolutely staggering amount of structure and constraint here. Area assignments refer to the fact that each Junior Whip is responsible for twenty-five to thirty-five Members ("which we call our flocks") from a par-ticular geographic area. The Conservative Party has fewer area groups than does Labour, and Conservative Members from some regions may not meet together at all. But when area groups do meet regularly, usually monthly, the Whips of course attend.

Area Whips try to see as much as they can of their flocks on a daily basis. Newcomers are brought under their wing for instruction in "the ropes, the

Table 7.1 Whips: Subtypes in the Government (Conservative) Whips' Office

Subtype and incumbents	General responsibilities	Area assignment	Committee (subject) assignment
Chief Whip (£9,500)			
Francis Pym	Overall direction of Whips' Office, relations with Ministers and Opposition Chief Whip		
Deputy Chief Whip (Treasurer of the Household) (£5,000)			
Humphrey Atkins	Management of Whips' Office, delegations, Select Committees, Courts and Garden parties		
Comptroller of the Household (£4,000)			
Bernard Weatherill	Private Member Bills and motions, accommodation, daily telegram to the Queen	Greater London	
Vice Chamberlain of the Household (£4,000)			
Walter Clegg	Pairing Whip, addresses to and from the Queen		
Lord Commissioners of the Treasury (£4,000)			
Victor Goodhew	Crown Estates Commission	South East	Defense, Housing and Construction
Paul Hawkins		Eastern	Agriculture, Broadcasting and Communications
Tim Fortescue	Government hospitality	North West	Aviation, Health and Social Security
Hugh Rossi	Council of Europe, Western European Union, Greater London Council		Foreign and Commonwealth, Arts and Amenities
Oscar Murton		East Midlands	Finance, Home Affairs

Table 7.1 (cont.)

Subtype and incumbents	General responsibilities	Area assignment	Committee (subject) assignment
Assistant Whips (£4,000)			
Michael Jopling		Yorkshire, Northern Ireland, Northern areas	Education, Transport Industries
James Gray		Scotland	Scottish
John Stradling Thomas		Wales, South Western	Employment, Trade and Industry
Marcus Fox		Wessex	Local Government and Development
Kenneth Clarke		West Midlands	Employment, Legal

do's and don'ts of the House." One Whip invited his intake down a day early to tour the building, "point out lavatories, explain where to meet constituents and how to take them about," and provide pointers on basic procedure. This same helpful orientation is apparent as Whips make their rounds through backbenchers' favorite haunts. Always listening, always soothing tempers and explaining difficulties, Whips serve as advocates for their backbenchers while remaining alert at all times for signs of dissent or rebellion. "I carry a list around with me and I tick them off." If the Whip overlooks one of his charges for several days, he may ring him up just to keep in touch. Junior Whips also sound out sources in the other parties for information that their Chief might find useful in planning strategy: "I have a very close line to a certain Labour Member whom I know very well and respect greatly. And I often have some very useful information which I can trust implicitly, as to the intentions of certain people on their own side."

Junior Whips are constant helpers. But their role also makes them occasional informers. Thus, the vast majority of the intelligence they gather concerns policy views of backbenchers that backbenchers themselves want transmitted. But Whips are at the same time ready to gather unguarded comments and intimate confidences: a report that a Tory had, in the Members' Bar, called his Prime Minister "a bloody fool," or gossip about personal matters such as excessive drinking and deviant sexual behavior.[9] Despite the Whips' vigorous denials that these "dirts" are collected and, as they once were, recorded on special forms, some backbenchers believe that they are still collected and filed away. According to cynics, this produces

Table 7.2 Whips: Subtypes in the Opposition (Labour) Whips' Office

Subtype and incumbents	General responsibilities	Area assignment	Committee (subject) assignment*
Opposition Chief Whip (£7,500)			
Robert Mellish	Overall direction of Whips' Office, relations with party Leaders and Government Chief Whip		
Opposition Deputy Chief Whip (£4,000)			
Walter Harrison	Management of Whips' Office, delegations, accommodation, Committee of Selection, Services Committee		
Assistant Whips (£4,000 for one of them)			
Donald Coleman	Council of Europe, Western European Union	Welsh	
John Cancannon	Pairing Whip	East Midlands	Power and Steel, Aviation Supply
John Golding	Statutory instruments, nationalized industries	Midlands	Post Office, Health and Social Security
Ernest Armstrong	Private Members' Bills and motions	North Eastern	Education and Science, Environment
Joseph Harper	Standing Committee manning	Yorkshire	
Tom Pendry	Government hospitality, Central Office of Information	Lancashire	
James Dunn	North Atlantic Assembly	Lancashire	Defense, Industrial Relations Bill Working Party
James Hamilton	Scottish Grand Committee	Scottish	Scottish, Trade and Industry
Ernest Perry		Greater London (Inner)	
James Wellbeloved		Greater London (Outer, Eastern, South, and South West)	

*Neither official nor semiofficial publications describe the assignments of Labour Whips to specific backbench subject committees. Entries in this column, which are incomplete, are based on information supplied by the Whip.

a sophisticated form of blackmail whereby the keepers of the information (if it exists) deny they have it and yet profit from suspicions that they do.

Committee (subject) assignments are distributed among the Junior Whips, who are expected to develop an active interest in the subjects and attend the committee meetings, which typically occur once or twice a fortnight. At these meetings, "one must be a total listener of course. It requires self-discipline to avoid coming out in a neurotic rash if two or three people fall off the left-hand edge or the right-hand edge." Afterward, the total listener reports back to the Chief or Deputy Chief on the direction of the discussion and what if anything is worrying Members. This information is then integrated with information from other committees to provide a summary for the party Leader.[10] Junior Whips are informal opinion leaders such that "in the course of committee discussions we will try to influence Members to where the balance is, where the Cabinet wants to move to deal with the matter." They maintain close contact with the officers of the committees and, when "misunderstandings" arise, suggest that the relevant Minister be invited to attend "so that he becomes more aware of their views and explains to them the nature of the problems he's dealing with."

Whips never lack for things to do. They are expected to be present in the Chamber when Questions arise in the area of their specialization. They arrange debates on their subjects and see that appropriate speakers are present in sufficient numbers to provide breadth and depth. On a rotational basis, they spend hours each day sitting on the frontbench in the Chamber to keep track of proceedings and move motions. Government Whips, in particular, are responsible for the complicated procedural maneuvers upon which the normal progress of the business of the House depends: "There is a sort of dialogue between the Speaker and the Whip on duty ... if it didn't go right, well, you'd have chaos in this place." Because their activities require continual coordination, Whips hold planning sessions on four out of five days of the week. On Wednesday mornings, Whips in the Heath Government gathered at No. 12 Downing Street for three hours to chart the progress of legislation. The Whip in charge of a Bill would report to his colleagues, sometimes marking up amendments to show how votes were expected to go on each. Then, on Mondays, Tuesdays, and Thursdays there would be meetings from 2:15 to 3:15 at the Whips' Office in the House to discuss the day's business along with the relevant procedure, the "day-to-day, hour-to-hour tactics," and approaches for persuading "difficult customers." When a Bill was produced in the Whip's subject area, he would usually be expected to follow it upstairs to Standing Committee.

One Junior Government Whip and one Junior Opposition Whip are assigned to each Standing Committee to ensure that the business runs smoothly with minimal inconvenience to Members. They manage the pairing carefully, arrange to telephone absentees, and discourage MPs from leaving the room:[11] "We sorted problems out behind the scenes, problems of personality between the Minister and Opposition Minister, problems of trying to get somebody away because he wanted to get a train for some reason. . . . And it just meant the whole committee went a lot better, a sweet temper; and, you know, one got the business through in a civilized way." Since it is the Government Whip's responsibility to get the business through, he carries the heaviest burdens. He must take care that a quorum is present on his side and, while allowing his backbenchers the opportunity to answer points from the Opposition, he attempts to keep them reasonably silent too so as not to prolong the committee's deliberations. At the same time, he must keep in touch with the Minister's thinking by seeing him before committee meetings to review the timetable and the point at which the work needs to be completed. Likewise, he ascertains which, if any, Opposition amendments the Minister is willing to accept; and he must also plan to instruct a backbencher to call out yes or no at the proper time.[12]

Conservative Whips are, in addition, expected to attend the weekly meetings of their party's 1922 Committee. When the party is in Government, Whips are the only Members of the Government with a standing invitation to this private backbench gathering. Not being members of the 1922, however, they "sit in the back of the room behind the bar from which you are not allowed to make any comments." Backbenchers welcome their presence "because one can get a bit of a feel for the thing," which backbenchers wish them to convey to party leaders.

Thus far, we have investigated beliefs and behaviors associated with the goals of liaison and management. Now we turn to discipline, which generates the principal puzzles in the Whip's role.

Discipline: Persuasion and Authority

Whips have always aroused curiosity. Their role's peculiar title, which suggests coercion and control, recalls the "Whipper-in" who keeps headstrong hounds running with the pack. The packs, that is to say, the parliamentary parties, are heterogeneous associations of independent and egocentric individuals, not the sort to shy away from dissent and rebellion. Indeed, backbench dissent increased markedly during the 1970s. The record is summarized in the first column of Table 7.3, where it can be seen that the

Table 7.3 Unanimity and cohesion in House of Commons divisions, 1945–1979

Parliament	Both parties: Unanimity (% of divisions)	Conservative: Cohesion (% of divisions)	Labour: Cohesion (% of divisions)
1945–1950	93.0	99.7	99.6
1950–1951	97.5	100.0	99.6
1951–1955	97.0	100.0	99.3
1955–1959	98.0	100.0	99.8
1959–1964	86.5	99.9	99.8
1964–1966	99.5	99.8	100.0
1966–1970	90.5	99.3	98.9
1970–1974	80.0	99.9	99.1
1974	77.0	98.2	95.5
1974–1979	72.0	98.3	94.4

Source: Richard Rose, "British MPs: A Bite as Well as a Bark?" *Studies in Public Policy* 98, University of Strathclyde, 1982: 24–26.

Unanimity = no votes at all against the party Whip. Cohesion = at least 90 percent of Conservative or Labour MPs voting with the party Whip.

proportion of unanimous party votes declined sharply after the 1966–1970 Parliament.

Yet even the 1970s, the decade of dissent, should not be "overinterpreted as a breakdown of the iron cage of party discipline."[13] When the time came to march, and regardless of the issues involved, most Members were ready to follow a lead. Even in the most rebellious years, the Whips delivered perfect unanimity (i.e., not a single dissenting vote on either side) in three out of four divisions. Nor was the dissent widespread. The second and third columns of the table show that rebellions rarely included as much as 5 percent of the party's MPs.[14] Discipline, not dissent, was before, remained then, and is still today the dominant and remarkable pattern. And it has never been explained satisfactorily. I would like to sketch a central component of such an explanation based on the Whips' interpretations of their roles.

Whips like to argue that cohesion is produced by good communication.[15] The parliamentary parties, they say, are bound together by solidarity of interest and outlook; all that is needed from the Whips is a little information to fill in the details and point the way. Yet, one wonders whether solidarity and information alone can account for the remarkable lack of deviance in the division lobbies. Most outside observers think not, for they suspect that political dispositions require reinforcement. And the Whips seem to concur; their "communication" explanations are hedged by corollaries and qualifications. In fact, they are much more convincing about what is *not* the explanation: backbenchers are not controlled by autocratic discipline. In the first place, Whips rarely use it: "Oh it's too crude. If anybody thinks that I am able to say to Gerald Nabarro, 'Well, come on, into the No Lobby,' they've got a completely wrong idea of how it is done." Second, Whips do not have as much power as people suppose: they cannot proscribe a rebel's readoption, constituency work, attendance at the House, or voting.[16] Finally, raw power simply doesn't work very well: "If you started to try to run the party on strong-arm methods, you wouldn't succeed for ten minutes," or, "If a chap says, 'No, I'm not going to,' absolutely nothing we can do about it. Well, not absolutely nothing but very nearly." It is that "not absolutely nothing" that has intrigued political commentators and sustained their suspicions.

The puzzle is captured best in the Deputy Chief Whip's principal goal: "I am paid to ensure that people do vote according to the party's wishes"; and in his closely related belief that "we can't make the people go and vote in the lobbies when they don't want to do so." The point is that effective supervisors try to create conditions whereby subordinates are likely to want to do what their superiors wish them to do. The supervisor's chief resource is indeed good communication—information and reasonable explanation of the thinking behind leadership policies. To this extent, the Whips are correct in their public claims. But the key is not so much the information they provide as the persuasion that accompanies it, the fact that *the information is packaged in cues and requests that are received sympathetically because the Whips, working as agents of the leadership, have accumulated considerable authority.* And, giving the cynics their due, these relationships and their characteristic attitudes and behaviors rest ultimately upon power, upon rewards and punishments that remain in the back cupboard and, paradoxically, seem ineffective when applied to individual troublemakers.

The "decision rule" is the thread that runs throughout the entire process: when you have no firm opinion and are not a specialist on the subject, the most rational rule of thumb is to support party colleagues, usually in the leadership, who have devoted themselves to the matter because, "if you're not an expert in a particular field, you try and trust the judgement and integrity of your colleagues who are." This decision rule is widely accepted on both sides of the House; Whips believe in it and cultivate it just as they cultivate other "natural processes" that economize their efforts by ensuring that most Members, most of the time, will be pleased to proceed through the proper division lobby without special encouragement. Still, even the most reasonable politicians sometimes disagree. On many issues there may be at least a dozen MPs in doubt; on controversial matters their ranks may swell to sixty or more. In a closely balanced House, backsliding by even a small minority can threaten the Government's existence or at least undermine the Leader's authority. Besides, what if the cancer should spread? All this is perfectly clear to the Whips, who resort to persuasion as their first and most important line of defense.

PERSUASION: DISPELLING DOUBTS

Whips are often more upset at a Member failing to warn them in advance about his or her dissent than by the actual dissent itself.[17] The reason is clear: lack of warning denies them the opportunity to change the Member's mind before it is too late. Morrison had it right when he stressed that such persuasion is the Whips' main tactic for guiding backbenchers; they rely in their behavior primarily upon friendly reasoning rather than threatening bullying.[18] Indeed, a friendly chat is usually sufficient to dispel doubts and secure voluntary compliance. Members will be approached by Area Whips who are anxious to explain the leadership's reasons for the policy or tactic in question and, if the backbencher is not fully convinced, to articulate claims of interest and duty that may oblige him to go along this time around.

The dissenters who are most difficult to deal with in this way are the congenitally rebellious spirits. But Whips believe that these cases too should be approached through reasonable discussions. The first duty is to try to convince Members intellectually. They will seek to show how the policy fits into a broader picture of key party ideals and tactics or, if it doesn't, why this particular about-face is necessary at this particular time. On important issues, the arguments are rehearsed beforehand in the Whips' Office, where individual backbenchers are sometimes discussed in terms of the particular sources of their disagreements and the reasons most likely to prove effective in moving them. Ordinarily, however, the "policy explanation campaign" is conducted on the run: "They come to us and say, 'I'm sorry, I can't vote with the party tonight.' And the Whip says, 'Oh, really, I'm sorry to hear you say that, but can you tell me what your difficulty is?' And they say, 'Well yes, it's so and so, and so and so, and so and so.' And you say, 'Well the answer there is this and that,' whatever it is. And sometimes it works."

But sometimes it doesn't. Then the Whip brings forward his list of general reasons for supporting the party despite honest misgivings about the intrinsic wisdom of this particular policy. He offers arguments of interest, arguments of duty, or both—whatever he believes will win through in the circumstances and discourage abstention or rebellion.

Arguments of interest refer to the good of the individual and of the party. On relatively minor issues, *conserve your strength* is the first and most important argument of interest. This advice seems to meet the situation head-on. Discontented with party policy, the backbencher would presumably like to see it modified. And yet, counsels his Whip, this will certainly not be the only issue where you find you have doubts; there may well be others, including more important ones, in the future. Therefore, "I have learnt that you should keep your rebellions for very special occasions; otherwise you just become branded as a rebel and you don't have the influence"—you risk impotence on the matters about which you care most. Ministers do not take the constant complainers seriously. Likewise, fellow backbenchers will understandably be annoyed: they will feel that while they support leadership policies with which they disagree, you shirk these burdens. So conserve your strength for the days when you will really need it.

Not surprisingly, when those days arrive, another argument awaits the patient and now discerning dissenter. Characterized as *don't rock the boat,* the reasoning shifts from individual interests to party interests. This argument, however, carries conviction only for Government parties with small majorities: "It isn't much use using that argument when you have a majority of one hundred because the boat takes a good deal more rocking."[19] By voting against the Government on "a real three-liner," you will at the least embarrass the party and at the worst precipitate a General Election with adverse consequences for everyone on our side. Not only may some of us lose our seats, but there might be a change in Government, "because in modern politics, unfortunately, any Government now after about nine months becomes unpopular. Therefore, although you may enjoy exercising your conscience, you will in fact also be helping to embarrass and perhaps even to change the party in power." Few politicians relish the thought of helping their own side lose.

Should these interest arguments prove inapplicable or fail to persuade, the Whips have another shot in their lockers: arguments of duty that invoke obligations to party, voters, and groups affected by the policy. *You owe it to your party* presses the point that MPs are not elected as autonomous individuals. You are not here because you are Mr. X, but because you were the Conservative or Labour candidate in your constituency. On your own, you wouldn't have won a thousand votes, "you'd be nothing without the system and the party." Furthermore, scores of unpaid party activists in your constituency worked very hard indeed to send you here under the assumption that you would support party policy. And, if that isn't enough, it would be well to remember that you are indebted not just to the extraparliamentary party and its activists—you also owe a decent loyalty to your colleagues in the House. Finally, there is an argument for all seasons put to persistent dissenters and to new Members who seem headed in their direction. Known as *Are you on the right side?*, this insinuates disturbing doubts about the individual's fundamental political identity: "There is an old phrase about this, isn't there? Unless you agree with your party ninety percent of the time, you should consider your position. And if you disagree with it ninety percent of the time, you should join the other side."

In accounting for discipline in the division lobbies, reason and intelligent discussion have long been vastly underestimated. In part, this is because whipping has, since the 1950s, lost its rough edges gradually and quietly. Largely unnoticed, the system tipped farther toward reasonable persuasion than had been supposed. By the 1980s, the better commentaries recognized this fact and suggested that the most serious disciplinary sanctions had disappeared.[20] Still, if this revisionist view is carried too far, it becomes as misleading as the autocratic stereotype it overturned. What both accounts overlook are social learning processes about which many Whips and backbenchers are well aware. What is suspicious about the revisionist view is that the Whips' arguments are so routinely accepted despite being so contestable.

Thus, the arguments of Whips contain many ambiguities and dubious assumptions. Backbenchers can and sometimes do disagree, for they are often specialists on the topics of their dissent and may simply not find persuasive the leadership's explanations. Much the same can be said for the Whip's stock of claims about interest and duty. Each has its obvious rejoinder: (1) Conserve your influence for important matters: "This for me is an important matter," or, "That is a recipe for excessive timidity"; (2) Don't rock the boat: "I don't believe that the PM will call a General Election on this," or, "If he does, I think we will win"; (3) Duty to party and electorate: "I wasn't elected to be a cipher," or, "I also have a duty to follow my conscience"; and (4) Are you on the right side? "I certainly am," or, "It is the leaders who have abandoned party principles." Just as the Whips have their points, so dissatisfied backbenchers have counterpoints. But even the backbenchers who retort successfully in these little duets usually recoil from the final rebellion: "Sometimes they say, 'Well that's just not good enough.' And you say, 'All right, that's your business. You're a free agent; you vote any way you like.' Then they usually vote with the party." Why?

AUTHORITY: TRADING ON THE NORM OF RECIPROCITY

Because he starts from a comparatively weak base of *formal* authority, the Whip must strengthen conventions and forge support to nurture his *informal* authority and thereby increase the probability of success. By servicing subordinates' needs, Whips create good will and trade on the norm of reciprocity: "It certainly paid dividends because I knew that when a really difficult vote arose, I could rely on the complete good will and support of Members. . . . There were a considerable number of instances when people came back to vote at great personal inconvenience and told me that they had done so because they were so appreciative of the understanding I had shown of their problems at other times."

Every day Whips dispense benefits to backbenchers. They offer free information and generosity: "That door is always open, and anybody can come in at any time and ask for anything. It's really like the enquiry office at Charing Cross Station." By bestowing minor favors, making exceptions to rules, and tolerating delinquency, Whips accumulate reserves of informal authority that are based upon indebtedness and gratitude. There is nothing sinister about it at all. The exchanges are conducted with genuine cordiality and good will: "We had a tremendous task with practically one hundred new Members on our side, to settle them down and establish a working relationship with them, 'If you want any help, for God's sake come and ask me.' It's almost a sort of father-confessor relationship." The father-confessor image was commented on by many Whips who described backbenchers coming to them for "guidance, advice, help, or support." This is what Whips are there to give. And this is what they talk about when they discuss their roles.

They have more to give than is generally realized. Party leaders ensure that virtually every conceivable privilege is funneled through the Whips' Office. In fact, the Whips' Office is organized for giving. Its gifts, or investments, include minor favors, exceptions to the rules, and tolerating delinquency.

Minor favors are at the heart of exchange relationships. "Foreign visits, that's one type of reward—direct. You can go to the West Indies." During their careers in Parliament, some MPs have traveled the world; and nearly everyone remembers these expeditions as pleasant and informative.[21] The Whips regard places on trips as attractive patronage and distribute them accordingly. Such trips are not bribes (backbenchers are not prepared to sell their votes for weekends in Malta). But they are one of the fruits in a cornucopia of favors that, over time, cultivates good will and gratitude. Domestic delegations are another. After a long and timid preface, the backbencher explains that he wishes to join an all-party delegation selected to visit an RAF base and inspect a new airplane. The Deputy Chief Whip will see what he can do. Whips ease the lives of backbenchers through office accommodations, committee assignments, and government hospitality. They dispense places, for example, on Select Committees, which are not a right, but a privilege: "If he wants to be on that committee he says, 'Go on, do me a favour,' and he gets it."

In the same vein, some backbenchers are not much interested in the annual Garden Parties at Buckingham Palace, but others regard them as pleasant opportunities to treat family and friends: "I brought my mother to the Garden Party and she met the Queen and that was marvelous." Whips bestow the invitations. Much more important is the Whip's ability to make backbench views heard at the top. By maintaining close relationships with their flocks, Whips collect and aggregate backbench opinion for presentation to Ministers. The least tangible of all the Whip's offerings is sympathy, an inexpensive investment that can pay greater dividends than most. By continuing to listen to a Member's objections, even after it is clear that his complaints cannot be rectified, Whips demonstrate serious regard for the Member's views.[22]

The minor favors are indeed minor. None of these "plum things" really amounts to much by itself. But, taken together, they build a structure of obligations with the mortar of good will. Other opportunities to use the norm of reciprocity can be created by making exceptions to the rules and by tolerating delinquency.

Creative supervisors do not insist that the rules be followed at all times. Instead, they forge obligations by granting exceptions in individual cases. Subordinates tend to be indebted for these personal considerations and become dependent upon those who have the discretion to ease their lot when the going gets heavy.[23] Both parties, for instance, operate a pairing system that institutionalizes this strategy of exceptions. Whenever the House is sitting, Members have an obligation to be present at Westminster. But the House sits at very peculiar hours (from 2:30 P.M. till 10 P.M.) that were designed for past eras when eliteness was associated with lateness. Life would quickly become intolerable if excused absences were not permitted.[24] They are permitted, so long as the MPs who excuse themselves are paired. They are permitted by the Pairing Whip, who legitimates and records these arrangements. Another exception to the rules is granting permission to abstain on issues where an individual has a history of sincere doubts about the party's position. This prophylactic strategy helps avoid the crime of cross-voting by sanctioning a misdemeanor: "It may be that Whips realize they have no hope of persuading the Member to follow their lead. In these circumstances, admitting defeat would only demonstrate . . . weakness."[25]

If the situation is handled properly, supervisors enhance their authority by absolving and overlooking rule violations that have already occurred. By choosing not to apply their sanctions, they may foster guilt, gain hostages to fortune, and trigger recognitions of dependency. Guilt is evoked when the offender realizes he has been granted an impunity denied his colleagues; hostages to fortune are created when the evidence can, in the future, be used against him; and dependency is promoted when repetition of the act relies upon the supervisor's willingness to look the other way.[26] Opportunities to tolerate delinquency occur daily, since there is much delinquency needing toleration. Each week, for instance, there are more unexcused absences than is generally realized, some due to indifference, some to genuine dissent and rebellion. Whips lack the resources to stamp them out, but they can discourage them and let the delinquents know that they are aware of what is going on. Those who are indifferent to the Whips will, nevertheless, have to face their colleagues who held up the side while they were out. Those who relish telling the Whips to "stuff it" will, nevertheless, be giving hostages to fortune, for the Whips will then have the option of bringing their truancy to the attention of party leaders, party meetings, or constituency associations.

Nurturing party discipline requires much time because it requires more voluntary compliance than can be achieved by formal authority alone. Hence, the Whips seek to build up informal authority by trading upon the norm of reciprocity. The broad outlines of this process are familiar to observers of many other complex organizations. What is unusual here is the doggedness with which it is pursued; from free lunches to selective rule enforcement, Whips seem to inventory everything that backbenchers desire. The Whip's cornucopia has something for everyone, and even trivial benefits accumulate to build indebtedness under the norm of reciprocity. There are no crude bargains being struck here. Instead, reciprocity is seen by most of those involved simply as decent behavior, as a norm that, not surprisingly, tends to be policed by peers.

AND POWER

Authority without power has no bite. Most Whips, like Trollope's Chief Whip Mr. Ratler, recognize that reciprocity alone cannot win all the respect they require. Mr. Ratler had "known many docile Members of the House of Commons who had . . . lost all regard for him as soon as they were released from the crack of the whip."[27]

It is important to distinguish power as a system of control from implicit power threats, which are more-subtle tools. Power as a system of control uses punishments and rewards to produce *involuntary* compliance. Implicit power threats, by contrast, are used by Whips to facilitate *voluntary* compliance. Raw power is, in fact, rarely seen in the House of Commons and generally backfires when rolled out for use. That is why some observers conclude that the Chief Whip has no clothes.[28] Crude images of power as a control system do not describe accurately what Whips do, and do not explain convincingly the maintenance of party discipline. Yet, at the same time, the Whips use and depend upon subtle power threats to strengthen their informal authority and thereby nurture consensus and voluntary compliance.

The sturdiest authority is built upon both good will and power threats. This was one of Machiavelli's most astute insights.[29] Good will alone leaves too much in the hands of subordinates and creates an influence that is unreliable in times of stress. The addition of power threats gives a better grip. According to Machiavelli, successful leaders command both love and fear; and successful Whips practice his advice. Their threats are hidden in the shadows and consist of minor punishments, promotion evaluations, and "excommunication." The more unpleasant the threats, the less often they see the light of day. It is easy to understand how raw power can produce involuntary compliance. But how can subtle power threats promote a compliance that is genuinely voluntary?

By hinting at what might be done to delinquents, by referring to what has been done in the past, or by applying the odd thumbscrew, Whips remind backbenchers of the unequal power situation in their parliamentary party. These reminders are unwelcome. One obvious way that backbenchers can react is to listen more sympathetically to the views of the leadership.[30] To the extent that they adopt the leadership's attitudes, they will be in a position to follow their own preferences safely. With power threats in the background, it is rational to try to see things a bit more from the party's perspective. The accommodations lighten the discomforts of unequal power and defuse potential sanctions, and compliance becomes largely voluntary.

To retain their credibility, power threats need to be carried out from time to time. But frequent applications must be avoided, for that would suggest that voluntary compliance is not expected. Furthermore, backbenchers resent frequent displays of power that illuminate the submission they are avoiding by trimming their outlooks.[31] Instead, we should expect to see only occasional reminders, which is usually what we do see. One such reminder is the withdrawal of patronage to emphasize that reciprocity is a two-way street: "Some people have said to me, 'Well I'm not going into that lobby, I'm not doing you a bloody favour. . . .' And if the party are then expected to do favors for them, the favour, as far as they are concerned, is removed. And I remove it." Favors occasionally removed in this way include committee assignments, trips abroad, and pairing privileges.[32]

These minor punishments are usually little more than annoying raps on the knuckles. Nor, for good reason, are they applied consistently: "It isn't done consistently because there would be a real cry in this place, they would really band together." Moreover, it would be an imprudent Whip who flaunted his uncertain power over promotions, for rebels are known to have been co-opted into positions as Junior Ministers. Far better to keep this threat obscure and allow backbenchers to feel vaguely aware of the perils. Thus, the point of minor punishments is not so much to punish as to remind backbenchers of the Whips' *potential* power, of "what they could do if they wished."

The last reminder is "excommunication." This behavior cannot count as a direct application of power either, because suspension from party meetings is very unusual, while withdrawal of the Whip is so rare that by the 1970s it was losing credibility even as a threat. Pressure from constituency associations, which do have the power to "excommunicate," is more credible; and these threats can be triggered by the Whips. In fact, there may be more such cases than is generally realized. Leading Conservative anti-Marketeers, for instance, were under pressure from their constituency associations to stop damaging the Conservative Government. Constituency officers and executive committees, who were said to have been alerted by the Whips, reminded their Members about who put them in the Commons in the first place. Whips cannot instruct constituency parties to discipline their Members. But they can increase the likelihood of such discipline by discreet signals and by general talks about the need for it.[33]

In sum, Whips are expected to accumulate in their roles an informal authority that is grounded in good will and ensured against failure by the crack of the whip. Revisionist commentaries underestimate the importance of power in this process because it works subtly and second-hand. Nevertheless, when power threats lose their credibility, authority always suffers. And Whips know it. When, on one occasion, so many Labour frontbenchers and backbenchers disregarded a three-line Whip that nobody could be punished, the Chief Whip felt this undermined his authority so much that he considered stepping down.[34] More common illustrations of the power of power threats are older Members who intend to retire at the next General Election, or professional rebels who disdain promotion and patronage. People like these are beyond power threats—and they are not so easily persuaded: "That's when a Whip's powers are absolutely rock bottom. When a guy is going to go out next time or when he considers himself a failure or that he's got no chance, and he still wants to catch the limelight, he still wants to rub somebody in it, then all your persuasion will not alter that."

Raw power is rarely seen at Westminster. At the same time, power threats support reciprocity's informal authority by reminding subordinates of their subordination. The bitter taste can be neutralized by adjusting one's outlooks to the leadership's perspectives. Then one follows one's own convictions and avoids trouble too. Self-delusion is not required, for most backbenchers agree with the leadership most of the time and need only make minor modifications in their views. Nurturing these gentle adjustments was not always so clearly the core of the Whip's role: "Well, there was a time when the Whips just bludgeoned people into things," whereas today, "this is just not on. I mean we'd forfeit all *respect* in the House if we were to do things like that."

PARTY DIFFERENCES

After Patrick Buchan-Hepburn left the Conservative Chief Whip's Office in 1955, the party exchanged the crack of the whip for a modern human relations approach. The collective memory of its Whips' Office regards this as a historical fact and a necessity. Sanctions simply did not work as well as in the past when Whips like Buchan-Hepburn and Captain Margesson could treat dissenters as "defaulters on parade."[35] The role of the Conservative Whip has definitely come to rely more upon informal authority and less upon raw power: "I now talk to Whips who have operated in earlier years, and there's no doubt about it: the party has moved more and more along the lines of easing restraints, of accepting differences, of trying to take account of them in policy . . . there is a decline of authoritarianism, it's diminished."

On the Labour side, whipping underwent a similar evolution: "The old idea was that the Whips went around sort of cracking the whip and saying, 'You've got to vote and if you don't, ―――― ――――,' you know. Well, it doesn't work that way with us today. I think the books have an old-fashioned view of the job of a Whip. The books say the Whips say what you've got to do and the Members toe the line. This is balls, they don't, not in our party." Labour Whips talked about the changes even more than did their

Conservative counterparts: "a very, very tolerant organization, very tolerant indeed. And I think it's a good thing." But unlike the Conservative Office, the Labour Whips' Office was during the 1970s staffed by sturdy trade union types whose experiences had made them wary of sparing the rod and spoiling the child. They recited the new catechism repeatedly to overcome temptation and convince themselves of the necessity of the new approaches.

Although both parties have been changing in the same direction, the attitudes and behaviors that characterize their Whips' roles are still easily distinguished. In particular, Conservative roles are more likely than Labour roles to deploy carrots rather than sticks and to build informal authority through good will rather than through power threats. Conservative Whips develop amicable relationships within which it seems natural to provide assistance and seek help in return. Labour Whips try the same sort of thing, but the Tories do it better and believe that this makes them more effective: "It's much looser and more informal on the Conservative side. It proves in the end to be more effective. I mean we don't try to impose prefect-like discipline on the schoolboy in the way that occasionally the Labour Whips' Office seems to me as an outsider to work."[36]

Thus, even position roles that are as institutionally overdetermined as the role of the Whip leave room for variations across parties. And even within parties individual Whips employ different mixtures of reciprocity and power threats in their behavior. They also react differently to role conflict.

Role Conflict

When the machine runs smoothly, backbench views are communicated to sympathetic Ministers. Then Whips are doubly blessed: they enjoy the confidence of their subordinates and the gratitude of their superiors. Yet these backbench views often represent dissent, usually minor and constructive, but at times destructive and threatening. Whips therefore try to keep serious dissent as private and individual a matter as possible: "The sort of thing that infuriates me is a bloke abstaining or even voting against the Government and then coming and telling me afterwards." As dissent goes public, it easily escalates into confrontations that, whether won by Ministers or by backbenchers, are lost by the Whips, who are caught in the middle.

THE PROBLEM

The Whip's role can be as awkward as it is tiring, because Whips are marginal people assigned to sensitive negotiations between the worlds of superiors and subordinates. Neither fully leaders nor fully followers, they have a foot in each camp. They are committed to pushing through their masters' policies; but they are also closely associated with backbenchers, among whom they spend most of the day and whose confidence must be maintained if the job is to be done properly: "We are odd people. I mean we are Ministers, Junior Ministers of the Crown, but we are also part of the parliamentary party." Their situation is a striking example of role conflict, of "intra-role" conflict in which the individual occupies a position for which different groups have conflicting expectations.[37] Thus, Whips are expected by party leaders to be their agents and to deliver the votes of backbenchers. But they are, at the same time, expected by backbenchers to be their friends and to represent them to party leaders. This role conflict is frequently acute, because party leaders and backbenchers are well placed to observe what, from their perspectives, might seem to be disloyal or disappointing attitudes and behavior.

Ultimately, of course, the Whips serve their party's leaders, for they have been appointed "from above" in order to guarantee their efficient service as leadership agents. Thus, each party Leader chooses his Chief Whip, who, in turn, selects Junior Whips to work under him. Although Junior Conservative Whips are formally appointed by the party Leader, in practice they are selected by the Chief Whip. And, although in Opposition the Labour Chief Whip is formally elected by the Parliamentary Labour Party, the Leader's choice almost invariably prevails. Appointment "from above" is a cardinal principle of bureaucratic authority.[38] If Whips were elected by those for whom they would be responsible, as in the United States Senate, they would derive their position "from below" and might be tempted to take liberties with their superiors. The significance of this distinction between appointment and election should not be underestimated.

Elected leaders are usually chosen because they articulate basic group goals; and they continue as leaders only so long as they do not stray too far from these goals. As creatures of the group, their position first emerges through informal social relationships: "Ah, in those days Ted Carpenter was regarded as the sort of King of the Tea Room." But Ted Carpenter, the informal leader, was subsequently *appointed* as a Labour Whip and invested with new authority by superiors whose interests he was expected to serve, even when those interests clashed with the wishes of former backbench colleagues. And it was soon observed that "since he's been a Whip, he doesn't hold court like he did." His masters had issued him with power threats to brandish in pursuit of their goals. The new role didn't take. Too much the democratic leader, Carpenter found himself unable to crack the Whip and before long resigned his post with this complaint: "I believe there should be justice and equality in pairing arrangements and equal sharing of committees. I regret to say that doesn't happen, and that's the reason why I'm no longer a Whip." In accepting the appointment, he mistakenly assumed he could continue his informal leadership role as a spokesman for subordinates' goals. Carpenter had failed to grasp the nature of his new situation.

The common assumption that role players are unable to alter the circumstances of the role conflicts in which they find themselves exaggerates the force of institutional constraints.[39] Yet this assumption fits some situations fairly well, particularly when it is impossible to avoid performing the conflicting scripts at the same time. In such situations (and the Whips are in just such a situation), there is no escape; and the consequences for the role players include excessive self-control, tension, and alienation.[40]

CONSEQUENCES

Good Whips rarely lose their tempers; they struggle to maintain an outward calm and good humor in handling both superiors and subordinates. When new recruits are sought for the Whips' Office, self-control is accorded very high priority because, "to keep the machine working, Whips must suppress their own emotional reactions to events and discipline themselves to a job that is, after all, operating as a go-between or an intermediary. Therefore a Whip has to suppress a lot of his own feelings in the interests of being seen to be an impartial negotiator." When conflicting expectations become intense, successful negotiation requires a great deal of self-control indeed. But self-control and impartiality can be wearisome ("Well, sometimes you've got to bite your tongue"). And beneath their benign exteriors, Whips may suffer tension and unease: "I, uh, outwardly I don't seem to worry. But I do at times, I have my worries, yes. It gets intense, but I suppose it would depend on your own psychology—some people can withstand pressures, others can't. I don't get too worried when people want to disagree with me, and I don't get too happy when they want to applaud me."

Whips take pains to be on their best behavior and cannot afford to let down their hair, even when bleary-eyed at 3 A.M.: "The effect of being a Whip really is to make one think in the central position *all* the time. I mean it wouldn't do for him to behave unreasonably." Whips step on stage whenever they step outside the Office. They must exercise self-control to avoid offending anyone and must always remember that they are expected to set a good example: "The Whip has got to set an example, definitely. I've got thirty-two Members, and if I lose their confidence. . . . I think that could happen if you did something which you feel rather ashamed of."

When conflicting expectations compound the burdens of exemplary behavior, tension and anxiety build up quickly.[41] "Sometimes when I see people walking around very calmly, I think I must be the exception to the rule. I do get a fair amount of, shall I say, a tenseness." Or, when a session has been completed, "at the beginning of each recess I am absolutely dead beat, and this is partly the tension of being in the Whips' Office the whole time. My wife says, 'You come home and you're just like a cabbage.'" Nearly all the Labour Whips interviewed, and half the Conservatives, identified personal strain as an unpleasant side effect of their duties.[42] They talked about the emotional energy required to keep their flocks together, waking up at odd hours of the night worrying about something that is hanging on, "taking half a pill" to get back to sleep. The difficulties are particularly burdensome on the Labour side, where Whips are more often buffeted by rows: "I do get tension. And sometimes I blow my top. But I can relax easy enough— I suppose I'm a man for a Guinness."

The tensions and anxieties are exacerbated by the long hours. First to arrive and last to leave, Whips cannot escape the consequences of their role conflicts by playing truant or otherwise reducing significantly the time they put in on their tasks. They spend up to seventy hours a week in the Palace of Westminster. Monday through Thursday, they open the shop around nine in the morning and generally stay till midnight or later. When zealous backbenchers complete a twelve-hour day, the Whips may soldier on for sixteen or eighteen. Bench duty late at night brings lack of sleep, and squeezing constituency work into weekends leaves little time for family and social life. Some say they get used to the grind, and some thrive on it; but others describe this as the most tiring job they have ever had:

I, for instance, arrived here this morning at nine o'clock, as I practically always do. And then I take the count at half past nine and I do my constituency correspondence for, well, as long as it takes—this morning it took till about eleven. Then I had a Whips' meeting at eleven fifteen which went on till lunch time. And then the House sits at two thirty. We're going to be here all night tonight, I think, on the Ireland Bill. And as long as the House is sitting, the Whips have to be here, we never get away. And so by the time I get home I'll have been in this House for twenty-four hours. And then tomorrow morning again; normally my secretary comes in at half past nine, but I told her not to come till ten or eleven tomorrow morning, because I shall want to have a shave or a bath. And then off we go again. Yes, the hours are very long, but an awful lot of those hours are spent, as a Whip, sitting around—because you have to be here. And the hours just tick away and through the night and the division bell goes or there's a crisis of some kind and you have to rouse yourself and rush around the place looking for your flock, rousing them into action.

The pressure also occasionally leads them to boil over in ways that may alienate them from fellow Members. Auberon Waugh's puckish report in *Private Eye* regretted the state of affairs whereby Whips were no longer able to manhandle Members and regretted in particular the dismissal of a Deputy Chief Whip for shaking by the lapels a disloyal backbencher he found drinking in Annie's Bar.[43]

ADAPTATIONS

It is difficult to imagine role conflicts in political life that would be more acute than those facing Whips. Both Ministers and backbenchers have very clear expectations about how Whips should behave. And the conflicts between these expectations are serious conflicts of interest. To adapt, Whips develop strategies that include compartmentalization, deflection of resentment upward, and withdrawal.

Those who handle the conflict best compartmentalize their social relationships: they look to other Whips for emotional support and become detached from backbenchers. Within the Whips' Office they find comradeship, a brotherhood that provides reassurance ("Most of the people I mix with would think highly of the Whips. I mean I live in the Whips' Office") and helps its members tolerate the emotional detachment from backbenchers that is the other side of the coin. One after another, Conservative Whips paid glowing tributes to the companionship of the Office. They spoke about the candor, the warmth, and the generosity of their fraternity: "In the Whips' Office the comradeship is quite exceptional. I mean I have never been able to reproduce quite this sort of almost brotherly feeling. I mean we refer to each other as 'the Brothers,' 'the Mafia.' Since I left my regiment I sought it; I tried to join all kinds of organizations like Rotarians and never found it again till I got here."

Although Labour Whips did not characterize their team as quite so intimate, they too enjoyed a special conviviality that helped to compensate for some of the discomforts with backbenchers and for other unpleasant consequences of their roles: "The conversation is good, you know, the banter usually very cynical. The Whips' Office is a very interesting place to be, a great bunch of cynics, an enjoyable experience. Nobody is really concerned to trample on the personalities of others. I mean there's a lot of banter, pull your leg, pull my leg." Asked to name their closest personal friends in the House, two-thirds of the Labour Whips named only other Whips, and four out of five Conservative Whips did the same.

Since Whips must tilt toward the frontbench, they tend to relieve the strain of their role conflict by creating a subtle social distance between themselves and the backbenchers for whom they are responsible: "A Whip, I suppose, is a pretty lonely sort of guy in many respects, you know." This is part of their social compartmentalization, part of their strategy for riding over the rough patches. Supervisors in other organizations go further and withdraw from informal gatherings, dine apart from the men, and so on. But the Whips cannot use such tactics because they must oversee backbenchers' opinions and keep acquainted with their personal problems. It is an essential part of their role to meet backbenchers informally most days and to participate in social gatherings while reconciling themselves to the realization that "I think there's a lot of banter about Whips and so on in the Tea Room and in the bars." The task is delicate because they must always be there and must cultivate confidences without reciprocating in a way that would undermine their position as the leadership's men.[44] The Whip's adroitness in distributing favors can help sweeten these exchanges but cannot entirely bar the resentments: "The experience is tremendous. But I think myself that the Members may dislike you; after all, you can't be everybody's pin-up boy. I tell my wife, she's my greatest supporter, that you can't be everybody's pin-up boy."

Compartmentalization is a defensive reaction to role conflict. A more aggressive strategy is to deflect backbenchers' resentments upward toward the Ministers who are calling the shots. Thus, Whips may explain to backbenchers that they have no choice, that their masters require them to lean on subordinates in this way: "You've got to talk to them about the problems of the job—'It's a bloody terrible job, isn't it, that I've been lumbered with and cor, I bet you're glad you haven't got it, but anyway I've got to see that the East Midlands plays its part, you know.'" Yet, these are dangerous games, for they target party leaders as scapegoats and, in the long run, may damage the party's morale and discipline. If compartmentalization can be interpreted as an expression of "loyalty" to the leadership, and deflecting resentment upward as a form of "voice," then surely withdrawal from the role is a type of "exit"—one that becomes attractive to those who value their relationships with the rank and file more than their associations with the Great and the Good. During the period of the interviews, several Whips besides Ted Carpenter resigned voluntarily from the Office, and several others announced that they were worn out and would be leaving Parliament altogether at the next General Election.

Willingness to do it again provides insight into a job's difficulties. Many MPs who voluntarily leave other leadership positions later come back to them. But none of the former Whips interviewed in this study ever came back to the treadmill after having left it behind. Moreover, since 1906 less than 5 percent of all Whips have had a second go, most of them before 1945.[45] Despite the fact that those in harness express satisfaction and even enthusiasm about the role, their duties and responsibilities entail significant sacrifices: endless hours, remarkable self-control, and considerable tension. In other organizations, the strains produced by role conflict are balanced by advantages such as special privileges, ego enhancement, or improved future prospects.[46] Such advantages used to hold Whips for an average of five years, but today nearly half of them move on before the end of three.

Sources of Role Choice

Many backbenchers understand the role of the Whip very well—and wouldn't touch it with a barge pole.[47] Indeed, given all the tribulations and tensions, one wonders how any sane backbencher could possibly be lured into the Office. Yet, according to former Conservative Chief Whip Francis Pym, it has never been difficult to recruit Whips, for there has never been a shortage of willing candidates.[48] Who, then, does the Chief Whip look for, and why do they agree to serve?

OPPORTUNITIES: PSYCHOLOGICAL ATTRIBUTES

The opportunities that affect the selection *of* backbench roles are factors, like constituency characteristics, that *actors* take into account in making their own choices. By contrast, the opportunities that affect the selection *for* frontbench roles are factors that *gatekeepers* use to choose recruits. The mix varies according to each Chief Whip's predilections and the availability of candidates to fit his plans. Nevertheless, it is possible to identify some standard guidelines, the psychological aspects of which concern personality traits, attitudes, and values.

Gregariousness is an essential personality trait for people who will be required to develop convivial relationships.[49] This is recognized as the common denominator on both sides: "We have this ability to get on with people; we're just a gregarious sort of lot." Whips must be approachable and ready to serve as good listeners whose modesty and sympathy will attract frank discussion. In the Labour Office, gregariousness implies a talent for the chatty humor of working-class banter: "But of course I'm a humourist as you might know; and I always see humour in every situation. I've a story to fit every situation, and I often relate that you know." Conservatives have their own peculiar style of banter and stress that newcomers must be able to fit in comfortably with Office colleagues. Gregariousness is a ticket to backbench social circles; it opens the door to relationships that can be used to pick up political intelligence, to pick up both explicit information and cues implicit in what is left unsaid.

Whips must also be capable of emotional detachment, for they will be expected to hold themselves aloof from party factions, though not from the party itself. Party loyalty is, in fact, a sign of suitability for work that entails building unity behind the leadership's program. One Conservative Whip, for example, explained that he had recently declined an invitation to join an ideological group because he believed that Whips should not push particular outlooks but should aim instead for reasonable neutrality. They must, he suggested, set aside any strong views they may hold, in order to maintain confidence in their reliability as honest messengers: "Otherwise a back-bencher may think that you wouldn't be honest in putting forward any view he'd expressed that was contrary. And I think that's right. I think one should be a sort of quasi-professional." Nothing would undercut his effectiveness more than giving the impression that "there's an element in the party which is not acceptable to me, which I wouldn't have anywhere near me." The only Whip who saw his role otherwise ("My most important responsibility is to ensure that the point of view of the Right is held in all the party") was a misfit who left after having served only a few months.

Although true believers must be kept out, representative values must be brought in. "Balance," several Whips suggested, is an important recruitment consideration: "I think our Office has a great range of people; politically you've got every range of the political spectrum: we have right-wing Members, we have left, and everybody in-between in our Office. That's deliberate actually." The claim can be examined by comparing the political values of Whips with those of their party colleagues. During the interviews, respondents were asked to rank-order, according to personal preferences, an inventory of political values that had been culled from parliamentary debates, memoirs, and political commentaries and presented in four lists of nine values each.[50] Difficult as it may be to represent the party's principal opinion groups in the bland Whips' Office, they must nevertheless each have kindred spirits on deck if they are to be reached effectively.

The Conservatives' Right and Left flanks divide most sharply over seven values: authority, compassion, free enterprise, patriotism, public order, community, and intelligence.[51] Labour factions are most at odds over participatory democracy, freedom, socialism, fellowship, empirical approach, economic equality, and security. The Whips' distributions for these key political values were plotted alongside those of other Members of their parties, with results that strongly support the argument that each side's broad value spectrum is well represented in its Whips' Office. The distributions were remarkably similar in every case. This is illustrated by Figure 7.1, which compares, for two of the seven values in each party, the percentages of Whips and non-Whips who ranked these values first, second, third, and so on in their lists. Thus, "You need a whole range of people so that every kind of Member, every section of the party, has somebody in the Whips' Office who's on their own terms and to whom they can talk and make their views known to them."[52]

OPPORTUNITIES: SOCIAL BACKGROUND ATTRIBUTES

Without standardized personality tests of the kind used in some business organizations, it would obviously be difficult to evaluate according to psychological criteria the entire backbench. Fortunately, there is no need to scan the entire backbench. Economy of effort can be achieved by focusing upon people with particular background characteristics of social-class origin, education, previous occupation, and gender.

From this perspective, Conservative Whips are as thoroughly middle class as their Labour colleagues are working class. Most Tory Whips' fathers were small businessmen, farmers, or modest professionals, such as chartered surveyors. Virtually all Labour Whips were raised in solidly working-class families. There is a conspicuous absence of upper-class background on the Conservative side and of middle-class background on the Labour side. The one has a middle-management tone, the other a shop-steward cadence.

One possible reason for this lies in the relationship between Whips and backbenchers. Any Whip's authority creates some distance from subordinates. Reinforcing his position with high social status might extend the distance and therefore add unnecessary impediments to comfort and confidence. Though perhaps it is not a critical consideration, the Whip's path will be smoothed when he and his flock share similar life experiences. Thus, Conservative backbenchers, who are overwhelmingly middle class themselves, are served by middle-class Whips. Where the match cannot be made, the rule of thumb is that supervisors should hail from more humble origins

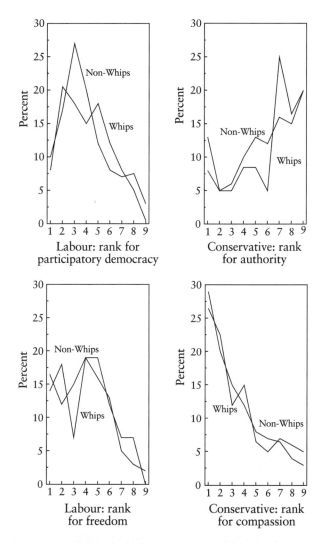

Figure 7.1 Illustrative value rankings of Whips and Non-Whips in the Labour and Conservative parties. (*Note:* Whips are both serving and former Whips who were interviewed and completed value ranking data: Labour $N = 28$; Conservative $N = 27$. Non-Whips are respondents who completed value ranking data but were neither serving nor former Whips: Labour $N = 188$; Conservative $N = 189$.)

than those of the subordinates whose confidence they must maintain. It is easier for most backbenchers to be chummy with Joe Bloggs than with Sir Alec. This rule can be seen more clearly on the Labour side, where matches between Whips and backbenchers are difficult because a Labour Whip's flock will usually mix Members from both middle- and working-class backgrounds. Thus, twelve of the fourteen serving Labour Whips were not the offspring of schoolmasters or civil servants but rather of miners and railwaymen.

Some would deny that social class is a salient consideration in the search. Evaluating MPs by their preparliamentary status violates an important Westminster taboo. The difficulty is that other variables, for other reasons, guide the selection process toward the same class outcomes.[53] For example, university graduates are rare additions to the Labour team. House gossip had it that graduates rarely entered the Labour Whips' service, and when they did, they did not last. Among the fourteen Labour Whips interviewed, three had been at university, but only one at Oxbridge (Oxford or Cambridge); the second departed before long for a higher post; and the third had, through trade union scholarships, attended university as a mature student, which seems to have preserved his talent for working-class banter. On the Conservative side, middle management has swept out the traditional regimental-headquarters atmosphere: "Fifteen years ago, most of the Whips were good, sound military gentlemen. And when they'd finished their duty, they either went to the Lords or they became Governor of Bengal or somewhere. That's totally changed." Today the Office is staffed by mild-mannered merchants, only one of whom has had a military career—and even he left it for the business world twelve years before entering Parliament. If the Tories seek recruits who can pursue a human relations approach to personnel management, and therefore look to businessmen rather than to brigadiers, Labour worries about party unity and therefore passes over intellectuals to give trade unionists first priority.[54]

Gender is the only background factor that does not reinforce middle- and working-class outcomes. Prior to the mid-seventies, only one woman had served as a Whip, Harriet Slater, who was appointed in 1964.[55] Women have been Ministers since the 1920s. Why did it take another forty years to break into the Whips' Office? The standard answer is that they wouldn't be suitable; for, unlike ministerial work, whipping is inseparable from life in the House of Commons, from the gentlemen's club of leather and liquor. This explanation is not fully convincing, because women have been Parliamentary Private Secretaries and performed many of the same liaison duties as Whips. A more plausible explanation notes that Whips are disciplinarians and, although male backbenchers accept women as Ministers or PPSs, the prospects of being disciplined by them might be another matter altogether.[56]

Social background criteria narrow the opportunities by narrowing the search. They enable gatekeepers to look for psychologically suitable candidates among manageable numbers of potential recruits. This screening frame is further compressed by considerations of parliamentary experience.

OPPORTUNITIES: PARLIAMENTARY ATTRIBUTES

Since Assistant Whips must shepherd flocks from particular regions of the country, it makes sense to find candidates who already know many of these Members and who will be familiar with their problems: "I mean naturally the sort of things like areas which you would represent, and the fact that we haven't got anybody in the North, or we haven't got anybody in the South West, comes into it." These considerations alone can narrow the search process more swiftly than any other.

Similarly, it is reasonable to pass over Members who are either very old or very young. The settled routines of older MPs may make them reluctant to accept such a demanding role. And, even if willing, they may be unable to adapt. Newcomers present other drawbacks, such as insufficient acquaintance with parliamentary procedures, folkways, and factions within the parliamentary parties. Thus, F. M. G. Willson found that between 1906 and 1966, the average Whip spent approximately four years in the House before being appointed to his post.[57] A similar pattern can be seen in Table 7.4, which reports prior tenure data for the serving and former Whips interviewed in the present study. There is ample spread around the mean but a clear bias toward younger rather than more senior Members.

Since they cannot make political speeches in the House, Whips lose this opportunity for local publicity and visibility in their constituencies. Thus, there is a danger that constituents may forget them, and their electoral sup-

Table 7.4 Length of tenure before becoming Whips

| Party | Years in the House | | | | | | | | Total N |
	1 (or less)	2	3	4	5	6	7	8 (or more)	
Labour	5	7	7	3	5	3	1	0	31
Conservative	8	8	5	5	1	4	2	3	36

port may decline over the years. Tories tend not to worry about this so much, because a posting in their Whips' Office can be regarded as a brief passage on the way to ministerial careers. Labour Whips stay longer and must therefore be protected by larger majorities. They do, in fact, have safer seats than their Conservative counterparts: twice as many serving Labour Whips sit atop majorities of 20 percent or more, though a substantial minority are in precarious electoral circumstances.

Experience and behavior at the House are also signs of suitability. Given that Whips must spend very long hours at Westminster, it makes sense to look for people who are already there a good deal of the time and whose personal or business commitments will not compel them to reject an offer. More helpful still is the experience that comes from a turn as a Parliamentary Private Secretary. Although the PPS is an apprentice Minister, his liaison tasks are similar to part of the Whip's role. Not surprisingly, therefore, Willson found that approximately half the Conservative Whips appointed between 1906 and 1966 had previously been Parliamentary Private Secretaries, as had fifteen of the thirty-six Conservative Whips interviewed in the present study.[58]

The last parliamentary attribute to be considered is rather puzzling, particularly on the Labour side. Despite Labour's emphasis on party loyalty as a psychological prerequisite, nearly half its Whips are reformed mavericks. And many of them seem proud of their former reputations as rebellious spirits in school, industry, or the House: "I voted against the Labour Government on prescription charges, defence and industrial relations." Or, "I have been known to go it alone. And if there were implied threats, that didn't impress me too much. I'm just that sort of character." It is recognized that certain types of rebels can successfully be harnessed to the team—which has the dual advantage of ensuring their future loyalty and adding people who may prove talented at mollifying insurgents.[59] One way of putting it is that poachers make good gamekeepers: "I wasn't the sort of chap who came into the Whips' Office and suddenly, you know what I mean, became a poacher turned gamekeeper." There are fewer former poachers in the Conservative Whips' Office, but one or two strays have had similar experiences: "Nobody told me anything when I first came in. I mean, well it was a bit silly, a thing I laugh about now, but I voted against my party. And I was invited to have a little conversation with the Chief Whip. I've never been so frightened in my life. I was shaking all over. And he said he'd never forgive me. Then he said, 'Who's your Whip?' So I said, 'I don't know.' And not long afterwards he invited me to join the Whips' Office."

Because the Whip's role is so critical to the party's success, and to the efficiency of the parliamentary machine, it is important that candidates possess the necessary character and social skills. Scanning the backbenchers for appropriate individuals would be extremely difficult were it not possible to concentrate on subgroups identified by background characteristics and parliamentary experience. This produces a selection frame within which the remaining individuals can be examined carefully and ranked according to key psychological attributes.[60]

Before the offer is made, the Chief Whip must consider whether or not it is likely to be accepted; frequent refusals will tarnish the gift and undermine the Whips' authority. Francis Pym has assured us that there are always willing candidates. Why are they interested?

INFORMATION AND EXCITEMENT

The motivational approach reconstructs roles by focusing on actors and by providing an integrated account of their goals, beliefs, and behaviors. The role of the Whip is highly crystallized because its principal goals—liaison, management, and discipline—are thoroughly specified by the institution. In taking up the role, Whips adopt these goals as their primary foci of interest. Even this motivational structure, however, leaves room for personal goals and emotional incentives—without which the role of the Whip cannot be satisfactorily understood.

Most politicians covet inside information. As the communications channel between front- and backbenches, the Whips' Office has more than enough inside information to satisfy the most addicted of newsmongers. "Well, I mean the great big advantage really is knowing what's happening all the time; one is told 90 percent of the time exactly what's happening in the party." Yet Whips are "doers" rather than observers, and they do things with the information they soak up. They tend to be gregarious people whose political voyeurism is a prelude to persuasion and an alternative to the lonely tasks of policy research. It gives them a finger on the party's pulse and foreknowledge of what will likely happen next week: "So when all the sort of crises occur, it's the Whips who know right across the board, ahead of almost everyone else, even sometimes ahead of Cabinet members." Gossip touching the strengths and weaknesses of every MP is part of the routine, "and you've always got something interesting to talk about."

For those who enjoy being at the center of things, the Whips' Office is "the cockpit of the political struggle," which puts you "right in the nerve centre" of the parliamentary body politic. Quite apart from the inside information, this venue offers an education in the subtleties of persuasion, power, and parliamentary procedure. There is an absorbing excitement in being associated, even as a factotum, with power and the powerful ("You really are in Government in the Whips' Office, you really are"), which confers an agreeable status upon the chosen few.[61]

INFLUENCE AND BROTHERHOOD

But Whips are not merely factotums; their Office is a brokerage house for the influence trade. The attractions of trading in influence are an important motivation for Whips. Because they are exponents of ministerial policy and monopolize inside information, Whips become opinion leaders to back-benchers. Many identify this as a key satisfaction in the role. "You see, the Whips know what is going on more than other Members do. So that when there's a Whip in any group of people discussing affairs of Parliament, this is regarded as an informed opinion." And Whips are keenly aware of their potential influence: "If you keep saying it often enough, they'll adopt it and adopt it as their own."[62]

Conservatives say that no important policies are put forward, no White Papers published, until a Whip has sifted each proposal for snags that may arise from the party's backbenchers. Since they are regarded as ministerial material, Tory Whips may be involved here more than their Labour counter-parts. "You talk about things that actually matter with people who will have quite a big say in the decision. I enjoy that." In this way, Whips some-times sound like Policy Advocates who feel they are achieving modest suc-cess by influencing the influential. And all of them, Labour and Conservative alike, are usually consulted about whipping arrangements, strategies, and tactics for getting Bills through the House. Playing the central link in a chain of authority is particularly attractive to people who enjoy the responsibility of weighing subordinates' criticisms and cajoling the troops into line.[63]

Whips are, in fact, driven by many different desires; it should not be sur-prising to hear, in addition to the echoes of Spectators and Policy Advocates, the sounds of Club Men pursuing conviviality. The Whips' brotherhood indemnifies them against unpleasantness with backbenchers and helps ex-plain the peculiarity of sociable people voluntarily joining a team that has been called "an unpopular group of men."[64] Actually, by joining "the club within the club," Whips can improve the range and intensity of their con-tacts with backbenchers. And in the Whips' Office they find a comradeship that backbench social circles often lack. Assistant Whips are always on the lookout for suitable comrades and will say to the Chief Whip or party Leader: "We want so and so because we can work with him." They also apparently exercise a veto over candidates proposed by others: "The Whips' Office will not have anybody in it whom somebody would object to, because it is such a closely knit group and has to be put under a tremendous lot of strain as a group, a team working together."

This cohesiveness is reflected in friendship patterns that center on office colleagues: "No better friend will you ever find than one's colleagues in the Whips' Office, I think. And you are a lifelong friend forever." Moreover, among Conservatives, the "Old Whip Tie" certainly doesn't harm promotion prospects that, for other reasons, already seem quite bright.

PROMOTIONS AND POUNDS

The desire for promotion is a significant incentive on the Conservative side, where tours in the Whips' Office are regarded as apprenticeships for ministerial work: "I think on our side we're picked as a Whip looking a little ahead that you might possibly be material for ministerial promotion at some future time."

In deciding whether to accept the offer of a Whip's post, backbenchers will examine the present and the recent past in order to project their prospects. Thus, the Conservative backbencher Julian Critchley observed that "not only have former Chief Whips made good, but it has become clear to us all that the road to the top runs straight through the Whips' Office. Those who would gain life must first lose it."[65] In addition to the Prime Minister, former Whips Anthony Barber, William Whitelaw, Gordon Campbell, and Joseph Godber had all risen to the Cabinet.[66] If it is suggested to prospective candidates that the role might be a stepping stone, how many former Whips can they themselves see around the House who have actually stepped up to high office? It would be difficult to misinterpret the signs in Table 7.5. Among former Conservative Whips still walking the corridors, 75 percent attained positions as at least Junior Ministers or Opposition Spokesmen.

Asked about their own promotion prospects, two out of three Conservative Whips said that they expected to find a place on the frontbench. This can be a substantial reason for taking up the role, just as it can be a serious motive for choosing similar roles in the House of Lords or the United States Senate.[67] In exploratory conversations with the Chief Whip or Assistant Whips, it might be hinted that "the normal healthy Whip will have to advance sometime," and "the Chief Whip takes the line, you know, that if a Whip is at all promotable, then a Whip should have a crack at it. And the Chief Whip has a great deal of influence." But promotion considerations are not relevant for every Conservative candidate. Some Whips must preserve

Table 7.5 Highest position attained after leaving Whips' Office, in percent

Position	Labour*	Conservative*
Backbencher	44	19
Parliamentary Private Secretary	24	6
Junior Minister or Junior Opposition Spokesman	20 ⎫ 32	47 ⎫ 75
Senior Minister or Senior Opposition Spokesman	12 ⎭	28 ⎭
Total	100	100
	(N = 25)	(N = 25)

*p ≤ .01

continuity and be able to mix comfortably with the older backbenchers. It would not do to field a team composed entirely of ambitious young men. Hence, there tend to be two types of Tory Whips, those who are upwardly mobile and others for whom service in the Office constitutes a career: "It is a stepping stone for some people to Government office. It wouldn't be in my case because I'm too old. One has certain Whips you bring in, I think, for stability purposes, and other people who are passing through and going on to promotion. I think there have always been the two sorts in the Whips' Office. Some people make the Whip's job a career."[68]

So most Conservative Whips go onward and upward. But how exactly do they manage it? How, without a policy specialization, will they attract the leadership's attention? How, without speaking in debates, will they achieve recognition in the parliamentary party? The answer to the first dilemma is easy: behind the scenes, Whips have ample opportunity for direct contacts with Ministers.[69] Exposure as a speaker is more difficult; one place that provides visibility before large audiences is the weekly meeting of the 1922 Committee where, by rotation, Whips take their turn on stage to explain the next week's business.

Labour backbenchers, by contrast, accept that promotion is a far from inevitable outcome of service in their party's Office (see Table 7.5). Promotions may have been more common in the past, Labour Whips say, whereas Conservatives believe that prospects on their side are better than ever. And Labour Whips recognize that "the Conservatives use their Whips' Office more as a springboard than what Labour do. You'll find that there's more promotions from the Tory Whips to Ministers of State and so on than what there is from the Labour Whips' Office. The Labour Whips don't get the same privileges in that respect." Only four of fourteen serving Labour Whips anticipated advancement to the frontbench, each of them with considerably greater uncertainty than their Conservative counterparts. And those without ambitions included both the young and the old, whereas only older Conservatives had withdrawn from the race.[70] In fact, the Labour Whips' Office rarely recruits ministerial material. This is reflected in its preference for trade unionists over graduates who might make more likely administrators. Most candidates for the post of Labour Whip see the service as an interlude in their backbench careers. They seek satisfactions other than promotion and stay on the job longer than their Conservative colleagues.

An alternative consideration for Labour recruits is the Whip's salary supplement, which can substantially improve their parliamentary income. Since Conservative backbenchers often have outside business interests, they may face the prospect of reducing their total income by accepting a paid office which requires that such interests be relinquished. By contrast, Labour candidates are more likely to be living mainly on their modest parliamentary salaries. The supplement for Assistant Government Whips at the time of the interviews would have increased a backbencher's parliamentary income by more than half. And a recruit who eventually rose to become Deputy Chief Whip could expect still more.[71] The additional salary is woefully inadequate compensation for the additional hours, but for people without outside incomes it must look helpful.

There isn't much else, since during the 1970s honors became a thing of the past: "Even on the Labour side Labour Whips got the CBE (a minor honour) in turn according to seniority each year. Wilson put the kibosh on as Prime Minister, which met with my approval. That's gone." Whips' minor incentives became limited to trips abroad and hospitality. Unable to promise promotions, the Labour Chief Whip distributed trips as patronage: "A Whip can go on foreign visits if he wants. I mean I've been offered a lot of foreign visits. That's one type of reward you know." A few also appreciated the hospitality, though none took it very seriously: "You get more than your share of free lunches which are a bore. But you can choose, you know, 'Well, the Ambassador from Panama is here, OK, you go and have lunch with the Ambassador.' "

To assure the recruitment of loyal leadership agents, Whips are appointed by their superiors. While curious mistakes have occasionally been made ("Geoffrey Bing . . . was appointed a Junior Whip in 1945 by accident. Attlee's instructions to Whiteley, the Chief Whip, included the name of Joe Binns. . . . Luckily for Bing, Whiteley misread Attlee's scrawl"),[72] selection and motivation mechanisms are usually efficient in finding the right person for the role. To understand this role, one must realize that the Whip is, above all, a leadership agent: "I am paid to ensure that people do vote according to the party's wishes." To understand the Whip's success, one must remember that "we can't make people go and vote in the lobbies when they don't want to do so."

The role is important, perhaps the most important in the House. Its principal goals are liaison, management, and discipline. Liaison builds consensus within the parliamentary party and thereby creates unity and strength. Thus, Whips try to see their backbench flocks daily in order to explain difficulties, soothe tempers, help with problems—and listen. They listen for backbenchers' views, which they report back to the Chief or Deputy Chief Whip. The Whips are also managers. Without their diligent efforts, Parliament could never "tick over." The "usual channels" plan the flow of parliamentary activity, while the Deputy Chief Whip runs the Office, assigns tasks to Junior Whips, and is assisted by the Comptroller and the Vice Chamberlain in arranging accommodation, committees, and pairing. In the Chamber, Junior Whips take turns watching over procedure and making sure that the right motions are moved at the right times. When they are not in the Chamber, corridors, or bars, they can be found managing committees. Whips' roles keep them running from morning till night and sometimes throughout the night as well.[73]

Party discipline is the key to effective government in Britain. And party discipline is the Whips' principal responsibility. Their success rates are truly remarkable: considering the ideological uproar in both major parties during the 1970s, even the rebellious surge during that decade looks quite modest. Whips are efficient truant officers and effective supervisors who build informal authority in order to persuade. The secret of their success has much to do with their application of Machiavelli's insights. Thus, the Whips' messages are received sympathetically because they trade successfully on the norm of reciprocity with a steady stream of minor favors, exceptions to the rules, and toleration of delinquency. This reciprocity is backed by subtle power threats that remind backbenchers of their position in the hierarchy and of what they might risk by reckless defiance.

Because the role of the Whip is so important, its duties and responsibilities are amply specified, and Whips are selected with great care. Recruitment is in the hands of gatekeepers who focus on social background and parliamentary attributes that help them reduce the field to a manageable number of backbenchers who can then be scrutinized for psychological characteristics. Clearly, the role of the Whip is not for everyone. Nor is everyone interested, for the costs are considerable. Whips open the shop in the morning, lock it up late at night, and describe the job as the most tiring they have ever had. Whips are bound by collective responsibility to refrain from publicly criticizing party policy; but unlike Ministers, they cannot speak at all in the Chamber, nor can they raise controversial issues in the press.[74] Nor can they raise constituency matters through debate or adjournment motions, since this might involve criticizing Government policy. Instead, Whips must look after their constituents' problems entirely by correspondence with Ministers.

Considering the many disadvantages, one wonders how anyone could possibly be persuaded to take up the role. Yet, though the costs are significant, so too are the attractions. Many recruits are drawn in by the prospects of inside information and the excitement of being in the real cockpit of the political struggle. Many more are attracted by the influence. They can become opinion leaders to backbenchers and may also be able to direct a little influence toward Ministers. Furthermore, the brotherhood attracts gregarious people. And, last but hardly least, Conservative backbenchers are well aware that a turn in their Whips' Office can greatly enhance their promotion prospects.

Compared with backbench roles, the motivational core of the role of the Whip seems multifarious. It encompasses the inside dopesterism of Spectators, the sense of achievement of Specialists, the promotion hopes of Ministerial Aspirants, and the Generalist's love of action and diversity. Recruits are also aware that contact with party leaders and with inside information can make good the Whip's silence and loss of policy specialization, and that the brotherhood can compensate for detachment from backbenchers. In fact, some recruits see nothing but the silver lining. Most susceptible to the job's seductions are, on the one hand, Conservative high flyers hoping to advance their careers and, on the other, working-class Labour MPs hoping to become involved, rub elbows with power, and confirm their adaptation to the world of Westminster. Whips enjoy building up informal authority and successfully promoting the leadership's program. Unlike PPSs, Whips are far more than messengers—they are craftsmen in the art of managing Members.

MINISTERS: LEADERSHIP IN
WESTMINSTER AND WHITEHALL

One tries to behave in the way in which
one's colleagues, and the House of Commons,
generally expect Ministers to behave.

A Minister

Two institutional tasks, checking the Executive and selecting leaders, shape the relationship between the Government and the House of Commons and thereby shape the role of the Minister. The House of Commons "checks" the Government by criticizing its Bills and its Ministers. The House of Commons "selects" the Government by formulating judgments about Members of Parliament who would like to become Ministers.

Ministers and Members

"Being a Minister is not just being a good administrator and running your department well, but it's also dealing with all of the things in *parliamentary* life." Ministers are Members of the Government and, at the same time, Members of Parliament. The two sides of this role are inseparable because, unlike "the American situation where the executive is ranged against the legislative, in Britain the executive is part of the legislature." Because Ministers are Members, they connect Government and Parliament—a "buckle" was how Walter Bagehot characterized the dual nature of their role. Today's analogies may be different, but the point is much the same: "I describe myself very often as the springs of a motor car, the car being very heavy and being the Government, the road being very bumpy and being Parliament."

In reconstructing the role of the Minister, it is easy to overdo the departmental administration, since so much power rests on the departmental side.

And yet, "If he's not a good parliamentarian, however good his policies may be, he won't effectively be able to put them over in the House of Commons—and that is essential in our system." Parliament is the test. If Ministers don't succeed here, their policies may fail, and their careers may fail as well. "Whether that is necessarily the right test, I don't know. But that is in fact the test":

> The House of Commons is very important. . . . A Minister can be awfully good in his department. . . . He can be very good on television and so on. But if he fails to put it across in the House of Commons, he will be doing very great damage. On the other hand, however bad he is elsewhere, if he is effective in the House of Commons, it will, it will carry him through a lot of mistakes . . . because this is, this is really where he draws his authority from, and if he is supported by the House of Commons, he will last for a good deal longer than if he wasn't.

In addition to the very full-time jobs they do in Whitehall, Ministers devote a great deal of time to their parliamentary responsibilities. This is the side upon which I will focus in examining the roles of Junior Ministers, Ministers of State, Ministers Outside the Cabinet, and Cabinet Ministers. All are position roles defined primarily by institutional arrangements and crystallized gradually through centuries of differentiation.

The Structure of the Role

D. J. Heasman has traced the steps whereby a nominal cabinet within the Privy Council evolved into today's specialized executive structure.[1] This process of differentiation began during the eighteenth century when the nominal cabinet developed an "inner" cabinet (the *conciliabulum*) of all those who held the great offices of state. Eventually, the First Lord of the Treasury and the Secretaries of State were distinguished from Members of the Ministry who were "Not of the Cabinet." A hundred years later, political undersecretaries were reclassified as Junior Ministers and added to the Ministry. Then the postwar period saw the creation of the position of Minister of State and saw all Ministers become increasingly specialized. Finally, the structure was rationalized during the 1980s by increasing the number of Ministers of State and collapsing into them Full Ministers Outside the Cabinet. Throughout this developmental process, the Ministry grew in size, mainly as a result of growth in the numbers of non-Cabinet Ministers who emerged as real power wielders in a newly decentralized and specialized system.

Hierarchical career ladders appeared as it became increasingly difficult to reach higher posts without first serving in lower ones.[2] Today the usual pattern is two posts at the level of Junior Minister and then either out or up to Minister Outside the Cabinet, where one serves for two or three years and then moves either out or up to the Cabinet. The positions on this ladder are associated with roles whose responsibilities are defined much more by official assignments than by their actors' attitudes. Institutional structure at this level is both more influential and more complex than on the back-benches.

Table 8.1 presents the official ranks, positions, subtypes, salaries, and incumbents in the ministerial hierarchy in 1972. It includes all seventy-four Members of the Government and excludes only the Whips and the Second Church Estates Commissioner. Three basic levels of authority were then and are now generally recognized: highest, intermediate, and lowest. Thus, there are three levels of Ministers; within the higher levels, there is also an order of precedence suggested by the relative positions of posts in official lists. These levels of authority are clearly reflected in the organization of official lists and in salaries as well.[3]

At the highest level, of course, are the Cabinet Ministers, who are responsible for leading the major departments of state and for guiding policy programs through the House of Commons. In addition, they are expected collectively to direct the Government as a whole and to respond to the will of the people as represented in Parliament. Unless otherwise obvious (e.g., Chancellor of the Exchequer), the Cabinet Minister's title is usually Secretary of State for ———. In 1972 there were eighteen such Cabinet Ministers, each paid £13,000, with the exception of the Prime Minister and the Lord Chancellor, whose special positions were recognized by the considerably higher salaries of £20,000. While not recognized by further salary differences, there exists a further pecking order within the Cabinet that is very well recognized by Ministers.[4]

Ministers Outside the Cabinet constitute the intermediate rank of authority and responsibility and, unless otherwise obvious (e.g., Paymaster-General), are known by their title of Minister or Minister of State. This is the most heterogeneous of the three basic levels, since it subsumes Law Officers as well. Its heterogeneity was recognized by the Review Body on Top Salaries, which recommended a range of salaries (£9,500–£7,500) to allow for flexibility with regard to individual posts. What is clear, however, is that in general, Ministers (£9,500) were ranked above Ministers of State (£7,500). It is also clear that Law Officers were and are a special category whose remuneration is inflated a bit above what would normally be due their rank in order "to attract lawyers of the right quality to Parliament." A few Minis-

Table 8.1 Ministerial hierarchy

Rank, position, subtype, and salary	Incumbent
Cabinet Ministers (£13,000)	
Prime Minister (£20,000)	Edward Heath
Home Department	Reginald Maudling
Foreign and Commonwealth	Sir Alec Douglas-Home
Lord Chancellor (£20,000)	Lord Hailsham*
Chancellor of the Exchequer	Anthony Barber
Northern Ireland	William Whitelaw
Defense	Lord Carrington*
Leader of the House of Commons	Robert Carr
Social Services	Sir Keith Joseph
Chancellor of the Duchy of Lancaster	Geoffrey Rippon
Education and Science	Margaret Thatcher
Scotland	Gordon Campbell
Leader of the House of Lords	Earl Jellicoe*
Environment	Peter Walker
Wales	Peter Thomas
Agriculture, Fisheries, and Food	James Prior
Trade and Industry	John Davies
Employment	Maurice Macmillan
Ministers Outside the Cabinet	
Ministers (£9,500)	
Posts and Telecommunications	Sir John Eden
Paymaster General	Viscount Eccles*
Trade	Michael Noble
Aerospace	Michael Heseltine
Overseas Development	Richard Wood
Housing and Construction	Julian Amery
Transport Industries	John Peyton
Local Government and Development	Graham Page
Industrial Development	Christopher Chataway
Industry	Tom Boardman
Ministers of State (£7,500)	
Home Office	Mark Carlisle
Northern Ireland	Lord Windlesham*
Northern Ireland	Paul Channon
Foreign and Commonwealth	Joseph Godber
Foreign and Commonwealth	Baroness Tweedsmuir
Chief Secretary, Treasury (£9,500)	Patrick Jenkin
Parliamentary Secretary, Treasury (£9,500)	Francis Pym**
Financial Secretary, Treasury	Terrence Higgins
Treasury	John Nott
Defense	Lord Balniel

Table 8.1 (cont.)

Rank, position, subtype, and salary	Incumbent
Ministers of State *(cont.)*	
Defense Procurement	Ian Gilmour
Health and Social Security	Lord Aberdare*
Employment	Robert Chichester-Clark
Scottish Office	Lord Polwarth*
Welsh Office	David Gibson-Watt
Minister without Portfolio	Lord Drumalbyn*
Agriculture	Anthony Stodart
Law Officers (£14,500–7,500)	
Attorney General	Sir Peter Rawlinson
Lord Advocate	Norman Wylie
Solicitor-General	Sir Geoffrey Howe
Solicitor-General for Scotland	David Brand***
Junior Ministers: Under Secretaries of State or Parliamentary Secretaries (£5,500)	
Agriculture	Peter Mills
Civil Service	Kenneth Baker
Defense—Royal Navy	Peter Kirk
Defense—R.A.F.	Anthony Lambton
Defense—Army	Geoffrey Johnson Smith
Education and Science—Schools	Lord Belstead*
Education and Science—Universities	William van Straubenzee
Employment	Dudley Smith
Environment—Housing and Construction	Reginald Eyre
Environment—Transport Industries	Keith Speed
Environment—Local Government and Development	Eldon Griffiths
Environment—Countryside	Lord Sandford*
Foreign and Commonwealth	Anthony Royle
Foreign and Commonwealth	Anthony Kershaw
Health and Social Security	Michael Alison
Health and Social Security	Paul Dean
Home Department	David Lane
Northern Ireland	David Howell
Scotland—Home Affairs and Agriculture	Alick Buchanan-Smith
Scotland—Health and Education	Hector Munro
Scotland—Development	George Younger
Trade and Industry—Industrial Development	Anthony Grant
Trade and Industry—Trade	Earl of Limerick*
Trade and Industry—Industry	Peter Emery
Trade and Industry—Aerospace	Cranley Onslow

*Member of the House of Lords
**Chief Whip
***Not a Member of the House of Commons or the House of Lords

ters, mainly in small departments such as Posts and Telecommunications, directed their departments themselves, but most were assigned a specific range of important responsibilities under their Secretaries of State. The responsibilities of the Ministers of State vary widely from one department and one Secretary of State to another. All, however, function as Ministers in their departments rather than as trainees like the Junior Ministers. They were "Ministers of State" rather than "Ministers" because, during the 1970s, the importance and breadth of their duties were usually less than those of Ministers.[5] At the time of our interviews, there were ten Ministers, seventeen Ministers of State, and four Law Officers, a total of thirty-one Ministers Outside the Cabinet.

Junior Ministers, known officially as Under Secretaries of State or Parliamentary Secretaries of State, are apprentices whose positions constitute the third and lowest tier of authority among Ministers. Their roles vary considerably from one department to another and from one Minister under whom they work to another.[6] They differ from the other obvious apprentices at Westminster, the PPSs, as follows: they are official Members of the Government and receive a ministerial salary; they have offices in their departments and have civil servants under them; and they have more influence than PPSs over departmental policy, albeit this may not amount to very much. Viewed either from below or from above, the role of the Junior Minister seems sufficiently distinctive to require separate treatment here. In 1972–73, there were twenty-five Junior Ministers with salaries (£5,500) that placed them between Ministers of State (£7,500) and Assistant Whips (£4,000).

Junior Ministers

The political role of Junior Minister was created when, under Lord Liverpool, Parliamentary Secretaries were separated from Permanent Secretaries, who began to take over their work.[7] Hence, the emerging Junior Ministers no longer had very precise duties or automatic powers—and some ambiguity in expectations for their role's performance has continued down to the present.

SUBTYPES: PLACEMEN AND JOURNEYMEN

Although the role of Junior Minister was not originally an apprenticeship, it eventually became one. Apprenticeship training is not, however, the only institutional function that the role serves, since some Junior Ministers are appointed as a reward for past services rather than with a view to the future.

Upon this distinction, Junior Ministers have constructed two preference roles, Placemen and Journeymen, which are not well defined in the minds of MPs nor well discussed in the transcripts. Nevertheless, they are important, and our material is adequate for brief accounts of each.

Most Placemen express either uncertainty, pessimism, or defeatism about their prospects. Uncertainty persists because where there is life, there is hope: "I would have thought, um, well, you can—you can never tell, can you?" Yet pessimism usually prevails because they are realistic about their chances of achieving further positions—"I mean . . . not very high." There is also defeatism because, in the end, "I quite accept my present place . . . and accept that I would never be more than a Junior Minister." Placemen were made Junior Ministers either to reward them for past services or to restrain them with the collar of collective responsibility. They were not typical backbench Aspirants. Furthermore, those who take up the role often have mixed feelings about it, expressed in signs of insecurity. Placemen sometimes become a little pompous and touchy when they suspect that others regard their position as a sinecure. In a world dominated by eager beavers, they are a little embarrassed about it, concerned that they might be "found out." Thus, one Placeman described himself more than half a dozen times as "a long-standing and highly respected Member of Parliament," while the self-importance of another was expressed through his self-conscious use of pronouns: "In our case, we've just set up this ———, the Minister and I, because we're responsible effectively for ———, and we've got ———. We've seen ——— informally, and we met with him. . . . We also make the point. . . ."

Another attitude characteristic of this subtype is that the identities of the role players sometimes seem to have more to do with being a Member of Parliament than with being a Junior Minister. One describes himself as a "farmer MP," which was his primary self-image before he became a Junior Minister, and apparently still is. Another explains that although he "has now got some little Chancellery fame inasmuch as I'm a Junior Minister," his real satisfactions come from membership in the House of Commons. Such Placemen talk as though they were outside the Ministry looking in: "I am actually in Government . . . er, not necessarily in the heart of the Cabinet . . . [but] on the fringe of getting something done and seeing changes taking place."

They feel like outsiders because their role concentrates more on "House work" than on "department work." In the House, they are expected to deal primarily with the problems that MPs bring to the department on behalf of constituents. Most Placemen have lots of time for their own constituents too: "We can be very high-minded wondering what is going to happen in

Europe. . . . But in the end the reality is that somebody writes to me as they did today saying, 'My neighbors are horrific, they bang on the walls, they abuse my children, they actually struck my wife.' This is the reality, the life that my constituents are leading. And therefore I must go into this in some detail."

"When I first came in here seventeen years ago," one frank Placeman explained, "I think there were more people like myself, a bit older . . . you know, Knights of the Shires . . . or in the Labour Party halfway up the NUM [National Union of Mine Workers] ladder . . . And whenever they were fifty, if they were fortunate, they would be elevated to a minor post in the Government." Placemen enter late and leave early. In and out in three years is the common pattern, for they are loyal "old wood," destined to be cut down after they have served their time, and grateful for having been rewarded in this way.[8]

The subtypes in Table 8.2 have been coded on the basis of respondents' reports about their prospects for promotion and about the character of their current duties. Since these codes are very impressionistic and the number of respondents is very small, Placemen and Journeymen will not be pursued any further through quantitative analyses.[9] The table is intended simply to provide rough estimates of their proportions among Junior Ministers and of the connections between these subtypes and the age variable that is said to be their marker.

According to my reading of the transcripts, and much to my surprise, approximately half (twelve out of twenty-five) of the Junior Ministers appear to think of themselves as Placemen. That leaves only thirteen out of twenty-five who are serious competitors in the ministerial race. It should be recalled that some Parliamentary Private Secretaries, the Auxiliaries, are not running either. It is essential, therefore, to take such considerations into account when one studies the proportions of MPs who move from one rung of the leadership ladder to the next. Everyone who has examined this subject

Table 8.2 Junior Ministers: Subtypes by age at appointment

Subtype	Age				
	Under 40	40–44	45–50	Over 50	N
Placeman	0	0	7	5	(12)
Journeyman	5	5	3	0	(13)

Note: Entries are numbers of respondents. $p \leq .01$.

has calculated gross "failure" rates in moving from PPS to Junior Minister and from Junior Minister to Minister. But these may be distorted by the fact that two quite different types of MPs are recruited to each role, one of them expected to pass through and the other to pass out. Likewise, contrary to many popular models of political ambition, it is utterly misleading to assume that everyone in a given position on the career ladder is reaching for the next rung. Table 8.2 suggests that age may have much to do with this state of affairs. All those who were appointed as Junior Ministers after their fiftieth birthdays regard themselves as Placemen, whereas all those who were appointed before they turned forty-five think of themselves as Journeymen and harbour ambitious plans.

Journeymen construct their role interpretations around the desire to rise: "I mean I just want to go on, I can't envisage giving up the climb, you know." They are often very ambitious, like the aggressive former business-man who claims he has "an unusual capacity for taking big decisions." Journeymen believe that they are leaders: "I've been trained since I left school, um, to . . . take responsibility, my whole training, my whole background has been to take responsibility." They expect to lead in minor posts today, in major posts tomorrow. They are ready to "go wherever the Prime Minister sends me," but expect to go upward. Thus, they save their uncertainty for the question of *which* "department of state would interest me." The role of the Junior Minister is an opportunity for learning, an apprenticeship for bigger and better things.

A busy professional approach to the job also distinguishes Journeymen from Placemen. Journeymen seem almost proud of how infrequently they dine out or attend the theater, proud that they have had to give up the sort of social life they used to lead before: "You have to make some kind of sacrifice, and if you find you haven't been to a play for a year, or that you're losing out on the number of days you go to Wimbledon, that's just hard luck." They think of themselves as professional politicians, as members of a special professional subculture. And in their professional approach, they highlight the role's departmental side. They spend more time than Placemen do in the department and are more likely to be delegated serious responsibility for specific policy matters. A Journeyman at the Home Office, for example, might be delegated responsibility for examining individual cases involving paroles and life sentences.

BEHAVIOR AT WESTMINSTER

Thus, all Junior Ministers put in many hours at Westminster. The adjective "Parliamentary" in the title "is no accidental one . . . you are meant to be closely in touch with Members of Parliament in the House of Commons about the affairs of your department." Until the postwar period, this was virtually the Junior Minister's only function—defending and explaining to Parliament the position of his or her department.[10] The goal is to be accessible to backbenchers, on behalf of the department; to be around the House, "in the Smoking Room or the Tea Room or having meals there so that other MPs can buttonhole him about their problems." Most don't mind all the time spent on these glorified PPS type of responsibilities, because Westminster is their element: "The essence of this place is that it is a market. It's like the Stock Market or the cattle market or Christies, where all the experts come to market ideas, to pick each other's brains, to argue, and to swap information." As Junior Ministers, they play a central role in this market, collecting information, selling ideas, and smelling the political atmosphere. "If you don't like being in the market, then there's no point in being here at all."

Nonetheless, some would rather be back at the department with Ministers and civil servants than here at Westminster with backbenchers; but they find themselves at Westminster because their role is structured more by its assigned responsibilities than by their own preferences. To fulfill the goal of liaison with backbenchers, they must be where backbenchers can come and talk to them, explain their views, tell them what they are feeling, and listen to the department's case. "A prudent Minister like Sir Keith Joseph must keep in very close touch with opinion in the House, and that is one of my principal tasks as his Parliamentary Secretary." A prudent Minister sees to it that his Junior Minister spends, whether he likes it or not, a great deal of time in the House. He sends him there to take the temperature and to pay particular attention to those backbenchers who have a continuing interest in the affairs of the department. The Secretary of State may meet privately with the officers of the backbench committees that focus on his department's subjects. But the Junior Minister will attend the committees' meetings regularly and appear before them formally. Usually it's a pleasant exchange, for the Junior Minister will be regarded as well informed and will be speaking with some authority. But on "what we might call the rather excitable issues of policy," it can sometimes be very trying indeed: "I had a very, very difficult time with them over the decision to bail out the Upper Clyde Shipbuilders, where the views of this Government or this department and the party committee were completely at loggerheads. I mean there was simply a hundred-and-eighty-degree split, er, and in the end of course the views of the Government had to prevail, but, er, not until after there'd been a great deal of very vigorous—and very painful—discussion."

The serious work involves Standing Committees, Adjournment Debates, and Written and Oral Questions.[11] But it also involves an endless series of informal contacts with Members of Parliament who come to chat, ask questions, make points, raise constituency issues, or inquire about a letter that hasn't been answered. The point is to deal satisfactorily with all these approaches and, perhaps more important, to do a little public relations, to give Members "the feeling that they are important and an important part of the policy-making processes as they affect this department." If Junior Ministers fail to accomplish this, their departments may develop an image of being administered by cold and distant bureaucrats. This image will appear, Junior Ministers are told, first in the House and then in the press. And then even policies based on the best intentions may be misunderstood. Blunders will be magnified, and the Secretary of State may come under fire. Of course all this does not pivot on the role of the Junior Minister; but Junior Ministers can certainly help their departments and Secretaries of State from becoming unstuck.

Like the PPS, the Junior Minister is at the House to listen. But, like the Whip, he or she is also at the House to persuade. They seek to convince their parliamentary colleagues that the department's "line of action is good and valid and proper" by drawing attention to "aspects of the question which they haven't seen before or understood properly."

One of the best opportunities that Junior Ministers have to distinguish themselves arises when they represent their departments at the Despatch Box. For big debates, "the big shots are wheeled in, as it were, the Secretaries of State come down." But for routine occasions, it is the Junior Ministers who cope with the House: "You have at least two parties to convince" in your audience. "You have your own backbenchers, who will include a number of positive enthusiasts about some contrary course of action, and you have to convince them. Much more difficult, you have to convince a probing Opposition which is out to find fault, out to cut down the impact you're making to a smaller size." When speaking at the Despatch Box, they are regarded as "spokesmen" for their senior colleagues, albeit everyone is aware that most of them do not have important decision-taking responsibilities. Allowances are often made, therefore, such that "it's assumed that he's, you know, you don't have to look for his weak spot."

Junior Ministers must find a convincing way to express self-confidence, for only then will their listeners genuinely have confidence in them: "Above all [he must] try and give the impression that he is confident—even if he isn't—and that he knows what he is doing," said one of the least-confident Junior Ministers. It isn't easy. Even the readily articulate admit that "one is a little nervous obviously if you're going to take a debate, if you are going to open and close it, or if you've got a particularly rough question to deal with." It isn't easy because, although the House sometimes makes allowances, Junior Ministers are always being judged and facing the chance that if "he slips up and in a speech makes a rather silly remark . . . they'll give him stick." They have watched the House cut pompous Ministers down to size, and know that Junior Ministers who are unable to master the arguments "get the sack."

All in all, the role can be an intriguing but narrowing experience. "The most narrowing period," commented a Cabinet Minister looking backward, "is when you're a Junior Minister." Cabinet Ministers can be concerned "about government policy as a whole." And "Whips know more about what is going on than most Ministers except those in the Cabinet." Even backbenchers can be "concerned right across the political spectrum." By contrast, Junior Ministers are fenced-in within the fields of their departments. These fences are built by the doctrine of collective responsibility and by the fear that the Junior Minister's opinions on any political topic might be interpreted as those of his superiors. He is required therefore to be quiet and constrained—which is not easy for Junior Ministers like Norman St. John-Stevas who, as a backbencher, had been described as "the Conservative Party's gift to the media." The role of the Junior Minister wasn't always such a narrowing experience. During the early nineteenth century, Junior Ministers were not subject to the norms of collective responsibility—because their positions held too little authority to warrant it.[12]

Today Junior Ministers have more authority. But they are still "Junior" Ministers. They may have offices in Whitehall, but they mainly carry their department's cans at the House, where, given their junior status, they may have to double up. This means that "if, for example, I'd been seeing you over there today, [the other] would have to get out of the office, and he might have an appointment, and you know this is damned difficult." The fact that this Junior Minister shares an office at the House but has his own office in Whitehall indicates, however, the direction in which the role's assigned duties have recently been moving. "Parliamentary" Under Secretaries are still embedded in Westminster, but they are being increasingly relied upon to help their Ministers in the departments.

BEHAVIOR IN THE DEPARTMENT

Before the war it was unusual for Junior Ministers to have serious departmental responsibilities, but by the 1970s it had become quite common.[13] "I've had responsibilities now for the last two and a half years on European

Affairs," explained a Junior Minister at the Foreign Office, "and I've been very much involved in the evolvement of our European policy." Throughout the postwar period, Junior Ministers have increasingly been assigned specific administrative tasks in order to lighten the load on the Ministers above them. The amount of work delegated in this way, however, varies widely by department and by the dispositions of their Secretaries of State.

The Service departments, the Foreign Office, and the Scottish Office have usually taken the lead. But in the Heath Government, the model for delegation came from the Department of the Environment, a mega-Ministry under the direction of megamanager Peter Walker. Walker and his Ministers, and this included Junior Ministers, ran the department as a team. They met together every morning at nine-fifteen to discuss the big issues of the day. These meetings made delegation less dangerous for Walker than it might otherwise have been, because they provided a daily opportunity for his Ministers to assess his thinking and to be guided by it. The team had been put together in Opposition. And it produced some of the strongest Junior Ministers in the Government. Keith Speed, for example, was given unusual responsibility for new road schemes; it was he who at the end of the day made most of the decisions about whether or not such schemes would go ahead. In fact, Junior Ministers in the Walker team sounded more like Ministers than like Ministers' apprentices. When they went to the House, it almost seemed that they were there on their own behalf: "Since I've been a departmental Minister, I take the view very strongly . . . that it's critical that I'm across in that place as often as possible because I'm dealing with things that are very sensitive. . . . All these things are very much of constituency interest to MPs. And so I'm normally over there every evening from six o'clock onwards. I dine over there . . . and people come into my room, and they see you in the lobby and they say, 'Oh, what about ————.' If I get a feeling that we're getting a bit out of touch . . . it's, you know, up to me to try and take remedial action."

Other Ministries offered their Junior Ministers much less responsibility, albeit delegation in specific areas was widespread: "You're getting the same now in the Department of Industry, where you're seeing Parliamentary Secretary–level Ministers delegated, handed specific blocks of work." Another department where delegation was frequently mentioned was Northern Ireland, whose Junior Minister was "sort of Acting Minister of Commerce, of Finance, of Agriculture." The institutional stimulus to delegation is overload; and the psychological stimulus is a desire to control the civil service. To facilitate this control, Ministers decentralize to Junior Ministers. Ultimately, of course, senior Ministers retain responsibility for the affairs of their departments. Delegation is not devolution. Junior Ministers must always refer important and sensitive matters back to the chief.[14]

Furthermore, senior Ministers are reluctant to delegate authority to those Junior Ministers who are not as ideologically compatible with them as they might like, or whom they fear as potential rivals;[15] for the brighter the Junior Minister shines in the department and at the Despatch Box, the greater the danger that he may replace one of his Minister's favored lieutenants. At the same time, senior civil servants try to discourage their Secretaries of State from delegating to Junior Ministers, because they don't like taking orders from "small fry" who may, in the end, be overruled by their masters anyway. Thus, there is delegation, but typically not as much as in the well-knit Walker team. "To be absolutely realistic . . . one's influence is limited as a junior member. But at least you have some chance of making your views known at the, at the level where decisions are actually taken."

It isn't easy being an *Under* Secretary, "being number four in a department when you have so often been on top in your business experiences. I've been a very active director of many companies and trade associations." Some subordinates don't at all enjoy the subordination. And most, from this perspective, are uneasy about their relationships with civil servants. They "didn't come across civil servants" much when they were backbenchers, and so they start off without much personal knowledge: "Well . . . it's, it's different from any other form of business organization, quite obviously." The alleged uniqueness compounds the mystery and increases the likelihood that the new Junior Minister may feel a little overwhelmed: "You are looked after by highly qualified professional men whose work is to concentrate on a narrow area and to be extremely well informed and expert about it. . . . You're more dangerous as a Minister if you think you know as much about it as they do. But if you recognize your limitations and appreciate your role . . . indeed, I would say it's a disadvantage for a Minister to be an expert in the field which he is helping to administer. He thinks he's up to date, in fact he's not. . . . He thinks he knows as much as his professional advisors do, which is not true."[16]

Junior Ministers are not sure what exactly their standing is with regard to the department's senior civil servants. In the departments, it is generally known that Junior Ministers have less income, less respect, and less influence than the senior civil servants who "serve" them.[17] At best, their situation might be understood as an ambiguous one, in which they stand outside the normal chain of command.[18] This interpretation saves face for Junior Ministers without irritating civil servants, but it may also encourage civil servants, "when they are able, to isolate and exclude Junior Ministers as they like to do with PPSs." Senior Ministers find that they must seek to ensure time and time again that their Junior Ministers are invited to meetings and are in line to receive documents. This tone is actually set by the Prime Minister, who, for constitutional reasons and to reinforce collective responsibility, distributes a memorandum of important instructions that includes the following statement: "The Junior Minister is not subject to the direction of the Permanent Secretary." "But equally," this peculiar instruction continues, "the Permanent Secretary is not subject to the direction of the Junior Minister."[19]

Not surprisingly, there are ambitious Junior Ministers who are not so easily satisfied by this specious reciprocity. They may put up with not being able to give orders to the Permanent Secretaries, but the interpretation that makes them unable to give orders to any civil servants at all is unacceptable. For example: "I mean, after all, I'm a political animal, and sometimes civil servants get the thing wrong and, you know, I say, 'Look, we're to take a decision, this is a political decision, we're going to do this, to hell with the fact it may not be administratively the best decision.'" But when that doesn't work, there isn't much they can do besides making sharp comments about civil servants being out of touch with the people and out of control.

They also have responsibilities for liaison with interest groups. In busy departments, Junior Ministers handle most of "the encounters that are fairly ritualised, part of the process, . . . you're always seeing them." Thus, on behalf of his or her Minister, the Secretary of State for Health and Social Security, the Junior Minister will be "in touch with the big professional bodies like the General Nursing Council, the BMA, and so on . . . discussing the terms and conditions of service, the rates of pay, and so on. . . . This is one of the jobs of a Junior Minister . . . we keep very much in touch." Occasionally they get a hot potato: "If there is a great concern nationally about, let us say, mental hospitals, then you will find yourself spending a lot more time with psychiatric people, mental nurses, the neurologists." But the most delicate tasks are usually handled by senior Ministers, leaving to Junior Ministers mainly the routine exchanges, which include "eating for the Minister." Associations and interest groups concerned with the department's responsibilities hold dinners and invite the Minister to attend. Obviously the Minister cannot attend them all, and some Ministers prefer to attend very few, so they send Junior Ministers in their place.

Good liaison with interest groups is essential for the success of policies, Ministers, and departments: "I've learned that one cannot get one's policies right unless one is in contact with them, unless they feel they have had a chance to have their say while policy is being formulated. . . . Before making up your mind, you want to have a pretty clear indication as to the way in which the policy is eventually going to be received." This is another apprenticeship lesson, in which the Junior Minister, who may formerly have been a businessman or a trade unionist, suddenly finds himself thinking more like a Minister than like a businessman or a trade unionist who isn't "sufficiently sophisticated to understand the problems which the politicians are actually grappling with." Interest groups may be after a grant for a firm or a factory, "whereas the politician is not, he's trying to hold the line between all sorts of interests . . . he may be trying to stimulate investment or employment or something like this . . . a very complex relationship." Most Journeymen are keenly interested in the work with interest groups, because it is stimulating and does seem to be a sort of training for the ministerial roles they hope to play.

A great variety of additional activities are assigned to the role of the Junior Minister. One is inspections and visits: "For example, you know the Rank organisation who are making some of our motorway signs, well I went up recently to Leeds to look at the factory, to see what was going on. I mean I met everybody from the factory floor people up to the, you know, the Chairman of the appropriate company." Many Junior Ministers enjoy doing it. They also enjoy getting involved in White Papers and especially in Cabinet Committees, despite the fact that their contributions are usually confined to the departmental brief and matters of direct interest to the department.[20] Several also do a little public relations, mainly in the provinces, such as holding a press conference about a new White Paper on noise from motorways, or about plans for hospitals and road schemes. Finally, some Junior Ministers find their satisfactions in the diversity of tasks that their role provides, "the enormous variety in the work . . . from say a Cabinet Committee to the chat we are having now, giving my Tory women tea when they come from their conference in a few moments' time. . . . The tremendous variety of the work is the thing which I find most attractive."

But what every Junior Minister finds most fascinating is the opportunity to watch senior Ministers in action. For Placemen, this offers a vicarious sense of participation behind the scenes. For Journeymen, it offers the best possible opportunity to learn about the role for which they are preparing themselves.[21] Using analogies, they try hard to interpret what they see:

The analogy I find most applicable is that of the farmer. A farmer is a professional man, but he is a professional manager. A farmer doesn't have to be a chemist, he doesn't have to be an engineer, he doesn't have to be a horticulturalist, but he has to know enough about these subjects to draw in these specialists when he needs them. The Minister is in exactly this position. He's a manager, he has to be able to assemble the data he needs, he has to know enough about the subject to know what the ingredients are for a clear picture, he has to evaluate, to make judgements—he is a professional man in his own right, he's not a stumbling amateur.

Ministers

We turn now to the Ministers—Ministers of State, Ministers Outside the Cabinet, and Cabinet Ministers—and to their roles in the department and at Westminster. I shall focus less on the department (which has already been covered well by Bruce Heady)[22] and more on the aspects of ministerial roles that are central to political life in Parliament.

RELATIONS WITH CIVIL SERVANTS

Ministers spend much time with senior civil servants who are impressive and who aim to impress. In these relationships, new Ministers need all the help they can get, for many cross their new departments' thresholds ill at ease.

They worry about being overwhelmed by a professional team that has been working together for some time, under several previous Ministers. The team will be familiar with the major academic studies of the department's subjects and with the major departmental facilities round the country. Furthermore, these civil servants may be the intellectual cream of their generations at Oxford and Cambridge, skimmed by a process that selects for first-rate social and administrative skills as well. To counter this image, the Head of the Home Civil Service wrote to assure the political world of the 1970s that departments do not, in fact, dominate their Ministers.[23] Many new Ministers aren't so sure, however, and remain wary of being "taken over." Even the formidable and combative former Oxford don Richard Crossman was, upon becoming a Minister, struck by "the tremendous effort it requires not to be taken over by the civil service. My Minister's room is like a padded cell . . . they know how to handle me . . . the civil service is profoundly deferential—'Yes, Minister! No, Minister! If you wish it, Minister!'—and combined with this there is a constant preoccupation to ensure that the Minister does what is correct. . . . Of course, all through I've had an underlying anxiety caused by my complete lack of contact (thank god they can't quite realize it) with the subjects I'm dealing with."[24]

The House, Ministers believe, likes firm leaders who appear to be in charge of their departments, because the House likewise "is very suspicious of the civil service." To make it easier to take charge, one in three Ministers suggested (unsuccessfully) that their salaries be raised "over the salaries of the most senior civil servants with whom they dealt."[25] At the time, Cabinet Ministers were paid £8,500, whereas their Permanent Secretaries were paid £14,000. "Being in charge" means that the Minister is imposing his party's objectives on the department and is himself choosing among meaningful alternatives: "You must remain absolute master of policy," claimed a Minister who professed to be strong, "and if you decide that the policy that they want you to adopt is wrong, you must say so . . . they're extremely efficient at changing it, as long as you know what you want to do." The formal division of responsibilities between the Minister and his Permanent Secretary makes the Minister primarily responsible for "the policy-making process" and the Permanent Secretary primarily responsible for "the execution of policies." Ministers make policy and therefore in their roles give first priority to the department, certainly over Parliament, and usually over the Cabinet too, because the department is where policy is made.

The irony for those who are most determined to "take charge," to wield "decisive power over policy," is that this power nearly always seems just beyond reach. They came to Westminster to find it, but found instead that they were small backbench cogs in a big machine. They accepted potentially humiliating posts as PPSs in order to get closer, but discovered instead that they were unwelcome in Whitehall and could hardly glimpse the goal. So they became Whips and won a better view, such a good view, in fact, that it intensified their awareness of how very little power they themselves still possessed. And then, at last, those who were fortunate became Junior Ministers—only to learn that this too was strictly an apprenticeship and that the power of decision was located above. With further good fortune the fortunate few rose to run departments, where they discovered that, even at the top of the ladder, the power available to full-fledged Ministers "often isn't so very much decisive power after all."

Along the way they also found that the potential for policy innovation varies by department as a function of departmental tasks, departmental traditions, and the department's senior civil servants. New Ministers in some departments, for instance, quickly come to suspect that their choices are being restricted by the Whitehall procedure of presenting proposals that are agreed upon beforehand, both interdepartmentally and within the department, agreed upon before they are presented to the Minister. Suspicions arise when Permanent Secretaries try to centralize advice giving in their own hands and to review all the papers that the Minister will see. Although such suspicions are not much discussed in academic commentaries about White-hall, they are very much a factor in the minds of Ministers and in their relationships with their senior officials. It was, in fact, as counterweights to the senior officials that Ministers insisted during the 1970s on bringing special advisors into their departments.

Some Ministers attempt to take charge by the "key-issues" approach. A key-issues Minister concentrates all his energy on a few specific projects that he and his Government would like to see implemented.[26] Others go with the flow and toss a coin, figuratively in most cases, literally in at least one: "I mean I used to have a tossing coin that I used when the arguments were very evenly balanced. . . . I just used to toss up and say, 'I give you a 50–50 chance of being right'—on the arguments that they [the civil servants] had put forward, there was nothing in it anyway. If you said, 'Well this is so evenly balanced that I must call them all together and discuss it,' you would stop the whole machine [from] working and this would be deadly."

If deciding policy is the first goal in the Minister's role package, then managing the department must be the second. Yet Ministers who take management seriously encounter even more frustrations than do those who concentrate on policy. Such Ministers set out to control the department by checking to see that policy objectives are being carried out, by motivating their civil servants, and by organizing personnel.[27] The key is organizing personnel. And the first frustration is that Ministers have surprisingly little control over appointments. Senior Ministers do occasionally "sack" their Permanent and Deputy Secretaries, but this is unusual and very difficult to accomplish. It requires convincing the Prime Minister to make an exception to the usual assumption of "permanence," an assumption closely linked to others about the neutrality and professionalism of civil servants. Consequently, they have little power of appointment over their top officials. And they have none whatsoever over civil servants further down the departmental tree. Some Ministers don't seem to mind, but others are quite irritated by it.

They are also irritated by the petty bureaucracy and by the patronizing attitudes that they sense behind the deference, behind the mandarins' references to them as their "masters."[28] The Permanent Secretary may seem too busy to take part in the less important policy discussions held by the Minister. An Under Secretary clearly thinks that the new Minister is unrealistic and abrupt. An Assistant Secretary is politely reluctant to question the Minister's premises but appears to regard them as rather muddled.

Ministers are expected to manage their departments by managing these civil servants. Yet sometimes their civil servants manage them, as in this remarkable story told by a Cabinet Minister who considers himself unusually lucky to have started off on such a good footing with his "extremely able chaps":

> The very first submission that I had on my desk as Secretary of State seemed to me to be the most utter rubbish. And so, without quite remembering that I was now supposed to be an important person, I just wrote "Balls!" on the top and initialed it. And then I lost my nerve. . . . My Private Secretary came in, and I said to him, "Mr. ———, is this all right?" So he looked at the submission and looked at my comment and said, "Unusual, Secretary of State, but in this case quite right." And by a pure bit of good luck this happened to get me off on rather a good foot with this particular civil servant, who was an extremely able chap. I met him later and he said again that he quite agreed with my comment, but that I hadn't exactly said *why*. "Well," I said, "there are three reasons why I thought it was balls"—and a great grin spread across his face. And he said, "Well, you realise that the submission was not written to you, it was written to your predecessor. I thought you might spot the first two reasons, but I'm delighted that you spotted the third. We'll get on very well." Well, this was, I think, a bit of luck for me.

No wonder so many Ministers worry that their Private Office may isolate them from the world outside. The Minister sees his Permanent Secretary and his Private Secretary far more each week than he sees representatives of interest groups, other Ministers, the Prime Minister, the public, the party's backbenchers, or even all of them together.[29] Many feel isolated from most of the Ministry as well. Under Secretaries and Assistant Secretaries who prepare briefings and correspondence for them submit these to the Private Office. The Permanent Secretary channels through his hands the important submissions and the Minister's contacts with the rest of the department. Thus, the Private Office is a little world within the larger world of the Ministry. And many Ministers wonder, at least some of the time, whether this little world is comfortably arranged to isolate them, watch them, and encourage them to accept established routines and programs.

RELATIONS WITH INTEREST GROUPS

Civil servants and Junior Ministers carry out most of the department's contacts with interest groups. But Ministers participate too, for this is one of the responsibilities assigned to their roles: "As a Minister, one has a large area of defined responsibilities. As a result of one's departmental portfolio, one is brought of necessity into contact with all the relevant associations, groups, trade interests, and others with whom one must keep in touch, as well as with individuals. This is a constant and continuing operation which never ends." Ministers spend a great deal of time "selling" departmental policies and priorities to interest groups.

They make time to see, for example, "a lot of the powerful organisations that are concerned with taxation and the management of the economy . . . from the CBI [Confederation of British Industries] downwards, the City organisations . . . the Building Societies." They may even feel obliged to meet with the Clerk of the Oxfordshire County Council to discuss the problem of the toilets in Bladon village. The point of these endless meetings is sometimes public relations, sometimes functional representation. But during the 1970s it was definitely corporatism: close collaboration among the top trade unions, business organizations, and Government Ministers on economic matters, close collaboration to bring "inside" the leaders of the TUC (Trade Union Congress) and the CBI, to attach them to the same broad church, to the same broad goal—sustained economic growth. One characteristic behavior was to cultivate cozy personal relations: "I do see Vic Feather [Chairman of the TUC]. . . . He's an old friend and we've been on Christian-name terms for fifteen years at least. I wouldn't hesitate to, um, discuss things privately with him."[30] Another was to work through groups like the National Economic Development Council, where representatives of Government, trade unions, and business met regularly.

The Heath Government began by pushing the much-hated Industrial Relations Act through Parliament; but within two years it was on the defensive, denying "union bashing" and entertaining the National Economic Development Council at No. 10 Downing Street. Heath became determined to create cooperation among "the big three" (Government, TUC, and CBI) in the form of an effective system of wage negotiations and industrial relations. By July 1972 the Government announced that it would resort less to the law if the unions would be more cooperative. Heath was very explicit about his aims: "What we have really embarked upon is *the management of the economy by the three parties*—the Government, the CBI and the TUC."[31] Thus, in the space of three years, Conservative Ministers moved from union bashing to corporatism. Our interviews caught them in the middle of this U-turn, when they were learning from experience and applying their new goals to readjust these parts of their roles.

The first learning experience was the realization that industrialists, for whose views in general "I, um, have a good deal of respect," were too frequently, "uh, opposed to the interests of the whole," were too frequently pushing "a rather badly presented argument as to why the selfish interests of their trade should be pursued in the greater national interest." In Opposition, these Conservative Ministers had seen the unions as the problem, but now they found themselves "discounting" *both* sides, albeit the most dangerous counterplayers from their perspectives were still the trade union leaders. Hence, Ministers were asked the following question: "And what about the trade unions? To what extent do you think that trade union leaders are well intentioned and not wholly selfish?"

Their responses, which were tape-recorded, transcribed, and coded, reflect the fact that Conservative Ministers were becoming more determined than Conservative backbenchers to treat trade union leaders well and to think well of them. Ministerial self-interest as well as ministerial experience stimulated the creation of new beliefs that would become characteristic of their roles during the Heath period. The Conservative Ministers in Table 8.3 did not, therefore, share the perception of 42 percent of Conservative backbenchers that trade union leaders "always" put their sectional interests before the public interest. They needed to see these trade union leaders as people with whom collaboration was at least feasible. Conservative Ministers were also asked to compare, from this perspective, trade union leaders with leaders of business organizations. They proved much more likely than their backbenchers to evaluate the character and intentions of trade union and business leaders as *much the same*: "By and large business leaders are well intentioned and not governed solely by profit motives. And, er, likewise trade union leaders—I think they are well intentioned in the sense that they

Table 8.3 Assumptions about motivations of trade union leaders, by rank, in percent

Assumptions	Conservative Ministers*	Conservative backbenchers*
Sometimes put sectional interests before public interest	8	2
Usually put sectional interests before public interest	78	56
Always put sectional interests before public interest	14	42
Total	100 (N = 37)	100 (N = 119)

*$p \leq .001$

are doing or seeking to do what they regard as in the interests of their members."[32]

Several were amused to find themselves attributing equal selfishness to the business side. But they did it, and sounded as though they more than half meant it too: "You know, the bankers and, and, and people in the Bank of England and industrialists and stockbrokers and all these people—these are people trying to chip a bigger piece of the cake off for themselves, just as the trade unions are." Trade union leaders are not free agents, Ministers further observed. They are bound to be oriented toward their short-term interests because they are elected to their positions and must respond to pressures from the shop floor. They look weaker than their counterparts in business mainly because of the more dogmatic and prejudiced views of their mass memberships. But they are coming along. Corporatism is possible because you can work with these people, so long as you are careful to take into account their obligations and constraints: "I mean they will . . . tell you that you're absolutely dead right and that you should go on doing it because they see why you're doing it. And then they'll go out and say you're the biggest shit they've ever met, and you're a complete ass. You know. But this you've got to live with. I mean they've, they've got to get votes. . . . The TUC are dependent on being elected. And if they move out of step with their colleagues and so on, they may lose their jobs . . . and, and it may be difficult, uh, to get any, uh, comparable employment outside."[33]

Although discussions about pressure groups usually focus on the CBI and the TUC, this is only the tip of the consultation iceberg. Whitehall is filled with advisory committees and other arrangements for meetings between Ministers and pressure groups. Departmental Ministers are negotiating with interest groups all the time. The Minister of Housing, for instance, has regular meetings with representatives of builders, building societies, and groups like the National Association of Property Owners—for it will be a major blow if they oppose his national housing plans. Most departments recognize certain groups as central to their work. At the Home Office, for instance, "there are people that one is directly responsible for, like the police, the probation service, the fire brigades. One's main contacts would be with them." Most also recognize a secondary tier of interest groups that have special and often nonrecurring concerns.

Constant consultation strengthens the legitimacy of the Ministry's programs and, at the same time, provides fresh ideas: "I think one must, where one can, keep in touch with as many people outside as possible . . . because you get very well advised by your department—but you need other ideas as well, otherwise you just get all the conventional ideas." And so Ministers have their rounds of drinks and lunches and dinners, "where you make a few ill-chosen words in a short speech to them afterwards."

RELATIONS WITH OTHER MINISTERS

The professionalization of politics in postwar Britain has eroded conviviality and collegiality among Ministers.[34] There have always been animosities, but today they are less ameliorated than they used to be by commitments to a common enterprise. Today, Ministers become colleagues but "not real friends." They become potential allies but also potential rivals who play their roles through shifting alliances with one another. Sometimes they all succeed together; but often one's gain is another's loss. Therefore, most Ministers trust their colleagues only a little and socialize with them only occasionally. At the same time, they pay careful attention to their reputations in these relationships; for in order to succeed, each needs the support of others who "are more likely to support him if they like him and respect him than they are if he has treated them abominably and arrogantly—they are not going to be much interested in his survival if that is the case."

The principal aim is to avoid "weight loss," "the downward spiral" that makes you a less useful Member of the Government, a Minister who "is, erm, less likely to remain one." The norms are less powerful than they used to be, but they still shape careers: "Well . . . I'm certainly not going to mention names, but I think one's seen . . . Ministers, um, as it were losing the ear of their colleagues, because they were thought to have departed in some way from, er, what was generally thought to be decent behavior." "I think if one is keen to influence one's colleagues," continued this same Minister, who was good at it, "one tries to behave in the way in which one's colleagues, and the House of Commons, generally expect Ministers to behave." She is reminding us that leadership roles are more constrained by informal rules than are backbench roles, and that these rules discourage destructive conflicts and enable ambitious competitors to conspire together.[35]

They conspire together to get for their departments the most of whatever there is to get from Cabinet, Cabinet Committees, and interdepartmental relations. Ministers are expected to fight to minimize cuts in their departments' existing programs and to secure authorizations for new ventures—and their efforts are evaluated carefully by political colleagues. A Minister's ability to get his way is said to be a function of two variables: his department's standing in Whitehall and his own personal "political weight."[36] Ministers cannot do much about the former, but they do have some control over the latter. British political history is full of brilliant Ministers who, because of prickly personalities, were regularly defeated in the Cabinet. It is also full of boring Ministers who, because of their personalities, succeeded in bringing home the bacon. Unfortunately, there are so many ways to win "weight," and so many ways to lose it, that the only universal law here is that losers are displeased.

Collective responsibility is the most important formal rule that restrains relations among Ministers. During the 1970s, MPs believed that this constitutional convention was fading but still obligatory.[37] It formalizes the notion that "there must be a limit to, um, what you can say and do . . . otherwise the idea of a corporate responsibility of Government would simply collapse." Collective responsibility is an old rule, and an important one. How is it understood by the senior Ministers in whose hands its interpretation ultimately rests? The dominant tone is pragmatic. The dominant theme is "teamwork":

> A Member of the Government under our system is obliged to support the Government . . . because our principle is teamwork. Everybody operates as a team. . . . There can be occasions where a Cabinet is divided on some important matter; er, eventually the majority decide the line to be taken, and the minority may have argued cogently against it, but they then have to accept it. . . . If a Member feels very strongly that he cannot support the policy, then that is the moment when he resigns. . . . If it is . . . not so much a matter of principle . . . but one of how the Government should handle a situation, then the minority will support the Cabinet view and will vote in the House of Commons in support of the Cabinet view. The Cabinet proceedings are confidential, and therefore nobody will know until 30 years later that they didn't wholly agree with what they were supporting.

Ministers pay special attention to their relations with the Prime Minister. It always helps to have him or her on your side when you are trying to get more time and money for your department. Usually, however, the Prime Minister is quite happy to leave most Ministers alone, to leave them to get on with their own work. And most Ministers are usually quite happy to be left alone in hopes that they will then be left in place.

PUBLIC RELATIONS

The roles of Ministers also require them "to sell to the public" their department's policies and their Government's general themes and programs. Ministers regard this as one of their most important goals, particularly if they feel they lack the time or the expertise to intervene successfully in the policy process.[38] They may feel swamped by routine tasks, for example, or out-gunned by civil servants. But the same parliamentary apprenticeships that prepare them poorly for policy making prepare them extremely well for representation: they are usually good speakers who know how to put a case to the public. These public-relations activities include media performances as well as direct contacts with citizens during visits to departmental sites round the country.

Ministers pursue good public relations wherever they go, even in their own constituencies: "I go round my towns and villages . . . public meetings . . . I kick off normally with a couple of subjects. . . . One is a local subject, maybe the local hospital, . . . and one is a national subject . . . what the Government is doing and what it should or shouldn't be doing. . . . We don't get vast crowds, but . . . I think as a Minister it's important. . . . I think a very important job of a Minister is to involve himself . . . explaining to people what the Government is trying to do . . . and, you know, seeing what people are thinking about things." Backbenchers, of course, do the same, but what makes Ministers different is their ability to capture national attention through the media.[39] Whenever all is not well, the first remedial steps are for top Ministers to make public speeches round the country.

To use the press, however, Ministers must court, entertain, and "manipu-late" it. They court the press by giving briefings and by dribbling out attrac-tive drops of information to individual journalists. They entertain the press with a little whisky for journalists who like it, and with lunches at private clubs for journalists who can do them the most good. Ministers manipulate the press by seeing that it is "favorably informed," that the information it receives is weighted in a favorable direction. When you brief journalists "on lobby terms . . . you can discuss things far more openly than if they were attributable—*and far more selectively too.*" Likewise, press conferences can be structured very carefully. Good news value is good value indeed; and it is not surprising that Ministers want first-rate press officers at their minis-tries. A first-rate press officer can influence the news significantly even if he cannot control it quite as much as the Minister might like: "A glance at the papers and I knew that Peter Brown had scored another of his tremendous successes. He knows exactly when to call a press conference, how to brief the press, and how to make it a success. We managed to get a front-page story in *The Mail* and *The Telegraph* . . . and a good story in *The Times* and *The Guardian.* . . . A department can, with a good press officer, make the news it wants."[40]

Television and radio broadcasts present powerful images to the public and to colleagues at Westminster. A single botched performance on the box may not destroy a department's program or a Minister's reputation, but it can accelerate a slide, just as a single superb performance can accelerate a climb. Ministers also attribute to these performances powerful electoral consequences. Hence, the Prime Minister sends the Leader of the House to negotiate with the BBC and ITV for "fair" (which is to say "favorable") treatment.[41]

Ministers become extraordinarily sensitive about the press and public opinion because they fear that both are fickle and cannot easily be managed. They observe flip-flops in press treatments of colleagues that transform overnight a Minister's image from "brilliant success" to "bumbling failure."[42] They become alarmed because such images cripple careers and send parties plummeting in the opinion polls. Ministers are always vulnerable, and so is the Government. There are too many situations, they explain, where, once a slip occurs, nothing can be done to repair the damage. Reginald Maudling, Home Secretary, Deputy Leader, and potential future Prime Minister, provided an unwelcome illustration. Although no one doubted his honesty, Maudling's image was permanently tarnished by news about his relationship with John Poulson, an architect whose bankruptcy case filled the headlines in 1972 with rumors of corruption in high places.[43] Further rumors were soon heard that Maudling would resign, rumors fed by gloomy statements from his Cabinet colleagues that "it was for Mr. Maudling to decide."

New Ministers who underestimate the representational side of the role soon learn that they are required to perform as public-relations officers. They are expected to create the impression that they and their departments are doing important things. They are expected to motivate people. Some Ministers make their role's characteristic public-relations work a predominant goal, but everyone does at least the minimum—which requires a lot of time.

Behavior at Westminster

Ministers spend nearly as much time at Westminster as do backbenchers. But they use this time differently. Our mailback data show that they are less likely to be found in the Chamber. They also spend less time on party meetings. And they devote fewer hours to constituency work.

What, then, do Ministers do at Westminster? Formally, they speak on behalf of their departments in the Chamber and in committees. Informally, they "keep in touch" with the House and particularly with their party's backbenchers who specialize in their area. The informal duties draw Ministers into the lobbies, dining rooms, and bars, where, the mailback data further show, they spend considerably more time than the average backbencher. Here they try to create consensus, build confidence, and boost the party's image. Here they try to see that their departments and their careers get as smooth a ride as possible. When they are not in the lobbies, dining rooms, or bars, Ministers are usually in their rooms working, for they have comfortable rooms off the quiet ministerial corridor, good places to review correspondence and papers in the evenings.

Ministers come to Westminster to vote, to perform in the Chamber and in committee, to "keep in touch," and to do correspondence. The most important goal that guides these activities is the goal of persuading the House. And the most persuasive Ministers are those with the most effective presentations of self.

PRESENTATIONS OF SELF

James Callaghan "is an extremely interesting example of how important image is in modern politics," commented one of his colleagues after viewing a Callaghan performance on television. "He has a good public image outside Parliament, his presence in Parliament is exactly right, his personality on T.V. is just right, and he also has a good image inside his own department in the sense that they like him."[44] The importance of such images in British political life cannot be overestimated. Ministers believe, correctly, that success in the House "depends to a very large extent on the sort of corporate view the House of Commons has of him." If the House doesn't respect the "self" behind the title, then that self isn't going to be a very useful Member of the Government. But if a Minister can become a figure whose image the House does respect, "a Minister like Willie Whitelaw or Robert Carr," then he or she will be very well positioned indeed.

How does one develop an agreeable image? What sorts of presentations of self will be "exactly right"? This question recalls the Ministerial Aspirant's concerns about how exactly one makes a mark. And the answers recall his absorption in ambiguity.

The press, Ministers believe, plays a surprisingly significant part in the evolution of images at Westminster. The press creates a feedback loop that was described as follows by a Cabinet Minister who was having difficulties and was keen to improve his image: "The press are very influential because on the whole you will find most opinions about Ministers reflected sooner or later in articles in the press, and then that comes back again to Members.

So it's a two-way business: the Members putting their views to the press and then likewise reading the press and taking views which they would not have taken very seriously but for some press articles."[45] This account is intriguing, but incomplete. Other factors shape Members' opinions of Ministers. And other factors besides Members' opinions shape the images that appear in the press.

First among such factors is one over which Ministers have some control: their own performances at Westminster. A series of successes in putting the department's case or in dealing with pressure groups or backbenchers can trigger a chain reaction of positive impressions among MPs, flattering stories in the press, and then still more favorable impressions in the House. It seems odd that MPs should be influenced by second-hand images in the press, since they see the Ministers' performances first-hand at Westminster. Nonetheless, when the quality newspapers and television profiles depict a Minister as doing a particularly good job, it becomes fashionable among MPs to say that the Minister is indeed doing a particularly good job and to begin regarding him or her as one of the successes of the present Government. Yet, there are so many other factors involved beyond these performances that Ministers wonder whether they have any significant control over the process at all. Thus, when they talk about the subject, they sound like outside observers watching, with fascination and with a little fear, as their images sway one way and then another. The volatility keeps them on edge.

The principal performances take place at the two Despatch Boxes that serve as lecterns in the Chamber. And these *are* performances: Ministers feel very much as though they were on stage and under spotlights. Backbenchers want the performances to count because this strengthens the House as a check on the Executive and as a school for Ministers.[46] It also makes backbenchers feel important, for they are the judges. Most of the time the process is very low key, but it can suddenly become very heated. The right speech can have an extraordinary impact on party morale: "By the time he sat down they were all cheering and laughing behind him, and the Tories were totally discomfited. It was a tremendous show."[47] The party's morale had reached a low ebb, and by wit, agility, and "hitting the level of the House exactly," this Minister's speech reinvigorated his backbenchers.

Because these performances are a constant topic of conversation at Westminster, Ministerial careers are always on the line. In fact, "there is probably no other political system in the world where a politician's career depends so much on his ability at the Despatch Box."[48] Performances at the Despatch Box matter so much "because it so affects his reputation through the press if he doesn't put up a good show." The ritual has many odd rules. For instance, newspapers that are normally unsympathetic to a party nevertheless like to be the first to tell the outside world that the inside world has awarded laurels to one of that party's leaders.[49] But when Ministers fluff debates, particularly on important occasions when the Chamber is full, "then people will instinctively note that down against them." And if they do it more than twice, they themselves begin to worry that they may not survive long as Ministers. Their vivid language conveys the intensity of their feelings: "I really needed to restore my reputation with my own backbenchers and get on top of the Tories. . . . They wanted a kill in the chase for the Minister of Housing . . . I had to fight for my life, and by means of a conscious rhetorically—and demagogically—forced row with the Opposition I won back both their respect and my popularity among my own party."[50]

Some can do it, Ministers say, and some can't. Those who can't sooner or later sink, because all Ministers must engage the enemy in duels or struggles. Thus, they talk about "annihilating attacks," "sheer debating skills," and "destroying the opposition." It is a world of single combat, reputation, and honor.[51] When he became Leader of the Opposition, Edward Heath at first had considerable difficulty holding the House, till late one night during a crisis and before a packed Chamber he "took on Michael Foot, one of the giants in Parliament . . . a superb speaker." Heath launched "a very powerful attacking speech against him." It was judged "an outstanding good performance," a performance of the kind whereby "the House begins to respect you." That was in 1968, and memories of the speech lingered on into the 1970s.

The Opposition is quick to test the mettle of new Ministers, but usually not till after their "Maiden Speeches." Although the ministerial Maiden Speech lacks the formality of Maiden Speeches for new backbenchers, ministerial neophytes feel the same peculiar combination of nervousness and insecurity that they experienced years before.[52] Not this time, but tomorrow they will have to stand their ground and fight. Then they will have to show that they are able to defend a weak case as well as a strong one and do it with a conviction that convinces at least their own side. Tomorrow they will have to appear to be the confident masters of their subjects, never at a loss, speakers whose self-confidence makes their audience confident in them. "He's also got to be prepared if necessary to hit and hit hard if he's being attacked," added a gentle Minister who wished he could. "A good Minister will sit down to a resounding cheer from his own side, and they'll mean it—he's really scored."

This impression management is difficult to analyze satisfactorily, for the audience and its criteria of judgment are always changing. There are, however, some regular ingredients, one of which we have already noted: the wish that the Minister appear to be "running his department" rather than vice versa. Backbenchers would like to believe that Ministers are creatures of the House. They are therefore very sensitive to signs that a Minister may be becoming a creature of his or her own department. Another established expectation that Ministers try to satisfy is that they are "taking the House seriously." The best way to convey this attitude is by being there, by explaining carefully, by listening attentively, and by respecting the traditions. Prudent Ministers try to create the impression that the House is, in their view, the center of British political life.[53]

"Taking the House seriously" requires Ministers to give the appearance of explaining their conduct carefully, of taking the time to keep the House fully informed—respectfully, with "a sort of basic humility," for "there is nothing that annoys, rightly annoys, the House of Commons more than a Minister who lectures when, when he makes speeches." Equally important is "listening attentively" ("He must listen to what *the House* thinks"), which likewise conveys an impression of respect. The Minister "must seem to pay a lot of attention to the House" because he believes that the House embodies collective wisdom in its ancient traditions and current opinions. Here is a Cabinet Minister whose presentation of self was, at the time, widely regarded as "just right": "We are all Members of something that is far bigger than the sum total of six hundred and thirty of us. There is something important there. And I think therefore that as Ministers we should listen with respect to, um, not only to what other people say or to criticisms they may have of our speeches or our actions, but that we should also have a healthy respect for the, er, the wisdom not only of the present House of Commons but of Houses of Commons in the past, stretching back, and all the great traditions of it."

"Showing regard to critics" is important too. Critics may be backbench Specialists whose expertise can be used to derail parts of your legislation. Or they may be backbench Generalists whose shots from the hip can damage your image and your career. Critics are dangerous and therefore require patience, "an almost unending courtesy, and patience, and tolerance, which mustn't be confused with being ready to give way over a point. What is needed is the *appearance* of readiness to listen to everybody's point of view, even when it is, er, a point of view which is so obviously a nonstarter." Patience. You know that they are just trying to delay the proceedings or goad you into mistakes. Nevertheless, you "must always *give the impression of having a serious regard for these points that you know are not serious*"; you must "be able to maintain, er, keep your cool in these situations." You

respect their efforts even when they are wrong because they are "representatives of the ordinary mass of the population, and even if they don't know
all the details about nuclear submarines or anything like that, their opinions
must be listened to." If the impression gets around "that you don't care . . .
well, if you're doing a good job perhaps they'll put up with it, but there'll
come a time when the judgement about you has to be made."

Patience, courtesy, respect, and care all help to convey the most important
impression of all: that you think of yourself as *one of them*. You have risen
into the ministerial pantheon and won a grand office and great authority in
Whitehall—but there is nothing that those left behind like better than being
told that you are all still equals. That's why "it's so dangerous to appear
arrogant." That's why it's so prudent to have dinner at the House several
times a week and sit next to anyone you see. That's why it helps to talk
with colleagues, even or perhaps particularly about their personal problems.[54] The point is to present yourself, and "indeed to think of yourself,"
such "that you feel that you are, so to speak, one of them," such that you
feel you are a Minister but "also an ordinary Member of Parliament."

Thus far, we have examined how at Westminster Ministers present themselves in the role of the Minister. They also characteristically "take soundings" and conduct important transactions, mainly with backbenchers, occasionally with Opposition Spokesmen.

TAKING SOUNDINGS

Ministers "take soundings" to help guide their legislation through the
House. "The essence of a Minister's job," explained a senior Minister, "is
to *get* his legislation." "You get your legislation by having the support of
your own party." And you get the support of your own party by "trying
to avoid introducing legislation which your own people then are going to
kick up hell about." Soundings help Ministers avoid trouble.

The term "soundings" refers to measuring the depth of water or to examining the atmosphere by sending up instruments attached to balloons. Ministers measure the depth of feeling in the House of Commons, which is important because backbenchers "are much more independent now than certainly
they were when I first came into the House twenty or thirty years ago." So
Ministers protect themselves by these soundings, and also by sending up
balloons. Thus it is "absolutely essential to test constantly the parliamentary
atmosphere," particularly with regard to new and controversial policies.
There is something wrong with a Government, they said, when it gets itself
into a situation where, in public, it is defeated by its own backbenchers.

"They shouldn't get into the position . . . they should, they should know in advance what the feeling is."[55]

The principal responsibility for collecting the data is, as we have seen, assigned to the role of the Whip. "The whole job of a Whip, in a way, is to be a sounding board." Whips speak to backbenchers regularly and work hard to understand what they will support and oppose, as well as what they think about Ministers' performances, "how they are presenting the issues, whether Ministers are making the wrong sort of speeches, and so on." "And there is terrific feedback," which leads to strategic alterations in Bills before they reach the Chamber. Parliamentary Private Secretaries provide the backup. "Your PPS can play a great part in this too, and a good PPS, erm, I think is invaluable in this respect."

Ministers also measure the feelings themselves at, for instance, the specialist backbench committees where they discuss the sorts of policies they would like to pursue: "By the rules of privilege and so on, you can't disclose in advance to your own party things that you can't disclose in public. But you can discuss in advance proposals you may have; and you can, therefore, form some idea of what the reaction of your own party will be." Other opportunities for examining the atmosphere include "answering Parliamentary Questions not with just the sort of tight-fisted statement about what the situation is, but sort of letting some further thought about what you're considering be drafted into the answer"—and watching the reactions. Actually, "there are a thousand and one ways of hinting at where you're going, and a thousand and one ways of getting their reactions to that."

Soundings help Ministers chart a safe course only if they can interpret these data accurately. Ministers who are unable to recognize when they "are coming up against the limits of the possible, what goes, and what can be achieved in the system" don't get very far, for "there is only a certain room for manoeuvreability. More likely than not you will have the information available. What you need to do is to *interpret* it." "The best Ministers have . . . a quick way of knowing what is likely to be acceptable and what they may have to compromise on" if they want to get the main part of the policy through.

Ministers believe that an ability to sense and to interpret the changing moods of the House is crucial. The least successful of their colleagues are, in their view, "the ones who seem to be out of touch with the sort of, er, mood of the House of Commons. And of course the mood changes, so it's quite difficult at times. . . . One's seen Ministers who missed this mood, and it really is, um, I mean it's rather like . . . rubbing a knife down a window and making a nasty noise. It's as awkward as that and as uncomfortable as that."

RELATIONS WITH BACKBENCHERS

Legislation is ordinarily initiated within the Whitehall machine. But "with the more headline-making operations, where there is public pressure for some action," the initiative can come, if you let it, up through the House of Commons, through backbenchers returning on a Monday morning from their constituencies and saying, "This intolerable situation! The Government's not doing anything." Ministerial responses to such pressures help generate support by making backbenchers feel part of the team. "Trickle-up" gives backbenchers "a chance to express their views which may influence your reactions." It also gives "Ministers a chance to say to their civil servants, 'Well, the party just wouldn't accept that. We can't do it. The backbenchers have explained it to me and that's that.'"

Ministers in the Heath Government talked trickle-up but, in the end, it was mostly trickle-down. They did listen. But they came to the House mainly "to discuss with Members the sort of things that he's concerned with and *to get their support* for his point of view." "I mean this is absolutely an essential part of a Minister's role. He must, must be able to do this." "You've got to try and explain and carry people with you." Ministers overestimate their effectiveness at trickle-down. They need to be persuasive and would like to believe that they are.[56]

Trickle-down uses both formal and informal channels. On the formal side are the White Papers and Green Papers through which Ministers present their ideas to backbenchers. White Papers are government policy, "but a Green Paper is a statement of government policy which is very much open to discussion." Green Papers can serve as a basis for discussion before the Government commits itself to specific policy proposals. They are, in effect, draft proposals that allow Ministers to test responses and discover the modifications needed to avoid trouble. Green Papers test the climate of opinion and at the same time shape it, for they are designed to define the debate and persuade the skeptics.

Standing and Select Committees offer another formal opportunity "to persuade people by argument." Here, the Minister will try to respond intelligently to the Opposition's attacks, to persuade the backbenchers that he has been thoroughly briefed, or, if they are not persuaded, that he at least has his reasons. These can be arduous tests, particularly for Ministers whose

departments have heavy legislative schedules, and particularly when the Opposition decides to oppose a Bill clause by clause.[57] Select Committees are
the most difficult. One way to try to bring them round is by drowning them
with inside information: "We have given them much more information than
Parliament as a whole has ever been given before about defence policy, but
we've given it on the condition that it is restricted to that subcommittee and
to the chairman of the main committee." Select Committees that are not
persuaded can usually be disregarded—but not always: when the Heath
Government disregarded an important report from the Select Committee
on Science and Technology, there was such a fuss on the backbenches that
Ministers felt obliged to make amends.[58]

Answering letters from MPs is yet another formal opportunity for persuasion.[59] But the most effective formal channel between Ministers and backbenchers is the backbench party committee. Prudent Ministers keep on good
terms with the backbench party committees that deal with their subjects.
The Conservative backbench committees meet weekly or fortnightly to discuss policy and administration and are usually run by Policy Advocates.
Conservative Ministers take them seriously because the backbenchers who
attend include those who are best informed about the subject and feel most
strongly about it. "They are the people who play the biggest part in the
debates. And those people I meet regularly. And when I'm not meeting them,
my PPS is meeting them, virtually every other day, you know, very frequently. They would be, I suppose, my main source of political contact,
apart of course, from the other Ministers."[60] Ministers meet committee officers regularly "to go through anything they like with me, and I go through
anything I like with them." Several give these officers their home telephone
numbers and urge them to call "if at any moment of time they wish to
discuss something with me." It is important "to keep a close relationship
with the officers of the parliamentary committee" because their views will
be influential in shaping the views of their colleagues who do not follow the
subject so closely.

The informal channels for persuasion encompass a myriad of settings
where "one has a lot of informal discussions," and you explain your reasons,
"and people tell you frankly that they think . . . the line you're going along
is wrong or they support it and so on." Ministers use these "less formal
means of communication" to rehearse options and drum up support. "It is
very important actually in your own interests" to do this "because otherwise
one does get out of touch with what your people are thinking." During the
Heath Government, the Leader of the House was constantly dipping into

these informal channels, partially because Heath himself was so uncomfortable there. Heath was not good at small talk—which did not endear him to his backbenchers, who complained, "and bearing in mind, on a nonattribution basis," that they were "very disappointed with his difficulty in communicating on a person-to-person basis with his supporters . . . on a person-to-person basis with those other than in the Cabinet."

Many Ministers work as much as they can in their rooms at the House of Commons so that they can venture out "and go into the Smoking Room . . . where Members, particularly of my own [Conservative] party, can have words and talk to me." The same role expectations send Labour Ministers to the Tea Room. These are the best-known places in the Palace of Westminster where one pours oil on troubled waters and keeps in touch with parliamentary tempers. Many Ministers also eat regularly in the Dining Room. "I mean I have lunch or supper in the House of Commons certainly twice a week, and one meets colleagues and talks about matters with them. . . . And you argue with them and you hear what's going on." Some characterize it as "doing a lot of lobbying over the dinner table" and alternate between sitting with the troops and sitting at the table for Ministers and Privy Councillors.

Others do their lobbying in the lobbies, including the division lobbies. "This is the one great point in having to be here in person—you see your own people in the lobby, oh quite a lot." "Terrific contact with people in the House every night," added another Minister; "people want to talk to me in the lobbies . . . it's important to keep in touch with one's backbenchers." The division lobbies, the rooms through which MPs walk in order to vote by having tellers tick off their names as they exit, have long been used as important informal channels: "I mean in a curious way the division lobbies are a place for exchanging advice and ideas. . . . The fact that there are three-line Whips means that we all must vote, and this means that you cannot avoid your supporters even if you want to avoid them . . . and they are always full of ideas—usually unhelpful—and you have got to, um, stay in touch with them, and give them your ideas too."

Ministers see these exchanges mainly as trickle-down, as persuasion. They listen, but they listen mainly to deepen their understanding of backbenchers the better to guide them. Their backbenchers, by contrast, see these same exchanges mainly as trickle-up, as influence. How much influence do they actually have upon their Ministers and how much should they have? The view from the backbenches is that this influence is real and that there ought to be more of it: "I mean I think backbenchers are here to make Governments change their mind." For Ministers, by contrast, backbench influence is expedient, since "when any party ceases to be responsive to its backbenchers, it's soon in trouble."

Ministers have their own ideas about how such processes work. It is instructive to compare their accounts with those of Whips and backbench Policy Advocates. Compared to Ministers, Whips attribute to the Whip's Office a more active role. Compared to Ministers, Policy Advocates characterize their campaigns as more elaborate and subtle. It seems simpler to Ministers because they focus on the bottom line: "How much must I give way in order to get my way?" Since expediency conditions their viewpoints, many are cynical about backbench influence ("You must . . . make them *feel* that they have a significant part") and inclined to think that there is more than enough of it already: "Backbenchers, like the public at large, always want the impossible. They want everything . . . but they must be prepared to accept that they can't get everything. . . . It's the Government that carries the responsibility ultimately."

In Chapter 2 backbench influence was probed by several questionnaire items. One focused on Private Members' Bills ("There should be fewer obstacles to Private Members' Bills"), which cut into the time available for a Government's own legislation. Ministers might therefore be expected to be less enthusiastic than backbenchers about them. They are indeed: whereas a majority of backbenchers would like to reduce the obstacles to Private Members' Bills, only one in four Ministers is prepared to go along—and, among senior Ministers, 97 percent would oppose such a move.

"All power to the Government," a belief characteristic of the role of the Minister, can also be seen in ministerial reactions to investigatory Select Committees. Thus, in Table 8.4 a proposal to increase the number of such committees is resisted by three out of four Ministers. Again, senior Ministers are most opposed to increasing backbench influence in this way. They thought they had already been generous; and, compared to their predecessors, they had been generous. But this generosity was begrudging and self-interested: "Mind you, to be absolutely candid I wouldn't want to put my hand to my heart and say that we would necessarily have changed our view on these things had our majority been a hundred." With a majority of about fifteen, they needed all the support they could get. Several Junior Ministers were sympathetic because they remembered what it was like. For most Ministers, however, images of active and influential backbenchers did nothing to warm their hearts.

"Leave it to the Executive" is an attitude that clashes with the expectations of backbenchers who want Ministers "to take a lot of time looking at

Table 8.4 Backbench influence: Increasing the number of Select Committees, in percent

Response*	Conservative Ministers**	Conservative backbenchers**
Agree without reservation	6	17
Agree, but with reservations	19	35
Disagree, but with reservations	25	23
Disagree without reservation	50	26
Total	100	100
	(N = 32)	(N = 139)

*Q. The number of specialist Select Committees in the House should be increased.
**$p \leq .01$

the ideas I put forward and the cases I put to him." Backbenchers want Ministers to be in the Palace of Westminster so that "if I badly want to see the Minister for X, he'll be there, he can't escape . . . and I'll say, 'Look, what about . . . ?'" They are best pleased when Ministers are there and also behaving like members of the crowd. Some Ministers disappoint them. And these disappointments are noticed:

> The chairman of the [backbench] committee was very pleased with the meeting and said, "Come and have a drink. . . ." And he automatically started off down to the Harcourt Room, where you take a *visiting* speaker. And I sort of paused and smiled and said, "You know, of course, that I am a Member of the House, ha, ha." And they all laughed . . . and somebody made a remark and said, "Of course, we don't see you about the House very much." I said "Well, I do try to come. . . ." But, I, I took this in a sense as, er, er, a mild criticism, that, er, as a Minister I hadn't been getting around among the Members and talking as much as I should.

RELATIONS WITH THE OTHER SIDE

Ministers' relationships with the other side are overlooked by outsiders, who regard them as unimportant. They are not, however, overlooked by Ministers, who regard them as very important indeed.

There are Ministers who go out of their way to "give stick" to the other side in order to win cheers from their own. But their colleagues doubt that this is the wisest strategy for getting legislation through.[61] "We got it through the Standing Committee in just a day and a half," one of them explained, "and I put that down entirely to wheedling the other side all the time, giving way to them, and saying, 'Alright, we'll stop now if you want to stop, but we must make progress.' And they'd say, 'Alright, alright, we'll see,' and so on. In the end I got my Bill when I wanted it." He goes out of his way to appreciate serious people on the other side, and finds that he is himself appreciated in return: "When I was promoted to this job, I had some very charming and very warm and nice letters from some of the Opposition Front Bench. . . . I mean this is, you know, it's, it's nice, you get a nice sort of feeling about it."[62]

During the interviews, we asked: "To what extent can one trust and rely on members of the other parties? How confidently can you work with them personally and politically?" Compared to backbenchers, Ministers have much more experience of negotiations with political opponents. Contacts "on a Privy Councillor basis" and "through the usual channels" are common and necessary, and Ministers have a self-interest in seeing that they go well. Compared to backbenchers, then, their beliefs about the other side should be conditioned by these experiences.

Table 8.5 suggests that Ministers are comparatively sympathetic toward members of the other parties. Three-fourths believe that they can trust and

Table 8.5 Trust of and reliance on members of other parties, in percent

Response*	Conservative Ministers**	Conservative backbenchers**
Always	8	10
Most of the time	65	39
Some of the time	24	36
Only in very special circumstances	4	12
Not at all	0	3
Total	101	100
	(N = 51)	(N = 162)

*Q. In your experience in Parliament, to what extent can one trust and rely on members of the other parties? How confidently can you work with them personally and politically?
**$p \leq .01$

rely on their political opponents at least "most of the time," whereas only half their backbenchers concur. This Cabinet Minister's view is typical: "There are people on the other side of the House of Commons I have enormous respect and regard for, and with whom I discuss things very freely. . . . I have in the past discussed with leading members of the Opposition things which, um, are of great importance . . . discussed in a confidential way, which I think is tremendously helpful." This topic of trust in political opponents was also probed by items in the mailback questionnaire, and responses to these items point consistently in the same direction. Thus, Ministers more than backbenchers accept without reservation the proposition that "confidential cooperation between Government and Opposition is essential for the effective management of parliamentary business." Although only a minority of all MPs regards compromise with political adversaries as dangerously disloyal, Ministers are three times less likely than backbenchers to express such views.

Since backbenchers tend to regard the Opposition as "the opposition," they bring some of these attitudes with them when they first rise to the role of Junior Minister. "I think one should beware of taking a Member of the other side into your confidence." But with time, "and, er, I mean if one has never been let down," most Junior Ministers eventually find, "I suppose, one becomes less, less partisan," and the characteristic ministerial attitude of cooperation seems easier and easier. "I think he's got to be liked by the Opposition," said a Junior Minister who was beginning to get the message. "It's no good having a Minister who, whenever he gets up at the Despatch Box, creates a most frightful row because he's so disliked by the Opposition." The Opposition "can help one achieve one's political aim." "It saves parliamentary time, strain, and effort all round."[63] Sometimes "you simply have to depend to a very large extent upon the other side."

In sum, your own backbenchers feel obliged to support you when you are in trouble, but Members opposite do not. Therefore, "it is not advisable to be quite so quick to pick up the political acid and throw it at him"—or you may get more than you anticipated coming back at you. If you don't play according to the rules of the game, they can "fix" you: "This House can take it out of a Minister pretty badly if they want to. You can be dealt with. We call it 'fixing.' They 'fix' it, all right."

Position roles are recognized by formal titles and defined by assigned responsibilities. Yet even within their constrained boundaries preference roles can sometimes be created—such as the ministerial subtypes Administrators and Politicians, which are found at all three levels of the ministerial hierarchy.[64]

A reconstruction of these two types draws together and concludes this chapter.[65]

It is a reflection of the constrained character of ministerial roles that even their preference-oriented subtypes are rooted in assigned responsibilities: administrative responsibilities, which include departmental policy leadership, management, and representation to the Cabinet; and political responsibilities, which include parliamentary oratory, party leadership, and public relations.[66] All Ministers *must* perform *all* these responsibilities to some degree. And yet the "overload" is such that Ministers must concentrate on some much more than on others. This overload creates an opening for preference roles and opens the door to individual career goals and emotional incentives. Hence, "some people are inclined to become Administrators . . . and some people prefer the Despatch Box."

Administrators are people who "like *doing* things, not *talking* about them." There have always been Ministers who think of themselves as "seconded" civil servants, lawyers, or businessmen, and therefore see themselves primarily as Administrators. Despite the fact that political careers have become increasingly orthodox, this unorthodoxy has persisted.[67] Thus, one of the country's leading politicians, a senior Member of the Cabinet, told us proudly that he had, in fact, never taken any part in politics; that he never, in fact, had had any intention of going into politics; that he had, in fact, always disliked politics; and that he was "not an intriguer, a corridor politician, or a discusser of personalities." He much preferred instead those aspects of the role of the Minister that involve "being able to do a job in administration."

Administrators don't like debates in the House of Commons. Their goal is to get legislation through as quickly as possible "by keeping the temperature down and getting on with the work." Nor do they admire Ministers who, at the Despatch Box, are "good knock-about characters, you know, and everybody cheers"—because it takes such Ministers twice as long as necessary to get their legislation. Besides, they themselves are not good at "knock-about." The Administrators' distaste for debates usually reflects a more general ambivalence about the House of Commons. They find Whitehall more enjoyable than Westminster and far more enjoyable than dealing with their constituents. Compared to the Politicians, Administrators tend to be less sensitive (and sometimes insensitive) to the electorate.

The role of the Administrator is most often found in particular departments and positions ("in what I call a nonpolitical department like the Board of Trade and the Foreign Office, or the Ministry of Defence and the Scottish Office") where the work is not very party-political and where Ministers treat the other side with respect. These are basically administrative contexts:

"One's involved very much more in administration and policy as it relates to administration rather than policy as it relates to the party struggle in the House." In a similar vein, two out of the three Law Officers we interviewed hardly seemed political at all: "I'm a Minister, but I'm a lawyer first." Their particular position, they explained, reinforces a quasi-administrative interpretation of their role.

Institutional assignments can encourage potential Administrators, but they cannot create them, for Ministers' preferences are dominant in the construction of this role. Hence, Administrators can also be found in "political" departments since, "well, I was never a very strong party-political chap." One such Minister calls himself a parliamentarian in order to avoid the label "politician" and explains that, unlike most of his colleagues, he actually dislikes politics as a way of life. Another feels that she is different from other people in politics, because they are immersed in political issues and "seek to provoke political issues," whereas she spends her life trying to avoid political issues.

Administrators characteristically try hard to take account of reasonable points from the other side. It pleases them to have a reputation in the House for doing so. "One of the things that has given me great pleasure in the last three weeks," reported a satisfied Administrator who was about to step down, "is the number of my socialist colleagues who have come up, obviously very genuinely, saying, 'We're terribly sorry you've given up,' you know. And this is simply because one has taken trouble—even with the Arthur Lewis[es] of this world, and God knows, I mean he's a maverick." Conflict makes Administrators uncomfortable and, therefore, so does the House. They find the experience of being in Opposition particularly frustrating because it means spending so much time at Westminster. Should their party lose the next General Election, these are the Ministers who will seek other employment rather than return full time to Westminster's world.

Administrators live *off* politics, but they do not live *for* politics of the party-political kind. They are pleased, for example, if their constituency party recruited them rather than the other way round: "And when they wrote, they had to ask amongst other things if I was a Conservative." Now he is a Conservative Cabinet Minister, but more a Cabinet Minister than a Conservative. And he is served by a similarly apolitical Junior Minister who is similarly absorbed in Cabinet Government. The majority of Administrators have, like these two, entered Parliament late in life; and several have not, in their entire experience as MPs, spent more than a few months on the backbenches. They have always been either in Government or in Shadow Government.

Table 8.6 shows that Administrators are indeed the minority—approxi-

Table 8.6 Ministers: Administrator and politician subtypes by position roles

	Position roles			
Subtype	Junior Minister	Minister of State	Full Minister Outside Cabinet	Cabinet Minister
Administrator	3	2	4(2)	2
Politician	22	6	8	6
Total	25	8	12	8

Note: Entries are numbers of respondents.

mately one out of eight among Junior Ministers and approximately one out of four among Ministers.[68] Administrators are found at every level of the formal ministerial hierarchy, but more than half are either working or have worked in comparatively non-party-political departments: Board of Trade, Foreign and Commonwealth, Defense, or Scottish Office. In the same institutional vein, the proportion of Administrators among Junior Ministers may be so meager because this preference role may be most easily developed in higher ministerial positions whose role requirements tilt toward Whitehall.

Politicians, by contrast, are captivated by the politics of Westminster's political life. "Politics is my major preoccupation," this Minister of State explains; "I won't say it's my hobby, my hobby is country life . . . but politics is almost all-absorbing to me." Moreover, he and his fellow Politicians dismiss the Administrator's dismissal of them as "dashing round the country being photographed and saying things for the press." They think it is important to be in the public eye. And they like being in the public eye. As with Generalists, a little vanity and egocentricity drives the public-relations activities at which Politicians excel and which help produce successful Ministers, departments, and Governments. These public-relations activities are what the Politicians have in mind when they insist that "this is absolutely primary—I am a *political* animal. When anyone says to me 'What are you?'— I'm a *Politician*. There are those who describe themselves as 'Statesmen.' No! I am a *Politician*."

Also like Generalists, Politicians want to be involved in the big issues and crises of the day. "The whole exciting point of a Cabinet is that you can address the pressing political issues." Politicians are attracted to political crises because, unlike Administrators, they actually enjoy political conflict: "We are prize-fighters, you know. We can be quite friendly, but when we get into that ring our main aim is to knock the other side down, er, to be as brutal and bloody as possible."

The most striking contrast between Politicians and Administrators is the way that Politicians thrive in the House of Commons. Of course, "when one does become a Minister, one, uh, one appreciates it. . . . *But the other* side of the role is *extremely* enjoyable—the House of Commons side." The most enthusiastic Politicians find it difficult to imagine retiring voluntarily from the House, "because it's, it's in my blood." It's like drink to an alcoholic: "You don't enjoy it at the time, but you miss it terribly if the supply is cut off." This analogy suggests some ambivalence, which, as we shall see in the next chapter, can at times become quite sharp. But here let us listen to the bright side, to the genuine affection for "the life of the place"—to dispositions that many Administrators lack. This love of the life is captured in analogies that remind us of backbench Club Men and in verbs that depict the institution as an organism of which they are a part:

> Its organic nature. . . . You have to have been here a good bit of time to understand it. No two Parliaments are the same. After a few years . . . they get their own character. . . . And therefore it's living the whole time. I think one has to use analogies from biology much more than from mechanistic systems. . . . You develop a certain sort of intuition about things, about people's relationships and so on . . . this gives you the subtleties . . . the autumn tints rather than the blacks and whites. And this is really what the life here's very largely about.

The most wonderful feature of the place, the most successful Politicians say and try to believe, is that all Members, "including the Members of the Government, are equal." And all Members are judged equally for their ability and for their character. "You know, you all have drinks together and meals together and talks together and likes and dislikes and so on. There is a continuous cross-fertilization of feelings and ideas and understandings." Although the House can irritate them greatly, these Politicians "like the people in the House of Commons. Some of them are right bastards; some of them are very nice—and I like them all." They have been working together for years, "seeing one another with the screws really down," mingling outside the Chamber, going together for drinks, for lunch. These are the Politicians who see themselves most clearly as *both* Members and Ministers.[69]

Other Politicians have a love-hate relationship with the place, but they always share at least the excitement and enjoyment of the intense debates. This more than anything else gets into their blood—the dramatic debates, and especially the noisy debates in which they themselves are players: "I mean one has absolute kittens beforehand. Sometimes it goes wrong; sometimes it goes right. Sometimes you score; sometimes you're scored off. But, you know, this is really *the great fun,* it *really* is." This more than anything else distinguishes Politicians from Administrators. The more party-political such debates are, the better. Instead of trying to avoid rows, as Administrators do, Politicians go out of their way to create them. They know they are succeeding when the adrenalin flows and they sense the excitement of the troops: "I mean a Minister's job in Parliament is to rally the troops, to make them feel as they march through the lobbies that they are supporting a good cause. One has to be a pretty good orator, a pretty good debater. One has to have the power to, first of all, show that . . . the Opposition's objections are base and unfounded. A Minister who can do that can build up his reputation very quickly indeed."

Leadership in Whitehall may crown the ministerial role. But it is leadership in Westminster that keeps *these* players going.

MINISTERIAL ROLE STRAINS
AND ROLE CHOICES

> I mean . . . once you're a candidate . . . you
> think, "God, now I want to be a Member
> of Parliament." Once you're an MP, you
> say, "I'd like to be a Junior Minister."
> Once you're a Junior Minister, after a few
> months you say, "I'd like to be a rather
> more senior Minister."
>
> Journeyman voicing "progressive ambition"

This chapter examines the "role strains" that Ministers encounter and the role choices that shape their careers. The analysis of role strains is primarily interpretative, whereas the analysis of role choices is more naturalistic. Both inquiries focus on senior Ministers but consider Junior Ministers as well. Both also rely upon several neologisms that I believe illuminate more than they obscure. The first of these is role strain itself, which covers two different situations, role conflict and role overload. Role conflict refers to situations where one's associates disagree about how one should behave. Role overload refers to situations where role players are assigned more responsibilities than they can reasonably be expected to fulfill.

Role Conflict

Ministers encounter role conflicts in Parliament and also in their constituencies. At the House of Commons, their ministerial colleagues and civil servants expect them to act as agents of the Government and to push the department's legislation through unscathed in the shortest possible time. But backbenchers at the House expect these same Ministers to demonstrate loyalty to Parliament by including them in the legislative process and "by modifying Bills in response to their representations." Role conflicts inherent in

Ministers' relations with their constituencies are different, for they involve not so much incompatible goals inherent in Ministers' roles but instead the way in which Ministers divide their time.

MEMBER OF THE GOVERNMENT OR MEMBER OF PARLIAMENT

Even Politicians who find the House invigorating cannot ignore the institutional strains in ministerial roles and cannot avoid, therefore, some ambivalence about the parliamentary experience. Role conflict is set up by the constitutional rules that require most Ministers who serve in Whitehall as Members of the Government also to serve in Westminster as Members of Parliament. Since one of Parliament's principal functions is to criticize Ministers, this creates tensions between themselves and those Members of Parliament who are not Members of the Government. In the same vein, the rules further require Ministers, like Whips, to be appointed from above. Ministers therefore owe their positions and their primary allegiances to the Prime Minister and to their ministerial colleagues. This exacerbates the tensions by discouraging them from trying to balance the conflicting role expectations and encouraging them instead to tilt toward those who control their careers.

Thus, how Ministers think of themselves as Members of Parliament becomes conditioned by how they think of themselves as Members of the Government. Members of Parliament are sometimes called Honourable Members. And Members of the Government who are Members of Parliament sometimes think of themselves as the "Most Honourable Members":

> Of course things are different when one is a Minister. One enters the House of Commons by a different way. I drive in the car into Speaker's Yard. I go by the policeman and up in the lift and in at the back to answer a Question or make a speech at the time I want. I don't have to sit about and wait. And when I am there I have my Private Secretary in the box. It's a Rolls Royce way of being a Member of Parliament, all the wheels are oiled especially for you and your life is made extremely easy. The whole of our Parliament is geared not to help backbenchers criticize Ministers but to help Ministers overcome backbenchers.[1]

Ministers come to regard Parliament as merely one reference group among many. "As the complexity of government has developed," they say, "the more one tends to use as one's sounding board the, um, representative bodies outside Parliament." Parliament is insulated; and so they pay more attention to well-informed civil servants and to "the various associations and bodies involved in the legislation than to the views of the Members." The House seems peripheral to real power. One goes through the motions because the established institutional arrangements require it. But Ministers, particularly senior Ministers, have so many other reference groups and sources of headaches that they are always tempted to depreciate the House and to arrange their affairs so that it bothers them as little as possible.[2]

"As little as possible" is still of quite a lot, of course, for the Westminster side is firmly bolted to their ministerial roles and requires a great deal of time and patience. It frequently creates irritations, even among Ministers who are Politicians and basically like the House of Commons. Because Ministers are so busy, it's hard for them not to notice that the House often strays from reality, that backbenchers are often uninformed ("they stand up and they make a speech off the cuff . . . and they've completely wasted their time and everybody else's time as well") and that, when they are trying very hard to guide their legislation through very quickly, "the House of Commons . . . behaves like a boy's school on a bad day—not actually throwing paper darts at one another but very nearly getting to that point." Busy people become impatient with democracy, and busy Ministers become ambivalent about a Westminster that consumes too much of their time.

During the interviews, it was put to them that "the House of Commons has been described as having the atmosphere of a 'gothic club'—as stuffy, lifeless, and out of date. Do you think this description is true?" Junior Ministers, who had recently risen from the House to seats in Whitehall, were extremely positive about the institution. But senior Ministers, who were further from the House both physically and psychologically, and who had personally experienced more parliamentary obstruction, were less enthusiastic: three-fourths of the Junior Ministers expressed positive feelings toward the House without qualification, but only half the senior Ministers shared such views. Many seemed indifferent.

Indifference was most often expressed by those Ministers who also said that their most important responsibilities were in Whitehall. After "being in Government one realises that Parliament has a somewhat more peripheral role to perform. . . . Parliament is, in fact, not the centre of government. The centre of government is the Cabinet and the Cabinet Committees and the departments." Backbenchers, in fact, have delusions of grandeur: "If you're not a Member of the Government, you delude yourself in thinking you're the centre of the web—but you're not. There's an enormous amount that goes on that the average Member of Parliament knows nothing about at all, because in this context he's part of *the public*." These Ministers express an instrumental orientation toward Westminster and try to detach themselves emotionally from the place and its traditions.[3] Some would like to ignore it altogether—but of course they can't. They can't ignore it because, according to the constitutional rules of the game, "you've got to be able to get your policy through Parliament." Unable to dismiss Parliament, they regard it as "a burden," as "an obstacle to be overcome by Ministers."

Ministers who deride the House as a peripheral irritation are a minority and are also usually Administrators. The Politicians become irritated too, but in the end "develop a sort of love-hate relationship with it. It's terribly wrong in many ways, it's out of date, it needs reforming—but by God it's about the best in the world if you analyze it with all the rest." Still, most Ministers find the House at least a little irritating and disquieting, for this is the place where they endure public scrutiny, the place where their careers are on the line. Their natural inclination, therefore, is to try to minimize ministerial vulnerability by seeking to control the symbols of dissent and how dissent is treated.[4]

First of all, they say, the Government must make very clear that it not only *is* in charge, but that it *should be* in charge: "The Government has to . . . say this is what *we* were elected to do, and this is what *we* are going to do." Next, Ministers should encourage the view that the point of being a backbencher is, at the end of the day, to support the Government. Several Ministers were so excited about the growing dissent in the division lobbies that they seemed ready to create a new constitutional doctrine of collective responsibility for backbenchers: "On matters of policy, backbenchers should conform like you do in a Cabinet," they told their colleagues. "I mean you have your say and if you can't persuade people to agree with you, then you've *got* to conform to the majority view." Personal opinions are a luxury, they told backbenchers who were in rebellion over the Government's "U-turns": "A Member of Parliament . . . shouldn't be indulging in the luxury of personal views when he was returned to Parliament on the basis of a party organisation." Backbenchers should be *followers,* argued an irate Minister: "The basic fact is that a Government is *entitled* to call its supporters to support it. . . . If any follower with a conscience can't do it, then they'll just have to stop being a follower. . . . If you break the place up, then you get sent home."

Some of the former Whips among them sounded very much like Whips when they argued that although a little dissent suggests an independent mind, too much dissent suggests heresy. "It's dead easy to be disloyal," said one; "sometimes it's rather cheap." Another exaggerated the consequences: "And, er, if you vote against your party, you destroy the majority. The meaning of that is that you do not wish your party to continue to govern." Party discipline was still strong enough to do the job during the early 1970s, but it was obviously slipping. And just as Whips worried about credibility, so Ministers worried about vulnerability. Most held their fire and tried to spread the word through cautionary tales: "It's like the old Dean of my college at Oxford, Dean Thompson . . . the Clerical Dean of Magdalen. He officiated in the chapel. And he then wrote a book disproving the fact that miracles could ever occur. Well, the Visitor, the Bishop of Winchester, over- looked this. And he then produced another book saying that the Resurrec- tion couldn't have occurred. This—the Bishop of Winchester got a little perturbed at this and had a few words. Then he produced a book saying that in fact God did not exist—whereupon he was removed as Dean of Magdalen. He'd gone rather far down the line."

The data in Table 9.1 indicate that Ministers are more cautious about free-thinking on the backbenches than are those who sit there. This item, which offers a decision rule that could weaken party discipline, is turned down by 42 percent of the Ministers but only by 24 percent of the back- benchers. Where you stand on party discipline depends on where you sit: "I used to criticise the whipping system much more . . . as a backbencher. . . . But as a Minister one started to see that really you had to have this sort of system to make the thing work." The establishment embrace begets an establishment mind-set: "It would be naive to think that, er, er, as one be- comes a member of the establishment, as it were, that one doesn't get estab- lishment views."

Ministers accept the obligation to expose themselves to Parliament's scru-

Table 9.1 Undesirability of party discipline, by rank, in percent

Response*	Conservative Ministers**	Conservative backbenchers**
Agree without reservation	7	23
Agree, but with reservations	52	54
Disagree, but with reservations	32	18
Disagree without reservation	10	6
Total	101	101
	(N = 31)	(N = 142)

*Q. Individual MPs should decide for themselves in any particular division in the House how they should vote.
**$p \leq .05$

tiny and criticism. But they are not always enthusiastic about it, because this criticism threatens their Government's image and their own careers. Wariness was evident in ministerial responses to three mailback-item proposals that, if implemented, would increase ministerial vulnerability. Thus, twice as many Ministers as backbenchers dismissed without reservation the notion that "Ministers should be prepared to reveal to Parliament virtually all information on their department's affairs." Similarly, Ministers outdid backbenchers in turning down the proposal that "there should be more opportunity for debates in the House on urgent or topical issues." And twice as many Ministers as backbenchers rejected the suggestion that "there should be greater opportunities for Members to question Ministers on the affairs of their departments." Ministers may also try to manipulate rules of the game that are already in place, as did Julian Amery, the Minister for Housing, in 1972. Half the Questions he was answering at Question Time, it was discovered, had been fed to friendly backbenchers by Amery's own civil servants. "Unacceptable," declared the Commons Select Committee on Parliamentary Questions: "Question-rigging to restrict the Opposition at Question Time is not in order and should not happen again."[5]

MEMBER OF THE GOVERNMENT OR MEMBER FOR EASTLEIGH

Ministers also encounter role conflict between the expectations of virtually all the groups with whom they deal as Ministers on the one side (ministerial colleagues, civil servants, interest groups, and backbenchers) and the expectations of their constituents on the other. But unlike conflict between the claims of Government and the claims of Parliament, this conflict is not so much over conduct as over time.

Those with whom the Minister deals in his role as Minister demand so much time that he feels the strain even before he begins to think about his constituency. His constituents of course still expect him to make sufficient time to investigate their local concerns and to represent them properly at Westminster. They expect their Minister-MP to hold at least occasional surgeries in the constituency and to spend time at Westminster on constituency affairs. But Ministers allocate much less time *at Westminster* than backbenchers do to constituency work, because ministerial duties require them to allocate more time to the lobbies, dining rooms, Smoking Room, Tea Room, and ministerial corridor. Nearly two-thirds of them, compared to one-third of their backbenchers, report that they devote less than 20 percent of their evenings at Westminster to their own constituencies.

Moreover, although Ministers collectively seem to work as many hours *in their constituencies* as do ordinary backbenchers,[6] there is a striking difference between senior Ministers, especially Cabinet Ministers, and Junior Ministers, a difference overlooked in the survey done for the Review Body on Top Salaries. Junior Ministers actually spend much more time in their constituencies than the backbench average. Senior Ministers, by contrast, spend much less; half are there only five hours or less per week. The constituents notice, and senior Ministers notice the role conflict: "I'm very conscious that I don't do my, um, representative job nearly as well as my constituents . . . expect. And I think this is really inevitable. Of the last five weekends, I shall have spent four abroad. . . . And during the week one's obviously wholly in the House of Commons. And therefore the opportunities of even seeing one's constituents are rather rare now for me. I don't think I represent them nearly as well as they would like to be represented." However, even among Cabinet Ministers there is variation. At one extreme, constituency work is dismissed as a waste of time, and Ministers complain about being badgered by their constituency parties.[7] At the other pole, one of the busiest Cabinet Ministers likes to think that he also manages to be "what you'd call a sort of very active constituency member. . . . I have a large constituency post. . . . I live in my constituency at weekends; I've got a farm there, and I go down there normally on a Friday and come back on Monday, very early Monday morning. Every Saturday morning I always hold my surgery . . . where between fifteen and thirty people come every Saturday morning with problems. Once a month I hold a meeting in . . . a small town in my constituency. Then I suppose in the average week I also attend a constituency function on Friday evening."

He feels it is a sign of vitality in a parliamentary government when Cabinet Ministers, who deal during the week with the world's problems, deal during the weekend with Mr. Bloggs's gutters and lamp post. It keeps things in perspective. But Junior Ministers are more likely to follow his lead than are most of his Cabinet colleagues. Journeymen make time for constituents, while Placemen have time. Journeymen are so active in constituency affairs because they know what lies ahead. They would like to build up a reputation as a Member who cares, to build up a fund of good will upon which they can draw later when there is less time for surgeries. This is particularly true of Journeymen who are concerned about the safeness of their seats (for "once you are locked away in high office, your majority may erode") and about the distance of their constituencies from London.

Another, albeit less common, type of role conflict between ministerial and constituency responsibilities concerns conflicting loyalties. Under the doctrine of collective responsibility, Ministers may occasionally be obliged to support publicly (or at least not criticize publicly) a government policy that harms their constituents. Likewise, their freedom to lead campaigns on behalf of their constituency's collective concerns may be seriously curtailed. If a factory in their constituency is marked for closure, they cannot, like a backbencher, fight it out in public. To protect their constituencies they must work behind the scenes—where they may still encounter pressure to take the national rather than the local-constituency view. "I kept wondering," complained a Cabinet Minister about a critical cabinet colleague, "what she would have said if the plane concerned was manufactured in her constituency and her biggest factory was due to be closed down and could have been saved if we had accepted this last-minute offer."[8]

We have already seen that Junior Ministers are in their constituencies more than are Cabinet Ministers. Ministers between them (Ministers Outside the Cabinet and Ministers of State) are between them here too, which suggests that responses to this role conflict may have more to do with crowded diaries than with inclinations. Those who do devote time to their constituencies often see a broader purpose beyond the casework. For some, this is again the opportunity to keep in touch with the real problems of real people: "There is nothing like the discipline of going down to your constituency every Friday and having what apparently are stupid and irrelevant questions thrown at you, er, . . . until you realise that this is what people want, and Government is to give people what they want." Others use constituency visits to make national news (and flatter their constituents who are present at the making) by trumpeting recent Government successes, announcing policy innovations, or attacking the Opposition. For such purposes, even Prime Ministers will visit their constituencies and speak at the local ladies' luncheon club.

On the whole, however, Ministers above Junior Ministers are pulled away from their constituencies more than they are pulled toward them. Why then, do they spend even as much time there as they do? Beyond electoral considerations, the norms discussed in Chapter 4 have much to do with their behavior. Basic constituency service is a duty accepted by all Members of Parliament, including Ministers.

Governors and Governed

Since representation in Britain has a national rather than a local-constituency focus, Ministers have strong reasons to be attentive to the national electorate, to the dynamics of public opinion and its implications for winning elections and governing. In reconstructing these aspects of their roles, we find a collage of blurred and contradictory images. The constitutional position is unclear, and so too are the views of the Constitution's keepers.[9]

EARS TO THE ELECTORATE

The relationship between Ministers and the national electorate is, of course, determined by the rule that requires General Elections: "The whole of one's opportunity to do what one wants in politics depends upon winning . . . er, so I mean I am a democrat by conviction and also *by necessity*." Ministers can play their roles only if their party can win General Elections. Ministers therefore tell themselves that "as a Minister my function is to try and discover what people want, to try and work out how that is reconcilable with what . . . we can produce for them."

Britain is a democracy, and its Ministers must respond to the electorate. The process "is very subtle and unobvious and very British, but it does work." It works mainly through Parliament, whose Members, on behalf of the electorate, exert pressure on the Government "to make it go in a way perhaps slightly different to what it otherwise would have gone." Ministers talked about the Shops Bill, which was quietly dropped under backbench pressure because Ministers felt that this pressure represented strong views held by people across the country. "Now contrast that," they said, "with the Retail Price Maintenance Bill, which was also opposed by backbenchers, but which was pressed forward by the Government nevertheless, because the Government believed that the lobbies opposing it were more narrowly based."

Ministers are most sensitive to issues they believe will make a difference in their party's electoral fortunes. At the time of our interviews, unemployment was soaring, and Ministers were becoming very nervous about it: "I think that we may, erm, likely have to have a higher rate of unemployment than we have had, um, during the last few decades." Panic over the electoral implications of unemployment helped turn by 180 degrees the Heath Government's economic policy. "Governments have to run countries with a very great, er, awareness of public opinion," observed a Cabinet Minister. "This is democratic, but not in a way which is obvious to people. It's much more democratic than they think." The focus is on General Elections: "The people at a General Election are giving their verdict on, you know, the five-year stewardship. And if you've done basically what the people think is a good job, you'll be returned, and if you haven't, out you go." "The word 'Democracy' is often loosely used in talking about politics and government. What seem to you personally," we asked them, "to be the essentials of a real democracy?" Ministers talked more about the electorate than did their backbenchers.

Ministers want to win elections. But they also want to govern. And if they are more keen than backbenchers to keep their ears to the electorate, they are less keen to encourage the sort of public participation between elections that might impede their governing by limiting their scope for independent action. Thus, when they discuss political participation, twice as many Ministers as backbenchers refer *only* to voting at General Elections—which recalls Jean-Jacques Rousseau's claim that the British public is sovereign at General Elections but not between them. These two contexts, winning elections and governing the country, structure Ministers' images of the electorate.

IMAGES OF THE ELECTORATE

What images of the electorate are held by Ministers of the Crown? The overall picture seems muddled, for quite different beliefs are held by different Ministers, and also by the same Ministers in different contexts. Nevertheless there is a pattern. When they think about winning elections, Ministers call up more-flattering images of the public than when they think about governing the country.

As elections approach, Ministers become "far more sensitive not only to opinion polls, but also to the press, the media, television, radio . . . every comment that's made. It only has to be a small paragraph in even some obscure weekly paper . . . notice is taken of it." They scrutinize all the signs "to see what they've got wrong yesterday and react." In this context, Ministers listen closely to the public and typically think about the public in flattering terms. They attribute more rationality to voters than they do at other times, because a reasonable public is easier to understand and to address than is a capricious one.[10] Ministers would like to assume that if, in the run up to the election, they enact antieviction Bill X^2 rather than X, and if, during the campaign, they stress land-use plan Y^2 rather than Y, the electorate will notice and react accordingly. This public's image is remarkably sensible and well informed.

But once Ministers are back in Government, back in the context of governing, the public becomes less salient, and its image becomes less flattering. The stimulus for this new image is the belief that "democracy . . . really only refers to a method of electing Governments. It has little to do with participation between elections." In the context of governing, "our system of democracy is really a system of dictatorship—dictatorship by the party in power . . . tempered by public opinion. And that is tolerable if the public knows that every now and then the party is liable to change. That's the essence of it." This interpretation of the Constitution appeals especially to Conservatives and stresses that between elections the Governors ought to be able to govern and not be impeded by an irrational and ill-informed public.[11]

In the context of governing, the electorate becomes a passive audience. Of course it is "essential to have people governing the country who are in communion with" this audience, but "the people never really know what they want. I think the elected representative should lead them." In the context of elections, leaders become followers. But in the context of governing, leaders can be leaders. The public needs guidance, "and you've got gradually to persuade them that they are wrong, to see the error of their ways." It is the responsibility of the leader "to educate public opinion," "to, er, try and lead them to improve their views . . . if he thinks they need improvement." In the context of governing, "we err in being too readily pushed around by public opinion. . . . Ministers are far too susceptible and easily swayed by this, and I think they should have greater confidence in their own basic convictions, and greater determination to express their views. . . . And if they did that, democracy would be better served." The idea that fifty million people can have a say in governing "is sheer twaddle."

Role Overload

In most institutions, differentiation is the usual response to growing responsibilities. But the number of Cabinet Ministers has hardly increased at all during this century; and although the total number of Ministers has nearly doubled, the expansion of governmental services has grown far beyond that. During the 1970s "overload" began to be taken seriously.[12] Too much was now expected of Government, it was said. Too much was now expected of individual Ministers.

Role overload, the second type of role strain examined in this chapter, refers to situations where Ministers cannot reasonably be expected to do well everything that is expected of them. One set of goals conflicts with others, either because Ministers have insufficient time to accomplish them all, or because accomplishing them all requires being in different places at the same time. Busy senior Ministers must therefore concentrate on some of their role's goals and do only the minimum on others. Thus, overload creates choices as well as headaches.

It also varies by department and by rank. By department, role overload ranges from the difficult to the impossible. The merely difficult ministries like Defense have work cycles that offer relief: "It comes and goes in this department. There are some days or even weeks where one is very lightly loaded . . . a 9-to-5 job really. Then there are weeks where you go on till 10 or 11 at night and take the spare bits home." A good example of the impossible is the situation of the Law Officers who were involved in such a variety of responsibilities that the pace never let up: "Easter-time holiday, a helicopter arrived opposite my house and took me away. And this constantly happens. There's never a weekend. I think my role is particularly difficult because it covers so many different fields. . . . All the different departments come at some time, involve me some time in part of their business."[13]

Occasionally, even Junior Ministers encounter role overload. At least it seems that way because the contrast with backbench roles is so striking. "As a backbencher, one can decide if one wants to be busy," but as a Junior Minister, you are "busy more or less all the time because you have to be." Of course many Junior Ministers are assigned so few responsibilities that "I don't regard myself as overworked, um, I never myself overwork." But some, usually Journeymen, are immersed in responsibilities; and although they are delighted to have been appointed, they are also distressed by the load: "I work an 80-hour week. . . . If I were not paid on results but paid on time, I would do very well indeed. But I, I train myself and I—I do on six hours a night. You've got to be fairly tough constitutionally, and those that aren't fall by the wayside. I've seen it."

For positions above Junior Minister the burdens are nearly always heavy. Late nights at the House can drag on till 3 A.M., after which you must be up at 7 in order to catch the 8:10 "and arrive at meetings at 9 o'clock the next morning. There's a limit to how long one can go on doing that without one's brain getting very tired at night." Travel to open a new block of houses or a new hospital, to visit the department's units in the field, to make a speech at a university, can be very tiring too. And then there are the red ministerial boxes that your civil servants send home with you every night. During the 1960s and 1970s, the homework of British Ministers grew from one red box to three.

Perhaps the most difficult choices created by role overload are between ministerial assignments and family responsibilities. Since the number of hours in a week is insufficient to fulfill official responsibilities, "the biggest tension, I think, the biggest strain is our relations with our families. It is very difficult. There is no question about it, it is not easy to maintain a sensible family life." Many Ministers complain that they are unable to see their spouses and children, and that they have considered giving up their positions because "the greatest danger one has in Parliament, as you'll see from the records, is that it is the worst place for marriages breaking up, particularly for Ministers whose responsibilities mean that they feel . . . the strains on family home life more than most."

The data in Table 9.2 are drawn from the study's mailback questionnaire in which respondents were asked to estimate, for an average week, the time they spent on specific activities. Since the number of ministerial respondents is very low here, the results must be interpreted with caution. Moreover, since the questionnaire concentrated on Westminster, it is possible that the Whitehall time and therefore the total time is underestimated. Still, the number of hours that these Ministers estimate they work each week is certainly sufficient to produce stress. Seventy percent report sixty or more hours, while further inspection shows that half claim seventy-one hours or more. Backbenchers claim much less. And these data are consistent with a similar survey conducted a year earlier by the Review Body on Top Salaries.[14]

For senior Ministers, the peak periods can be truly staggering: "I have been working now for seventeen hours a day, seven days a week, for eighteen, nineteen months. . . . I don't think I've let up at all. . . . I'm doing a normal full-day's work at Westminster . . . and if you add on top of that being a Minister, and of course we have constituencies . . . it is I think one of the most exhausting jobs in the country . . . um, almost enough to break one down." This overload is exacerbated by the practice of shuffling Ministers about so much that they are frequently unfamiliar with the subject matters of the new departments they enter. It is said to require two years to master half a department's important subjects. Unfortunately, two years is

Table 9.2 Total working hours per week at Westminster and outside Westminster, in percent

Hours per week	Conservative Ministers*	Conservative backbenchers*
0–30	0	4
31–40	0	12
41–50	5	23
51–60	24	32
60+	71	29
Total	100 (N = 21)	100 (N = 112)

*$p \leq .01$

the average stay of a Cabinet Minister in a department.[15] No wonder so many feel they are running to stand still.

Even more striking than the magnitude of the overload is the variation in ministerial reactions to it—from the excruciating to the exuberant. There are Ministers for whom role overload creates very considerable psychological stress. Some take a pill: "I mean I never hesitate to take a sleeping pill when I need it—no problems there." Some take a day off: they try to keep one day on the weekend clear for doing nothing except what they want to do. Others schedule their escapes by the pressure rather than by the calendar: "Ministerial time schedules are less rigid than for Junior Ministers . . . Cabinet Ministers can and do scratch an afternoon's appointment, or series of appointments, or day's appointments when the pressure builds up on them. And they can therefore go for a walk or go for a sail from time to time."[16]

Everyone close to the situation seems to regard it as remarkable that "there is no great casualty list of Ministers. I mean they are not dying right and left, and they don't have many more coronaries than anybody else."[17] Why not? To get to be a Minister in the first place, Ministers say, you need to have a tough, strong physical constitution: "So anybody who becomes a Minister, whatever other qualities he has, he must have been a resilient person, somebody who can perk up after a great strain, a couple of hours' sleep and he will be right again." Health is the thing, they say. If you haven't got good health, then public life is impossible. Actually, many Ministers who work as hard as everyone else claim that they have "never felt the slightest bit overworked, in fact, most of the time underworked." "Yes there are masses of work, but it isn't work. I love every day. I thrive on it."[18]

The Ministers who thrive on it are those who delegate well and manage rigorously. "I think it's like anything else in life. One must learn to delegate responsibility. . . . If you can't delegate responsibility, you're going to kill yourself . . . and get heart attacks and things. I'm not going to do that." These politicians manage the work, manage their subordinates, and manage the tension. They refuse to be overworked. They understand that there is potentially "an endless amount of work, quite endless." Red boxes follow them everywhere; perhaps three red boxes arrive at their houses at the weekend. But "all this means is that the civil servants are trained to send your in-basket around with you. It doesn't mean you've got to do the damn thing, or that you have got to keep your in-basket free on a Saturday evening. . . . You know, you can clear it on Monday." So you say to your civil servants that if on top of the number-one box "there is anything that doesn't matter, I'm going to be very annoyed. . . . Of course if it's raining and you can't play golf, you get through all three boxes [chuckle]. But I wouldn't think of doing that if it was sunny the weekend."

By managing their work, they manage their time. This helps them feel that they have their roles under control, and that they can "live with the tension and therefore it doesn't worry me like it used to." They approach the overload as "a question of managerial planning," and gather round them teams of competent people so that they "don't get buried by the avalanche of paper which is constantly floating around Whitehall." It requires rigorous organization of the private office and the Junior Ministers. The best-organized Cabinet Minister in the Heath Government explained cheerfully how this was done:

> I have tried, very deliberately, to look at the life I'm now leading and to get on top of it. . . . I work set hours, I perform for a certain amount of time. I, I'm not prepared to throw my life away, er, to be someone who drives themselves into an early grave. I like my family, and they are entitled to see a lot of me, they are young children. I like the social life that I lead, erm, I am not prepared to give that up. . . . I have therefore evolved a pattern of work which is my own style of working . . . which suits the input that I feel capable of putting in. I mean, for example, the thing that can kill you in this business is the in-tray. I mean they would fill that up so fast that you don't know what hit you. Now I don't like in-trays, so the amount of paper that's allowed to come through here is very severely curtailed. Things have to be written in short, sharp summaries; and if too much comes in, I don't read it, I just chuck it, send it back, and tell them to do it again. And I have meetings . . . every morning with my top civil servants coming here for half an hour. . . . I know by the time that meeting is over that whatever we are going to do, someone is going to go and do it. . . . And I am very, very tough on the amount of work I'll take home at night. . . . You know, . . . if they've got a problem they can get it in during the day when I'm here. They are not going to pack the whole lot up at 7 o'clock and say, "Well, see you around if you finish by the morning." I work like everyone else a normal lengthy day, longer than most— much. But I am not prepared to sort of find myself sitting there at three o'clock in the morning trying to understand these hieroglyphics.

A more exotic explanation for exuberant reactions to role overload is called "energy elasticity." As a senior policy advisor to two Prime Ministers, Bernard Donoughue saw first-hand how "the adrenalin of high office makes light of the years." Many Ministers embarrassed him by their fourteen-to-sixteen-hour-per-day work schedules with which he, a much younger man, could not keep up.[19] This is not an unusual observation. Nor is this: When Harold Macmillan was appointed to three Cabinet posts in two and a half years, he became bored and worn out and ready for retirement. All this changed suddenly when he was made Prime Minister—"hidden energies" were released.[20]

The usual assumption about any individual's store of energy is that it can, in the course of a day's activities, be drained quite dry.[21] And yet the Ministers who thrive on ministerial overload do not seem to run out of energy when they perform the same tasks that drain their colleagues. This is usually cited as evidence that they have stronger constitutions. No doubt there are individual differences in such capacities. But it may also be the case that ministerial energy is simply a more "renewable resource" than is generally realized, and that the activities in which Ministers renew it best are those they find most challenging: "I think one does work harder than one does in any other sort of job," commented a busy Minister who was temporarily managing two Cabinet posts at the same time, "but for all that, I think it's *so* interesting and *so* much more enjoyable than the average type of job that I don't think the hard work really worries one. . . . It's so interesting that I don't really, I discount a lot of the complaints that Ministers make." They discover abundant energy for the activities to which they are highly committed, and sometimes still feel energetic afterward.

When Ministers complain about weariness, it is often weariness from activities they dislike: for Administrators, the long and heated debates in the House; for Politicians, the third red box full of departmental details. By contrast: "I started five fifteen on Monday morning from Devon, came up, was in the Ministry by nine twenty-five. I didn't get to bed until quarter to one Tuesday morning. And last night was twelve o'clock, and the night before was twelve o'clock. Mr. Wilson has said many things, but, er, one of the truer things I think he said is that if the kitchen's too hot for you, get out. There's nothing to stop us from going—*but we all like it too much.*" Those who like it so much seem to generate extra energy to deal with the role. And when the attraction wanes, so apparently does their stamina. Toward the end of his premiership, the same Mr. Wilson became "less interested and no longer excited by being Prime Minister" and, as a consequence, lost his legendary stamina and began to suffer bouts of minor illnesses such as stomach disorders and colds.[22]

The most exuberant Ministers also get by successfully with less sleep than their colleagues: "I don't need a great deal of sleep. . . . I get up very early, and I go to bed very late." Or, "I sleep like the bed—for about, um, oh between four and six hours a night. I'm perfectly competent to, um, cope with. . . ." No doubt they are. But others get tired and nod off at meetings. No one counts the number of times that chins sink to chests on the frontbench; nor do Ministers report on colleagues who fall asleep in Cabinet Meetings or Cabinet Committees—except Richard Crossman, whose memoirs offer amusing images of ministerial overload's occasional consequences. For example:

> This question of falling asleep is now getting serious. I am fifty-seven, or is it fifty-eight. . . . Certainly I find myself falling asleep on the frontbench next door to the PM when he is making a long statement. . . . Indeed, Douglas Houghton and I were quietly snoozing next door to each other.[23]

> I slept again through most of Cabinet just as Barbara Castle did a week or two ago when the Immigration Bill was being discussed on the morning after her all-night sitting on the Transport Bill. So I missed hearing Roy's exposition of the crisis which nearly brought us into catastrophe.[24]

Crossman's comments remind us that fifty- and sixty-year-old Ministers are playing roles that require extraordinary time, travel, and tension. Role overload can jeopardize the quality of their decisions and occasionally even put them to sleep. And yet, as we have seen, the reactions to these burdens vary remarkably from one Minister to another. Everyone copes, but those who love it best, who seem to be the majority, thrive by concentrating on the tasks they like best and generating new stores of energy to engage their enthusiasms.

Sources of Role Choice

For Ministers, just as for backbenchers, role choice is a function of both opportunities and incentives. But because ministerial position roles, unlike backbench preference roles, are assigned so many important duties and responsibilities, the opportunity side has been woven into a recruitment screen. Powerful gatekeepers do the screening, and "role choice" becomes a matter mainly of deciding whether or not to accept their offers.

THE HEAD GATEKEEPER

The head gatekeeper is the party Leader who, once chosen, chooses most everyone else. And when the party Leader is Prime Minister, he or she goes on selecting and reselecting, shuffling and reshuffling Ministers in order to make room for newcomers by removing deadwood. The Prime Minister is always under pressure to keep the hierarchy moving, for the party's rising stars and unoccupied heavyweights become impatient for office.[25] They want their turn, and if they conclude they aren't going to get it, they may leave for careers in business or the professions. Moreover, the Prime Minister has a duty to nurture the quality of the party and the Government by moving those who have proved most talented to positions where they can do the most good.

All this is complicated by a fairly rigid hierarchy among departments that is not recognized in the salary structure but is recognized in Ministers' minds. Thus, the PM will be reluctant to fill the post of, say, Foreign Secretary simply by promoting a Junior Minister in the same department. Instead, he will try to appoint either a senior Minister of "equal rank" (e.g., Home Secretary) or a senior Minister "one rank lower" in the departmental hierarchy (e.g., Secretary of State for Employment). And if he taps, say, the Secretary of State for Employment, he will similarly feel obliged to replace him with a Minister of equal rank or one rank lower. This is the reason that reshuffles often involve so many changes all the way down the line.[26] If these hierarchical norms are violated, there will be much consternation and possibly some resignation as well.

Obviously there are far too many posts for the PM to handle entirely on his or her own. So the Chief Whip proposes names, as do most senior Ministers. Senior Ministers are usually consulted about the choice of the Ministers and Junior Ministers to work under them, albeit the Prime Minister retains control.[27] Thus, although the PM may allow senior Ministers to negotiate over the package of appointments, and perhaps veto the odd Junior Minister, he will in the end make sure that he gets his way. Whenever the Prime Minister allows a veto, for instance, he will usually go on to *his own* next choice.[28]

The Prime Minister covets these patronage powers because they strengthen his authority over subordinates, but also because he has less freedom of choice in these matters than he would like. Only half the MPs in the party are, in fact, eligible, for office, because a PM cannot, it is said, realistically consider newly elected Members, Members unwilling to neglect their families and finances, Members below age thirty and above age fifty-five, Members with extreme ideological or social views, and Members with unsuitable personal characteristics of a mental, alcoholic, or sexual nature.[29] Among those who are left, the Prime Minister must promote approximately *one out of two*. "The Prime Minister does not have enough flexibility in appointing his chief Ministers," complained a former Prime Minister who went on to contrast his situation unfavorably with that of the American President. Britain's institutional arrangements, he said, virtually guarantee that the Prime Minister will remain a first among equals.[30] He or she must bring into the highest offices a collection of powerful colleagues of different views and doubtful loyalties. Margaret Thatcher's first Cabinet, for instance, included a majority of non-Thatcherites who had not wanted her to be the party Leader.[31]

Because the Prime Minister's powers of appointment are constrained, senior candidates are sometimes in a position to bargain over rank and status and over the policy options that will be available to them.[32] Many make a place in the Cabinet a condition of acceptance, and others bargain over their precise standing in the order of precedence within the Cabinet. Some insist on a particular Ministry, while others demand particular Junior Ministers. They negotiate as well over the precise responsibilities of the department they will lead, even over time for specific legislation or funds for specific projects. They don't always get what they want. But sometimes they do, because the PM either needs them or is genuinely indifferent to the requests. Casual observers underestimate the constraints on the Prime Minister's powers of patronage, and careful political scientists exaggerate them. The other side of the selection coin, sacking, keeps Ministers on edge regardless of the odds. It is a little like safe seats: margins of security that seem substantial to outsiders nevertheless worry those whose roles are on the line. Fear of the sack keeps ambitious Ministers very sensitive to their relationships with the PM. One Secretary of State worries that he hasn't forgiven him for siding with the Chancellor. Another frets because it has been a month since the PM has engaged him in a frank discussion.

From the perspective of the motivational approach to politicians' roles, we must ask how Ministers themselves understand the recruitment process. But we must also be concerned with how this process actually operates, with the actual criteria involved. Here the interview data are somewhat disappointing, for the gatekeepers are somewhat vague. Asked about the most important characteristics of a Good Minister, this is what the following people had to say, though not necessarily in the same order: Leader of the Opposition (and former and future Prime Minister) Harold Wilson; Secretary of State for Education (and future Prime Minister) Margaret Thatcher; future Labour Leader Neil Kinnock; and Deputy Chief Whip (and future Chief Whip) Humphrey Atkins.

> He must know his subject. . . . He must listen to the House, must listen to his own party, must attend the specialist group . . . and get the feel of the job. . . . Spend time . . . in constituencies, learn their problems, and understand them better.

The characteristic he shouldn't have is stubbornness. . . . Another characteristic he shouldn't have is pomposity. . . . He must command the House. . . . He has got to be intelligent. He must be prepared to give honest answers, direct answers.

Good performance in the House. At the Despatch Box always courteous, always helpful. . . . A good debater . . . good at answering Questions. . . . A good public image, and I'm afraid that often means far more than the decisions that are taken. Keeping in touch with your backbenchers too, and approachability.

He must be *here* a certain amount . . . and be available for people . . . and people can talk to them and so on. . . . To be a successful Minister, you've got to be good at the Despatch Box. . . . If you can't get your point of view and policies over by making speeches about them . . . you're not a good Minister—because the efficient administrators are hired, I mean they're the civil servants.

If what these gatekeepers say reflects what they think, then they are indeed not very particular in their preferences, perhaps no more particular than their gatekeeping predecessor, Trollope's Duke of St. Bungay: "For my own part I find that though Smith be a very good Minister, the best perhaps to be had at the time, when he breaks down Jones does nearly as well."[33] Still, there must be more to it than that.

A STRUCTURE OF OPPORTUNITIES

Actually, the pattern for selecting Junior and senior Ministers appears to be much the same as for selecting Whips: a population is sifted by social background frames, sorted by parliamentary attributes, and scrutinized for personal characteristics. The difference is that the scrutiny is less rigorous for Ministers than for Whips, partially because a wider range of personal characteristics is tolerable in these roles, partially because the gatekeepers cannot afford to be as choosy.

Social background frames sift out candidates who warrant a close look. Age and education have become key criteria as others, like aristocratic backgrounds, have faded during the postwar period. Table 9.3 presents data on age which show that, in the first year of the Heath Government, the typical Junior Minister was between forty and fifty, while the typical senior Minister was between fifty and sixty years old. These data are consistent with the claim that if an MP hasn't become a Junior Minister by his forties or a

Table 9.3 Opportunity: Distribution of age, by rank, in percent

Age	Backbencher	Junior Minister	Senior Minister*
Under 40	18	29	7
40–49	32	62	36
50–59	30	10	54
60+	21	0	4
Total	101	101	101
	(N = 458)	(N = 21)	(N = 28)

Source: Review Body on Top Salaries, *First Report: Ministers of the Crown and Members of Parliament,* Cmnd 4836 (HMSO, 1971): 49.

*Junior/senior Minister v. age ($p \leq .01$)

senior Minister by his fifties, then he is unlikely to do so. And when serving Ministers advance into their sixties, Prime Ministers come under great pressure to "trade them in." "Well, I'm, er, I'm getting to the, er, normal, toward, uh, in sight of the normal age limit," worried a sixty-year-old Minister who was not old enough to retire from Parliament but was old enough to be retired from the frontbench.

Stuart Elaine Macdonald's information, which spans most of the postwar period, likewise demonstrates that age is a critical consideration in promotions.[34] She finds that MPs who enter the House in their thirties rise two and one-half times as quickly as those who enter at age fifty or more. This reinforces Anthony King's findings for Cabinet Ministers.[35] Members who enter in their thirties have time to prepare themselves to become Junior Ministers while they are in their forties, that is to say, before it is too late. They may also be favored over older entrants because they have more years of service to give, and it is therefore more efficient to spend the time and resources required to train them in junior posts.

Macdonald further demonstrates that education, though still a significant social background characteristic in recruitment, is not as significant as might be expected, or as it perhaps once was. The advantage enjoyed by MPs who attended Eton and Oxford or Cambridge peaked at the turn of the century. Eton and the public schools generally have been losing ground ever since, although public school credentials continue to provide substantial help in climbing the Conservative promotion ladder. Likewise, with the recent rise of meritocrats from state schools and non-Oxbridge universities,[36] Oxbridge credentials are no longer so important either. Where one was educated is, in fact, becoming a less significant factor than the amount of education one has attained. The recent Conservative leaders, Mr. Heath and Mrs. Thatcher, attended state secondary schools and Oxbridge and thus represented bridges between the new system and the old.

Parliamentary attributes are used to sort out the candidates who pass through the social background frames. Key attributes include experience (previous posts), length of service (tenure), performance (making a mark), and loyalty to superiors.

Experience can be acquired in a variety of roles that Ministers regard both as training grounds for office and as testing grounds for candidates. "There is a rough career structure. . . . If you come in in Government, your first rung of the ladder is to be a PPS." Likewise for Whips on the Conservative side of the House. Those who have served in these roles "for a certain length of time . . . are likely to be offered the opportunity when these jobs [Junior Minister] become available." Another stepping stone in the Conservative Party, Ministers say, is service as an officer of a backbench party committee.[37] This puts one in a position to be noticed and gives one resources that warrant further notice.[38] Similarly, the role of the Opposition Front Bench Spokesman is "a fairly good grounding" for office. PPS, Whip, committee officer, Opposition Front Bench Spokesman, "that's the rough career structure . . . a very rough sort of ladder—but it doesn't mean that people can't jump up a series of snakes as well." The English board game "Snakes and Ladders" comes to mind because, although the career ladder is fairly well established, one finds cases where several or even all the rungs for PPS, Whip, committee officer, and Opposition Front Bench Spokesman may be passed over, contrary to the rules of the game, by "jumping up a snake." Whether or not one is invited to make such an unorthodox jump depends on length of service, performance, and loyalty.

E. Gene Frankland found that among those who became candidates during the 1950s, length of parliamentary service (tenure) was an outstanding predictor of attaining leadership positions.[39] His results underscore the importance of apprenticeships. Thus, when the average length of parliamentary service before entering the Cabinet is fourteen years, we conclude that long apprenticeships are required for Britain's top posts.[40] Likewise, when time *in ministerial office* before entering the Cabinet has not increased much, whereas length of service *on the backbenches* before entering ministerial office has increased a great deal, we conclude that professionalization has particularly affected training on the backbenches: "You see, people don't normally become Members of Government these days until they've been backbenchers for quite a time and they've had time to absorb the atmosphere and know the ways." But although these interpretations are generally correct—lengthy service is, in general, important—they should not be allowed to obscure the perhaps more important fact that the race to the *very* top, to the Cabinet, is won by those who climb the ladder most quickly.

Performance attributes refer to making a mark, to capturing the attention of gatekeepers by doing something that demonstrates parliamentary or managerial skills. Junior Ministers believe that success can be won by energetic parliamentary performances: "There was a gang of us (most of whom won promotion). . . . We used to work away at every aspect of food and forestry and agriculture. . . . Anything we could get ahold of we would make into a debate. . . . We had a lot of fun." Making such a mark can open the doors to the level of Minister of State. To rise further, however, one must pass managerial muster, which is dicey because senior Ministers find it difficult to assess the administrative performances of their juniors.[41] One may also have to survive several parliamentary ordeals, such as helping to take contentious Bills through the Commons successfully and with good humor. At this stage and the next, Ministers will be building up administrative track records.

About loyalty, our fourth and final parliamentary attribute, there is some controversy, which we examined in Chapter 3. The most obvious way to get ahead, we found, is by "loyalty to party leaders." And yet Ministers believe that rebels attain offices—distinguished rebels, and high offices: "They usually become Prime Minister, I mean Disraeli, Churchill, Macmillan—they were all mavericks in their way."[42] Several even claimed that "you're *far more* likely to get preferment, especially in the Conservative Party, by being a rebel than by being loyal."[43] But surely loyalty is the more effective path to success. Ministers pigeonhole mavericks into three subtypes, only one of which enjoys serious prospects. First is the incorrigible maverick who has no support on the backbenches and no chance of attaining office. Second is the ordinary maverick who is sometimes liked by the House and sometimes drawn into the role of Junior Minister, but who will not advance further unless he changes his spots. Third and most favored is the responsible maverick, "the man who makes a nuisance of himself in a sensible way," who takes care to make himself the sort of nuisance about whom Ministers will say, "Well so and so's got a jolly good case and he is very bright and very dangerous and difficult." This sort of maverick sometimes does succeed.[44]

Ministers mentioned several other parliamentary attributes that have been reviewed in previous chapters about people on the way up. Moderate specialization, being a good attender, and having a mentor-patron are regarded by Ministers as helpful. They also notice safe seats, for "if you haven't got that firm base, you're done." And, "if you don't adhere to the customs, traditions, and so on . . . you become regarded as someone who is not a serious candidate for ministerial office."

Personal characteristics are not well articulated, because gatekeepers are not in a position to be as selective as they would like or to assess such characteristics systematically. Nevertheless, those that Ministers mention most in judging a candidate's capabilities are affability, sensitivity, intelligence, and flexibility, all of which we have encountered previously. The ultimate goal here, they say, is to "establish your reputation . . . in the party and in Parliament, as someone of judgement . . . as someone who matters—and that's not easy." It's not easy because the personal characteristics that create such a reputation are vague and subject to change. Moreover, many different combinations of them can achieve the desired result. The best approach, therefore, is to find a combination that feels comfortable and convincing, and "that identifies one as sufficiently above average to stand out, but not so far above average to raise suspicions about one's reliability."

Among personal characteristics, political ideology is taken most seriously. Prime Ministers go to considerable lengths to make appointments that will balance their party's left and right wings; for they want to give the impression that all major viewpoints have some representation in the Government as a whole.[45]

For the Heath Government in 1972–73, Figure 9.1 traces the distributions of Conservative Ministers, Junior Ministers, and backbenchers across the party's ideological spectrum.[46] It can readily be seen that Heath's appointments covered the range. But it is not quite as important here as it is in the Whips' Office to mimic the parliamentary party's ideological distribution. Indeed, the Prime Minister has every reason to tilt the leadership in his direction—which is just what Heath appears to have done. The figure suggests that preference was given to kindred spirits. Thus, he drew the bulk of his Ministers from the "Centre-Right," definitely a tilt, albeit a more modest one than the "tampering" with which he might have been charged had he dipped deeper at the time into the "Heath Loyalists." Note, however, that the Heath Loyalists fared relatively better in the selection for Ministers than for Junior Ministers.

One further personal characteristic is emphasized by gatekeepers, although its significance lies less in the opportunity structure than in candidates' incentives. This is ambition, the desire for office. Successful politicians are expected to have it. Ambition is regarded as desirable, indeed as essential, for success as a Minister.

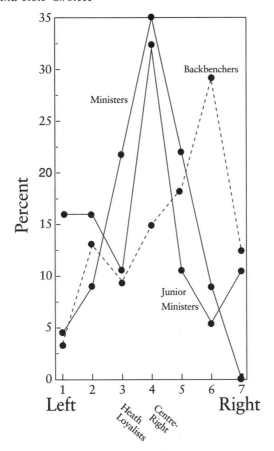

Figure 9.1 Conservative ministers and backbenchers
in 1972–73: ideological reputation, by rank

GOALS: AMBITION, THE DESIRE FOR OFFICE

In Chapter 3 I noted that MPs who have the strongest ambition for office are indeed most likely to attain it. Their ambition affects the process of recruitment to ministerial roles via three pathways, two controlled by the aspirants and one by the gatekeepers. Obviously individuals must themselves decide whether to accept or to decline offers that may come their way. And, on this first pathway, the more one desires office, the more likely one is to accept it. Those who decline may do so because they are insufficiently ambitious to accept offers they do not like, or insufficiently ambitious, period. The second path is the opportunity that individuals have to prepare and position themselves so as to increase the likelihood that offers will, in fact, come their way. People with a strong desire for achievement typically perform in ways that, other things being equal, increase their chances of emerging successfully as leaders.[47] Third, ambition comes into play when gatekeepers use it as one of the criteria by which they evaluate candidates. R. A. Butler is said never to have been offered the office of party Leader and Prime Minister, for example, because his ambition was judged inadequate.[48]

Ambition is a popular topic of conversation among politicians and political commentators. But this goal cannot provide a satisfactory motivational account until its ties are traced to the career structure within which it operates and to the other incentives with which it is intertwined. Ambition alone is not the motor. The topic is more complex than it at first glance appears—which has not been sufficiently appreciated by political scientists, who, for several decades before the mid-1970s, approached it with simplistic sociological models that linked the desire for approbation with norm-driven behavior. Since then, we have turned to equally simplistic economic models that link rational calculation with the pursuit of individual self-interest. What is needed instead are more-complex models that focus both sociological and economic perspectives on particular institutional contexts and make room for different mixtures of career goals and emotional incentives.

Table 9.4 begins our investigation by suggesting what those who would be Ministers might see if they had perfect information. The data in this table were compiled by Macdonald, who, for each of our 521 respondents, traced his or her career history back "retrospectively" to the point of entry into the House and forward "prospectively" to 1986.[49]

The prospects for promotion to ministerial office are surely adequate to attract the ambitious. Among *all* backbenchers, not just Ministerial Aspirants, it can be seen that 30 percent go up to become Junior Ministers.

Table 9.4 Incentives: Promotion prospects to ministerial positions, in percent

	Destination		
Origin	Junior Minister	Senior Minister	Cabinet Minister
Backbencher	30	11	4
Junior Minister		45	3
Senior Minister			52

Source: Stuart Elaine Macdonald, "Political Ambitions and Attainment: A Dynamic Analysis of Parliamentary Careers," Ph.D. diss., University of Michigan, 1987.

Among *all* Junior Ministers, not just Journeymen, 45 percent go up to become Ministers, almost exactly the same proportion that Frankland found in his study of cohorts who first became candidates during the 1950s.[50] And finally, among senior Ministers, 52 percent reach the top rung to become Cabinet Ministers. Furthermore, there are no significant party differences here; the results are very similar for Conservative and Labour MPs.

It should also be noted that promotion prospects increase substantially with each step up the ladder. Thus, if one is among the 30 percent of backbenchers who rise to Junior Minister, then one's chances increase to 45 percent for the next step to senior Minister. Similarly, the likelihood of attaining the next level, Cabinet Minister, increases again from the previous level— although the prospects for rising *all the way* from the backbenches to the Cabinet are still extremely slim. Many Members understand these odds. What they often do not understand, however, because they lack the necessary information, is that their actual promotion prospects are much better still, because at each level below that of Minister a substantial proportion of the "runners" are not running in the race. At least half the backbenchers are excluded by age and other factors reviewed earlier. A substantial minority of PPSs are Auxiliaries without prospects. And between a third and a half of the Junior Ministers are Placemen whom everyone expects to stay in place.

But what exactly is political ambition? Today it is usually defined as a desire for advancement or for office. And this simple definition of political ambition is frequently associated with the work of Joseph Schlesinger, who distinguished three different types: discrete, static, and progressive.[51] Progressive ambition refers to the desire not just for office, but for higher office. Recent research has further characterized progressive ambition as a career goal based on careful choice, on rational calculation.[52] Candidates are presumed to weigh the potential costs (such as time and effort) of seeking an office against the utility they expect to derive from holding the office, and then to factor in their probability of attaining this office. Hence: "A person will strive for advancement when the expected value of striving is greater than the expected value of not striving."[53]

Most Ministers would reject out of hand this reconstruction of their thinking, for it leaves out important variables and exaggerates the calculation. And yet they do think hard about their career prospects, which are of the utmost importance to them. Ministers may, in fact, underestimate the rationality with which they deliberate about the subject because so much of this deliberation is done casually, over drinks or on the run.[54] The truth is that

Ministerial Aspirants and Ministers alike assess as carefully as they can variables such as costs to family life; efforts that would be required at Westminster; steps they need to reach by given ages; possibilities if their party wins the next General Election or loses and leaves them in Opposition while their time clocks tick away; relationships with the present party Leader and with whoever the next Leader is likely to be; safeness of their seats; and, in the language of rational choice rather than their own, the utility they expect to receive if they win the higher office.

This is how Ministers think about their career prospects. They try to estimate how high they can go ("A Minister's got to realise what his ceiling is . . . often a painful appraisal to make") and what it will take to get there. They also consider the costs of failure and try to minimize them with defense mechanisms: "The only people who really enjoy politics are those who never worry about what the next job might be," said a successful Minister who protects himself by regulating the utility he anticipates from attaining higher offices. "And if tomorrow we're defeated and I become a backbench Member of Parliament, I shall thoroughly enjoy the freedom."[55] Political scientists treat the utility of higher office as a constant, but many Ministers make it into a *variable:* they modify their utilities to suit their changing situations. Some do this quite self-consciously, and some just do it. Thus, Ministers adjust their utilities to take account of new career experiences, changes in their family circumstances, and changes in their other incentives.

Ministers manage their ambition because ambition matters. And the fact that ambition matters suggests that standard sociological views of recruitment give too much weight to the institution and too little to the individual. Individual dispositions count even in contexts of formal, highly institutionalized leadership roles where gatekeepers would like to be very selective. Even here role choice is a function of *both* opportunities and incentives. Even here the individual's goals are well worth taking seriously.

Let us look more closely, therefore, by examining our Ministers' desires for office before they have assessed the probability of attaining these desires.[56] Two features are particularly striking. One is that Junior Ministers have the strongest ambitions: 72 percent either specified a particular position they would like or said that they would like further positions. The Placemen among them check these desires when they consider their chances of attaining them. But the Journeymen swim in a sea of progressive ambition: "I mean . . . once you're a candidate . . . you think, 'God, now I want to be a Member of Parliament.' Once you're an MP, you say, 'I'd like to be a Junior Minister.' Once you're a Junior Minister, after a few months you say, 'I'd like to be a rather more senior Minister'—and I would indeed because you're taking bigger and bigger decisions the whole time." It is not surprising that Journeymen are very ambitious, because ambition was a criterion in choosing them, and the very fact that they were chosen further fuels their aspirations. Ambition, like the utility of higher office upon which it is built, is a *variable*. And those Ministers with the strongest ambitions are very ambitious indeed: "Look, there aren't many people my age who work as hard as I work who do it believing that at the age of 43 they've reached the end of the road."

The second striking feature is how ambition fades among some of the most senior Ministers. Thirty-seven percent of them say, and seem to mean (even before assessing their chances) that they have no strong desire for further office. Their views range from ambivalence to an inclination to play out their present roles and then leave the game of snakes and ladders to others. Thus, at the very top of the tower, ambition may dim as well as glow. This is puzzling, because the fading flames are not obviously attributable to fading prospects. The explanations put forward by senior Ministers themselves emphasize instead family obligations and career experiences that wear them down, wear them out, leave them fulfilled, or lead them to seek other mountains to climb before it is too late.

Family can create "a feeling of contentment" that "moderates the sort of burning ambitions" and leaves Ministers wanting more than ministerial office allows: "I've got a young family, you see . . . and I'm beginning to feel now that, er, I would like to see more of them . . . I mean I, I hardly ever see them." Family obligations include duties to adolescent children or to a spouse who, after years of neglect, wants to retire to the country. More distracting are family difficulties, including separation or divorce. In the same vein, there are also family businesses to which one feels obliged to return or other businesses that one feels obliged, for financial reasons, to pursue.

Among career experiences, role overload more than anything else makes senior Ministers weary and ready to contemplate the end. "I've done, done nearly twenty years now. . . . At the moment I love it . . . but at this pace I don't know how long one can go on." When the PM asks them to stand down in order to make room for new people, they will be ready to go "and at last be able to get on with all the many other things I'd like to do in life instead of the very full-time job of being a Minister." No longer quite as hungry for office as they once were, they recognize this change and welcome it: "I mean I take a fairly relaxed view; if I was sacked now I wouldn't cry." Some say they have found a new satisfaction and peace of mind by looking for the end of the road and acknowledging that it is coming to an end.

More interesting still are Minister's claims that career experiences have left them fulfilled and reduced their desires for further fulfillment. "I've fulfilled my ambitions as a politician," they say, sometimes sounding remarkably like the Duke of St. Bungay. These senior Ministers find considerable satisfaction in the feeling that they have mastered the posts they have held, especially the important posts: "I've been Home Secretary, I've been Chancellor. It doesn't leave many others does it?" They've been in the Cabinet, "seen it from all angles," and don't wish to become Prime Minister—although this particular disclaimer may have more to do with probabilities than with utilities. They are facing the end with equanimity: "I shan't miss anything when I leave politics. . . . I've been very heavily engaged really for practically the whole of the, well, for 10 or 11 of the 15 years." They "thoroughly enjoy being in Government," but are no longer consumed with ambition. Filled with the feast that they sought for so long, they no longer seem as determined as they once were to sit at the high table.

Several senior Ministers who share these satisfactions contemplate moving on to other careers rather than to the end of the road. They have likewise climbed the mountain and enjoyed the experience, but they are younger and still restless. So if you "accept that, er, your enthusiasm as a Minister expires after a certain time, . . . I think I, I, I could see myself, quite without any deep regrets . . . returning to my old profession." As a barrister, he can return easily to the legal profession, where he would like to end his days as a senior Judge. Others contemplate greater risks, "whilst I am still relatively young [enough] to launch on another career in business." These prematurely mellow Ministers are still very ambitious, but their ambitions are leading them beyond Whitehall and Westminster. Their *political* ambition has apparently been satisfied, whereas their ambition writ large still seeks further fulfillment in other careers.

Before leaving fading ambition behind, we should remind ourselves that this phenomenon affects only a minority of those at the top. Political ambition is indeed a variable. And most senior Ministers have quite a lot of it, ranging from those who might like to move up a notch, courteously ("Well, I've always had a hope that one day I might possibly be Chancellor of the Exchequer. Yes. But not while Tony Barber still wants to hold the post, because he's absolutely superb"), to those who are enthusiastically eager ("Oh yes, there are *lots* of things I'd like to do in Government before I'm finished, I mean *many* things, there are *many* problems I find fascinating"), to those who are convinced, as was Iain Macleod, that "being a Minister is the only thing worth doing in the whole world. . . . A Minister's life is the only thing in the world worth having."

AMBITION'S ENGINES

Two emotional incentives, greed and sense of duty, can be eliminated straightaway. Ministerial salaries are insufficient to attract the avaricious. In fact, there are always senior Ministers who suffer financially by accepting their posts, and many Junior Ministers complain about what they earn.[57] Moreover, there is comparatively little financial corruption in British national politics. It is not Mammon who draws Members to ministerial office. Nor are they driven there by duty's demands. The sense of duty that sends many Constituency Members into their roles rarely sends aspirants into the Ministry. Exceptions exist: "I come from a military family . . . whose basic ideal was service, not only to . . . Britain but also to the British Empire . . . my family is one of those which has been steeped in a tradition of public service." But the professionalization of politics has been hard on such motivations.[58] By the 1970s, the principal incentives intertwined with ambition were status, stimulation, and power.

"Fame is the spur," wrote the Conservative MP Julian Critchley. "Anyone in public life who tells you differently is not telling the truth"—especially Ministers.[59] Although most Ministers wouldn't admit it quite so guilelessly, they very much like the admiration. It is flattering to be discussed in newspapers and interviewed on television, "to be listened to with respect even when talking at random,"[60] to be regarded as one of the handful of people who are governing the nation. The single most common emotional incentive in political life is this desire for status and for the publicity that accompanies it: "Every Member of Parliament is an extrovert. . . . He likes the opportunity to display his feathers and show himself off." This display is most impressive when made on the ladder's highest rungs. The importance that Ministers attribute to status compels us to take it seriously as an emotional incentive that can drive political ambition. Again: "What takes you into ministerial office? Well, you know Disraeli's famous phrase: fame brought us here."

A fulfilling sense of status can be derived from responsibility for major national issues. Although this Minister enjoyed his financial rewards in business, "really, was it very satisfying to think that you were spending your whole life making crisps and selling them to people? Is that really a *big* contribution to the world?" Now he deals every day with major national issues, which he thinks gives him a status that making crisps never did. Others derive similar satisfactions from the trappings of office, from the paneled walls, antique desks, paintings from the National Gallery, silver properly presented, and a ministerial car to whisk them round London and the country. Surely the nation wouldn't provide all this unless the Minister was a very important person. Some take care to look the part. They project their status by appearing well dressed, authoritative, and, where appropriate, a little bored. When they talk in this mode, they hardly move their arms, their bodies, or even their lips. They manage their presentations carefully and are delighted to find that people seem delighted to be in their company.

The desire for office is also driven by a taste for "intellectual stimulation. . . . Er, I like thinking about things. . . . It is this *stimulation* of new ideas from colleagues, from people from outside who come and talk to you. . . . There are moments of intense tedium, but yet on the other hand it's so very, very stimulating." From this perspective, former Whips find some continuity between the incentives for their present ministerial roles and the incentives in the Whips' Office. They say that once again they feel alive, vital, in touch with exciting people and events—with the difference that now, as Ministers, they are at the center of decision taking, not just of the House. Ministerial roles are so attractive because they are so fascinating: "A Cabinet Minister's work is extremely challenging . . . I mean, it's, it's much more fascinating, more obsessive in some ways than being the head of a very big business or of a great thing like the Confederation of British Industries. It's more tense, it's more difficult—but it's *much* more fascinating."

The variety of the problems and the rapid pace offer the stimulation. "This does make a call on *all* one's capabilities, really," both intellectual and physical. It can stretch these fifty- and sixty-year-olds to their limits, at a time when their contemporaries have slowed down. Most like the experience, and some find it exhilarating. Ministerial roles are not routine, for there are always crises and unexpected events. Ministerial roles are burdensome, but the burdens can be attractive too: "I'm a compulsive worker. I like having things to do. . . . Problems interest me and, er, I can't let them alone, you know, and the best thing is to harness that energy somehow if you can." Ministerial harnesses are made "for the whirl of activity that comes from being in the Government, from being in the sort of top stream of British politics." When they become ex-Ministers, they will miss those red dispatch boxes stuffed with the up-to-the-minute information that keeps them in touch with vital realities.

Those red dispatch boxes also symbolize power, the third emotional incentive that intensifies political ambition. According to Harold Lasswell, the need for power is fundamental for all politicians.[61] Lasswell's claims have been explored through case analyses of individual leaders,[62] and through aggregate analyses at various levels of government.[63] Although these studies have never been fully convincing owing to difficulties with their methodologies and data bases, they do consistently suggest that Lasswell's claims have a basis in reality: most politicians are more interested in power than are most nonpoliticians, and some politicians are very interested in power indeed.

Members who want power want to be Ministers because Ministers are "pursuing policies that will affect this country for the next two hundred years." They have all heard Ministers talking enthusiastically about how "we are slowly but surely changing this country for the better, and it's, you know, very exciting being involved in that. I make, I suppose, ten, fifteen decisions, some of them minor but one or two pretty major, every day." They want to play the role of the Minister because even Ministers with comparatively modest power drives say that,

> in the end, the things that are wildly exciting are the opportunities to influence the way in which society is evolving and to create frameworks which help it to evolve in different ways . . . to create new dimensions. And there are so many opportunities, especially in these big departments, where one absolutely knows, and this is the satisfaction of it, that one has made a contribution. No, you don't run the thing of course—there are too many of us, too many clever men. But there are times when . . . you've got something you want to see done, where you see it come about in a field where it is important, and you know you have actually succeeded in changing something . . . for the better.

Ministerial roles attract people who are "motivated by the sense of trying to secure important objectives in political life." Ministers measure their satisfaction by the events that would have developed differently had they not, as Ministers, intervened. They like to "feel that . . . I've been able to create some new institutions and procedures." This desire to control institutions, procedures, or policy programs is one type of power incentive. Another, less attractive, type of power incentive is the desire to dominate people. Thus, Westminster's political culture distinguishes between the man "who *wants to use* such power as comes his way" and the man "who wants to *enjoy* it,"[64] between the man who desires power to accomplish aims and the man who desires power "to lord it over fellow creatures." Unfortunately, ministerial roles provide many opportunities to "enjoy" power and many important people to humiliate: "I barged in and made it clear that I thought that what they were saying was pretty good nonsense. They were very angry with the way I treated them . . . I am very conscious . . . of taking it for granted that I have the right to be bloody-minded and have tantrums and pull people to pieces. I have got to be careful that I am not falling victim to the disease of Ministeritis, becoming corrupted by power."[65]

It is ironic that so many Ministers talk so much about power, for only a few of them, those at the very top, have much power at all. Nevertheless, this emotional incentive helps energize the desire for office, because aspirants don't absorb the lessons of power's elusiveness until it is too late. They tell themselves that the further they rise, the closer they will get to the place where major decisions are made. But at the very top, where senior Ministers "are able to steer the policy affecting your country the way you feel is right," senior Ministers find "that the idea that *one* person can have a *major* influence on policy is nonsense."

Westminster's Apprenticeships from Hindsight

The processes of recruitment and apprenticeship are often discussed together because they are often interconnected. We asked our senior Ministers to reflect upon these processes at Westminster and put them into perspective. Let us begin with what they had to say about the experience of serving as a Parliamentary Private Secretary. What, in retrospect, do Ministers think is learned here?

First, they think that the training a PPS receives depends on the Ministry, particularly when it comes to learning about Whitehall. Some departments are less "closed" to the eyes and ears of PPSs than are other departments, such as Defense, where everything seems secret. "It [the training] also depends to a large extent on, you know, how much the Minister actually chooses to draw you in." Parliamentary Private Secretaries spend most of their time on apprenticeships for the parliamentary side of ministerial roles, on relationships "between Minister and Parliament, Minister and backbenchers. You begin to see . . . the craftsmanship, the art of it." Most of the learning comes from work at the House. But the way that Ministers remember it, most of the *key* insights come from visits to the department. The way they remember it, "watching the Minister" in the department was the essence of this apprenticeship experience.

Whips are in a slightly poorer position than PPSs to learn about the departmental side but in a much better position to learn about Parliament. During the 1970s, the Conservative Whips' Office became a training ground for future Ministers. "The PM was a Chief Whip, er, the Chancellor of the Exchequer was a former Whip," observed a Minister who felt he had missed something by not having been one. "All the ones who really have that, er, sense and nuance of the House have had experience in that field." Service as a Whip teaches "virtually everything about handling the House," "about how to get legislation through and what is acceptable . . . how far you are going to have to have a struggle and just brazen it out." "All Ministers would be helped by this period in the Whips' Office, because then when you bring legislation forward, you are watching for the sort of snags which as a Whip you learn to watch for." Mastering Westminster's subtleties builds confidence. And "you've got to get confidence. I remember first coming to the House of Commons . . . I was dead scared, I was, I was dead scared," commented a Cabinet Minister who claimed that his four years in the Whips' Office taught him more about Parliament and more about himself than any other apprenticeship he ever had.

Ministers also point to experience on the backbenches. "There is a certain danger," they say, "in coming in and rocketing up to the top . . . without the hard grind on the backbenches." The hard grind gives you a feel for the debating chamber, a feel for the way backbench groups operate. Most important is the tacit understanding that backbench experience provides, since "a Minister cannot survive unless he can . . . understand the House and the people in it, how their minds work, how their emotions work." It is a matter of understanding that the House of Commons is a very moody place, that "if you just touch it wrong, it hits back at you and makes you look rather a fool." It is a matter of understanding dozens of little lessons such as where you will have to give way and where you will not, such as which sorts of Members you can attack with impunity and which you can't:

> I remember once when I was first a Member, I was thrown in debate and I followed, er, a Labour Member who was not the most articulate Member there ever was. He was a mining MP, and he made what I thought was a very foolish speech. And I followed him, and I tore it to pieces, shred by shred . . . um, and I was very pleased with myself . . . And when I walked out of the Chamber half an hour later, several of our Members were, uh, several of our Members came up to me and said, er, sort of, uh, "Filthy thing to do! Fred's one of the nicest chaps in the House of Commons." . . . Whereas if they'd thought old Fred was a nasty man, they'd . . . have been rather pleased if somebody sort of tore him apart.[66]

Committee work is a particular backbench experience that Ministers remember as tedious at the time but, in retrospect, very useful. Service in Standing Committees when one is on the Government side gets mixed reviews, since to save time "you must just sit there like a stuffed dummy, because, you know, they don't want you to speak." But backbench party committees and Select Committees were said to have much more to offer.

What Ministers emphasized most, however, was general experience as a backbencher *in Opposition*. "You have far greater opportunity as a back-bencher in Opposition than you have . . . as a backbencher in Government," because in Opposition backbenchers can criticize new Government legislation and, on the Conservative side, participate in the formulation of party policy. Here one can get to know the party's leaders, work with them, and learn from them. One can join teams working to oppose a Transport Bill or a Finance Act; and, by learning how legislation is best resisted, one can learn how legislation is best pushed through. "I've said over and over again," said a senior Treasury Minister, "that I simply do not understand how anybody can do the job properly who hasn't had a fairly long period of shadow in the Opposition." By comparison, "a backbencher in Government has much less of a real role to perform . . . I mean there is *nothing* to do"—nothing for a Ministerial Aspirant perhaps, but Constituency Members, Parliament Men, and Policy Advocates all find plenty to do. And they particularly resent Aspirants who become Members of the Government before they have done enough to become proper MPs.

DIFFICULTIES OF "LATERAL ENTRY"

Prime Ministers usually eschew "lateral entry," the option of appointing top outsiders to top ministerial positions. They are reluctant to appoint outsiders because their party's leading MPs want these positions for themselves, and also because they believe that parliamentary apprenticeships are prerequisites for understanding ministerial roles and performing them successfully: "In our way of doing things, Ministers have to be Members of the House of Commons. So they've got to know the House of Commons, they've got to know its ways, its customs, its procedures. And those Ministers who tend to get promoted straight from outside . . . none of these people have been really very successful Ministers. They haven't understood the strange animal that the House of Commons is."

Although lateral entry increased slightly after the First World War,[67] it has never been common enough to create an institutional anomaly, albeit its two most talked-about examples were anomalous enough each in his own way. One was Frank Cousins, brought by Harold Wilson directly from the Trade Union Movement into the Cabinet as Minister of Technology in 1964. The other was John Davies, brought by Edward Heath directly from the Confederation of British Industries into the Cabinet as Secretary of State for Trade and Industry in 1970.

Both Cousins and Davies were made Members of Parliament by finding them constituencies rather than by elevating them to life peerages. And both were much discussed by Ministers in this study as the exceptions that proved the rule against lateral entry. Their disastrous performances at Westminster "proved" that lateral entry is defective recruitment. Frank Cousins had been a powerful leader of his Trade Union and of the Trade Union Congress. But he had no feel whatsoever for the House and, at his age and position, no inclination to learn. Instead, he came to detest parliamentary life and, worse still, made no secret of this fact. "Frank Cousins was an absolute ass about this . . . so of course he was an absolute failure as a Minister. . . . It's the nice quirks which make the House of Commons what it is. And the people who purport to despise it, like Cousins, . . . who won't acknowledge these sorts of things . . . they will never get the respect of the House." Cousins' failure to connect with the House led to his resignation after two years in ministerial office.

John Davies had been Director General of the Confederation of British Industries. Like Cousins, he knew how to run many things—but not the House. He didn't have "the political feel," and he didn't like dealing with public scrutiny and with an Opposition. He didn't like the House much, period. And the House didn't like him. Eventually, he was demoted to a peripheral Cabinet post because his performances were embarrassing his party's backbenchers and his ministerial colleagues. Backbenchers would say, "They're wiping the bloody floor with him again." Ministers would say, more discreetly, "We can all think of recent examples of Ministers who have, er, suddenly emerged." The House resented both Cousins and Davies and put their feet to the fire: "I think the Conservatives certainly wanted to test Frank Cousins, and I believe the Labour Opposition went out of their way to give John Davies a particularly testing time." "Which you might argue was tit for tat," added an unsympathetic Conservative Cabinet Minister.[68]

In Britain, institutional hedgerows separate the fields of politics, business, trade unions, military, and media. Leaders cannot move readily between fields but instead typically enter one at a young age and explore slowly its established pathways. Even in politics, where the new recruits are not so young, they are still expected to begin near the bottom and, like new boys at school, serve the prescribed apprenticeships. Each field has its own peculiar norms and procedures that must be absorbed through experience: "If you haven't had the apprenticeship of working your way up here, you're a fish out of water . . . it's grossly unfair to a man to throw him into this, from business, without having the background." The rise of the career politician and the professionalization of politics have made it increasingly difficult for outsiders to enter directly at senior levels and increasingly unlikely that they will do so in the future.[69]

Taken together, Chapters 8 and 9 show clearly how ministerial roles are molded by institutional rules and detailed by the goals assigned to them. Even their subtypes tend to be positional, although it must be emphasized that some of them are significantly defined by the preferences of the players and therefore count as preference roles. Compared to the situation on the backbenches, however, these preference roles are so constrained that they leave little room for their players to create approaches as different as those, say, of Policy Advocates and Parliament Men.

The Constitution requires Ministers to be both Members of the Executive and Members of Parliament. This defines for their role its two distinct sets of goals and invites the creation of the preference roles of Administrators and Politicians. The most important aspect of this institutional arrangement is that it requires Ministers—Administrators as much as Politicians—to present themselves to Parliament for criticism and evaluation. All are required to persuade Parliament of the soundness of their policies and stewardship. If they cannot do that successfully, they cannot succeed. The parliamentary side of their roles is demanding and dangerous, which is why Ministers send Junior Ministers to Parliament to defend the department and to learn the trade. They expect them to keep in touch with backbench opinion and to learn how to present themselves as leaders. Back in the department, some are delegated administrative responsibilities. The role of the Junior Minister constitutes an advanced apprenticeship for the role of Minister, an advanced apprenticeship that builds upon whatever the candidate may have learned as a PPS, Whip, backbencher, or Opposition Spokesman.

At the same time, because Ministers have so very many responsibilities, they cannot avoid choosing among them. This creates somewhat more flexibility than might be expected, but also more headaches. Their workload is exacerbated by travel, late nights at the House, and the red-box problem: "I think a Minister is dreadfully overworked . . . by the time you get to bed at two and three in the morning, you are ready to do nothing but sleep." Yet many Ministers thrive on the same routines that drive others to their pills and into their gardens. This is, again, a consequence of the role's two very full sides, one in Whitehall, the other in Westminster. The two sides also create the principal role conflicts that Ministers encounter. The most common such conflict pits the expectations of the Minister's ministerial colleagues and civil servants against the expectations of his or her backbench supporters. Another common conflict pits those who would like them to immerse themselves in ministerial responsibilities against constituents who would like them to devote more attention to local concerns. The Ministers who succumb most completely to the ministerial embrace tend to become irritated with the House, and with their constituents as well.

Ministers are selected by Prime Ministers, who can't be too selective, for the candidate pool is greatly diminished by social background frames of age and education and by parliamentary attributes of previous posts, tenure, making a mark, and loyalty. Nonetheless, there is some flexibility for the PM, and some flexibility as well for the candidates, whose ambitions are powerful variables affecting their promotion prospects. These ambitions are driven by the emotional incentives of status, stimulation, and power. And the intensity of the package bears witness to the high "involvement" that Ministers have with their roles.

Ministers are at least as involved as Whips, sometimes more so. In Max Weber's words, they live "for" politics and make it their life in an "inward sense."[70] To assess the depth of this involvement, Ministers were asked the following question: "We are interested in how Members see themselves. If you were to describe yourself in a few sentences, how likely would you be to mention the fact that you are a Member of Parliament?" They offered responses along the following lines: "I'm, er, an absolutely extreme political-full-time-professional professional politician . . . I mean naturally as a, as a Member of the Government." This strong sense of involvement in one's role is the antipode to the "role distance" we found among some Welfare Officers and Auxiliaries. It suggests "embracing" the role, disappearing into the image of self that the role presents.[71]

Two standard indicators of "embracement" are statements that express attachment to the role and active involvement in the role's activities. Both can be seen in the transcripts of many Ministers. Another indicator of "embracement" is how, when we asked about identifications with the role of the "Member of Parliament," Ministers spoke instead about their identifications as "Ministers" and as "politicians": "I suppose I would have to say I was a Minister to the Crown or something." "Well, I'm a *politician* first, last, beginning, and end." When Ministers become deeply involved with their roles, the attitudes and activities characteristic of these roles begin to define who they are.[72] Particularly among senior Ministers, ministerial roles can be so absorbing that the role players find it difficult not to "become, er, well sort of absorbed. It was when I first came to the Foreign Office and I was abroad a great deal. . . . And it was after that that I really gave up trying to run the business at all. And I became completely immersed in politics. I then became a Member of the Cabinet. I became a Member of the Cabinet and became so deeply immersed."

It is difficult not to become involved, and difficult therefore to leave the role behind. Ministers relinquish their roles in four different circumstances: (a) when the electorate dismisses their party from Government; (b) when the Prime Minister sacks them in a reshuffle or (c) sends them down a snake to a less important position; and (d) when they cannot continue to support publicly government policies with which they disagree (resignation).

The electorate never dismissed the Government during the period of our interviews, but some of the Government's Ministers relinquished their roles under each of the remaining three circumstances. Several were sacked in reshuffles, including Paul Bryan and Frederick Corfield, who received knighthoods a few months later, and Richard Sharples, who was subsequently appointed Governor of Bermuda. The slide to a less important position was taken by John Davies, in the wake of negative comments from his ministerial colleagues such as, "There are those who say that the loss to British political life would not be intolerable."[73] Finally, Jasper More and Edward Taylor resigned over Britain's joining the European Economic Community. In accepting Taylor's resignation, the PM said that he respected his sincerity. But, as usual, it would be a long time and another Government before Taylor would again be offered a ministerial role.

How do the Ministers who are most involved in their roles react to losing them? "I think it's very interesting how people react to that situation," especially when they return to the backbenches and leave behind their antique desks, silver plate, magnificent offices, and ministerial cars. They return to a House of Commons where they must exchange power for influence, and where they may be expected to share a room and a secretary. It is difficult not to be disappointed.[74] As a recently sacked minister complained, somewhat indignantly: "I now think the idea that the House of Commons is the best club in London is a *myth*. . . . We ought to have better office facilities. . . . You can't do sitting in the Commons Library with your elbows squashed up with your next-door neighbour." In the same vein, a Cabinet Minister described a recent conversation with a former Cabinet Minister in which "I was asking him, 'Do you feel out of it?' And he said, 'One feels absolutely desolate, in having for years, having been the centre of the web. . . . You no longer know what's going on. . . . You miss the flow of papers, you miss. . . .'"

Most try to behave admirably, which is easier to do when you have resigned than when you have been sacked. Being sacked creates a temporary stigma that may be difficult to abide: "You have got to be rather careful that you don't appear to be motivated by bitterness at having been sacked. You have got to keep the appearance of bitterness out of things and, um, the disappointment and so on." Those who are most disappointed consider leaving the House altogether, because "I think you have to face the fact in our system that if you get sacked . . . you are not likely to get picked up again . . . and one begins to wonder whether one wants to go on much longer." Administrators find the loss most devastating and the roles of the backbencher least attractive. The Politicians, by contrast, are more likely to stay on, because though they loved Whitehall, they also love Westminster and know that respected positions are available to senior backbenchers. "I think I shall find a place as a chairman of a committee in the House, which is the sort of thing that senior people tend to do." They will stay on because they were always, in spirit as well as in title, Members of Parliament who were serving their turn as Members of the Government: "You know, I've had ten years of the frontbench. It's nice to be in Government. But it's also very nice to be here. I'm enjoying it again enormously."

CONCLUSION: INSTITUTIONAL STRUCTURE AND INDIVIDUAL CHOICE IN PERSPECTIVE

> I only act, as everyone does, the part in
> life that he's chosen for himself, or
> that others have chosen for him.
>
> Pirandello, *Six Characters in Search of
> an Author*

To govern liberal democratic states, politicians must accommodate themselves to the rules of parliamentary institutions. Their accommodations create political roles, which are composite patterns of goals, attitudes, and behaviors characteristic of people in particular positions. Explaining these
roles can help us explain the governing of liberal democratic states—but
only when we understand them as they are understood by their players.

For each established role, each player has his or her own individual interpretation. This is where I have begun, for political roles are composites constructed from such interpretations and, as such, are more abstract than the
accounts provided by any single individual. They are general interpretations
of individual interpretations, which, as Sir Lewis Namier emphasized, require generalization because they are each only partial views of the system
of meaning that interests us.[1] Thus, I have tried to understand Westminster's
principal political roles as they are understood by those who play them, but
with sufficient generality to reconstruct their composite patterns, explain
their origins and consequences, and illuminate their institutional contexts.
This is the book's contribution to the study of British politics and its principal contribution. At the same time, I have sought to address the study of
comparative political behavior. Hence the motivational approach, and some
of the concepts and mechanisms that it uncovers, can be used to compare
politicians' roles over time and across similar institutions.

In Britain, these roles have been quite stable throughout the postwar period and, in their basic outlines, throughout the century. They have evolved slowly because they are embedded in parliamentary institutions that have evolved slowly. And yet there has been change. Recent modifications of parliamentary roles follow a trend that has characterized most Western legislatures during the same period: the movement toward increasing professionalization. This movement has dominated institutional change at Westminster. In this chapter, I review the recent modifications and suggest how they might be explained by social, economic, and political factors. I also consider their constitutional consequences and thereby draw attention to the considerable political significance of relationships among roles, rules, and reasons.

The Direction of Change: Professionalization

The postwar convergence in the social and educational backgrounds of Members of Parliament highlights the professionalization of their roles. Thus, the number of working-class MPs in the Labour Party has declined, as has, on the Conservative side, the proportion of Members from public-school backgrounds and Oxbridge. Parliament, it is said, is no longer "a microcosm of the nation" but instead an assembly of middle-class professionals in which the aristocratic and amateur traditions of British politics are fast disappearing. But are MPs indeed professionals?[2]

Compared to many recent and convoluted strategies for identifying "professions," I think that A. M. Carr-Saunders and P. A. Wilson were closer to the mark in 1933 when they said simply that "the typical profession exhibits a complex of characteristics," and that "other vocations approach this condition more or less closely, owing to the possession of some of these characteristics fully or partially developed."[3] The practice of politics at Westminster is a vocation that has been approaching this condition by developing some of the characteristics that are commonly associated with the typical professions. It is a vocation that, like the ministry or the military, is synonymous with an organization—in this case, Parliament. When I review the evidence, I think it will become clear that although political work in Britain may in general not be very professional, and although British politicians may in general not be very professional either, *at Westminster* the roles and the role players have become quite professional after all.

Professionals enter their occupations early, rarely leave, and, above all, work full time. Today's Members of Parliament enter during their thirties and forties, infrequently leave, and, increasingly, work full time. "Full time" is a minimum forty-hour week and also a matter of perception. The 1970s were the watershed. Thus, two-thirds of our Members of Parliament indicated that they put in a forty-hour week at Westminster alone, while more than four-fifths claimed at least this much time when they added in political work outside Westminster.[4] By the 1990s, the perception had developed that the job of the Member of Parliament was clearly full time, and that it had become extremely difficult to combine with part-time occupations outside the House.[5] Those who played leadership roles, of course, put in more hours still.

Moreover, by the 1970s the job at Westminster had become the principal source of income for many backbenchers. Work outside the House was increasingly ancillary, occasional, or very occasional.[6] The subsequent rises in parliamentary salary and allowances came close to providing a convincing economic foundation for full-time public-service careers with modest standards of living.

Most professions are distinguished by professional associations. Those that are not are distinguished more informally by strong bonds among their members and by the sense of identity their members have with their roles.[7] MPs feel this way, if not about the world of politics writ large, then certainly about the world of Westminster. The fact that their average length of service has more than doubled since the war both reflects and reinforces this psychological commitment to the career.[8] Thus, High Flyers say that they propose to make a career in politics and don't see much point in being at Westminster otherwise; the more that Specialists specialize, the more they become committed to politics as a career; a Whip is a Whip, is a Whip; and among Ministers the commitments are every bit as intense.

Another central characteristic of a profession is dedication to serving the needs of clients and to placing their interests above one's own.[9] The principal clients of Members of Parliament are, nationally, the public and, locally, the constituents for whose grievances Members are expected to seek redress. Although the redress of grievances is one of Parliament's most ancient functions, it has not always been vigorously practiced.[10] But today, nearly all MPs, including those in the highest ministerial offices, do at least a little constituency *service*. And some of them, Constituency Members, make this service the principal preoccupation of their careers. They regard their "surgeries" (the analogy with the doctor's professional office is no accident) as a civic duty coupled, as we have seen, with the medieval conception of the role "as a lawyer [another common professional analogy], as an advocate for my constituents, the people I represent."

Professional occupations afford their members considerable autonomy in authority and judgment. The striving for autonomy in authority is reflected by a concern with formal titles to distinguish qualified members of the profession from unqualified outsiders—as in Chartered Accountant (CA), Member of Parliament (MP), or, as in the signs that control access throughout Westminster, "Members" and "Strangers."[11] The striving for autonomy in judgment draws our attention to the constitutional doctrine of Parliamentarism, which suggests that policy is best made through deliberation at Westminster rather than by seeking mandates from the public. Members of Parliament, it is often said, are more like doctors (again, the simile) than like delegates: they are expected to diagnose the public's ailments and prescribe remedies. And the public is expected, between elections, to accept these prescriptions. Policy Advocates devote more energy to such deliberations than do any other role players on the backbenches. Senior Ministers make the lion's share of the authoritative judgments, albeit during the 1980s Ministers of State and even Junior Ministers increased slightly the autonomy of their activities.[12]

According to Carr-Saunders and Wilson, the oldest and most important distinguishing characteristic of the professions is the application to ordinary life of special knowledge that has been acquired through specialized training.[13] This is the criterion that, more than any other, makes us reluctant to characterize politicians as professionals. Indeed, from this perspective, *most politicians are not* very professional. But *most MPs are*. Members of Parliament possess a special and important body of knowledge and apply this knowledge in their political work: knowledge about rules of the game (both constitutional and parliamentary); detailed knowledge about political ideologies (complex goals and the most effective means to reach those goals); and very considerable knowledge about the parliamentary roles reconstructed in this book. These are the principal components of Westminster's political culture, which is not, in anything like its fully developed form, acquired by anyone besides Members of Parliament.

MPs do not earn formal degrees or certificates in these subjects. But neither do the members of some standard professions earn formal degrees or certificates.[14] Instead, MPs acquire this special knowledge through apprenticeships—as, again, do the members of many standard professions. Their education frequently begins in preparliamentary apprenticeships in local government, which have become increasingly common as part of the trend toward increasing professionalization,[15] but also in political parties, trade unions, research departments, public-relations firms, and other organizations that deal directly and regularly with Parliament.

Their most important educational experiences, however, occur at Westminster, where they work full time in situations for which rules of the game are the constraints, ideologies the tests of policy programs, and parliamentary roles the frameworks for daily living. Without their rules of the game, ideologies, and informal roles, backbenchers would not know what to do. In the same vein, by helping Ministers prepare for Question Time, the PPS learns how dangerous it can be not to have learned to bell the cat. In the Whips' Office, Whips are taught about their party's ideological groups and about the nitty-gritty of the rules of the game. Likewise, Junior Ministers acquire through their roles a rigorous "postgraduate education" for the position of the Minister, a position that takes, on average, a total of fourteen years to reach, fourteen years that Ministers believe are absolutely essential to acquire the special knowledge and training needed to perform effectively.

Certain occupations are commonly characterized as "vocations," and certain vocations as "professions." Politics is a vocation, not a profession. But at Westminster, the vocation of politics has become increasingly professional. This is desirable because it serves Parliament's representational goals by making more effective its checks on an increasingly powerful Executive. But it can also be undesirable, for if professionalism is carried too far, Parliament could become a "house without windows," its representational goals undermined by insularity and the arrogance of expertise. Yet, in the end, professionalization refers simply to change, not to an inevitable progression. Parliamentary institutions are patently revisable, and their principal revisionists are the politicians who run them.

Role Choice and Recruitment

Role choice and recruitment are the gateways to change in parliamentary roles and particularly to their professionalization. "Role choice" is an economic concept that focuses on individual decisions and rationality. "Recruitment" is a sociological concept that focuses on a collectivity's needs and rules. Both are used by the motivational approach to explain why particular types of individuals end up in particular types of roles and why these roles have become increasingly professional. This is the explanatory context of the *origins* of roles, a context that invites naturalistic explanations, a politically important context in which theoretically oriented research has been surprisingly rare.

Role choice and recruitment are a function of *opportunities* and *incentives*. As Machiavelli put it, "fortune is the ruler of half of our actions, but she allows the other half or thereabouts to be governed by us."[16] Still, this very general model does not tell us much until we fill in the blanks for particular types of roles. The incentives are reviewed later in this chapter. Here I wish to examine the opportunities, which are usually either *constituency characteristics* (electoral insecurity, social-class composition, region, urban-rural) or *individual characteristics* (party, social class, education, ideology, age, tenure). For preference roles, the process is usually one of "role choice," in which the opportunities become conditions that structure desires and beliefs, which, in their turn, influence the choices that politicians make among alternative roles. For position roles, the process is more likely to be one of "recruitment," in which the same sorts of opportunities become criteria that gatekeepers use to select recruits. Here role choice becomes mainly a matter of accepting or rejecting their offers.

CONSTITUENCY CHARACTERISTICS

Role choice can be affected by any characteristic of a constituency that makes constituents' demands more compelling, direct, or visible.[17] *Electoral insecurity* makes them more compelling. Particularly in times of uneven and volatile swings, "a Member with a marginal seat may feel a greater inducement to work hard in his constituency."[18] And he or she would presumably then have less time for the busy backbench preference roles of the Policy Advocate or the Ministerial Aspirant. Indeed, in our data the backbenchers with marginal constituencies are somewhat less likely than their colleagues to choose the role of the Policy Advocate and much less likely to choose the role of the busiest of Policy Advocates, the Specialist. Yet there seems to be no linear relationship whatsoever between electoral insecurity and dispositions to become Ministerial Aspirants or, even more surprisingly, Constituency Members.

The *social-class composition* of one's constituency can likewise increase demands for constituency services and thereby reduce the time available for alternative pursuits. Such demands are said to be heaviest where the social-class composition is heterogeneous, for this produces a broader range of problems than those that arise in homogeneous working-class or middle-class areas. There is, in fact, a curvilinear relationship in our data between the percentage of nonmanual workers in each constituency and the choice of the role of the Policy Advocate, especially that of its busiest subtype, the Specialist. Moreover, the same heterogeneous-constituency conditions that turn a backbencher's desires away from policy advocate roles turn them toward the role of the Constituency Member (Constituency Members are frequently found in the heterogeneous constituencies where Policy Advocates are absent).

Demands can be made more visible by a constituency's *regional* and *urban-rural* character. Thus, many constituencies in the regions of Scotland, Wales, the North, and the Midlands are obviously much less prosperous than constituencies in the South. And they are believed by MPs to demand greater attention. Such conditions apparently dampen desires to become a Policy Advocate, for Policy Advocates are most prominent not in any of these regions but instead in the South. Furthermore, these are precisely the regions, particularly Scotland, with the greatest concentrations of Constituency Members.[19] In the same vein, rural areas are said to spawn Constituency Members, because Members in rural areas spend so much time attending local events where they are seen and can be approached by constituents.[20] There is some support in our data for these expectations, but not much; and it disappears in an analysis of the fifty most agricultural seats, where the proportion of Constituency Members is just about average.

Thus, constituency characteristics structure the desires and beliefs that influence choices about preference roles. The key is the electoral insecurity that the MP feels and the demands for constituency service being made upon him or her. Both increased during the 1970s and 1980s. These have been the most important recent changes in constituency characteristics related to role choice. Moreover, as Anthony Barker and Michael Rush foresaw in 1970,[21] a cultural multiplier has magnified their effects: the actions of vigorous Constituency Members stimulate among their constituents higher expectations for services. As the number and visibility of vigorous Constituency Members grow, the expectations of the constituents of less vigorous Members rise as well.

Now let us consider some of the individual characteristics involved in choices among preference roles.

INDIVIDUAL CHARACTERISTICS

Age, party, and ideology are often discussed in studies of backbench preference roles. *Age* has a particularly strong influence here, an influence created by the informal institutional rule that virtually bars from ministerial office backbenchers who have not by the age of fifty been appointed to a junior post. Thus, those who enter Parliament in their late forties or early fifties find that they are too old to get started and that, if they are interested in power, they should become interested instead in influence and become Policy Advocates. There is not much point in pursuing promotion unless it is indeed attainable. Age also has a substantial impact on the thinking of those who take up the role of the Parliament Man, which has become largely an exit role for those approaching retirement. Because "time clocks" are critical in constructing political careers, backbenchers think and talk about them a great deal.

Party differences have only a minor influence in the distribution of parliamentary roles, for these roles are usually embedded in institutional structures that are common to all Members, rather than in party structures that divide them. Thus, none of the principal backbench preference roles is dominated by partisan biases that would strongly attract Conservative rather than Labour backbenchers or vice versa. Party becomes important only in the subtypes and in the subcategories of these subtypes. Among the "strong" and "very strong" Specialists, for instance, Conservatives outnumber Labour by nearly three to one. But even these results with subtypes are not very significant, for they are less theoretically linked with the partisanship that divides the parties than with the recruitment patterns that bring in different kinds of people with different personal rather than political reasons for preferring one subrole over another. Conservatives are more likely to become "strong" Specialists, for example, because their occupational backgrounds are more likely to give them subjects in which to specialize.

Ideology is unlikely to be a dominant force either, since partisanship is not driving these relationships. No backbench preference role is aimed at promoting a particular ideological program. At the same time, being ideological, that is to say, standing on the Left or Right of one's parliamentary party rather than near its Center, is a less programmatic and more positional dimension of ideology that might nevertheless influence the desires and beliefs that determine role choice. It does indeed—for when one has an ax to grind, it makes sense to pursue a role that enables one to grind an ax. Thus, backbenchers who take up the role of the Policy Advocate are more likely than their colleagues to come from the poles rather than the midpoint of their party's political spectrum. Ministerial Aspirants are, by contrast, more likely to come from the midpoints because, while extreme views do not exclude backbenchers from office, they do dampen their prospects and thereby make striving less attractive.

Opportunities that affect the selection *of* backbench preference roles do so by helping backbenchers to make their own choices. By contrast, opportunities that affect the selection *for* frontbench position roles do so by helping gatekeepers to choose recruits. Throughout this century, the number of responsibilities assigned to leadership roles has increased steadily. This has raised the value of safe, steady, and reliable performances. At the same time, the career hierarchy has become a series of successive apprenticeships and filters that would, if they worked perfectly, ensure that no one who is unsafe, unsteady, or unreliable is ever appointed to a position where he or she can do any damage. They don't work perfectly. But they already work well enough for lobby correspondents to talk about "the rise of the grey suits."

Party Leaders are the head gatekeepers who, once chosen, choose almost everyone else. And when the party Leader is Prime Minister, the selecting and reshuffling of Ministers goes on continuously. The number of positions is, however, far too large for the Prime Minister to manage on his or her own; so the Chief Whip proposes names, as do senior Ministers. Moreover, senior Ministers are usually consulted about the choice of Ministers and Junior Ministers to work under them. And all Ministers select their own PPSs, a process much less rigorous than the selection of Whips, Junior Ministers, or Ministers, for PPSs are much less important to the effectiveness of the institution. Still, the procedures in all these cases are much the same: appropriate populations are sifted by social background frames, sorted by parliamentary attributes, and scrutinized for personal characteristics.

Social background frames. The search is narrowed by using individual social background characteristics to identify for careful examination a manageable number of potential recruits.[22] Thus, when Ministers and Whips scan the backbenches for potential PPS Apprentices, they focus on backbenchers who are well educated and in their late thirties or early forties. By contrast, when they look for PPSs to serve as Auxiliaries, education becomes less salient and they concentrate on backbenchers who are closer in age to Ministers and have served in the House long enough to know the ropes.

The importance of age in the selection of PPSs is matched by the importance of gender in the selection of Whips. Gatekeepers seek mainly men because, they tell themselves, Whips must cajole mainly male backbenchers. Conservative Whips also tend to be middle class (not upper class), whereas Labour Whips tend to be working class (not middle class) to facilitate the same sort of smooth relations with each party's backbenchers. As both parliamentary parties become increasingly middle class, however, this characteristic becomes increasingly irrelevant. Higher up the career ladder, it is less essential to narrow the search, for the field is already reduced, primarily to those one step below. Even for Junior Ministers, age (the critical age of fifty) is the only social background characteristic obviously used to frame the process. Age is again used alone, but less rigorously, in selecting Ministers, for Ministers are selected almost exclusively from among Junior Ministers who are Journeymen and therefore already within the desired range.

Parliamentary attributes. Prime Ministers are reluctant to appoint newcomers to leading posts because they believe that their vocation's apprenticeships are necessary to understand ministerial roles and perform them successfully. Hence, even the backbenchers tapped to become Parliamentary Private Secretaries are usually those with a little experience in the Chamber or in back-bench committees.

Future Ministers are likewise expected to "make a mark" in the Chamber. But when it comes to Whips, more emphasis is placed on good attendance, which suggests a willingness to spend long hours at Westminster. Service as a PPS is also a promising sign for prospective Whips, because the liaison tasks in these two roles are so similar. Finally, although constituency characteristics are generally unimportant in recruitment to leadership roles, they can enter here as individual characteristics: Whips need large majorities because their constituents may forget them; and it makes sense to seek Assistant Whips whose constituencies are from the same regions of the country as those of the flocks for whom they will be responsible. Turning to Ministers turns the gatekeepers to parliamentary performances (like good speeches) and managerial performances (like guiding a Bill through the Commons) that demonstrate parliamentary skills. For Junior Ministers they look to PPSs, Whips, committee officers, and Opposition Front Bench Spokesmen; for senior Ministers they look to Junior Ministers, whose roles provide the most serious education and training of all.

Personal characteristics. There are many personal characteristics by which potential Parliamentary Private Secretaries might be evaluated—but aren't. Instead, gatekeepers use the social background frames for a quick sort; and without too much further scrutiny, they make appointments. They are willing to "try people out" as PPSs because if some are duds, no great harm will have been done to the parliamentary machine. Reliable performances are not as important here as in more-institutionalized leadership positions. The position of Whip is more institutionalized; in fact it is as institutionalized as leadership positions get in parliamentary organizations. And, for recruiting Whips, personal characteristics are taken very seriously. First of all, the ideological sympathies of candidates must be determined, because the full range of the party's ideological spectrum must be represented in the Whips' Office. Personality traits must be considered carefully too. Gregariousness, for example, is essential for people who will be required to develop convivial relationships. Emotional detachment is also needed, so that Whips can remain aloof from party factions and thereby maintain the confidence that others must have in their reliability.

Political ideology is taken seriously in selecting Ministers, for most Prime Ministers want most major wings of their parliamentary parties represented in their governments. But personality traits are, surprisingly, not applied so seriously in choosing people for these posts. Gatekeepers and commentators mention traits like affability, sensitivity, intelligence, and flexibility; yet most of their talk sounds more like afterthoughts than like criteria by which candidates are actually scrutinized. Although the role of the Minister is as institutionalized as the role of the Whip, it also offers more choice (a consequence of role overload) and thereby tolerates a wider range of personality characteristics. The "grey suits" may be rising, but neither Parliament nor the parliamentary parties will collapse if ministerial roles are played with a little improvisation. Besides, at this level the gatekeepers cannot afford to be very choosy, since their choices are limited to Junior Ministers and Ministers of State.

Professionalization characterizes the principal direction of change in the recruitment characteristics and role choices that condition parliamentary roles. These are the conduits through which systemic and institutional changes on the "origins" side reach parliamentary roles, reshape them, and thereby stimulate institutional and systemic changes on the "consequences" side. If recruitment and role choice are the direct link between the origins and the roles, then it is the behavior of the role players that is the direct link between these roles and their consequences. Before we go on to consider the full explanatory field, it is necessary to clarify some of the conceptual confusion that surrounds this topic.

How Roles Work: Behavior

Nothing much happens in politics until politicians act. Their behavior and the desires and beliefs that explain it are essential components of most political explanations. Many claims that link their behavior to institutional and systemic consequences seem obvious as soon as they are stated. But what has not seemed so obvious are the antecedent claims linking role-related desires and beliefs to the role behavior itself. The skepticism that exists about these links is based on many unsuccessful attempts during the 1950s, 1960s, and 1970s to demonstrate relationships between role-related attitudes and behavior. It is also based on confusion about the nature of interpretative explanations in the study of roles.

This confusion underlies the conclusion that political roles are, in general, unrelated to behavior. Most contemporary philosophers of social science would find this conclusion very peculiar, because they regard desires, beliefs, and behavior as *inherently* intertwined—behavior is explained in interpretative explanations by identifying the desires and beliefs that lead to it. Therefore, if through empirical investigation one has not found relationships between the behavior and particular desires and beliefs, this simply suggests that one has not yet found the right desires and beliefs. In studying *purposive* roles, the motivational approach seeks to reconstruct characteristic clusters of desires, beliefs, and behaviors that are inherently intertwined. These are its roles. The behavior is part of these roles.

Let us lay to rest this peculiar conclusion by invoking both the nature of interpretative explanations and the numerous examples in this book where, for preference and position roles, relationships between attitudes and behavior have been perfectly clear and convincing. Most of the behaviors that are characteristic of these parliamentary roles are obviously driven by the desires and beliefs that are characteristic of these roles. The "obviously" here is based on my interpretations—which apply the rationality principle of situational analysis, backed in most cases by understandings of the situation that the role players themselves have articulated, and probed in many cases by quantitative analysis. No doubt I may have gotten some of them wrong. But if so, the criticism should be that I have identified the wrong desires and beliefs—not that I have discovered a new class of behaviors that are unrelated to any desires and beliefs and are in this sense inexplicable.

We have yet to consider, however, behaviors that are *not characteristic* but nonetheless common in parliamentary roles. These were identified as such in the preceding chapters. And here they may help us lay to rest another peculiar claim about role beliefs and role behavior. This claim takes up where the other leaves off but is likewise based on confusion about the nature of interpretative explanations. Relationships there may be, this new claim suggests, but the trouble is that these relationships are "tautological" and therefore trivial. It is tautological to demonstrate, for example, that backbenchers who think of themselves as Constituency Members spend more time in the constituency than do their colleagues.

A tautology is a redundancy, a needless repetition of the same idea in different words. Actually there is nothing tautological about finding that politicians who express certain characteristic desires and beliefs also behave in a manner consistent with those desires and beliefs. They don't always. And there is always a wider range of behaviors from which these particular behaviors have been selected. But the main point is as follows: When we say that the desires and beliefs inherently "lead" to the behaviors, we are simply saying that they are linked to them logically—not tautologically, for the behavior is in no sense a needless repetition of the same idea as the belief. Moreover, we should be very pleased that in the wake of so many studies in which "delegates did not behave like delegates" by voting their constituents' wishes, we have successfully reconstructed motivational preference roles like that of the Constituency Member, whose players actually behave like Constituency Members by tending to their constituencies. Perhaps what is meant by tautological in this context is not "redundant" but rather "banal." Interpretative explanations of political roles often do seem obvious, once they have been fully articulated. And since achieving some robustness in relationships between role-related attitudes and role-related behaviors is a desirable goal, it would be satisfying to find some relationships that were not quite so obvious. This is the point behind our reports in the chapters about uncharacteristic but common behaviors that role players perform. The fact that they are not characteristic suggests that other important desires and beliefs are also involved.

Thus, some Policy Advocates are frequent dissenters in the Chamber, in committee, and also in the division lobbies. This behavior is not characteristic of the role, either in their own eyes or in the eyes of their associates. But it is nonetheless related to the role because it is the role of the Policy Advocate that enables them to pursue their preferences so intensely. Some Constituency Members are uncharacteristically dissenters as well, albeit for them the connection to the role is quite different: a little reaction to a little resentment over their role's low status at Westminster. Other common but uncharacteristic behaviors include those of High Flyers "playing at" the role of the Minister; Welfare Officers taking up constituents' private problems, including cases of mental illness or attempted suicide; and perhaps Spectators collecting memories.

Further examples from frontbench position roles are as follows: Among Parliamentary Private Secretaries, a few Apprentices may be asked to serve as personal assistants in policy negotiations with other departments. These behaviors are not characteristic of the role, and not even very common; but they are certainly role related. What is quite common and role related but in no way characteristic of the role, and therefore likewise in no way banal, is the fact that, among Junior Ministers, Journeymen spend more time in their constituencies than do backbenchers. They are building up funds of good will upon which they can draw later when, as more-senior Ministers, they will have less time for surgeries. Among senior Ministers, it is similarly common, without being characteristic, to express privately to other senior Ministers the belief that Parliament has become peripheral to real power, and to act on this belief by arranging one's ministerial affairs so that Parliament bothers one as little as possible.[23] Political roles are *characteristic* patterns of desires, beliefs, and behaviors that are interrelated. These relationships are not causal, and often not calculational either, for most of the time politicians are, like the rest of us, typically responding to typical situations with typical reactions they have already learned.[24] But they can and should be investigated empirically and quantitatively in order to get them right and to make the interpretative explanations as persuasive as possible. The results of such investigations are no more tautological than are the results of investigations about links between these behaviors and their consequences.

"Professionalization" characterizes the direction of change in parliamentary roles. "Role choice and recruitment" links these changes back to their institutional and systemic origins. And "behavior" is the principal mechanism by which such role changes contribute to further institutional and systemic change. Now I would like to put together these strands from different sectors of the explanatory field to illustrate how roles are embedded in their contexts.

Roles and Rules in Context: Checking the Executive

The predominant direction of change in parliamentary roles, professionalization, strengthens both the Executive and Parliament's scrutiny of the Executive. It has intensified the tension between the two and made this struggle the predominant focus of parliamentary reform.

The contemporary Executive's dominance of Parliament is rooted in a predemocratic tradition that is, in fact, not recognized by the Constitution and is beginning to seem as outdated as did by 1911 the power of the House of Lords.[25] This executive dominance was most recently consolidated by the growth of mass parties outside the House, by the rise of party discipline within the House, and by the twentieth century's expansion in governmental responsibilities.[26] Today's reformers propose to redress the balance. They are led by Constituency Members and Policy Advocates, who are playing roles that hardly existed in Namier's eighteenth-century Parliaments or in Trollope's nineteenth-century political novels, but that today fill the backbenches of the House of Commons.

To study these topics, British political scientists don't much need the "new institutionalism," for their discipline was never overrun by either the behavioral or the public-choice revolutions, and they consequently never stopped writing about rules, roles, and rationality. Thus, their essays address many of the connections between roles and rules and can help us to understand concretely how political roles are embedded in institutional contexts. In particular, they can help us to map some of the principal origins and consequences of the three roles whose recent evolution has been most widely discussed: Constituency Members, Policy Advocates, and Ministers. For each we first review some of the principal changes and then consider their hypothesized origins and consequences.

CONSTITUENCY MEMBERS

Throughout the 1970s and 1980s, backbenchers began to pursue greater accountability from the Executive by pursuing energetically the redress of grievances. The proportion of Constituency Members on the backbenches may have increased during this period, but probably not by very much, because the roles of Policy Advocates and Ministerial Aspirants were becoming more popular at the same time. In fact, what is more likely than radical change in the distribution of these roles is a marked increase in the overlap among them such that, today, backbenchers who still may not see themselves primarily as Constituency Members are nevertheless doing more constituency service than ever before.

This trend has been noticed since the early 1960s and has been attributed to the postwar creation of the Welfare State, a systemic development that brought citizens into frequent contact with government and created a need for MPs to protect their interests.[27] It also created demands that were further stimulated by the rise of "community politics" during the early 1960s. Local parties began to campaign on local issues, often in response to local Liberals who were asking at meetings of community groups, "Where is the MP?"[28] During the 1970s and the 1980s, another systemic change, electoral volatility, began pressing backbenchers in the same direction by increasing the electoral value of constituency service.[29] Finally, the impact of such factors has been multiplied by a diffusion effect: the more that MPs are seen attending to these tasks, the more widespread become the assumptions in the constituencies that this is their proper role. Thus, the recent increase in backbenchers' attention to constituency member roles is said to be a function of these four systemic variables. This is a naturalistic or causal explanation of the *origins* of the role change, parts of which have been investigated empirically.

On the other side of the explanatory field, the *consequences* of increased attention to constituency member roles seem obvious: institutionally, Ministers and their civil servants have had to establish more procedures, assign more personnel, and devote more time to the ever-rising tide of letters that MPs write on behalf of their constituents; and systemically, the chief consequence has been to revive and relegitimize in the British Constitution the redress of grievances as an important mode of representation.

Another recent development deserves notice because it illustrates how changing just one institutional rule can change the character of parliamentary roles and thereby produce constitutional consequences. Thus, during the early 1980s the Labour Party introduced a new recruitment rule, the mandatory reselection of MPs. It is said that many constituency activists and some Labour MPs have, as a result of the threat of deselection by constituency activists, come to believe that the role of the Constituency Member should now encompass service as a sometime delegate for the policy opinions of constituency activists.[30] Although this view will probably never be incorporated into parliamentary roles, these are just the sorts of little acorns from which constitutional consequences can grow: in this case greater constitutional legitimacy than exists today for constituency-based policy representation.

It must be emphasized that satisfactory naturalistic explanations of institutional changes like the expanded civil service procedures for dealing with constituency cases, or of constitutional changes like the revival of the redress of grievances, cannot be constructed without including at the heart of those explanations interpretative accounts of the roles of MPs and of how the changes have been triggered by changes in these roles. Moreover, there is nothing inevitable about the impact of institutional and systemic forces upon parliamentary roles, just as there is nothing inevitable about the parliamentary roles' institutional and systemic consequences. Taking account of such forces, politicians analyze, evaluate, and shape their roles in accordance with their *own* desires—and these "person facts" can block as well as facilitate the flow of "group facts" from one side of the explanatory field to the other.

POLICY ADVOCATES

Over the past several decades the role of the Policy Advocate, like the role of the Constituency Member, has become increasingly important. Policy Advocates, the most professional of backbenchers, are more self-confident today than when they were first identified as backbench professionals in the 1950s and 1960s.[31] During the first Thatcher Government, they decided that their desire for independence was appropriate, that their long-standing belief that government defeats in the division lobbies would cause resignations was incorrect, and that their optimistic belief in the efficacy of such threats as a tool for checking the executive was, if anything, an underestimate.[32] They therefore began to scrutinize government policy more critically and aggressively than before. Led by Specialists, their role's dominant and most professional subtype, they pressed for reforms such as strengthening Select Committees, increasing research staff, and improving facilities. They pursued these goals through lobbying and also through Select Committees on Procedure and the All-Party Commons Reform Group.

The advance of the Administrative State is the systemic variable to which these role changes are most often attributed. Thus, the role of the Policy Advocate has grown more popular and professional as a function of the growth in government activities throughout the century. For Parliament as an institution, this has generated more legislation and committees, longer sitting days and parliamentary sessions, and more Policy Advocates.[33] At the same time, the Advocates' desire for independence has been fed by modifications in British political culture since the 1950s, in particular by a slightly stronger emphasis on the "democracy" in "liberal democracy." It is in the name of democracy as well as accountability that contemporary reform movements propose to redress the balance between Parliament and the Executive. These winds of cultural change have also encouraged the belief that effective government requires less deference than had previously been supposed.[34]

In addition, causal claims have been made for several institutional variables on this, the "origins" side of the field: professional lobbying, recruitment patterns, new facilities, and the new system of Select Committees. Thus when, during the 1970s and 1980s, interest groups sent professional lobbyists to Westminster in increasing numbers, backbenchers added to their duties service as parliamentary consultants for companies from British Airways to Kentucky Fried Chicken.[35] Throughout this same period, changes in recruitment patterns turned away those who might have become traditional part-time Members, while improvements in pay and research facilities provided the eager beavers inside with much needed resources. Finally, the parliamentary rule changes that created the new system of Select Committees in 1979 encouraged Policy Advocates by constructing better-equipped stages on which to play their parts. These are the principal systemic and institutional variables that have recently shaped the evolution of the Policy Advocate's role, which, in turn, is said to have contributed to the following institutional and constitutional "consequences."

During the 1970s the House of Commons seemed to be dismissing its deferential image as backbenchers inflicted more defeats on the Government than had been seen for a century. This was a consequence of backbench role changes that seemed at the time worth taking seriously, albeit they were reversed during the 1980s when government majorities grew larger and safer. Governments are most responsible to Parliament when their own backbenchers are willing to produce defeats in the division lobbies. Thus, as cross-voting became more common during the 1970s, Ministers became more anxious to explain themselves and their policies.[36] This new backbench influence, which was spearheaded by Policy Advocates, eventually modified the institutional rules of party discipline.[37] But as fast as Ministers made these concessions, they also devalued them by "clarifying" the constitutional rule of collective responsibility. The defeat of the Government on an important issue, they announced, would no longer be regarded as the litmus test for a loss of confidence and hence of a need for collective resignation.

Committee work was another route for pursuing influence through professionalization. Policy Advocates and particularly Specialists came to see committees, not the Chamber, as the most effective arena in which to check the Executive. It was as a result of their pressures that the new system of Select Committees was created in 1979 to monitor particular areas of government policy. But if these committees were a response to vigorous new interpretations of policy advocate roles,[38] once they were established, they made these roles more attractive still, which encouraged still more backbenchers to practice them. This is an example of a change in parliamentary rules that was both a consequence of changes in the role of the Policy Advocate and an origin of further changes in the same role. The point of these new committees was to strengthen the constitutional rule of ministerial responsibility by questioning Ministers and civil servants about departmental affairs.[39] They have not created as many waves as Policy Advocates hoped, but by strengthening the rights of parliamentarians to be informed and to criticize, they have taken a modest step toward redressing the balance between Parliament and the Executive.[40]

Although many changes in institutional rules are unintended consequences, others are introduced quite deliberately. Thus, the rise of the Administrative State and the recent sparks of democratic irreverence have stimulated changes in the behavior of Policy Advocates mainly because Policy Advocates had come *to believe* by the 1960s that the balance between the Government and the House of Commons was unbalanced.[41] In the same vein, the power of these systemic forces to produce (through the roles of the Policy Advocates) significant constitutional change was checked by Ministers who, in their roles as Ministers, *desired* to retain control of the House so that they could continue to push through it the policies that they themselves preferred. Until the 1979 Select Committee reforms, the dominance of the Executive was not modified in any serious way. Ministers didn't want it to be—and it wasn't.[42]

MINISTERS

Although Ministers sought to neutralize the new Select Committees by ignoring their reports, they were unable to ignore their invitations and, after some resistance, accepted giving evidence to these committees as a new duty in ministerial roles.[43] Because such appearances were now prescribed by institutional rules, they could not easily be avoided. But Ministers did not welcome the additional parliamentary scrutiny, for it increased their vulnerability and added to the burdens of role overload that continued to grow throughout the 1970s and 1980s.

Again, what Ministers gave with one hand they took back with the other. Behind the protection of large government majorities during the 1980s, they began to pay less attention to their own backbenchers and to the Opposition.[44] Hence, the most significant modifications in the role of the Minister over this period lie elsewhere: in its chief desire, ambition, which is said to have become stronger and more personal, and in the addition of two beliefs to the role's repertoire: that the intensity of competition for ministerial positions is rising, and that it is less necessary than it used to be to follow established norms. The result, John Mackintosh was already arguing by 1977, is that politicians were increasingly "willing to go along with almost anything rather than give up the prestige, the excitement, the sense of power, and the emoluments of office."[45]

These modifications in ministerial roles have been attributed to many different systemic and institutional origins. The first is a cultural variable, the declining force of convention in post-Victorian Britain. This has significant implications for the Constitution, which consists largely of conventions constructed when established rules were better established and had a firmer grip over politicians than they do today.[46] Moreover, changes in recruitment processes have produced increasingly partisan and personally ambitious parliamentary intakes. And such dispositions have been slowly climbing to high office to modify the typical desires and beliefs in ministerial roles.[47] The origins of role overload are easier to see: expansion of the Administrative State, and Britain's membership in the European Communities. Thus, legislation has become more complex, while the number of pages of the statute book devoted to public Acts has grown steadily. Membership in the European Communities has increased this complexity and thereby the work of most Ministers.[48]

The creation of the Central Policy Review Staff was an intended institutional "consequence" of these changes in ministerial roles, for it was created to strengthen the influence of Ministers by helping them to master their overloads.[49] Changes in ministerial roles during the 1970s and 1980s also produced, again intentionally, modifications in the protoconstitutional principle that interest groups have a right to be consulted about policy decisions that affect their interests. This type of functional representation was on its way to becoming constitutionally canonized during the 1970s by Ministers who had attached corporatist beliefs to their roles. But during the 1980s, they discarded the corporatist beliefs, attacked the principle of functional representation, and changed their role's characteristic behavior toward interest groups, particularly the trade unions.

Perhaps the most disturbing consequences that have been attributed to these changes in ministerial roles are (a) deterioration in the civility and character of debate in the House, and (b) the "evolution" of institutional and constitutional rules in directions that led Lord Denning, the Master of the Rolls, to warn that the politicians can no longer be trusted.[50]

Consider, for example, the collective and individual responsibility of Ministers. Collective responsibility requires Ministers, by voice and vote, to support government policy in public and to resign first if they wish to criticize their Government in public. But Ministers have frequently and with impunity leaked their dissatisfactions in order to curry favor with interest groups or party supporters.[51] Likewise, individual Ministers have disregarded with impunity the expectation that they should resign when an important policy fails with which they and their departments are identified. Increasingly, the resignation of a Minister has less to do with what the Constitution says than with what the Prime Minister and the Cabinet, for party-political reasons, decide.[52]

The stronger the Executive in a modern liberal democracy, the more it needs to be scrutinized by a strong Parliament and Opposition. Most commentators agree that Britain today needs some constitutional reform to reset this balance. But effective constitutional reform requires a theory about relationships between parliaments and parliamentarians and an account of parliamentary roles in context. It requires discovering how particular roles are affected by particular systemic and institutional conditions and what the consequences of changing such roles are likely to be. It requires, above all, understanding the principal career goals and emotional incentives that drive parliamentary roles and activate the reform process.

Motivations: Career Goals and Emotional Incentives

In this book I have tried to sort out the motivational components of parliamentary roles by listening carefully to the language and concepts of the role players. It has been a great advantage to be able to analyze verbatim transcripts of their discussions as a window to their own understandings. But the 521 Members of Parliament whose discussions have been analyzed in this way do not have consistent conceptual schemes, and using their language and concepts has left inconsistencies across the chapters. These need to be addressed, but addressed cautiously, for, as Pirandello never tired of reminding us through his plays: "I put in the words I utter the sense and value of things as I see them; while you must inevitably translate them according to the conception of things you have within yourself. We think we understand each other, but we never really do."

Pirandello's puzzle once drove psychologists to behaviorism and has recently driven some political scientists to rational choice theory. Both seek to avoid the difficulties of studying motivations by not studying motivations. But without satisfactory accounts of political motivations, it is impossible to construct satisfactory explanations of political roles, for these roles cannot be understood without understanding their players' purposes. It will not do to substitute for the empirical study of such motivations assumptions about operant conditioning or about egoistic utility-maximization. Even in cases where these strategies generate respectable *predictions,* they cannot generate *explanations* that will satisfy anyone except those methodological instrumentalists who declare predictive success the sole goal of social science.[53]

Cognitive career goals and emotional incentives are difficult to identify and more difficult still to unravel. Although we find it useful to talk about these desires and about the beliefs and actions with which they are associated as though they were all distinct entities, they are, in fact, not so easily distinguished from one another. Cognitions involve emotions and emotions involve cognitions—and actions are inherent products of the two.[54] This can be seen particularly clearly in the motivational structure of the role of the Specialist, where the cognitive goal of influencing the influential is intertwined with the sense of achievement, an emotional incentive. Both desires dwell on the same phenomenon, on the something that is done, on having "some effect on policy." But when Specialists think about this as a cognitive career goal, they think primarily about processes of influence and count up the strategies by which it is pursued. When they engage their emotional incentives, by contrast, they savor the results and contemplate the sense of achievement that it gives them.

CAREER GOALS AND POLITICAL VALUES

Moreover, although a limited number of goals and incentives appear to account adequately for the motivational structure of parliamentary roles, other variables are involved. Prominent among these are the political "values" that have appeared occasionally in this book. The values we have examined are either political "ideals," like capitalism and economic equality, or they are "means" by which ideal ends might be reached, like an empirical approach or social planning.[55] These very general constructs are neither career goals nor emotional incentives; but they might be associated with them and might have considerable motivational force of their own.[56] They might, but they don't, at least not in parliamentary roles at Westminster.

The correlations between the thirty-six political values in our rank-order measure and parliamentary roles are few and weak. There is enough there to suggest that values play some part in the roles, but not enough to suggest a consistent or dominant part. These results are similar to others reported in the literature.[57] Thus, the values that are connected to political roles are not the politically controversial ones, since parliamentary roles are framed by institutional structures that all MPs have in common, rather than by the more partisan parliamentary parties. Furthermore, the values that do the work are apparently related to self-conceptions:[58] "efficiency" for Policy Advocates who are full of projects and energy; "security" (but not "compassion") for Welfare Officers whose approach is practical and bureaucratic; and "intelligence" for Ministers who like to feel intelligent.[59]

Getting the career goals "right" is essential to successful interpretative explanation. The difficulty is that there are at least as many of them as there are roles and subtypes at Westminster. Thus, all Policy Advocates propose to influence the influential; but it is the Ideologues' predominant interest in abstract political ideas that sets them apart from the Specialists, whose goals entail specific pressures behind the scenes. The principal career goal of Constituency Members is redressing grievances; but it is the Welfare Officers' focus on individual constituents that distinguishes them from the Local Promoters, who concentrate on collective concerns. Aspirants likewise have an overriding goal: attaining office. But because High Flyers aim at the top, they play the role quite differently from the Subalterns who aim to become Junior Ministers. All Parliament Men are concerned with the institution. Yet one cannot understand them till one understands that Status Seekers are concerned with what the institution can do for their "visibility," Spectators with watching its dramas unfold, and Club Men with its agreeable atmosphere.

The career goals that guide leadership roles may be set by the institution but, as on the backbenches, they are many and, in the subroles, not so easily seen. Thus, all PPSs communicate with backbenchers and lighten ministerial loads, but Auxiliaries also propose to serve as confidants and Apprentices to learn the trade. Liaison, management, and discipline are the three general goals for Whips, whose subtypes are distinguished by their assigned aims. The Chief Whip, for instance, is required to organize and direct the Whips' Office, whereas the Deputy Chief manages it day-to-day. The goal of Junior Ministers is to assist senior Ministers; but this is interpreted quite differently by different Ministers, who use their Junior Ministers in quite different ways. In their own roles, Ministers focus on directing the Government in Whitehall and defending in Westminster the Government's policies. Yet within the context of these, their most general career goals, Politicians and Administrators pursue different paths.

EMOTIONAL INCENTIVES

Because emotional incentives are less cognitive than career goals, they are less well understood by role players and observers alike. Nevertheless, to identify them, we cannot do much more than rely on what the role players say and do. Some of our interview questions were semiprojective; and some of what our interviewees said was quite clear and convincing. These are highly intelligent people who think about and talk with one another about the incentives in parliamentary roles. I have done my best to listen, attentively and contextually, to their conversations.

Ideologues, for example, say they would "much rather be right than successful"; they talk about their desire for a sense of rectitude, for feelings of integrity, honesty, or uprightness. Generalists, by contrast, enjoy stirring coals and beating drums. They also like the action, the diversity, the publicity. And Specialists say they seek a sense of achievement, which is a motive not unlike the sense of competence or duty that intensifies the striving of Constituency Members. Although the ambition of Aspirants mixes cognitions and emotions more than most incentives, its emotional character is hard to miss in accounts of the attractions of moving ever "upwards" and of having "the driving force within" to do so successfully. These incentives are quite different from those that apparently move Parliament Men through their roles: a vicarious sense of importance, a desire for camaraderie, a tonic against boredom.

Parliamentary Private Secretaries discuss many similar emotional incentives, which is not surprising, since they are still in many respects backbenchers. Thus, the Apprentices among them talk about a vicarious sense of power, whereas the Auxiliaries discuss the satisfactions of being at the center of things. The desire for camaraderie also helps drive the roles of the Whip. But the motivational core here is, compared to backbench roles, multifarious. It encompasses the inside-dopesterism of Spectators, the sense of achievement of Specialists, the promotion hopes of Ministerial Aspirants, and the Generalist's love of action and diversity. In addition, ambition's emotional spurs are felt by some Whips—and by nearly all Ministers. Ministers have other desires as well, some of which drive the preference roles of Administrators or Politicians. But it is ambition that most fascinates them, and us.

Ambition, the desire for office, is distinguished in Westminster's world from the desire for influence. Unless we distinguish the two, it is easy to overestimate the proportion of MPs who have a serious, let alone dominant, desire for office. Their numbers have increased, but it remains true that a majority of backbenchers are either too busy, too old, too tired, or too eccentric for the race. Of course in addition to Ministerial Aspirants, there are upwardly mobile PPSs, Whips, Junior Ministers, Ministers, and Opposition Front Bench Spokesmen. Most of them are ambitious, and aware of it. They may not, as economic models suggest, always weigh the potential costs of seeking an office against the utility they expect to receive from holding the office while factoring in their probability of attaining the office. But neither are they the sleepwalkers of sociological theory. They think hard about their career prospects because these prospects matter to them.

The aspect of ambition that fascinates them most concerns a distinction between two interwoven motivational threads: an institutionally based focus on achieving public-policy goals, and an individually based focus on personal incentives. This is the distinction between the politician "who wants to use such power as comes his way" and the one "who wants to enjoy it," between the politician who desires power to accomplish aims and the one who desires power "to lord it over fellow creatures." The subject is so fascinating because it is so difficult to disentangle the two and because most ambitious politicians would like to believe, and would like us to believe, that they seek office mainly to introduce desirable public policies and not "primarily for reasons of *personal* ambition."

They know, and we know, that they do not simply pursue their private interests behind rationalizations about the public good.[60] But they also know, and we do too, that they do not simply desire "to use power for good" either. Most ambitious British politicians have ideas about public affairs and desire office to implement those ideas "on a grand scale." Yet they also appreciate Julian Critchley's comment that "fame is the spur. . . . And anyone in public life who tells you differently is not telling the truth." They may not put it quite so guilelessly, but Ministers make it clear that they very much like the admiration. They very much like the power as well, power to control institutions, procedures, policy programs—and people. Some are also attracted by the challenge, by the stimulation. They have a taste for the variety and even for the punishing pace. They find it exhilarating.

The aspect of this desire that should most fascinate political scientists is its *variability*. Politicians typically (not occasionally, but typically) adapt their ambitions to their changing circumstances. It is difficult to see this clearly from sociological viewpoints, because they give too much light to institutions and too little to individuals. Economic models help us see it better. Thus, Ministers modify their ambition by manipulating the utility that higher office holds for them. Some do this quite self-consciously, and some just do it. They do it to take account of new career experiences, changes in family circumstances, and changes in other incentives. This helps explain the fading ambition that we have seen among some of the most senior Ministers. It also helps explain the differences between High Flyers and Subalterns, Apprentices and Auxiliaries, Journeymen and Placemen. The less ambitious players in these pairs are often refreshingly realistic about their prospects. They minimize failure by managing ambition, by eschewing "an overwhelming ambition which, if unfulfilled, results almost always in a great feeling of bitterness, and you *sour your soul*." Perhaps equally remarkable is the fact that so many of their more ambitious colleagues succeed at the ministerial career game. They succeed because they are judged by the strength of their ambition, because they position themselves to be chosen, and because they eagerly accept whatever offers come their way.

One cannot but be impressed by the variety and complexity of the goals that guide parliamentary roles. This variety and complexity must be incorporated in interpretative explanations, for these goals are the central components of those explanations. To *predict,* it may sometimes be sufficient to posit a preference, even one "revealed" only by the actor's role behavior.[61] But unless this posited preference is the actual preference, all attempts at *explanation* are bound to fail, because the explanation cannot tell us what we want to know. The motivational approach is based on the economic assumption that role players are behaving rationally. Yet it only makes this assumption initially, since it also prepares us to find irrational and nonrational patterns such that the connections among a role's desires, beliefs, and actions are more "psychological" than "logical."[62] We need, therefore, wherever possible, to ask the actors themselves about their goals and to listen carefully as well as critically to what they say.

From the perspective of comparative political behavior, it may be the concepts of career goals and emotional incentives that travel best cross-nationally. The substance of these goals may, by contrast, be better suited to comparisons over time in their own evolving institutional and cultural contexts. Presumably that is why Members of Parliament read Trollope and Members of Congress do not. Let us now turn to other role concepts in our framework that have some potential for cross-national applications.

Politicians in Parliaments

The professionalization of parliamentary roles has strengthened institutional constraints and strained individual adaptations. Institutional constraints are reflected in the clarity, density, and power of the expectations that are associated with parliamentary roles. Individual adaptations concern the depth of psychological involvement in these roles and the experience of role strain.

EXPECTATIONS: CLARITY AND DENSITY

Constraint varies enormously from one parliamentary role to another. This is the first observation to emerge from our analysis and the most important guide for comparative research. Institutional constraints are applied through the clarity and density of the responsibilities that are attached to roles. Thus, the chief structural contrast between backbench roles and leadership roles is that the former are so much less constrained than the latter. Backbenchers have far more room for maneuver. They find a greater variety of informal roles associated with their position. And they are freer to pick and choose among these roles and to tailor them to suit their individual preferences. On the leadership side of the fence, by contrast, reliable performances are more vital to the institution, and responsibilities are precisely defined. Hence the greater constraint.

Even if we focus on the backbenches alone, we still find that constraint is plainly a variable, not a constant. The principal difference between Constituency Members and Parliament Men, for example, concerns the clarity of the expectations established for them. Thus, the Constituency Member is the best-known and most clearly defined role on the backbenches. Its name is recognized by constituents and Members of Parliament alike. Everyone understands its major goal: "serving one's constituency." Moreover, its subtypes, Welfare Officers and Local Promoters, are well known; and their different priorities (individual v. collective concerns) are familiar too. By contrast, the Parliament Man is the least clearly defined role that backbenchers play. It is not widely recognized, and its subtypes have subtypes of their own that would be recognized only by cognoscente of the Commons. Variety and eccentricity are the most striking impressions that Parliament Men create, for there are extremely few established expectations about how they should behave.

But although our backbench roles vary greatly among themselves in constraint, none of them is as constrained as sociological role theory would lead us to expect. Thus, Ministerial Aspirants are surprisingly uncertain about how their role might be played most effectively. Even the role of the Constituency Member, the clearest backbench role, has considerable ambiguities. Most Constituency Members do at least a little "social work," because it is hard to avoid. But many are uncertain about how appropriate this is; and some are certain that it isn't appropriate at all.

Leadership roles vary among themselves too, but they are arrayed across a sector of the spectrum that is more cordial to sociological stereotypes. Here we begin with the role of the Parliamentary Private Secretary, where the density of expectations is noticeably greater than the density found in backbench preference roles. Thus, the subtypes of the role of the PPS are few and fashioned more by the expectations of superiors than by the preferences of players. Parliamentary Private Secretaries may formally be backbenchers, but their role is nonetheless a position role with a common set of assigned duties.

The density of such duties becomes daunting in the role of the Whip. As the gears of the parliamentary machine, Whips' roles are so fully defined, so fully positional, that they leave room only for idiosyncratic interpretations, not for preference-based patterns of goals, attitudes, and behaviors. The expectations, which are clear and often written, keep out preference roles by keeping the Whips running from morning till night. Moreover, since reliable performances in their roles are critical, Whips are recruited very carefully. It won't do to stuff just any pegs into these carefully machined holes. Ministers are recruited carefully too, but not so much as Whips. Their subtypes are likewise dominated by formal assignments, but not so dominated as to exclude entirely the possibility of informal preference roles. The key to this difference between the institutional situations of Whips and Ministers is that Ministers are not on tap but instead are on top and have some authority to follow their own desires in emphasizing particular duties and deemphasizing others.

The institutional architecture of the House of Commons allows much more autonomy to backbenchers than to frontbenchers. It was, remember, a backbencher, not a Minister, who said, "Each man makes his own role." But even on the frontbenches, the existing expectations do not "determine" the way that roles are played. Even in the most constrained cases, these are still only scripts that must be interpreted by the politicians who play them.

EXPECTATIONS: POWER

When the expectations for how a role should be performed are clear and dense, their power can be considerable. "Power" refers to the control that such expectations exert over the individual. It varies primarily by how much others care about how the role is played and by the force of the rewards and sanctions involved.

From this viewpoint, what seems so peculiar about the role of the Ministerial Aspirant is that, although its expectations are quite unclear, its players cannot afford to play their parts as they please. The role is frustrating because their fate is in the hands of gatekeepers who do not say authoritatively what a good ministerial aspirant performance is, because they are not sure themselves. This frustration fades when Aspirants become Parliamentary Private Secretaries. But there is something unusual about the role of the PPS too. Clarity, density, and power promote uniformity. The role of the PPS has all three. And yet it is performed with so many different variations. The explanation here is that the most "relevant others," the Ministers who reward PPSs and can sack them at will, hold so many different expectations.

By increasing the power of parliamentary roles, professionalization has reduced the number of eccentrics at Westminster. Survivors are found mainly among Parliament Men and Policy Advocates. The roles of Parliament Men are relatively undefined because very few backbenchers, Ministers, or members of the public very much care about whether they are played one way or another. Hence, the proportion of quiet eccentrics is high. It is also high among Policy Advocates, although here the eccentrics are not so quiet, for they see in their role an opportunity to promote their unorthodox views. Actually, all four backbench roles have their "respected" and their "suspected" performances. The fact that respected types are not the only types that play these roles is evidence that the institutional power of established expectations is incompletely established in the House of Commons.

What is striking about the power behind the role of the Constituency Member is that the most forceful expectations come not from backbenchers but from outside the House, from the constituencies. This ancient parliamentary role was, in fact, revived by the demands of constituents, by a public that, as non-Constituency Members complain, has come to expect its MPs to be good Constituency Members, to be "county councillors at Westminster."[63] And yet these expectations are not powerful enough to be decisive when they clash with the individual preferences of the many backbenchers who become instead Policy Advocates, Ministerial Aspirants, or Parliament Men.

Ministers face powerful expectations from all quarters, since they are on stage and being judged all the time. Thus, they tell us that one of their role's most important goals is to persuade the House, and that the most persuasive Ministers are those with the most effective presentations of self. Ministerial careers are always on the line. The exaggerated accounts of structural role theory about how inadequate performances produce negative reactions in colleagues and traumatic reactions in role players[64] are not so very exaggerated when applied to Ministers. Even expectations from the other side have some power, because if one doesn't play according to the rules, "They" can "fix you." Likewise, ministerial colleagues are potential rivals among whom one needs to pay careful attention to one's reputation. To influence them, "one tries to behave in the way in which one's colleagues . . . generally *expect* Ministers to behave." Of course civil servants have expectations too. And then there are the department's key interest groups, and also the press, whose members have their own views about what constitutes appropriate ministerial behavior.

INVOLVEMENT AND IDENTITY

With "depth of involvement" we turn from institutional pressures to individual adaptations, to how much people care about the roles they are playing and how involved they become in them. In this context, Alasdair MacIntyre's notion of a "character role" draws attention to the important adaptations whereby players "fuse" their roles with their personalities, whereby their roles become involved with their self-esteem and with their images of themselves.[65]

At Westminster, professionalization has reduced to a minority the former majority of semidetached Members. But it is only in the most demanding roles, in those of Ministers and perhaps Whips, that we see signs of character roles that require their players to think and feel the part, to become psychologically dipped in the role and perhaps dominated by it. As with so many other aspects of roles, no one expresses the idea as brightly and playfully as does Pirandello: "A Character, sir, may always ask a man who he is. Because a character has really a life of his own, marked with his especial characteristics; for which reason he is always 'somebody.' But a man . . . may very well be 'nobody.'"

So "depth of involvement" is a matter of degree. Roles count as character roles when their depth noticeably affects the characters of most of their players. Moreover, depth of involvement varies within roles as well as across them. Most parliamentary roles have at least some players whose self-esteem and self-images become engaged. For instance, some Specialists, though not all or even a majority, seem completely immersed in their work and take it very seriously indeed. They are "workaholics," as are those Generalists (again a minority) who put down hundreds of Questions and talk about their "unquenchable thirst" for the chase. Such intensity is frequently associated with "identification," but not always. Not all intense High Flyers regard themselves as "politicians all the time." Identification with a role is easiest to spot when the players themselves describe their absorption through the language of "*I am* an originator," or "*I am* a right-wing politician." Some Ideologues speak this way—but others don't, like those who are simply waiting for the revolution or remembering things past.

The similarities between Parliamentary Private Secretaries and Whips are often noted, but on the dimension of involvement the contrasts are far more striking. Outside of a few cases, like PPSs to the Prime Minister, the role of the PPS is a part-time occupation. When PPSs talk about their work and life at Westminster, many do not talk at all about these roles. By contrast, when Whips are asked the same questions, they talk about little else besides. They become so absorbed with the life of the Whips' Office, with the strain, the strategy, and the brotherhood, that it colors their characters.

Many Ministers are at least as involved as Whips. They make the Ministry their life in an "inward sense," for ministerial roles are character roles, roles that are sufficiently all-embracing, and enticing, to tempt Ministers to disappear into the images of self that they present. When we asked Ministers about their identifications with the role of Member of Parliament, many answered by talking instead about their roles as Ministers, about how the attitudes and actions that are characteristic of their roles begin to define who they are, first perhaps in the eyes of others and then eventually in their own eyes. Particularly among senior Ministers, these roles routinely become so absorbing that the players "become, er, well sort of absorbed."

"Role distance" is the antithesis of involvement in a character role. Instead of fusing our self-images with the role's images, we try to insulate our self-images from them. This is done by letting others know that we are not really the sort of people for whom such images are suitable. It would be difficult to play our principal roles without involving our identities in them at all. But when negative stereotypes are associated with a role, this is precisely what we try to do. For example, it is the social-work aspects of the role of the Constituency Member that draw disdain from other MPs. Since

Welfare Officers do the most along these lines, they are the most vulnerable. And some react with role distance, which they express through jokes ("silly old man went to hear a pension tribunal"), apologies ("in a sense this is not perhaps what an MP should be doing"), and explanations ("all right, there is *nothing wrong* with that. The great thing is that you are able to do it"). The stereotypes are more negative in the case of the Parliamentary Private Secretary: the "dogsbody," the Minister's "fag," "a PPS is a total nonjob." And yet the typical Parliamentary Private Secretary seems more enthusiastic than humiliated. The explanation is that this role is very transitory. At the same time, some role distance is evident among a minority of PPSs—the Auxiliaries, who are much more likely than Apprentices to make the self-deprecating jokes ("My youngest daughter describes me as the 'Minister's Fag' ") and to offer the apologetic explanations.

In role distance, one plays at separating one's self from a role whose negative images one wants to avoid. In "role taking," by contrast, one plays at playing a role whose positive images one wants to adopt. This is done by imagining oneself in the role, by empathizing with the role players, and by practicing occasionally some of its characteristic desires, beliefs, or behaviors.

Taking a role in this way is a mode of "anticipatory socialization" and a common learning experience in apprenticeships. Junior Ministers, for instance, have many opportunities to imagine themselves as Ministers, because they are quite literally understudies and frequently on stage. On behalf of the Minister, they attend committee meetings and handle Adjournment Debates and Written and Oral Questions. Parliamentary Private Secretaries who are Apprentices are also licensed to take the role, for as part of their training they are expected to absorb attitudes that will facilitate their adjustment to the Ministry should they eventually come inside. Likewise, those Ministerial Aspirants who are High Flyers scrutinize Ministers' performances and occasionally try on aspects of ministerial outlooks. As they do so, they begin to think about the role of the Minister as a role for "Me" rather than only for "Them."

The last aspect of role involvement that we have considered concerns the adaptations of MPs who see themselves as outside the mainstream and sometimes as outsiders. These are the politicians who are playing "antiroles," roles that are themselves a little antiestablishment. This is certainly the way some Ideologues see it—"very much as *an outsider* within my party in the House." They are irritated by institutions in general and by this institution in particular. Status Seekers resent the place too and tend to see themselves as misfits or as marginal Members who are on the fringe and are seen by others as on the fringe. It is no accident that their general role type, Parliament Man, is an exit role, or that some Spectators sound like slightly detached supporters of the institution. In a similar vein, the Placemen among Junior Ministers can be painfully uneasy about their sinecures and occasionally talk as though they were outside the Ministry looking in.

The relationship between roles and identities has always been a central concern of sociological symbolic interactionists, a concern they trace back to work done at the turn of the century by the philosopher and psychologist William James.[66] But compared to modern sociological theory, which has its actors absorbing roles in response to the expectations of their associates, James's ideas were more rational and less complicated.[67] People are most likely to integrate new roles with their social conceptions of themselves, he argued, when the new roles are compatible with these conceptions and with the emotional incentives that drive them.

ROLE STRAIN: CONFLICT AND OVERLOAD

Role strain is the second general, individually oriented feature of parliamentary roles that we have examined. It addresses two different situations: role conflict, where players face conflicting expectations about how they should behave, and role overload, where players are assigned many more tasks than they feel they can reasonably accomplish. Both situations are more likely to be found in position roles than in preference roles.

Whips provide the most striking example of role conflict. They are expected by party leaders to be their agents and to deliver the votes of backbenchers in every whipped division. But they are expected by backbenchers to be their friends and to advocate their views to party leaders. It is difficult to imagine in political life role conflicts more acute than this: both Ministers and backbenchers have clear expectations about how Whips should behave; conflicts of interest between the two sides can be very intense; and both Ministers and backbenchers are very well placed to observe disappointing performances. The dismal prospects that structural role theory projects for adaptations to such situations fit remarkably well here: excessive self-control, tension, and enough discomfort to ensure that hardly anyone ever returns for a second tour of duty.

Interactionist theories, by contrast, expect people to adapt to role conflict by working out solutions that take account of their career goals and emotional incentives.[68] With a little license, this view can be reworked into a purposive account that fits fairly well the reactions of Ministers to the role conflicts that they encounter with Parliament and their constituencies.

At Westminster, their ministerial colleagues and civil servants expect Ministers to act as agents of the Government and to push through the department's legislation unscathed in the shortest possible time. But the party's backbenchers expect Ministers to demonstrate loyalty to Parliament by including them in the legislative process and by modifying Bills to take account of their contributions. Guided by individual goals and incentives, Ministers handle these conflicts by adopting the preference role of the Administrator or the Politician. At the same time, they still face incompatible expectations between virtually all the political groups with whom they deal as Ministers on the one side, and their constituents on the other. Thus, everyone in Westminster and Whitehall expects the Minister to think like a Minister who is engaged in national and international affairs. But the Minister's constituents expect him or her to think like a Constituency Member whose attention is at least occasionally engaged by their local concerns. Here Ministers lean one way or the other according to whether they see themselves primarily as Members of the Government in Parliament or as Members of Parliament in the Government.

Whips describe their job as the most tiring they have ever had. Tiring it may be, but "role overload" it is not, because most of them do not feel they have been assigned more tasks than can reasonably be accomplished. Ministers, by contrast, cannot accomplish everything that is expected, and most of them understand this dilemma. Either there is insufficient time to accomplish all their responsibilities, or accomplishing them all would require being in different places at the same time. Busy senior Ministers therefore concentrate on some and do the minimum on others. Thus, role overload forces choices as well as headaches and, more than anything else, wears Ministers down. More remarkable than the magnitude of this overload are the variations in ministerial reactions to it. For there are Ministers who, while their colleagues are swallowing pills and taking days off, are instead managing the work, managing their subordinates, managing the tension—and seeming to grow younger rather than older with the passing months and years. Those who thrive best on the overload are said to have strong constitutions; but it may also be that the "strain" in role strain is not always as stressful as it seems.

Clarity, density, power, identity, conflict, and overload—these role concepts have been brought to Westminster from other institutions to facilitate understanding parliamentary roles. Together with the sorts of general mechanisms that we have uncovered in perception, ambition, and authority, such constructs do valuable explanatory work in the study of political behavior, explanatory work that is too often confounded with the search for illusory covering laws or hidden in the construction of idiosyncratic narratives.[69] It is not possible to foresee which constructs will best fit particular situations. Nor is it possible to foresee how they will have to be modified to fit particular situations effectively. But it is possible to recognize their relevance and use their insights to help explain important political phenomena like parliamentary roles.

The more one studies parliamentary roles "up close," the more one is impressed by the fact that they both constrain and enable their players; and the more one is therefore puzzled by the either-or nature of the debate between those who argue that institutions shape individuals and those who argue the opposite point of view.[70] The sociological perspective in the study of roles has emphasized the former; the economic perspective, the latter.[71] I have drawn upon both to construct for the new institutionalism a motivational approach that analyzes the interplay between institutional contexts and rational individuals.

The sociological constraints in these institutional contexts can be seen clearly even in the evolution of backbench preference roles. For although individual desires and beliefs shape these roles, the fact is that backbenchers are at the same time adjusting to roles that already exist in an already-existing institutional context. Even here, where the formally prescribed duties and responsibilities are minimal and where actors tell themselves that they make their own roles, the outcome is four general roles that serve four of Parliament's established functions. Institutional constraints work by setting rules and by setting up situations. They also work by shaping the desires and beliefs of the politicians who encounter the rules and pass through the situations.[72]

Conversely, the economic tradition reminds us of the contribution of individual choice and of the very important fact that roles provide the material resources, the power, the legitimacy, and the cooperation to pursue successfully many actions that could never be achieved by the individual alone. The economic tradition emphasizes the malleability of established institutional arrangements, which can be modified by the rationally autonomous desires, beliefs, and behavior of individual role players. The idea that individuals can always to some degree make their roles and remake the institutional rules within which these roles are embedded may seem controversial to some philosophers; but in the end this idea seems very uncontroversial to political role players and to the observers who study them "up close."

APPENDICES

NOTES

INDEX

Interviewing Members of Parliament

The project began during the summer of 1971 when I established an office at the University of Essex. During that autumn, Elizabeth Crighton, Christopher Game, Janet Morgan, and I developed the survey instruments through pretests with former Members of Parliament and with students at Oxford, the London School of Economics, and the University of Essex. The first interviews were conducted at the House of Commons in January 1972. They were difficult to arrange, for MPs had recently been irritated by a run of academic studies. It took twenty-one months, till September 1973, to complete the project's 521 tape-recorded interviews. The transcriptions began after these interviews were safely under way and ended twenty-two months later in the spring of 1974. Finally, the coding process consumed yet another eighteen months, carrying on into 1975.

The study's design called for a "saturation sample" in order to provide sufficient numbers of respondents for analyses of Parliament's many subunits and subgroups. We set out to interview all 630 Members and succeeded in interviewing 521 of them, 83 percent of the population. It wasn't easy. The interviews were long and complicated because they sought conversational discussions on a series of general topics as well as detailed information on specific settings in the House about which particular interviewees were knowledgeable. Each Member of Parliament was approached, in other words, as a respondent whose general views would be used, along with the views of colleagues, to reconstruct the institutional context. But each was also approached as an expert informant whose particular experiences (which had been researched before the interviews began) could help illuminate specific aspects of the parliamentary system. This book relies on both types of information. From this perspective, the value of the saturation sample should be apparent. When there are only twenty-eight Whips, for instance, fourteen on each side, and when each side operates its whipping system somewhat differently, even a relatively large random sample of the 630 Members would have been unlikely to turn up enough Whips to reconstruct convincingly their work with backbenchers. In the same vein, given the dozens of very small and very important groups, committees, and offices to be examined, even an elaborately stratified random sample could not have provided enough informants in all these categories.

The interviews were conducted in a variety of settings at the Palace of Westminster, in Whitehall, and around the country. Most discussions with backbenchers, Whips, and Parliamentary Private Secretaries took place in the privacy of Westminster's interview rooms and meeting rooms, although some also took place in corridors, alcoves, cramped offices, or on the terrace. Ministers were usually interviewed either in their departments, where the privacy was good and the comforts better, or in their offices off the ministerial corridor at the House. Other interviews weren't so convenient. To achieve the required response rate, we met MPs at any time and any place that suited them. This took us from Edinburgh to Bristol and Norwich, from homes in London to homes in the constituency, from London offices to country houses and Saturday surgeries. Moreover, since MPs tend to have peculiar schedules, these meetings were conducted at all hours of the morning, afternoon, and evening and at late-night sittings. Late-night sittings worked well because some Members were so bored by one o'clock in the morning that even an academic interview looked attractive. The interviews lasted approximately one and a half hours on average, with a range between a half hour and five hours. Conversations with Ministers were usually shorter than average; conversations with backbenchers were usually longer. Our questions were designed to be answered adequately in forty-five minutes. Yet most respondents were very generous, and we got far more information than we had anticipated.

To prepare for these interviews, we took considerable trouble to compile background information on each Member of Parliament. This was collected and cross-checked from published sources that were sometimes inconsistent and required further checking. The effort was worth it, because it permitted us to take into each interview useful information about the Member's career, including data about previous positions and committee service. In addition, we had at hand basic facts about his or her constituency, social and educational background, and work outside Parliament. This saved time by saving questions. And it developed good rapport. Members were pleased that we had "done our homework" and knew so much about them and their careers.

The interviews followed a schedule, but MPs were encouraged to develop their thoughts on the topics that interested them most. Often, they could not be discouraged from doing so—which explains some of the five-hour interviews. They were asked, in addition, to fill out several printed forms (very unpopular) and to return a mailback questionnaire. The centerpiece of the exercise was the tape-recorded interview. Few Members objected to the tape recorder, and most seemed genuinely to ignore its presence on the table. This was a consequence, they told us, of the fact that MPs had themselves recently begun to do their correspondence with tape recorders much like those we carried.[1]

The interview schedule had been reworked through pretests with former MPs till it created reasonable approximations of conversational interviews. This was the format that several former MPs suggested would be most likely to make Members comfortable and win us the insights we sought. The conversational structure was enhanced by ordering the sequence of open- and closed-ended items so as to maximize the conversational flow. This structure was further developed by reworking the closed-ended questions until response categories like "many, some, few" would not have to be read aloud in order to elicit responses that fell into them, albeit they were printed on the interview schedule so the interviewers could check to see that they had obtained codable responses. The open-ended questions were accompanied by specific probes, which we discovered could also be used to good effect with the closed-ended questions. Such probes helped guide the conversations into the channels that were needed for coding purposes and, no less important, helped make our sometimes peculiar-sounding questions more acceptable than they might otherwise have been.

For studying the roles of politicians, open-ended questions are generally superior to closed-ended items. In particular, the use of closed-ended questions is likely to create distortions when little is known about a parliament's roles. It is all too easy to misinterpret the willingness of politicians to respond to such questions as evidence that the prefabricated roles measured by the questions actually exist in their minds.[2] Moreover, if roles are different in different parliaments, it seems best to work with this fact rather than try to squeeze them all into one cross-national mold. Of course open-ended questions have serious problems too. They require more time to administer, are more troublesome to code, and more likely to impede cross-national research. Further, respondents may not have much to say about certain roles in this context, not because they don't care about them, but because they do not normally think about them a great deal.[3] In the present study, fortunately, Members of Parliament had a lot to say about their roles and were as reflective about them as were the political commentators who wrote on the subject.

They told us about their roles. But did they tell us the truth about their roles? All the interviews were conducted on "a nonattribution basis." This phrase, which MPs use with political journalists, means that nothing they say can be attributed to them without their explicit permission. They assume that they will not be disappointed, for detection is likely and the penalties are severe.[4] This facilitated frankness. Besides, most of the interview's topics concerned institutional matters, career information, or beliefs that were simply too abstract to seem politically sensitive.[5] Members had little reason to disguise their views.

Along with the interviews, three other types of data were gathered: mailback questionnaires, records of behavior, and information from participant observation.[6] The mailback questionnaires were given to MPs, along with a self-addressed envelope, at the end of their interviews. These forms included some standard attitude scales, items about political issues, and questions about how MPs distribute their time. Since the form included a chart to be filled in, as well as fifty-eight items with Likert-type scales; since among all academic techniques the mail questionnaire is the most despised by MPs; and since we had already taken up a considerable bit of their time, it is not surprising that a significant minority did not return the material. One and in some cases two detailed follow-up letters raised the response rate for the mailback questionnaires to 79 percent.

Data about the respondents' behavior were gathered through these mailback questionnaires and also during the interviews. But the bulk of the project's records on behavior came from published sources. These included attendance at Standing and Select Committees; memberships in ideological groups and ginger groups such as the Tribune Group and the Monday Club; data on the Oral and Written Questions asked by MPs; records of crossvoting (voting with the other side); frequency of participation in divisions, which is a crude indicator of attendance; and information on ideological reputations based largely on conduct. Some of the most valuable information about behavior came from my experiences with what Richard Fenno calls the soaking and poking of participant observation. For nearly two years, I drank with Members in Westminster's bars, ate with them in the dining rooms, and during the summer months chatted with them over strawberries and cream on the terrace. From both the Strangers' Gallery and the Box, I watched Members perform in the Chamber. I also visited their homes and offices in London and in the country, and their surgeries in their constituencies. I spent mornings with Whips in the Whips' Office, afternoons with Ministers and their civil servants, and hours with backbenchers roaming the neo-Gothic lobbies, corridors, and committee rooms of the House. I interviewed a disgraced Whip in a pub in Leeds and a dispirited Minister in a park in Bristol. I rode in trains and cars with Members of the Cabinet and had breakfast with their children. I interviewed MPs in the clubs of Pall Mall and listened to them talk with their assistants on walks through the countryside.

My hosts were extraordinarily hospitable and introduced me to most of the places in the Palace of Westminster where Strangers are permitted to go. I poked about the Ministries in Whitehall a little too. I was therefore able to observe many typical role performances many times over. I observed relationships between PPSs and Ministers and backbenchers. I observed relationships between Junior Ministers and senior Ministers and between them and their civil servants. I sat in the background as Ministers played their parts with backbenchers, with representatives of interest groups, and with other Ministers. From the background I also watched backbenchers deal with other backbenchers on their own side and with those opposite. And I watched from the foreground as I helped MPs entertain their constituents. But my most instructive soaking, and that for which I am most grateful, took place in the Whips' Offices, where I sat by the file cabinets with my tape recorder off but with my eyes and ears opened wide as Whips plotted with other Whips and as backbenchers arrived for requests and reprimands. I am particularly grateful to these Whips, to these extraordinarily astute managers of men and women, for giving me the access that they did, for occasionally whipping-in reluctant backbenchers to face my tape recorders, and above all for sharing with me their insights and understandings about how roles are played out at Westminster.

Nevertheless, when all is said and done, perhaps these experiences are indeed properly described as soaking and poking rather than as systematic participant observation. For the more I became immersed in Westminster's many worlds, the more I realized how little of these worlds I was actually seeing. Participant observation is one of the most revealing methods of empirical investigation. I sometimes learned more from watching Whips and backbenchers play their parts, for instance, than I did from a week's worth of formal interviews. But at Westminster, most areas behind the scenes are off limits to Strangers—and many of the most important performances occur behind these scenes. My soaking and poking has been invaluable, but it has also been misleading. I have tried, therefore, to use it prudently as a source of hypotheses and as a background against which the interviews can be interpreted.

Beyond the pleasant interviews and participant observations lie the tedious tasks of transcription and coding. The transcription of the interview tapes was organized by me and run by the project's administrative secretaries. They supervised a pool of six typists who worked part-time on the materials for nearly two years at the University of Essex to produce approximately thirty thousand single-spaced pages, which were then checked and corrected against the tapes by myself or by one of the administrative secretaries. For these transcriptions, the typists were given detailed instructions, the most important of which was that we required every word on the tapes, the exact words, uncorrected for grammar and unaltered in any way. When words were inaudible, the typists were not to guess but instead to leave blank spaces. Long pauses were to be indicated by a series of periods, and "pause sounds" such as "um," "ah," "er," and "oh" were to be included as well.[7] Such attention to the conversational flow may seem excessive, but when used during the analysis along with other signs, it can signal boredom, confusion, and especially discomfort in the respondent's reactions to a question or topic. This has sometimes proved invaluable in interpreting and coding the transcripts.

Finally, assisted by graduate students of British politics, I coded the background data, mailback data, and data from the printed forms that had been filled out during the interviews. This work was then proofed against the original materials. The closed-ended interview data from the transcripts was more difficult to code, but not that much more difficult, owing to the structure built in during the pretesting. These codes were likewise proofed. The transcribed, open-ended conversations were coded at different times but usually by two people and, again, usually proofed through several stages.

APPENDIX B

Coding Preference Roles

Everyone needs typologies to think and talk intelligently about political life. Even historians who emphasize the unique cannot avoid terms that presuppose typologies, terms like "left-wing Tory" or "strong Prime Minister." This book has been organized around two typologies, one of formal leadership roles and one of informal backbench roles. Typologies make diversity intelligible by squeezing out the idiosyncratic. When they become too abstract, however, they lose their explanatory grounding. Thus, in studying political behavior, it is desirable to tether typologies to the constructs that are actually in the minds of the political actors being studied.

Typologies of formal position roles are constructed by their institutions. Moreover, there is no ambiguity about who is playing such roles at any given time. A special methodology is needed, however, to identify informal preference roles and their players. The most important, and problematic, preference roles in this book are the four principal roles played on Westminster's backbenches. The themes around which these roles are built dominate backbench political life writ large and the coding for the more concrete subroles that emerge within their frameworks. Coding criteria and intercoder reliabilities have been reported throughout the book. But the recovery of these four "architectonic" backbench roles required complex procedures that need further discussion. We developed a strategy to extract from the transcribed data empirical types based on central tendencies.[1] These are not Weberian ideal types that deliberately distort experience for theoretical pur-

poses. Yet they are not photographic representations either. The four principal backbench roles are instead "extracted types" constructed from the transcribed language and concepts of the role players themselves.[2] We set out
to abstract from the transcripts roles that would be somewhat more general,
and generally more revealing, than the particular views of particular actors.
The basic work was done by Edward Crowe, who created measures of
career-related goals and investigated their validity as part of his dissertation
research.[3] The motivational approach defines roles as patterns of goals, attitudes, and behaviors that are characteristic of people in particular positions.
Furthermore, the rationality principle of situational analysis leads us to presume that politicians' roles are usually driven by goals: career goals and
emotional incentives. Our coding efforts concentrated on such goals. We
wished to understand what backbenchers understood to be the motivational
foci of backbench roles, what they understood to be the set of desires that
guided them and their colleagues in organizing their work at Westminster.
The full-blown roles would be reconstructed in the book. Here the task was
to recover the motivational cores.

The situational model draws attention to role players' accounts of problem situations in which they find themselves. We used the accounts that
backbenchers presented in response to five questions that were formulated,
with probes, to elicit contextually based information about career goals and
emotional incentives. These open-ended questions had been developed
through pretests with former Members of Parliament. The first asked backbenchers to characterize the broadest and most significant aspects of their
work.[4] This often-used item taps what is appropriately called a purposive
role, since backbenchers typically respond by describing what they do in
terms of why they do it. They relate their activities to their goals. They also
discuss the symbolic system of roles within which their own role is situated.

The second question, introduced as a follow-up to the first, moved the
discussion beyond describing roles to evaluating their importance.[5] Its semiprojective format was designed to encourage respondents to elaborate on the
themes that they personally regarded as most significant. The third question
sought to explore more fully the emotional incentives in backbench roles.[6]
Accompanied by a series of follow-ups and probes, it was designed to create
a discussion of satisfactions that could be used for several different measures. The most successful result was a rich harvest of comments about motivations involved in those aspects of backbench roles that respondents liked
best and least. The fourth and fifth questions tapped ambition, a subject
that MPs were reluctant to introduce in the context of the first three general
questions, but were willing to consider when approached with direct ques-

tions, politely put.[7] The first of these questions asked about aspirations for attaining further positions and elicited comments about career ladders and what it took to move from one rung to the next. The other asked about the likelihood of attaining such positions and drew the discussion away from the general situation and back to the interviewees' own prospects.[8]

By using these five quite different questions, we hoped to avoid the common bias of coding responses that are peculiar to a single context. As we immersed ourselves, in a few sittings, in approximately half the transcripts, we sought to develop a sense of the major patterns being expressed there. In this way, Crowe and I independently identified four roughly similar backbench preference roles: Policy Advocates, Ministerial Aspirants, Constituency Members, and Parliament Men.[9] During the next few years, we examined the transcripts again and again. And neither of us found any reason to change substantially our interpretations of the major patterns in which these backbenchers thought about the subject.

At the same time, we identified the following motivational themes, which were eventually specified further in detailed coding instructions. Policy advocate themes: promoting political goals and issues; influencing party leaders and Ministers; campaigning to modify government policy or party programs. Constituency member themes: resolving problems of individual constituents; resolving collective problems of the constituency; influencing government policies to aid the constituency as a whole. Parliament man themes: being at the center of things; enjoying the status associated with MPs' roles; enjoying the traditions and atmosphere of the House of Commons. Returning to the transcripts, Crowe then coded instances of these themes in responses to the first three role questions, each in turn: Q1—descriptions; Q2—evaluations; Q3—motivations. This work was designed to generate composite scores that would enable us to associate particular individuals with particular roles.

Our procedure extracted from each backbencher's response to each question three distinct scores, one for each role. These scores used four values: "theme central to discussion—example used" (value = 3);[10] "theme central to discussion" (value = 2); "theme present in discussion" (value = 1); "theme absent" (value = 0). Since the fourth and fifth questions (which tapped ambition) were considerably more focused than the others, the material they produced was inadequate for the same thematic coding. Hence, they were scored on their own two dimensions. One coded in detail the particular positions that respondents desired. The other coded, again in detail, the respondents' assessments of their chances of achieving these positions.

Next, each backbencher was assigned a summary score for the roles of the Policy Advocate and the Constituency Member by summing his or her respective coded values (3–0) across the first three questions. These "composite scores" therefore varied between 9 and 0. We soon realized, however, that for the role of the Parliament Man this procedure was introducing a bias toward underestimating the role's frequency: only one of the three questions (Q3—motivations) in practice elicited the Parliament Man's themes.[11] And if only one question was tapping this role, then its composite scores could vary only between 3 and 0 and would not be comparable with the composite scores for the policy advocate and constituency member themes (which, because they combined scores from all three questions, varied between 9 and 0). We resolved this difficulty by multiplying by 3 the scores for Parliament Man themes in Q3. It was more difficult still to achieve comparability in coding motivational themes for the role of the Ministerial Aspirant. To generate the composite scores here, two sets of preliminary scores were constructed from the transcripts. One coded the positions that backbenchers desired according to the standing of these positions in Westminster's hierarchy. The other coded their assessments about their chances of achieving these positions. Permutations of the combinations of these two scores were then assigned to summary composite scores that varied between 9 and 0.[12]

The purpose of these complicated procedures was (a) to construct systematically a map of the motivational cores of backbench roles, which would help resolve a problem that has long been confounded by overlapping labels and definitions, and (b) to construct a method for matching backbenchers with particular motivational themes, which would facilitate reconstructing the roles and investigating their origins and consequences. Both purposes converge on the construction of the empirical typology. Thus, each backbencher had, up to this point, been assigned four composite scores, one for each of the sets of motivational themes associated with the roles of Policy Advocate, Ministerial Aspirant, Constituency Member, and Parliament Man. The empirical typology was generated by comparing each respondent's composite scores and assigning him or her to that role for which his or her composite score was highest.[13] To assess the results produced by this procedure, two questions must be addressed. First, are the role assignments reasonably valid? Second, are the role categories reasonably mutually exclusive?

Because backbench preference roles are framed by institutional goals, it is perhaps not surprising that Crowe and I independently identified from the transcripts roughly similar general roles and motivational themes. But from the perspective of validity, our measurement procedure segmented the role phenomena and then constructed wholes from these segments. Immersed in parts rather than wholes, a coder might have lost perspective and produced scores that in the end added up to a peculiar set of classifications. This does not, however, appear to have happened. One important check is whether another coder, using a yardstick rather than a ruler, would, for example, regard as Constituency Members those who had been classified as such by the additive procedures. Thus, the principal investigator, who had not done the original coding, examined three years later each backbencher's responses to all of the role questions and made "global" coding judgments about appropriate role assignments. These qualitative classifications matched extremely well the assignments generated by the additive procedures (Scott's $\pi = .87$).[14]

We can also count as validity probes many of the quantitative analyses in the chapters on backbench roles; analyses of relationships between the motivational cores and characteristic attitudes and behaviors; and analyses of relationships between the roles themselves and attitudes and behaviors beyond their borders. These can be interpreted as validity checks in the sense that they investigate whether the motivational cores, or the roles constructed around them, do indeed structure the sorts of attitudes and behaviors that they would, as organizing principles, be expected to structure.

From the quite different perspective of epistemological rationalism, interpretative accounts of roles win certification when they seem intelligible to those who are familiar with the institutional worlds they purport to explain. Thus, the fact that backbenchers recognize our four architectonic backbench roles buttresses their plausibility. The All-Party Reform Group of MPs, for instance, produced a list of roles nearly all of which fit neatly under the umbrellas of Policy Advocates, Ministerial Aspirants, and Constituency Members.[15] Likewise, most political observers who have written about backbench roles mention Policy Advocates (e.g., "Educator and Explainer," "Promoter of Causes and Interests"), Constituency Members (e.g., "Constituency Welfare Officer," "Constituency Representative"), and Ministerial Aspirants (e.g., "Ministerialists," "High Flyers").[16] The role of Parliament Man is the only one missing from such lists. Still, this may be less because it is unrecognized (e.g., "Good House of Commons Man," "Squire," "Knights of the Shires") than because it is played today by so few Members of Parliament.

But are the role categories reasonably mutually exclusive? Are they, in other words, sufficiently distinct from one another to justify characterizing most backbenchers, at any given stage in their careers, as primarily playing one of these roles rather than several?[17] The roles are constructed around motivational goals much like David Mayhew's "reelection" goal or Richard Fenno's "making good public policy."[18] Such goals have been suspected of misleading us by definition to assume incorrectly that one chief goal guides a politician's behavior across several different contexts. Actually, I think that career goals tend to be robust in just this way. They are particularly likely to be arranged hierarchically and to carry across contexts, for they are developed to serve the "cross-contextual" purpose of guiding the politician's career.

Still, we already know that our four principal backbench roles are not completely mutually exclusive. Backbenchers play several at the same time and, in the course of their careers, transfer their predominant interest from one to another. Indeed, since these are empirical rather than ideal types, it would be peculiar if they were completely mutually exclusive. Nevertheless, to justify themselves for present purposes they must be reasonably distinct. And an indication that they are reasonably distinct is the fact that only 6.5 percent of the backbenchers had ties among their composite scores. In other words, nearly all of them had only one top score. Moreover, although the remaining three scores were rarely negligible, they were not systematically interdependent. The interitem correlations among them were very low.[19] The composite scores for the role of the Policy Advocate, for example, show that most backbenchers do dabble in this role. But the highest scores in policy advocacy are built up by backbenchers with the widest interests or the keenest specializations, by backbenchers who see the role of the Policy Advocate as the principal part they are playing on Westminster's stage. Much the same pattern applies to the role of the Constituency Member: nearly everyone does some, but only a minority makes it a principal preoccupation.[20]

The integrity of the role categories was explored further by a confirmatory factor analysis of the items from which the roles were generated. This analysis, the results of which are presented in Table B.1, investigated (a) whether the four role dimensions created by the additive indices actually structured the original data, and (b) whether the sets of items that were used to construct each composite score actually dominated their own separate factors. From an oblique rotation of the original eleven items, five factors were generated with eigen values above 1.00, the first four of which explained 57 percent of the variance. These factors correspond well to the general role dimensions that were constructed with the additive indices. And, with the exception of the measures for Parliament Men, each set clusters together to define a different factor. The interfactor correlations, presented at the bottom of the table, are low and therefore consistent with the hypothesis that the factors are fairly distinct and do not fade into one another.

Table B.1 Factor analysis of indicators from which composite scores for MP roles were constructed*

Indicators	Factor 1	Factor 2	Factor 3	Factor 4	Factor 5
Ministerial Aspirants					
Question 1	.925	−.067	−.077	−.064	−.068
Question 2	.923	−.074	−.072	−.053	−.050
Policy Advocates					
Question 1	−.080	.686	−.040	−.083	.072
Question 2	−.082	.783	−.034	−.044	−.150
Question 3	.387	.501	.218	.142	.273
Constituency Members					
Question 1	−.096	.068	.731	−.159	.100
Question 2	.088	−.274	.383	−.580	.288
Question 3	−.051	−.131	.748	.021	.088
Parliament Men					
Question 1	−.097	.027	−.143	.064	.891
Question 2	−.082	−.215	−.078	.836	.169
Question 3	−.091	−.071	−.071	−.279	.212
Percent variance explained	18%	15%	13%	10%	09%

		Interfactor correlations			
Factor	Factor 2	Factor 3	Factor 4	Factor 5	
1	.05	.12	−.00	.03	
2		.05	.07	−.09	
3			.01	−.01	
4				−.03	

*Based on data from all backbenchers. Oblique rotation used.

Factor 1 clearly represents the Ministerial Aspirants' dimension. It is dominated by the two aspirant themes and produces no other notable loadings except for Q3 from the advocate set.[21] In the same way, factor 2 is dominated by the Policy Advocates' themes. And factor 3 offers a similarly unambiguous picture, defined in this case by the thematic measures for Constituency Members. Each of these first three factors demonstrates its distinctiveness by a pattern of weak negative relationships with measures for the other role types. The measures for the motivational themes of Parliament Men are the odd ones out in this analysis, since they load on two different factors, 4 and 5. Factor 4 is dominated by one parliament man item. But it is disappointing that this role type's Q3 does not load positively on any dimension except factor 5, the least crystallized factor in the set. These difficulties may be a consequence of both measurement error and heterogeneity.[22]

With the exception of the measures for Parliament Men, then, the factor structure matches well the number and character of the role dimensions that we generated through the use of additive indices. And the sets of items that were used to construct the composite scores tend to dominate distinct factors. Certainly backbenchers act in roles beyond their primary roles; but they do not do so systematically enough to produce strong associations or vigorously enough to undermine the presumption that four reasonably distinct motivational cores have been isolated.

NOTES

Preface

1. In this process, sociology and political science have often been out of synchronization. Thus, since the mid-1970s, formal institutional analysis has been enjoying its turn with political scientists who study legislatures, while sociologists have moved back toward the informal, subjective aspects of organizational culture. During the 1950s and 1960s it was the other way round: political scientists concentrated on the culture of legislatures, while sociology was dominated by more formal and institutional approaches to organizations. William G. Ouchi and Alan L. Wilkins, "Organizational Culture," *Annual Review of Sociology* (1985): 458–68.

2. Clifford Geertz, *The Interpretation of Cultures* (New York: Basic Books, 1973): chap. 1.

3. David Braybrooke, *Philosophy of Social Science* (Englewood Cliffs: Prentice-Hall, 1987).

4. "It is with the kind of material produced by long-term . . . and almost obsessively fine-comb field study in confined contexts," Geertz argued, "that the mega-concepts with which contemporary social science is afflicted . . . can be given the sort of sensible actuality that makes it possible to think not only realistically and concretely *about* them, but, what is more important, creatively and imaginatively *with* them." *Interpretation of Cultures,* 23. This also involves, for the type of social science that I like best, the analysis of mechanisms, such as reciprocity and role distance, that may be found across institutions as well as cross-nationally. Although it is difficult to predict exactly where or when such mechanisms are likely to be uncovered, familiarity with their typical structure and dynamics can greatly facilitate the explanation, after the fact, of important instances of phenomena such as authority

and representation. Jon Elster, *Political Psychology* (Cambridge: Cambridge University Press, 1993): 2–7.

5. Nevil Johnson, *In Search of the Constitution: Reflections on State and Society in Britain* (Oxford: Pergamon, 1977): 42.

6. For example: Julian Critchley, *The Palace of Varieties: An Insider's View of Westminster* (London: Faber and Faber, 1990); Edward Pearce, *Hummingbirds and Hyenas* (London: Faber and Faber, 1985).

7. Hugh Berrington's comments on the subject are still apt: "A cynic might aver that the amount of intellectual energy devoted to understanding the behaviour of political participants varies inversely with their importance. In the last twenty-five years, scholars and polling organizations have accumulated a vast amount of information about the motives and opinions of ordinary electors. We know, however, very little of a *systematic* kind about top decision-makers, except that they are drawn disproportionately from the well-educated and the well-to-do." "The Fiery Chariot: British Prime Ministers and the Search for Love," *British Journal of Political Science* 4, 3 (1974): 347.

8. Sir Lewis Namier, *Skyscrapers and Other Essays* (London: Macmillan, 1931): 53.

9. Edward Crowe, "Purpose in Politics: The Influence of Career Goals on Attitudes and Behavior in the House of Commons," Ph.D. diss., University of North Carolina, Chapel Hill, 1982.

10. Peter Winch, *The Idea of a Social Science* (London: Routledge and Kegan Paul, 1958).

1. Introduction

1. Bruce J. Biddle, "Recent Developments in Role Theory," *Annual Review of Sociology* 12 (1986): 67.

2. James G. March and Johan P. Olsen, *Rediscovering Institutions: The Organizational Basis of Politics* (New York: Free Press, 1989); Kenneth A. Shepsle, "Studying Institutions: Some Lessons from the Rational Choice Approach," *Journal of Theoretical Politics* 1 (1989): 131–47; Karen Schweers Cook and Margaret Levi (eds.), *The Limits of Rationality.* (Chicago: University of Chicago Press, 1990): Part III.

3. March and Olsen, *Rediscovering Institutions,* 5.

4. Richard L. Hall, "Participation in Congressional Committees," Ph.D. diss., University of North Carolina, Chapel Hill, 1985; Barbara Sinclair, "Purposive Behavior in the U.S. Congress: A Review Essay," *Legislative Studies Quarterly* 8, 1 (1983): 117–32; John A. Ferejohn and Morris P. Fiorina, "Purposive Models of Legislative Behavior," *American Economic Review* 65, 2 (1975): 407–14.

5. David R. Mayhew, "Congressional Elections: The Case of the Vanishing Marginals," *Polity* 6, 3 (1974): 295–317; Richard F. Fenno, *Congressmen in Committees* (Boston: Little, Brown, 1973); Kenneth A. Shepsle, *The Giant Jigsaw Puzzle: Democratic Committee Assignments in the Modern House* (Chicago: University of Chicago Press, 1978); Steven S. Smith and Christopher J. Deering, *Committees in Congress* (Washington, D.C.: Congressional Quarterly Press, 1984).

6. March and Olsen, *Rediscovering Institutions.*

7. Herbert Simon, *Administrative Behavior* (New York: Free Press, 1957).

8. Philip Selznick, "An Approach to a Theory of Bureaucracy," *American Sociological Review* 8 (1943): 47–84. Norms prescribe particular attitudes and behaviors. Roles are more complex for, as we shall see, they prescribe *sets* of attitudes and behaviors and can vary even more than do norms in their prescriptive force.

9. Shepsle, "Studying Institutions," 135.

10. James G. March and Johan P. Olsen. "The New Institutionalism: Organizational Factors in Political Life," *American Political Science Review* 78, 3 (1984): 734–49. More irritating still for rational choice models is the fact that many informal rules are actually designed to encourage people to behave some of the time as though they were *not rational egoists*. See Jon Elster, *The Cement of Society: A Study of Social Order* (New York: Oxford University Press, 1989); and M. W. Jackson, "Chocolate-Box Soldiers: A Critique of 'An Economic Theory of Military Tactics,' " *Journal of Economic Behavior and Organization* 8 (1987): 1–11.

11. Elster, *Cement of Society.*

12. R. M. Punnett, *Front Bench Opposition* (London: Heinemann, 1973): 287ff.

13. Selective recruitment is the most obvious alternative explanation for the greater voting cohesion on the Conservative and Labour frontbenches than on their respective backbenches. This explanation would suggest that those recruited to the frontbenches are mainly MPs who either agree with their party leaders or are psychological conformists, or both. However, further analyses of the respondents' political values and policy preferences show that, within each party, the distribution of opinion on the frontbenches resembles the distribution of opinion on the backbenches. This is perhaps not surprising, because each party needs, for the sake of party unity, to represent on the frontbench most of its significant parliamentary groups and factions. The frontbenches also include their share of difficult characters, for they always take in some potential troublemakers to silence them under the collective responsibility rule.

14. Jerold Heiss, "Social Roles," in Morris Rosenberg and Ralph H. Turner (eds.), *Social Psychology: Sociological Perspectives* (New York: Basic Books, 1981): 94–127; Bruce J. Biddle, *Role Theory: Expectations, Identities and Behaviors* (New York: Academic Press, 1979): 55–58.

15. Some of the worst muddles were resolved early on. But these efforts had little impact on subsequent research. See Lionel J. Neiman and James W. Hughes, "The Problem of the Concept of Role: A Re-Survey of the Literature," *Social Forces* 30, 2 (1951): 141–49; and Neal Gross, Ward Mason, and Alexander McEachern (eds.), *Explorations in Role Analysis* (New York: Wiley, 1966). I will in this chapter argue for the general (though certainly not exclusive) utility of a "politician-focused" definition of roles as configurations of goals, attitudes, and behaviors that are characteristic of people in particular positions.

16. Sheldon Stryker and Anne Statham, "Symbolic Interaction and Role Theory," in Gardner Lindzey and Elliot Aronson (eds.), *The Handbook of Social Psychology*, 3rd ed., vol. 1 (New York: Random House, 1986): 312; Biddle, "Recent Developments in Role Theory," 86.

17. Stryker and Statham, "Symbolic Interaction and Role Theory," 349.

18. For a fuller discussion see Donald Searing, "Roles, Rules and Rationality in the New Institutionalism," *American Political Science Review* 85, 4 (1991): 1239–61. The examples in Table 1.2 are drawn from the following sources: Joel D. Aberbach, Robert D. Putnam, and Bert A. Rockman, *Bureaucrats and Politicians in Western Democracies* (Cambridge, Mass.: Harvard University Press, 1981); James David Barber, *The Lawmakers: Recruitment and Adaptation to Legislative Life* (New Haven: Yale University Press, 1965); Bruce E. Cain, John A. Ferejohn, and Morris P. Fiorina, "The House Is Not a Home: British MPs in Their Constituencies," *Legislative Studies Quarterly* 4, 4 (1979): 501–23; Philip E. Converse and Roy Pierce, *Political Representation in France* (Cambridge, Mass.: Harvard University Press, 1986); Roger H. Davidson, *The Role of the Congressman* (New York: Bobbs-Merrill, 1969); Richard F. Fenno, "U.S. House Members in Their Constituencies," *American Political Science Review* 73, 1 (1977): 883–917; Ralph K. Huitt, "The Outsider in the Senate: An Alternative Role," *American Political Science Review* 55, 3 (1961): 566–75; Malcolm E. Jewell and Samuel C. Patterson, *The Legislative Process in the United States,* 3rd ed. (New York: Random House, 1977); Anthony King, *British Members of Parliament: A Self-Portrait* (London: Macmillan, 1974); John F. Manley, "Wilbur D. Mills: A Study in Congressional Influence," *American Political Science Review* 63, 2 (1969): 442–64; Donald R. Matthews, *U.S. Senators and Their World* (New York: Random House, 1960); K. Newton, "Role Orientations and Their Sources among Elected Representatives in English Local Politics," *Journal of Politics* 36, 3 (1974): 615–36; James L. Payne, "Show Horses and Work Horses in the United States House of Representatives," *Polity* 12, 3 (1980): 428–56; John Wahlke, Heinz Eulau, William Buchanan, and Leroy Ferguson, *The Legislative System* (New York: Wiley, 1962); Oliver H. Woshinsky, *The French Deputy* (Lexington, Mass.: D. C. Heath, 1973).

19. Ralph Linton, *The Study of Man: An Introduction* (New York: Appleton, 1936); Robert K. Merton, *Social Theory and Social Structure* (New York: Free Press, 1967); Robert K. Merton and Elinor Barber, "Sociological Ambivalence," in Edward A. Tiryakian (ed.), *Sociological Theory, Values, and Sociological Change: Essays in Honor of Pitirim A. Sorokin* (New York: Free Press, 1963): 91–120; Robert K. Merton, "The Role-Set: Problems in Sociological Theory," *British Journal of Sociology* 8 (1957): 106–20; Florian Znaniecki, *Social Relations and Social Roles* (San Francisco: Chandler, 1965); Talcott Parsons, *Social Structure and Personality* (New York: Free Press, 1964).

20. George C. Homans, "Bringing Men Back In," *American Sociological Review* 29, 5 (1964): 809–820.

21. Dennis H. Wrong, "The Oversocialized Conception of Man in Modern Sociology," in Neil J. Smelser and William T. Smelser (eds.), *Personality and Social Systems* (New York: Wiley, 1963): 68–79; Malcolm E. Jewell, "Attitudinal Determinants of Legislative Behavior: The Utility of Role Analysis," in Allan Kornberg and Lloyd D. Musolf (eds.), *Legislatures in Developmental Perspective* (Durham, N.C.: Duke University Press, 1970): 460–500.

22. Stryker and Statham, "Symbolic Interaction and Role Theory," 331. Struc-

tural-functional analysis proposed to study the polity, economy, and society as vast blueprints of roles with each of these "basic units" (roles) clearly specified, and with each individual associated with a series of basic units.

23. Biddle, "Recent Developments in Role Theory," 70–71. The tendency of the structural approach to create "oversocialized" images of people in worlds of homogeneity and conformity was corrected somewhat by Robert Merton's observation that the expectations established for a role often involve inconsistencies. Merton and Barber, "Sociological Ambivalence"; Merton, "Role-Set." Recent structural research has built on these observations and now takes it for granted that some confusion and inconsistency are the usual state of affairs rather than a departure from normality. Warren Handel, "Normative Expectations and the Emergence of Meaning as Solutions to Problems: Convergence of Structural and Interactionist Views," *American Journal of Sociology* 84, 4 (1979): 855–81; Heiss, "Social Roles."

24. Sheldon Stryker and Richard T. Serpe, "Commitment, Identity Salience, and Role Behavior: Theory and Research Example," in William Ickes and Eric S. Knowles (eds.), *Personality, Roles and Social Behavior* (New York: Springer Verlag, 1982): chap. 7.

25. George Herbert Mead, *Mind, Self and Society* (Chicago: University of Chicago Press, 1934); Ralph H. Turner, "Role: Sociological Aspects," in David L. Sills (ed.), *International Encyclopedia of the Social Sciences,* vol. 13 (New York: Macmillan and Free Press, 1968): 552–57; Ralph H. Turner, "Role-Taking: Process versus Conformity," in Arnold Rose (ed.), *Human Behavior and Social Processes* (Boston: Houghton Mifflin, 1962); Herbert Blumer, "Sociological Implications of the Thought of George Herbert Mead," *American Journal of Sociology* 71 (1966): 535–44; Herbert Blumer, "Society as Symbolic Interaction," in Rose, *Human Behavior and Social Processes,* 179–92; Erving Goffman, *The Presentation of Self in Everyday Life* (Garden City, N.Y.: Doubleday, 1959).

26. Bernard N. Meltzer, John W. Petras, and Larry T. Reynolds, *Symbolic Interactionism* (London: Routledge and Kegan Paul, 1975); Handel, "Normative Expectations and the Emergence of Meaning as Solutions to Problems."

27. Biddle, "Recent Developments in Role Theory," 71–72.

28. Mead, in *Mind, Self and Society,* argued that social interaction creates one's mind as well as one's self in an ongoing process. From this viewpoint, personality becomes no more than a set of social roles that the individual is currently playing.

29. Interactional approaches reject the assumption that behavior is determined by the external force of established norms. Instead, they argue that behavior is determined by the ongoing flow of interactions with one's associates. The individual's basic goals and emotional incentives are, however, frequently overlooked in the interactionists' empirical accounts, which are typically sociologistic and depict people far more as social products than as social producers. See Stryker and Serpe, "Commitment, Identity Salience and Role Behavior." This tendency to submerge the rational individual in the flow of interaction has been corrected by attributing motivational significance to "chance desires" (Ralph H. Turner, "The Real Self: From Institution to Impulse," *American Journal of Sociology* 81, 5 [1976]: 989–1015) and by attributing conditioning effects to institutional contexts: Handel, "Normative

Expectations and the Emergence of Meaning as Solutions to Problems"; Stryker and Statham, "Symbolic Interaction and Role Theory," 313. But neither corrective has been carried far enough to secure for the individual a convincing autonomous viewpoint.

30. Stryker and Statham, "Symbolic Interaction and Role Theory," 311–78.

31. Roland Cayrol, Jean-Luc Parodi, and Colette Yamal, "L'Image de la fonction parlementaire chez les députés français," *Revue français de science politique* 21, 6 (1971): 1173–1206.

32. The methods used by motivational studies have been varied, but the most successful has usually proved to be the semistructured interview, an alternative between the structuralists' detailed questionnaires and the "soaking and poking" of the interactionists. The numbers of individuals studied is frequently in-between too, since convincing motivational accounts require substantial samples, but the need for elaborate discussions makes it difficult for these samples to become very large.

33. Bruce Headey, *British Cabinet Ministers: The Roles of Politicians in Executive Office* (London: Allen and Unwin, 1974). In the same vein, when Ian Budge and his associates examined the role of councillors in Glasgow, they, like their respondents, interpreted this subject to mean "the question of what councillors should do." The role types they produced were therefore constructed around career goals. *Political Stratification and Democracy* (London: Macmillan, 1972). See also Austin Mitchell, M.P., "Consulting the Workers: MPs on Their Job," *The Parliamentarian* 66, 1 (1985): 9–13; and Charles L. Clapp, *The Congressman: His Work as He Sees It* (Washington, D.C.: Brookings Institution, 1963).

34. For example: Peter G. Richards, *The Backbenchers* (London: Faber and Faber, 1972); Richard Rose, "British MPs: A Bite as Well as a Bark?" *Studies in Public Policy* 98, University of Strathclyde, 1982; and Kenneth O. Morgan, *Labour People: Leaders and Lieutenants, Hardie to Kinnock* (Oxford: Oxford University Press, 1987).

35. Sir Lewis Namier, *The Structure of Politics at the Accession of George III* (London: Macmillan, 1968).

36. John Wahlke, Heinz Eulau, William Buchanan, and LeRoy Ferguson, *The Legislative System* (New York: Wiley, 1962). See also John R. Johannes and John C. McAdams, "Entrepreneur or Agent: Congressmen and the Distribution of Casework, 1977–1978," *Western Political Quarterly* 40 (1987): 535–54; Chong Lim Kim, Joel D. Barken, Iltef Turan, and Malcolm E. Jewell, *The Legislative Connection: The Representative and the Represented in Kenya, Korea and Turkey* (Durham, N.C.: Duke University Press, 1983); William Mishler and Anthony Mughan, "Representing the Celtic Fringe: Devolution and Legislative Behavior in Scotland and Wales," *Legislative Studies Quarterly* 3, 3 (1978): 377–408; Allan Kornberg and William Mishler, *Influence in Parliament: Canada* (Durham, N.C.: Duke University Press, 1976); Peter Gerlich, "Orientations in Decision-Making in the Vienna City Council," in Samuel C. Patterson and John C. Wahlke (eds.), *Comparative Legislative Behavior: Frontiers of Research* (New York: Wiley, 1972): 87–106.

37. Donald R. Matthews, *U.S. Senators and Their World* (New York: Random House, 1960).

38. Malcolm E. Jewell, "Legislator-Constituency Relations and the Representative Process," *Legislative Studies Quarterly* 8, 3 (1983): 303–38.

39. Oliver H. Woshinsky, *The French Deputy* (Lexington, Mass.: D. C. Heath, 1973); James David Barber, *The Lawmakers: Recruitment and Adaptation to Legislative Life* (New Haven: Yale University Press, 1965).

40. Fenno, *Congressmen in Committees.*

41. Ronald D. Hedlund, "Organizational Attributes of Legislative Institutions: Structure, Rules, Norms, Resources," in Gerhard Loewenberg, Samuel C. Patterson, and Malcolm E. Jewell (eds.), *Handbook of Legislative Research* (Cambridge, Mass.: Harvard University Press, 1985): 326.

42. Wahlke, Eulau, Buchanan, and Ferguson, *Legislative System,* Ronald D. Hedlund and H. Paul Friesema, "Representatives' Perceptions of Constituency Opinion," *Journal of Politics* 34, 3 (1972): 730–52; H. Paul Friesema and Ronald D. Hedlund, "The Reality of Representational Roles," in Norman Luttbeg (ed.), *Public Opinion and Public Policy,* rev. ed. (Homewood, Ill.: Dorsey Press, 1974): 413–17; Donald A. Gross, "Representative Styles and Legislative Behavior," *Western Political Quarterly* 31, 3 (1978): 359–71.

43. Converse and Pierce, *Political Representation in France,* 681.

44. Kent C. Price, "Instability in Representational Role Orientation in a State Legislature: A Research Note," *Western Political Quarterly* 38, 1 (1985): 162–71.

45. Eugene J. Alpert, "A Reconceptualization of Representational Role Theory," *Legislative Studies Quarterly* 4, 4 (1979): 587–603.

46. James H. Kuklinski with Richard C. Elling, "Representational Role, Constituency Opinion, and Legislative Roll-Call Behavior," *American Journal of Political Science* 21, 1 (1977): 135–47; Donald J. McCrone and James H. Kuklinski, "The Delegate Theory of Representation," *American Journal of Political Science* 23, 2 (1979): 278–300; Glenn Abney and Thomas A. Henderson, "Role Orientations toward Subconstituencies: State Legislators and Local Officials," *Polity* 15, 2 (1982): 295–304; Converse and Pierce, *Political Representation in France.*

47. Martin Hollis and Steve Smith, "Roles and Reasons in Foreign Policy Decision Making," *British Journal of Political Science* 16, 3 (1986): 272.

48. Alasdair MacIntyre, *After Virtue,* 2nd ed. (Notre Dame, Ind.: University of Notre Dame Press, 1984): 31–33.

49. Hollis and Smith, "Roles and Reasons in Foreign Policy Decision Making," 278.

50. See, for example, Karl Popper, "The Rationality Principle," in David Miller (ed.), *Popper Selections* (Princeton: Princeton University Press, 1985): 357–65; Karl Popper, "The Logic of the Social Sciences," in Theodore Adorno et al. (eds.), *The Positivist Dispute in German Sociology* (New York: Harper and Row, 1976): 87–104.

51. James Farr, "Resituating Explanation," in Terence Ball (ed.), *Idioms of Inquiry* (Albany: State University of New York Press, 1987): 45–64; James Farr, "Situational Analysis: Explanation in Political Science," *Journal of Politics* 47, 4 (1985): 1085–1108.

52. Farr, "Resituating Explanation," 52. See also Jon Elster, "When Rationality

Fails," in Karen Schweers Cook and Margaret Levi (eds.), *The Limits of Rationality* (Chicago: University of Chicago Press, 1990): 19–59. This is less restrictive than the rationality principle that Karl Popper recommended, though what exactly Popper recommended is not at all clear: some say an unfalsifiable assumption; some say a universal law that is known to be false; some say a methodological principle used to generate predictions. Bruce J. Caldwell, "Clarifying Popper," *Journal of Economic Literature* 29 (1991): 1–33. The confusion arises because Popper wrote so little about the subject and because economists have such a large stake in how the ambiguity is resolved. The new institutionalism might best be served by saying "none of the above" and adopting Farr's reconstruction.

    53. Shepsle, "Studying Institutions," 135.

    54. March and Olsen, *Rediscovering Institutions*, 48.

    55. Simon Evnine, *Donald Davidson* (Stanford: Stanford University Press, 1991); Alexander Rosenberg, *Philosophy of Social Science* (Oxford: Oxford University Press, 1988); David Braybrooke, *Philosophy of Social Science* (Englewood Cliffs: Prentice-Hall, 1987); Brian Fay and J. Donald Moon, "What Would an Adequate Philosophy of Social Science Look Like?" *Philosophy of Social Science* 7 (1977): 209–27; Donald Davidson, "Actions, Reasons and Causes," *Journal of Philosophy* 60 (1963): 685–700.

    56. Their thinking is used as the point of departure here, because although ignoring it may be necessary for certain theoretical purposes, such strategies often create role concepts that have little to do with the political behaviors we seek to explain. In particular, it seems desirable to avoid definitions of roles that include only observable behavior, since politicians understand the concept to mean far more than that. See Biddle, *Role Theory*, 58. Politicians want to know what is going on in the *minds* of their associates—and so do we. This politician-focused perspective also suggests that although the alternative rational choice strategy of using unrealistic assumptions about politicians' motivations as theoretical premises (the "as if" strategy) may help to predict events or clarify normative claims, it is usually ill-suited for constructing satisfactory *explanations* of *empirical* phenomena. Empirical explanations are unlikely to be convincing when their basic theoretical premises are presumed incorrect: Terry M. Moe, "On the Scientific Status of Rational Models," *American Journal of Political Science* 23 (1979): 215–43; Timothy J. McKeown, "The Limitations of Structural Theories of Commercial Policy," *International Organization* 40 (1986): 43–64.

    57. Jerome Bruner, *Actual Minds, Possible Worlds* (Cambridge, Mass.: Harvard University Press, 1986). Thus, Sir Lewis Namier often argued that politicians are "rational beings . . . who are never (rarely?) moved by reason alone." *Avenues of History* (London: Hamish Hamilton, 1952): 1. See also his *Skyscrapers and Other Essays* (London: Macmillan, 1931).

    58. Charles Taylor, *Philosophy and the Human Sciences* (Cambridge: Cambridge University Press, 1985): 23.

    59. Bruner, *Actual Minds, Possible Worlds*, 110–11.

    60. See March and Olsen, *Rediscovering Institutions*, 6.

    61. The motivational approach does not ignore questions about relationships be-

tween role attitudes and role behaviors. Wherever possible, these linkages must be established empirically in order for specific items to be counted as part of the definition of a specific role.

62. As Hollis and Smith put it, this rationality involves much more than the calculation of expected utilities for means to achieve ends that remain unquestioned: "Our actors *interpret* information, *monitor* their performance, *reassess* their goals. The leading idea is that of reasoned judgment, not of manipulation." "Roles and Reasons in Foreign Policy Decision Making," 283.

63. Braybrooke, *Philosophy of Social Science,* 12.

64. Braybrooke, *Philosophy of Social Science,* 98.

65. Farr, "Resituating Explanation," 51–52.

66. Giovanni Sartori, "Comparing and Miscomparing," *Journal of Theoretical Politics* 3, 3 (1991): 252.

67. This is still an unchallenged assumption in most discussions of explanation in comparative politics. See David Collier, "New Perspectives on the Comparative Method," in Dankwart A. Rustow and Kenneth Paul Erikson (eds.), *Comparative Political Dynamics: Global Research Perspectives* (New York: Harper Collins, 1991): 7–31.

68. See the very diverse list compiled by Malcolm E. Jewell, "Legislator-Constituency Relations and the Representative Process," *Legislative Studies Quarterly* 8, 3 (1983): 316–17.

69. Alexander Rosenberg, *Philosophy of Social Science* (Oxford: Oxford University Press, 1988); Fay and Moon, "What Would an Adequate Philosophy of Social Science Look Like?" Giovanni Sartori, "Concept Misformation in Comparative Politics," *American Political Science Review* 64, 4 (1970): 1033–53. Despite the fact that the inspiration for the American-crafted, theoretically oriented concepts of "delegates" and "trustees" was drawn from Edmund Burke, even British politicians do not see themselves in these terms—or share with Americans anything like equivalent denotations for them. Compare Heinz Eulau, John Wahlke, William Buchanan, and LeRoy Ferguson, "The Role of the Representative: Some Empirical Observations on the Theory of Edmund Burke," *American Political Science Review* 53 (1959): 742–56, with John P. Mackintosh, M.P., "Attitudes to the Representative Role of Parliament: Introduction," in John P. Mackintosh, M.P. (ed.), *People and Parliament* (London: Saxon House, 1978): 1–9.

70. See Taylor, *Philosophy and the Human Sciences,* vol. 2, chap. 1.

71. Richard J. Bernstein, *The Restructuring of Social and Political Theory* (Philadelphia: University of Pennsylvania Press, 1976): 1.

72. Rosenberg, *Philosophy of Social Science,* 109–11.

73. Rosenberg, *Philosophy of Social Science,* 92.

74. Taylor, *Philosophy and the Human Sciences,* 17.

75. Farr, "Resituating Explanation," 54.

76. Max Weber, *The Theory of Social and Economic Organization* (New York: Free Press, 1947): 111–12.

77. Lord Wigg, *George Wigg* (London: Michael Joseph, 1972).

78. March and Olsen, *Rediscovering Institutions.*

79. Despite all the institutional changes that we as academics are so careful to chronicle, Anthony Lester could still claim confidently in 1989 that "an MP who sat in the Commons in 1900 would find little in the present framework of operations to surprise him." "The Constitution: Decline and Renewal," in Jeffrey Jowell and Dawn Oliver (eds.), *The Changing Constitution,* 2nd ed. (Oxford: Oxford University Press, 1989): 345–69. See also Harris N. Miller, "Future Research on Parliament," in Dennis Kavanaugh and Richard Rose (eds.), *New Trends in British Politics: Issues for Research* (London: Sage, 1977): 123, and Lisanne Radice, Elizabeth Vallance, and Virginia Willis, *Member of Parliament: The Job of a Backbencher,* 2nd ed. (London: Macmillan, 1990). The House has increasingly become a busier place, much busier. Consequently, leadership roles have become increasingly constrained, while overlaps among backbench preference roles have increased and their distributions have tilted to favor Policy Advocates and Constituency Members. Nevertheless, the similarities, particularly throughout the postwar period, are far greater than the differences.

80. The 1970s transformed Britain's collectivist polity through what Samuel Beer characterized as pluralistic stagnation, class decomposition, and "populism." Pluralistic stagnation refers to political immobility over a benefits scramble among workers and a subsidy scramble among employers. Class decomposition refers to crumbling bonds between social class and party support as the cracks of dealignment began to appear. And populism refers here to the fact that constituents were demanding more from their MPs and respecting them less, while new MPs were becoming increasingly reluctant to get along by going along. *Britain against Itself* (New York: Norton, 1982).

81. Harold Wilson, *The Labour Government, 1964–1970: A Personal Record* (London: Weidenfeld and Nicolson and Michael Joseph, 1971): 224.

82. Colin Mellors, *The British MP: A Socio-Economic Study of the House of Commons* (London: Saxon House, 1978): 123–24; Michael Rush, "The Members of Parliament," in S. A. Walkland and Michael Ryle (eds.), *The Commons Today* (London: Fontana, 1981): 39–63.

83. Philip Norton, *Conservative Dissidents: Dissent within the Parliamentary Conservative Party, 1970–1974* (London: Temple Smith, 1978): 212–13. The term "professionalization" refers to the adoption by members of an occupation of some of the characteristics that are commonly associated with the typical professions. Prominent among these characteristics is the attempt to use special knowledge to claim authority over decisions that concern particular areas of ordinary life. See Andrew Abbott, *The System of Professions* (Chicago: University of Chicago Press, 1988): chap. 1; A. M. Carr-Saunders and P. A. Wilson, *The Professions* (Oxford: Oxford University Press, 1933): 4.

84. *The Times,* 24 September 1971.

85. *The Daily Telegraph,* 6 March 1972.

Part I. Backbench Roles

1. The role concept itself implies that roles are "played" more than they are "made," that a script is already written, that expectations are established. Sheldon

Stryker and Anne Statham, "Symbolic Interaction and Role Theory," in Gardner Lindzey and Elliot Aronson (eds.), *The Handbook of Social Psychology*, 3rd ed., vol. 1 (New York: Random House, 1985): 323.

2. See Maurice Natanson, *Phenomenology, Role and Reason* (Springfield, Ill.: Charles C. Thomas, 1974): 213.

3. Malcolm E. Jewell, "Legislators and Constituents in the Representative Process," in Gerhard Loewenberg, Samuel C. Patterson, and Malcolm E. Jewell (eds.), *Handbook of Legislative Research* (Cambridge, Mass.: Harvard University Press, 1985): 10.

4. See Appendix B.

5. Compare these backbench roles to those suggested by MPs in response to the 1983 survey conducted by the All-Party Reform Group: Lisanne Radice, Elizabeth Vallance, and Virginia Willis, *Member of Parliament: The Job of the Backbencher*, 2nd ed. (London: Macmillan, 1990): 130.

6. For a description of the goals of the House of Commons that is close to that presented here, see Philip Norton, *The Commons in Perspective* (Oxford: Martin Robinson, 1981): chap. 4. See also Michael Rush, *Parliament and the Public*, 2nd ed. (London: Longman, 1986): 24ff.

7. Walter Bagehot, *The English Constitution* (London: Collins/Fontana, 1963 [1867]): chap. 5.

2. Policy Advocates

1. Anthony King, "The Rise of the Career Politician in Britain—and Its Consequences," *British Journal of Political Science* 11 (1981): 249–85; John E. Schwarz, "Exploring a New Role in Policy Making: The British House of Commons in the 1970s," *American Political Science Review* 74 (1980): 23–37; Richard Rose, "British MPs: A Bite as Well as a Bark?" *Studies in Public Policy* 98, University of Strathclyde, 1982.

2. Philip Norton, "Party Committees in the House of Commons," *Parliamentary Affairs* 36 (1983): 7–10.

3. Gavin Drewry, "The New Select Committee System at Westminster," *The Parliamentarian* 64 (1983): 57–63.

4. D. H. Close, "The Growth of Backbench Organization in the Conservative Party," *Parliamentary Affairs* 27 (1974): 372; King, "Rise of the Career Politician in Britain," 249–86.

5. *The Times*, 22 July 1971; Gavin Drewry, "The 1979 Reforms—New Labels on Old Bottles?" in Gavin Drewry (ed.), *The New Select Committees: A Study of the 1979 Reforms* (Oxford: Oxford University Press, 1985): 368.

6. Andrew Abbott, *The System of Professions* (Chicago: University of Chicago Press, 1988): 315–16; Robert A. Rothman, "Deprofessionalization: The Case of Law in America," *Sociology of Work and Occupations* 11 (1984): 183–206; Douglas Klegon, "The Sociology of Professions: An Emerging Perspective," *Sociology of Work and Occupations* 5 (1978): 259–83; Wilbert E. Moore, *The Professions: Roles and Rules* (New York: Russell Sage, 1970); J. A. Jackson, *Professions and Profes-*

sionalization (London: Cambridge University Press, 1970); A. M. Carr-Saunders and P. A. Wilson, *The Professions* (Oxford: Oxford University Press, 1933).

7. The contrast between these outlooks and those of Constituency Members constitutes the most important fault line among backbench roles: a division between politicians who are immersed in constituency matters and politicians who pursue wider issues in Chamber and committee. This is the key distinction that backbenchers themselves are most likely to put forward whenever they consider "the different types of Member. You see, there are a large number of chaps who are totally immersed in purely constituency matters . . . and they would never dream of going outside that. Others look wider. . . . Therefore I think you've got to subdivide people between the Constituency Member, who is dedicated to his job as a Constituency Member, as distinct from those who want to influence wider issues of national and international politics."

8. John P. Mackintosh, *The British Cabinet,* 3rd ed. (London: Stevens and Sons, 1977): 613.

9. Richards, *Backbenchers,* 49–54.

10. "Members of Parliament are completely different," they say. "Some have ambitions to be Ministers, some will act as Welfare Officers." By contrast, they want to achieve things on the fields of influence and policy: "I've always wanted to get something done. I've always wanted to influence. I'm not interested in playing games, I'm interested in something achieved."

11. Scott's measure of intercoder agreement (π), which corrects for the number of categories and for the frequency with which they are used, is 0.86 for the coding of Ideologues, Generalists, and Specialists. This measure varies between 0.00 and 1.00 and is comparable to a "percentage agreement" score. William A. Scott, "Reliability of Content Analysis: The Case of Nominal Scale Coding," *Public Opinion Quarterly* 19, 3 (1955): 321–25. See also Robert T. Craig, "Generalization of Scott's Index of Intercoder Agreement," *Public Opinion Quarterly* 45, 2 (1981): 260–64; and Graham Kalton and Richard Stowell, "A Study of Coder Variability," *Applied Statistics* 28, 3 (1979): 276–89.

12. The most significant Ideologue of the 1970s was certainly Enoch Powell, who was often characterized as "distinctly fundamentalist in his approach in contrast to his more pragmatic colleagues." Andrew Roth, *Enoch Powell: Tory Tribune* (London: Macdonald, 1970): 50. Robert D. Putnam, *The Beliefs of Politicians: Ideology, Conflict and Democracy in Britain and Italy* (New Haven: Yale University Press, 1973), found more Ideologues than I do on the backbenches because his search was not limited to Policy Advocates and because he used a stylistic definition that emphasized analytic thinking. Here I focus instead on the substance of what respondents say—which leaves mainly Marxists on the Labour side and Tory populists across the floor, backbenchers who say emphatically that the character of their role is determined by the fact that "I personally have these right-wing (or left-wing) views which I endeavour to propagate."

13. Since Conservative Ministers paid more attention to their backbenchers during this period than did Labour Ministers, specialization promised greater gratification on the Conservative side. Another factor is that Conservative MPs are likely to

have business backgrounds that provide expertise in particular areas such as chemical industries, foreign trade, or finance. By contrast, recent Labour MPs are more likely to come from backgrounds that give them intellectual tools rather than trades—lecturers, teachers, or journalists, for example, whose broad outlooks are unsuited to "overspecialization."

14. Roth, *Enoch Powell*, 361; Robin Oakley and Peter Rose, *The Political Year 1970* (London: Pitman, 1970): 133–43.

15. Ideologues usually graze on the far slopes of the Labour Left and Conservative Right. But because we have defined them as people captivated by abstractions, not just by Marxism or Tory populism, it should not be surprising to find an occasional moderate here as well: "I think that a Member ought to devote his time to thinking of long-range issues. I do that a lot. . . . I'm interested in the whole relationship of the individual and the state. . . . And I try to think of the philosophical ramifications and the reason that we've got where we are, and whether the Tory Party really believes in the free economy, or whether that's something we've caught as an infection from the Liberals . . . we don't have to swallow free trade–Manchester School notions intact. And I rather tend to reject them."

16. Ideologues appreciate that "it is of course much easier to do all this as an MP than as a private man, because everyone seems to insist on having an MP on the platform." "There is a certain magic about being a Member of Parliament which gives you a certain entrée to discussions, and groups, and opportunities, and contact with the media. . . . You attract attention to your ideas simply by virtue of being a Member of Parliament."

17. Or, as Aneurin Bevan put it: "The House of Commons is . . . an elaborate conspiracy to prevent the real clash of opinion which exists outside from finding an appropriate echo within its walls. It is a social shock absorber placed between privilege and the pressure of popular discontent." *In Place of Fear* (London: Macgibbon and Kee, 1961): 26. These views echo the "mission incentive" discussed by James L. Payne and his associates, *The Motivation of Politicians* (Chicago: Nelson-Hall, 1984): 163ff. But no one in our sample could even remotely be said to be driven by the "twisted" and "dogmatic" fervor that the Payne study describes.

18. "You see, this is regarded as being a sort of club where everybody is matey and that sort of thing. To me it isn't. . . . The first impression I had when I approached the building was that it was a museum. And I suddenly found after I'd been in a couple of days that it was a menagerie, that there were all sorts of queer animals in this place. And the longer I've been here, the more I'm convinced that this was correct. . . . That's how I look at it. I have no what you might call personal friends. I think politicians are very difficult to be friendly with . . . because they have . . . no basic principles." Even Enoch Powell, who loved the *idea* of Parliament as an institution, was regarded by his colleagues as a classic case of an Ideologue who was "unclubbable" and "no mixer." Roth, *Enoch Powell*, 361.

19. Valentine Herman, "Backbench and Opposition Amendments to Government Legislation," in Dick Leonard and Valentine Herman (eds.), *The Backbencher and Parliament* (London: Macmillan, 1972): 141–55.

20. Sir Gerald Nabarro, M.P., *NAB1: Portrait of a Politician* (London: Robert

Maxwell, 1969): 289–90. "I wasn't the least bit interested in just having a Ten Minute Rule," explained a very active Conservative backbencher who had recently succeeded with a Private Members' Bill, "because I was only interested in seeing it appear *on the statute book.*"

21. Peter G. Richards, "Private Members' Legislation," in S. A. Walkland and Michael Ryle (eds.), *The Commons Today* (London: Fontana, 1981): 137–53; Dick Leonard, "Private Members' Bills since 1959," in Leonard and Herman, *Backbencher and Parliament,* 126–40.

22. Richards, *Backbenchers,* 142–49; P. A. Bromhead, *Private Members' Bills in the British Parliament* (London: Routledge and Kegan Paul, 1956): 26–41. If it is thought that "the Government would never, ever swallow this thing," then everybody, for good reason, assumes it is "a dead duck." During the Wilson Governments (1964–1970), the scope for Private Members' Bills was increased, and important reform measures were introduced successfully by backbenchers. But the Heath Government seemed to be trying to narrow the opportunity for these initiatives. In November 1970 the Leader of the House, William Whitelaw, reduced the number of days for Private Members' Bills from sixteen to twelve, thereby reducing the number that could be introduced. He also made it clear that the Government did not intend to encourage them. Dick Leonard, M.P., "A Freshman's Look at Parliament, or, Neophyte in the House," unpublished paper, 1971: 1032–33.

23. Such proposals were actually put forward in 1971 and 1972 by the Select Committee on Procedure and by a handful of backbenchers. *The Times,* 18 August 1971; *The Guardian,* 12 February 1972.

24. The success rate was only one in four. Dave Marsh, Peter Gowin, and Melvyn Read, "Private Members' Bills and Moral Panic: The Case of the Video Recordings Bill (1984)," *Parliamentary Affairs* 39, 2 (1986): 180. Private Members' Bills introduced by supporters of the Government stand a much better chance of being passed than do those introduced by the Opposition. Not only is it nearly impossible to put through a Bill that the Government dislikes, but success often requires government assistance with drafting and provision of parliamentary time. Leonard, "Private Members' Bills." Since the Conservative Party was in Government at the time of the interviews, Conservative backbenchers might be expected to show more interest in Private Members' Bills than their Labour counterparts. Actually, it is Labour Advocates who are most keen to reduce the obstacles to Private Members' legislation. An explanation for this state of affairs may be found both in the fact that increasing the time for such Bills decreases the time controlled by the (Conservative) Government and in the strong expressive and symbolic attractions of the Private Members' enterprise, for it is Labour Members whose Bills are more likely to have considerable scope, controversy, and publicity value with little chance of practical success.

25. There was during the 1970s a feeling that the House was "standing up," that it was going to scrutinize and influence the Executive more than it had before, and that the heavy hand of party discipline was loosening, though certainly not losing, its grip. Philip Norton, *The Commons in Perspective* (Oxford: Martin Robinson, 1981): 247–48.

26. King and Sloman, *Westminster and Beyond,* 133.

27. "A lot of people think we are part of the Government because we are Conservative MPs. But of course we are not. We are really here as backbenchers who try and check the Executive and keep it within bounds."

28. Julian Critchley, *The Palace of Varieties: An Insider's View of Westminster* (London: Faber and Faber, 1990).

29. The sting in the label "Publicist" comes from its suggestion of a stronger interest in publicizing oneself than in publicizing one's causes. Jean Mann, *Woman in Parliament* (London: Odhams Press, 1962): 139. That is partially why MPs voted, while our interviews were under way, against a motion to televise the House of Commons on the grounds that it would have an adverse impact on the character and atmosphere of the House.

30. This is facilitated by being in the Tea Room, Smoking Room, or corridors, contributing gradually to the development of opinions. It is also facilitated by being respected, since "if a Member isn't respected by his colleagues in the House, he has very little influence no matter how great an orator he may be."

31. Or getting them to go along anyway: "For example, nothing gives me greater pleasure than when I go with an Early Day Motion to various people and say, 'Sign this.' They say, 'I don't want to, but if you're backing it, I'll sign it,' half-jocular, but half-meant. And people sign it. Well, that gives me great pleasure indeed."

32. King, *British Members of Parliament*, 69–70.

33. Judge, *Backbench Specialisation*, 181.

34. "After the war, somebody came to me and said, 'Do you remember Derek ———?' I said, 'Yes, jolly good bow and only decent one who ever rowed at Magdalen.' And this fellow said, 'His blessed research psychiatrists haven't got any money for research.' So what remained of the boat club, and the rugger club, whipped up 700 pounds, and we founded the Mental Health Research Fund. . . . And, in view of the fact that 49 percent of the beds in this country are for the mentally ill, we in the All-Party Mental Health Group believe that more can be done about it."

35. King, *British Members of Parliament*, 77.

36. Richards, *Backbenchers*, 115–34.

37. If he seems to be trying to convince himself, it may be because Policy Advocates at the time worried that these new Select Committees might, in the end, amount to less than promised when they were created as an expression of parliamentary innovation and reform. Thus, there was, in the early 1970s, a shortage of Members willing to serve on them. However, committee investigations of broad policy areas such as race relations and immigration began to receive attention from the press and to look as though they might amount to something after all. Backbenchers appointed to these committees were often those with special interests and qualifications in the area, that is to say, Specialists who were willing to devote a great deal of energy to parliamentary affairs. Drewry, "1979 Reforms," 358.

38. Nevil Johnson, "Select Committees as Tools of Parliamentary Reform: Some Further Reflections," in S. A. Walkland and Michael Ryle (eds.), *The Commons in Perspective* (London: Martin Robinson, 1977): 175–201; King and Sloman, *Westminster and Beyond*, 145.

39. See, for example, *The Independent,* 14 July 1992.

40. One Conservative Member of its Executive Committee, for instance, says he uses the association to persuade foreign leaders "that one can have right-wing views and still not confuse them with race" and "to cut down on abrasion . . . when the Chinese Ambassador was appointed here, he's so far been only to one private house, and that's mine." Or "the new Australian High Commissioner is a dedicated Labour Man, and yet when he arrived here he just rang me up and said, 'This is John. I've heard I must get in touch with you.' Mine was the first house he came to to have dinner."

41. King, *British Members of Parliament,* 49. If Ministers aren't present to listen, they will hear about it eventually from the Whips who are assigned to attend these committees, take notes, and report back to the Chief Whip about storms that may be brewing. Ministers will also hear about it from their PPSs, their "eyes and ears," who typically go along to any committee that is discussing a problem their Minister should know about and then report back directly to him.

42. Richards, *Backbenchers,* 45–49; Richard Hornby, M.P., "The Influence of the Backbencher: A Tory View," *The Political Quarterly* 36, 3 (1965): 286–94.

43. King, *British Members of Parliament,* 53–54.

44. G. R. Strauss, M.P., "The Influence of the Backbencher: A Labour View," *The Political Quarterly* 36, 3 (1965): 277–85.

45. Many Specialists become members of NEC committees on their particular subjects, because they regard these committees as more significant than backbench party groups. King, *British Members of Parliament,* 54.

46. See the comments about Humphry Berkeley's decision to specialize in African affairs: *New Statesman,* 1 December 1972: 804.

47. Specialists enjoy the corridors of power and are determined to make the most of their opportunities: "I very much like being in the corridors of power. . . . If you are not going to walk up and down the corridors and do something, you are wasting your time . . . try to influence governments . . . try to influence them to do things which you want." The Specialist's desire for influence is similar to the "program incentive" discussed by Payne and his associates, *Motivation of Politicians.* MPs ought to be working, Specialists believe, working behind the scenes instead of sitting in the Chamber listening to other MPs "debate on drains . . . where one Member scores a point about main drains, and another scores a point about subsidiary drains. It's like playing tennis, and they quite enjoy that."

48. "I look on it as a means of influencing a smaller circle of people." And if one does not seek to influence circles within circles, then, "if you are a Specialist, you have got a hell of a barren life in front of you." But if one does, then the process can be as enjoyable as the results: "I'm fond of being a political animal. I do like influencing the actions of others." It is difficult not to be "impressed by the way that Ministers do occasionally appear to come and listen to what one has to say."

49. The threat of rebellion became a very serious factor for the Government during the early 1970s and continued to be a serious factor till 1983, when the large Conservative majority of 144 reduced the Government's need to make concessions to backbenchers. Norton, "Backbench Independence."

50. Mackintosh, *British Cabinet,* 592–94. In 1972, Conservative backbenchers turned up the heat by electing a "tough" chairman of the 1922 Committee, Edward Du Cann, who, they believed, would "stand up" to the Prime Minister and the Cabinet. *The Daily Telegraph,* 17 November 1972.

51. Ministers give way either because they believe that their backbenchers may carry objections into the division lobbies or because they find the arguments reasonable. Valentine Herman, "What Impact Do Backbenchers Have?" *New Society,* 27 April 1972: 169–71. But to maintain their authority, Ministers disguise the scope of their concessions: "The way Parliament works is to disguise from Members of Parliament that Parliament has anything to do with power. Ministers may do what one is pressing for, but they never tell you, never say, 'Oh thank you, that was a wonderful idea.' But they do it."

52. King, *British Members of Parliament,* 68.

53. David McKie, "Tigers of the Order Paper," *The Guardian,* 31 May 1972. In this, Lewis succeeded Colonel Harry Day, who, during the 1930s, had established an equally undisputed claim on the title. James Griffiths, *Pages from Memory: An Autobiography* (London: J. M. Dent and Sons, 1969): 55.

54. At the same time, differences among groups will be reduced by the fact that so many different goals may be served by this activity. Sir Norman Chester, "Questions in the House," in Walkland and Ryle, *Commons Today,* 175–202. Constituency Members, for example, typically use Oral Questions to pursue constituency matters rather than general policy concerns.

55. Judge, *Backbench Specialisation,* 88–91, by contrast, found no relationship between degree of specialization (measured by the number of topics covered in Questions) and the number of Questions asked.

56. G. W. Jones, "The Prime Minister and Parliamentary Questions," *Parliamentary Affairs* 26 (1973): 262.

57. David Judge, "Backbench Specialisation: A Study in Parliamentary Questions," *Parliamentary Affairs* 27 (1974): 180.

58. Bernard Levin, "A Lesson in the Delicate Art of Throwing Coconuts in Parliament," *The Times,* 20 March 1973.

59. Humphry Berkeley, *Crossing the Floor* (London: Allen and Unwin, 1972). See also Donald McI. Johnson, *A Cassandra at Westminster* (London: Johnson, 1967). For a very clear example of how one very articulate backbencher self-consciously chose to develop this interpretation of the role, see Julian Critchley, *Westminster Blues* (London: Future Publications, 1985): 1–14.

60. See Julian Critchley, *The Palace of Varieties: An Insider's View of Westminster.* (London: Faber and Faber, 1990): 95–98.

61. Nigel Nicolson, "Freelance," *New Statesman,* 14 April 1972: 493.

62. "Sydney Silverman died on Saturday . . . he was vain, difficult and uncooperative. No one could get him to work in any kind of a group. All his life he remained an individualist backbencher, rather like my friend Tam Dalyell." Richard Crossman, *The Diaries of a Cabinet Minister,* vol. 2 (London: Hamish Hamilton and Jonathan Cape, 1976): 675.

63. Donald D. Searing, "Measuring Politicians' Values: Administration and As-

sessment of a Ranking Technique in the British House of Commons," *American Political Science Review* 72, 1 (1978): 65–80. For this analysis, the ordinal scales were recoded into three ranks: 1–3, the values respondents placed at the head of the lists; 4–6, the middle ranks; and 7–9, the values liked least.

64. These ideological reputations were coded from journalistic assessments presented in Andrew Roth, *The MP's Chart* (London: Parliamentary Profile Services, 1971). The data should not be taken for more than what they are: a journalist's generally well-informed but rather casual ideological sketches.

65. The same results were found using, instead of ideological reputations, memberships in the following ideological groups. Labour: Tribune Group, Fabian Society, social democrats. Conservative: P.E.S.T., Bow Group, Monday Club.

66. The handicaps of late entry, and the processes of adjustment to them, are expressed very clearly by this Labour Member shortly after his arrival in the House through a by-election victory: "Well, I'm not entirely devoid of political ambition, though I try to give the impression of being so. The only, the problem I think is this: that I've come into the House at the age of 48. . . . I don't lack the convictions that I used to have . . . but what I do lack is the capacity that I used to have to sling mud, for example, at the other side. . . . I wouldn't like to be a PPS to some . . . publicly known colleague of mine who was younger than me. . . . I know myself, I know my limitations. I know that, that those sort of dreams I used to have of, uh, being a Disraeli of the Labour Party, uh, were simply stuff and nonsense as things turned out. I missed the boat by not coming into the House rather earlier when I might still have retained the hard core of ambition to make a career out of being in the House. But now I have, you know, I would like to do useful things here. But I don't feel any enormous urge to occupy a whole page in *Who's Who,* as compared to three lines."

3. Ministerial Aspirants

1. Sir Lewis Namier, *The Structure of Politics at the Accession of George III* (London: Macmillan, 1968): 7.

2. Anthony King, *British Members of Parliament: A Self-Portrait* (London: Macmillan, 1974): 114. Or, as Richard Crossman succinctly put it, "I wanted to *run* things and not to be merely running a committee criticizing somebody running things." *Inside View: Three Lectures on Prime Ministerial Government* (London: Jonathan Cape, 1972): 104.

3. Julian Critchley, M.P., "How to Get on in the Tory Party," *Political Quarterly* 49, 4 (1978): 467–73.

4. Robert H. Miles, "Role-Set Configuration as a Predictor of Role Conflict and Ambiguity in Complex Organizations," *Sociometry* 40, 1 (1977): 21–34.

5. The intercoder agreement score for the three subtypes (High Flyers, Mixed, Subalterns) is Scott's $\pi = .84$. See also Appendix B.

6. This Mixed group is heterogeneous because it includes both those who were genuinely undecided about their level and those who probably had decided but were not prepared to say.

7. This tendency is further reflected within the High Flyer subgroup, where Labour MPs show signs of more intense ambition than do Conservatives.

8. Stuart Elaine Macdonald, "Political Ambition and Attainment: A Dynamic Analysis of Parliamentary Careers," Ph.D. diss., University of Michigan, 1987: 92–117.

9. Peter Winch, *The Idea of a Social Science* (London: Routledge and Kegan Paul, 1958): 115.

10. Critchley, "How to Get on in the Tory Party," 470.

11. Of course this message too is ambiguous. According to Lord Butler, if one shows that he doesn't much mind whether or not he has power, then "power would come to him." *The Art of the Possible: The Memoirs of Lord Butler* (London: Hamish Hamilton, 1971): 115. Ironically, Butler's colleagues claimed that it was precisely because Butler practiced what he preached that he did not succeed, as everyone had expected he would, to the leadership of the Conservative Party. See Anthony Howard, *RAB: The Life of R. A. Butler* (London: Jonathan Cape, 1987): 304.

12. Anthony Trollope, *Phineas Finn* (London: Oxford University Press, 1973 [1869]): 44–45.

13. A Scot on the Labour side explained it this way: "Well you see I'm 47, I'm getting old and doddery, and if Labour were to be returned, say at the next election, I'd be 51. I think I'd, well I wouldn't have a chance under Harold . . . I think that if, on the other hand, Labour were to get in under Roy Jenkins, I would probably get a very junior thing, say Parliamentary Secretary to the Scottish Office."

14. Some have entered late, others have changed careers. But whatever the basis of their modest assessment of their talents, they see themselves in "the lower echelons," as does this former secretary to a Liberal MP who has now herself won a seat: "I think as a woman, again, you do have a certain advantage—at least for a minor job."

15. They aren't the only ones who notice and talk about "the whole number of Members walking around here who are bitterly disappointed at never having been made a Government Minister," but they are the ones who manage their ambition by reminding themselves regularly that grand ambitions are likely to "be thwarted and you become a very bitter person indeed."

16. It is widely known in the House that not everyone desires promotion, that some backbenchers have no interest whatsoever in ministerial office, and that others accept that they are, for one reason or another, barred from the race. As a general motivation for refraining from cross-voting, "hope of future promotion" should therefore be expected to come rather low on the list. Hence, Table 3.3's entry "Significant motivation" includes all responses that give the motivation any serious consideration at all: those that rank it in the upper third (ranks 1–3) or middle third (ranks 4–6) of the list of nine reasons. The other category, "Not a significant motivation," reflects the view that ambition for office is not such a major factor in voting behavior (ranks 7–9).

17. King, *British Members of Parliament*, 70.

18. Thus: "A Member of Parliament is around when . . . quite fundamental decisions about society are being taken and . . . certainly has a much better chance of

being able to influence the way those decisions go than somebody of equivalent status in commerce, or the law or anything else."

19. "We lunch together, we dine together. I sat down at lunch today with one Cabinet Minister, the Chief Whip, and three Ministers of State. Well now, there are no holds barred. If you make yourself the club bore, you won't be very popular. But I mean if I had anything to say to any of those people I could have said it, and this is the best time to say it. . . . I think this is the feeling that is perhaps uppermost in the consciousness of MPs."

20. John Dickie, *The Uncommon Commoner: A Study of Sir Alec Douglas-Home* (London: Pall Mall Press, 1964): 179. In Plato's *Republic,* which has been read in university by those Ministerial Aspirants who have read Classics, Socrates argued that the desirable leaders are rarely eager to take office, for in office they will feel obliged to pursue the advantage of the community rather than status or wealth for themselves.

21. Still, Aspirants are also aware that motives are usually mixed, and that even when the end product of good policy is the primary aim, it is usually accompanied by satisfactions of a more personal kind: "Yes I, well I suppose one does have those feelings [satisfactions of status and power], although I think that's rather blatantly put, you know. I mean I suppose, you know, it's a rationalisation . . . but I set out because I want to do certain things. . . . I don't say to myself consciously, 'I'm now going out to influence others.' I am much more interested in influencing the end product, and if that means influencing others, so be it."

22. "The worrying aspect is that . . . you are tied up with much more routine matters . . . people come to the MP with every problem. . . . It takes up an awful amount of time. And while I think it's important . . . I'm not convinced it's the most important thing an MP ought to be doing." If you let them, constituents will take advantage of you till you are impelled to become "more of a Welfare Officer than I think is proper. . . . One is not only the last port of call, but sometimes the first port of call for a terrific range of rather obvious welfare questions."

23. *The Times,* 26 June 1972.

24. While most seem self-confident, the ambiguity makes some feel like the fledgling storks in Grimm's fairy tale who were told that, although the proper flying techniques for storks could not be explained to them, they were nonetheless expected to learn these techniques and would eventually be judged by the chief storks. Those who passed would fly up with the adults; those who didn't would be speared through their hearts by the leaders' beaks and left behind.

25. Namier, *Structure of Politics,* 7.

26. Anthony Trollope, *Can You Forgive Her?* (London: Penguin, 1972 [1864–65]): 268.

27. Aspirants try to speak regularly in the House because, even if not many other Members are there to listen most of the time, the Whips are always there, and Aspirants assume that they need their good opinion. Critchley, "How to Get On in the Tory Party." See also Richard Needham, M.P., *Honourable Member* (Cambridge: Patrick Stephens, 1983): 105.

28. Jorgen Rasmussen, "Will I Like It the First Time? The Maiden Speech in the

British House of Commons," *European Journal of Political Research* 16 (1988): 529. See also Peter G. Richards, *Honourable Members: A Study of the British Backbencher* (London: Faber and Faber, 1959): 82.

29. According to Julian Critchley's observations of several decades, "A brave speech witty, pithy and unkind to the other side is the quickest way to achieve a reputation and with it the attention of the Whips." *The Palace of Varieties* (London: Faber and Faber, 1990): 68. Perhaps more than any other backbencher during the decade of the 1970s, Conservative MP Norman Tebbit made his mark and brought himself to the attention of party leaders by ferocious attacks on Labour Ministers in the Chamber. Edward Pearce, *Hummingbirds and Hyenas* (London: Faber and Faber, 1985): 127.

30. Those who might have been tempted to turn their guns on their own side had before them the constant example of Enoch Powell, former Aspirant and former Minister who had been frozen out and who was ensuring that he would continue to be frozen out by frequent attacks on his Government that were described by the press as bitter and savage. "Has he taken leave of his senses?" Powell thundered at his Prime Minister in the Chamber, "as Tory MPs whistled in amazement." *The Times,* 7 November 1972. See also *The Observer,* 1 October 1972 and 6 August 1972.

31. Critchley, "How to Get On in the Tory Party," 471. See also *New Statesman,* 1 December 1972: 803. As Barrington Erle put it: "There is nothing on earth that I'm so afraid of in a young Member of Parliament as convictions. There are ever so many rocks against which men get broken. . . . I've had to do with them all, but a fellow with convictions is the worst of all." Trollope, *Phineas Finn,* 273. Barrington Erle, a successful "ministerialist," "believed in men rather than measures. . . . He never broke his heart because he could not carry this or that reform." Trollope, *Prime Minister,* 124.

32. "The modest interruption can lead to election as secretary, and with it a growing reputation for expertise." Critchley, "How To Get On in the Tory Party," 471. See also Richards, *Backbenchers,* 207.

33. Keith Ovenden, "Policy and Self-perception: Some Aspects of Parliamentary Behaviour," in Dick Leonard and Valentine Herman (eds.), *The Backbencher and Parliament* (London: Macmillan, 1972).

34. Very strong specialization (1 issue area); strong specialization (1–2 issue areas); moderate specialization (2 issue areas); weak specialization (1–3 issue areas). The unspecialized code was as follows: weak (2–4); moderate (4); strong (5); very strong (5+).

35. In the same vein, in two provincial Canadian legislatures Michael Atkinson ("Policy Interests of Provincial Backbenchers and the Effects of Political Ambition," *Legislative Studies Quarterly* 3, 4 [1978]: 629–45) found that the most ambitious members, those who regarded themselves as aspirants for ministerial office, were much more likely than nonambitious members to gravitate toward broad policy areas rather than narrow ones.

36. Trollope, *Phineas Finn,* 28. For views about iconoclasm and promotion prospects at the time of our interviews, see Rasmussen, "Will I Like It the First Time?"

541–42, and the *New Statesman,* 13 August 1971: 204. The kicking and bowing metaphor is often attributed to Aneurin Bevan. See Crossman, *Inside View,* 46. On how Bevan practiced what he preached, see James Griffiths, *Pages from Memory: An Autobiography* (London: J. M. Dent and Sons, 1969): 131.

37. "Kicking" is kept credible through stories such as those told by George Brown, who, as a young Labour MP, collected signatures in the Tea Room demanding the resignation of his party's Prime Minister, Clement Atlee. As Brown explains in his memoirs, which were widely read at Westminster during the 1970s, he was dressed down first by the Foreign Secretary (Ernest Bevin, whom he had proposed to put in Atlee's place), then by the Chief Whip, and was then summoned to appear before the Prime Minister himself: "I went to Downing Street to receive the biggest surprise of my life. I was duly received by the Prime Minister who proceeded to offer me the job of Under-Secretary of State at the Ministry of Agriculture." *In My Way: The Political Memoirs of Lord George-Brown* (London: Victor Gollancz, 1971): 50–51. George Wigg's memoirs, likewise widely read at the time, also helped to keep the idea alive. "Indeed," wrote Wigg only half in jest, "the more violent and loud-mouthed an opponent had been, the better was his chance of being included in the Wilson administration." *George Wigg* (London: Michael Joseph, 1972): 259.

38. Macdonald, "Political Ambition and Attainment," chap. 8. Schwartz and Lambert, who studied the 1959 Parliament, and Philip Norton, who studied the 1970 Parliament, both found that career aspirations had virtually no impact upon cross-voting in the division lobbies. John E. Schwartz and Geoffrey Lambert, "The Voting Behavior of British Conservative Backbenchers," in Samuel C. Patterson and John C. Wahlke (eds.), *Comparative Legislative Behavior* (New York: Wiley, 1972): 65–84; Philip Norton, *Conservative Dissidents: Dissent within the Parliamentary Conservative Party, 1970–74* (London: Temple Smith, 1978): 217–21. However, in the absence of interview data, their measures of career aspirations were quite indirect (age and length of service), compared to the more direct measures that were used by Macdonald and produced positive results.

39. Everyone accepts that Aspirants have consciences and that there will be extraordinary occasions on which their consciences (or their constituencies) will compel them to vote against their party. See George Thomas, *Mr. Speaker: The Memoirs of Viscount Tonypandy* (London: Arrow Books, 1986): 58–59.

40. Trollope, *Can You Forgive Her?,* 480–81. "My trouble," wrote Humphry Berkeley in support of this view, "was that I was physically incapable of flattery or fawning. I could never join a group around Harold Macmillan or some other senior figure in the party and laugh without restraint at their inferior jokes." *Crossing the Floor,* 142.

41. It isn't necessary to read between the lines to realize that Aspirants like this young Labour High Flyer simply don't know much at all about the role to which they aspire: "I think it's essential that to be a good Minister one should . . . know what's going on in one's field, and make sure that one's colleagues are in the same position . . . because obviously if one's controlling a Ministry, one's got to be able to rely on one's colleagues . . . and also I think to generally act responsibly." The good Minister appears, at this stage, as an impressive but vague figure who, one

would like to believe, embodies a proper proportion of proper virtues such as "I mean courage . . . really. And secondly I think good sense. . . . And thirdly . . . perhaps humanity."

42. Studies in the United States have suggested that ambition affects the attitudes and behaviors that politicians adopt. See, for example, John R. Hibbing, "Ambition in the House: Behavioral Consequences of Higher Office Goals among U.S. Representatives," *American Journal of Political Science* 30, 3 (1986): 651–65.

43. Even while eschewing the term "social psychology," they talk about social psychological aspects of leadership the way Trollope did, and the way Thomas Mann did in his short story "Mario and the Magician," about the magic between the magician and his audience.

44. Robert K. Merton, "The Role-Set: Problems in Sociological Theory," *British Journal of Sociology* 8 (1957): 265. Richard Rose too has noticed the concept's applicability to the present case: "self conscious and ambitious backbenchers looking for their first appointment can show the outlook of a ministerialist by virtue of *anticipatory socialization,* hoping that their adoption of this outlook while not yet in receipt of patronage will help gain them a government appointment." "The Making of Cabinet Ministers," *British Journal of Political Science* 1, 4 (1971): 400.

45. Philip Williams, *Hugh Gaitskell: A Political Biography* (London: Jonathan Cape, 1979): 383–84, 775–76.

46. These flickers of role taking did not, however, appear on the Labour side, possibly because parties in Opposition are less keenly sensitive than parties in Government to potential electoral fallout.

47. Ministerial Aspirants who study these examples suggest that the foundation is a self-control that permits one to be soothing on the outside but, at the same time, determined and calculating on the inside. Thus, the most effective frontbenchers "have a soothing way of putting things," while they are "absolutely strong willed and firm and determined." They are accomplished actors who have mastered the arts necessary "to not be afraid of the House of Commons, to talk to it, and be listened to and accepted."

48. "Control of the Government should pass from one party to another every so often rather than one party having control for a long time."

49. "By constantly criticizing the Government, the Opposition is performing a constructive public duty."

50. Some interpret this relationship in ways that favor their own talents and limitations. This Subaltern who feels that he himself is weak in debate argues, for instance, that what counts most in playing ministerial roles is really "the [Minister's] ability to run his own department and get results. And in doing this he doesn't necessarily have to be a good debater, or good at answering Questions."

51. Club Men, one of the subtypes of Parliament Men, and Ministerial Aspirants tend to take opposite views of the House and its Members. Thus, whereas 39 percent of the Club Men express extremely favorable attitudes toward the members of other parties (they have no reservations about "trusting and relying" upon them), only 8 percent of Aspirants hold similar attitudes.

52. Here, once again, Ministerial Aspirants differ most noticeably from the Club

Men, the institution's principal patriots, 43 percent of whom score at the very top of the positive scale, whereas only 10 percent of the Aspirants put forward such positive views.

53. John P. Mackintosh, *The British Cabinet*, 3rd ed. (London: Stevens and Sons, 1977): 608.

54. Miles, "Role-Set Configurations."

55. Trollope, *Prime Minister*, 367–68.

4. Constituency Members

1. David R. Mayhew, "Congressional Elections: The Case of the Vanishing Marginals," *Polity* 6, 3 (1974): 295–317; Richard Fenno, *Home Style: House Members in Their Districts* (Boston: Little, Brown, 1978); Glenn R. Parker, "Sources of Change in Congressional District Attentiveness," *American Journal of Political Science* 24, 1 (1980): 115–24; Morris P. Fiorina, "Congressmen and Their Constituencies: 1958 and 1978," in Dennis Hale (ed.), *Proceedings of the Thomas P. O'Neill, Jr., Symposium on the U.S. Congress* (Boston: Eusey Press, 1982): 33–64; Albert Cover and Bruce S. Brumberg, "Baby Books and Ballots: The Impact of Congressional Mail on Constituent Opinion," *American Political Science Review* 76, 2 (1982): 347–59; Bruce E. Cain, John A. Ferejohn, and Morris P. Fiorina, "The Constituency Service Basis of the Personal Vote for U.S. Representatives and British Members of Parliament," *American Political Science Review* 78, 1 (1984): 110–25; Bruce E. Cain, John A. Ferejohn, and Morris P. Fiorina, *The Personal Vote: Constituency Service and Electoral Independence* (Cambridge, Mass.: Harvard University Press, 1987).

2. R. E. Dowse, "The MP and His Surgery," *Political Studies* 11, 3 (1963): 333–41; Anthony Sutcliffe, "The British Member of Parliament and Local Issues," *The Parliamentarian* 51, 2 (1970): 87–95; Ronald Munroe, "The Member of Parliament as Representative: The View from the Constituency," *Political Studies* 25, 4 (1977): 577–87; John P. Mackintosh (ed.), *People and Parliament* (London: Saxon House, 1978); Bruce E. Cain and David B. Ritchie, "Assessing Constituency Involvement: The Hemel Hempstead Experience," *Parliamentary Affairs* 35, 1 (1982): 72–83; Philip Norton, " 'Dear Minister . . .': The Importance of MP-to-Minister Correspondence," *Parliamentary Affairs* 35, 1 (1982): 59–72; James W. Marsh, "Representational Changes: The Constituency MP," in Philip Norton (ed.), *Parliament in the 1980s* (London: Basil Blackwell, 1985).

3. See Malcolm E. Jewell, "Legislator-Constituency Relations and the Representative Process," *Legislative Studies Quarterly* 8, 3 (1983): 303–4, who notes that "traditionally the term 'representation' has referred to the relationship between legislators and constituents on policy matters, but in recent years we have defined the topic more broadly." The "we" refers primarily to American political scientists, for constituency service has been at the forefront of British conceptions of representation since at least the thirteenth century. This reflects differences in the theory and practice of representation in the two political systems. Heinz Eulau and Paul D. Karps have defined the key constituency dimensions as service responsiveness and allocation responsiveness and discussed the theoretical and conceptual issues involved. "The Puz-

zle of Representation: Specifying Components of Responsiveness," in Heinz Eulau and John C. Wahlke (eds.), *The Politics of Representation* (Beverly Hills, Calif.: Sage, 1978): 55–72. Cross-national empirical literature on this subject is reviewed by Michael L. Mezey, *Comparative Legislatures* (Durham, N.C.: Duke University Press, 1979): 159–93, and Jewell, "Legislator-Constituency Relations," 319–21.

4. Peter G. J. Pulzer, *Political Representation and Elections in Britain,* 2nd ed. (London: George Allen and Unwin, 1972): 9, 136–40; Donald D. Searing, "Rules of the Game in Britain: Can the Politicians Be Trusted?" *American Political Science Review* 76, 2 (1982): 239–58.

5. F. F. Ridley, "The Citizen against Authority: British Approaches to the Redress of Grievances," *Parliamentary Affairs* 37, 1 (1984): 2; A. H. Birch, *Representative and Responsible Government* (London: Unwin, 1964): 12–13; J. E. A. Jolliffe, *The Constitutional History of Medieval England* (London: Adam and Charles Black, 1937); John P. Mackintosh, M.P., "The Member of Parliament as Representative or as Delegate," *The Parliamentarian* 52, 1 (1971): 14–21.

6. Walter Bagehot, *The English Constitution* (London: Collins/Fontana, 1963 [1867]): 152–53; Nevil Johnson, *In Search of the Constitution* (New York: Pergamon, 1977): 50–51.

7. George L. Haskins, *The Growth of English Representative Government* (London: Oxford University Press, 1948): chap. 2; Jolliffe, *Constitutional History of Medieval England,* 340; A. F. Pollard, *The Evolution of Parliament* (London: Longmans, Green, 1926): 34–38.

8. Mackintosh, *People and Parliament,* 141–44.

9. As Col. Sir Charles Ponsonby recalls it: "Before 1939, unless there was some controversy afoot, I rarely received more than ten or twenty letters a week. . . . But after the election of 1945, everything was changed . . . suddenly the M.P. ceased to be a politician and potential statesman and became an official of the welfare state. Thousands wanted houses; old people wanted pensions; ex-service men wanted jobs; everybody wanted something, and 'write to your M.P.' became a cliché . . . the wretched M.P. was snowed under." *Ponsonby Remembers* (Oxford: Alden Press, 1965): 11. See also Julian Critchley, M.P., "Returning to the House," in Dick Leonard and Valentine Herman (eds.), *The Backbencher and Parliament* (London: Macmillan, 1972): 242; Cain, Ferejohn, and Fiorina, "Constituency Service Basis," 115.

10. They understand their role well and understand the choices they have made: "When one comes in this place, one has to decide what one is going to do. . . . I'm, I chose a Constituency MP."

11. "After all, the most rewarding thing for *me* is not to make a good speech in the House, but to get a woman a house."

12. Cf. David Wood, "The Conservative Member of Parliament as Lobbyist for Constituency Economic Interests," *Political Studies* 35, 3 (1987): 393–409. The intercoder agreement score for the three subtypes (Welfare Officers, Mixed, Local Promoters) is Scott's $\pi = .81$. Moreover, all three codes encompass a four-point scale from "very strong," a pure statement of the subtype across all responses, to "weak," in which the subtype theme is dominant overall but mixed with others or expressed with half-hearted interest.

13. Malcolm E. Jewell, "Attitudinal Determinants of Legislative Behavior: The

Utility of Role Analysis," in Allan Kornberg and Lloyd D. Musolf (eds.), *Legislatures in Developmental Perspective* (Durham, N.C.: Duke University Press, 1970): 460–500; Donald A. Gross, "Representative Styles and Legislative Behavior," *Western Political Quarterly* 31, 3 (1978): 359–71.

14. They are only 9 percent more likely. The probability in Table 4.1 refers to the probability that Local Promoters would be this different by chance alone. The probability that Welfare Officers would be this different by chance alone is weaker: $p \leq 10$. It is often assumed that the gap between the parties is much larger than this: that Labour MPs constitute a still more disproportionate share of Constituency Members because they are more elderly, have fewer outside responsibilities, and have constituents who are more likely to need help (Sutcliffe, "British Member of Parliament and Local Issues," 89). The fact is that there are many more Conservative Constituency Members than is generally recognized—even during periods when the Conservative Party is in Government and Conservative backbenchers might be expected to be most likely to gravitate toward the roles of Policy Advocate and Ministerial Aspirant.

15. Anthony Barker and Michael Rush, *The Member of Parliament and His Information* (London: Allen and Unwin, 1970): 192–95, also found that Labour MPs were more likely to express satisfaction with the welfare officer aspects of the Constituency Member's role than were Conservative MPs. Those who have no outside jobs to go to easily have an extra incentive to become deeply involved in the welfare officer role. This is typical of the type of social situation that stimulates commitments to occupational roles. Becker, "Notes on the Concept of Commitment."

16. Marsh, "Representational Changes," 69–70.

17. Dowse, "MP and His Surgery"; Barker and Rush, *Member of Parliament and His Information;* Cain, Ferejohn, and Fiorina, "Constituency Service Basis," 115.

18. Munroe, "Member of Parliament as Representative"; Dowse, "MP and His Surgery" Rosemary Dinnage, "Parliamentary Advice Bureau," *New Society,* 24 February 1972: 392–93.

19. Bryan Gould, M.P., "The MP and Constituency Cases," in Mackintosh, *People and Parliament,* 84–85.

20. Cain and Ritchie, "Assessing Constituency Involvement," 74–75.

21. Fred Willey, M.P., *The Honourable Member* (London: Sheldon Press, 1974): 154; Anthony King and Anne Sloman, *Westminster and Beyond* (London: Macmillan, 1973): 3–12.

22. MPs have a relatively low rate of success with such cases, since waiting lists are established by a "points system" and unjustified favoritism is neither possible nor desirable. Still, there are a few cases in which mistakes have been made that the MP can put right. And these few cases are apparently sufficient to keep constituents coming and pressing these MPs, if the MPs allow them to do so, into their roles as local ombudsmen or social workers. Gould, "MP and Constituency Cases."

23. He also contacts the local authority about the problems of individuals; but he is particularly drawn toward group concerns such as "finding a proper site with proper water and things like that" for gypsies who are being harassed in his biggest ward.

24. Richards, *Backbenchers,* 156–57.

25. See David M. Wood, "The Member of Parliament and Economic Policy: Is There a Territorial Imperative?" paper presented at the Annual Meeting of the American Political Science Association, 1985: 9–11. One Labour Member had statistics comparing government investments during the six years he had represented his constituency with investments during the previous six (12.5 million pounds more), "and I took that to be a tremendous achievement."

26. "The difference between a Constituency MP and a non-Constituency MP," said a Constituency MP, "is that a Constituency MP is one who does quite a lot of advice bureau, is in the constituency a lot. A non-Constituency MP would do the minimum." During the 1980s, both Constituency and non-Constituency MPs increased the time they spent in their constituencies. Compare the data in Table 4.2 to Austin Mitchell, M.P., "Consulting the Workers: MPs on Their Job," *The Parliamentarian* 66, 1 (1985): 12.

27. It is obvious from the diaries of London MPs like John Grant, who was not a Constituency Member, that London Members find it very easy to make brief but frequent visits to local factories or housing associations and then return to the House for parliamentary work. *Member of Parliament* (London: Michael Joseph, 1974). In fact, whatever facilitates travel to the constituency can have this effect. For example, in the United States, increases in the travel allowances of Senators have increased their attention to their constituencies. Glenn R. Parker, "Stylistic Changes in the U.S. Senate: 1959–1980," *Journal of Politics* 47, 4 (1985): 1190–1202. The introduction of travel allowances in Britain may likewise be related to the rise in attentiveness to constituency matters during the 1970s and 1980s.

28. Electoral security ("marginality") is the difference between the winner's percentage of the total vote and that of the candidate who came second. Constituency location ("distance") measures the constituency's distance from the House of Commons by means of the concentric circles just discussed. "Value-security" enters, from a rank-order instrument, the political value with the closest ties to constituency service.

29. Bruce E. Cain, John A. Ferejohn, and Morris P. Fiorina, "The Constituency Component: A Comparison of Service in Great Britain and the United States," *Comparative Political Studies* 16, 1 (1983): 67–91.

30. To investigate whether extreme cases on the dependent variable might be distorting the performance of electoral security or other independent variables, the regression was rerun with these cases recoded. There was no change in the results. In the same vein, because of the important part played in role choice by "distance from London" as a control, the regression was rerun introducing "role × distance" as an interaction term. Again, there was no change.

31. *The Evening Standard,* 27 June 1972.

32. May McKisack, *The Parliamentary Representation of the English Boroughs during the Middle Ages* (London: Oxford University Press, 1932): 134–36; Derek Hirst, *The Representative of the People?* (Cambridge: Cambridge University Press, 1975): 160–63.

33. McCartney described Sir Gerald as "one of the most loathsome persons I

know." *The Evening Standard,* 27 June 1972. "Perhaps this is a sign of an inferiority complex," observed another Constituency Member, "but sometimes you're regarded as a slightly inferior type of Member compared to the Member who is floating off to the Councils of Europe and foreign parts. I resent anybody who thinks that a grass-roots Member is a second-class type of Member. I think we've all got something to contribute."

34. Cain, Ferejohn, and Fiorina, "Constituency Service Basis," 115.

35. Norton, " 'Dear Minister,' " 61–62; Barker and Rush, *Member of Parliament and His Information,* 189–91.

36. King and Sloman, *Westminster and Beyond,* 118–19.

37. Norton, " 'Dear Minister,' " 63.

38. Gould, "MP and Constituency Cases"; Dowse, "MP and His Surgery."

39. Richards, *Backbenchers,* 167–71.

40. This is the point at which representation as redress of grievances can intersect with representation of political opinion on matters of national importance.

41. *New Statesman,* 15 September 1972: 363.

42. Richards, *Backbenchers,* 167–71; Gould, "MP and Constituency Cases."

43. King and Sloman, *Westminster and Beyond,* 119–20. Tabling questions can also serve as harassment: "The Minister was going to let an airplane factory in my constituency close. The factory employed nearly four hundred people, so I put down two hundred detailed Questions in the House—two hundred! I brought the Ministry to a complete stop. So Fred fetched me up in the middle of the night and says, 'What the bloody hell do you think you're doing?' . . . So I sat up all night and in the morning put down another fifty. In the end, Fred fetches me in again and says, 'All right, you win, I give up.' Four hundred jobs, and I saved them." King, *British Members of Parliament,* 79–80.

44. Valentine Herman, "Backbench and Opposition Amendments to Government Legislation," in Leonard and Herman, *Backbencher and Parliament,* 141–55.

45. The principal difficulty with this strategy is its uncertainty. Members compete in a ballot for the privilege. By the time the Constituency Member wins the right to move the adjournment and debate the topic, the topic may no longer be topical. Sutcliffe, "British Member of Parliament and Local Issues," 88.

46. It may not be part of the job, but there have always been Constituency Members who have performed this sort of constituency service. In the fourteenth century, for instance, many parliamentary burgesses were expected by their communities to undertake for them errands and other local business in London. This included tasks such as buying wine, collecting debts, paying farm fees, and concluding agreements about tolls. McKisack, *Parliamentary Representation of the English Boroughs,* 136–39.

47. John R. Johannes, "Explaining Congressional Casework Styles," *American Journal of Political Science* 27, 3 (1983): 530–47.

48. William Mishler and Anthony Mughan, "Representing the Celtic Fringe: Devolution and Legislative Behavior in Scotland and Wales," *Legislative Studies Quarterly* 3, 3 (1978): 391–92; King, *British Members of Parliament,* 27–28; T. F. Lindsay, *Parliament from the Press Gallery* (London: Macmillan, 1967): 70.

49. At the same time, Conservatives appear to shoulder more than their share of the load in Scotland and Wales. Perhaps this is because Conservatives are attracted to the promotion of constituency interests, and Scotland and Wales have the most distinct regional interests to promote. Similarly, Labour Constituency Members, who prefer welfare officer work with individuals, also seem to be found where they are most needed—in the Midlands, Yorkshire, and the North, regions that have serious socioeconomic problems. See Lisanne Radice, Elizabeth Vallance, and Virginia Willis, *Member of Parliament: The Job of a Backbencher,* 2nd ed. (London: Macmillan, 1990).

50. Weakening the relationship still further, a separate investigation of the fifty most agricultural seats finds the proportion of Constituency Members at 29 percent, only 4 percent above average for all backbenchers' constituencies.

51. Bruce E. Cain, John A. Ferejohn, and Morris P. Fiorina, *The Personal Vote: Constituency Service and Electoral Independence* (Cambridge, Mass.: Harvard University Press, 1987); David M. Wood, "The Role of the British MP as Lobbyist for Constituency Economic Interests, as Seen by Potential Users of this Service," paper presented at the Annual Meeting of the American Political Science Association, 1986.

52. Ridley, "Citizen against Authority," 23; Richards, *Backbenchers,* 160; Richard Hornby, M.P., "The Influence of the Backbencher: A Tory View," *The Political Quarterly* 36, 3 (1965): 286–94; King and Sloman, *Westminster and Beyond,* 13–14.

53. The reason that no linear relationship exists between marginality and choosing the role of Constituency Member is that there are too many Constituency Members like this one: "Sometimes people will say that the Constituency MPs are those that [are in marginal seats] and therefore have to do a lot of constituency work in order to maintain their vote. But it doesn't affect me, because I have a very large majority. Whether I did it or not wouldn't make a scrap of difference to my vote. I get 28,000 votes every time. My majority goes between 12,000 and 8,000, but my vote remains 28,000 whatever happens—the others go up and down."

54. Like thwarted ambition, however, electoral insecurity does have its effects. There are backbenchers who serve energetically as Constituency Members in hopes of collecting votes. One of them is even reported to have perused local newspapers for announcements of births, deaths, and other events so that he might improve his image as a good Constituency MP by sending personal messages of congratulations or condolence. Willey, *Honourable Member,* 157. Another claimed that the trust of constituents is the key to electoral security and that "if they feel they can trust you," you have secured your base. Still another argued that being a good Constituency Member has, since he entered the House eighteen years ago, increased his majority at each election: "I'm the only one who has had a bigger majority each time." But altogether it is not enough, and not systematic enough, to create a generally important impact upon role choice.

55. Johannes, "Political Culture and Congressional Constituency Service."

56. The ideological groups used in this analysis correspond roughly to each party's Left, Center, and Right. In the Labour Party these are the Tribune Group, the Fabian Society, and the social democrats. In the Conservative party they are P.E.S.T., the

Bow Group, and the Monday Club. This absence of structuring is also apparent in an analysis of backbenchers' ideological reputations, which were coded from journalistic assessments presented in Andrew Roth's *The MP's Chart* (London: Parliamentary Profile Services, 1971).

57. Donald D. Searing, "Measuring Politicians' Values: Administration and Assessment of a Ranking Technique in the British House of Commons," *American Political Science Review* 72, 1 (1978): 65–80. For this analysis, the ordinal scales were recoded into three ranks: 1–3, the values respondents placed at the head of the lists; 4–6, the middle ranks; and 7–9, the values liked least.

58. The greater the problem, the greater the satisfaction. "Helping people is the most fascinating job in the world," explained a Member from a rural constituency, "and during one of the great storms in Scotland, where we went through a dreadful time, I was able full-time to assist and help people who possibly gave up hope. You're able to step in . . . it's a special relationship."

59. James W. Marsh, "Representation Changes: The Constituency MP," in Philip Norton (ed.), *Parliament in the 1980s* (Oxford: Basil Blackwell, 1985): 69–93.

60. Although few Local Promoters are as sentimental as this union-sponsored Labour MP who, despite a limited education, worked effectively for decades to help turn a decaying community into a prosperous borough, most of them would understand his sense of accomplishment: "And I take that to be a tremendous achievement, and I would say amongst the best. . . . And I used to walk the hills surrounding Bradford, where I live, near to what is called the Matlock Golf Links, and I could look down into Bradford, and I had a hell of a job to stop the tears coming into my eyes. They were not tears of pride, unless pride is associated with humility. And it could be summed up in one sentence, and the thought used to be in my head, it used to stimulate my being, 'Well, you see, it's a better place lad, since you've been here.' "

61. This sense of duty is not such an unusual motivation in political life. James L. Payne and his colleagues found that it was present among politicians in a wide range of countries. *The Motivation of Politicians* (Chicago: Nelson-Hall, 1984): 103ff. They likewise noted its relationship to self-reinforcement, to satisfactions derived from comparing one's behavior with how one believes one should behave— seeking rectitude and avoiding guilt.

62. Lawrence A. Blum, *Friendship, Altruism and Morality* (London: Routledge and Kegan Paul, 1980): 120.

63. In fact, most MPs feel this way, though not as intensely perhaps as Constituency Members; for example, Labour Front Bench Spokesman John Grant: "Running a 'surgery' and handling a post bag properly would seem to me to be part of my unwritten contract of employment." *Member of Parliament*, 127.

64. See King and Sloman, *Westminster and Beyond*, 13.

65. Another Constituency Member explained that people stand up when he walks into the room ("I don't think that's necessary at all, and I tell them so"), while others talked more directly about respect: "You get a great deal of respect. You get more respect probably in the provinces than in the London area."

66. King and Sloman, *Westminster and Beyond*, 1.

67. After explaining that "individual MPs are elected to *represent* their constituen-

cies as a whole," and that "their job is to be the permanent voice of their electors," Francis Pym, who was Conservative Chief Whip at the time of the interviews, made clear what in his view these duties entailed: redress of grievances; judging the overall performance of the Government; scrutinizing specific legislation; and contributing to debates on the major issues of the day. What Pym "left out" was representing the policy views of individual constituents. This didn't occur to him with regard to individual MPs, because this is something that Parliament does "collectively." *The Politics of Consent* (London: Sphere Books, 1985): 95–96.

68. Barker and Rush, *Member of Parliament and His Information,* 174–76.

69. Ian Gilmour, *The Body Politic* (London: Hutchinson, 1969): 275.

70. This is why many Welfare Officers were uneasy about the Ombudsman, and hesitant about supporting the Bill that set up his office. See Ridley, "Citizen against Authority," 7. For if Members begin to "just send it off to the Ombudsman and say, 'This case is in your hands,' " they may be giving away the heart of the Welfare Officers' role.

71. At the same time, many Constituency Members, particularly among the Local Promoters and strong Welfare Officers, are among those backbenchers who are most deeply involved in their roles.

72. Erving Goffman, *Encounters* (Indianapolis: Bobbs Merrill, 1961): 85–152.

73. See George Herbert Mead, *Mind, Self and Society* (Chicago: University of Chicago Press, 1934); Maurice Natanson, *Phenomenology, Role and Reason* (Springfield, Ill.: Charles C. Thomas, 1974): 195; Martin Hollis and Steve Smith, "Roles and Reasons in Foreign Policy Decision Making," *British Journal of Political Science* 16, 3 (1986): 277.

74. Norton, " 'Dear Minister,' " 59.

75. Birch, *Representative and Responsible Government,* 14.

76. See, for example, Lynda W. Powell, "Issue Representation in Congress," *Journal of Politics* 44, 3 (1982): 658–78.

77. Birch, *Representative and Responsible Government,* 227.

78. Jolliffe, *Constitutional History of Medieval England.*

5. Parliament Men

1. Sir Samuel Roberts, M.P., "Politics," unpublished paper; 1940. Even up to the 1960s, the Leader of the Conservative Party still felt he needed to be concerned about the views of his Parliament Men. See Cecil King, *The Cecil King Diary, 1965–1970* (London: Jonathan Cape, 1972): 24. But by the 1970s, they had become an endangered species on the backbenches. Colin Mellors, *The British MP: A Socio-Economic Study of the House of Commons* (London: Saxon House, 1978): 124.

2. Anthony Trollope, *Phineas Redux* (London: Oxford University Press, 1973 [1873]): 26–27.

3. Sir Lewis Namier, *The Structure of Politics at the Accession of George III* (London: Macmillan, 1968).

4. Namier, *Structure of Politics,* 12. It distinguishes women too. But women choose the role of the Parliament Man less frequently than any other backbench

preference role because they are much less comfortable than their male counterparts with Parliament's club-like atmosphere of leather and liquor. Elizabeth Vallance, *Women in the House: A Study of Women Members of Parliament* (London: Athlone Press, 1979): chap. 6.

5. See James David Barber, *The Lawmakers: Recruitment and Adaptation to Legislative Life* (New Haven: Yale University Press, 1965); Anthony King, "The Rise of the Career Politician in Britain—And Its Consequences," paper presented at the Annual Meeting of the American Political Science Association, 1980.

6. The intercoder agreement score for these three subtypes is Scott's $\pi = .82$.

7. Julian Critchley, *Westminster Blues* (London: Futura Publications, 1985): 41. James L. Payne and his associates have also found that the desire for status is a very common goal in political life. Politicians usually have ample opportunity to pursue this goal by projecting their names and images in the media. These status concerns may be reflected in interviews when politicians raise topics that put them in a favorable light, talk about the public recognition they have won, or evaluate others primarily in terms of their political or social standing. *The Motivation of Politicians* (Chicago: Nelson-Hall, 1984): 19ff.

8. Namier, *Structure of Politics,* 12.

9. You don't even get it from the Strangers' Gallery: "I had many times looked down upon our rulers from the dizzy heights of the Strangers' Gallery, but in the close up view from the third seat above the gangway they looked very different, some larger and some not so large." James Griffiths, *Pages from Memory: An Autobiography* (London: J. M. Dent and Sons, 1969): 53. Nor did you during the nineteenth century: "You have heard the debates from the Gallery," he explained to the new Member. "Now you'll hear them from the body of the House, and you'll find out how very different it is. There's no man can know what Parliament is who has never had a seat." Anthony Trollope, *Can You Forgive Her?* (London: Penguin, 1972 [1964–65]): 482.

10. These are the sorts of Parliament Men whose disappearance the lobby correspondents are most likely to regret: "What is lacking is that old-fashioned kind of disillusioned MP, who has long abandoned hope not just of office but even of getting his name in the national press, but who has retained a passionate interest in finding out what the Government or his own party leadership is up to. . . . They could be primed with a hint, a clue, a bit of gossip, whereupon they would disappear into the labyrinthine corridors to return later triumphantly bearing a succulent morsel of real, printable news. Oh where are they now?" Wilfrid Sendall, "A View from the Bridge," *The Spectator,* 4 August 1973: 146.

11. Conservatives are more likely to talk about being "a good communicator . . . a link between Parliament and the people," about the importance of explaining to one's constituents what the Government is trying to do, and about bringing back information to Westminster about what the people are thinking: "I *do* know what people are thinking. And when I go to some of my, my little ward meetings and address them, I've had old ladies come up to me and say, 'Oh, Mr. Turnbull, you've said *exactly* what I'm thinking.' You get that power to judge the audience."

12. This is also an "exit role," and the last Parliament, for the lawyer who doesn't

fit in and doesn't think he is ever going to be offered anything. Although only forty-two, he "wouldn't really want to stay much longer. I mean I've got lots of things to do. . . . There are a lot of elderly old bores here, I don't really want to join that category particularly."

13. At the time of our interviews, for instance, Charles Pannell, M.P., wrote a brief historical sketch for *The Times* arguing that Parliament's reputation for rowdiness is nothing new and that, in fact, the British Parliament is "a marvel—genuinely one of the political wonders of the world." *The Times,* 15 April 1972.

14. From a Policy Advocate: "[In the Chamber] . . . some older ones sit and watch, but gradually everyone finds better things to do, except a few oddities who never grow out of it or who find some perverse satisfaction in what is going on." Austin Mitchell, *Westminster Man: A Tribal Anthropology of the Commons People* (London: Thames Methuen, 1982): 107.

15. Peter G. Richards, *The Backbenchers* (London: Faber and Faber, 1972): 70.

16. Namier, *Structure of Politics,* 12.

17. Sir Lewis Namier, *Skyscrapers and Other Essays* (London: Macmillan, 1931): 47.

18. Frank Allaun, a Labour Policy Advocate, once asked the Lord President of the Council, presumably as an objection to the exclusiveness implied by the term "Strangers," to replace this label throughout the House with the word "Visitors." He was refused with the curious explanation that "Visitors" would be imprecise since it would not, of course, cover secretaries. *The Times,* 3 August 1972.

19. It has long been said that some barristers come to the House partly to make their practices outside still more busy: "Mr. Low the barrister . . . who was now himself in the House of Commons . . . with a view to his further advancement . . . and thus a proper and sufficient number of real barristers finds its way into the House." Anthony Trollope, *Phineas Finn* (London: Oxford University Press, 1973 [1869]): 225.

20. Earlier in the century, such part-timers were even more part-time than they are today. Their public silences were even more prolonged and, like the young businessman Max Aitken, they rarely even bothered to vote. See A. J. P. Taylor, *Beaverbrook* (London: Penguin Books, 1974): 88.

21. For example, a hard-working working-class Constituency Member who has never much liked the patrician themes at Westminster has this to say: "The playboy is the type that, er, goes down to the club and, er, you know, sort of 'Terribly interested in politics,' but he spends most of his time away from the House, usually in a fairly safe seat. He doesn't really contribute much."

22. His rough edges have been smoothed off by years in the Palace of Westminster. The extensive experience of the Good House of Commons Men, it is said, leads them to appreciate "tolerance and understanding and forgiveness." Jean Mann, *Woman in Parliament* (London: Odhams Press, 1962): 26. Moreover, not only is the Good House of Commons Man himself not very partisan, but others tend to soften the party political edge of their criticisms of him and his positions. Emanuel Shinwell, *I've Lived through It All* (London: Victor Gollancz, 1973): 136.

23. *New Statesman,* 21 July 1972: 91.

24. A year after the Lambton affair, the Committee of Privileges struck again by finding that a firm of solicitors had committed "an affront to the House" and a contempt by entering the precincts of the House and sending for a Member for the purpose of serving him with a copy of a writ alleging slander and libel. *The Times,* 23 February 1973.

25. These are also the people who, if they see themselves as candidates for anything further, look toward the posts of Speaker or Chairman or Deputy Chairman of Ways and Means. Richards, *Backbenchers,* 70. "The only thing I would aspire to," commented one of the most active among them, "would be a Deputy Chairman of Ways and Means. That's the only thing I would aspire to."

26. Another described the MP's most important duties and responsibilities this way: "To *prevent* stuff going through the House of Commons. All the changes are bad, basically. And I spend my whole life stopping things from happening. And that's the truth. . . . The Government has much too much legislation. I mean it's not like the end of the war—there's not an awful lot of things that need doing. One Government is just as bad as another. And one doesn't want to facilitate any more legislation."

27. Namier, *Structure of Politics,* 12.

28. Most rational choice models assume that all politicians will become highly ambitious whenever the opportunities to succeed seem good. See Paul Abramson, John H. Aldrich, and David W. Rohde, "Progressive Ambition among United States Senators: 1972–1988," *Journal of Politics* 49, 1 (1987): 3–35.

29. *The Daily Telegraph,* 4 March 1972 and 23 October 1972.

30. The principal fear of those who opposed televising Parliament was always that this would trivialize the proceedings, change the nature of the debate, and thereby reduce the esteem in which Parliament was held. Bob Franklin, "A Leap in the Dark: MPs' Objections to Televising Parliament," *Parliamentary Affairs* 39, 3 (1986): 286.

31. Donald D. Searing, "Rules of the Game in Britain: Can the Politicians Be Trusted?" *American Political Science Review* 76, 2 (1982): 239–58.

32. Roberts, "Politics," 1940.

33. Payne et al., *Motivation of Politicians,* 79ff.

34. Club Men enjoy the agreeable social life so much that they sometimes overestimate the institutional patriotism of their colleagues and assume that it is just this sort of enthusiasm, for instance, that explains why "most people who lose their seats here during an election are very anxious to get back. It's an extraordinarily nice place to be in from the point of view of association with others, group activities, cooperation."

35. Anthony Trollope, *The Prime Minister* (London: Oxford University Press, 1970 [1876]): 357.

36. Or it can come through a reputation for being knowledgeable: "If you are in Parliament, through some mysterious process you find yourself becoming extremely well informed . . . I suppose because you read more, discuss things, listen to debates. And I find . . . with other people in conversation I usually know more than they do. It's nice to know a lot, it's nice to feel that, even if one is not in Government. . . . I think, uh, that one would have to be very pure-minded to say that this was of no importance to one."

Part II. Leadership Roles

1. The striking difference in constraint between frontbench and backbench roles has also been commented on by Radice and her associates, who characterize the Minister's role as *well-delineated* and the backbencher's role as something to be *carved out* by the individual actor, albeit within Westminster's institutional context. Lisanne Radice, Elizabeth Vallance, and Virginia Willis, *Member of Parliament: The Job of the Backbencher*, 2nd ed. (London: Macmillan, 1990): 3. There is no question about whether position roles are related to behavior—because so much specific behavior is *required* of those who perform them. See Bruce J. Biddle, *Role Theory: Expectations, Identities and Behaviors* (New York: Academic Press, 1979): 73.

2. Thus, Parliamentary Private Secretaries, Junior Ministers, and Ministers all have subtypes that, compared to backbench roles, may be quite uncrystallized and overlapping but are nonetheless "preference" driven. Likewise, Whips have subtypes that may be defined primarily by "positional" criteria but nonetheless permit expressive conduct undertaken with comparatively little calculation. See Fred I. Greenstein, "Personality and Politics," in Fred I. Greenstein and Nelson Polsby (eds.), *Handbook of Political Science*, vol. 2 (Reading, Mass.: Addison-Wesley, 1975): 21.

6. Parliamentary Private Secretaries

1. For example, Norman Wilding and Philip Laundy, *An Encyclopedia of Parliament*, 4th ed. (London: Cassell, 1971): 541.

2. *The Daily Telegraph*, 26 October 1972.

3. Between 1900 and 1960 the number of Parliamentary Private Secretaries generally grew along with (a) the creation of new departments with more senior Ministers and therefore more PPSs, and (b) the increase in the number of Ministers appointed per department, particularly the creation in 1943 of the new rank of Minister of State to fill in below the level of Secretary of State but above Junior Minister. R. K. Alderman and J. A. Cross, "The Parliamentary Private Secretary: A Danger to the Free Functioning of Parliament?" *Political Studies* 14, 2 (1966): 202.

4. See David Butler and Gareth Butler, *British Political Facts, 1900–1985* (London: Macmillan, 1986).

5. Peter G. Richards, *Honourable Members: A Study of the British Backbencher* (London: Faber and Faber, 1959): 215.

6. "Get me a sandwich James." "Oh yes, of course, Rhodes, certainly." . . . "You know I don't like asparagus. Get it off." "Oh, yes, Rhodes, sorry Rhodes." Edward Pearce, *Hummingbirds and Hyenas* (London: Faber and Faber, 1985): 159.

7. J. Hoelter, "The Effects of Role Evaluation and Commitment on Identity Salience," *Social Psychological Quarterly* 46 (1983): 140–47; Erving Goffman, *Encounters* (Indianapolis: Bobbs Merrill, 1961): 85–152; W. Coutu, "Role-Playing vs. Role-Taking: An Appeal for Clarification," *American Sociological Review* 16 (1951): 180–87.

8. Some PPSs, in fact, say that they automatically look to the Whips "to tell *me* what the leadership expects of Members," and, likewise, "when I've got a genuine complaint I go and see my Whip and say, 'Look, I don't like the way this is going.'"

9. Of course this is an experience largely missed by Apprentices to Ministers who do not have formal departments: PPSs to the Leader of the House, Attorney General, and Solicitor General, for example. Such Apprentices often have less work than do their colleagues who serve departmental Ministers and have a bureaucracy to be explored.

10. Like most other politicians, PPSs think about their careers clearly, rationally, and often. Because PPSs are so clear about their goals, the only ambiguous cases in the coding were a few Apprentices who were beginning to doubt that they were ever going to be promoted and beginning to realize that they liked being PPSs anyway. Scott's $\pi = .92$.

11. Since published sources, especially prior to the 1970s, are disappointingly incomplete and inconsistent about service as a PPS, we cross-checked our records with several sources and then entered them into career inventories that were subsequently checked again and revised during the interviews by the MPs themselves. These data included all PPSs who were serving at the time of the interviews, as well as all MPs, including Ministers, who had served as PPSs earlier in their careers.

12. In Philip W. Buck's data for 1918–1955, six out of ten served no more than two years, compared to 65 percent and 62 percent here. *Amateurs and Professionals in British Politics, 1918–59* (Chicago: University of Chicago Press, 1963): 116.

13. See R. K. Alderman and J. A. Cross, "The Parliamentary Private Secretary," *The Parliamentarian* 48, 2 (1967): 71.

14. PPSs are like "butlers of my father's generation . . . [who] tended to see the world in terms of a ladder—the houses of royalty, dukes . . . at the top. . . . Any butler with ambition simply did his best to climb as high up this ladder as possible, and by and large, the higher he went, the greater was his professional prestige." Kazuo Ishiguro, *The Remains of the Day* (London: Faber and Faber, 1990): 155.

15. Eight respondents identified themselves as Opposition PPSs, which suggests (by our response rates) that there were at least ten Opposition PPSs serving Opposition Front Bench Spokesmen at the time.

16. A salient example for them all was "Jim Prior, for instance, who was Ted Heath's PPS in Opposition and went straight from the backbenches to Cabinet rank when Ted Heath formed a Government." Very strong suggestions about promotion prospects are needed to attract Apprentices in Opposition. And it is mainly Apprentices who will be attracted, for Auxiliaries aren't much interested once the power is out of their master's role.

17. *The Times,* 6 May 1972.

18. Alderman and Cross, "Parliamentary Private Secretary," 70–71.

19. For example, Margaret Thatcher's PPS, Ian Gow, was sometimes referred to by his fellow backbenchers as a "Supergrass," a two-faced informer. Hugo Young, *One of Us: A Biography of Margaret Thatcher* (London: Macmillan, 1989): 244–45. See also Edmund Marshall, *Parliament and the Public* (London: Macmillan, 1982): 98.

20. Sixty-four percent of them spend ten or more hours per week in such settings, compared to only 40 percent of Conservative backbenchers. These data are derived from respondents' estimates, which were reported on a mailback questionnaire given to them at the end of the interviews.

21. Peter G. Richards, *The Backbenchers* (London: Faber and Faber, 1972): 45.

22. Opposition PPSs are freer to integrate such activities with their responsibilities. Francis McElhone, PPS to Anthony Wedgwood Benn, for instance, served as Chairman of the Regional Policy Committee of his party's Trade and Industry Committee while Benn was Shadow Minister for the same department and Chairman of the parent committee.

23. Colin Seymour-Ure, "The Cabinet and the Lobby," in Valentine Herman and James E. Alt (eds.), *Cabinet Studies: A Reader* (London: Macmillan, 1975): 159–63; Richards, *Backbenchers*, 198–99.

24. "The Shadow Minister and I were involved from the outset, from the very first day of the hospital workers' trouble. We went to meet them, 6 o'clock in the morning, coming off the special train. . . . I arranged parades and demonstrations, I was probably you might say 'the coordinator.' "

25. Either "you run round trying to get him a pair" or you maintain regular contact with the member of the Opposition with whom he usually pairs so that arrangements can be made and unmade quickly. Marshall, *Parliament and the Public*, 98; Richards, *Honourable Members*, 217.

26. Marshall, *Parliament and the Public*, 98–99.

27. Marshall, *Parliament and the Public*, 98–99; Richards, *Honourable Members*, 217.

28. This applies particularly to PPSs who serve Cabinet Ministers and especially Prime Ministers. When he was PPS to Harold Wilson as PM, Gerald Kaufman, for instance, was said to have been part of an inner circle of friends who influenced speeches, junior appointments, and matters of style. John P. Mackintosh, *The British Cabinet*, 3rd ed. (London: Stevens and Sons, 1977): 520.

29. He "is expected," at least, "to conform especially in respect of his own boss's particular responsibility, and I couldn't get up and say rude things about the Overseas Development program. . . . Obviously, if you're at loggerheads with the Minister in the pursuit of his policy, the answer is to stop being his PPS." Alderman and Cross, "Parliamentary Private Secretary," 199; Richards, *Backbenchers*, 206. These restraints on the conduct of PPSs are at the heart of concerns about the growth in their numbers. When the obligation to support the Government is extended "in large measure" to PPSs, that increases the Government's opportunities to stifle criticism in the Commons by increasing the size of its captive vote. It reduces the extent to which the Executive is likely to be checked by backbenchers.

30. Alderman and Cross, "Parliamentary Private Secretary," 203.

31. So on departmental subjects, the voice of the PPS is not heard in the House. A major concern is the extent to which the PPS must maintain silence on such topics in the country too. Some say that since these are issues they have long been concerned with, "I can speak in the country and I do." But most say that they have been given to understand that they must not speak on these matters, not "even outside the House of Commons without a very detailed brief, because on these subjects I am considered, even in the country, to be a Member of the Government if I speak. I speak, as it were, in the Minister's name, and so I have to be terribly careful."

32. Mackintosh, *British Cabinet*, 532.

33. *The Times*, 25 July 1983.

34. For example, "PPSs can today be maverick in what you might call a legitimate sense on other subjects because the whole atmosphere is much looser than it was. In the old days, the PPS really did toe the party line in respect of other subjects. . . . Nowadays they do obviously for the most of the time, if they can. But sometimes a PPS will kick over the traces, and this will be regarded as not particularly terrifying or wrong."

35. *The Spectator,* 11 November 1972.

36. Mackintosh, *British Cabinet,* 531, observed from the backbenches that it was not clear *to what extent* this convention covered cross-voting by PPSs, except that it had less force than for Ministers, but more, of course, than for backbenchers.

37. The sanctions for not doing so seemed to become stronger during the 1980s. In the notes that the Chief Whip was by then sending to Ministers telling them that they needed to be present to vote at such and such a time, he was also asking them to make sure that their PPSs were there as well. If a PPS did not wish to vote as a Member of the Government, he was expected to resign. *The Times,* 25 July 1983.

38. See Lord Wigg, *George Wigg* (London: Michael Joseph, 1972): 156. The role of the PPS includes an introduction to the doctrine of collective responsibility. It is a probationary role in which recruits are tested to see if they can accept the discipline.

39. William James, *Psychology* (New York: Henry Holt, 1892): 191.

40. Robert A. Stebbins, "A Note on the Concept of Role Distance," *American Journal of Sociology* 73 (1967): 247–50.

41. Sheldon Stryker and Anne Statham, "Symbolic Interaction and Role Theory," in Gardner Lindzey and Elliot Aronson (eds.), *The Handbook of Social Psychology,* 3rd ed., vol. 1 (New York: Random House, 1985): 342; Goffman, *Encounters,* 109–10; Chad Gordon, "Development of Evaluated Role Identities," *Annual Review of Sociology* 2 (1976): 405–33.

42. Richard Crossman, *The Diaries of a Cabinet Minister,* vol. 1 (London: Hamish Hamilton and Jonathan Cape, 1975): 303.

43. Apologies were defined as explicit statements denigrating the role of the Parliamentary Private Secretary. Tensions were coded from the responses to an explicit question that was, during the project's pretests, checked for validity against Taylor's manifest anxiety scale (Q. Many of the people we've talked to mention being overworked and, in consequence, they experience considerable tension and sleep fitfully. How often would you say *you* experience this sort of thing?). The exercise is crude because the codes are binary and the measures indirect: apologies may be an expression of role distance, but they may express other attitudes as well; tensions may arise from humiliation, but they may arise from other sources too. Nevertheless, such measurement errors should reduce rather than magnify the group differences we examine, for there is no reason to think they are systematically related to one's status as an Auxiliary or an Apprentice.

44. P. J. Burke and D. Reitzes, "The Link between Identity and Role Performance," *Social Psychological Quarterly* 44 (1981): 83–92; Peter J. Burke and Judy C. Tully, "The Measurement of Role Identity," *Social Forces* 55, 4 (1977): 881–97; Maurice Natanson, *Phenomenology, Role and Reason* (Springfield, Ill.: Charles C. Thomas, 1974): 210.

45. It was observed of Frank McElhone, for example, who was Opposition PPS to Tony Benn, that in the Commons and on public platforms he seemed to be trying increasingly to sound like his intense and sober mentor. *The Spectator,* 10 June 1972: 889.

46. The range of variation in such behaviors is likely to be considerable. Some PPSs do little beyond run the occasional message and attend the one essential party committee, while others are so busy that they see all their favorite outside interests disappear. Thus, *The Times* (31 July 1972) reported that Nick Scott, who had topped the Lords and Commons cricket club batting averages the previous season was, after being appointed PPS, able to turn out only twice for the Lords and Commons.

47. Morrison, *Government and Parliament,* 129.

48. The Chief is most likely to perform this service for Junior Ministers or for senior Ministers who are taking up posts in areas where they have little experience. First, the Ministers are given the information and the opportunity "to say, 'Well, I won't have him,' or 'I'll have a go at him.' " Then the Whips sound out the PPS. And then the Minister "rang me up . . . the ground having been sounded out for him . . . so I . . . wouldn't have rebuffed him." The lack of soundings can create "a slightly embarrassing Monday this week when I got two offers. And I've just had to resolve that particular problem this week. . . . I'm going to join Patrick Jenkin. I was also offered, uh, Michael Heseltine asked me if I'd look after the work there. And, uh, I said no to him."

49. Conservatives, for instance, tend to have comparatively few Scottish and Welsh MPs. Yet the Secretaries of State for Scotland and Wales want to have backbenchers from these regions as their Parliamentary Private Secretaries: "I'm PPS to the Secretary of State for Wales. I am Welsh, and there are not, uh, we hold seven seats out of thirty-six in Wales. So it is a bit of a special situation you know. . . . They wanted me to be a PPS, and I could see that they didn't have much choice."

50. The data were gathered from published sources and then checked by the respondents themselves. They are more accurate than the published sources (which are often inconsistent), but are not completely accurate because of missing data. In particular, the table underestimates the number of PPSs who had been officers of backbench party committees. This is the information least likely to be recorded in published sources and most likely to be overlooked, especially if it is old, by the MPs.

51. The proportion of backbenchers following this route in the table is smaller than is suggested by House lore; the lore may be closer to the truth.

52. Three others did too, but they are not included in the table, because the table records only immediately prior positions. One of them had been appointed directly to the Opposition Front Bench but was then "heaved out by an ungrateful electorate." When he was later reelected, he began as a backbencher and went from there to become a PPS. The other two, also Auxiliaries, had once before been PPSs in Government, but then moved up to Junior Opposition Front Bench Spokesmen when their party moved into Opposition. When it returned to Government, they returned to their PPS positions.

53. According to Buck's (*Amateurs and Professionals,* 116) data for 1918–1955,

only a third of all MPs were thirty-nine years old or less at the time of their election, whereas two-thirds of the PPSs were this age.

54. Others include similar social background to the Minister who seeks an Auxiliary; a self-confident demeanor that helps prospective Apprentices to look the part; a gregariousness that gives both Apprentices and Auxiliaries access to backbench circles; a verbal fluency that combines a talent for public debate with an ease in private conversation; and intelligence, which has become increasingly essential for service in Governments that have become increasingly complex.

55. Buck, *Amateurs and Professionals,* 47–48, 115. Published data on service as a PPS are extremely unreliable.

56. These data were collected and cross-checked from several published sources and then checked again by the respondents themselves. They are probably more accurate than Buck's data, but it is difficult to know whether this explains why the results are less sanguine than Buck's, or whether the promotion prospects of PPSs have declined as their numbers have risen.

57. They may underestimate slightly the proportions who served as PPSs because in many cases these experiences occurred ten to twenty years before, were of brief duration, and were not very salient to senior Ministers as they checked over our long lists of all the ministerial and Opposition Front Bench appointments they had held throughout their careers. Another source of bias is that Ministers who were young backbenchers when their party was in Opposition would not, in most cases, have had an opportunity to become PPSs.

58. Critchley, "How to Get on in the Tory Party," 472. Furthermore, although acceptance of the offer may boost one's chances only a little, rejecting this recognition may reduce one's chances a lot. Such refusals have been interpreted by Ministers and Whips as indicating a lack of ambition—and one might not be given a second chance. *The Times,* 25 July 1983.

59. Alderman and Cross, "Parliamentary Private Secretary," 203.

60. Anthony Trollope, *Can You Forgive Her?* (London: Penguin, 1972 [1864–65]): 492.

61. Richard Rose, "The Making of Cabinet Ministers," in Herman and Alt, *Cabinet Studies,* 6–7.

7. Whips

1. During the 1964–1970 Labour Governments, Government Whips introduced a forerunner of the personal computer, an electronic machine that stored the information about backbenchers that came into the Office each day. "At the touch of a switch," this provided up-to-the-minute information on any backbencher's whereabouts and activities. When Conservative Whips returned to office in 1970, however, they found the machine cumbersome and replaced it with "the time-honoured technology: a piece of chalk and a list of Members."

2. Donald D. Searing and Chris Game, "Horses for Courses: The Recruitment of Whips in the British House of Commons," *British Journal of Political Science* 7,

3 (1977): 361–86; F. M. G. Willson, "Entry to the Cabinet, 1959–68," *Political Studies* 18, 2 (1970): 71.

3. See Philip Norton, "The Organization of Parliamentary Parties," in S. A. Walkland (ed.), *The House of Commons in the Twentieth Century* (Oxford: Oxford University Press, 1979): 11–13; Peter G. Richards, *The Backbenchers* (London: Faber and Faber, 1972); Robert J. Jackson, *Rebels and Whips* (London: Macmillan, 1968); Lord Morrison, *Government and Parliament,* 3rd ed. (London: Oxford University Press, 1964): 116.

4. Martin Redmayne, interviewed by Norman Hunt, "The Power of the Whips," in Anthony King (ed.), *British Politics: People, Parties and Parliament* (Boston: D. C. Heath, 1966).

5. Jackson, *Rebels and Whips,* 35–37.

6. Thus, the Comptroller may be assigned to send the Queen the daily telegram that summarizes events in Parliament, while the Vice Chamberlain brings to the Queen Addresses from the Commons and brings back to the House her replies, which, with his white staff, he reads aloud in the House and delivers to the Clerk. Morrison, *Government and Parliament,* 114–15.

7. Many have regular pairs, often colleagues on the other side with similar work schedules, such as lawyers, or similar travel schedules, such as Scottish Members. The pairing compacts permit them to meet their constituency obligations and other commitments outside Westminster, or simply to escape the hothouse atmosphere for a day.

8. In addition, the Pairing Whip arranges pairs for Ministers who are abroad or committed to dinners and official engagements, as well as for backbenchers who are ill. With overseas delegations, Pairing Whips will be concerned to see that equal numbers from each side travel together or that proper pairs have been arranged. Anthony King and Anne Sloman, *Westminster and Beyond* (London: Macmillan, 1973): 113–14.

9. Jackson, *Rebels and Whips,* 42.

10. Richards, *Backbenchers,* 59. From the backbenchers' perspective, such reports are opportunities to modify party policy. From the perspective of the leadership, they are opportunities to identify both rebels who need surveillance and loyalists who deserve promotion.

11. Philip Norton, *Conservative Dissidents: Dissent within the Parliamentary Conservative Party, 1970–74* (London: Temple Smith, 1978): 164–65. Most Junior Whips are very good at the management of committees. The Government rarely loses a vote as a result of poor management, and the Opposition rarely feels it has been denied its opportunity to criticize.

12. His negotiations with the Junior Whip on the other side will cover how much business can be done in a sitting and whether a certain number of votes will be allowed. The Government Whip also handles procedural matters such as moving closures and arranging extra sittings as required.

13. Richard Rose, "British MPs: A Bite as Well as a Bark?" *Studies in Public Policy* 98, University of Strathclyde, 1982: 29. Indeed, the amount of dissent is likely to vary over time as a consequence of changes in leadership, norms, formal rules,

the size of the Government's majority, and, last but not least, the pace of reform: "When men combine to do nothing, how should there be disagreement? When men combine to do much, how should there not be disagreement? . . . The wonder is that there should ever be in a reforming party enough of consentaneous action to carry any reform." Trollope, *The Duke's Children* (London: Oxford University Press, 1970 [1880]): 162.

14. And, in most cases, the rebels were upholding more-orthodox positions than were their party's leaders. Just as important as ensuring that backbenchers choose the proper division lobby is ensuring that they are present to vote. When the Whips are off, a party's voting strength can be halved. The roles of the Government Whips require them to be vigilant truant officers so that the Government's supporters will always outnumber the forces on the other side. Even when the Opposition has gone home for the night, Government Whips must hold approximately 120 supporters in order to move "that the question now be put" and provide a margin of safety. To prevent backbench escapes, they are occasionally posted at House exits—according to one backbencher who was apprehended slipping out a back door. See Richards, *Backbenchers,* 57; Peter G. Richards, *Honourable Members: A Study of the British Backbencher* (London: Faber and Faber, 1959): 83–84.

15. For a good example of the Whip's "communication explanation," see Francis Pym, *The Politics of Consent* (London: Sphere Books, 1984): 98–101.

16. Anthony King, *British Members of Parliament: A Self-Portrait* (London: Macmillan, 1974): 59; Douglas Houghton, "The Labour Backbencher," *Political Quarterly* 40, 4 (1969): 454–63. Nevertheless, "power-explanations" were very popular among commentators at the time: T. F. Lindsay, *Parliament from the Press Gallery* (London: Macmillan, 1967): 22–23.

17. Norton, *Conservative Dissidents,* 165.

18. Morrison, *Government and Parliament,* 119. And, recently: "The Whips were nothing but absolute reason," said the Member for Colchester North. "There were enormous pressures but sweet reason was a more painful pressure." *The Independent,* 6 November 1992.

19. Redmayne, "Power of the Whips," 144.

20. For example, Philip Norton, *The Commons in Perspective* (Oxford: Martin Robinson, 1981): 30–31.

21. "Join the House of Commons and see the world!" was how one MP began a paragraph on the subject in her memoirs: Jean Mann, *Woman in Parliament* (London: Odhams Press, 1962): 141. Although it is a common mistake to assume that Whips control every trip abroad, they do select Members for most official delegations.

22. This discourages dissidents from feeling neglected and possibly becoming professional rebels; even persistent offenders appreciate a good listener because they "hate not to be noticed." Jackson, *Rebels and Whips,* 299.

23. Peter M. Blau, *The Dynamics of Bureaucracy* (Chicago: University of Chicago Press, 1963): 215–16.

24. Strict adherence to the attendance rule would disrupt modern families, interfere with constituency work and social activities, and make it impossible to pursue

the outside employment that many backbenchers require to maintain their living standards.

25. Sometimes, however, backbenchers cross-vote anyway. And then it may be prudent to express tolerance after the fact: "You say, well yes, indeed you agree, they have every right to dissent." Badgering people who have violated party discipline may in certain circumstances be counterproductive and set off an epidemic. As with exceptions to the rule, tolerance for delinquency may make the best of a bad situation: "I simply told my Whip, and he said to me, very kindly, 'I've told the Chief Whip we must never approach you because you make up your mind and, if we do approach you, it can only make things worse.'" King, *British Members of Parliament,* 57. Tolerating delinquency mops up what exceptions to the rules fail to prevent.

26. Blau, *Dynamics of Bureaucracy,* 215–17.

27. Anthony Trollope, *Phineas Finn* (London: Oxford University Press, 1973 [1869]): 274. This is presumably the main reason that there is considerably less party discipline in the Lords than in the Commons.

28. Norton, *Conservative Dissidents,* 166–68, for example, argues that when persuasion fails, there is nothing else to be done, because the Whip's coercive powers are so few and weak. As far as it goes, this account is correct. The punishments and rewards available to contemporary Whips are not sufficient to produce involuntary compliance, which is nonetheless occasionally demanded. Rupert Allason, for example, got a card from his Whip informing him that he had been assigned to a Standing Committee that would meet on Wednesday mornings. "Very kind of you to invite me," Allason replied, "but alas, I'm booked up for the mornings." Back came a very curt reply: "You clearly do not understand. It's not an invitation. It's a demand." *The Independent,* 9 August 1988.

29. Niccolo Machiavelli, *The Prince and the Discourses* (New York: Random House, 1940 [1520]): 60–63. Love, he wrote, "is held by a chain of obligation." But this chain by itself is not sufficiently strong to guarantee successful influence unless it is reinforced by a fear of punishment, albeit not by a fear that inspires hatred.

30. See Blau, *Dynamics of Bureaucracy,* 219–20.

31. At the time of the interviews, the Conservative Whips' informal authority was strained when backbenchers began to feel "that they are in the hands of, and regarded as servants of, a Leader who has little regard for their affection or their principles, and who considers them as cattle to be driven through the gates of the Lobby." Patrick Cosgrave, "The Winter of their Discontent," *The Spectator,* 28 September 1972: 878. The result was a great deal of dissension and disobedience.

32. Soon after two Labour MPs missed several important divisions in 1972, for example, they faced motions from Labour Whips that they be discharged ("sacked") from their Select Committees. This was widely interpreted on the backbenches as a message about what the Whips can do if they wish. *The Daily Telegraph,* 27 March 1972.

33. Humphry Berkeley, *Crossing the Floor* (London: Allen and Unwin, 1972): 26. They can also release to newspapers, and thereby make public, the names of delin-

quents who abstain without permission—which they were said to have done during the Common Market votes. *The Times,* 5 July 1972.

34. *The Times,* 29 October 1971. The next day it was announced that if he did resign, the Deputy Chief Whip and the Junior Whips would go with him for the same reason. *The Times,* 30 October 1971.

35. Norton, "Organization of Parliamentary Parties," 18–21; Norton, *Conservative Dissidents,* 168.

36. This difference in emphasis arose from different assessments of the nature of each parliamentary party. Whips on both sides seemed to agree that Conservative MPs were bound together mainly by feelings of community; Labour MPs, by feelings of contract. Thus, reason and reciprocity were suitable techniques for the comparatively homogeneous Conservative parliamentary community—until it became more disputatious after the overthrow of Margaret Thatcher, that is, for then the balance began to tilt in the other direction: *The Independent,* 6 November 1992. By contrast, Labour's heterogeneity in background and ideology has always required a firmer hand. And that may be why so many Labour experiments in relaxing discipline have backfired. Labour MPs are said to need to feel a little more white heat before the velvet touch can bring out a willing response. See Charles Perrow, *Organizational Analysis: A Sociological View* (London: Tavistock, 1970): 37–49.

37. See M. Van Sell et al., "Role Conflict and Role Ambiguity: Integration of the Literature and Directions for Future Research," *Human Relations* 34 (1981): 43–71.

38. Max Weber, "Bureaucracy," in H. H. Gerth and C. Wright Mills (eds.), *From Max Weber: Essays in Sociology* (New York: Oxford University Press, 1958): 196–244.

39. Sheldon Stryker and Anne Macke, "Status Inconsistency and Role Conflict," *Annual Review of Sociology* 4 (1978): 57–90. Moreover, people differ markedly in the extent to which they are aware of these role conflicts. Sheldon Stryker and Anne Statham, "Symbolic Interaction and Role Theory," in Gardner Lindzey and Elliot Aronson (eds.), *The Handbook of Social Psychology,* 3rd ed., vol. 1 (New York: Random House, 1985): 350.

40. See Robert H. Miles, "Role-Set Configurations as a Predictor of Role Conflict and Ambiguity in Complex Organizations," *Sociometry* 40, 1 (1977): 21–34.

41. See Miles "Role-Set Configuration"; Robert H. Miles, "Role Requirements as Sources of Organizational Stress," *Journal of Applied Psychology* 1 (1976): 172–79; R. L. Kahn et al., *Organizational Stress: Studies in Role Conflict and Ambiguity* (New York: Wiley, 1964).

42. During the brief period of the interviews, one Whip was divorced because of his adultery, one ran off with a Minister's wife, one became ill and died, and one (Labour) Whip found succor by reminding himself that things could be worse: "It is a worrying job; it is a hard job. But when I compare it to the job I used to do, well, it's a piece of cake. When I really feel depressed I just make myself sit down for two minutes and think about the thirty-four years I spent in the pits—and I'm a refreshed man."

43. Auberon Waugh, "The Broken Whip," *Private Eye,* 31 December 1971: 16. The party's Leader reinstated him, but he was nonetheless "enraged and sickened by the disloyalty of so many colleagues," and could be found, Waugh further

claimed, "sitting alone in obscure corners of the House looking emotional and muttering to himself about revenge."

44. Charges of duplicity and insincerity are the occupational hazards; it is difficult for backbenchers genuinely to like someone whose normal approach is a personal interview conducted with hints of aloofness and undertones of detachment. Not surprisingly, some backbenchers characterize them as "double agents." Andrew Roth, *Heath and the Heathmen* (London: Routledge and Kegan Paul, 1972): 103.

45. F. M. G. Willson, "Some Career Patterns in British Politics: Whips in the House of Commons, 1906–1966," *Parliamentary Affairs* 24 (1970–71): 36.

46. Sam D. Sieber, "Toward a Theory of Role Accumulation," *American Sociological Review* 39 (1974): 567–78.

47. See, for example, the comments of Humphry Berkeley, *Crossing the Floor* (London: Allen and Unwin, 1972): 142, and of William Hamilton in King and Sloman, *Westminster and Beyond,* 109.

48. King and Sloman, *Westminster and Beyond,* 112.

49. See James Stuart, *Within the Fringe: An Autobiography* (London: Bodley Head, 1967): 80.

50. This measure, which has successfully passed a variety of validity tests, distinguishes the ideals of right-wing and left-wing factions within each parliamentary party. Donald D. Searing, "Measuring Politicians' Values: Administration and Assessment of a Ranking Technique in the British House of Commons," *American Political Science Review* 71, 1 (1978): 65–80.

51. All these political values were defined in the rank-order lists by their first definitions in the *Shorter Oxford English Dictionary.*

52. Common Marketeer James Wellbeloved was said to have been appointed, for example, in hopes of healing wounds and reestablishing contact with Labour's pro-Market group. *The Daily Telegraph,* 4 February 1972.

53. Prominent among these variables is the desire for cozy relationships in the Whips' Office. Being bound to work together day and night, Whips are keen to ensure that newcomers will fit in with the fellowship. It is not surprising that Conservative Whips can sustain a Billy Bunter banter when twelve out of fourteen attended public schools, most of them minor ones, and almost all were boarders. Five of the six who went on to university were at Cambridge, all but one at the same college (Kings). If anything, Labour Whips are even more compatible: not only are they working class, but six out of fourteen of their fathers were miners.

54. The assumption is that trade union experience teaches people to submerge their differences behind a united front. This trade union stamp is often said to be the single most salient characteristic of the Labour Whips' Office.

55. It has surprised some observers that the Whip's Office was one of the last male preserves in the House to be entered by women: Elizabeth Vallance, *Women in the House* (London: Athlone Press, 1979): 103. And, surprisingly, it was Labour, the more punitive of the parliamentary parties, that appointed two women to its whipping staff, Betty Boothroyd in 1974, followed by Margaret Jackson in 1975.

56. Julian Critchley, *The Palace of Varieties: An Insider's View of Westminster* (London: Faber and Faber, 1990): 66.

57. Willson, "Some Career Patterns in British Politics," 35.

58. Willson, "Some Career Patterns in British Politics," 35–36. Compared with Labour, Conservatives bring more Parliamentary Private Secretaries into the Whips' team because they regard whipping as the next step up the ladder to ministerial office. Former Ministers, by contrast, would regard the Whip's job as a step down and are not asked for this reason. Even the most junior of Junior Ministers rarely slips back into the Whips' Office; only a handful have done so in this century, and none in the present sample. The major exceptions are Ministers, such as Whitelaw and Mellish, who moved over into the Chief Whip's chair, a seat that confers substantial ministerial status.

59. For an illustration of this time-honored strategy, see Viscount Chilston, *Chief Whip: The Political Life and Times of Aretas Akers-Douglas, First Viscount Chilston* (London: Routledge and Kegan Paul, 1961): 27.

60. If each criterion were applied rigidly, the selection frame would quickly squeeze out all possible candidates. This, of course, does not happen. The criteria are weighted and applied according to the preferences of the Chief Whips and their junior colleagues, who, at any given time, are constrained by the distribution of these attributes on the backbenches.

61. King and Sloman, *Westminster and Beyond*, 112. This can be especially attractive for Labour MPs from working-class backgrounds who, as backbenchers, found in the House "a new life full of stresses and strains. It's an overwhelming place, this." The role of the Whip offers a confirmation of their successful adaptation to Westminster's world: "I think the fact of your doing something makes you real confident, and at the same time you get a satisfaction that you're really on the ball—and that's something, believe me."

62. Henry Fairlie has described this subtle and satisfying process as follows: "Indeed, the majority of politicians probably begin to use new concepts and new categories without properly realizing what they are doing. They pick up a phrase from their leaders and, without understanding its full implications, repeat it. . . . Slowly, by repetition and modification, the phrase and the idea which it represents, become part of the common language and common assumptions of their party." *The Life of Politics* (London: Methuen, 1968): 28–29.

63. Many Labour Whips held analogous jobs before entering Parliament: shop stewards, factory foremen, headmasters, and Whips in local government. For them, service in the Whips' Office offers scope to exercise talents that brought success earlier in life.

64. King and Sloman, *Westminster and Beyond*, 102. It is not at all unusual for supervisors to develop close ties among themselves in order to replace the emotional support formerly provided by colleagues who have now become subordinates. Peter M. Blau and W. Richard Scott, *Formal Organizations: A Comparative Approach* (San Francisco: Chandler, 1962): 159.

65. *The Times*, 15 October 1971.

66. Backbenchers prefer this sort of rough assessment over the political scientist's more precise data on career patterns spanning previous decades. They prefer their own data, but do not gather it systematically. Instead, they look around the House and listen to others who are knowledgeable in such matters, to insiders like Lord

Swinton, who advised the young Edward Heath to "take the chance to get into the machine at however squalid a level." Andrew Roth, *Heath and the Heathmen* (London: Routledge and Kegan Paul, 1972): 80.

67. Philip Norton, "The Forgotten Whips: Whips in the House of Lords," *The Parliamentarian* 57, 2 (1976): 89; Walter J. Oleszek, "Party Whips in the United States Senate," *Journal of Politics* 33, 4 (1971): 967.

68. The minority of Conservative Whips who did not anticipate promotion were all over fifty—too old, they said, to strike out as Junior Ministers.

69. Besides, Chief Whips can be relied upon to press their vassals' claims: as Patrick Buchan-Hepburn championed Edward Heath during the 1950s, so Heath helped further the careers of Whitelaw and Barber during the 1960s.

70. If Labour Whips do go on to something else after working in the Office, likely as not it will be a job as Parliamentary Private Secretary (see Table 7.5), wherein they can further utilize the liaison skills they have acquired. But that will usually be the end of it, in contrast to Conservatives who are PPSs *before* entering the Whips' Office and who treat the role of the Whip as a further apprenticeship for ministerial positions.

71. In Opposition, only two Whips (besides the Chief Whip) receive remuneration, and they are usually senior members of the Office. Yet, even if prospective Opposition Whips cannot expect an immediate salary increase, they will have staked out a position to receive this supplement later, either when their party returns to Government or when they have accumulated seniority in Opposition.

72. Lord Wigg, *George Wigg* (London: Michael Joseph, 1972): 165.

73. To ask, therefore, whether a link exists between the attitudinal and behavioral sides of their position roles would be absurd. If Whips don't behave like Whips, they are dismissed. And if they can't behave like Whips, they resign.

74. These restraints are eased in Opposition, where Whips participate in Question Time, make speeches, introduce Private Members' Bills, and enjoy some of the normal backbench activities. Basking in this relative freedom, an Opposition Whip forecast that when his party returned to Government, he would probably resign rather than "accept the monastic vows of silence." Still, Opposition Whips are not free: they must avoid strong policy commitments and accept the obligations of an informal collective responsibility. Even Opposition Whips must "be very selective in what we do, obviously."

8. Ministers

1. D. J. Heasman, "The Prime Minister and the Cabinet," *Parliamentary Affairs* 15, 4 (1962): 307–12.

2. D. J. Heasman, "Parliamentary Paths to High Office," *Parliamentary Affairs* 16, 3 (1963): 315–22.

3. Review Body on Top Salaries, *First Report: Ministers of the Crown and Members of Parliament*, Cmnd 4836 (HMSO, 1971). For this reason, Table 8.1 includes information about the salaries of Ministers who, when they simultaneously serve as Members of the House of Commons, as most of them do, also receive a parliamen-

tary salary. As Prime Minister, Harold Wilson characterized the three levels of authority as his *first* (Cabinet Minister), *second* (Full Ministers Outside the Cabinet and Ministers of State), and *third* (Parliamentary Secretaries) teams. *The Governance of Britain* (London: Weidenfeld and Nicolson and Michael Joseph, 1976): 32.

4. Senior Cabinet Ministers consider those lower down in this order as their "juniors" in the Cabinet. This pecking order was still a little muddled in 1972 as a result of the previous Labour Government's amalgamations of ministries, which led at the time to the unusual situation of several departments having several representatives in the Cabinet. R. L. Leonard, "Snakes and Ladders," *New Society,* 9 October 1969: 558.

5. They usually did not, in 1972, work for Ministers, because in most of the departments that had a Minister of State there was no Minister, and the Minister of State served directly under the department's Secretary of State. They may have been the functional equivalent of Ministers in such circumstances, but they still had, on the whole, less weighty responsibilities and were still, on the whole, less weighty members of their party.

6. Even when they are given specific areas of responsibility, this is usually in connection with "helping," "assisting," or "supporting" the Minister who is actually in charge of the policy. R. S. Milne, "The Junior Minister," *Journal of Politics* 12, 3 (1950): 437–49. This is what the Review Body on Top Salaries, *First Report,* 32–33, had in mind when it described the role of the Junior Minister as "an apprenticeship to higher Ministerial office." It is a weakness of Kevin Theakston's otherwise excellent book *Junior Ministers in British Government* (Oxford: Basil Blackwell, 1987) that he lumps together Ministers of State and Parliamentary Secretaries, for this makes his account of the "average" duties and responsibilities of Junior Ministers seem more important than they actually are and leads us to lose sight of the "trainee" character of the role.

7. D. J. Heasman, "Ministers' Apprentices," *New Society,* 16 July 1960: 16. The best available account of the role's institutionalization can be found in Theakston, *Junior Ministers in British Government,* chap. 1.

8. They are "people who should be given three years of fat ministerial life as reward for services rendered but whom one shouldn't keep longer than that." Crossman, *Diaries of a Cabinet Minister,* 761. See Harold Wilson, *The Labour Government, 1964–1970* (London: Weidenfeld and Nicholson and Michael Joseph, 1971): 713.

9. Although the intercoder reliability here is acceptable (Scott's $\pi = .80$), the material leaves more room for doubts about validity than is the case with the other preference roles.

10. Milne, "Junior Minister," 440–41; Duff Cooper, *Old Men Forget* (London: Rupert Hart-Davis, 1957): 161.

11. Theakston, *Junior Ministers in British Government,* 136.

12. By 1869, however, Anthony Trollope's Phineas Finn was beginning to worry about the growing constraints that were moving beyond votes in the division lobbies ("where he knew that it would be his duty as a subaltern to vote as he was directed") to words in the other lobbies: "He had taught himself to understand that Members

of Parliament in the direct service of the Government were absolved from the necessity of free-thinking. Individual free-thinking was incompatible with the position of a Member of the Government." *Phineas Finn* (London: Oxford University Press, 1973 [1869]): 47.

13. Theakston, *Junior Ministers in British Government,* 77–87.

14. Milne, "Junior Minister," 442–43. Kevin Theakston, "The Use and Abuse of Junior Ministers: Increasing Political Influence in Whitehall," *The Political Quarterly* 57, 1 (1986): 21. The importance that senior Ministers place on retaining ultimate control is reflected in the fact that, when they are away from London for a time, their responsibilities are not taken up by their Junior Ministers but are instead delegated to senior Ministers in other departments.

15. Heasman, "Ministers' Apprentices," 17.

16. Placemen are particularly likely to feel intimidated. One of them insisted that his Private Secretary, who was nearly half his age, be present throughout our interview, and, at the end of every lengthy response, looked to him for approval. Another Junior Minister, who was in much the same boat, was very pleased that his civil servants gave him his due: "I like working with them because there is good mutual respect." And yet another coped with the "authority of *their* expertise" by working very hard "to maintain all the outside contacts which I built up whilst I was specializing on the backbenches—by no means all of which I'm prepared to, to reveal to my civil servants."

17. Richard Rose, "The Making of Cabinet Ministers," *British Journal of Political Science* 1, 4 (1971): 396.

18. Junior Ministers aren't "Ministers," senior civil servants have been heard to say. They are "Parliamentary Under Secretaries," underlings, a form of political life not to be taken very seriously. Edward Pearce, *Hummingbirds and Hyenas* (London: Faber and Faber, 1985): 150–51.

19. See Theakston, *Junior Ministers in British Government,* 70–75.

20. Bruce Headey, *British Cabinet Ministers: The Roles of Politicians in Executive Office* (London: George Allen and Unwin, 1974): 104–05; Theakston, *Junior Ministers in British Government,* 119–21; Wilson, *Governance of Britain,* 67.

21. Social learning theory in psychology suggests that the most effective way to learn roles is to observe models, to observe the conduct and attitudes of others who are playing these roles. Jerold Heiss, "Social Roles," in Morris Rosenberg and Ralph H. Turner (eds.), *Social Psychology: Sociological Perspectives* (New York: Basic Books, 1981): 102.

22. Headey, *British Cabinet Ministers.*

23. Sir Douglas Allen, "Ministers and Their Mandarins," *Government and Opposition* 12, 2 (1977): 135–36.

24. Richard Crossman, *The Diaries of a Cabinet Minister,* vol. 1 (London: Hamish Hamilton and Jonathan Cape, 1975): 21–23. Margaret Thatcher was never convinced; so much so that when she became Prime Minister, it was thought wise to arrange a dinner party at No. 10, where she could exchange views with all the Permanent Secretaries. But when she rose to speak, she began by saying that together she and they could "beat the system"—to which they replied, "But we are the sys-

tem." It was an experience that, contrary to the plan, confirmed her worst fears. Hugo Young, *One of Us: A Biography of Margaret Thatcher* (London: Macmillan, 1989): 229–31.

25. Review Body on Top Salaries, *First Report,* 30. This was not the only way that Ministers expressed their concern about being in charge. Peter Walker, for instance, made it known that not only did he meet personally with his six Ministers every morning, but that his Permanent Secretary was not present. "And this demonstrates to my mind the relative success of that Ministry in the sense that it's been run by a politician, and it hasn't been all that time influenced by civil servants," said an MP back at Westminster who was duly impressed. See *The Spectator,* 30 September 1972: 495; R. K. Alderman and J. A. Cross, "Ministerial Reshuffles and the Civil Service," *British Journal of Political Science* 9, 1 (1979): 48.

26. Richard Rose, "The Making of Cabinet Ministers," *British Journal of Political Science* 1, 4 (1971): 405–06.

27. Headey, *British Cabinet Ministers,* 68.

28. For example, on the matter of appointments Sir Douglas Allen ("Ministers and Their Mandarins"), Head of the Home Civil Service, writes that if the minister (not capitalized) and his Permanent Secretary (capitalized) cannot get on with one another, then "somebody has to be moved." To the Minister, it may seem that if it isn't immediately apparent that it is his subordinate who must be moved, then perhaps the subordination isn't so apparent either. In the same vein, when a classroom of sixty young civil servants at the Civil Service College was asked what they thought the principal differences were between civil servants and Ministers, waves of nervous laughter filled the room in response to the first answer: "Intelligence."

29. Headey, *British Cabinet Ministers,* 159.

30. Similarly, when George Brown was in charge of the DEA [Department of Economic Affairs], he tried to build rapport between the Labour Government and leading industrialists by having the industrialists to monthly dinners where he would seek their advice. *In My Way: The Political Memoirs of Lord George Brown* (London: Victor Gollancz, 1971): 100–02. See also Wilson, *Labour Government,* 174.

31. *The Times,* 27 September 1972. This proved more difficult than Heath had anticipated. But he kept at it—and soon his Conservative critics were worrying about "the beginning of a corporate state." *The Times,* 26 March 1973.

32. Senior Ministers, who had more at stake and had more direct contact than Junior Ministers, were more likely than Junior Ministers to express such views.

33. "It's a little like the Tory Party," commented a Minister who was more involved than most in the party machine. "Central Office can't control the constituency associations. And you get the most God-awful people chosen." Likewise, in the trade union movement "you get the most God-awful people like Bernie Steer operating as shop stewards in the docks—and there's damn all that Jack Jones can do about it."

34. Anthony King, "The Rise of the Career Politician in Britain and Its Consequences," *British Journal of Political Science* 11, 3 (1981): 282.

35. Among these rules, the most obvious is the use of titles to depersonalize debates in the Cabinet and in Cabinet Committees. Just as civility is promoted by the

use of titles in the House of Commons, so civility is promoted in the Cabinet by addressing one's colleagues as "First Secretary," "Minister of Defence," or "Prime Minister." Another way to reduce conflict is to communicate with one another through confidential minutes that can be written in an informal and personal style that facilitates consensus when policies are being formulated.

36. Headey, *British Cabinet Ministers,* 164.

37. Donald D. Searing, "Rules of the Game in Britain: Can the Politicians Be Trusted?" *American Political Science Review* 76, 2 (1982): 239–58.

38. Rose, "Making of Cabinet Ministers," 410–11.

39. Ministers always assume that the public wants them "to explain the case," certainly a more comforting assumption than the alternative possibility that the public understands the case and rejects it. The Chairman of the Conservative Party, Peter Thomas, was merely treading in the familiar footsteps of his predecessors when he explained to the party's annual conference in 1971 that "in spite of all the achievements of the Conservative Government since their return to office, the Conservatives, as a party, were dismally failing to make proper use of the splendid ammunition which they could be using to deploy their case to supporters and potential supporters." *The Times,* 14 October 1971.

40. Crossman, *Diaries of a Cabinet Minister,* 497.

41. Since the press is by nature critical, many Governments come to believe that the BBC is politically prejudiced against them. Sometimes they are correct. Yet, Ministers understandably tend to see more political bias in journalistic criticism than might an outside observer whose survival is not at stake. It is instructive to note that the loudest complaints have come from both a Labour Government (Harold Wilson's during the 1960s) and a Conservative Government (Margaret Thatcher's during the 1980s).

42. In the press, reputations go up and down like the stock market: "It is perhaps time this week to take note of the political stock market—who's up, who's down, how are they doing? . . . Mr. Heath is up slightly . . . so to a greater extent are Mr. Whitelaw, Mr. Peter Walker . . . and Sir Geoffrey Howe. . . . Mr. John Davies, I am afraid, is going down slowly but steadily. . . . Further down still—so far down that she demands separate and fairly extended treatment—we have Mrs. Margaret Thatcher. All governments have their statutory albatross. It is Mrs. Thatcher's misfortune to combine the role of statutory albatross with that of statutory woman." Alan Watkins, *New Statesman,* 10 December 1971: 810.

43. As *The Observer,* 9 July 1972, put it when the case first broke: "The Poulson bankruptcy case has certainly damaged and may have destroyed Mr. Reginald Maudling's credibility as Home Secretary . . . even though nothing he has done, or is alleged to have done in this case, can be declared disreputable let alone illegal."

44. Crossman, *Diaries of a Cabinet Minister,* 466.

45. For example, a typical comment in *The Spectator* (24 June 1972): "Puzzle regrets to report that Tory backbenchers are not enthusiastic about the performance, so far, of Mr. Maurice Macmillan." Or *The Economist* (11 November 1972): "The 40-year-old Mr. Walker . . . is thought by many good judges . . . to be a likely next-prime-minister-but-two."

46. Its value as a method for seriously scrutinizing government policy is widely doubted. But its value as a method for testing and retesting Ministers is reflected in the exodus from the Chamber when it is over. Lisanne Radice, Elizabeth Vallance, and Virginia Willis, *Member of Parliament: The Job of the Backbencher*, 2nd ed. (London: Macmillan, 1990): 59.

47. Crossman, *Diaries of a Cabinet Minister*, 295–96.

48. Headey, *British Cabinet Ministers*, 72.

49. Thus, the normally anti-Conservative *Guardian* (30 November 1972) rushed to announce that Prime Minister Heath, who hadn't been doing well against Harold Wilson, had suddenly developed a command of Question Time: "The Prime Minister, once so despised as a parliamentary performer, is becoming almost indecently accomplished." Similarly, *The Daily Telegraph* (17 November 1972), which is normally anti-Labour, described at the same time Labour's Shadow Environment Secretary, Anthony Crosland, as "the most elegant pneumatic drill in the Commons" and went on to echo recent Westminster judgments that his recent performances were "by any standard superb."

50. Crossman, *Diaries of a Cabinet Minister*, 209–11. And conversely: " 'I can't stand it any longer,' he said, 'not from old colleagues.' " Emanuel Shinwell, *I've Lived through It All* (London: Victor Gollancz, 1973): 81.

51. Women in the House have had difficulty developing successful styles at the Despatch Box because the images that seem "exactly right" are embedded in a world of rugby fields and gentlemen's clubs with which they are not comfortable. Elizabeth Vallance, *Women in the House* (London: Athlone Press, 1979): 107–08.

52. John Grant, *Member of Parliament* (London: Michael Joseph, 1974): 104–05.

53. From the backbenches before the war, David Kirkwood observed carefully who was respected by the House and who was not. One of his principal conclusions was that those who fail to take the House seriously are never forgiven. They are treated as outsiders. *My Life of Revolt* (London: George C. Harrap, 1935): 214.

54. That's why it was said during the 1970s that Roy Jenkins could never be the Leader of the Labour Party. His arrogant manner gave people the impression, as the *New Statesman* (19 May 1972: 666) unkindly put it, "that the only thing he has ever really fought for is a table in a fashionable restaurant."

55. By the third year of the Heath Government, Conservative Ministers were being defeated by their own backbenchers and were working hard to reassess the way the policy process ideally should work.

56. During their interviews, Ministers were asked to rank-order a list of nine reasons that had been put forward to explain why most backbenchers refrain from cross-voting most of the time. Leaders of organizations tend to see their team as more consensual than it actually is. Thus, the Ministers were more likely than their backbenchers to give "basic agreement with party leaders' positions" top marks. And senior Ministers were much more likely than backbenchers to do so. See William D. Crano, "Assumed Consensus of Attitudes: The Effect of Vested Interest," *Personality and Social Psychology Bulletin* 9, 4 (1983): 597–608.

57. Headey, *British Cabinet Ministers*, 168–69.

58. *The Times*, 7 August 1972. After the 1979 reforms of the Select Committee

system, ministerial performances in these forums became increasingly important—as important and sometimes more important for departments and for ministerial reputations than performances at Question Time in the Chamber. Peter Hennessy, *Whitehall* (New York: Free Press, 1989): 335–36; Stephen J. Downs, "Select Committees: Experiment and Establishment," in Philip Norton (ed.), *Parliament in the 1980s* (Oxford: Basil Blackwell, 1985): 65.

59. Great care is taken over correspondence with MPs because Ministers believe that this greatly affects the department's reputation in Parliament, which greatly affects its success and its Minister's success as well. See, for example, William Whitelaw, *The Whitelaw Memoirs* (London: Aurum Press, 1989): 166.

60. They are such an important reference group because they are the opinion leaders for other Conservative backbenchers. Conservative Ministers like to think of these committees as their private listening posts and centers for persuasion. The discussions are private, and the results can therefore "be taken into account before a division is forced on the floor of the House."

61. Ministers learn through experience that success in the House depends on reasonable working relationships between the parties. Whitelaw, *Whitelaw Memoirs*, 51; Wilson, *Governance of Britain*, 143. For example, 78 percent of all government legislation is not opposed by the Opposition on principle at the Second Reading Debate. It is, in other words, consensual—and this reflects the fact that Ministers usually spend much more time conciliating the Opposition than insulting it. Richard Rose, "British MPs: A Bite as Well as a Bark?" *Studies in Public Policy* 98, University of Strathclyde, 1982: 10.

62. The general feeling during the early 1970s was still one of camaraderie across the frontbenches, which was promoted by Privy Councillor relationships and by the usual channels. Privy Councillors, who are normally leaders in their parties, talked to one another frequently and frankly on "a Privy Councillor basis."

63. Conservative Ministers were weary from Labour's withdrawal of all cooperation in the passage of the Industrial Relations Act during the previous year. Of course, in the end the Government of the day can usually get its way regardless, but "in fact life got hell for everybody . . . life became so unpleasant, people couldn't get away, people got irritable and tetchy, and the House of Commons I think started to deteriorate."

64. These subtypes echo the task-oriented versus relationship-oriented performances that are so often heard in leadership studies. See Mark R. Leary, Byron D. Barnes, Rebecca B. Robertson, and Rowland S. Miller, "Self-Presentations of Small Group Leaders: Effects of Role Requirements and Leadership Orientation," *Journal of Personality and Social Psychology* 51, 4 (1986): 742–48.

65. They will not be pursued quantitatively because, even more than the junior ministerial preference roles, Placemen and Journeymen, they are less crystallized than virtually any of the backbench subtypes. Moreover, the number of cases of Administrators and Politicians that I have been able to code confidently is too small to support quantitative investigations. For the entire set, Scott's $\pi = .62$.

66. See Headey, *British Cabinet Ministers.*

67. Heasman, "Parliamentary Paths to High Office." Administrators may be in

the minority, but their existence has been widely recognized in observations, like those of Peter Hennessy (*Whitehall*, 493–94), that some Ministers seem to wish to be civil servants, can easily be imagined to be civil servants, and often sound like civil servants when performing their roles.

68. The codes here were generated from "global judgments" on entire transcripts rather than from specific responses to specific questions. The entry for Full Ministers Outside the Cabinet (4[2]) indicates that two of the four Administrators at this level are Law Officers, "professional advisors" who do not regard themselves as politicians, nor do they regard themselves as Administrators in quite the same sense as their colleagues.

69. "And you've got friends and all the excitement of mixing this strange body of people all together. I love the House, and whenever we rise for the long recess, and I have to go back into the House when it's empty for some papers or something like that . . . the echoes of the past you know, you know, it's like, it's like, and suddenly it'll all erupt and all your friends will be back there together and we'll all be engaged in things. . . . I adore the House."

9. Ministerial Role Strains and Role Choices

1. Richard Crossman, *The Diaries of a Cabinet Minister*, vol. 1 (London: Hamish Hamilton and Jonathan Cape, 1975): 628.

2. By the 1960s, observers like Bernard Crick noted that Ministers were beginning to feel that they were "not in any real sense Members of Parliament, but simply remote and all-powerful trustees for the electorate, only answerable to anyone at general elections. The prejudice grows that the proceedings of Parliament are a waste of ministerial time." *The Reform of Parliament* (London: Weidenfeld and Nicolson, 1968): 4.

3. Their dilemma is recognized in role studies as a situation where the individual works in one organization (Parliament) but owes primary allegiance to a different reference group (Government). A very common strategy for dealing with such dilemmas is to withdraw emotionally from one of the roles. Sheldon Stryker and Anne Statham, "Symbolic Interaction and Role Theory," in Gardner Lindzey and Elliot Aronson (eds.), *The Handbook of Social Psychology*, 3rd ed., vol. 1 (New York: Random House, 1985): 336–38.

4. Many examples of attempts to minimize ministerial vulnerability can be found in George Thomas, *Mr. Speaker* (London: Arrow Books, 1985). Among the more ironic were the efforts of William Waldegrave, the Cabinet Minister responsible for open government, to help "Whitehall departments *block* requests to provide more information about policy decisions." *The Independent*, 14 July 1992.

5. *The Times*, 3 August 1972. "A ventriloquist talking to his backbench puppets," *The Guardian* (14 December 1971) complained, "Mr. Amery was thus able to reserve a considerable part of the Commons' precious Question Time for what amounted to self-congratulation." Actually, modest versions of this practice were quite common. It was only the scale of Amery's efforts that provoked outrage. In the same vein, Ministers give uninformative and evasive answers to Parliamentary

Questions; they waffle in their conversations with the new Select Committees; and they schedule many important announcements for the parliamentary recess: Colin Turpin, "Ministerial Responsibility: Myth or Reality?" in Jeffrey Jowell and Dawn Oliver (eds.), *The Changing Constitution,* 2nd ed. (Oxford: Oxford University Press, 1989): 80.

6. These data are consistent with those reported from the survey undertaken by the Review Body on Top Salaries, *First Report: Ministers of the Crown and Members of Parliament,* Cmnd 4836 (HMSO, 1971): 51, which indicated that both Ministers and backbenchers spent approximately ten to twelve hours per week on constituency work outside the House.

7. Like Iain Macleod, they think their constituents should be pleased to be represented by a Cabinet Minister rather than by an undistinguished backbencher, even if the Cabinet Minister is unable to attend to all "their small disputes and differences." Nigel Fisher, *Iain Macleod* (London: Andre Deutsch, 1973): 69–70.

8. Crossman, *Diaries of a Cabinet Minister,* 152–53. Furthermore, even when Ministers succeed in constituency battles behind the scenes, they do not get the local publicity they would win were they fighting in public. They sometimes feel at an electoral disadvantage and, like the Whips, worry that their majority may erode with each successive General Election.

9. Donald D. Searing, "Rules of the Game in Britain: Can the Politicians Be Trusted?" *American Political Science Review* 76, 2 (1982): 239–58.

10. See, for instance, Harold Wilson, *The Labour Government, 1964–1970* (London: Weidenfeld and Nicolson and Michael Joseph, 1971): 572.

11. Thus, virtually all Conservative Ministers rejected without reservation the notion that "the electorate ought to have the opportunity to vote in a referendum on crucial matters affecting the nation's vital interests." They rejected it much more decisively than did their backbenchers, presumably because it is from ministerial hands that such referenda take policy decisions and give them to the public.

12. On the history of the problem of ministerial overload, see Peter Hennessy, *Cabinet* (Oxford: Basil Blackwell, 1986): chap. 2. By the 1990s the workload seemed even heavier, and it seemed even clearer that "stamina" and "high horsepower" were essential qualifications for the job. Julian Critchley, *The Palace of Varieties: An Insider's View of Westminster* (London: Faber and Faber, 1990): 8.

13. The variety itself can be a strain: "One has got to jump from, you know, I'm working on this Bill just now, I've already had a meeting this afternoon on a totally different matter. And, er, before the night is finished I'll no doubt have one or two discussions about some, some totally disconnected things." The worst situation for the "ulcer-ridden executive" is when he *believes* that the duties are too multifarious and complex to be managed successfully. David Coburn, "Job-Worker Incongruence: Consequences for Health," *Journal of Health and Social Behavior* 16 (1975): 198–212.

14. Review Body on Top Salaries, *First Report,* 52. The Review Body's results differ only in that they find slightly higher proportions of respondents in the categories for sixty or more hours per week. This difference is consistent with the assumption that our study's questionnaire underestimated total time and also with the fact

that their study's questionnaire was known to be part of an effort to build a case for higher salaries.

15. Rose, "Making of Cabinet Ministers," 406–08.

16. One senior Minister slips away to his London townhouse for a little "English therapy": "I've been getting away recently in the middle of the afternoon . . . and it's very pleasant when I can go home and do a little gardening."

17. They have less sleep, less exercise, and fewer holidays than other Members but, collectively, no greater instances of the symptoms of ill health (such as headaches, indigestion, insomnia, or fatigue) that might be produced by stress. H. Beric Wright and G. Pincherle, *British Heart Foundation Enquiry into Health and Work in the House of Commons* (London: British Heart Foundation, 1967).

18. Or: "I always think I'm overworked, but it does seem to do me a power of good. I only regret actually that there aren't twenty-five hours in the day. No, I have always worked terribly hard, and er, as life goes on I seem to work harder and harder. But it doesn't, er,—I seem to thrive on it. I sometimes feel like a little more sleep, but apart from that it doesn't matter."

19. Bernard Donoughue, *Prime Minister: The Conduct of Policy under Harold Wilson and James Callaghan* (London: Jonathan Cape, 1987): 11. Likewise, according to a former Permanent Secretary who worked with many Ministers in a number of different departments, it is the "adrenalin-rousing" stimulus of high office that generates anew the energy "to cope" with role overload. Leo Pliatzky, "Mandarins, Ministers and the Management of Britain," *Political Quarterly* 55, 1 (1984): 27.

20. Anthony Sampson, *Macmillan: A Study in Ambiguity* (London: Pelican, 1968): 102.

21. See Stephen R. Marks, "Multiple Roles and Role Strain: Some Notes on Human Energy, Time, and Commitment," *American Sociological Review* 42 (1977): 921–36.

22. Donoughue, *Prime Minister*, 12; Joe Haines, *The Politics of Power* (London: Jonathan Cape, 1977): 10.

23. Crossman, *Diaries of a Cabinet Minister*, 562.

24. Crossman, *Diaries of a Cabinet Minister*, 712. See Barbara Castle, *The Castle Diaries, 1964–70* (London: Weidenfeld and Nicolson, 1984): 377–78.

25. D. J. Heasman, "The Prime Minister and the Cabinet," *Parliamentary Affairs* 15, 4 (1962): 473.

26. Bruce Headey, *British Cabinet Ministers: The Roles of Politicians in Executive Office* (London: George Allen and Unwin, 1974): 98.

27. They are usually consulted, but not always: "The Minister of Transport and Civil Aviation then was Jack Maclay. . . . I went and knocked on the door of his room and was bidden to enter. 'Hello Reggie,' he said, 'What can I do for you?' 'Well, Jack,' I replied, 'I am your new Parliamentary Secretary.' 'Oh,' he said, somewhat aghast, 'are you?' The truth is that Winston had not bothered to tell him." Reginald Maudling, *Memoirs* (London: Sidgwick and Jackson, 1978): 52.

28. Examples of such negotiations can be found in Barbara Castle, *The Castle Diaries, 1974–76* (London: Weidenfeld and Nicolson, 1980): 34–39. One important

problem with the PM's monopoly of this patronage is that, as with the reshuffles, what may be advantageous from the perspective of pleasing the party's leadership echelon may be less desirable from the perspective of sound administration. Senior Ministers frequently find that their subordinates are not personally or politically compatible with them. And this makes it difficult to delegate to these subordinates assignments that might more readily be given to people they selected themselves.

29. Richard Rose, "The Making of Cabinet Ministers," *British Journal of Political Science* 1, 4 (1971): 400–02.

30. There are always important party barons whose independent power bases in the party are such that they must be included in the Cabinet. Donoughue, *Prime Minister,* 12; D. J. Heasman, "The Prime Minister and the Cabinet," *Parliamentary Affairs* 15, 4 (1962): 464. They must be included because of the rules that make the Government responsible to the House, and thereby dependent on the solidarity of its own backbench supporters. It would be foolhardy for a Prime Minister to leave powerful, disgruntled notables on the backbenches, where they might lead revolts. Headey, *British Cabinet Ministers,* 69.

31. It must sometimes seem to Prime Ministers that they more often select posts for people rather than the other way round. For instance, there is a convention that Ministers in the Scottish and Welsh Offices should represent constituencies from those regions. This greatly narrows the choices for Conservative Prime Ministers, since the Conservative Party normally wins very few seats in these areas. Another restriction of this kind is the arrangement in the Labour Party whereby Shadow Ministers are elected by the Parliamentary Labour Party and, thus legitimized, have a strong claim on a place in the Cabinet. R. K. Alderman, "The Prime Minister and the Appointment of Ministers: An Exercise in Political Bargaining," *Parliamentary Affairs* 29, 2 (1976): 110.

32. Alderman, "Prime Minister," 101.

33. Anthony Trollope, *The Prime Minister* (London: Oxford University Press, 1970 [1876]): 5.

34. Stuart Elaine Macdonald, "Political Ambition and Attainment: A Dynamic Analysis of Parliamentary Careers," Ph.D. diss., University of Michigan, 1987.

35. Anthony King, "The Rise of the Career Politician in Britain and Its Consequences," *British Journal of Political Science* 11, 3 (1981): 264–65.

36. Martin Burch and Michael Moran, "The Changing British Political Elite, 1945–1983: MPs and Cabinet Ministers," *Parliamentary Affairs* 38, 1 (1985): 1–15.

37. D. J. Heasman, "Parliamentary Paths to High Office," *Parliamentary Affairs* 16, 3 (1963): 323.

38. If an ambitious young Member "can get himself elected Chairman of the committee, he will often be the one who takes the chair when Ministers come to talk to the committee, and he will be in touch with the department telling the Ministers what the committee thinks. . . . And as he's recognized as being very much *au fait* with this particular subject, when they're looking for a Junior Minister, the Prime Minister or the Chief Whip . . . might say, 'Well, who's the Chairman of the committee?' "

39. E. Gene Frankland, "Parliamentary Career Achievement in Britain and West

Germany: A Comparative Analysis," *Legislative Studies Quarterly* 2, 2 (1977): 143–45.

40. F. M. G. Willison, "The Routes of Entry of New Members of the British Cabinet, 1868–1958," *Political Studies* 7, 3 (1959): 222–32, and "Entry to the Cabinet, 1959–68," *Political Studies* 18, 2 (1970): 236–38.

41. Headey, *British Cabinet Ministers,* 89–90.

42. See Lord Butler, *The Art of the Possible* (London: Hamish Hamilton, 1971): 30–31.

43. These Ministers were perhaps overimpressed by an unusual cluster of recent examples. Thus, Peter Mills was said to have been promoted to Parliamentary Secretary in the Heath Government because he had so successfully given the Department of Agriculture a difficult time as an officer of the backbench party committee. Robin Chichester-Clark's "promotion came exactly a fortnight after he had expressed doubts to the Prime Minister in the Commons about whether he had a mandate to remain in Parliament." *The Daily Telegraph,* 8 June 1972. And, in his reshuffle of April 1972, Heath was alleged to have taken into the Government four aggressive right-wingers (Tom Boardman, Peter Emery, John Nott, and Cranley Onslow) in order to stifle backbench revolts over the U-turns in the Government's economic policies. *The Spectator,* 15 April 1972: 580–81.

44. See Kevin Theakston, *Junior Ministers in British Government* (Oxford: Basil Blackwell, 1987): 9, and Castle, *Castle Diaries, 1974–76,* 411.

45. Theakston, *Junior Ministers in British Government,* 49; Harold Wilson, *The Governance of Britain* (London: Weidenfeld and Nicolson and Michael Joseph, 1976): 30; Emanuel Shinwell, *I've Lived through It All* (London: Victor Gollancz, 1973): 237. This can extend to appointments within departments as well. For example, in his reshuffle of April 1972, Prime Minister Heath appointed the left-wing Tory Christopher Chataway as a Minister in the Department of Industry and appointed, at the same time, a right-winger, Tom Boardman, to counterbalance him. *The Guardian,* 8 April 1972.

46. The data on which this figure is based were coded from reputational assessments of the ideological positions of MPs presented in Andrew Roth's *The MP's Chart* (London: Parliamentary Profile Services, 1971). These data have consistently proved useful in other analyses, but they should not be taken for more than what they are, a political journalist's generally well-informed but rather casual ideological sketches.

47. Richard M. Sorrentino and Nigel Field, "Emergent Leadership over Time: The Functional Value of Positive Motivation," *Journal of Personality and Social Psychology* 50, 6 (1986): 1091–99.

48. Anthony Howard, *RAB: The Life of R. A. Butler* (London: Jonathan Cape, 1987): 304ff.

49. Macdonald, "Political Ambition and Attainment."

50. Frankland, "Parliamentary Career Achievement," 139.

51. Joseph Schlesinger, *Ambition and Politics: Political Careers in the United States* (Chicago: Rand McNally, 1966).

52. Gordon S. Black, "A Theory of Political Ambition: Career Choices and the

Role of Structural Incentives," *American Political Science Review* 66, 1 (1972): 144–59; David W. Rhode, "Risk-Bearing and Progressive Ambition: The Case of Members of the United States House of Representatives," *American Journal of Political Science* 23, 1 (1979): 1–26; Paul Brace, "Progressive Ambition in the House: A Probabilistic Approach," *Journal of Politics* 46, 2 (1984): 556–71.

53. Macdonald, "Political Ambition and Attainment," 86.

54. For example: James Callaghan, *Time and Change* (London: Collins, 1987): 231; Lord Williams, *Digging for Britain* (London: Hutchinson, 1965): 109–10; and Robert Harris, *The Making of Neil Kinnock* (London: Faber and Faber, 1984): 73.

55. The people who unnecessarily risk painful disappointments, he further explains, are those who "first of all worry most about what they're going to get. When they get it, they worry about the next job. And when they get the next job they worry about losing either of them—and they never really *enjoy* politics. So I try not to be involved in that particular fact."

56. Near the end of the interviews, Ministers were asked: "And finally, your own plans? Are there any further positions in the House that you would like to seek sometime in the future?" Their responses were coded for ambition as follows: specific positions named (e.g., Chancellor); positive responses with no positions named; coy but positive-leaning responses (e.g., "I take what comes, we'll have to see"); and no further position desired. These codes were later treated as an ordinal scale of degrees of ambition and weighted according to the respondent's assessment, elicited by the next question, of his or her chances of attaining such positions.

57. For example, see the comments in *The Economist,* 11 December 1971.

58. King, "Rise of the Career Politician in Britain," 249–86.

59. Julian Critchley, *Westminster Blues* (London: Future, 1985): 41. See also Henry Fairlie, *The Life of Politics* (London: Methuen, 1968): 45, and Nicholas Henderson, *The Private Office: A Personal View of Five Foreign Secretaries and of Government from the Inside* (London: Weidenfeld and Nicolson, 1984): 124–25.

60. Oliver Lyttelton, Viscount Chandos, *The Memoirs of Lord Chandos* (London: The Bodley Head, 1964): 431.

61. Harold D. Lasswell, *Psychopathology and Politics* (Chicago: University of Chicago Press, 1930), and *Power and Personality* (New York: Norton, 1948). Furthermore, Lasswell claimed, this need is especially strong in an important subgroup of politicians among whom it is linked to low self-esteem, anxiety, Machiavellianism, and rhetorical skills. See also Douglas Madsen, "A Biochemical Property Relating to Power Seeking in Humans," *American Political Science Review* 79, 2 (1985): 448–57.

62. Alexander L. George and Juliette L. George, *Woodrow Wilson and Colonel House: A Personality Study* (New York: Dover, 1964); Sigmund Freud and William C. Bullitt, *Thomas Woodrow Wilson: A Psychological Study* (London: Weidenfeld and Nicolson, 1966); Arnold A. Rogow and Harold D. Lasswell, *Power, Corruption, and Rectitude* (Englewood Cliffs, N.J.: Prentice-Hall, 1963); Erik H. Erikson, *Young Man Luther* (New York: Norton, 1962); E. Victor Wolfenstein, *The Revolutionary Personality: Lenin, Trotsky, and Gandhi* (Princeton: Princeton University Press, 1967); Robert N. Kearney, "Identity, Life Mission, and the Political Career: Notes

on the Early Life of Subhas Chandra Bose," *Political Psychology* 4, 4 (1983): 617–36; William McKinley Runyan, *Life Histories and Psychobiography: Explorations in Theory and Method* (New York: Oxford University Press, 1982); Marvin Rintala, "The Love of Power and the Power of Love: Churchill's Childhood," *Political Psychology* 5, 3 (1984): 375–90.

63. J. B. McConaughy, "Certain Personality Factors of State Legislators in South Carolina," *American Political Science Review* 44 (1950): 897–903; Robert M. Rosenzweig, "The Politician and the Career in Politics," *American Journal of Political Science* 1, 2 (1957): 163–72; Bernard Hennessey, "Politicals and Apoliticals: Some Measurements of Personality Traits," *Midwest Journal of Political Science* 3 (1959): 355–66; Rufus P. Browning and Herbert Jacob, "Power Motivation and the Political Personality," *Public Opinion Quarterly* 28, 1 (1964): 75–90; James W. Clarke and Marcia M. Donovan, "Personal Needs and Political Incentives: Some Observations on Self-Esteem," *American Journal of Political Science* 24, 3 (1980): 536–52.

64. *The Spectator,* 30 September 1972. See also Philip M. Williams, *Hugh Gaitskell: A Political Biography* (London: Jonathan Cape, 1979): 288, 757.

65. Crossman, *Diaries of a Cabinet Minister,* 514–19. Other notable if mild cases of this malady can be detected in the hubristic rectitude of Hugo Young's Margaret Thatcher and in the hubristic self-importance of George Brown's own George Brown: Hugo Young, *One of Us: A Biography of Margaret Thatcher* (London: Macmillan, 1989); George Brown, *In My Way* (London: Victor Gollancz, 1971).

66. In the same vein, "I mean if you committed the most appalling and atrocious crime," explained a senior Minister only a little tongue-in-cheek, "and you went down and said to the House of Commons, 'I would like permission to speak, I would like to make a personal statement. I regret to say that last night I murdered my wife, left my daughter. . . . I deeply regret this behaviour of the day when I bring discredit on the House as a whole.' So long as you said it *sincerely,* all the House would say would be 'Yae, yae, yae,' and leave it at that." It is a peculiar crowd, and spending a number of years as a backbencher in this crowd is the surest way to develop the right touch.

67. See F. M. G. Willson, "The Routes of Entry of New Members of the British Cabinet, 1868–1958," *Political Studies* 7, 3 (1959): 222–32, and "Entry to the Cabinet, 1959–68," *Political Studies* 18, 2 (1970): 236–38.

68. Unlike Frank Cousins, however, after a period of considerable unhappiness John Davies decided at age sixty to try to become "sensitive to the way in which this place works and what makes it tick, what you can get away with and the ways in which you can get away with it. It takes quite a long time to learn."

69. Anthony King, "The Rise of the Career Politician in Britain and Its Consequences," *British Journal of Political Science* 11, 3 (1981): 277.

70. See Arthur B. Gunlicks, "Max Weber's Typology of Politicians: A Reexamination," *Journal of Politics* 40, 2 (1978): 498–509.

71. Erving Goffman, *Encounters* (Indianapolis: Bobbs-Merrill, 1961): 106. See also Sheldon Stryker and Richard T. Serpe, "Commitment, Identity Salience, and Role Behavior: Theory and Research Example," in William Ickes and Eric S. Knowles (eds.), *Personality, Roles, and Social Behavior* (New York: Springer Verlag, 1982): chap. 7, who sought to study this subject with a question similar to ours.

72. See Ralph H. Turner, "The Role and the Person," *American Journal of Sociology* 84, 1 (1978): 1–23.

73. *The Guardian*, 1 June 1972.

74. See Brown, *In My Way*, 187, 199.

10. Conclusion

1. Sir Lewis Namier, *Personalities and Powers* (New York: Harper and Row, 1965): 10–11.

2. Lisanne Radice, Elizabeth Vallance, and Virginia Willis, *Member of Parliament: The Job of a Backbencher*, 2nd ed. (London: Macmillan, 1990); Anthony King, "The Rise of the Career Politician in Britain and Its Consequences," *British Journal of Political Science* 11, 3 (1981): 249–86.

3. A. M. Carr-Saunders and P. A. Wilson, *The Professions* (Oxford: Oxford University Press, 1933): 4.

4. Compare Anthony Barker and Michael Rush, *The Member of Parliament and His Information* (London: Allen and Unwin, 1970); H. Beric and G. Pincherle, *British Heart Foundation Enquiry into Health and Work in the House of Commons* (London: British Heart Foundation, 1967).

5. Radice, Vallance, and Willis, *Member of Parliament*, 52. Many Members were still "moonlighting," but in most cases these pursuits were more like academic consulting than like a second job.

6. Radice, Vallance, and Willis, *Member of Parliament*, 114–15.

7. Carr-Saunders and Wilson, *Professions*, 298; J. A. Jackson, *Professions and Professionalization* (London: Cambridge University Press, 1970): 6.

8. Radice, Vallance, and Willis, *Member of Parliament*, 24, 37.

9. Wilbert E. Moore, *The Professions: Roles and Rules* (New York: Russell Sage Foundation, 1970): chap. 1; Carr-Saunders and Wilson, *Professions*, 471.

10. John P. Mackintosh, "Parliament and the Public: The Effects of the Media," in John P. Mackintosh, M.P. (ed.), *People and Parliament* (London: Saxon House): 141–42.

11. Andrew Abbott, *The System of Professions* (Chicago: University of Chicago Press, 1988): 7; Carr-Saunders and Wilson, *Professions*, 360.

12. Colin Turpin, "Ministerial Responsibility: Myth or Reality?" in Jeffrey Jowell and Dawn Oliver (eds.), *The Changing Constitution*, 2nd ed. (Oxford: Oxford University Press, 1989): 63.

13. Carr-Saunders and Wilson, *Professions*, 491. The best recent work on the professions comes to similar conclusions: "professions are somewhat exclusive groups of individuals applying somewhat abstract knowledge to particular cases." Abbott, *System of Professions*, 318. See also William J. Goode, "Community within a Community: The Professions," *American Sociological Review* 22 (1957): 194–200.

14. Abbott, *System of Professions*, 318.

15. They were always common in the Labour Party, but since 1945 they have become common in the Conservative Party too at the expense of the amateur Tory

politicians who typically jumped into politics in midlife at the national level. Radice, Vallance, and Willis, *Member of Parliament,* 33.

16. Nicolo Machiavelli, *The Prince and the Discourses* (New York: Random House, 1950 [c. 1520]): 91.

17. Malcolm E. Jewell, "Attitudinal Determinants of Legislative Behavior: The Utility of Role Analysis," in Allan Kornberg and Lloyd D. Musolf (eds.), *Legislatures in Developmental Perspective* (Durham, N.C.: Duke University Press, 1970): 480.

18. Bryan Gould, M.P., "The MP and Constituency Cases," in Mackintosh, *People and Parliament,* 84.

19. Compare William Mishler and Anthony Mughan, "Representing the Celtic Fringe: Devolution and Legislative Behavior in Scotland and Wales," *Legislative Studies Quarterly* 3, 3 (1978): 391–92.

20. John P. Mackintosh, M.P., "The Changing Role of the M.P.: Introduction," in Mackintosh, *People and Parliament,* 76. They do seem to receive more letters from constituents: Barker and Rush, *Member of Parliament and His Information,* 174–77.

21. Barker and Rush, *Member of Parliament and His Information,* 387.

22. Donald R. Matthews notes in his review of the literature on legislative recruitment that few consistent relationships have been found between social background characteristics and legislative role orientations. Social background characteristics do not dominate recruitment here either, but they are an important starting point. Age, in particular, can be quite consequential. "Legislative Recruitment and Legislative Careers," in Gerhard Loewenberg, Samuel C. Patterson, and Malcolm E. Jewell (eds.), *Handbook of Legislative Research* (Cambridge, Mass.: Harvard University Press, 1985): 25.

23. There are also common behaviors that are role related but too transitory to become characteristic. A good example is the senior Ministers who, during the latter half of the Conservative Heath Government, began speaking sympathetically about the situations of trade union leaders, and for several years tried to persuade them of the desirability of "corporatistic" economic planning.

24. James G. March and Johan P. Olsen, *Rediscovering Institutions: The Organizational Basis of Politics* (New York: Free Press, 1989): 21–25.

25. Samuel H. Beer, *Britain against Itself: The Political Contradictions of Collectivism* (New York: Norton, 1982): 190–91; Bernard Crick, *The Reform of Parliament,* 2nd ed. (London: Weidenfeld and Nicolson, 1968): 4.

26. Philip Norton, "Introduction: Parliament in Perspective," in Philip Norton (ed.), *Parliament in the 1980s* (Oxford: Basil Blackwell, 1985): 8–11.

27. Radice, Vallance, and Willis, *Member of Parliament,* 65, 168; R. E. Dowse, "The MP and His Surgery," *Political Studies* 11, 3 (1963): 333–41.

28. Mackintosh, "Changing Role of the M.P.," 77–80.

29. Bruce E. Cain, John A. Ferejohn, and Morris P. Fiorina, *The Personal Vote: Constituency Service and Electoral Independence* (Cambridge, Mass.: Harvard University Press, 1987): chap. 4.

30. Radice, Vallance, and Willis, *Member of Parliament,* 5.

31. See James L. Lynskey, "The Role of British Backbenchers in the Modification of Government Policy," *Western Political Quarterly* 23, 2 (1970): 333–48.

32. Philip Norton, "Behavioural Changes: Backbench Independence in the 1980s," in Norton, *Parliament in the 1980s,* 22–47.

33. Michael Ryle, "The Commons Today: A General Survey," in S. A. Walkland and Michael Ryle (eds.), *The Commons Today,* rev. ed. (London: Fontana, 1981): 27–28; Edmund Marshall, M.P., *Parliament and the Public* (London: Macmillan, 1982): 6–7.

34. Turpin, "Ministerial Responsibility," 55; Beer, *Britain against Itself,* 180–84.

35. Julian Critchley, *The Palace of Varieties: An Insider's View of Westminster* (London: Faber and Faber, 1990): 71–80; Radice, Vallance, and Willis, *Member of Parliament,* 117–18.

36. Turpin, "Ministerial Responsibility," 71.

37. Norton, "Behavioural Changes"; John E. Schwarz, "Exploring a New Role in Policy Making: The British House of Commons in the 1970s," *American Political Science Review* 74 (1981): 23–37.

38. King, "Rise of the Career Politician," 280.

39. Turpin, "Ministerial Responsibility," 73.

40. Turpin, "Ministerial Responsibility," 71–73. Many Policy Advocates would like to see these Select Committees fortified by new parliamentary rules that would require, for instance, that their reports be debated and that these debates be accompanied (and this would be a genuinely radical reform) by free votes. Radice, Vallance, and Willis, *Member of Parliament,* 163–64.

41. Philip Norton, *The Constitution in Flux* (Oxford: Basil Blackwell, 1982): 284–85.

42. Nevil Johnson, *In Search of the Constitution: Reflections on State and Society in Britain* (Oxford: Pergamon, 1977): 52–59; Crick, *Reform of Parliament,* xv.

43. Stephen J. Downs, "Structural Changes: Select Committees: Experiment and Establishment," in Norton, *Parliament in the 1980s,* 59.

44. Radice, Vallance, and Willis, *Member of Parliament,* 133–36. They also sought to deny them money for researchers, secretaries, computers, and other facilities needed to keep in check "this swollen and overweening executive." *The Independent,* 19 July 1992.

45. John P. Mackintosh, *The British Cabinet,* 3rd ed. (London: Stevens and Sons, 1977): 535–36. See also King, "Rise of the Career Politician"; and Radice, Vallance, and Willis, *Member of Parliament.*

46. Johnson, *In Search of the Constitution,* 32–33.

47. Radice, Vallance, and Willis, *Member of Parliament,* 20; King, "Rise of the Career Politician."

48. Radice, Vallance, and Willis, *Member of Parliament,* 8.

49. Norton, *Constitution in Flux,* 82–87. But the Central Policy Review Staff has, unintentionally, in practice strengthened the influence of the civil service instead. Ministers have become not less but more dependent on civil servants than they were several decades ago.

50. Donald Searing, "Rules of the Game in Britain: Can the Politicians Be Trusted?" *American Political Science Review* 76, 2 (1982): 239–58. As with functional representation, these consequences often seem more intended than unintended, and more intended to promote the self-interest of Ministers than a responsi-

ble interest in constitutional development. The situation sparked a widely supported movement for constitutional reform and an informal constitutional convention in Manchester in 1991.

51. Their individualistic and self-interested behavior has substantially weakened this constitutional rule to the point where Prime Ministers have been reduced to suspending it in order to save face. Turpin, "Ministerial Responsibility," 81–83.

52. If they do decide to defend the Minister, then the pressure to resign is deflected by a shield of collective responsibility that permits him or her to continue to enjoy the emoluments of office. Norton, *Constitution in Flux,* 56.

53. Alexander Rosenberg, *Philosophy of Social Science* (Oxford: Oxford University Press, 1988): 79.

54. Jerome Bruner, *Actual Minds, Possible Worlds* (Cambridge, Mass.: Harvard University Press, 1986): 117–18.

55. Donald Searing, "Measuring Politicians' Values: Administration and Assessment of a Ranking Technique in the British House of Commons," *American Political Science Review* 72, 1 (1976): 65–80.

56. James L. Payne and Oliver H. Woshinsky sought to exclude values from their incentive variables, but that may not be so easy to do. "Incentives for Political Participation," *World Politics* 24, 4 (1972): 518–46.

57. Malcolm E. Jewell and Samuel C. Patterson, *The Legislative Process in the United States,* 3rd ed. (New York: Random House, 1977): 369–71.

58. See Ralph H. Turner, "The Role and the Person," *American Journal of Sociology* 84, 1 (1978): 1–23.

59. "Most like to give the impression that they are cleverer, deeper, wiser than they are." *The Independent,* 14 July 1992.

60. Contrary to the claims of Harold D. Lasswell, *Politics: Who Gets What, When, How* (New York: Meridian Books, 1958).

61. March and Olsen, *Rediscovering Institutions,* 6.

62. James Farr, "Situational Analysis: Explanation in Political Science," *Journal of Politics* 47, 4 (1985): 1085–1108.

63. Jenny Jeger, "The Image of the MP," in Mackintosh, *People and Parliament,* 10–29; Mackintosh, "Changing Role of the M.P.," 75; Bruce E. Cain, John A. Ferejohn, and Morris P. Fiorina, "The House Is Not a Home: British MPs in Their Constituencies," *Legislative Studies Quarterly* 4, 4 (1979): 501–23.

64. Sheldon Stryker and Anne Statham, "Symbolic Interaction and Role Theory," in Gardner Lindzey and Elliot Aronson (eds.), *The Handbook of Social Psychology,* 3rd ed., vol. 1. (New York: Random House, 1985): 311–78.

65. Alasdair MacIntyre, *After Virtue,* 2nd ed. (Notre Dame, Ind.: University of Notre Dame Press, 1984). See also Sheldon Stryker and Richard T. Serpe, "Commitment, Identity Salience, and Role Behavior: Theory and Research Example," in William Ickes and Eric S. Knowles (eds.), *Personality, Roles, and Social Behavior* (New York: Springer Verlag, 1982): chap. 7.

66. Peter J. Burke, "The Self: Measurement Requirements from an Interactionist Perspective," *Social Psychology Quarterly* 43, 1 (1980): 18–29.

67. William James, *Psychology* (New York: Henry Holt, 1892). Compare Bruce

Biddle et al., "Social Influence, Self-Referent Identity Labels, and Behavior," *The Sociology Quarterly* 26, 2 (1985): 159–85.

68. Stryker and Statham, "Symbolic Interaction and Role Theory," 350.

69. Jon Elster, *Political Psychology* (Cambridge: Cambridge University Press, 1993).

70. See Rosenberg, *Philosophy of Social Science*, 92–95.

71. Robert N. Bellah et al., *The Good Society* (New York: Knopf, 1991): 40.

72. Bruner, *Actual Minds, Possible Worlds*, 66–67. The preferences of politicians are not exogenous. And economic models in politics will lack verisimilitude so long as they continue to assume that they are exogenous. Politicians do bring their own goals and incentives to their organizations—but then they reconstruct them there, sometimes consciously, sometimes half-consciously, sometimes unconsciously, as they adapt to these institutional environments. March and Olsen, *Rediscovering Institutions,* chap. 3.

Appendix A

1. It was very common, for example, to see Members dictating into their tape recorders in corridors, alcoves, and meeting rooms around the House.

2. Philip Converse and Roy Pierce, *Political Representation in France* (Cambridge, Mass.: Harvard University Press, 1986): 676. See also Malcolm E. Jewell, "Legislators and Constituents in the Representative Process," in Gerhard Loewenberg, Samuel C. Patterson, and Malcolm E. Jewell (eds.), *Handbook of Legislative Research* (Cambridge, Mass.: Harvard University Press, 1985): 104.

3. Bruce J. Biddle, *Role Theory: Expectations, Identities, and Behaviors* (New York: Academic Press, 1979): 79–83.

4. The rule, which is very rarely violated, is "Say what you want and we won't say you said it." Austin Mitchell, *Westminster Man: A Tribal Anthropology of the Commons People* (London: Thames Methuen, 1982): 205–06. Since the interviews were granted on this nonattribution basis, names have been used only when the information comes from published sources such as newspapers rather than from the transcripts. Likewise, in quotations from these transcripts, the names of places and other distinguishing characteristics have been changed whenever they would make it possible to identify the interviewee. In the same vein, names have occasionally been invented when it would have been inappropriate to use the names of MPs being commented upon by their colleagues but awkward not to use any names at all.

5. The sensitive questions from their perspective were certainly not about the roles but about friends and family, albeit toward the end of the interview when these topics were introduced, rapport was often sufficiently strong that they were remarkably forthcoming about these subjects too.

6. Experimental studies, the other possible source of data about roles, are just not on for politicians in most circumstances. Many MPs suspect that the academics who study them are a little peculiar to begin with. They already dislike questionnaires, many of whose items they find ludicrous, intellectually insulting, or impertinent. And they would laugh out of the Central Lobby suggestions that they should,

in the name of science, participate in controlled experiments under laboratory conditions.

7. Compare James L. Payne, Oliver H. Woshinsky, Eric P. Veblen, William H. Coogan, and Gene E. Bigler, *The Motivation of Politicians* (Chicago: Nelson-Hall, 1984): 192.

Appendix B

1. On coding qualitative data of this sort, see John G. Geer, "What Do Open-Ended Questions Measure?" *Public Opinion Quarterly* 52, 3 (1988); Anselm Strauss, *Qualitative Analysis for Social Scientists* (Cambridge: Cambridge University Press, 1987).

2. See John C. McKinney, *Constructive Typology and Social Theory* (New York: Appleton-Century-Crofts, 1966): 6–21. The principle is similar to that applied by Joel D. Aberbach, Robert D. Putnam, and Burt A. Rockman, *Bureaucrats and Politicians in Western Democracies* (Cambridge, Mass.: Harvard University Press, 1981).

3. Edward Crowe, "Purpose in Politics: The Influence of Career Goals on Attitudes and Behavior in the House of Commons," Ph.D. diss., University of North Carolina, Chapel Hill, 1982.

4. "Thinking about your broad role as a Member of Parliament, what are the most important duties and responsibilities involved?" This item elicited very articulate characterizations of roles and proved most effective in identifying the concepts in Members' minds.

5. "Thinking for a moment very broadly about British society, how do your duties and responsibilities fit in with the work of society as a whole?—How important is your work as an MP to the functioning of society as a whole?" Some respondents objected to this question's vagueness and spent time questioning the question. Yet even their objections often provided valuable information. And most of them did, as planned, elaborate themes from their previous discussion and offer detailed examples to illustrate their points. They told, for instance, about how helping a constituent made a major difference in her life. Or they introduced new themes, such as influence at Westminster, which the question's stress on "importance" brought out.

6. "Thinking over your political activity, what do you personally find most satisfying about it? What would you miss most if you left politics?" Some backbenchers talked, for instance, about gratifications from modest successes in modifying policy. Others discussed at length the satisfactions they derived from helping their constituents. Similar questions have been used in other studies to analyze incentives through tape-recorded interviews. See James L. Payne et al., *The Motivation of Politicians* (Chicago: Nelson-Hall, 1984): 191. For a more cognitively oriented approach, see William Hampton, *Democracy and Community: A Study of Politics in Sheffield* (London: Oxford University Press, 1970): 192–93.

7. "And finally your own plans? Are there any further positions in the House that you would like to seek sometime in the future?" (If yes) "What would you say are your chances of achieving [highest position mentioned]?"

8. The first three questions were easier to discuss than these two and were there-

fore introduced earlier in the interviews. The two questions on ambition were reserved till the interviewer had time to build rapport. Even then, some backbenchers understandably regarded the questions as impertinent, while others requested reassurance about the nonattribution arrangements. Most, however, responded readily in a straightforward manner, albeit a significant minority were as indirect as Trollope's MP who, when asked about his ambitions, said coyly, "The schoolboy, when he sits down to make rhymes, dare not say even to his sister, that he hopes to rival Milton; but he nurses such a hope." Anthony Trollope, *Can You Forgive Her?* (London: Penguin, 1972 [1864–65]): 492–93.

9. We were not seeking four roles any more than we were seeking two or seven. But we were seeking more than one. It seemed to both of us that these four roles permeated Members' discussions of their tasks and responsibilities. They also permeated the language involved: names of three of the four roles, or synonyms for them, appeared throughout the transcripts. Only the term "Parliament Man" is unfamiliar at the House (although "Good House of Commons Man" is close). We adopted it from Sir Lewis Namier's famous study of an earlier era: *The Structure of Politics at the Accession of George III* (London: Macmillan, 1968).

10. Although it may seem odd to distinguish between using and not using an example, we found that backbenchers who seemed to care most about a theme not only made it central to their discussions but also reinforced it with striking examples.

11. Only half the backbenchers scored 0 for instances of these themes in their responses to Q3, whereas virtually all did in their responses to Qs 1 and 2. In the age of democracy and active government, the role of the Parliament Man might appear inappropriate, indeed anachronistic, a remnant from the eighteenth century. Understandably, then, MPs seemed reluctant to use such themes to characterize their general role in Q1 and even more reluctant in Q2, which asked them to evaluate the importance of their role as an MP. It was only after responding woodenly to these first two questions that they explained, in the context of savoring satisfactions (Q3), that parliament man themes characterized their understandings of the parts they played. Such measurement difficulties are not at all unusual in research on roles—which underscores the desirability of using a series of different questions and tape recording the discussions.

12. See Crowe, "Purpose in Politics," chap. 3. These summary composite scores, which were constructed in this way to make them comparable to the other thematic measures, are equivalent to the product of the two variables, aspirations and chances (correlation = .993) and are theoretically consistent with economic approaches to the subject. See Stuart Elaine Macdonald, "Political Ambition and Attainment: A Dynamic Analysis of Parliamentary Careers," Ph.D. diss., University of Michigan, 1987: 33.

13. In 11.5 percent of the cases, role assignments could not be made due either to ties (6.5%) or missing data (5%). These cases were dropped from the analysis.

14. William A. Scott, "Reliability of Content Analysis: The Case of Nominal Scale Coding," *Public Opinion Quarterly* 19, 3 (1955): 321–25. See also Graham Kalton and Richard Stowell, "A Study of Coder Variability," *Applied Statistics* 28, 3 (1979): 276–89. Many of the inconsistencies between the results of the additive and global

procedures fell into two categories. One concerned backbenchers who had been identified as Policy Advocates by the additive procedure, but who looked more like Constituency Members in the global view. This reflects the ambiguity in cases where the
"causes" that Policy Advocates put forward when responding to one role question
are linked closely to constituency matters, but where these links become clear only
when they respond to other questions. The second category involved backbenchers
who were classified as Ministerial Aspirants by the additive method, but who seemed
to the second coder, who compared their responses to all five questions and read a
bit between the lines, to be insufficiently serious about their ambitions to justify this
classification.

15. Austin Mitchell, M.P., "Consulting the Workers: MPs on Their Job," *The
Parliamentarian* 66, 1 (1985): 10.

16. See, for example, Lisanne Radice, Elizabeth Vallance, and Virginia Willis,
Member of Parliament: The Job of a Backbencher (New York: St. Martin's Press,
1987): 1–20, 45–46; Richard Rose, *Politics in England,* 3rd ed. (Boston: Little,
Brown, 1980): 87–89; Richard Rose, "British MPs: A Bite as Well as a Bark?" *Studies in Public Policy* 98 (1982): 13–19; Anthony Barker and Michael Rush, *The Member of Parliament and His Information* (London: Allen and Unwin, 1970): 21–22;
Bruce Cain, John A. Ferejohn, and Morris P. Fiorina, "The House Is Not a Home:
British MPs in Their Constituencies," *Legislative Studies Quarterly* 4, 4 (1979):
501–23; Michael Rush, "Political Recruitment, Representation, and Participation,"
in John P. Mackintosh, M.P. (ed.), *People and Parliament* (London: Saxon House,
1978): 29. What does not appear at all in our typology, but appears often in typologies published by both MPs and political commentators, is the "role" of the Party
Politician or Party Loyalist. This is obviously one of the most important dispositions
on the backbenches. But it is a *disposition,* not a role, a disposition like "delegate"
or "trustee," a disposition that functions like a decision rule and can be applied by
MPs *in any role.* One could conceive of building around this decision rule a full-
blown role, a broadly scripted part for people to play. But this part *qua* role isn't
prominent in the minds of Westminster's backbenchers—which is the template with
which we have done our work.

17. See Lisanne Radice, Elizabeth Vallance, and Virginia Willis, *Member of Parliament: The Job of a Backbencher,* 2nd ed. (London: Macmillan, 1990), who report
(p. 132) that backbenchers from the intakes of the 1980s understood their career
choices in very much these terms: roles that they would for any given period of time
make *predominant.*

18. David R. Mayhew, *Congress: The Electoral Connection* (New Haven: Yale
University Press, 1974); Richard F. Fenno, *Congressmen in Committees* (Boston:
Little, Brown, 1973).

19. Four of these six correlations were below .10 (gamma) and none were significant at the .05 level. The two correlations that were significant at this level were
weak and negative ($-.12$, $-.23$).

20. By contrast, many backbenchers give the roles of Parliament Man and Ministerial Aspirant short shrift. Activity as a Policy Advocate or Constituency Member
is simply more difficult to avoid.

21. As we have seen in Chapters 2 and 3, the resemblance between Policy Advocates and Ministerial Aspirants is stronger than the resemblance between any other pair of roles.

22. Since the first two of the parliament man measures tapped so few of the relevant themes, the index construction relied on the third question. This may be the principal reason that the three items do not cluster together on a single dimension. In the same vein, we have seen in Chapter 5 that Parliament Men are certainly the most heterogeneous of our categories. Their subtypes are quite distinct.

INDEX